INTERNATIONAL LAW

INTERNATIONAL LAW

By

D. W. GREIG, M.A., LL.B.,

of the Middle Temple, Barrister-at-Law,
Senior Lecturer in Law at Monash University

LONDON
BUTTERWORTHS
1970

ENGLAND: BUTTERWORTH & CO. (PUBLISHERS) LTD.
                LONDON: 88 KINGSWAY, W.C.2
AUSTRALIA: BUTTERWORTH & CO. (AUSTRALIA) LTD.
                SYDNEY: 20 LOFTUS STREET
                MELBOURNE: 343 LITTLE COLLINS STREET
                BRISBANE: 240 QUEEN STREET
CANADA: BUTTERWORTH & CO. (CANADA) LTD.
                TORONTO: 14 CURITY AVENUE, 374
NEW ZEALAND: BUTTERWORTH & CO. (NEW ZEALAND) LTD.
                WELLINGTON: 49/51 BALLANCE STREET
                AUCKLAND: 35 HIGH STREET
SOUTH AFRICA: BUTTERWORTH & CO. (SOUTH AFRICA) LTD.
                DURBAN: 33/35 BEACH GROVE

First Edition   1970
Reprinted   1971

©

Butterworth & Co. (Publishers) Ltd.
1970

Standard Book Numbers: Casebound: 406 59180 6
Limp: 406 59181 4

Made and printed in Great Britain by
Compton Printing Ltd., London and Aylesbury

PREFACE

This book has two principal aims. First, it has as its object a survey of both the general law of peace and the law of international institutions within the same framework. Hence aspects of the law of international institutions are discussed in the chapters on international personality, recognition, and jurisdiction, in addition to the wide coverage contained in the chapters on international organisations towards the end of the book. Secondly, it is designed to provide a far more detailed overall treatment of the subject matter than is given in most one-volume texts.

Throughout a good deal of use has been made of United States practice and of decisions of American courts. It was felt that to present primarily the United Kingdom view and the decisions of English courts would be harmful to what must be a basic consideration in writing a book on international law—that is, to be as "international" in outlook as possible. While it is not possible within the confines of a single volume to cover in detail how other legal systems deal with such problems as the relationship between international law and municipal law, recognition, or sovereign immunities, nevertheless brief descriptions have been included of the approaches to be found in a number of other common law jurisdictions and in the states of continental Europe towards such matters.

This work is fundamentally a lawyer's book, aimed primarily at students taking final year courses as part of their degree, or studying general aspects of international law as part of an initial postgraduate degree, or diploma, by examination. It is hoped, however, that much of it will also be suitable for students of international relations who take something more than a brief introductory course in international law as part of a politics degree. Without losing sight of the object of writing a book on international law, the attempt has therefore been made to demonstrate wherever appropriate that international law is only one aspect of the conduct of international relations.

Because of the wide range of jurisdictions and of areas of state practice from which illustrations and authority have been drawn, it is not possible to "state the law" as at any particular date. In any case, international law being a subject given to evolution and development rather than to amendment by statute or judicial decision, such a date would be inappropriate. All that can be said is that the attempt has been made to include important materials that have become available as late as the proof-reading stage.

I am particularly grateful to early criticisms of the first few chapters by my then colleague at Birmingham, J. A. Andrews, now Professor of Law at the University College of Wales, Aberystwyth, and to the reading of much of the typescript by my colleague at Monash, Mr. H. B. Connell. Both brought home to me the difficulties that a reader might encounter in understanding parts of the text; the difficulties that remain cannot be attributed to their efforts. Any errors and heresies there may be are entirely my own responsibility. My thanks is also extended to a number of other colleagues for a variety of helpful comments on various parts of the book; to those members of the Monash Law School secretarial staff, Miss Jenny Neil, Mrs. Dolour Warneke and Mrs. Valda Pugh, for their valiant efforts in typing from illegible manuscript and to Mrs. Frances Hanks, Research Assistant in the Law School, whose careful reading of the proofs has done so much to eradicate errors, particularly in the references. Finally, I must express my gratitude to the publishers for the speed with which they accepted the book for publication and succeeded in getting it into print.

August 1969   D. W. GREIG

TABLE OF CONTENTS

TABLE OF CASES

PAGE

PAGE

Table of Cases

PAGE

CHAPTER ONE

THE NATURE AND SOURCES OF INTERNATIONAL LAW

1 INTRODUCTION

International law provides a system of rules governing the conduct of inter-state relations. Thus, diplomatic intercourse between states is greatly facilitated by legal principles concerning the inviolability of embassy premises and of communications with the home state, and the immunity from legal process of foreign diplomatic representatives in the courts of the receiving state. International law can also offer an answer to the majority of international disputes, though in some cases the dispute may not be susceptible of settlement by the application of legal rules. In the dispute between India and Portugal over the remaining Portuguese possessions on the Indian sub-continent, the major issue was not the validity of Portugal's legal title, but whether it was politically acceptable in present-day circumstances that one colonial power should retain sovereignty in an area from which other colonial powers had withdrawn. It is this inter-action of the political with the legal which must be kept in mind throughout any study of international law. Therefore, although this book is designed primarily as an introduction to international law, it will pay particular attention to the fact that international law cannot exist in isolation from the political factors operating in the sphere of international relations.

It does not follow that the influence of political factors in some way destroys the claim of international law to be considered as "law". The political decision by a state to withhold a dispute from judicial settlement, or to act in a way contrary to a particular legal rule, is no more a denial of the existence of the relevant legal principles than is the breach of the provisions of an American or British statute by an individual a rejection of the statute as part of American or English law. International law certainly differs from municipal systems of law in a number of significant details. The lack of a legislature with the power of making new laws, the absence of courts with compulsory jurisdiction over all disputes, and the failure of the international community to provide any but the most primitive system of sanctions for the punishment of the law-breaker are the most obvious distinguishing features. But international law does have one

---

1. The dispute in this form was resolved by India's seizure of Goa and the other territories in December 1961: for the issues raised by this action, see below.

major similarity with municipal law which far outweighs these points of difference: it depends for its efficacy upon the general will of the community to abide by its rules. In the last resort, both international law and municipal law depend upon the underlying acceptance by the community of the duties imposed upon individuals, whether they be persons or states. Furthermore, international law can usefully be considered as law because it is treated as law by the members of the international community. Even the state which wishes to escape from an inconvenient rule of law will not argue that international law as a whole does not exist, but will seek to justify its actions by denying the existence of the particular rule as part of international law, or by claiming that, though such a rule does exist, it is not applicable to the circumstances of the case or should be altered to meet a new situation. If states look upon international law as governing their relations *inter se*, it would be pedantic to deny the term "law" to such a body of rules.

Historically, international law was a by-product of the gradual increase in the power of the nation states which emerged from European feudalism. As the rulers of Europe secured their own internal position, their policies were increasingly directed towards the field of foreign affairs. More frequent contacts, and the resulting conflicts of interest, led to the mutual acceptance of rules applicable to a variety of situations. Legal pronouncements upon the privileges and immunities of diplomatic agents were common by the seventeenth century, and the following century saw the foundation of many of the rules of maritime warfare. After the Napoleonic Wars, the Vienna settlement of 1815 made the first attempt at "organising" peace under the direction of the major European powers. A series of international treaties established the neutrality of Switzerland (1815) and of Belgium (1831); laid down general rules for the navigation of international rivers (1815), and more specific regulations *inter alia* for the Rhine (1831) and for the Danube (1856); codified much of the law of maritime warfare (the Declaration of Paris, 1856); and created special régimes for the Suez Canal (1888) and for the Panama Canal (1901). During the same period, state practice produced the general framework of modern international law dealing with the recognition of states, which had achieved prominence from the attitudes of Great Britain and the United States to the independence of Greece and to the break-away of the Spanish colonies in Central and South America. A similar development took place in the principles governing the responsibility of a state for injuries suffered by aliens within its territory. The present century has seen repeated efforts to make the conduct of warfare more humane (at the Hague in 1899 and 1907, and at Geneva in 1925 and 1949); and to limit or abolish war altogether as an instrument of national policy (by the Covenant of the League of Nations, by the Kellogg–Briand Pact of 1928, and by the Charter of the United Nations). Indeed, the creation of various international organisations operating in economic, social and political fields, and the adoption of international conventions granting rights directly enforceable against states by individuals, have added new dimensions to the concept of international relations, and consequently to the scope of international law.

The notable feature in the development of international law has been the importance of the notion of agreement. In the preceding paragraph a number of examples were given of important aspects of international law which were dealt with in the course of the nineteenth century by the express agreement of states in the form of international treaties, or conventions as multilateral treaties are usually called. At the same time, state practice as a source of rules of law was justified on the ground that it was based upon the implied agreement of the members of the international community. As one of the Legal Advisers to the United States Department of State has recently explained:[2]

> "International law has been defined as those rules of international conduct which have met general acceptance among the community of nations. It reflects and records those accommodations which, over centuries, states have found it in their interests to make. It rests upon the common consent of civilised communities."

The emphasis on the consensual nature of international law, i.e., that a state could only be bound by a rule to which it had in some way consented, was re-enforced by the doctrine of sovereignty which came into prominence in the political philosophy of the sixteenth and seventeenth centuries, and was later readapted to justify the late nineteenth- and twentieth-century concept of statehood. Both Bodin (1530–96) in France, and Hobbes (1588–1679) in England, saw in the authority of the sovereign the best guarantee of the well-being of the subject by protecting him from the evils of civil strife. Although the former was not preaching a doctrine of absolute sovereignty, indeed he clearly stated that "all the princes of the earth are subject to the laws of God and of nature, and even to certain human laws common to all nations",[3] this limitation has largely been ignored in favour of his subsequent observation that

> ". . . it is the distinguishing mark of the sovereign that he cannot in any way be subject to the commands of another, for it is he who makes law for the subject, abrogates law already made, and amends obsolete law. No one who is subject either to the law or to some other person can do this. That is why it is laid down in the civil law that the prince is above the law, for the word *law* in Latin implies the command of him who is invested with sovereign power."[3]

Similarly, although Hobbes based sovereignty on the prior covenant of the governed, once the sovereign had been granted this status, neither abdication nor deposition from that power was possible in the interests of the people's own safety. Without a sovereign, endowed with absolute powers, life would soon degenerate into primitive chaos.[4]

---

2. Phleger, Legal Advisor to the U.S. State Department, quoted Whiteman, *Digest of International Law*, Vol. I, at p. 2.
3. *Six Books of the Commonwealth*, Book I, Chap. 8.
4. *Leviathan*, Chap. XVIII.

Eighteenth-century political philosophy was mainly concerned with the contractual nature of sovereignty. The revolt of the American colonies had drawn much of its inspiration from the theory, used by Locke as a justification for the English revolution of 1688, that by breaking his duty to the subject the sovereign could forfeit his right of obedience. It was Hegel (1770–1831) who employed the theory of a social contract between the sovereign and the subject as the starting point for the attempt to identify the State as the realisation of individual freedom. Once individual freedom became enmeshed in a theory of state supremacy, it became inevitable that the individual will would be subordinated to the general will, i.e. the "will" of the State. The intoxicating effects of the cult of the divine State, when harnessed to the forces of nationalism, as in the nationalistic and authoritarian writings of Del Vecchio and Binder, can be seen in the actions of the fascist dictatorships in Italy and, more particularly, Germany prior to, and during, the Second World War.

However, it was not only the freedom of the individual subject in totalitarian states which suffered from extreme doctrines of sovereignty. The acceptance of the premise that sovereignty was absolute power had equally serious implications for any theory of obligation in international law. The state was under no internal limitation in the exercise of its authority, and, being sovereign, could be subject to no external limitation. The transfer of the concept of sovereignty in its internal application unaltered into the sphere of external relations involved a denial of the existence of any rules of international law, because a state could not bind itself even by agreement. For an agreement to be binding there would have to be a prior rule that treaties are binding, but the existence of such a rule would be inconsistent with the doctrine of sovereignty.

Such an extreme view of the sovereignty of states is clearly untenable because it is inconsistent with the practice of states. Treaties *are* binding, and are treated as creating obligations by all members of the international community. Nevertheless, the absolute nature of sovereignty still remains as the foundation of the "positivist" view of international law (as it is called). In order to bring this notion of sovereignty more into line with reality, the positivist calls in aid what is termed the principle of "auto-limitation"—sovereignty is absolute except in so far as a state agrees to its limitation. Thus, a state has absolute freedom of action except in so far as it has agreed to rules restricting that freedom. Such a statement has a deceptive appeal until the question is asked, how does a state "agree" to rules of international law? To this, the positivist might reply that it is not necessary for a state to agree to every principle: "it is sufficient . . . that consent is given to international law as a system rather than to each and every relationship contained in it."[5] But even this explanation is not entirely satisfactory because there are situations in which states reject the application of certain rules altogether, but it does not necessarily follow

---

5. Jaffe, *Judicial Aspects of Foreign Relations*, p. 90. For a strong criticism of the consent theory, see Brierly, *The Basis of Obligation in International Law*, pp. 1–67.

that, in such circumstances, the rules no longer exist. Nevertheless, the consent theory does illustrate the practical limitations on the role of law in international relations. As a political reality, international law can only develop in so far as states acknowledge its existence and make use of its rules in the regulation of their affairs. In the absence of some community interest in, and of a general consent to, the application of its rules, international law would have no function, and therefore only the pretence of an existence, in the field of inter-state relations. In this sense, as a political fact, international law does depend on the consent of states.

As has already been stated, international law, like any other system of law, depends upon the general acceptance of the community. Its basic tenets, such as the principle that treaties are binding, *pacta sunt servanda*, cannot be created by a prior legal rule: they are the legal rules upon which all else rests. In the words of Salmond,[6] the law "is the law because it is the law and for no other reason that it is possible for the law itself to take notice of". Although community acceptance is the basis of the international legal system, it does not follow that all problems of contemporary international law may be answered by reference to the consensual theory. The theory is at best a descriptive generalisation, too broad to be applied to many of the problems concerning the binding nature of international law. In what circumstances, if at all, can a state dissent from a developing or established rule of international law? What is the position if a new state declares that it will not consider itself bound by certain principles of international law? These and other similar questions will be considered in the following discussion of the sources of international law; and it will become clear that the answers do not depend solely on any *a priori* theory of consent as the basis of international obligation.

2 THE SOURCES AND EVIDENCES OF INTERNATIONAL LAW[7]

The identification of the sources of the law of a state may give rise to difficulties in the precise analysis required by the writer on jurisprudence, but to the layman it is possible to talk in terms of statutes and judicial decisions with both a degree of accuracy and the likelihood of being understood. And if the request is made to state the law on a particular matter, the relevant rules may be ascertained with confidence from the statute book or the law reports. The question of identifying the sources of international law and of explaining where the relevant rules can be found cannot be so readily answered. In a dispute between two states before the International Court of Justice, Article 38 of its Statute directs the Court to apply:

6. *Jurisprudence*, 11th ed., p. 137.
7. For a recent discussion of the subject see the book with this title by Parry.

> "(a) international conventions, whether general or particular, establishing rules
>   expressly recognised by the contesting states;
> (b) international custom, as evidence of a general practice accepted as law;
> (c) the general principles of law recognised by civilised nations;
> (d) ... judicial decisions and the teachings of the most highly qualified publicists
>   of the various nations, as subsidiary means for the determination of rules of
>   law."

Although it will be necessary to go into these provisions individually at a later stage, it can be seen that, while Article 38 may have something to do with sources, it is primarily a statement of how the Court is to approach a particular dispute. Is there a treaty obligation relevant to the subject matter of the dispute? If there is, the Court should apply the terms of the treaty. If there is no such treaty obligation, is there evidence of a custom between states which the two disputants have accepted as binding on themselves? If there is such a custom, then it should be adopted to give an answer to the question at issue between the parties.

At this stage, the framers of the Statute were faced with a difficulty, because situations might arise in the relations between states in which no treaty exists, and no settled practice among states has become apparent upon which an international tribunal could base a decision. Has the Court simply to announce that international law was silent on the issue? Earlier arbitral tribunals and claims commissions had not had to resort to such a drastic acknowledgement of the deficiencies of international law. If the law was uncertain, it was still for the tribunal to pronounce its decision on the basis of existing international law. The answer provided by the framers of the Statute was to lay down that if there was no treaty and no international custom, the Court should call an aid "general principles of law recognised by civilised nations". Despite the shortcomings of the actual wording used, it can be seen that the Court's search for the relevant principles takes it to treaties the terms of which the parties have expressly recognised; to general practice accepted as law (by the states) or to general principles of law (recognised by states). However, if the conventions, practices and principles, are not clear from evidences of the behaviour of states, the Court may resort "to judicial decisions and the teachings of the most highly qualified publicists of the various nations, as subsidiary means for the determination of rules of law."

Article 38 is thus a direction to the Court of where to look for international law, and it offers a guide to any individual person whose task it is to discover the rules of international law. But it is only when the attempt is made to answer the question "what are the sources of international law?" that the difficulties which face the Court in attempting to carry out the directions of Article 38 become apparent. International treaties are not frequently of direct relevance to the subject-matter of a dispute, but does it necessarily follow that all conventional rules are irrelevant? If international custom is a source of law, based upon the actions of states, what actions are evidence of a state's acceptance of a particular practice as law? The adoption of sub-paragraph (c) relating to the general principles of law and the mention of "judicial decisions" in (d) as a subsidiary means for the determination of rules of law, seems to perpetuate the theory that judges do not make law but only apply that which is law already. Cannot it be said that international tribunals play a creative role? Or are their pronouncements simply applications, and evidence, of (existing) customary international law, or perhaps of "general principles of law"? And because Article 38 was originally drafted in 1920 at a time when the proliferation of international institutions, with their own specialised field or "international administrative law", was unimagined and unforeseen, Article 38 provides only the most general suggestion through the presence of "general principles of law" of the method that should be adopted in the settlement of a dispute in the field of international administration, and little guide at all to the sources of this new branch of international law.

TREATIES

A. Treaties as law

Because of the absence of a legislative organ with the power to lay down principles of law binding on all states, it will often be a matter of some difficulty to ascertain what rules of law exist in a particular case. In deciding between conflicting claims, the first step would obviously be to consider whether the parties have made any express agreement concerning the subject matter of their dispute. Of course, if there were a provision directly in point in a treaty to which the contesting states were both parties, there would normally be no area of dispute, unless one of the states was urging that the treaty was for some reason no longer binding. It is more likely that the provisions of the treaty are not altogether clear, and the decision in the case will depend on how the relevant provisions will be interpreted in the light of the situation which has in fact arisen.

In the *Wimbledon* case,[8] the Permanent Court of International Justice had to consider the effects of Article 380 of the Treaty of Versailles which guaranteed that the Kiel Canal should be "free and open" to vessels of all nations at peace with Germany. German officials had stopped the s.s. *Wimbledon*, a British ship carrying munitions through the Canal to Poland, then at war with Russia, on the ground that a customary rule of international law did not allow the passage of armaments of war through the territory of a neutral state to the territory of a belligerent. While there was no doubt as to the existence of such a rule, the Court nevertheless held that the treaty provision must take precedence: the stopping of a vessel sailing under the flag of a state at peace with Germany was a breach of Germany's obligations under the Treaty of Versailles.

---

8. (1923), P.C.I.J. Rep., Ser. A, No. 1.

However, in interpreting a treaty which appears to alter the existing rights and duties of states under customary international law, it is a rule of construction that "treaty provisions must be so construed as best to conform to accepted principles of international law rather than in derogation from them", unless the intention to effect such an alteration is apparent from the unambiguous wording of the relevant provision. In the case of *The Wanderer*,[9] an arbitral tribunal had to decide whether the seizure of this British vessel by the American authorities was lawful under a British Act of Parliament passed in order to carry out the award in an earlier arbitration between the two states. Under the Act, specified United States officers had the same powers of arrest over British vessels breaking the regulations contained in the award, and annexed to the Act, as British commissioned officers. In the regulations, it was an offence to use nets, firearms and explosives in fur-seal fishing. *The Wanderer*, which was suspected of being in breach of this regulation, was stopped and searched on the high seas, and, on discovery of an unsealed gun and ammunition, the vessel was taken into custody. *Prima facie*, the American authorities had committed two acts contrary to customary international law: they had exercised the right of visit and search over, and had then seized, a foreign vessel on the high seas. The tribunal pointed out that it was a fundamental principle of international maritime law that no state could exercise a right of visit and search over foreign vessels "pursuing a lawful avocation on the high seas", except in time of war or by special agreement. It was for the United States, therefore, to show that their naval authorities had acted under such an agreement which, "being an exception to the general principle, must be construed *stricto jure*". As the regulations incorporated in the Act of Parliament prohibited only the use of firearms, the possession of them alone could not be justification for the seizure of the vessel, nor could it be any justification of the prior visit and search.

As has already been stated, the procedure for determining the legal position of the parties to a dispute of looking first to any treaty obligations which they might have undertaken towards each other is emphasised by the direction contained in Article 38 (1) of the Statute of the International Court by which the Court is first to apply in any dispute submitted to it "international conventions, whether general or particular, establishing rules expressly recognised by the contesting states". In other words, where the two parties to the dispute have recognised the rules established by the relevant treaty, the Court should apply those rules in reaching its decision. The usual way in which states "expressly recognise" treaty rules is by being parties to the treaty, in which case there would exist a contractual obligation between the contesting states. Treaties, whether they have only a few parties, or have a large number of parties, are basically sources of obligation between the signatories, in much the same way as a private law contract grants rights to, and imposes duties on, the parties to the

---

9. (1921), 6 U.N.R.I.A.A., 68.

agreement. In this sense it is inaccurate to talk of treaties as a source of international law in the way that a statute is a source of municipal law, because treaties, being contractual in nature, do not normally have any legal effect on third parties. Indeed, it will be recalled that Article 38 itself does not refer to "international conventions" as sources of law, although it does refer to them as sources of "rules", not to parties to the convention—for that is not wide enough—but to any states expressly recognising such rules. In this respect, the framers of Article 38 were attempting to define in precise terms for the new Permanent Court of International Justice the approach already adopted by arbitral tribunals to the problem of deciding on the relevant rules of international law to be applied in a particular case. If two states are not both parties to a treaty, but expressly recognise the applicability of its provisions to the conduct of their relations, clearly, an international tribunal, called upon to settle a dispute arising in a sphere of operations regulated by the treaty, would look first to the terms of the treaty to discover whether they offered any solution to the dispute.

However, Article 38 seems to fall short of providing an adequate definition or description of treaties which are commonly referred to as "law-making". This epithet has been applied to multilateral conventions which are designed to lay down rules of conduct for general application, and, to some jurists at least, treaties of this type are regarded as having quasi-legislative effect. But how can a treaty, which is primarily a source of contractual obligation, develop into a source of legal obligation for non-parties?

When one talks of legislation under a municipal system, the reference is to the power of the law-giver to create rules applicable to all persons within the territory of the state irrespective of individual consent. Obviously, there is no legislative power in this sense available to an international conference given the task of codifying and developing a particular field of international law. In carrying out its tasks, such a conference is attempting to define rules of general application, so that there is a difference in practical terms between the "law-making" treaty and other inter-state agreements. Both are sources of obligation for those states which have become parties to them, but the former have more likelihood of tacit acceptance by the majority of states. As Brierly has explained:[10]

> "The only class of treaties which it is admissible to treat as a source of general law are those which a large number of states have concluded for the purpose either of declaring their understanding of what the law is on a particular subject, or of laying down a new general rule for future conduct, or of creating some international institution. Such treaties are . . . the substitute in the international system for legislation, and they are conveniently referred to as 'law-making'. . . ."

---

10. *Law of Nations*, 6th ed., p. 58.

B. Codification and the law-making process

The process of codifying existing law and of developing new rules for
regulating future conduct has been a feature of international life for more
than a century. The first phase, which continued until after the First
World War, was largely taken up with attempts to revise various aspects
of the law relating to the settlement of disputes and to the conduct of
warfare. The Declaration of Paris, 1856, on the regulation of naval warfare has already been mentioned. In 1864, the first Geneva Convention
on the amelioration of the condition of the wounded in armies in the
field was signed. In 1899 and 1907, a series of Hague Conventions provided for the Pacific Settlement of International Disputes, regulated the
conduct of warfare on land and adapted the 1864 Convention to maritime
warfare; made a declaration of war obligatory, dealt with the rights and
duties of neutral states and laid down a variety of rules for the conduct of
naval warfare. In 1920, the Committee of Jurists, appointed by the
Council of the League of Nations to prepare a draft statute for the Permanent Court of International Justice, also submitted a resolution calling
for an inter-state conference to re-establish existing rules, and to formulate and approve modifications, primarily of the laws of war; and again,
after the Second World War, the Geneva Conventions of 1929 had their
counterpart in the Geneva Conventions of 1949.

The second phase developed from the proposals of the 1920 Committee
of Jurists concerning the law of peace. In 1924, the Assembly of the League
created a Committee of Experts for the progressive codification of international law, and an inter-state conference did meet at the Hague in 1930
to consider nationality, territorial waters, and state responsibility, on
"bases for discussion" drawn up by the Committee of Experts. Although
some progress was made in relation to nationality, the conference was
such a great disappointment that the experiment was never again repeated
by the League.

The third phase concerns the means adopted by the General Assembly
of the United Nations to fulfil its duty under Article 13 (1) of the Charter
to "initiate studies and make recommendations for the purpose of . . .
encouraging the progressive development of international law and its
codification". In 1947, as a result of recommendations made by a committee set up by the Assembly to study the methods by which it could
implement its obligations under Article 13, the Assembly created the
International Law Commission to consider, either on its own initiative, or
through proposals submitted to it by members of the United Nations,
or, primarily, as a result of express directions from the Assembly, various
aspects of international law with a view to formulating draft conventions.

The method usually adopted by the Commission is to appoint a
rapporteur to receive information supplied by various governments at
the request of the Commission, and to draw up a draft convention for
consideration by the Commission. When the Commission is satisfied
with the draft, the draft is submitted to governments for their comments

and then reconsidered in the light of those comments. The final text is adopted by the Commission and submitted, along with the Commission's recommendations, through the Secretary General of the United Nations to the General Assembly. It is for the Assembly to decide whether there is a sufficient measure of agreement on the draft proposals to make it worthwhile convening a conference of states in order to draw up a convention on the particular subject.

Article 15 of the Commission's Statute adopted, and attempted to define, the distinction inherent in Article 13 of the United Nations Charter between "codification" and "progressive development". Thus, "progressive development" is taken to mean the preparation of draft conventions on subjects which have not yet been regulated by international law or in regard to which the law has not yet been sufficiently developed in state practice; while "codification" is interpreted as the more precise formulation and systematisation of rules of international law in fields where there has already been extensive state practice, precedent and doctrine. It is, of course, doubtful whether such a theoretical distinction can be maintained in practice. Whatever the subject of a draft convention, even in fields where there is a wealth of state practice, certain rules might require modification, or disagreement will exist as to the exact interpretation of the relevant precedents. In its report on the final text on the law of the sea, the Commission admitted that the distinction could "hardly be maintained", at any rate with regard to maritime law: several proposed articles did not fall wholly into either category.[11] Furthermore, it is interesting to note that the rapporteur was prepared to recognise that the distinction had already been abandoned in the work of the Commission:[12]

> "During the eight years of its existence the Commission has become more and more convinced that the very clear distinction established in the Statute between these two activities cannot be maintained in practice. Not only may there be wide differences of opinion as to whether a subject is already 'sufficiently developed in the practice of states', but also several of the provisions adopted by the Commission, and based upon a recognised principle of international law, have been framed in such a way as to be suitable for inclusion in the category of the 'progressive development of international law'. At first the Commission tried to draw a distinction between articles in the one category and those in the other but has had to abandon the attempt; few of the rules adopted belong purely to codification and many belong partly to one and partly to the other category."

The process of codification, of preliminary discussion by legal experts followed by consultations with and between governments in the hope of achieving an international convention ratified by a large number of states, has been slow to produce worthwhile results outside the laws of war. True, the patient labours of the Commission did produce draft

11. Eighth Report (1956), para. 26.
12. Doc. A/CN. 4/L. 68/Add. 1, para. 20, conveniently quoted (1960), 36 B.Y.B.I.L., at pp. 143–4, fn. 6.

conventions sufficiently acceptable to states in the non-contentious fields of Diplomatic and Consular Intercourse and Immunities; but for the most part the political implications of such topics as the state responsibility, and the rights and duties of states, have made it unlikely that agreement would be reached. Indeed, in these fields, the General Assembly has not considered it worth while calling a conference to discuss the Commission's proposals.[13]

Perhaps the most strenuous efforts of the codifiers have been directed at obtaining a measure of agreement on different aspects of the law of the sea, and it is in this context that the chief obstacles to effective codification can be seen most clearly. The failure of states to agree on a formulation of what is believed to be existing customary law makes the uncertainty greater than if codification had not been attempted. The discussion of territorial waters at the Hague in 1930 foundered on the inability of States to accept the traditional three mile limit which many had considered a settled principle of international law. The cumbersome codification procedure can also be the cause of confusing compromises and omissions. To take a striking illustration from the 1958 Geneva Conference: there was considerable support for some restriction being imposed on the right of foreign warships to proceed unauthorised through territorial waters (other than territorial waters forming part of an international strait where there would be no restriction). The International Law Commission therefore drafted a provision under which, although warships would normally be granted the right of innocent passage, the coastal state would have the power to make the right subject to prior authorisation or notification. The "authorisation" requirement was voted separately, and because of the objection of the maritime powers it failed to gain a majority of the votes cast. The redrafted text, providing only for prior notification, though acceptable to a majority of states, failed to obtain the necessary two-thirds vote. As a result, no special provision for warships appears in the final text of the convention, an outcome much in line with the United Kingdom's view of the law, though clearly contrary to the views of a majority of the states represented at the Conference. Finally, the four draft Conventions adopted by the Geneva Conference laid down that they should come into effect between the states ratifying them once twenty-two ratifications had been received, although the number of states attending the Conference was nearly four times that number. All four Conventions have been ratified by more than twenty-two states, and the provisions of the Convention are therefore operative between those states, but what is the position as regards states which have not ratified? It is this question which must now be considered.

---

13. The law of treaties has always been considered too contentious a subject matter, but, following the Commission's final draft of 1966, the Assembly convened two conferences to consider the draft. The text of the Convention was finalised and opened for signature in May, 1969.

C. Treaties and non-signatories

For treaties, even those to which a large number of states are parties, to be regarded as in any way "legislative" they must affect the rules of international law applicable to non-signatories. There is evidence to suggest that a number of what are sometimes termed "constitutive treaties", treaties establishing a special régime or an international institution do create rights and obligations under international law which non-parties cannot ignore. But as far as treaties in general are concerned, the development of a treaty rule binding only on parties into a general rule of international law depends upon the political and other extra-legal factors operating in the international sphere which together influence the acceptance or rejection of a particular rule by the rest of the world community.

a TREATIES CREATING INTERNATIONAL ORGANISATIONS

The constitutional treaties establishing international organisations, e.g. those provisions of the Treaty of Versailles which created the League of Nations and the International Labour Organisation, the United Nations Charter and the basic texts of the various specialised agencies, and, possibly, the Treaty of Rome and the other instruments establishing the European Communities, not only imposed obligations upon member states, they have also created legal entities with powers to operate as subjects of international law. In the *Reparations* case, the International Court was asked whether the United Nations had the capacity to bring a claim under international law against a state which was not a member of the Organisation in respect of an injury suffered by a United Nations official. In holding that the United Nations did have this capacity, the Court commented[14] that:

> ". . . fifty states, representing the vast majority of the members of the international community, had the power, in conformity with international law, to bring into being an entity possessing objective international personality, and not merely personality recognised by them alone, together with capacity to bring international claims."

In other words, an international organisation, certainly one with a large membership, may possess a status recognised by international law, and binding on states not parties to its constitutional treaty; and, because of that status, it may also be endowed with rights, similarly recognised by international law, which it can enforce even against non-member states.

b TREATIES CREATING SPECIAL TERRITORIAL RÉGIMES

Only in exceptional circumstances has international law recognised the binding nature of a treaty as a direct source of obligation to third parties.

---

14. *Reparations for Injuries Suffered in the Service of the United Nations*, Advisory Opinion, I.C.J. Rep. 1949, at p. 185.

However, it has long been accepted that a treaty (often termed a "disposi-tive treaty") can create a special territorial régime which goes beyond a purely contractual relationship. In the *Aaland Islands* dispute, 1920, between Sweden and Finland, a committee of jurists appointed by the Council of the League of Nations had to decide whether Finland, as successor state to Russia, was bound by a convention of 1856, made by Russia with France and Great Britain, by which Russia had agreed to the permanent demilitarisation of the islands. The Committee reported[15] that the terms of the 1856 convention created "a special international status" for the islands. It followed "that until these provisions are duly replaced by others, every state interested has the right to insist upon compliance with them" and "that any state in possession of the Islands must conform to the obligations binding upon it".

c TREATIES IN GENERAL

Whether in normal circumstances a particular treaty will give rise to obligations on third parties would seem to depend largely on political factors. The statement in Article 2 (6) of the United Nations Charter that the Organisation "shall ensure that states which are not members . . . act in accordance" with the principles of the Charter "so far as may be neces-sary for the maintenance of international peace and security" depends for its implementation on the amount of pressure that the Organisation is able and willing to exert, and the extent to which the offending state is influenced by such pressure. Article 2 (6) is principally a guide to political conduct, and even without it the obligations of the Charter relating to international peace and security would have come to be regarded as part of general international law. Whereas this provision is a justification for conscious political action by the parties to the United Nations Charter, the process whereby the provisions of a treaty may give rise to legal duties binding on third parties often involves the far less conscious pressure of a large group of states applying the terms of a treaty amongst themselves, and, in so far as the treaty lays down rules of conduct, tending to apply the same principles in their relations with non-parties. If a third state falls in with the assumption that it should also conduct itself in a like manner, there will come a time when conformity with the terms of the treaty will be expected from that state, not as a matter of courtesy, but as a matter of law. Furthermore, even if the third state has not been involved in direct dealings with parties to the treaty, the general acceptance of its terms by other non-parties will be taken as establishing these terms as general rules of international law.

The difficulties facing a state which wishes to enforce a treaty provision that creates a new rule of law against a non-signatory were considered in the recent *North Sea Continental Shelf* cases.[16] Denmark, the Netherlands and the Federal Republic of Germany agreed to the determination by the

---

15.   L.o.N. Off. J., 1920, Sp. Sup. No 3., p. 3.
16.   (1969), 8 I.L.M. 340, esp. at pp. 359 *et seq.*

International Court of the rules governing the allocation of their respective areas of continental shelf under the North Sea. One of the arguments advanced by Denmark and the Netherlands was that all three states were bound by the median line rule contained in Article 6 of the Geneva Convention on the Continental Shelf of 1958. Both Denmark and the Netherlands had ratified the Convention, but the Federal Republic, although a signatory of the Convention, had not ratified it. Their argument was that the Federal Republic had by its conduct recognised the application of the Convention either generally, or at least to the delimitation of continental shelf areas. The Court rejected this contention. Only "a very definite, very consistent course of conduct" on the part of a state could be the basis of a finding that it was bound by provisions in a treaty to which it was not a party. And even if such conduct existed, there was the additional factor in this case that the Federal Republic was a signatory of the treaty. If it wished to become bound by the provisions of the Convention, why had it not ratified? In order to show that a signatory was bound by the provision of a Convention that it had refrained from ratifying, it was necessary to establish the "existence of a situation of estoppel" in which the state concerned was precluded from denying the applicability of the provision in question.

The expression "law-making" as applied to treaties is, therefore, misleading. It is a useful shorthand expression for treaties, usually with a large number of signatories, which attempt to lay down rules of general application, as long as it is remembered that a treaty obligation will only give rise to a rule of law either in so far as it is clearly declaratory of an existing rule, or in so far as, by acceptance or acquiescence, it becomes binding on non-parties as a principle of customary international law. Perhaps the best illustration of a combination of both these factors is to be found in the Nuremburg and Tokyo judgments in the trials of the major German and Japanese war criminals. It was argued for the defence that the Hague Rules concerning the conduct of war on land did not apply to the Second World War because of the "general participation clause" contained in the 1907 Convention which made it inoperative in any conflict involving states not parties to the Convention. Both tribunals rejected this contention on the ground that the Convention, even in 1907, was based on existing principles of international law, and, certainly "by 1939, these rules laid down in the Convention were recognised by all civilised nations and were regarded as being declaratory of the laws and customs of war."[17]

CUSTOM

In the international community in which the nearest approach to legislation is the cumbersome, and often inefficient, multilateral convention,

---

17. Nuremberg Judgment, p. 83.

custom must continue to play a significant role in the development of
international law. By using the term "custom", the reference is clearly
to some habitual course of conduct. But when custom is considered as a
source of law, the problem has to be solved of how a particular course of
conduct comes to be regarded as based on a rule of law, and not simply
on convenience. In other words, at what stage does the usual become the
obligatory?

In laying down a guide for the Permanent Court to what was believed
to represent the view of earlier international tribunals, Article 38 of the
Statute suggested that the Court should apply "international custom, as
evidence of a general practice accepted as law". Though this provision is
worded rather imprecisely (it is difficult to see how the Court can apply a
custom), it does emphasise that it is only a practice "accepted as law"
which the Court is to apply. This dual requirement that there should be a
sufficiently uniform practice *and* the belief that such a practice is obligatory
has been well expressed as follows:[18]

> ". . . almost all the doctrine on the subject is limited to the statement that inter-
> national custom results from similar and repeated acts by states—repeated with the
> conscious conviction of the parties that they are acting in conformity with law.
> Thus there would be two factors in the formation of custom:
> (1) a material fact—the repetition of similar acts by states, and
> (2) a psychological element usually called the *opinio juris sive necessitatis*—the feeling
>   on the part of the states that in acting as they act they are fulfilling a legal
>   obligation."

What amounts to state practice for the purpose of creating a customary
rule of international law, and the extent to which it would also be necessary to establish the "psychological" element, will depend entirely on the
circumstances of the case. The "local remedies" rule requires that before a
state can take up a claim on the international level against a foreign state
for an injury suffered by one of its nationals while in the territory of that
foreign state, the national must first of all take advantage of all remedies
open to him under the law of the foreign state. This rule is supported by
such a wealth of practice that there would be no need for a state relying
on it to show any "acceptance" of the practice as a rule of law: as the
International Court has commented,[19] the rule has been "generally
observed in cases in which a state has adopted the cause of its national."

On the other hand, where state practice establishing the rule contended
for is lacking, or ambiguous, the psychological element will assume
greater significance. In the *Lotus* case,[20] the French ship *Lotus* had collided
on the high seas with the Turkish vessel *Boz-Kourt*. When the *Lotus*
arrived in Turkish waters, criminal proceedings were instituted in the
Turkish courts against the French officer of the watch on duty on the

---

18. Kopelman, *Custom as a Means of the Creation of International Law* (1937), 18
B.Y.B.I.L., at p. 129.
19. In the *Interhandel* case, I.C.J. Rep. 1959, at p. 27.
20. (1927), P.C.I.J. Rep., Ser. A, No. 10.

Lotus at the time of the collision. The French government intervened diplomatically on behalf of the officer, and the dispute was eventually submitted to the Permanent Court. The French argument was that there was a customary rule of international law granting exclusive criminal jurisdiction to the state the flag of which a vessel is flying. Evidence of this alleged rule was to be drawn from the fact that conflicts of jurisdiction had often occurred in civil courts, but seldom in criminal courts. As there had been few disputes over jurisdiction in criminal cases, it could be assumed that prosecutions had normally taken place in the courts of the flag state, a practice which demonstrated a tacit acceptance by states that the courts of the flag state were entitled to exclusive jurisdiction in such cases. The Court, however, refused to accept this line of reasoning:

"Even if the rarity of the judicial decisions to be found among the reported cases were sufficient to prove . . . the circumstance alleged by . . . the French government, it would merely show that states had often, in practice, abstained from instituting criminal proceedings, and not that they recognised themselves as being obliged to do so; for only if such abstention were based on their being conscious of having a duty to abstain would it be possible to speak of an international custom. The alleged fact does not allow one to infer that states have been conscious of having such a duty. . . ."[1]

In contrast, one of the issues raised in the *Corfu Channel* case[2] was whether warships had the right of innocent passage through the territorial waters of a foreign state where it could be shown that those waters formed part of an international strait. Although warships had in the past made use of territorial waters for purposes of navigation, the International Court was reluctant to rely specifically on diplomatic precedents or the generality of state practice. The Court preferred to reach its decision on the ground that freedom of transit through international straits was "generally recognised and in accordance with international custom".[3]

A. State practice

Hitherto, "state practice" has been referred to in general terms, but what precisely is meant by the "practice of states"? It would seem that the expression can cover every activity of the organs and officials of a state in an international context.

a INTERACTION OF RIVAL CLAIMS

Claims at the expense of the position of other states followed by acquiescence by those states; protests at what is regarded as the encroachment by other states on a state's own rights; compromises and mutual tolerances; all play a part in the development of new rules and the

---

1. *Ibid.*, at p. 28.
2. I.C.J. Rep. 1949, p. 4.   3. *Ibid.*, at p. 28.

modification of existing principles. In discussing the legality of hydrogen bomb tests involving the closing of large areas of the high seas to shipping, McDougal explained this process of interaction of rival claims as follows:[4]

> ". . . the international law of the sea is not a mere static body of rules but is rather a whole decision-making process. . . . It is . . . a process of continuous interaction, of continuous demand and response, in which the decision-makers of particular nation states unilaterally put forward claims of the most diverse and conflicting character to the use of the world's seas, and in which other decision-makers external to the demanding state and including both national and international officials, weigh and appraise these competing claims in terms of the interests of the world community and of the rival claimants, and ultimately accept or reject them. As such a process, it is a living, growing law, grounded in the practices . . . of . . . state officials, and changing as their demands and expectations are changed by the exigencies of new interests and technology and by other continually evolving conditions in the world arena."

b PRACTICE OF INTERNATIONAL ORGANISATIONS

State practice will also include the actions and reactions of international institutions:

i *In developing their own internal law*

The attitude of the permanent members of the Security Council of the United Nations to the application of Article 27 (3) of the Charter (requiring that decisions of the Council on non-procedural matters can only be adopted by a qualified majority "including the concurring votes of the permanent members") has led to the acceptance of a practice whereby the abstention of one of the permanent members does not prevent the Council from adopting a resolution which otherwise satisfies the provisions of Article 27.

Because the Security Council has not been able to fulfil adequately its tasks in the field of international peace and security in the manner intended by the framers of the Charter on account of disagreements among the permanent members, the General Assembly has assumed a vital role in the creation, or control, of United Nations peace-keeping operations. This power it has claimed by reference to Articles 11 and 24 of the Charter. Under Article 11, the Assembly may "discuss any questions relating to the maintenance of international peace and security . . . and may make recommendations with regard to any such questions. . . ." Article 24 confers on the Security Council "primary responsibility for the maintenance of international peace and security", but by using the expression "primary responsibility" the Charter clearly implied that a secondary, or residual, responsibility rested with the Assembly. The setting up of the United Nations Emergency Force by the Assembly in 1956 to superintend the withdrawal of foreign troops from Egypt was a development quite unforeseen in 1945 when the Charter was created, and

---

4. (1955) 49 A.J.I.L., at pp. 356–357.

illustrates clearly how the constitution of an international institution may be altered in practice, though not formally amended, to meet the exigencies of new situations.

ii *In developing the law governing the relations between the organisations themselves and states*

In 1949, the advisory opinion of the International Court in the *Reparations* case affirmed the international personality of the United Nations, and established its right to present claims on the international plane to enforce obligations owed by states to the Organisation. It follows that if the United Nations can bring claims against states, it can also be subject to claims presented by states, and there is a wealth of practice concerning the adjustment of claims arising out of damage to private property particularly in the course of peace-keeping operations.

One of the attributes of international personality is the capacity to enter into treaty arrangements with other members of the international community. Treaties to which the United Nations, or the specialised agencies, are parties, provide a wealth of practice in a variety of fields. Technical assistance agreements usually provide for the immunity from judicial process of United Nations officials in the territory of the state where they are employed. The creation of peace-keeping forces has necessitated the negotiation of agreements between the United Nations and states providing troops, those providing services, and with the state of the territory on which the force is to operate. And, usually, such agreements are the subject of debate and analysis in the General Assembly, which provide further evidence of the attitudes of states towards their relations with the United Nations. As the International Law Commission commented in 1950, "records of the cumulative practice of international organisations may be regarded as evidence of customary international law with reference to states' relations to the organisations."[5]

iii *By developing or modifying general rules of international law*

Many of the contemporary illustrations concerning the concept of statehood have arisen out of applications for membership in the United Nations which, according to Article 4 (1) of the Charter, is open to states only. Objections have been raised that an applicant did not have a defined territory (as happened in the case of Israel) or had not attained a sufficient degree of independence (which was the argument raised in the cases of South Korea and South Vietnam).

In the field of treaty law, the International Court in the *Reservations* case[6] held that there was no rule of customary international law that a reservation prevented a ratification of a multilateral treaty from being effective against other parties even if those other states did not expressly consent to the reservation. The Court was influenced in reaching this

---

5. Y.B.I.L.C., Vol. II, p. 372.   6. I.C.J. Rep. 1951, p. 15.

conclusion by what it believed to be the absence of the necessary *opinio juris* as demonstrated by the "profound divergence of views" expressed in the course of a debate on reservations to multilateral treaties that had taken place in the Legal Committee of the General Assembly.

c THE LAWS OF INDIVIDUAL STATES AS STATE PRACTICE

In some situations, it may be necessary to investigate the decisions of municipal courts, or the acts of national legislatures, in order to ascertain the existence of a particular rule of international law. It will be recalled that in the *Lotus* case, the French government attempted to rely on the absence of disputes relating to criminal jurisdiction as a reason for concluding that in criminal cases jurisdiction over matters occurring on the high seas belonged exclusively to the flag state. Although the Permanent Court rejected the conclusion advocated by the French government, the Court made no attempt to deny the relevance of municipal decisions to questions of jurisdiction under international law.

The legislative acts of various states played a significant evidentiary role in the *Scotia*,[7] a decision of the United States Supreme Court. The *Scotia*, a British steamer, had been in collision with the American sailing ship, *Berkshire*, which had sunk. As the collision had occurred on the high seas, the Court could not apply the law of the United States, nor indeed the laws of any other state: the law of the place where the accident occurred was international maritime law. The defendants, the owners of the *Scotia*, contended that their crew had mistaken the *Berkshire* for a steamer because it had been carrying the wrong navigational lights according to both English and American law, and by the laws of most other maritime states. In holding that the defendants were not liable for the loss of the *Berkshire*, the Supreme Court accepted that the enforcement of a particular system of warning lights by "nearly all the commercial nations of the world" was sufficient to make such regulations "in part at least . . . the laws of the sea". Although this decision is by a municipal, and not an international tribunal, it nevertheless provides a useful illustration of the approach adopted by a court to the problem of ascertaining the relevant rule of international law from one aspect of state practice, the activities of the legislative organs of various states.

The evidence of state practice may, therefore, cover a wide range of activities. Indeed, the range is so wide that it might prove difficult in a particular case to establish a sufficient degree of consistency in the practice of states in favour of the rule of international law alleged to exist. In the *Asylum* case,[8] for example, Haya de la Torre, a Peruvian national, was due to appear on a charge of "military rebellion", but instead sought sanctuary in the Colombian Embassy in Peru. By a Convention on Political Asylum between the two states, a political fugitive legitimately granted the right of asylum in the Embassy of the other state was entitled to a safe-conduct to enable him to leave the country. The Peruvian government refused to

---

7. 81 U.S. 170 (1872).   8. I.C.J. Rep. 1950, p. 266.

accept the Colombian contention that it was for the state granting asylum to make a decision binding on the territorial state as to the nature of the offence for which the fugitive was to be charged. The International Court held that Colombia had failed to produce any clear evidence to support its argument:

> "The facts brought to the knowledge of the Court disclose so much uncertainty and contradiction, so much fluctuation and discrepancy in the exercise of diplomatic asylum and in the official views expressed on various occasions, there has been so much inconsistency in the rapid succession of conventions on asylum, ratified by some states and rejected by others, and the practice has been so much influenced by considerations of political expediency in the various cases, that it is not possible to discern in all this any constant and uniform usage, accepted as law, with regard to the alleged rule of unilateral and definitive qualification of the offence."[9]

Providing there is consistency, the length of time over which a particular practice has been adhered to will be a relevant, though seldom a vital factor. Obviously, a long-established usage will more readily be accepted by a tribunal as giving rise to a rule of law, but the principle of national sovereignty over airspace (despite previous writings based on the Roman Law precept that "the sea, like the air, is free to all men") was rapidly accepted. The first cross-Channel flight took place in 1909. Between 1906 and 1913, the Institute of International Law retained the freedom of air navigation as the basis of its draft recommendations to governments for the future development of air law. But, already, the United Kingdom had come out in favour of national sovereignty over airspace, and, by the Aerial Navigation Act of 1913, a Secretary of State was empowered to prohibit the navigation of aircraft over any areas he might designate, including "the whole or any part of the coastline of the United Kingdom and the territorial waters adjacent thereto." Finally, the experiences of the First World War, in which aircraft assumed an important role as an offensive weapon, persuaded all governments of the need to claim exclusive jurisdiction over its airspace. Article 1 of the Convention of Aerial Navigation signed at Paris in 1919 was probably already declaratory of existing law when it asserted "that every Power has complete and exclusive sovereignty over the air space above its territory."

B. Must be acceptance of the practice as law

The discussion of the *Lotus* case demonstrated that the psychological element—the feeling on the part of states that in acting as they had acted they had been fulfilling a legal obligation—though essential to the creation of a new rule of international law, will only become crucial in establishing the existence of a particular rule when the practice relied upon does not itself point unequivocally to the existence of such a rule.

---

9. *Ibid.*, at p. 277.

It will be recalled that in the *Lotus* case, even if states had refrained from exercising jurisdiction over crimes committed on the high seas in deference to the flag state, the French government was unable to prove that states had acted in this manner from a sense of legal obligation.

In order for a customary rule to develop, it must at some stage be possible to imply from the conduct of a group of states that between them it is regarded as a matter of legal duty that they should act in a certain way. Such a rule will only attain the position of a general rule of international law if a sufficient number of states accept it as binding on them, and if the rest of the international community fail to register an effective protest to the extension of the rule to the conduct of relations in which they are involved. It is because of this emphasis on the acceptance of, or acquiescence in, a developing rule that international law retains its theoretically consensual foundation. As Fitzmaurice has commented:[10]

> "Where a general rule of customary international law is built up by the common practice of states, although it may be a little unnecessary to have recourse to the notion of agreement (and a little difficult to detect it in what is often the unco-ordinated, independent, if similar, action of states), it is probably true to say that consent is latent in the mutual tolerations that allow the practice to be built up at all; and actually patent in the eventual acceptance (even if tacit) of the practice as constituting a binding rule of law."

But how far is the proposition that international law is based on the consent of states a useful guide to understanding the nature of international law and the way in which its rules develop? It must be realised, of course, that the consensual theory should not be taken to its ultimate logical conclusion. For example, the fact that the practice relied upon to prove the existence of a customary rule is limited to a group of states does not necessarily prevent the development of a rule of universal application. The actions of the chief maritime powers could clearly create a universal principle of the law of the sea, and it would not be open to a state, hitherto without a coast, if it acquired access to the sea and built up a shipping fleet, to refuse to recognise the principle because it had developed without that state's consent. In such a situation, it would be difficult to imply the acceptance of the rule by the inland state, and equally difficult to establish acquiescence on its part. The rule is part of universal international law because it would be totally destructive of any principle of obligation to allow a state to decide that it was not bound by an existing rule of international law.

As long as this limitation on its scope is kept in mind, the consensual theory does provide an explanation of the fact that, in certain circumstances, rules of international law can exist which are not binding on all states, either because the practice on which they are based is limited to a small group of states, or because a fairly uniform practice has been

---

10. *The Law and Procedure of the International Court of Justice, 1951–4: General Principles and Sources of Law* (1953), 30 B.Y.B.I.L., at p. 68.

expressly dissented from by a particular state. In the *Asylum* case, the International Court recognised that Colombia could succeed in its claim by showing that a particular rule relating to diplomatic asylum was binding on Peru, even though such a rule was nowhere recognised outside Latin-America. In the words of the Court:

"The Colombian government has finally invoked 'American international law in general' . . . it has relied on an alleged regional or local custom peculiar to Latin-American states. The party which relies on a custom of this kind must prove that this custom is established in such a manner that it has become binding on the other party. The Colombian government must prove that the rule invoked by it is in accordance with a constant and uniform usage practised by the states in question, and that this usage is the expression of a right appertaining to the state granting asylum and a duty incumbent on the territorial state. This follows from Article 38 of the Statute of the Court, which refers to international custom 'as evidence of a general practice accepted as law'."[11]

Then, having commented on the uncertainties and contradictions in the practice of the states concerned, the judgment continued:

"The Court cannot therefore find that the Colombian government has proved the existence of such a custom. But even if it could be supposed that such a custom existed between certain Latin-American states only, it could not be invoked against Peru which, far from having by its attitude adhered to it, has, on the contrary, repudiated it by refraining from ratifying the Montevideo Conventions of 1933 and 1939, which were the first to include a rule concerning the qualification of the offence in matters of diplomatic asylum."[12]

This last statement by the Court explicitly recognises that a state will not be bound by a rule of international law if it has positively asserted its refusal to follow the practice from which the rule has developed. Indeed, as the development of a new customary rule depends upon the actual acceptance of a practice, or acquiescence in that practice, by states, it would seem logical that, during the time a rule is evolving, it is open to a state or group of states to disassociate itself from the rule. In submitting the *Fisheries* case to the International Court, the United Kingdom acknowledged the Norwegian right to rely on a four-mile limit to territorial waters as the Scandinavian countries had traditionally rejected the three-mile limit in favour of a limit of four miles. However, in the *Fisheries* case itself[13] is to be found even stronger authority for the proposition that a state can expressly dissent from a developing rule of international law. It was argued on behalf of the United Kingdom that the ten-mile rule (i.e. that the base-line from which territorial waters were to be measured could be drawn across the neck, or otherwise the widest part, of a bay which did not exceed ten miles in width) was an established principle of customary international law. In addition to rejecting this contention, the Court went on to state that even if it had acquired the

---

11. I.C.J. Rep. 1950, at pp. 276–277.   12. *Ibid.*, at pp. 277–278.
13. I.C.J. Rep. 1951, p. 116.

authority of a general rule of international law it "would appear to be inapplicable as against Norway inasmuch as she had always opposed any attempt to apply it to the Norwegian coast."[14]

C. The application of customary international law to new states

One of the major problems of contemporary international law concerns its application as a system to newly independent states. The fact that international law developed largely among the states of Western Europe, and reflects their economic and social interests, has led the states of Africa and Asia to raise the argument that, as the rules of international law developed without their consent, they are free to consider as binding only those rules which reflect their own notions of what is politically just and desirable in the circumstances of the second half of the twentieth century. However, even if the criticism that traditional doctrines of international law give too much weight to what are essentially the interests of the developed communities of Western Europe and North America is valid, it does not follow that a new state of Africa or Asia has the right to choose which rules of international law it will regard as binding.

The traditional positivist approach, which regarded consent in some form as essential to the existence of rules of international law, met the difficulty of ascribing consent to a new state, that could have taken no part in the creation of international law, with the theory that the recognition of a new state was conditional on that state accepting the rules of the international community. But this is to introduce a fiction to support the consent of states as the explanation of the binding nature of international law. It is the basis of the international legal order that international law is binding on all states. The point has already been made that a state cannot declare itself unaffected by a particular rule simply because it did not take part in the rule's creation, the example being given of a land-locked state, subsequently acquiring access to the sea and a navy, not having the right to reject rules of international maritime law. The same principle applies equally to a new state which is bound by existing customary international law irrespective of any manifestation of consent.

It is true that the universal nature of international law is subject to certain exceptions where international law has itself recognised the realities of state practice, i.e. that a particular rule may only apply to the relations of a small group of states, or that a particular rule has never become binding on an individual state because that state has always dissented from it. Hitherto, no exception has been recognised in favour of new states for historically new states entered the primarily European community of nations almost as a favour. Thus, the new states which

---

14. I.C.J. Rep. 1951, p. 131.

came into existence in 1919, mostly as a result of the break up of the Austro-Hungarian Empire, "became subject to international law as a matter of course, without their consent being either asked or given".[15] However, the political climate of today is very different from that of 1919. The favour of community membership is now regarded more as a right. The increasing tendency to regard certain traditional notions of international law, with their basic assumptions of a certain economic and property order, as being no longer applicable to the problems of Africa and Asia may well oblige the more highly developed states, particularly the former colonial powers, to reconsider their attitudes towards such matters as state succession and state responsibility. The developing countries feel keenly their position as debtors of more fortunate, developed, states, and this sensitiveness will only give rise to resentment if their territory is subject to a large number of concessions in favour of foreign businesses, or to agreements allowing the use of military bases to the former colonial power. In such circumstances, seizure of foreign property is seen more as an essential assertion of independence than as a breach of international law, and if such an act is contrary to international law, then it is international law which must be altered to meet the needs of the under-privileged members of the international community.

If a dispute arises between two newly independent states, it may be possible for them to argue that the relevant rules of traditional international law have been modified by their own attitude and by the practice of other new states. For example, there was a strong feeling among the new states of Africa that boundaries created by the European colonial powers in disregard of geographical and ethnical divisions could not be imposed on them by the normal rules of state succession. The immediate problem was solved temporarily by an agreement by the Conference of African States at Addis Ababa in 1963 that the existing boundaries should be retained, but that individual states should negotiate with their neighbours for the revision of their boundaries. Should such negotiations prove abortive, it would hardly be likely that one of the states involved could rely on the traditional principles of state succession to enforce the existing boundary against its neighbour.

Should the dispute arise between a new state and a European state which has for long been a member of the international community, the position is less easily reconciled. As no exception to the rule that international law is binding on all states has yet been recognised in favour of new states, the traditional rules of international law are clearly applicable. Yet, and this is a political rather than a legal factor, it will only be possible to continue to regard international law as a unifying factor in the world community if it is sufficiently flexible to meet the reasonable demands of its newer subjects. The working of the resources of a new state by foreign interests under concessions granted by the former sovereign may be regarded as exploitation. But the principles of state

---

15. Brierly, *Basis of Obligation in International Law*, p. 12.

succession lack the refinement to distinguish between what is a reasonable
burden for a new state to bear and what is unreasonable. To an under-
developed state, the taking over of all natural resources and means of
production may seem essential in the interests of the future economic
well-being of the country. The traditional view of international law is that
the expropriation of foreign assets must be accompanied by adequate
compensation. If a new state is prepared to expropriate the property of
its own nationals without compensation in the national interest, it will
view with disfavour any rule of international law which requires that
compensation be paid to aliens in the same situation. The arguments on
either side are clear enough: it is for the international community to work
out in practice or by agreement how to reconcile these conflicting
interests for the prospects of international law. A failure to do so—the
too rigid attempt to apply traditional rules to new situations, or the
refusal on the part of new states to compromise their often extreme
claims to exemption from many of the rules of international law—could
well lead to a complete breakdown of law as a part of international
relations.

GENERAL PRINCIPLES OF LAW RECOGNISED BY CIVILISED NATIONS

This third heading for the sources of international law is taken directly
from Article 38 of the Statute of both the former Permanent Court and
the present International Court. If there is no treaty relevant to the dispute, or if there is no rule of customary international law that can be
applied, the Court is directed to apply these general principles of law.
As far as treaties and custom were concerned, the Statute was designed to
guide the Court in the normal procedures of international adjudication.
In 1920, the inclusion of "general principles" was regarded by many as an
innovation, but the better view would seem to be that it was only giving
expression to a practice which had already become accepted by earlier
arbitral tribunals.

The need to rely upon something akin to "general principles" (whatever terminology is used) can best be explained in answering the question
of what action an international tribunal should take if there is no treaty
applicable to the issue presented to it, and there is no generality of state
practice giving rise to a customary rule of law. Should there be no precedent directly relevant to a case before a municipal court, the judge would
be expected to rely upon certain basic legal notions of justice and equity
in order to deduce a new rule for application to the novel situation: he
could not simply refuse to give judgment on the ground that there was
no law available. An international judicial body is similarly under a duty
to adjudicate, a proposition affirmed by the Administrative Tribunal of
the I.L.O. which stated that one of the "fundamental tenets of all legal
systems is that no Court may refrain from giving judgment on the

ground that the law is silent or obscure."[16] As the international judge may therefore be called upon to create a rule of law to fit the circumstances of the case before the court with fewer and less clearly defined existing rules at his disposal than are normally available to the municipal judge, the likelihood is that he too will resort to general notions of justice and equity in deducing the new rule or in refining an existing rule. In either case, the new rule or the modified rule will often be referred to as a general rule of international law, or as a customary rule, and the traditional fiction will be preserved that the judge is in no way creating law, but simply applying existing international law. The question of whether judicial decisions can correctly be considered as sources of international law in their own right will be dealt with in a subsequent section, but for the moment the important issue is whether or not the process of judicial adaptation and development of the law has any relevance to the "general principles" under discussion.

The difficulty in evaluating the role of these "general principles" appears to be that Article 38 of the Statute does not make clear if it is referring to general principles of international law which are recognised by civilised nations, or to general principles of law in the most general sense, including principles of private law which have their counterpart in most developed legal systems. The reason for the ambiguity is not hard to discover. In its infancy, international law barely touched upon a number of important aspects of inter-state relations. To take the obvious illustration of territorial claims, the practice of states had accepted that territory could be acquired from another state by annexation or by cession, but some method was required for the acquisition of areas of the world unoccupied by "civilised" peoples. The writers of the seventeenth and eighteenth centuries, trained exclusively in the Roman law tradition, turned therefore to the rules of Roman private law—to *occupatio*, the acquisition of ownership by the taking of physical possession of a thing belonging to no one (a *res nullius*), and to *praescriptio*, the acquisition of rights over a thing by long possession which would in time supersede all previous rights in that thing. Although this example of borrowing from private law was blatant, two directly opposed views of the nature of international law helped create the fiction that international law was not dependent on municipal law for its doctrines. To the writer of the naturalist school, the rules of international law, like the rules of municipal law, rested ultimately on principles of natural law. If there appeared to be a gap in the rules of international law, or of municipal law for that matter, recourse could always be had to general principles of law, i.e. to natural law. On the other hand, as to a positivist international law depended entirely on the consent of states,

---

16. The controversy between Lauterpacht (whose views are expressed in *The Function of Law in the International Community*, Part II; and in *Symbolae Verzijl*, pp. 196–221) and Stone (*Legal Controls of International Conflict*, pp. 153–164; (1959), 35 B.Y.B.I.L., pp. 124–161) is too detailed for analysis here. It is believed that the text represents the attitude that an international tribunal would adopt, though it does not answer the question of whether a tribunal *should* decline to exercise jurisdiction rather than exercise a legislative function.

and general principles of natural law, or of municipal law could not be considered as relevant to questions of international law without some manifestation of consent on the part of states, the absence of a treaty rule or some customary rule that could be ascribed to a particular course of state conduct, would be glossed over by reference to general principles of international law which had in some undefined way been acknowledged by states as basic notions of the international legal order.

Any analysis of the use made by international tribunals of general principles of law is likely to be hampered by the fact that these tribunals, and particularly the Permanent Court and the International Court, have been reluctant to cast any light on the processes whereby they reach the conclusion that a particular rule is a rule of international law. Thus, on a number of occasions, the Permanent Court used "general principles" in a context which could only refer to principles of international law, but whether these references were to "general principles" within the meaning of Article 38 of the Statute, or to general principles of customary international law, was not explained. In the *Chorzow Factory* case,[17] which concerned a claim by Germany against Poland for the seizure of two companies in Upper Silesia contrary to Poland's international obligations, the Court described the rule that a breach of an engagement involved a duty to make reparation as "a principle of international law, and even a general conception of law".[18] And in the *Eastern Carelia* case,[19] in which the Court was asked for an advisory opinion on whether the Council of the League of Nations could adjudicate in a dispute involving a non-member of the League which refused to recognise the Council's competence in the matter, the Court referred to the "independence of states" as a "fundamental principle of international law", and deduced from this principle that no state could "without its consent, be compelled to submit its disputes . . . to mediation or to arbitration, or to any other kind of pacific settlement".[20] Similarly, the International Court held Albania liable to the United Kingdom for failure to notify British ships of the presence of mines in the Corfu Channel, by basing the obligation to inform all shipping of the presence of the minefield "on certain general and well-recognised principles, namely: elementary considerations of humanity, even more exacting in peace than in war; the principle of the freedom of maritime communication; and every state's obligation not to allow knowingly its territory to be used for acts contrary to the rights of other states."[1]

Recourse to municipal law analogies on the other hand has always been a matter of controversy for adherents of the positivist view that international law depends on the consent of states. But it is obvious that certain principles of municipal law were applied originally to deal with problems arising in the international sphere because they supplied the

---

17. (1928), P.C.I.J. Rep., Ser. A, No. 17.   18. *Ibid.*, at p. 29.
19. (1923), P.C.I.J. Rep., Ser. B, No. 5.   20. *Ibid.*, at p. 27.
1. *Corfu Channel* case, I.C.J. Rep. 1949, at p. 22.

most satisfactory answers. For example, when questions of treaty interpretation first arose, governments and their advisers turned to principles of construction well known to private law. It is a matter of little practical importance whether the rule of construction that the words of a document should be given their normal meaning unless to do so would give rise to ambiguity or manifest absurdity, is a general principle of law recognised by civilised nations or whether it only became a rule of international law through its adoption in the practice of states.

It seems a simple enough proposition that an international tribunal should, if necessary, be able to apply principles of municipal law which have achieved general acceptance to the settlement of an international dispute. All that the tribunal has to do is to look at the major legal systems of the world and rely upon those rules which they have in common. As the United States Military Tribunal said in the course of its judgment in a war crimes trial:[2]

> "The tendency has been to apply the term 'customs and practices accepted by civilised nations generally', as it is used in international law, to the laws of war only. But the principle has no such restricted meaning. It applies as well to fundamental principles of justice which have been accepted and adopted by civilised nations generally. In determining whether such a fundamental rule of justice is entitled to be declared a principle of international law, an examination of the municipal laws of states in the family of nations will reveal the answer. If it is found to have been accepted generally as a fundamental rule of justice by most nations in their municipal law, its declaration as a rule of international law would seem to be fully justified."

Although major differences exist between municipal systems in many areas of private law, i.e. rules governing domestic relations, or private property, international tribunals, and particularly the International Court itself, have frequently been able to make use of general principles of a procedural nature. Thus, it has been recognised that "any body possessing jurisdictional powers has the right in the first place to determine the extent of its jurisdiction".[3] Furthermore, once a decision has been reached, it becomes binding on the parties in relation to the issue submitted to the tribunal. In the course of its opinion in the *Administrative Tribunal* case,[4] the International Court referred to the "well-established and generally recognised principle of law" that "a judgment rendered by a judicial body is *res judicata* and has binding force between the parties to the dispute." In the *Northern Cameroons* case,[5] an application was made by the government of Cameroons against the United Kingdom seeking what amounted to a declaration that the latter had failed to carry out its obligations under the Trusteeship Agreement under which it had formerly administered the territory of the Cameroons. The International Court was clearly applying a general principle inherent in the judicial function in refusing to exercise its jurisdiction over a dispute the substance of which had disappeared with the independence of the Cameroons and the

---

2. *In Re List* (1948), 8 W.C.R., at p. 34; 15 A.D., at p. 633.
3. *Interpretation of the Greco-Turkish Agreement* (1928), P.C.I.J. Rep., Ser. B, No. 16, at p. 20.　　4. I.C.J. Rep. 1954, at p. 53.　　5. I.C.J. Rep. 1963, p. 15.

termination of the Trusteeship Agreement. In the Court's own words:[6]

> "The function of the Court is to state the law, but it may pronounce judgment only in connection with concrete cases where there exists at the time of the adjudication an actual controversy involving a conflict of legal interests between the parties. The Court's judgment must have some practical consequence in the sense that it can affect existing legal rights or obligations of the parties, thus removing uncertainty from their legal relations. No judgment on the merits in this case could satisfy these essentials of the judicial function."

Turning to what might be termed the substantive rules of international law, one of the more fruitful principles that has been adopted in international adjudications is that of estoppel, or preclusion as it is usually called in Roman law systems. The extent of its field of application is as yet uncertain, and the most that can be attempted here is a general description together with a few illustrations of the use made of it in practice.

Estoppel is based upon the principle that a state which has "slept upon its rights" will not be allowed subsequently to revive them. A state would be precluded from contesting a "state of affairs" in which it has acquiesced.

It has often been applied in circumstances where there is a dispute between the claimant and the defendant states as to the nationality of the injured individual. In the *Canevaro* case,[7] for example, the arbitration tribunal held that, as one of the Canevaro brothers, all of whom were nationals of both Peru and Italy, had "on several occasions acted as a Peruvian citizen, both by running as a candidate for the Senate, where none are admitted except Peruvian citizens . . . and, particularly, by accepting the office of Consul-General for the Netherlands", he was precluded, and so therefore was the Italian government, from denying his Peruvian nationality in a claim presented on his behalf by Italy against Peru. Conversely, on a number of occasions the principle of estoppel has been invoked to prevent a defendant state from setting up the fact that an injured individual was one of its own nationals when the individual's property has been seized under legislation applicable only to foreigners.

Estoppel has also been frequently adapted to meet problems of territorial sovereignty. In the *Eastern Greenland* case, the Permanent Court held that, in accepting a number of treaties which contained references to Danish sovereignty over the disputed territory, Norway had "debarred herself from contesting Danish sovereignty".[8] The recent *Temple* case[9] provides a series of illustrations of how estoppel can be applied in practice. The disputed frontier between Cambodia, formerly part of French Indo-China, and Thailand, depended upon the report of a frontier commission, but its survey was inconclusive on the sovereignty of the area round the Temple of Preah Vihear. Cambodia successfully relied upon a map of 1907 which the predecessor French authorities had produced at the

6. I.C.J. Rep. 1963, at pp. 33–34.   7. U.N.R.I.A.A., Vol. XI, p. 397.
8. (1933), P.C.I.J. Rep., Ser. A/B, No. 53, at p. 69.   9. I.C.J. Rep. 1962, p. 6.

request of the Siamese Government. The map clearly showed the Temple area as part of French Indo-China, but the Siamese, far from protesting at the error, thanked the French and requested a further fifteen copies. Furthermore, in 1930, a Siamese Prince paid a state visit to the disputed area and was officially received there by the French Resident at a ceremony at which the French flag was flown. Together, these two events were, in the opinion of the international Court, conclusive. "Even if there was any doubt as to Siam's acceptance of the map in 1908, and hence of the frontier indicated thereon, the Court would consider, in the light of the subsequent course of events, that Thailand is now precluded by her conduct from asserting that she did not accept it."[10]

The principle of estoppel is an application of the general duty incumbent upon states to act in good faith, or, as Judge Hudson considered it in his Separate Opinion in the *Diversion of Water from the Meuse* case, the duty to pay regard to the principles of equity which "have long been considered to constitute a part of international law and as such . . . have often been applied by international tribunals".[11] Thus, in the arbitration[12] arising out of the notorious *Naulilah* incident, one of the precedents Judge Hudson would certainly have had in mind, Portugal claimed damages for the invasion by German forces of Portuguese territories in Africa under two heads: (a) the direct damage caused, i.e. the destruction of property and the killing and wounding of soldiers and civilians, and (b) the indirect damage resulting from tribal warfare which flared up as soon as Portuguese troops withdrew in the face of the German attack. The tribunal held that it would not be equitable to restrict the damages awarded to the direct consequences of the German action when many of the results of the attack were clearly foreseeable, and might even have been desired.

D. Decisions of international tribunals

Although there are thus numerous examples of international tribunals making use of principles which have a place in most legal systems, it is less certain how far these "general principles" may in themselves be regarded as international law, or whether they are more what might be termed "sources of inspiration" from which an international tribunal might formulate rules of international law. Attention has already been drawn to the fiction that judges do not make law but are only applying existing principles to novel situations. However, if an international tribunal is unable to discover an existing treaty or customary rule relevant to the dispute, in theory at least the conclusion seems inescapable that

---

10. *Ibid.*, at p. 32. In the *Continental Shelf* cases, the International Court suggested that for an estoppel to arise the party relying upon a representation or course of conduct must be able to show that, as a consequence, it has detrimentally changed its position (8 I.L.M. 340, at p. 360, para. 30). Although this detriment requirement has support in juristic writings, it is inconsistent with some of the authorities cited in the text. Estoppel in international law probably has more in common with recognition than it has with municipal law notions of estoppel based upon detriment.

11. (1937) P.C.I.J. Rep., Ser. A/B, No. 70, at p. 76.

12. (1927-8) 4 A.D. Case No. 179, U.N.R.I.A.A., Vol. II, p. 1013.

the rule which the tribunal adopts, even if it is stated in the form of an existing principle, is a new rule of international law. But is this new rule a rule of customary law, or is it possible to regard the tribunal's decision itself as a source of international law?

The fiction that tribunals can only apply existing rules is preserved in the wording of Article 38 of the Statute of the International Court which goes on to state that, in addition to conventions, custom and general principles, the Court can apply *inter alia* judicial decisions as "subsidiary means for the determination of rules of law". The explanation of the use of the expression "subsidiary means" would seem to be that in the normal conduct of international relations each state must decide for itself the relevant rules and attempt to justify them in its contacts with other members of the international community. As, by this process, state practice is responsible for the creation of new rules and the clarification of existing rules of international law, state practice is also the primary means for the determination of those rules. Only infrequently will tribunals be called upon to arbitrate on inter-state disputes, so that judicial decisions are "subsidiary means" of determining rules of law. When an international court is called upon to decide a particular legal issue, it will largely be concerned with applying directly or by analogy existing rules. The further the process of analogy is taken, however, the more creative is the court's role, and when there is no sufficiency of state practice and therefore no pre-existing rule, the decision reached by the court will serve as a direct source of international law for the future: to consider the new rule as the "determination" of a customary rule would be totally unrealistic.

There is an additional difficulty that must be faced before it is possible to accept unreservedly the proposition that decisions of international tribunals are sources of international law. According to Article 59 of the Statute of the International Court, the Court's decisions have no binding force except between the parties and in respect of the particular case. Although in theory there is this barrier to the adoption of any general doctrine of precedent, in practice it is difficult to refrain from treating decisions of the International Court as of the highest authority. One has only to consult the pleadings presented by states parties to cases before the Court to realise how frequently reference is made to the decisions of various international tribunals. The International Court refused to exercise jurisdiction in the *Nottebohm* case,[13] brought by Liechtenstein against Guatemala, because it was not prepared to hold that Liechtenstein had the right under international law to regard Nottebohm as a Liechtenstein national. It had been part of the Liechtenstein argument that Guatemala, as a belligerent in the Second World War, had been in breach of its duties towards Nottebohm, a national of a neutral state. The section in the Liechtenstein pleadings dealing with the obligations of a belligerent with regard to the treatment of the person and property of

---

13. I.C.J. Rep. 1955, p. 4.

nationals of a neutral state was replete with illustrations from international jurisprudence. Even more striking were the pleadings of Israel in the *Aerial Incident* case,[14] which arose out of the shooting down of an Israeli passenger aircraft by Bulgarian fighters. Although the Court held that Bulgaria was not subject to its jurisdiction, so that it was not able to pass upon the merits of the dispute, the substantive rules upon which Israel's case depended were supported in the Israeli pleadings by a wealth of authority drawn particularly from previous decisions of the International Court itself.

Not only has the Court found itself obliged to refer to its own previous decisions, it has also on occasions had to resort to "distinguishing" them from the case actually being heard. It will be recalled that in the *Eastern Carelia* case,[15] the Permanent Court declined to give an advisory opinion because of the refusal of Russia, one of the parties to the dispute, to have any part in the proceedings: the Court could not depart from the fundamental principle that a state could not, without its consent, be forced to submit its disputes to arbitration or judicial settlement. The *Peace Treaties* case[16] of 1950 concerned a request for an advisory opinion in a dispute over whether the arbitral tribunals under the Peace Treaties with Bulgaria, Hungary and Roumania had been properly constituted within the terms of those Treaties. These tribunals were intended to look into breaches of certain human rights provisions of the Treaties. The reason for attempting to constitute the tribunals, and this was the underlying issue of the dispute, was that allegations had been made that breaches of the provisions had occurred in all three states. The three states refused to co-operate in constituting the arbitral tribunals, nor would they take any part in the proceedings before the International Court beyond presenting the argument that the Court should not depart from the ruling of the Permanent Court in the *Eastern Carelia* case: as the three states had not consented to the Court's jurisdiction, it should decline to give an advisory opinion. The Court rejected this objection on the ground that the *Eastern Carelia* principle related to the investigation of the merits of a dispute, whereas the matter presented to the Court in connection with the Peace Treaties related solely to the procedure for the settlement and not to the substance of the dispute between the parties.

The great reliance upon pronouncements of the Court and of other international tribunals can be explained on the ground, not that they are themselves sources of international law, but that they are the best evidence available of the existence of the rules of international law referred to in the course of the decision. And too much should not be read into reference to, for example, the "Eastern Carelia principle". The power to give an advisory opinion laid down in the Court's statute was stated sufficiently widely to have enabled the Court in the circumstances of the *Eastern Carelia* case to have given an opinion, and undoubtedly its decision to

---

14. I.C.J. Rep. 1959, p. 127.   15. (1923) P.C.I.J. Rep., Ser. B, No. 5.
16. I.C.J. Rep., 1950, p. 65.

decline to exercise its jurisdiction created a precedent against which to measure future requests involving the advisory procedures of the Court, but, as a general proposition, the consensual basis of the jurisdiction of any international tribunal had been a basic tenet of international litigation from its inception.

However, there have undoubtedly been situations in which the Court's decision has been so strikingly different from what was considered to have been existing customary law that the conclusion seems inescapable that the decision may be regarded as a source of international law in its own right. Probably the best known illustration of "law-making" by the International Court was its decision in the *Fisheries* case.[17] Norway had promulgated a series of decrees claiming as the base line of Norwegian territorial waters the general line of the *skaegaard* or rock rampart which stretches along Norway's north-western coast, often at considerable distances from the mainland. The effect of the decrees, the legality of which had been contested by the United Kingdom, was to enclose large areas of what the United Kingdom contended were high seas as part of Norwegian national waters, and therefore subject to exclusive Norwegian jurisdiction, to the grave detriment of British fishing interests. The refusal of the International Court to hold that the method adopted by Norway of drawing these base lines was contrary to international law in effect created a new rule of international law for the delimitation of maritime frontiers in parts of the world where unusual geographical and economic factors are present. The implications of the Court's decision have been analysed by Fitzmaurice as follows:[18]

> "Theoretically the United Kingdom is only bound by this decision to accept the *Norwegian* base-line system, as approved by the Court. It is not (formally) bound to accept a similar system instituted by any other country. Furthermore, no country *other than* the United Kingdom is (formally) bound to accept even the Norwegian delimitation. In practice, it is obvious that neither the United Kingdom nor any other country could now successfully contest the general principle of straight base-lines. . . ."

Another excellent example of law-making by the International Court is to be found in the field of international organisations. In the *Reparations* case,[19] the Court was asked whether the United Nations had the right to present a claim on the international plane against a state for injuries suffered by United Nations' officials in the performance of their duties. The Court held that, under the provisions of the Charter, the Organisation had been granted extensive powers of acting on the international plane; but in order to carry out its various functions effectively its officials must feel that they were in no way dependent for protection on the state of which they were nationals. To answer this need, it was

---

17. I.C.J. Rep. 1951, p. 116. For a wider discussion of the judicial process in the International Court, see Carlsten-Smith, *The Relation Between Proceedings and Premises.*
18. *Symbolae Verzijl*, p. 170.   19. I.C.J. Rep. 1949, p. 174.

therefore necessary that the Organisation should be able to offer its personnel adequate protection in the performance of their duties. The power to bring claims under international law against any state responsible for an injury to an individual was an essential part of that protection, and could therefore be implied from the express functions entrusted to the Organisation under the Charter. The Court's decision that such a power could be implied was clearly an extension of the rights of the Organisation as laid down in the Charter, and, as such, can only be regarded as creating a new principle of international law.

The *Fisheries* case and the *Reparations* case are exceptional in international jurisprudence in that they are impossible to disguise as applications of preexisting rules of international law. It is perhaps because of the status of the International Court, and the eminence of the jurists who form the judicial bench, that the Court while stating its adherence to the convention that its duty is to apply, and not create, the law has nevertheless not always felt bound by it. It is true that the Court in the recent *South-West Africa* case[20] expressed the view that it was not "a legislative body" and that its duty was "to apply the law as it finds it, not to make it",[1] but this restrictive view of the judicial function is inconsistent with other decisions of the Court, and may be explained by reference to the subject matter of the dispute presented to the Court in the *South-West Africa* case. The applicant states, Ethiopia and Liberia, were among the few African states which had been members of the League of Nations. The respondent state, South Africa, held South-West Africa under a Mandate from the League. Under Article 7 (2) of the Mandate agreement, it was agreed that any dispute between the Mandatory and another Member of the League of Nations relating to the interpretation or the application of the provisions of the Mandate should, if it could not be settled by negotiation, be submitted to the Permanent Court. *Prima facie*, this provision gave any state which had been a member of the League a sufficient *locus standi* to bring a matter before the International Court as successor to the Permanent Court under Article 37 of the present Statute, and this view had been accepted by the International Court on the hearing of South Africa's Preliminary Objections to the Court exercising jurisdiction in the case.[2]

However, on the hearing of the merits of the dispute the Court held that, while the applicant states had sufficient standing to initiate the proceedings, a closer examination of the substance of the dispute disclosed that they did not have sufficient interest of their own in the dispute to enable the Court to proceed to judgment. In other words, Article 7 (2) required a dispute involving the parties to the litigation, while what in fact existed was a general disagreement between South Africa on the one side and the majority of member states on the other. Liberia and Ethiopia had no greater interest in the substance of the dispute than any

20. I.C.J. Rep. 1966, p. 6.   1. *Ibid.*, at p. 48.
2. I.C.J. Rep. 1962, p. 319.

other member of the United Nations upon which the duties of supervising the Mandate had devolved after the dissolution of the League of
Nations. It was the Court's view, therefore, that it could not "legislate"
to apply Article 7 (2) to a situation that it was never intended to cover,
that is to a dispute involving the Mandatory on the one hand and the
League, as an institution, on the other. Seen in this perspective, the
Court's view that it had no power to alter the effect of Article 7 (2) of
the Mandate by "judicial legislation" is hardly surprising: it is fully consistent with its attitude in other cases involving the interpretation of
treaties. But the Court's statement that it is not a legislative body cannot
invalidate what has already been said about the significance of the Court's
role in the development of rules of international law. Even in "applying"
existing law the Court will in certain situations be called upon to exercise
a quasi-legislative function. This function is well described by Judge
Tanaka in his dissenting opinion in the *South-West Africa* case:[3]

> "Undoubtedly a court of law declares what is the law, but does not legislate. In
> reality, however, where the border-line can be drawn is a very delicate and difficult
> matter. Of course, judges declare the law, but they do not function automatically.
> We cannot deny the possibility of some degree of creative element in their judicial
> activities. What is not permitted to judges, is to establish law independently of an
> existing legal system, institution or norm. What is permitted to them is to declare
> what can be logically inferred from the *raison d'être* of a legal system, legal institution
> or norm."

Whatever may be the position with regard to the Court's judgments,
international arbitrations, often the decision of one man, or at the most of
a small group of jurists, are not usually regarded as providing illustrations
of judicial law-making. However important these arbitrations may be to
the student or practitioner of international law, they are at the most the
best materials available of the existence or application of a particular
principle, and not the origins or sources of international legal rules. It
must be admitted that such an assertion can be supported on no really
strong logical ground. The difference between pronouncements of an
arbitral tribunal and the rulings of the International Court in this regard is
related primarily to the standing of the two bodies. A decision of an
arbitral tribunal, however significant for the future development of
international law, or however widely and approvingly cited, is evidence,
often the strongest evidence, of the relevant customary rule. The same is
true of most decisions of the International Court, but in certain unique
situations a decision of the Court has assumed a more fundamental
significance. The difference may be one of emphasis, but the difference in
emphasis is so great in a limited number of cases, that in those cases
decisions of the International Court have attained a higher status in the
law-making process.

If there is an exception to be found to this general proposition it may
lie in the judgments of international administrative tribunals. The exact

---

3. I.C.J. Rep. 1966, at p. 277.

status of the administrative rules which govern the relations between members of the United Nations Secretariat and the Organisation itself may be difficult to describe with precision. As members of the Secretariat, these individuals may be described as forming an international civil service, and the law relevant to their position is part of the internal law of the United Nations. "International administrative law", as it is often called, may properly be regarded as a new branch of international law, and no discussion of sources would be complete without some comment upon its development, particularly through the work of the U.N. Administrative Tribunal. Although the interpretation of the Charter of the U.N. and the constitutions of the various specialised agencies are continuously the subject of debate and interpretation in the day to day workings of those institutions, and have seldom been the subject of judicial determination, the contracts between members of the Secretariat and the United Nations have repeatedly come under the scrutiny of the Administrative Tribunal. A contract must create rights and duties cognisable under some system of law, because an agreement without such a reference would create no enforceable obligations whatever. However, as the U.N. Administrative Tribunal was created to consider claims arising under such contracts, the contracts must be legally binding; but legally binding by what system of law? The Tribunal has not attempted to apply any particular system of municipal law, but has consistently applied what it considers the appropriate "general principles" to give substance to the provisions of these agreements. These "general principles" seem to rely heavily upon the rules of administrative jurisprudence best known to Continental Europe, but in adapting these principles to the needs of an international civil service, the Tribunal is playing a creative role in a minor and unspectacular way.

E. Decisions of municipal tribunals

So far the discussion of the pronouncements of courts as a "source", or as "evidence", of international law has related exclusively to international tribunals, but Article 38 contains no such limitation: it refers simply to "judicial decisions . . . as subsidiary means for the determination of rules of law". Obviously the occasions on which a municipal court will be called upon to decide questions involving issues of international law will be infrequent (unless the court is a prize court dealing with the legality of the seizure of ships and cargoes in time of war). But how can the decisions of a municipal tribunal be a means of determining the rules of international law?

The decision of a municipal court would seem to be relevant to international law in two ways, though the distinction between the two situations might not be easily maintained in practice. In the first place, and this aspect of the work of a municipal court would clearly qualify for consideration under Article 38 (1) (d), the decision might provide a statement of what the court considered to be a rule of international law. The value of such a statement would necessarily depend upon factors like the "standing" of the court concerned, and the availability of other evidence relating to the existence of the rule of international law in question. The august deliberations of the United States Supreme Court have long been highly regarded. In the case of the *Schooner Exchange*[4] in 1812, Marshall, C.J., laid down what came to be accepted as the classic statement on the immunity of ships belonging to a foreign sovereign from the jurisdiction of the territorial state. Disputes between the various states of the Union over their respective boundaries have led the Supreme Court to apply and develop the relevant principles of international law. In the field of prize law, the pronouncements of the English Prize Court have held a pre-eminent position; and in maritime law in general, decisions of English courts have been regarded with great respect. Where existing authorities are scanty, or the evidence in favour of a particular rule is uncertain, the role of a municipal decision will be that much more important. On the other hand, a wealth of state practice which seems to support a contrary view of international law will obviously detract from the value of a particular decision as a "determination" of the relevant rule of international law, whatever the standing of the court concerned. In *Polites* v. *The Commonwealth*,[5] a majority of the members of the High Court of Australia were prepared to accept the existence of a rule which "prevented the imposition upon resident aliens of an obligation to serve in the armed forces of the country in which they resided, unless the state to which they belonged consented to waive this ordinarily recognised exemption." Whatever uncertainty existed in the practice of states, the significance of the view adopted by the High Court is greatly diminished by the fact that it was based on the authority of the opinions expressed by a limited number of writers without reference to the records of British practice which showed the reluctance of the United Kingdom government to protest on behalf of those of its nationals who had chosen permanent residence in the conscripting state.

The second way in which municipal decisions might be relevant to international law is not as a direct statement of the law as envisaged by Article 38, but indirectly as evidence of the practice of the state of the *forum*. The most obvious illustrations of an area of law in which the practice of states is largely evidenced by acts of the judiciary rather than of the executive deal with the limits of a state's jurisdiction. Although national courts often purport to be applying a particular rule of international law in such cases, significant differences of opinion exist between the courts of one state and the courts of another. In relation to sovereign immunity, the English courts have hitherto refrained from exercising jurisdiction over a foreign state-owned merchant vessel engaged on a normal trading venture, but no such immunity is accorded by, for example, the French courts. In the *Lotus* case,[6] the Permanent Court was

4. 7 Cranch 116.   5. (1945) 70 C.L.R. 60.
6. (1927), P.C.I.J. Rep., Ser. A, No. 9.

referred to a number of municipal decisions (on the question of criminal jurisdiction in cases of collision on the high seas) but, as municipal jurisprudence was divided, the Court commented that it was "hardly possible to see in it an indication of the existence of the restrictive rule of international law which alone could serve as a basis for the contention of the French Government."[7]

Whether a municipal decision can be regarded as a subsidiary means for determining a particular rule of international law or simply as evidence of the practice of states would seem to be primarily a matter of emphasis. If there exist numerous decisions from the courts of a number of states, these decisions are likely to be considered primarily as evidence of the practice of the states concerned. If, on the other hand, a particular municipal decision finds favour among those whose duty it is to apply international law, whether because there is a dearth of authority, or because, though there is a conflict of state practice, it represents in an outstanding way the view that the international tribunal wishes to adopt, the tendency will be to regard the municipal decision as determining the relevant rule of international law. This difference in emphasis can be seen in the *Lotus* case itself. To the majority, the relevant municipal decisions were in conflict and therefore provided no indication of the rule contended for by the French Government. To the minority, on the other hand, criminal jurisdiction over events occurring on board a vessel on the high seas depended entirely on the flag that the vessel was flying, and this principle could not be extended by holding that a collision causing damage to a ship flying the flag of another state could also give jurisdiction to the courts of that other state. And, in his dissenting judgment, Lord Finlay accepted as an authoritative statement of the applicable rule of international law the decision of the English judges in the Court of Crown Cases Reserved in the case of the *Franconia*.[8] To Lord Finlay, the judges, in deciding that the English Courts did not have jurisdiction over the captain of the German ship, *Franconia*, who had been held guilty of the manslaughter of a passenger on board a British ship with which the *Franconia* had been in collision, were applying not English municipal law, but an established rule of international law.

F. Writers on international law

The inclusion of judicial decisions under Article 38 (1) (d) has been shown to be misleading in the sense that it tends to conceal the importance of international decisions as sources of international law in their own right and the position of municipal decisions as evidence of state practice. It would seem, however, that the contribution of writers to the development of international law is more limited. By drawing analogies with existing rules, and by deductions from the generality of, or trends in, state practice, the writer provides a statement of what he considers to be

---

7. *Ibid.*, at p. 29.   8. *R.* v. *Keyn* (1876), 2 Ex. D. 63.

international law in a particular field. In this way he fulfils the function ascribed to him by paragraph (1) (d) which refers to "the teachings of the most highly qualified publicists of the various nations . . . as subsidiary means for the determination of rules of law".

But how influential are juristic writings in the development of international law? Historically, before there existed any great wealth of state practice or judicial precedent, writers on international law held a preeminent position and it was impossible not to rely heavily on the writings of Suarez and Gentilis in the sixteenth century, of Grotius (volume III of whose *De Jure Belli ac Pacis* earned him the title of "Father of the Law of Nations"), Zouche and later Pufendorf in the seventeenth century, and the so-called "positivists", Bynkershoek, Moser and Van Martens, and the "Grotian", Vattel, of the eighteenth century. Even today, particularly where the law is uncertain, the advocate before an international tribunal, or the legal adviser to the foreign affairs department of a state, will make occasional reference to the works of these writers, the so-called "Classics of international law", though more frequent citation is made to contemporary writings, particularly to Oppenheim's treatise, and to various monographs and articles on specialised fields of international law. Even if it is possible to demonstrate the significance of international juristic writings to the advocate or legal adviser from the frequency with which use is made of such writings in written and oral pleadings submitted by states parties to cases before the International Court, it is less apparent what impact these citations have either on the practice of states, or on actual decisions.

In so far as the views of writers reflect the practice of states, those views will be used to reinforce the majority opinion, and add pressure on the minority to conform. And the object of a state in including the wealth of citations in the pleadings before the Court is to persuade the Court that its case is supported by the practice of states as explained by the preponderance of juristic writing. Where the writings of publicists are not supported by the weight of evidence of state practice, they may yet influence a particular state or states to adopt a different practice in their relation with other members of the international community and so bring about a new development in the law. This possibility may be illustrated by reference to the contention of Lauterpacht that states were under a legal duty to recognise a newly established state or government once that state or government fulfilled the conditions required by international law. Apparently influenced by this view a British Foreign Secretary stated the view of the British Government that it was international law which defined the conditions under which a government should be recognised, and that such recognition should not depend on whether the British Government approved of the character of the régime.[9] If this is the policy followed by the British Government, it is not one that has met with approval among other states, particularly the

---

9. See below, p. 99.

U.S.A., and cannot therefore be said to represent current international law. In the absence of a general adherence by states to the exposition of the law by a writer or writers, juristic writing can in no way be said to create or establish rules of international law.

As far as the Court is concerned, it has studiously refrained from making mention of specific writings, contenting itself with occasional references to "all or nearly all writers" or "the writings of publicists". If separate or dissenting opinions can be regarded as throwing light upon the Court's deliberations in preparing its judgment, it appears that the Court will take notice of significant contributions from writers to the science of international law. The reason for the tentative nature of this statement may be seen from a reading of the separate opinions of Judges Alfaro and Fitzmaurice in the *Temple* case.[10] On the issue of preclusion or estoppel, Judge Alfaro was obviously greatly influenced by the relevant sections of Lauterpacht's *Private Law Sources and Analogies of International Law* and by an article of MacGibbon's entitled *Estoppel in International Law*.[11] Judge Fitzmaurice, on the other hand, while making reference to an article by Bowett on *Estoppel before International Tribunals and its Relation to Acquiescence*[12] largely adopted the approach of the Court in its majority judgments of stating the law without reference to authorities or precedents. The most that can be stated, therefore, is that individual judges will pay greater or less regard to the writings of publicists as authoritative statements of the law, although as a matter of policy the Court will not disclose in its judgment the secondary means of determining the relevant rules which have most influenced its deliberations.

3 CONCLUSIONS

The distinction between what is a source and what is only evidence of the state practice giving rise to a particular rule of customary international law may seem unsatisfactory, particularly when it is overlaid by the attempted separation in Article 38 of the Statute of the International Court between rules that the Court should apply—treaty rules, customary rules, and general principles—and the "subsidiary means" for the determination of those rules—judicial decisions and the writings of publicists. However, the existence of the directive to the Court contained in Article 38 should not obscure the helpfulness of the distinction between sources and evidences.

The legal adviser, the advocate before an international tribunal, or the writer on international law, must first examine all the materials relevant to the matter in issue. Decisions of courts, statements by government officials, the legislation of national parliaments, the deliberations or resolutions of an international conference or organisation, will be referred

---

10. I.C.J. Rep., 1962, p. 6, at p. 39 and p. 52 respectively.
11. (1958), 7 I. & C.L.Q. 468.   12. (1957), 33 B.Y.B.I.L., 176.

to as evidence of the attitude of states. The conclusions of jurists from their examination of the relevant precedents of state practice will be quoted to reinforce the interpretation favoured by the adviser, advocate or writer. If there exists a decision of an international tribunal which is at all relevant, the attempt will be made to apply it to, or distinguish it from, the circumstances of the case in issue. In order to establish a particular rule as a "general principle of law recognised by civilised nations", it may be necessary to indulge in a comparative survey of various legal, even moral, systems, before the principle can be accepted. Thus, to take an extreme illustration (and not one that can be recommended to the student), the United States written pleadings to the International Court in the *Aerial Incident* case included a series of extracts from the writings of Grotius, the judgment of the International Court in the *Corfu Channel* case, Oppenheim's treatise on international law, the Koran, a book on anthropology, the Ten Commandments, and the Sermon on the Mount, in order to establish killing as an international wrong!

The International Court, on the other hand, although it must sift the evidences in a manner similar to that of the adviser, advocate, or writer, must, in addition, state the basis, and content, of a rule or of a number of rules, to be applied to the circumstances of the case being litigated. As international law is largely unwritten, being primarily dependent for the creation of its rules upon the uncertainties and vicissitudes of state practice, the evidences of the existence of a particular rule are more important than its source (whether it is a customary rule, or a general principle of law). In this context judgments of the Court are a misleading example of the application of international law. The mass of evidence of the relevant rules presented to the Court in the arguments and pleadings of the parties is not dealt with in detail: the judgments are conclusions stated in the form of existing rules, which are then applied to the fact-situation in issue.

This approach has tended to give the impression that the Court is, in stating the content of a particular rule, in fact creating that rule. However, it is clear that in the absence of some clear statement of a rule (for example, in an international convention that was intended to codify existing law, or which has come to be accepted by the international community as a whole), the legal adviser, or the writer, as well as the Court, is pronouncing what he believes is the rule to be deduced from the relevant evidence. If the pronouncement is by a writer, it will qualify for consideration by the Court as a subsidiary means for the determination of the content of the rule being considered. If the pronouncement is by the Court, then Article 38 also refers to it as a subsidiary means, but, because of the standing of the Court, its decision on the existence of a particular rule of law will provide the best evidence of the content of that rule. If the same legal issue is involved in a subsequent case before the Court, the generalisation of state practice will be stated in the form of that previous decision as a readily accessible statement of the content of the rule. In reality it was the practice of states which created the rule, and which by a subsequent change in direction could alter the rule, but this fact is obscured by the reference to the judgment of the Court as if it were the source and not just the statement of the rule.

Finally, and this point is worth re-emphasising, Article 38 carefully preserves the notion of consent as the basis of legal development. An international convention is only relevant to the case before the Court if it establishes rules "expressly recognised by the contesting states"; the general practice to be considered as an international custom, must be "accepted as law"; and the general principles of law must be "recognised by civilised nations". As long as a dispute was handled by diplomatic methods, the state, as the law determining body, retained its control over the rules that could be applied in resolving the dispute. Once the matter came before a judicial tribunal, however, it was for the tribunal to decide what rules should be applied, a fact which tended to increase the suspicion that the Court would, if no clear rule of existing law presented itself, create a new principle without paying too much attention to the "consent" of the parties to the dispute. Only by reaffirming the notion of consent, not only as the basis of its jurisdiction, but also as the basis of the rules of international law, which it can apply, will the Court allay this suspicion. For the Court to depart on a process of "law-creation" not based upon the consent of states would be contrary to "the very nature" of the international legal order, which the Permanent Court described in the following terms:[13]

> "International law governs the relations between independent states. The rules of law binding upon states therefore emanate from their own free will as expressed in conventions or by usages generally accepted as expressing principles of law and established in order to regulate the relations between those co-existing independent communities. . . . Restrictions upon the independence of states cannot therefore be presumed."

---

3. The *Lotus* case (1927), P.C.I.J. Rep., Ser. A, No. 9, at p. 18.

CHAPTER TWO

INTERNATIONAL LAW AND MUNICIPAL LAW

Any discussion of the relationship between international law and municipal law must concern itself with two main problems. First, there is the theoretical question of whether international law and municipal law are part of a universal legal order (monist doctrine), or form two distinct systems of law (dualist doctrine). Secondly, a court may be faced with the practical difficulty of reaching a decision where there exists a conflict between the rules of international law and the rules of municipal law relevant to the particular situation. Before an international tribunal, the question is one of *primacy*—whether international law takes primacy over municipal law, or *vice versa*. If the conflict arises before a municipal court, the answer depends on how far the constitutional law of the state allows international law to be applied directly by the courts.

1 MONISM AND DUALISM

Much of the difficulty of the theoretical approach arises from the fact that monism and dualism are not so much theories of the relationship of international law and municipal law as explanations of the underlying basis of legal obligation. Thus, monism, which had its origins in the Middle Ages and Renaissance philosophies of the unity of Western Europe under the twin hegemony of the Pope and Emperor, supported by the naturalist doctrine that authority and legal duty were alike subject to the universality of natural law, has again found favour amongst a number of writers, notably those of the so-called "Vienna School",[1] in the present century. To their basic principles of the completeness of the legal order, they added the postulate that the boundaries of municipal law and jurisdiction were delimited by international law. These contemporary adherents of monist theories are, however, although still positivists rather than believers in any concept of natural law, part of a reaction against the main nineteenth-century positivist philosophy which saw international

---

1. Of which Kelsen was the leading figure. For a brief discussion of the theoretical aspects of monism and dualism, see Starke in (1936), 17 B.Y.B.I.L. 66.

law solely as a creation of the "will" of states. Dualism, as a cornerstone of positivist doctrine, placed its emphasis on the differences between international law and municipal law, the former being a body of rules based on the common will of states and functioning solely between states, the latter being the will of the State itself operating upon individuals within its jurisdiction. However, not only is it impossible to fit the wealth of judicial decisions, both of municipal courts and of international tribunals, into either of the conflicting doctrines, but the attempt to do so can give rise to misunderstanding. International law and municipal law have so many points of contact, especially with the gradual extension of the rules of the former to cover situations hitherto considered solely the concern of the latter, that the adoption of an *a priori* approach will either result in the over-simplification, or the distortion, of what is basically a complex problem. It is important, therefore, to concentrate, not on whether a theoretical framework can be constructed to demonstrate the similarities or differences of the two legal orders, but on the view that a court will be most likely to take in a given case.

2 MUNICIPAL LAW BEFORE INTERNATIONAL TRIBUNALS

a THE QUESTION OF PRIMACY

The role of municipal decisions as evidence of international law has already been considered,[2] but if a dispute comes before an international tribunal, and the issue is whether a state is in breach of international law, it is only to be expected that preference will be given to the rules of international law rather than to the rules of the municipal systems of the states involved in the litigation. A state cannot therefore plead its municipal law as an excuse for failing to fulfil its international obligations.

An early, though well known, authority for this proposition was the *Alabama Arbitration* of 1872.[3] During the American Civil War, a number of ships were built in England for private buyers. Although the vessels were unarmed when they left English ports, it was known that they were to be fitted out as warships by the Confederate states in order to attack the Union's maritime trade. These raiders, of which the *Alabama* was the most famous, caused considerable damage to American shipping, and it was for these losses that the United States sought to make Britain liable under the so-called "Three Rules of Washington", which set out the neutral duties accepted by Britain for the purposes of settling the dispute. One of the arguments put forward by the British Government was that, under English law as it then stood, it had not been possible to prevent the sailing of vessels constructed under private contracts. In allowing the United States' claim for compensation, the arbitrators had no hesitation in upholding the supremacy of international law. "It is plain that to satisfy the exigency of due diligence, and to escape liability, a neutral

2. Above, pp .37–39.   3. Moore, *International Arbitrations*, Vol. 4, p. 4057.
CIL

government must take care . . . that its municipal law shall prohibit acts contravening neutrality."[4] The jurisprudence of the International Court has been similarly emphatic:

> ". . . a State cannot adduce as against another state its own Constitution with a view to evading obligations incumbent upon it under international law or treaties in force. Applying these principles to the present case, it results that the question of the treatment of Polish nationals or any other persons of Polish origin or speech must be settled exclusively on the bases of the rules of international law and the treaty provisions in force between Poland and Danzig."[5]

The principle applies to all aspects of municipal law, to its constitutional provisions, to ordinary legislation and to decisions of the courts. Thus, it would not be open to an individual charged with having committed war crimes to plead that his actions were lawful, or even encouraged, by the municipal law in force in his own state at the time when the acts were performed. The Nuremberg Tribunal, which tried the major Nazi war criminals, stated that "the very essence" of its Charter was that individuals were subject to international duties which transcended "the national obligation of obedience" imposed by their own state.[6] In fact, municipal legislation, far from providing an excuse for a state failing to fulfil its obligations under international law, might constitute the breach of duty complained of by other states. As Judge Lauterpacht pointed out in a case before the International Court, there is "little difference between a government breaking unlawfully a contract with an alien and a government causing legislation to be enacted which makes it impossible for it to comply with the contract."[7]

b THE QUESTION OF VALIDITY

It does not necessarily follow that, in a case of conflict between a state's municipal law and its international obligations, the rules of its municipal law are in some way "invalidated".

As far as internal effect is concerned, it is not the function of international law to interfere in the application of a state's own law in accordance with its constitution. In the *Statute of Memel* case,[8] the Permanent Court had to decide whether the dissolution of the Diet of the Memel Territory by the Governor was compatible with Lithuania's obligations under the Territory Statute which was annexed to, and formed part of, the Convention of Paris of 1924 between Lithuania and the Principal Allied Powers. The Statute fulfilled two distinct juridical roles: on the international plane it was part of a treaty, and in the municipal sphere it formed the constitu-

---

4. Per Sir Alexander Cockburn, *ibid.*, at p. 4076.
5. *Treatment of Polish Nationals in Danzig* (1932), P.C.I.J. Rep., Ser. A/B, No. 44, at p. 24.
6. 22 I.M.T., at p. 529.   7. *Norwegian Loans* case, I.C.J. Rep. 1957, at p. 37.
8. (1932), P.C.I.J. Rep., Ser. A/B, No. 49. It may be, of course, that, *by a state's constitutional law*, international law takes precedence over its own laws, but this possibility is considered below, pp. 68–71.

tion of the Memel Territory. However, the case as submitted to the Court related solely to the extent of Lithuania's international obligations, and to the effect of the breach of those obligations on the internal law of the Territory as laid down in the Statute. While holding that the Governor's actions did constitute a breach of Lithuania's obligations under the Treaty, the Court was careful to avoid suggesting that this fact had any effect on the internal validity of the dissolution of the Diet.

While international law does not deny the internal validity of an act which is in breach of a state's international obligations, it does not impose a duty on other states to recognise the external effects of acts contrary to international law, or which do not conform to the standards required by international law. In the *Nottebohm* case,[9] the issue before the International Court was whether Liechtenstein could take up a claim on behalf of one of its naturalised subjects, with whom it had only the most tenuous connection, against Guatemala where Nottebohm had spent most of his life. The effect of the Court's decision in favour of Guatemala was to establish that, though a state could validly pass legislation which enabled an individual to acquire its nationality without having to show any particular link with that state, such naturalisation might be without effect as far as other states were concerned. Only if a state had acted in conformity with the general requirement of international law that the "legal bond of nationality" should "accord with the individual's genuine connection with the state"[10] could the state claim that its nationality rules were entitled to be recognised by other states.

3 INTERNATIONAL LAW IN MUNICIPAL COURTS

A. In the English Courts

a CUSTOMARY INTERNATIONAL LAW AS PART OF ENGLISH LAW

The classic doctrine that international law is part of the law of England, or the *adoption* theory as it is termed, was stated by Blackstone in the words: ". . . the law of nations . . . is here *adopted* in its full extent by the common law, and is held to be a part of the law of the land."[11] In its origins, the doctrine owed much to the medieval theory that all law, whether the law of nations, or the common law, was part of natural law. This influence of natural law can be seen from the arguments presented to the Court in *Palachies* case.[12] According to Coke, Palachie, a Moroccan subject who claimed to be the Moroccan Ambassador to the United Provinces, had seized a Spanish vessel in the course of hostilities between Morocco and Spain. When he came to England, Palachie was charged with piracy and it was contended by a number of civil lawyers that an

---

9. I.C.J. Rep. 1955, p. 4.   10. *Ibid.*, at p. 23.
11. *Commentaries*, Book IV, Chap. 5.
12. Discussed by the Court in *Marches Case* (1615), 1 Roll. Rep. 175.

ambassador enjoyed immunity both by natural law and by international law; but if he committed an offence against the law of nature or reason, though not if the offence was simply against the laws of the state in which he happened to be, he forfeited his immunity. Long before the passing of the Diplomatic Privileges Act in 1707, therefore, the immunity of diplomatic agents had been accepted by the English courts, and it is clear that this acceptance could only have been on the basis that international law was part of English law.

In a series of cases[13] in the period 1764–7, Lord Mansfield reaffirmed the principles of diplomatic immunity as depending "upon the law of nations; which is part of the common law of England". The immunities of consuls were recognised early the following century as an application of the identity of international law with the common law.[14] The immunity of foreign states and heads of states, though implicit in the immunities of their representatives, was judicially established during the nineteenth century, and was expressly stated to be based upon rules of international law: as the court said in *De Haber* v. *The Queen of Portugal*, "to cite a foreign potentate in a municipal court . . . is contrary to the law of nations."[15]

Even more striking were cases in which international law was invoked to invalidate transactions carried out without any apparent contravention of rules of English law. In 1824 in *De Wutz* v. *Hendricks*,[16] the plaintiff sought to recover from the defendant certain papers relating to the plaintiff's attempt to raise a loan in support of a Greek rebellion against the Turkish Government: in dismissing the action Best, C.J., said:[17]

> "It occurred to me that it was contrary to the law of nations . . . for persons in England to enter into engagements to raise money to support the subjects of a government in amity with our own, in hostilities against their government, and that no rights of action could arise out of such a transaction."

The case of *Emperor of Austria* v. *Day and Kossuth*[18] went further: not only did the Court pronounce against the legality of the defendant's actions in printing money for the rebel Kossuth in derogation of the public rights of the Emperor, but it was held that the Emperor was entitled to the positive remedy of an injunction to prevent repetition of acts contrary to international law.

Although historically there is substantial support for the general proposition that international law is part of English law, its value as a legal principle is subject to a number of qualifications.

(1) The first is more apparent than real, and is based on the contention

---

13. *Triquet* v. *Bath* (1764), 3 Burr. 1478, expressly relying upon the authority of Lord Talbot in *Barbuit's Case* (1737), Cas. t. Talb. 281; *Lockwood* v. *Coysgarne* (1765), 3 Burr. 1676; *Heathfield* v. *Chilton* (1767), 4 Burr. 2015.
14. *Viveash* v. *Becker* (1814), 3 M. & S. 284.
15. (1851), 17 Q.B. 171, at p. 207.   16. (1824), 2 Bing. 314.
17. *Ibid.*, at pp. 315–16.   18. (1861), 2 Giff. 628.

that the earlier authorities must be reconsidered in the light of the decision of the Court for Crown Cases Reserved in *R. v. Keyn*,[19] which, it is said, established that international law is only part of English law in so far as it is "incorporated" into English law by a decision of the courts or by an Act of Parliament. In other words, according to this argument, the adoption theory has been replaced by a doctrine of *incorporation*.

In *R. v. Keyn*, the *Franconia*, a German ship, collided with a British vessel less than three miles from the English coast. The British vessel sank with the loss of one life. The German master of the *Franconia* was convicted of manslaughter, but the case was referred to the judges on the question of whether the English courts had jurisdiction over such an incident occurring within British territorial waters. The decision of the judges, that the English courts did not have jurisdiction in the absence of an Act of Parliament granting such jurisdiction, has been too readily interpreted as a denial that international law is part of English law. The true *ratio decidendi* is difficult to establish because the thirteen judges gave in all eleven different judgments. However, only a minority seemed to favour the view that the English courts no longer accepted the adoption theory: a majority were either willing to uphold the court's jurisdiction by applying "international law", or felt that the difficulty arose from the fact that under international law the extent of the jurisdictional rights of littoral states over territorial waters was not beyond dispute, while there was a far more strongly established principle reserving to the flag state exclusive rights of jurisdiction over its own nationals. Indeed, in the light of subsequent English cases[20] which, despite some hesitation on the part of the judges, seem to reiterate the direct application of international law, *R. v. Keyn* cannot be considered as in any way detracting from the traditional doctrine.[1]

---

19. (1876) 2 Ex. D. 63. For the meaning of "territorial waters" in the Wireless Telegraphy Act, 1949, see *R. v. Kent Justices, Ex p. Lye*, [1967] 2 Q.B. 153.

20. Notably *West Rand Central Gold Mining Co. v. R.*, [1905] 2 K.B. 391, in which Lord Alverstone, C.J. said at p. 406:

"... Whatever has received the common consent of civilised nations must have received the assent of our country, and that to which we have assented along with other nations in general may properly be called international law, and as such will be acknowledged and applied by our municipal tribunals when legitimate occasion arises for those tribunals to decide questions to which doctrines of international law may be relevant."

This passage was cited with approval in *Commercial & Estates Co. of Egypt v. Board of Trade*, [1925] 1 K.B. 271, at p. 283, per Bankes, L.J., who added that a particular rule was so well established as part of international law that it must be part of English municipal law (at p. 284).

See also *The Cristina*, [1938] A.C. 485, at p. 490 (per Lord Atkin), and at p. 502 (per Lord Wright). But for a categoric statement by an Australian judge that Blackstone's view that international law is part of English law is "now regarded as without foundation", see per Dixon, J. in *Chow Hung Ching v. R.* (1948), 77 C.L.R. 449, at p. 477.

1. Parliament seemed to have no doubts as to the jurisdictional rights of the courts within three miles of the coast. The *Territorial Waters Jurisdiction Act*, 1878, which was passed to reverse the effects of the decision in *R. v. Keyn*, stated in its Preamble that "the rightful jurisdiction of Her Majesty . . . has always extended over the open seas adjacent to the coasts of the United Kingdom", and s. 5 provided that nothing in the Act should "be construed to be in derogation of any rightful jurisdiction of Her Majesty . . . under the law of nations".

(2) A more significant objection is that, although in origins international law might have been applied directly in the English courts, the underlying principles of international law became overlaid by the English doctrine of precedent, so that the English courts were no longer applying developing principles of international law but what might be termed an "anglicised" version of those principles.

During the nineteenth century, the English courts expressly recognised that they would not exercise jurisdiction over the head of a foreign state, nor would they exercise jurisdiction over his property and thus compel him to enter an appearance to protect his rights. As long as the foreign sovereign and the foreign state were synonymous, and the most that a foreign sovereign might attempt by way of commercial adventure was to run a fleet of mail ships, English law could be said to be in accord with international law. However, whereas in Europe, for example, the immunities of foreign states have been limited to meet twentieth-century economic realities,[2] typified by the creation of state trading corporations and trading fleets, with worldwide business connections, the English courts have continued to apply a rule of absolute immunity. As a result, when an English court upholds a plea of immunity from a foreign state agency or trading corporation, what it is applying is not a rule of international law, but a rule of English municipal law.[3]

(3) As a matter of English constitutional law (and on this point Scots law is identical) international law must yield precedence to an Act of Parliament.

The leading case is *Mortensen* v. *Peters*,[4] in which a Danish subject, the master of a Norwegian ship, was convicted for otter trawling in the Moray Firth. The relevant statute prohibited this method of fishing without permission anywhere within a line drawn from Duncansby Head to Rattray Point, the distance thus measured being more than seventy miles. A Scottish court held, *inter alia*, that even if there did exist a rule of international law limiting territorial waters to bays and estuaries of no greater breadth than ten miles, all that a court could do with an unambiguous statutory provision was to apply it. In the words of Lord Dunedin:[5]

> "In this Court we have nothing to do with the question of whether the legislature has or has not done what foreign powers may consider a usurpation in a question with them. Neither are we a tribunal sitting to decide whether an Act of the legislature is *ultra vires* as in contravention of generally acknowledged principles of international law. For us an Act of Parliament duly passed by Lords and Commons and assented to by the King, is supreme, and we are bound to give effect to its terms."

The basic constitutional principle of English law is the supremacy or sovereignty of Parliament: as Parliament can make or unmake any law whatsoever, it follows that it may disregard or alter, for the purposes of

---

2. See below, pp. 213 *et seq.*   3. See below, pp. 169 *et seq.*
4. (1906) 14 S.L.T. 227.   5. *Ibid.*, at p. 230.

internal application as part of English municipal law, any rule of the common law or of international law. In the same way as there is a presumption that, in case of ambiguity, the particular statute did not intend to alter the common law,[6] there is a similar presumption that it did not intend to prevent the application of international law. It was the effect of this presumption which was the chief point at issue in *Mortensen* v. *Peters*, and its existence was not doubted: as Lord Kyllachy commented:[7]

> "A legislature may quite conceivably, by oversight or even design, exceed what an international tribunal (if such existed) might hold to be its international rights. Still there is always a presumption against its intending to do so. I think that is acknowledged. But then it is only a presumption; and as such it must always give way to the language used if it is clear. . . ."

(4) The direct application of international law is also denied in circumstances where such matters as the status of a foreign state, or government, or the existence of a state of war, are in issue.

Although there is early authority for the view that it was for the defendant himself to establish by evidence his right to diplomatic privilege, with the beginning of the nineteenth century the procedure became established that the court should apply to the Crown for a statement concerning the defendant's status. Similarly, after some hesitancy in other cases, *Taylor* v. *Barclay* (1828) established that the same principle applied in relation to the status of foreign states: in the words of Shadwell, V.C.[8]

> "I have had communication with the Foreign Office and I am authorised to state that the Federal Republic of Central America has not been recognised as an independent government by this country . . . I conceive it is the duty of the judge in every court to take notice of public matters which affect the government of the country. . . ."

The effect of the Foreign Office Certificate, as it is usually termed, is to substitute the view of the British Government for an independent judicial determination on the facts of the claim to be entitled to the particular status involved. Thus, although individual judges during the nineteenth century,[9] and even in the present century,[10] did survey the actual situation giving rise to the claim in addition to receiving the Crown's statement of the position, the House of Lords finally established in *Duff Development Co., Ltd.* v. *Kelantan*[11] that it was "the settled practice of the Court to take judicial notice of the status of any foreign government, and for that purpose, in any case of uncertainty to seek information from a Secretary of State, and the information so received is conclusive."[12] The Govern-

---

6. "It is a well established principle of construction that a statute is not to be taken as effecting a fundamental alteration in the general law unless it uses words that point unmistakably to that conclusion." Per Devlin, J. in *National Assistance Board* v. *Wilkinson*, [1952] 2 Q.B. 648, at p. 661.
7. 14 S.L.T., at p. 232. 8. 2 Sim. 213, at p. 220.
9. Notably Sir Robert Phillimore in *The Charkieh* (1873), L.R. 8 Q.B. 197.
10. See *Statham* v. *Statham & The Gaekwar of Baroda*, [1912] P. 92.
11. [1924] A.C. 797. 12. *Ibid.* (headnote).

ment of Kelantan was held entitled to immunity from process as a foreign
sovereign in the English courts on the strength of the certificate issued by
the Colonial Secretary, despite the fact that the Sultan of Kelantan had
undertaken by treaty to have no political relations with any foreign state
except through the Crown and to follow the advice of a British Resident
on all matters of administration except those concerning the Mohamme-
dan religion and Malay custom. Lord Sumner acknowledged that "it was
not the business of the Court to inquire whether the Colonial Office
rightly concluded that the Sultan was entitled to be recognised as a
sovereign, by international law."[13]

b TREATY RULES AND THEIR RELATION TO ENGLISH LAW

While it is possible to regard customary international law as part of
English law, a similar principle does not apply to treaty rules. Although
a treaty duly ratified by the Crown will be binding under international
law, if the treaty is to have internal effect in the sense of changing legal
rights, it will require enabling legislation by Parliament. Of course, not
all treaties have any bearing on rights under municipal law, but where
they do, such treaties will require specific enactment, because there is no
general rule of English law (comparable to the constitutions of some states)
which gives them internal effect.

In the case of the *Parlement Belge* at first instance,[14] it was held that the
Anglo-Belgian "Convention regulating Communications by Post" of
1876 could not affect the rights of a British subject by conferring upon
mail-boats belonging to the Belgian Crown an immunity from jurisdiction that they did not enjoy under customary international law. Although
the decision was reversed by the Court of Appeal[15] on the ground that
the *Parlement Belge* was entitled to immunity from suit under international
law, the first instance decision still stands as authority for the proposition
that the Crown, by entering into a treaty, cannot alter the law of
England.

More recently, in the *Republic of Italy* v. *Hambros Bank, Ltd.*,[16] the
plaintiff state claimed that the residue of the late King Victor Emmanuel's
estate should not have been transferred to the defendant bank as adminis-
trators of the estate, but should have been made available for the payment
of Italian debts in the United Kingdom as provided by a Financial Agreement of April, 1947, between the two Governments. Vaisey, J., dismissed

---

13. *Ibid.*, at p. 824. The fact that the prerogative powers of the Crown in foreign affairs
are largely unfettered by judicial control is further evidenced by the English "act of state"
doctrine that neither the Crown nor its agents incur liability under English law for harmful
acts committed against foreigners abroad: *Secretary of State for India* v. *Kamachee Boye
Sahaba* (1859), 13 Moo. P.C. 22; *Buron* v. *Denman* (1848), 2 Ex. Ch. 167; *Johnstone* v. *Pedlar*,
[1921] A.C. 262; *Nissan* v. *Attorney-General*, [1967] 2 All E.R. 1238.
14. (1879) 4 P.D. 129. The judge at first instance was Sir Robert Phillimore. His conclusion was that the defence raised was "a use of the treaty-making prerogative of the
Crown . . . without precedent, and in principle contrary to the laws of the constitution" (at
p. 154).
15. (1880) 5 P.D. 197.   16. [1950] Ch. 314.

the plaintiff's claim on the ground that, in the absence of statutory authority, the Agreement was not "cognizable or justiciable in this Court".[17]

c INTERNATIONAL LAW AS A REASON FOR NOT APPLYING THE RELEVANT FOREIGN LAW

The principles of English private international law might require that transactions involving a foreign element should be decided according to a foreign system of law and not to English municipal law. For example, a transfer of property is governed by the *lex situs*, the law of the place where the property is situated; and the rights and obligations arising out of a contract are governed primarily by its *proper law*, which, in the absence of an express choice of the proper law by the parties, is the law of the place with which the contract has the most real connection. The rule that a transfer of property is governed by the *lex situs* is reinforced in the case of governmental acts by the principle, known in the United States as the "Act of State" doctrine, that a legislative, executive, or other act of a foreign state over persons or property situated in that state should be recognised by the courts of the *forum*.

The fact that, as far as property is concerned, the "Act of State" doctrine is but a specific application of the *lex situs* rule may be illustrated by the case of *Luther* v. *Sagor*,[18] in which timber belonging to the plaintiff, a Russian company, had been seized in Russia by Russian officials acting in pursuance of legislation nationalising all such property. The timber was sold to the defendants who shipped it to England, where the plaintiff company commenced proceedings to obtain a declaration that it was still the owner of the timber. The Court of Appeal held that the defendants had acquired a good title. In the view of Bankes, L.J., the law of Russia was the *lex situs* and therefore governed the seizure of the timber and its transfer to the defendants: by Russian law the defendants had acquired a valid title which would be recognised by the English Courts.[19] Warrington, L.J., on the other hand, preferred to base his reasoning on the principle that "the validity of the acts of an independent sovereign government in relation to property and persons within its jurisdiction cannot be questioned in the Courts of this country."[20]

In *Luther* v. *Sagor*, the property seized belonged to a national of the confiscating state, so that no possible reference to principles of public international law could arise; but what is the position if the territorial sovereign seizes the property of an alien without offering adequate compensation, an act which is *prima facie* a breach of international law? Such a situation came before the Supreme Court of Aden in the case of

17. *Ibid.*, at p. 329.   18. [1921] 3 K.B. 532.
19. *Ibid.*, at pp. 544–545. It is clear that Bankes, L.J., was dealing specifically with the question arising "as to the title to goods lying in a foreign country which a subject of that country, being the owner of them by the law of that country" has sold for export to England (at p. 545).
20. *Ibid.*, at p. 548.

Anglo-Iranian Oil Company v. *Jaffrate*.[1] The plaintiff company had been entitled under an agreement of 1933 with the Persian Government to work an oil concession for a period of 60 years. In 1951, the government nationalised the company's assets in Persia with, in the opinion of Campbell, J., no more than a vague offer to consider the question of compensation. A consignment of oil from the company's confiscated installations was purchased by an Italian concern and part of it was sold to the charterers of a tanker called the *Rose Mary*. When the *Rose Mary* called at Aden, the company commenced proceedings to recover the oil or its value from the captain of the vessel, the ship-owner, and the charterers. Campbell, J., upheld the plaintiff's claim on the ground that "following international law as incorporated in the domestic law of Aden, this Court must refuse validity to the Persian Oil Nationalisation Law in so far as it relates to nationalised property of the plaintiffs which may come within its territorial jurisdiction."[2]

This final conclusion that the Persian Law was invalid "following international law as incorporated in the domestic law of Aden" seems to be based upon the following line of reasoning: (i) that a confiscation of alien property without adequate compensation is contrary to international law; (ii) that if an act is contrary to international law it is invalid; (iii) that, as international law is part of the law of Aden, the act is also invalid by the law of Aden. While it is possible, in principle, to accept propositions (i) and (iii), proposition (ii) is less easily supported. In discussing the effects of municipal law in international courts, it was suggested that international law did not question the internal validity of a state's municipal laws, even if those laws constituted a breach of the state's international obligations. Indeed, in relation to property rights, it is difficult to see how international law can deny validity to any particular aspect of municipal law. As international law is primarily concerned with the relations between states, it contains no concept of private ownership: it leaves the determination of title entirely to the sphere of municipal law. What international law does admit is that, although a state can pass its own nationality laws, or define the rules governing the acquisition of ownership of private property, and although the internal validity of such acts will not be questioned, if those acts are contrary to international law, or do not meet the requirements of international law, it is open to other states to refuse to give effect to them. Although the decision in the *Rose Mary* may be based upon the line of reasoning suggested by propositions (i), (ii) and (iii), and the use of the expression "following international law . . . this Court must refuse validity" supports this view, the significance of the conclusion is limited by the qualification that the court should only refuse validity to the Nationalisation Law in so far as it related to nationalised property which came within the court's territorial jurisdiction. If the court had restricted itself to saying that it could, in accordance with international law, refuse to give effect to the Nationalisation

---

1. [1953] 1 W.L.R. 246; (1953) 20 I.L.R. 316.　　2. *Ibid.*, at p. 259.

Law, even over property situated in Persia at the relevant time, once that property had left Persia and had come within the court's jurisdiction, its conclusion could, as a statement of international law, be supported. But as the rule of international law is permissive (the courts of other states *may* refuse to recognise the effectiveness of the Nationalisation Law), and not mandatory (the courts of other states *must* refuse to recognise its effectiveness), even if international law did apply as part of the municipal law of Aden, it could not in itself justify the court's decision. International law left the court free to decline to apply the Nationalisation Law: in order to refuse to apply it there would have to be some rule of municipal law enabling the court to take this course. Is there a rule of English law (which was the system of law applied by the Supreme Court of Aden) that the courts will not give effect to a foreign decree on the ground that the decree is in breach of that foreign state's obligations under international law?

Of the cases cited to the Supreme Court, the most relevant decision was that of the Court of King's Bench in *Wolff* v. *Oxholm*.[3] On the eve of the outbreak of war with Great Britain, the Government of Denmark issued an ordinance seizing and detaining all assets belonging to British nationals, and requiring all debts payable to British subjects to be paid to certain comissioners established to receive such payments. An action commenced in the Danish courts by a British creditor against his Danish debtor was quashed on the production of a receipt for the payment of the debt to the commissioners. Subsequently the debtor came to England and proceedings were instituted in the English courts for the recovery of the debt. At a time when the notions of private international law were in the earliest stages of development, it is not surprising that the issues of the proper law of the contract and of the law governing the discharge of the debt were not considered. The plaintiff's "principal point" was that the Danish Confiscating Ordinance, "being contrary to the law of nations", afforded no grounds of defence to the action. The court accepted the plaintiff's argument: the English courts were not bound to respect the quashing of the plaintiff's suit in Denmark under an ordinance which was "not conformable to the usage of nations".[4]

Wolff v. *Oxholm* clearly supports the proposition that, according to English law, the fact that the legislation of a foreign state is in breach of that state's obligations under international law is sufficient reason for an English court refusing to apply it, and would therefore have been reason enough for the decision of Campbell, J., in the *Rose Mary*. However, in *Re Helbert Wagg*,[5] Upjohn, J., joined issue with Campbell, J.'s interpretation of the decisions of the Court of Appeal in *Luther* v. *Sagor* and *Princess Paley Olga* v. *Weisz*.[6] Both cases concerned the seizure by the territorial state of property of its own subjects: for this reason, Campbell, J. held

---

3. (1817), 6 M. & S. 92.   4. *Ibid.*, at p. 106.
5. [1956] Ch. 323; (1955) I.L.R. 480.
6. [1929] 1 K.B. 718; (1925–30) A.D. Case No. 60.

that they were distinguishable from the situation where the property con-fiscated belonged to a non-national. The view of Upjohn, J. was that no such distinction could be read into the judgments, as the proposition that the English courts would not enquire into the legality of acts done by a foreign government in respect of property situated in its own territory, was stated in the most general terms. Implicit in the statement of this rule was the belief that it was based upon international comity: it would be "a serious breach of international comity" for the courts of one state to sit in judgment on the legislation of another state. But if the legislation in question constituted a breach of international law, it could hardly be argued that a principle of good neighbourliness between states should preclude an English court from considering the breach of international law as a reason for not giving effect to the legislation.

Upjohn, J., did suggest that the decision in the *Rose Mary* case could be justified on the facts by reference to the doctrine of public policy: inter-national law, as a reason for not recognising the legislation of foreign states, could be relevant only in so far as it qualified for consideration as a matter of public policy. However, if the normal rule of English law is to give effect to foreign legislation over persons and property within the foreign state at the relevant time, the notion of public policy will only hesitatingly be used to deny the effectiveness of the legislation in the English courts. A clearly established exception to the application of foreign law in situations where the law in question is in breach of the foreign state's international obligations would not give rise to the same hesitations. As there is no reason in principle, or established by authority, why the English courts should give effect to foreign legislation that is contrary to international law, it is an unsatisfactory alternative to have to rely upon the vagaries of the notion of public policy.

B. In the American Courts

a CUSTOMARY INTERNATIONAL LAW AS PART OF AMERICAN LAW

The fact that American law developed from the same historical origins as English law was reflected in a number of early decisions which simi-larly regarded both the common law and international law as parts of the law of nature. Even after independence, American courts did not hesitate to apply the "law of the land" doctrine. In 1784, a Philadelphia court convicted the accused for the specific offence of violence against the person of the Secretary of the French Legation, M'Kean, C.J., observing that "the first crime in the indictment is an infraction of the law of nations" which "law in its full extent, is part of the law of this state."[7] Similar statements are to be found throughout the nineteenth century, and in 1900 the Supreme Court in *The Paquete Habana* treated the prin-ciple as established beyond doubt: in the words of Judge Gray:[8]

---

7. *Respublica* v. *de Longchamps* (1784), 1 Dall. 111.   8.   175 U.S. 677, at p. 700.

"International law is part of our law and must be ascertained and administered by the courts of justice of appropriate jurisdiction, as often as questions of right depending upon it are duly presented for their determination."

Thus, in *State of Netherlands* v. *F. R. Bank of New York*,[9] when the decision depended on the validity of the decrees of the Netherlands Government-in-Exile set up in London after the occupation of Holland by the German army in 1940, it was held, on the strength of cases heard by American, Dutch, Norwegian, Belgian and Polish courts, that contemporary international law required the enforcement of the legislative acts of the absent sovereign in so far as these acts did not interfere with the authority vested in the occupying power by Article 43 of the Hague Regulations of 1907 concerning the Laws and Customs of Land Warfare

The adoption theory, as practised by the American courts, is subject to similar limitations in its application as those discussed in the context of English law.

(1) The same criticism can be levelled against the American courts that was made against the English decisions relating to sovereign immunity —far from applying rules of international law, English and American courts have in fact been relying upon rules derived from their own precedents.

In the case of the *Pesaro*,[10] the Supreme Court was called upon to decide whether the defendant ship, arrested under a libel *in rem*, was entitled to immunity from process in the courts of the United States. The *Pesaro* was owned by the Italian Government which operated the vessel as a carrier of merchandise between Italian and overseas ports. The Court refused to distinguish its own earlier decision in the *Schooner Exchange* which had laid down the general principle of immunity in relation to a French warship. The reason for applying the principle of the *Schooner Exchange* was that if a state, for the purpose of expanding its trade, or increasing its revenue, operated a shipping fleet, such vessels were as much public ships as warships would be: the Court knew "of no international usage which regards the maintenance and advancement of the economic welfare of the people in time of peace as any less a public purpose than the maintenance and training of a naval force." The *Pesaro* case was the basis of a rule of American law which differed substantially from the view gaining ground among the states of Continental Europe, and finding expression in the Brussels Convention of 1926, that the legal position of state operated merchant vessels should be assimilated to that of privately owned ships.[11]

---

9.   201 F. (2d) 455 (1953).

10.   *Berizzi Bros.* v. *The S.S. Pesaro*, 271 U.S. 562 (1925); (1925–6), 3 A.D. 186.

11.   Though the authority of this decision has been substantially affected by the Tate letter, see below, p. 59, and pp. 192–194. It is also noticeable that the American courts, when faced with deciding upon a rule of international law to be applied to the circumstances of a case, do show considerable freedom in looking at decisions from other municipal systems as evidence of the current rule of international law. In *Dexter* v. *Kunglig Jarnvagsstyrelsen* [43 F. (2d) 705 (1930); (1929–30), 5 A.D. 109], for example, a Circuit Court of Appeals considered European, as well as English and American cases, before upholding a plea of immunity from execution by a department of a foreign state.

(2) As far as legislation is concerned, the American courts apply the same rule as that employed by the English courts: a statute takes precedence over, but should be interpreted, as far as possible, so as not to conflict with, the rules of customary international law.

In *Schroeder* v. *Bissell*,[12] a District Court had to decide whether s. 447 of the Tariff Act, 1922, which contained no express territorial limitation to its scope could be applied to the unloading of part of a cargo of whisky some 19 miles off the American coast. Judge Thomas stated the principles to be applied to the question in the following terms:[13]

> "If we assume for the present that the national legislation has, by its terms, made the acts complained of a crime against the United States even when committed on the high seas by foreign nationals upon a ship of foreign registry, then there is no discretion vested in the federal court, once it obtains jurisdiction, to decline enforcement. . . . The act may contravene recognised principles of international comity, but that affords no more basis for judicial disregard of it than it does for executive disregard of it. . . . If, however, the Court has no option to refuse the enforcement of legislation in contravention of principles of international law, it does not follow that in construing the terms and provisions of a statute it may not assume that such principles were on the national conscience and that the congressional act did not deliberately intend to infringe them. In other words, unless it unmistakably appears that a congressional act was intended to be in disregard of a principle of international comity, the presumption is that it was intended to be in conformity with it."

Bearing that presumption in mind, the Court proceeded to examine the provisions of the Tariff Act and concluded that, being a criminal statute, jurisdiction under which was normally territorial in extent, the Act could not apply to events taking place on the high seas.

More recently, in *Tag* v. *Rogers*,[14] the appellant, a German national, impugned the Trading with the Enemy Act 1917, as amended in 1941, and the vesting orders made thereunder against his property, on the ground *inter alia* that the relevant provisions of the Act were in conflict with international law. The District Court of Appeals had no doubt that the existence of the rule of international law could not undermine the authority of the Federal statute: "there is no power in this Court to declare null and void a statute adopted by Congress . . . merely on the ground that such provision violates a principle of international law."[15]

(3) The relationship between the judiciary and the executive in the field of foreign affairs in the United States has resulted in the virtual surrender of all initiative by the courts to the State Department. The tendency is for the executive's statements to the court to lay down conclusions of law to a much greater extent than occurs in British Foreign Office certificates. This tendency is most noticeable in dealing with claims to immunity. The normal procedure in the American courts is for a representative of the foreign state involved to request the Secretary of State to inform the court of the defendant's immunity from jurisdiction. A copy of the

---

12. 5 F. (2d) 838 (1925); (1925–6) 3 A.D. 154.
13. 5 F. (2d), at p. 842.   14. 267 F. (2d) 664 (1959).   15. *Ibid.*, at p. 666.

request is handed on to the Federal Attorney-General whose duty it is to inform the court that the State Department" accepts as true" the statement of fact contained in the request. The effect of this "suggestion", as it is called, is conclusive on the particular issue. As the "suggestion" is a pronouncement on the merits of a particular claim, for example, in respect of a state-owned merchant ship, it goes much further in excluding the investigation of matters of law than does the British Foreign Office Certificate which, although conclusive as to the status of a particular state or government, does not attempt to lay down conclusions of law on whether the state or government is entitled to the claim of immunity in respect of the subject-matter of the action.

Being an executive act, the granting or withholding of immunity is not subject to the need to follow previous precedents. In 1952, the State Department issued what has always been referred to as the "Tate Letter",[16] the most significant passage in which stated:

> "the Department feels that the widespread and increasing practice on the part of governments of engaging in commercial activities makes necessary a practice which will enable persons doing business with them to have their rights determined in the courts . . . it will hereafter be the Department's policy to follow the restrictive theory of sovereign immunity in the consideration of requests of foreign governments for a grant of sovereign immunity."

However, in a number of recent cases, the State Department has blatantly departed from this declared policy, the most notorious example arising out of the case of the *Bahia de Nipe*.[17] This cargo ship had been nationalised by the Castro régime in Cuba, but, later, it was taken over by the master and ten of the crew, who sailed it into American waters. Immediately a series of actions were commenced against the vessel. The Cuban Government requested that the vessel should be granted immunity from the jurisdiction of the United States Courts, and the Secretary of State notified the Attorney-General of the wish of the United States Government that the ship should be released. The reason for the State Department acceding to the Cuba request had nothing to do with legal principle. On the eve of the arrival of the *Bahia de Nipe* in American waters, Cuba and the United States had exchanged an Eastern Air Lines aeroplane that had been seized and flown to Cuba, for a Cuban naval vessel that had been taken to Florida by Cuban opponents of the Castro régime. This exchange was part of an understanding between the two governments based upon Cuban protests and an undertaking given by the United States to the Security Council of the United Nations. Faced with this change in policy by the State Department, the court felt itself obliged to follow authority: the suggestion of the State Department in a matter of foreign relations withdrew it "from the sphere of litigation".

Although the State Department is not reluctant to use its power to

---

16. See Bishop's comment in (1953) 47 A.J.I.L. 93.
17. *Rich* v. *Navicra Vacuba, S.A.*, 295 F. (2d) 24 (1961).

interfere with the scope of judicial review of claims to immunity, there are examples of situations in which a "suggestion" has not been forthcoming, and the courts have felt themselves free to apply legal criteria to the issue. In the case of the *Navemar*,[18] the Spanish Ambassador, unable to obtain the support of the State Department for the plea that the vessel was a public ship in the possession of the Spanish Republic, himself filed an application challenging the Court's jurisdiction. The Supreme Court held that the absence of a communication from the State Department was not fatal to the plea of immunity: it was open to the Ambassador to take this step and leave the Court to decide on the merits of the issue. On the facts, however, the Court held that the evidence did not support the claim that the ship had been in the possession of the Spanish Government.

b TREATY RULES AND THEIR RELATION TO AMERICAN LAW

By English law treaties are negotiated by the Executive, and ratified by the Executive in the name of the Crown. As, at no stage, is Parliamentary intervention necessary in the making of a treaty, the English courts have taken the view that such a treaty cannot affect private rights without enabling legislation. By American law, the treaty is negotiated by the Executive, but the Constitution provides that it can only be ratified by the President if two-thirds of the Senate approves. The Constitution also lays down that "all Treaties made, or which shall be made, under the Authority of the United States, shall be the supreme law of the land" and that "the Judges in every state shall be bound thereby" whatever might be the law of the particular State of the Union.

Although, clearly, a treaty will take precedence over State laws, the Constitution places treaties on an equal footing with Federal Statutes. In situations where an Act of Congress and a treaty are in conflict, the rule is that the later instrument has the effect of repealing the earlier so far as the two are inconsistent. In *Edye* v. *Robertson*,[19] the Supreme Court was called upon to consider whether a statute imposing a fifty cent charge on owners for every foreign national brought into American ports by their vessels was invalidated by the alleged fact that the charge was contrary to a number of treaties of friendship between the United States and numerous other countries. In upholding the validity of the statute, the Court stated that there was nothing in treaty law which made it "irrepealable or unchangeable": the Constitution gave it "no superiority" over an Act of Congress, which could always be "repealed or modified by an Act of a later date."[20]

i *Self-executing treaties*

It is not all international agreements which are the law of the land, for a distinction has been made between those which are, and those which

---

18. *Compania Espanola de Navegacion Maritima* v. *The Navemar*, 303 U.S. 68 (1938); (1938–40), 9 A.D. 176.

19. 112 U.S. 580 (1884).   20. *Ibid.*, at p. 599.

are not, "self-executing". In *Edye* v. *Robertson*, the Court pointed out that a treaty was "primarily a compact between independent Nations": only when it contained "provisions which confer certain rights upon the citizens or subjects of one of the Nations residing in the territorial limits of the other, which partake of the nature of municipal law, and which are capable of enforcement as between private parties in the courts of the country" did the Constitution place it "in the same category as other laws of Congress."[1]

The difficulty of distinguishing between provisions that are self-executing and those which are not, has been particularly vexing in relation to contemporary multilateral treaties containing guarantees of human rights. In *Sei Fujii* v. *State of California*, a State Appeal Court[2] had held that legislation forbidding aliens to "acquire, possess, enjoy, use, cultivate, occupy, and transfer" real property was invalid as being in conflict with the United Nations Charter. The Supreme Court of California,[3] while upholding the decision on another ground, rejected the view that the Charter provisions on human rights were self-executing. Part of the judgment of Gibson, C.J. admirably described the judicial approach to the problem:

> "A treaty . . . does not automatically supersede local laws which are inconsistent with it unless the treaty provisions are self-executing. . . . In determining whether a treaty is self-executing, courts look to the intent of the signatory parties as manifested by the language of the instrument, and, if the instrument is uncertain, recourse may be had to the circumstances surrounding its execution. . . . In order for a treaty provision to be operative without the aid of implementing legislation and to have the force and effect of a statute, it must appear that the framers of the treaty intended to prescribe a rule that, standing alone, would be enforceable in the Courts. . . ."[4]

The Chief Justice went on to point out that the language used was not of the type usually to be found in treaties held to be self-executing and contrasted, it with the clear language employed in Articles 104 and 105 of the Charter. He concluded:

> "The provisions in the Charter pledging co-operation in promoting observance of fundamental freedoms lack the mandatory quality and definiteness which would indicate an intent to create justiciable rights in private persons immediately upon ratification. Instead, they are framed as a promise of future action by the member nations."[5]

ii *The Treaty making power and the Constitution of the United States*

Although a treaty would be ineffective to make a fundamental alteration to the Constitution itself, it can offer a means of evading some prohibition contained in that document. Thus, in 1914 an Act of Congress passed the previous year to protect migratory wild fowl was declared

---

1. *Ibid.*, at p. 598. It had early been decided that a treaty took precedence over the laws of any of the States of the Union: *Ware* v. *Hylton*, 3 U.S. 199 (1796).
2. 217 P. (2d) 481 (1950).   3. 242 P. (2d) 617 (1952).
4. *Ibid.*, at p. 620.   5. *Ibid.*, at pp. 621–2.

outside the powers delegated to the Federal Government. In 1916, the United States concluded a treaty with Great Britain for the protection of such birds, in which both parties undertook to adopt legislation to enforce the agreement. In *Missouri* v. *Holland*,[6] the Supreme Court held the Migratory Bird Treaty Act of 1918 valid on the ground that the enforcement of Treaty obligation was a matter exclusively within the powers of the Federal Government, but Holmes, J., was careful to point out that, though "Acts of Congress are the supreme law of the land only when made in pursuance of the Constitution, while treaties are declared to be so when made under the authority of the United States" this did not mean that there were "no qualifications to the treaty-making power".[7]

This decision has far-reaching implications for the balance of constitutional powers between the federal government and the states. It seems to suggest that, by making use of its exclusive powers in the field of foreign relations, the federal executive might erode the jealously guarded rights of the individual states. But even if one disregards the federal aspects of the case,[8] *Missouri* v. *Holland* does offer the executive a means of legislating indirectly in a way that it cannot do directly.

Various attempts have been made, notably by the so-called Bricker Amendment, to prevent treaties having internal effects in the absence of enabling legislation. Although this proposed amendment to the Constitution has not succeeded in obtaining the necessary majority even in the Senate, in one field, that of taxation, Congress has always jealously regarded any attempt to usurp its functions through the use of the treaty-making power. Thus, the House of Representatives has continuously asserted its right to deliberate upon, with a view to deciding upon the desirability of, any request for funds needed to implement a treaty: it has refused to accept the view that it was bound automatically to give effect to such a treaty. Indeed, there is judicial support for the proposition that a treaty requiring the appropriation of money for its enforcement would not be regarded as internally effective without enabling legislation.[9]

iii *Executive agreements*

Although the theory of the Constitution is that agreements with foreign powers should be made by the President with the approval of

---

6. 252 U.S. 416 (1920).   7. *Ibid.*, at p. 433.
8. Which are apparently in contradiction to the principle laid down in *Geofroy* v. *Riggs*, 133 U.S. 258, at p. 267 (1890):
"The treaty power, as expressed in the Constitution, is in terms unlimited except by those restraints which are found in that instrument against the action of the government or of its dependants, and those arising from the nature of the government itself and of that of the States."
As Lauterpacht commented, the decision in *Missouri* v. *Holland* did give to treaties a status "dangerously approaching that of a constitutional amendment": *An International Bill of Rights of Man*, p. 179.
9. See the comments of the District Judge in *Aerovias Interamericanas de Panama* v. *Dade Commissioners*, 197 F. Supp. 230 (1961), at p. 246:
"Inasmuch as treaties calling for expenditure of funds are ineffective without an accompanying appropriation, they are uniformly considered to be not self-executing."

two-thirds of the Senate, the Constitution itself, in granting the widest powers over external affairs to Congress and, by implication from its terms and by subsequent practice in the implementation of those terms, to the President, has provided the legal basis for the use of so-called "executive agreements" made by the President on his own authority, or with the approval of Congress as expressed in a statute. Far from being in any sense "inferior" to treaties assented to by two-thirds of the Senate, executive agreements are endowed with all the attributes of formal treaties. Under international law, they are effective to bind the United States, and during the successive terms of President Franklin D. Roosevelt, they were used extensively, "at times threatening to replace the treaty-making power, if not formally yet actively, as a determinative element in the field of foreign policy."[10]

As a matter of constitutional law, the validity of these agreements was upheld by the Supreme Court in two cases[11] arising out of the famous Litvinov Agreement of 1933.[12] in which the United States accorded recognition to the Soviet Government in return for the assignment to the United States of certain debts owing to the Soviet Union and for an undertaking that the Soviet Union would restrain any persons or groups of persons in any way under its control from any act likely to injure the prosperity, order or security of the United States. In *United States* v. *Belmont* it was held that the Government had the right to sue, as assignee of the Soviet Government, for the recovery of assets of a company appropriated by the Soviet Government. The President's recognition of that government, and the rights granted to the United States under the Litvinov Settlement, constituted an "international compact" which the President, "as the sole organ" for the conduct of United States foreign policy, could enter into without the approval of the Senate.[13]

c INTERNATIONAL LAW AS A REASON FOR NOT APPLYING THE RELEVANT FOREIGN LAW

While the emphasis in English law is on whether reason exists for not applying the *lex situs* to changes in ownership, including those brought

---

10. *The Constitution of the United States of America*, Senate Doc. No. 170, 82nd Congress: U.S. Govt. Printing Office, 1953, p. 437.

11. *U.S.* v. *Belmont*, 301 U.S. 324 (1937); (1935–7), 8 A.D. Case No. 15. *U.S.* v. *Pink*, 315 U.S. 203 (1942); (1941–2), 10 A.D. Case No. 13.

12. The various documents are reproduced in the document section of (1934) 28 A.J.I.L., 1–21.

13. 301 U.S., at p. 330. *Belmont* and *Pink* seemed to settle by implication any doubts as to the status of executive agreements. As they were endowed with all the attributes of a formal treaty they should also take precedence over existing legislation. However, *U.S.* v. *Capps*, 204 F. (2d) 655 (1953), and *Seery* v. *U.S.*, 127 F. Supp. 601 (1955), both seem to support the proposition that an executive agreement cannot alter a prior inconsistent statutory provision. But neither case is altogether satisfactory. In the first, when the appeal was heard, the Supreme Court expressly dissociated itself from this aspect of the lower courts decision (348 U.S. 296); while, in the second, the decision of the Court of Claims can more easily be justified on another ground. It is interesting to note that in *Hawaii* v. *Ho*, 41 Hawaii 565 (1957); (1958), 26 I.L.R. 557, the Supreme Court of the Territory of Hawaii applied a subsequent executive agreement in preference to a previous statute.

about by the confiscatory decrees of foreign governments, it is the public law aspect of such acts which has been the primary consideration of the American "Act of State" doctrine. The classic statement of the doctrine was that of Fuller, C.J. in *Underhill* v. *Hernandez*:[14]

> "Every sovereign state is bound to respect the independence of every other sovereign state, and the courts of one country will not sit in judgment on the acts of the government of another done within its own territory. Redress of grievances by reason of such acts must be obtained through the means open to be availed of by sovereign powers as between themselves."

This change of emphasis has tended to make it a matter of public policy that foreign "acts of state" should be respected. Considerations of public policy tend, therefore, to reinforce, rather than create an exception to, the application of the doctrine. In *Bernstein* v. *Van Heyghen Frères*,[15] the plaintiff had been the owner of all the shares in a shipping line, one of the assets of which had been a ship called the *Gandia*. As the plaintiff was a Jew he had been imprisoned for two years by the Nazis and had been in fear of his own life and the lives of his family. He was only released when he assigned all the assets of the shipping company to a Nazi nominee and his family had paid a ransom. He was then allowed to leave Germany. The defendant company had obtained the assets of the line including the *Gandia* from the Nazi nominee, and after the outbreak of war the *Gandia* had been chartered by the British Government. In addition to the proceeds of the charter, the defendants had received £100,000 insurance money when the *Gandia* was sunk. The court held that the plaintiff's claim must fail. Although it was "a well-settled exception to the usual doctrine that a Court of the forum will take as its model the rights and liabilities which have arisen where the transactions took place, that the foreign rights and liabilities must not be abhorrent to the moral notions of its own state", the plaintiff was unable to escape from the application of the "other doctrine"—"that no court will exercise its jurisdiction to adjudicate the validity of the official acts of another state."[16]

The contention that the act of state principle did not apply in cases where the act complained of constituted a breach of international law has similarly fallen upon unreceptive ears. In the *Sabbatino* case,[17] the decision depended upon the effectiveness of the notional seizure by the Cuban Government of a consignment of sugar which had just been loaded on board a ship at a Cuban port. The government refused to allow the ship to sail until the consignee agreed to pay a Cuban state bank, and not a Cuban corporation most of the capital stock of which was owned by U.S. residents, for the sugar. The principal reason put forward on behalf of the dispossessed corporation was that the law under which the Cuban

---

14. 168 U.S. 250 (1897), at p. 252.
15. 163 F. (2d) 246 (1947); (1947), 14 A.D., Case No. 5.
16. 163 F. (2d), at pp. 249–50.
17. *Banco Nacional de Cuba* v. *Sabbatino*, 376 U.S. 398 (1964); (1964), 58 A.J.I.L. 779.

Government had acted, having created a discretionary power to nationalise by forced expropriation property or enterprises in which American nationals had an interest, was a flagrant breach of international law. Despite the fact that the State Department itself had characterised the Cuban legislation as "manifestly in violation of . . . principles of international law", the Supreme Court concluded its judgment on this point by stating that "however offensive to the public policy of this country . . . an expropriation . . . may be, we conclude that both the national interest and progress toward the goal of establishing the rule of law among nations are best served by maintaining intact the act of state doctrine".[18]

The *Sabbatino* decision was attacked from two different points of view. The legal argument was that it hardly fostered respect for international law if the American courts, despite paying lip-service to the law-of-the-land principle, refused to consider international law in the context of foreign expropriation. The political attack was based on the decision's apparent disregard of the policy, embodied in the Foreign Aid Assistance Act, which provided for the suspension of aid to countries illegally expropriating the property of U.S. nationals, of encouraging and protecting foreign investment. As a consequence, Congress passed the "Sabbatino Amendment"[19] to the Act which stated that:

> "no court in the United States shall decline on the ground of the . . . act of state doctrine to make a determination on the merits giving effect to the principles of international law in a case in which a claim of title or other right to property is asserted by any party including a foreign state (or a party claiming through such state) based upon (or traced through) a confiscation or other taking after January 1, 1959, by an act of that state in violation of the principles of international law. . . ."

These "principles of international law" are to apply unless the President "determines that application of the act of state doctrine is required in that particular case by the foreign policy interests of the United States and a suggestion to this effect is filed on his behalf."

The object of the amendment was to "reverse" the Supreme Court's decision in the *Sabbatino* case while an examination was made of the need for more widely drafted legislation. Until such legislation is forthcoming, the result is that, in the absence of Presidential intervention, the courts are free, in relation to claims to property, to adopt the decisions of the lower courts in the *Sabbatino* litigation. The District Judge, for example, held that the U.S. courts had "the obligation to respect and enforce international law" not only by virtue of America's "status and membership in the community of nations", but also because "international law is part of the law of the United States."[20] As has been stated in the discussion of English law, the fact that an act is contrary to international law is not

---

18. 376 U.S., at pp. 436–437.
19. The Amendment was originally limited in time by a provision that it was not to apply to proceedings commenced after January 1, 1966, but this limit has been extended.
20. 193 F. Supp., at pp. 381–382; for the Appeals Court decision, 307 F. 2d 845, at pp. 859–869.

decisive on its ineffectiveness in the municipal law of other states. International law provides a reason why the courts of other states need not recognise the acts of the expropriating state; but it does not provide the answer to the question of whether the municipal courts of a state shall refuse to recognise an expropriation that is contrary to international law. The answer suggested by the lower courts and since accepted by a circuit Court of Appeals and apparently by the Supreme Court as well in the *Sabbatino* case, is that the law of the land doctrine requires that the rules of international law should not only be applied but should be enforced by the American courts. If an act is contrary to international law, the American courts should supply the necessary sanction by declaring the act ineffective.

C. In the courts of other states with common law systems

The basic principles of common law still apply in most states of the Commonwealth, and in a number of other states which were once part of the British Empire, like Eire or Burma, or which expressly adopted English law, like Israel.

a CUSTOMARY INTERNATIONAL LAW AS PART OF MUNICIPAL LAW

Not surprisingly, the rule that customary international law is part of the law of the land is generally accepted, and in cases of conflict with municipal legislation, the statutory provision prevails. One of the best known authorities for this proposition is the decision of the Australian High Court in *Polites* v. *The Commonwealth*,[2] in which it was held that, though there was a rule of international law that aliens should not be compelled to serve in the military forces of the foreign state where they happened to be, and though such a rule was therefore part of the law of the land, the rule of construction that, in the interpretation of statutes, it must be presumed that Parliament did not intend to act in derogation of the principles of international law was ousted in this case by the express provisions of the National Security Act.

---

1. See *Banco Nacional de Cuba* v. *Farr, Whitlock*, 383 F. (2d) 166; *certiorari* denied, 390 U.S. 956.
2. (1945), 70 C.L.R. 60; (1943–5), 12 A.D., Case No. 61. For the opinion of the High Court on whether international law is part of the law of Australia, see *Chow Hung Ching* v. *The King* (1948), 77 C.L.R. 449. "International law is not as such part of the law of Australia . . . but a universally recognised principle of international law would be applied by our courts": per Latham, C.J., at p. 462. Starke, J. was content to quote the advice of the Judicial Committee of the Privy Council in *Chung Chi Cheung* v. *R*. that on "any judicial issue" the courts will seek to ascertain the relevant rule of international law and "will treat it as incorporated into the domestic law, so far as it is not inconsistent with rules enacted by statutes or finally declared by their tribunals" ([1939] A.C. 160, at p. 168), cited 77 C.L.R., at p. 471. Dixon, J., having stated that the Blackstone view was "now regarded as without foundation" suggested that international law was only one of the sources of English law, and therefore of Australian law, *ibid.*, at p. 477.
For the Indian view on the relationship between international law and an Indian statute: *Sharma* v. *West Bengal* (1954), 21 I.L.R., at p. 275.

The same status is accorded to statements of the executive. Before a colony attains independence, the rules are applied as part of English law. In *Re Wong Hon,*[3] for example, the question whether the High Court of Hong Kong had jurisdiction over an offence committed in Kowloon was predetermined by certain Orders-in-Council which, by dealing specifically with the "City of Kowloon", afforded "little foundation upon which to rest an argument that the area was intended to be excluded from Her Majesty's jurisdiction", particular reliance being placed on the decision of the Court of Appeal in the *Fagernes*, in which Lord Atkin said:[4]

> "What is the territory of the Crown is a matter of which the Court takes judicial notice. The Court has, therefore, to inform itself from the best material available; and on such a matter it may be its duty to obtain its information from the appropriate department of Government. Any definite statement from the proper representative of the Crown as to the territory of the Crown must be treated as conclusive."

Following the granting of independence to a particular territory, its courts, in applying the former rules, naturally continue to accept any statement that the government might make as conclusive on the extent of national territory. The Federal Court of India has held[5] that the fact that the subject matter of the dispute related to land claimed by both India and Pakistan was no bar to its exercising jurisdiction, for it was bound by the views expressed by the Indian Government.

b TREATIES AND THEIR RELATION TO MUNICIPAL LAW

The position in relation to treaties was well summarised by Lord Atkin giving the Privy Council's advice in *Attorney-General for Canada* v. *Attorney-General for Ontario:*[6]

> "Within the British Empire there is a well-established rule that the making of a treaty is an executive act, while the performance of its obligations, if they entail alteration of the existing domestic law, requires legislative action. Unlike some other countries, the stipulations of a treaty duly ratified do not within the Empire, by virtue of the treaty alone, have the force of law."

The only states where the position might not be altogether certain are those which have adopted written constitutions, although, even in the cases of Burma and Eire which have written constitutions, the relevant provisions clearly state the need for legislation to give internal effect to treaties.[7] The only reference to treaties in the Indian Constitution is in

---

3. (1959), 27 I.L.R. 49.   4. [1927] P. 311, at p. 324.
5. *Midnapore Zemindary* v. *Province of Bengal* (1949), 16 A.D., Case No. 6. For the same principle as applied in Israel, see *Attorney-General* v. *El-Turani* (1951), 18 I.L.R. 164.
6. [1937] A.C. 326, at p. 347.
7. Article 25 (5) of the Irish Constitution provides:
"1. Every agreement to which the state becomes a party shall be laid before *Dail Eirann*.
2. The State shall not be bound by any international agreement involving a charge upon public funds unless the terms of the agreement shall have been approved by *Dail Eirann*.

Article 51 (c) which stipulates that "the State shall endeavour to . . . foster respect for international law and treaty obligations . . ." and this has given rise to some dispute as to whether the general pre-independence rule requiring enabling legislation to give internal effect to treaties is still firmly adhered to. The most that can be suggested in the light of the decision in *Menon* v. *Collector of Customs*,[8] in which the Supreme Court of Madras considered not only two statutes, but also the Customs Convention on the Temporary Importation of Private Road Vehicles, is that the Indian courts are tending towards a more flexible approach to the internal application of international agreements.

D. In the courts of states with civil law systems

a CUSTOMARY INTERNATIONAL LAW AS PART OF MUNICIPAL LAW

In the legal systems based upon Roman Law, mainly the states of Continental Europe, rules of customary international law are normally regarded as part of domestic law. This principle has either been established directly or indirectly by constitutional provision—as with Article 9 of the Austrian Federal Constitution, and Article 10 of the Italian Constitution of 1947 respectively—or it has developed by judicial application—as in the Netherlands, Switzerland and France.

As in common law systems, the direct application of customary international law may be precluded in a particular situation.

1. In general, ordinary municipal legislation takes precedence over rules of international law. Thus, although Article 9 of the Austrian Constitution provides that "the generally recognised rules of international law are held to be component parts of the Federal Law", it was held by the Constitutional Court[9] that, even if the nationalisation of all means of production and distribution without compensation were contrary to international law, the Statute under which this expropriation was carried out would, as far as Austrian municipal law was concerned, take precedence over any rule of international law for Article 9 only conferred on

---

3. This section shall not apply to agreements or conventions of a technical and administrative character."

By Article 29 (6):

"No international agreement shall be part of the domestic law of the State save as may be determined by the *Oireachtas*."

The *Dail* is the lower house of the Irish Parliament; the *Oireachtas* is defined by Article 15 (1) 2 as comprising "the President and two Houses" i.e. the Dail and the Senate. In view of this definition, Article 29 (6) must intend legislation as the means of incorporation. Also under the Constitution, international law is considered as part of Irish law because of Article 29 (3), which states:

"Ireland accepts the generally recognised principles of international law as its rule of conduct in its relations with other States."

The provisions of the Burmese constitution are virtually identical: see Sections 213, 214 and 65.

8. (1962) A.I.R. Madras 404; 2 I.L.M. 648.
9. *In re Rhein-Main-Donau* (1954), 21 I.L.R. 212.

international law the status of ordinary Federal Law and not the higher status of federal constitutional law. In contrast, Article 25 of the Basic Law of the German Federal Republic is unusual in that international law is granted a status superior to municipal legislation:

> "The general rules of international law shall form part of federal law. They shall take precedence over the laws and create rights and duties directly for the inhabitants of the federal territory."

2. The practice of obtaining a certificate from the Foreign Ministry of the state concerned is generally adopted, though of course with slight differences of procedure from one state to another. The type of question dealt with by such certificates includes the same issues as in the case of common law jurisdictions. The status of diplomatic and consular agents is normally dealt with in reliance on the attitude of the executive.[10] As far as the position of states and state corporations is concerned, continental courts are similarly reluctant to encroach upon the purely political issue of whether or not a state or government exists, but, because of the distinction between acts *jure imperii*, which entitle the defendant state or corporation to immunity, and acts *jure gestionis*, to which sovereign immunity does not apply, the courts do have a wider discretion than exists under English, and most certainly, American law, to decide into which category a particular transaction falls.[11] For example, in *Lakhowsky v. Swiss Federal Government*,[12] the Paris Court of Appeal held that the defendant government was entitled to immunity in proceedings relating to a shipment of cocoa. As the transaction had been arranged by a Transport Office specially created by the government to ensure the maintenance of supplies with Switzerland during the First World War, it could not be considered as a commercial venture but was a political act wholly remote from any idea of profit or speculation.

b TREATY RULES AND THEIR RELATION TO MUNICIPAL LAW

The attitude of the courts in the continental states of Europe is governed by the provisions of each state's constitutions, and these are, generally speaking, favourable to the direct application of treaties.

In the German Federal Republic, the courts will give precedence to a treaty rather than to municipal legislation. In the *Town and Country Planning* case,[13] the Federal Supreme Court allowed claims by United States nationals to compensation for land compulsorily acquired under the German-American Treaty of Friendship of 1954 rather than under the less favourable German Town and Country Planning statutes. On the

---

10. Though not always, for in *Re Armenian Chargé d'Affaires* (1923–4), 2 A.D., Case No. 172, a Greek court held that it was for the judiciary, and not for the executive, to ascertain whether the conditions of diplomatic status under international law existed in a particular case.
11. See below, pp. 213–219.   12. .(1919–22) 1 A.D., Case No. 83.
13. (1957) 24 I.L.R. 8. And for the effects of German ratification of the European Convention of Human Rights, see *Expulsion of Alien Case* (1956), 23 I.L.R. 393.

other hand, a treaty cannot bring about a change in the constitution of the state: in the *Concordat* case,[14] the Federal Constitutional Court held that the absence of constitutional provision to give effect to a treaty was fatal to the internal application of that treaty where it was clear that the constitution did not intend to give the Federal Government such a power.

The Netherlands Constitution was modified in 1956, but, although the approval of the States-General is now required for the final promulgation of a treaty as part of Dutch law, it is still for the courts to decide whether or not a particular treaty provision is self-executing. However, the requirement of approval, which can be express or tacit, does not mean that legislation is required to give the treaty internal effect. As the Supreme Court stated in connection with the Constitution of 1887:[15]

> "Article 59 authorises the Queen to conclude and to ratify treaties with foreign powers under the *proviso* that, whenever treaties affect the rights of Netherlands nationals, they shall not be ratified except after having been approved by the States-General. Prior approval would make no sense if Article 59 were to be regarded as meaning that the legal rights of nationals can be changed only by amending statutes as a consequence and in conformity with such treaties. Rather, it should be accepted that Article 59 entitles the Queen to make binding upon Netherlands nationals treaties that affect the legal rights of those nationals, provided that they have previously been approved by the States-General."

In France, the Constitution of the Fifth Republic has departed from the provisions of the 1946 Constitution which made clear the supremacy of treaties over internal law. Influenced largely by President De Gaulle's more nationalistic attitudes to foreign commitments, the 1958 Constitution lays down that a wide range of treaties (peace treaties, commercial treaties, treaties or agreements relating to international organisations, those that involve a financial commitment on the part of the State, those that contain provisions of a legislative nature, etc.) can only be ratified or approved by legislation. Furthermore, the Constitutional Council has the power to declare that an international undertaking, referred to it by the President of the Republic, the Premier, or the President of either of the Chambers of the legislature, contains a clause contrary to the Constitution, in which case the treaty in question may only be ratified after the Constitution is amended to conform to the undertaking. Once a treaty has been duly ratified or approved, it shall, upon publication, have an authority "superior to that of laws" subject to its application by the other party.

The Italian Constitution provides in Article 10 (1) that the Italian legal system should be in conformity with the generally recognised rules of international law. The Court of Cassation has held[16] that the effect of

---

14. (1957) 24 I.L.R. 592. And see McWhinney, *Constitutionalism in Germany and the Federal Constitutional Court*, pp. 46–9.

15. Order W.8383 of 25th May, 1906, quoted Erades and Gould, *The Relation between International Law and Municipal Law in the Netherlands and the United States*, p. 191.

16. *Ente Nazionale per la Cellulosa* v. *Cartiera Italiana* (1957), 24 I.L.R. 12.

this provision is to introduce customary international law as part of Italian law, but not to introduce rules laid down in treaties. The Court explained that reliance could not be placed upon Article 10

"because the automatic reception provided for . . . applies only in the case of generally recognised rules of international law, that is, the general customs of international law, and not those obligations which become part of positive law by virtue of the ratification of international treaties providing for such obligations. The latter require . . . the enactment of a municipal measure of enforcement."

c INTERNATIONAL LAW AS A REASON FOR NOT APPLYING THE RELEVANT FOREIGN LAW

There have been a number of decisions dealing with the effectiveness of foreign confiscations in breach of international law, but, unless the property seized belonged to nationals of the same state as the court of the forum, the courts have been reluctant to give relief to the expropriated owners. This unsatisfactory situation may be illustrated by a comparison between a number of German and Dutch decisions.

In the *Confiscation of German Property in Czechoslovakia* case,[17] the plaintiff sought to recover his property, a quantity of furniture, when it was brought to Germany from Czechoslovakia. The defendant claimed that the furniture had been given to him by the Czechoslovak authorities. The Supreme Court of the Federal German Republic ordered a new trial on the ground that the findings of fact by the trial judge had not made it clear whether a law of the Allied Control Commission placed the subject matter of the dispute outside the jurisdiction of the Federal Courts. However, both the Court of first instance and the Court of Appeal had held that the confiscation, being contrary to German public policy, was ineffective to deprive the plaintiff of his property.

The emphasis in the decisions of the two lower courts was on the criterion of public policy, and not on the issue of public international law. Public policy, however, is a principle of justice more likely to be applied for the benefit of a state's own nationals than for the benefit of nationals of other states. In a case [18] before the Bremen Courts, arising out of the seizure of Dutch tobacco plantations in Indonesia by the Indonesian Government, the District Court and the Court of Appeal refused to accept the argument that the Indonesian Nationalisation Act, being discriminatory and not providing for adequate compensation, was contrary to international law and therefore should not be recognised as effective in Germany in view of Article 25 of the Federal Constitution which declared that the general rules of international law formed part of federal law. Both Courts were of the opinion that even if the Nationalisation Act was contrary to international law, the remedy available under international law was not to regard the Act as invalid, but to allow the

---

17. (1953) 20 I.L.R. 31.
18. *N.V. Verenigde Deli-Maatschappijen* v. *Deutsch-Indonesische Tabak-Handelsgesellschaft* (1959), 28 I.L.R. 16.

state the national of which had suffered loss, to present a claim for compensation at the international level. The Court of Appeal held that it was "entitled to adhere to the opinion which, starting from the positive effect of the territorial principle, permits the . . . Court to recognise a foreign Act of State, even though it be contrary to international law." On the question of public policy, the Court found that there was not such a "serious violation" of the purposes of German law and *ordre public* as to require the non-recognition of the Indonesian legislation.

Before the Dutch Courts[19] on the other hand, the "Act of State" doctrine was held inapplicable. Although the courts should normally refrain from determining the legal effectiveness of the acts of a foreign state over matters within its territory, an exception must be made if the acts constituted a flagrant breach of international law. The main emphasis, however, was placed on the issue of public policy, and the extent to which public policy could be invoked to protect Dutch interests. Irrespective of any question of international law, it could not be presumed that Dutch public policy would allow any legal effect to a measure which discriminated against the rights and interests of Dutch nationals and which seriously affected the national economy.

The conclusion from these cases seems inescapable. International law does not seem to be directly relevant to the non-recognition of foreign acts of state, although public policy would be invoked in order to protect the property of nationals of the state of the forum. Whether the fact that an act is contrary to international law would be a ground for applying the doctrine of public policy does not seem to have been viewed with any great favour. In the *German Property in Czechoslovakia* case, the Court considered the fact of confiscation as reason enough for applying public policy in favour of a dispossessed German national. On the other hand, in Italy,[20] although the Civil Court of Rome refused to characterise the Persian seizure of the Anglo-Iranian Oil Company's assets in Persia as contrary to public policy as the Court was not convinced that compensation was not going to be paid, the Court did state that the Italian concept of public policy included a requirement that foreign legislation, to be recognised by the Italian Courts, must be compatible with the rules of international law. Although the Rome Court seemed to accept the proposition that, because of the wording of Article 10 of the Italian Constitution, it might refuse to give effect to foreign acts of state that constituted a breach of international law, the authority of the decision is lessened by the conclusion of a Venice Court on identical facts that it was not possible for an Italian Court to call in question the "principles adopted by a foreign Legislature" on the ground that they were contrary to public policy because "the proceedings before the Italian Court deal only with the juridical consequences of these acts, the acts themselves having—from a legal point of view—been finally concluded abroad."

---

19. *Bank Indonesia v. Senembah Maatschappij* (1959), 30 I.L.R. 28.
20. *Anglo-Iranian Oil Co.* v. *S.U.P.O.R.* (1955), 22 I.L.R. 19.

CHAPTER THREE

INTERNATIONAL PERSONALITY

Legal personality is primarily an acknowledgment that an entity is capable of exercising certain rights and being subject to certain duties on its own account under a particular system of law. In municipal systems, the individual human being is the typical "person" of the law, but certain entities, such as limited companies or public corporations, are granted a personality distinct from the individuals who create them, and can enter into legal transactions in their own name and on their own account. Under international law, the State is the typical legal person, and other entities may be considered as the "subjects" of international law in so far as they can enter into legal relations on the international plane.

Before the proliferation of international organisations, particularly following the establishment of the United Nations in 1945, the traditional view was that "only states are subjects of international law". Since 1945 it has become obvious that international law is no longer centred exclusively on the rights and duties of states, but has recognised the independent existence of a variety of international institutions, and, in a number of situations, has imposed obligations on, and granted rights to, individuals. The consequence of this trend has been the widespread acceptance of the view that both international organisations and other non-state entities, together with individuals, are the "persons" of the international legal system.

It is undoubtedly possible to frame a definition of international personality that would be sufficiently broad to include both non-state entities and individuals, but such a definition would not be an accurate reflection of the practice of states. International relations are the concern of the principal actors on the international scene, and any definition of international personality should distinguish their position from the position of those whom international law affects only in a subsidiary capacity. The brief statement that *an international person is an entity having the power of independent action on the international plane* has the obvious advantage of including not only states, but also communities like "protected states", which lack some attribute of statehood, such as complete independence, but which nevertheless are regarded as endowed with their own separate identity. Furthermore, it serves to distinguish between on the one hand international institutions which, even if their constitutional origins were

73

"derivative" from the will of the states which created them, have attained an independent existence no longer legally subject to the consent or approval of any particular state or group of states; and on the other hand, various entities of an international character and individuals, neither of which have the power of independent action on the international plane, except in so far as the latter may from time to time have been granted the limited right to prosecute claims directly against states before some specially constituted arbitral tribunal.

1 THE STATE AS AN INTERNATIONAL PERSON

Despite the growth of international institutions with the power of independent action on the international plane, the state is still the typical and most obvious example of an international person. But what is a state? However easy to answer such a question might seem, in certain cases it can be a matter of great difficulty to decide whether a particular entity is or is not a state. For example, is there a German state today, or are there two German states? What is the status of Formosa? Is the Ukraine a state? How should Rhodesia be categorised? Was Katanga an independent state in 1961? Or Biafra in 1967?

Traditional definitions, or perhaps more accurately, descriptions, with their emphasis on the "characteristics" of a state (territory, population, government) are not precise enough to answer such questions. Typical of these "descriptions" of the characteristics of statehood is the often quoted provision of the Montevideo Convention of 1933:

> "The state as a person of international law should possess the following qualifications: (a) a permanent population; (b) defined territory; (c) a government; and (d) capacity to enter into relations with the other states."

Both the German Democratic Republic (East Germany), and, during the time of its secession from the Republic of the Congo, the province of Katanga, would seem to fulfil the requirements of this provision, but it does not mean that the German Democratic Republic *is* a state, or that Katanga *was* a state.

More in keeping with present-day circumstances, in which a number of governmental authorities exist which have not been recognised as states even though they exercise exclusive administration over large areas of territory, would be the following definition:

> *a state, for the general purposes of international law, is a territorial unit, containing a stable population, under the authority of its own government, and recognised as being capable of entering into relations with other entities with international personality.*

a FOR THE GENERAL PURPOSES OF INTERNATIONAL LAW

This proviso is necessary because, in the application of the term "state" in the constitutions of certain international organisations, the criteria of statehood have not always been rigidly applied. Under Article 3 of the Charter of the United Nations, two of the individual Republics of the Soviet Union, the Ukraine and Byelorussia, were accepted as original member states of the Organisation. Yet neither of these Soviet Republics can be classified as a state within the above definition. It is the requirement of recognition that the government has the capacity to carry on international relations for an acknowledged state which distinguishes the position of the central government of a federal state and the position of the governments of the various parts of the federation. However great their internal authority, governments of the individual members of the union, as in the case of the states of the United States of America or of the Commonwealth of Australia, do not operate on the international plane, partly because they have no constitutional power to do so,[1] and partly because they are not considered by foreign states as representing entities with international personality. Even if the national constitution allows individual members the right to conduct their own external relations, as with the Soviet Republics, because of the attitude of other states, their status under international law is similar to that of the states of the United States of America. The position of the Ukraine and Byelorussia as member "states" of the United Nations must therefore be considered as anomalous and of no significance to a general consideration of the concept of statehood.

b A TERRITORIAL UNIT, CONTAINING A STABLE POPULATION

The existence of a shifting element in the population (for example, the wandering tribes which are the source of conflict on the Kenya–Ethiopian border) or the lack of clear definition of the boundaries, are not sufficient to affect the existence of a state. The State of Israel had been recognised by a majority of members of the United Nations when it was admitted to membership in 1949, though the final delimitation of its boundaries had not yet been settled. A distinction can therefore be made between situations in which there is substantial dispute over a "state's" boundaries (i.e. whether there are boundaries), and those in which the uncertainty has little affect on the *corpus* of the state (the question being where the boundaries are situated). Many of the states created after 1918 were recognised by the Allied Powers although their boundaries were finally drawn only by the Peace Treaties. On the other hand, recognition was withheld from Lithuania on the express ground that, because of the dispute over Vilna, its frontiers had yet to be fixed with any certainty.

c UNDER THE AUTHORITY OF ITS OWN GOVERNMENT

The absence of governmental authority does not necessarily deprive an existing state of its right to be considered as a state. "States have frequently survived protracted periods of non-government, civil war,

---

1. For the view that the Australian states have a residual power in the field of external affairs, see O'Connell (Ed.), *International Law in Australia*, pp. 36–39.

anarchy and hostile occupation."[2] But in order for a territory, which has not already achieved the status, to be considered as a state, it must have a government *of its own*, and not be subject to the control of another state. One of the more notorious examples of a "puppet state" was the Chinese province of Manchuria, which was conquered by the Japanese in 1931. The Japanese placed in control a government of their own nomination and proceeded early in 1932 to recognise the province as the "new state of Manchukuo". Both the United States and the Assembly of the League of Nations independently adopted a principle of non-recognition.

A problem of some nicety presents itself with regard to territorial units like Andorra, Liechtenstein, Monaco and San Marino. *Andorra* has most in common with a protectorate, and should perhaps be classified as such. It is subject to the protection of both France and Spain which have inherited their position from the feudal rights of the Count of Foie and the Bishop of Urgel.

Liechtenstein has placed the conduct of its foreign relations in the hands of Switzerland, and, from the economic standpoint, is virtually part of the Swiss confederation. When Liechtenstein applied for membership of the League of Nations in 1920, the Committee on Admission advised[3] the Assembly of the League that, although retaining sovereignty, Liechtenstein had delegated a number of its sovereign powers to Switzerland, and would not therefore be able to carry out its obligations under the Covenant if admitted to membership. The position would seem to be that Liechtenstein is a state, even though, on account of its size, it entrusts many state functions to Switzerland. Liechtenstein was allowed to become a party to the Statute of the International Court under the provisions of Article 93 (2) of the Charter which enables a "state which is not a Member of the United Nations" to become a party to the Statute "on conditions to be determined in each case by the General Assembly upon the recommendation of the Security Council." And in the *Nottebohm* case, the International Court did not draw any distinction between Liechtenstein and any other state in approaching the question of whether a state's nationality rules were conclusive on other states for the purposes of the rule of nationality of claims.

The status of *Monaco* stems from a treaty of 1918 between Monaco and France whereby France "assured to the Principality of Monaco the defence of its independence and sovereignty and guaranteed its territory". In the event of the Crown Prince of Monaco not having an heir, Monaco is to come directly under French protection. This provision suggests that, for the present, Monaco retains an independent status, though one that for reasons of political and economic necessity is largely dependent upon French good-will.

San Marino, like Monaco, is under the general protection of a larger

---

2. Quincy Wright, *The Status of Germany and the Peace Proclamation* (1952), 46 A.J.I.L., p. 307.
3. Hackworth, *Digest of International Law*, Vol. I, p. 48.

state, in this case Italy. However, it does accede to treaties in its own name, and, like Liechtenstein, it has become a party to the Statute of the International Court in accordance with Article 93 (2) of the Charter.

It may be largely a question of degree whether these principalities are regarded as states or as protectorates. They do retain a larger measure of control over their foreign policy than is the case in protectorates of the colonial model.[4] And, in the last resort, it is the conduct of the policy, rather than the control of the policy, which they have deputed to larger states. In the colonial protectorates, the protectorate was subject to the direct control of the protecting power in both conduct and content of the policy. The general consensus of opinion is, therefore, to regard these principalities as states under the authority of their own governments.

d RECOGNISED AS BEING CAPABLE OF ENTERING INTO RELATIONS WITH OTHER ENTITIES WITH INTERNATIONAL PERSONALITY

Although the new entity may have a government capable of acting on its behalf, in order for its claim to be a state to succeed, the entity itself must be accepted as capable of entering into relations with other states. No definition can be complete unless it takes into account that, as far as states are concerned, recognition plays a constitutive role in their creation. The appearance of a new entity, and the ability of that new entity to prolong, or perpetuate, its existence, will depend on political factors, perhaps the most important being the approval of existing states. It is only reasonable to suppose that individual states will demonstrate their approval by recognising the new state, that is, by formally acknowledging its independent existence. In so far as absence of recognition is a sign of general disapproval, it would be difficult, in the present international situation, for a new entity to establish and maintain its separate identity without being recognised.[5] In July, 1960, Belgium granted independence to its former Congolese territories, but, within a few days, there was a complete breakdown in internal law and order. Encouraged, it was alleged, by Belgian troops, and supported by Belgian mining interests, the province of Katanga purported to secede from the Congolese Republic. Its attempt to establish itself as a separate state failed because no member of the international community was willing to accord recognition to Katanga, and, as a last resort, the Security Council was prepared to authorise the use of force to bring an end to the civil war.

In a situation of uncertainty, therefore, recognition by other states may prove decisive in an entity's claim to statehood. In this narrow context, recognition may be said to "constitute" the state. On the other hand, if the absence of recognition does not connote disapproval, and there is

---

4. See below, pp. 80–82.
5. The position of Rhodesia is unusual in that it had achieved complete control over its internal administration, including its armed forces, long before the Unilateral Declaration of Independence of November, 1965. Although legally still a dependent territory, it had already achieved independence in all but name. Until it is recognised, however, Rhodesia cannot be considered as a state.

general acquiescence in the creation of the new state, pending some multilateral act of acceptance, then, even prior to formal recognition, the entity may properly be considered as a state. For this reason, it is not possible to accept the full implications of the constitutive theory that through recognition only and exclusively a state becomes an international person and a subject of international law. Though the state of Czechoslovakia was only formally recognised under the Treaty of Saint Germain which was signed in September, 1919, and came into operation in July, 1920, it had clearly been in existence with the approval of the Allied Powers since the beginning of 1919, a fact acknowledged in the decisions of a number of municipal courts. In a German case, it was held that the appellants had been rightly convicted of counterfeiting Czech stamps in May, 1919. Their argument that in May, 1919, the Czechoslovak Republic had not been legally constituted was rejected. In the court's opinion, the decisive consideration was that, at the critical date, the Republic was in fact established and its government had been effectively in power since January, 1919: the question of recognition was therefore irrelevant.[6]

The need to take into consideration more general criteria than the mere fact of recognition becomes clearly apparent when the new entity has been tacitly accepted, or expressly recognised, by only a small number of states. Critics of the constitutive theory suggest that, in such a situation, its logical application leads to the absurd conclusion that the new entity is a state for the few members of the international community which have recognised it, but is not a state for the majority. Although this conclusion may be accurate so far as the municipal law of the various states is concerned, international law is capable of providing a more objective answer. Between the extremes of total non-recognition and disapproval on the one hand, and of general recognition and approval on the other, this objective analysis is not solely a matter of "head-counting". That is to say, it is not a matter of deciding that an entity recognised by more than twenty or forty states, or by half or two thirds of the members of the United Nations, must be a state. As the *Counterfeiting* case, and other similar decisions illustrate, some attempt must be made to evaluate the reasons for recognition or non-recognition, and the general attitude of states, in the light of whether the new entity possesses the factual characteristics (territory, population, government, and ability to enter into international relations) of statehood.

It is only by objective analysis along these lines that it may be possible to answer the vexed problem of the status of the German Democratic Republic, established originally as some sort of subordinate authority by a "People's Council" under the aegis of the Russian military authorities in 1949. In 1954, its independent existence was recognised by the Soviet Union in a statement of 25th March, whereby the latter established "the same relations with the German Democratic Republic as with other

---

6. (1919–22) 1 A.D., Case No. 24. See also, *Establishment of Czechoslovak State Case* (1925–26), 3 A.D., Case No. 8.

sovereign states" and announced that the Democratic Republic should be "free to decide on internal and external affairs". The reply of the three "western" powers (France, United Kingdom and the United States) still represents their official policy. The Soviet statement did not alter the position. "The Soviet Government still retains effective control there. The western powers will continue to regard the Soviet Union as the responsible power for the Soviet Zone of Germany"; they "do not recognise the sovereignty of the East German régime which is not based on free elections, and do not intend to deal with it as a government."[7]

The position of the German Democratic Republic is that it has been recognised by the Communist States of Eastern Europe, by the People's Republic of China, and by various entities like North Korea and North Vietnam, the status of which is also in doubt. As the western policy of non-recognition includes a total refusal to deal with the Eastern Zone of Germany, except through the Russian military authorities, the question of whether the Democratic Republic is a state or not would seem to depend for objective determination on the attitude of the so-called uncommitted nations. The attitude of these states seems to be in the process of change, from the general attitude of apathetic non-recognition (Germany, for geographical reasons, is hardly a matter of fundamental concern to states of Africa and Asia), to the more equivocal state of tacit acceptance, taking the form of state visits by leading East German politicians to India in 1959, and to the United Arab Republic in 1965, or to the more formal exchanges of Consulates-General, as with Burma, Indonesia, Ceylon, and other states and even, more recently, to actual recognition by a limited number of stakes such as Iraq and Cambodia. Until this trend gains momentum, however, the status of the Democratic Republic must remain doubtful. For the moment, the most that can be suggested is that part of the territory of the former German Reich is under the *de facto* administrative and legislative control of the East German Government which, for political reasons, remains unrecognised by the western powers. But even if the "western" powers were prepared to recognise the *de facto* control of the East German régime, it is unlikely that they would be prepared to accept the perpetuation of a divided Germany by recognising East Germany as a separate state.

2 NON-SELF-GOVERNING TERRITORIES

There still exist, though the numbers are dwindling, a number of territories—principalities, protectorates, mandates, trusteeship territories, and various colonies—which have restricted powers of control over their

---

7. And in the House of Commons, a spokesman for the British Government said on 19th May, 1958:
"Her Majesty's Government do not consider that the so-called 'German Democratic Republic' has the characteristics of an independent State. It has been created and artificially maintained by the Soviet Government. Her Majesty's Government continue, therefore, to hold the Soviet authorities responsible for the conduct of affairs in Eastern Germany." (588 H.C. Deb., col. 876.)

foreign relations. Although international law may lay down a number of rules governing their position in the world community (and this is particularly so in the case of mandates and trusteeship territories), such entities might appear to lack the power of independent action on the international plane. Whether, in a particular case, the power of independent action would be denied to a particular territory (for example, if it wished to be represented in the hearing of complaints against the state by which it was administered in proceedings before a United Nations organ), must be doubtful in view of the political impetus given to the developing legal status of such territories by the United Nations General Assembly's resolution of 14th December, 1960, known as the *Declaration on the Granting of Independence to Colonial Countries and Peoples.* The Resolution expressed the conviction that all peoples had the inalienable right to complete freedom, the exercise of their sovereignty, and the integrity of their national territory, and went on to declare that—

> "immediate steps shall be taken, in trust and non-self-governing territories or all other territories which have not yet attained independence, to transfer all powers to the peoples of those territories, without any conditions or reservations, in accordance with their freely expressed will and desire, without any distinction as to race, creed or colour, in order to enable them to enjoy complete independence and freedom."

The political pressures, of which this resolution is a symptom, in favour of the rapid advancement to self-government and complete independence of all non-sovereign territories, must be borne in mind in any discussion of whether, prior to independence, non-self-governing territories can be considered as possessing a measure of international personality.

a COLONIES

For the most part, colonial territories are closely controlled by the colonial power, either under the type of relationship created by France and Portugal of constitutionally amalgamating the overseas possessions with the metropolitan state and allowing colonial representatives to attend the central parliament, or under the British system of local semi-autonomous legislatures and a representative of the Crown as head of the executive, usually with extensive prerogative powers to be used in emergency. It is difficult to regard colonies as possessing international personality, because the control of their foreign relations has been kept entirely in the hands of the colonial power. Even discussions of the political situation in such territories has been regarded by the colonial power as a matter exclusively within its own domestic jurisdiction and not subject to the competence of United Nations organs.[8]

b PROTECTED TERRITORIES

International law would seem to recognise three types of protection by a state. In the first place the protection might be exercised over a territory

---

8. For the concept of domestic jurisdiction, see below, pp. 314–322.

which did not have international personality before the "protectorate" was created, or which, if it did have a measure of personality, lost its personality by the terms of the agreement which created the "protectorate". Secondly, where a territory already existed as a state before the creation of the protectorate, but the agreement defining its status did not altogether extinguish its personality, the status of the protected territory is usually termed that of a "protected state". The third situation arises where one state exercises a general protective power over a much smaller state without destroying its position as a state. This description applies to the principalities like Liechtenstein, Monaco and San Marino, which have already been dealt with. However, it is necessary to examine in more detail the characteristics of the first two categories, protectorates and protected states.

i *Protectorates*

A number of European states have at various times created "protectorates" over unexploited and underdeveloped areas by entering into agreements with the local rulers. The effect of the relationship was to restrict the power of the local rulers over internal affairs to the extent of making its exercise subject to the consent of a local "resident" (typical of British practice),[9] and to take the conduct of foreign relations out of their hands altogether. The status of agreements of this type is not altogether clear because an agreement between two entities, one of which lacks international legal capacity, is not a treaty, a point made by Max Huber, the Arbitrator in the *Island of Palmas* case:[10]

> "As regards contracts between a state or a company such as the Dutch East India Company and native princes or chiefs of peoples not recognised as members of the community of nations, they are not, in the international law sense, treaties or conventions capable of creating rights and obligations such as may in international law arise out of treaties."

As such an entity was not originally an international person, a measure of international personality will only exist when it begins to operate on the international plane on its own behalf, and is recognised as having the capacity to do so. Recognition by the protecting state alone would not be sufficient. Many of the so-called "protected states", recognised by the United Kingdom as "Independent states in special treaty arrangements with Her Majesty" were in no sense independent as a fact, nor could they be classified as states under international law. On the other hand, once a protectorate does begin to operate on the international plane, and its competence is recognised, it must clearly be "reclassified" at least as a

---

9. And by Order in Council, it was customary to extend the provisions of the Foreign Jurisdiction Act, 1890, to such territories.
10. (1928), 2 U.N.R.I.A.A. 829, at p. 858, though, of course, as the Arbitrator went on to admit:
    "Contracts of this nature are not wholly void of indirect effects on situations governed by international law; if they do not constitute titles in international law, they are none the less facts of which the law must in certain circumstances take account."

protected state or even, if the control of the protecting power is sufficiently restricted, or removed, as a state in its own right. For example, Kuwait, which became a British protectorate in 1899 was gradually given responsibility for the conduct of its international relations, a development formally recognised by an exchange of notes between the United Kingdom and Kuwait in 1961. But it is clear that Kuwait had already achieved statehood independently of formal recognition by the United Kingdom. As Edward Heath stated in the House of Commons in June, 1961:[11]

"For some time past the state of Kuwait has possessed entire responsibility for the conduct of its own international relations, and, with the full support of Her Majesty's Government, Kuwait has already joined a number of international organisations as an independent sovereign state."

ii *Protected states*

These exist where the personality of the protected entity existed prior to the agreement establishing its dependent status, and by the terms of the agreement (which, because it was between two international persons, was a treaty cognisable, and giving rise to rights and duties, on the international plane) this personality is not extinguished. Whether or not an entity had achieved the status of an international person will depend on an analysis of the circumstances existing when the treaty was made, and whether that status will survive the treaty will depend on an interpretation of its terms.

Morocco, which existed as an independent Empire until the beginning of the present century, became a focal point of the struggle between European powers seeking fresh spheres of influence. The territory was divided into three units, the City of Tangier, the international status of which was guaranteed, and the French and Spanish Zones. The treaties which created these two protectorates vested complete control of each territory's foreign affairs in the hands of the protecting power. Despite the overall control exercised by the protecting state, it was nevertheless assumed by the International Court in the *Rights of U.S. Nationals in Morocco* case[12] that Morocco retained its personality as a state under international law. It would seem therefore that, providing an entity once possessed the criteria of statehood, and was recognised as being a state, it could by treaty allow another state to exercise some of its sovereign rights without loss of *personality*, though whether it is useful to continue to consider the entity as a *state*, as assumed by the International Court, would appear to be doubtful.

c MANDATES AND TRUSTEESHIP TERRITORIES

The Mandate System of the League of Nations, which still applies to one territory, South-West Africa,[13] and the Trusteeship System of the

---

11. 642 H.C.B., col. 955.   12. I.C.J. Rep. 1952, at pp. 185, 188.
13. It is believed that the General Assembly has no power unilaterally to terminate South Africa's mandate over the territory, although by G.A. Res. 2145 (xxi) of 27th

United Nations, which applies to the Pacific Islands, to New Guinea and until recently to Nauru, are not susceptible of exact definition in traditional terms of sovereignty. As Judge McNair said in his separate opinion in the *Status of South-West Africa* case,[14] the international community had established in the mandates system "a new institution—a new relationship between territory and its inhabitants on the one hand and the government which represents them internationally on the other—a new species of international government, which does not fit into the old conception of sovereignty and which is alien to it." To this new system "the doctrine of sovereignty" had no application: sovereignty was in abeyance until "the inhabitants of the Territory obtain recognition as an independent state." The important question in considering this new institution was not where does sovereignty lie, but "what are the rights and duties of the Mandatory in regard to the territory being administered by it."

The Mandate System was established by the Covenant of the League of Nations to provide for the administration of "those colonies and territories which as a consequence of the late war have ceased to be under the sovereignty of the states which formerly governed them and which are inhabited by people not yet able to stand by themselves under the strenuous conditions of the modern world": Article 22 went on to divide the former "Axis" colonies into three categories "according to the stage of their development."

Class A comprised communities, formerly part of the Turkish Empire, which were sufficiently advanced for their independence to be "provisionally recognised" subject to the administrative advice and assistance of the Mandatory "until such time as they are able to stand alone." Of the "communities" involved, only Iraq achieved early independence in accordance with the mandate treaty between Iraq and Britain, but, as no provision was made in the Covenant, nor was any date for independence laid down in the respective instruments of mandate, the other four, Palestine, Transjordan, Syria and Lebanon, only achieved statehood with the collapse of the dominating influence of the Mandatory Powers (France and the United Kingdom) in the Middle East as a result of the Second World War.

Class B comprised peoples, "especially those of Central Africa", still at a stage where the Mandatory must be responsible for the administration of the territory, subject to a variety of guarantees and to the obligation to allow equal trading opportunities to other Members of the League. The areas concerned—Tanganyika, British and French Togoland, the British and French Cameroons, Ruanda-Urundi—have only attained independence, following transfer to the trusteeship system under the United Nations, in the last few years.

October, 1966, the Assembly purported to declare that the mandate was terminated because South Africa "has failed to fulfil its obligations in respect of the administration of the Mandated Territory and to ensure the moral and material well-being and security of the indigenous inhabitants of South-West Africa, and has, in fact, disavowed the Mandate".

14. I.C.J. Rep. 1950, at p. 150.

Class C was composed of certain territories "which owing to the sparseness of their population, or their small size, or their remoteness from the centres of civilisation, or their geographical contiguity to the territory of the Mandatory" were "best administered under the laws of the Mandatory as integral portions of its territory, subject to the safe-guards above mentioned in the interests of the indigenous population." Territories in this category have given rise to the most problems, partly because of the nature of the territories themselves: Nauru for example, being little more than an island phosphate deposit, was until recently not considered capable of an independent existence as a sovereign state; and partly because of the integration with the Mandatory allowed under the Covenant, as with South-West Africa.

It was clearly hoped by those who drafted the Charter that the new trusteeship system would supplant the mandate system completely and might well be a means of modifying, by Article 77 (1), the whole concept of dependent territories:

> "The trusteeship system shall apply to such territories in the following categories as may be placed thereunder by means of trusteeship agreements:
> (a) territories now held under mandate;
> (b) territories which may be detached from enemy states as a result of the Second World War; and
> (c) territories voluntarily placed under the system by states responsible for their administration."

Only in the case of South-West Africa did the problem have to be faced of what the position was if the Mandatory Power refused to negotiate a trusteeship agreement. The International Court[15] rejected the South African argument that the mandate had lapsed with the dissolution of the League of Nations in 1946 and pointed out that, as the rights exercised by the South African Government over the territory depended on the Mandate, if that had lapsed the government's powers must equally have lapsed. Nor was it possible for South Africa to alter its relationship with South-West Africa without the consent of the General Assembly of the United Nations, as successor to the Assembly of the League. However, as Article 77 (1) of the Charter stated that the trusteeship system would apply "to such territories . . . as *may* be placed thereunder", there was no duty on the mandatory to effect the change by negotiating a trusteeship agreement.

In outline, the procedure for the creation of a trusteeship agreement was for its terms to be "agreed upon by the States directly concerned" and to be "approved" by the General Assembly (or, in the case of a trusteeship of a "strategic area", by the Security Council). In practice, the agreement with states directly concerned was replaced by agreement between the administering authority and the United Nations, acting through the General Assembly, while the most that the designated

---

15. *International Status of South-West Africa*, Advisory Opinion, I.C.J. Rep. 1950, p. 128.

administering power did in deference to Article 79 was to circulate the draft agreements more often for information purposes than out of a genuine desire to "negotiate".

As far as the machinery for supervision is concerned, in all territories but "strategic areas" where the supervisory functions are assigned to the Security Council, the General Assembly exercises an overall control of the trusteeship system's operation, though most of its means of super-vision—set out in Article 87—the Assembly leaves to the Trusteeship Council to carry out. This latter body is supposed to comprise, under the provisions of Article 86, an equal number of administering and non-administering states members of the United Nations,[16] but must also include the five permanent members of the Security Council. The Trustee-ship Council's functions, apart from its exclusive competence over the formulation of "a questionnaire on the political, economic, social, and educational advancement of each trust territory" the answers to which should be included in the administering authority's annual report to the General Assembly, mainly concern its assistance to the Assembly or the Security Council. As has already been stated, the initial consideration of these annual reports and of petitions from inhabitants of the trust territories is left to the Trusteeship Council which then reports to the Assembly or the Security Council.

The object of the system is to enable dependent territories to proceed to self-government under the guarantee of international supervision. It was also thought, and emphasised by Article 76 (a) of the Charter, that the effect of such supervision would be to promote international peace and security by the elimination of "wars of independence". Although terri-tories under trusteeship have passed peaceably enough to self-government, it should be realised in attempting to evaluate the significance of the system that it was only applied to eleven territories—ten former man-dates and one territory, Somalia, detached from Italy as a result of the Second World War. In no case were other dependencies (protectorates or other colonial possessions) brought under the system of international supervision as envisaged by Article 77 (1), and the most that the Trustee-ship Council has been able to do in relation to such territories has been to provide a forum for the exercise of political pressure against colonial powers, and in this capacity its functions were largely superseded by the increased use of the Trusteeship Committee of the General Assembly as a forum for ventilating "anti-colonialist" spleen.

As the object of the system was to provide a peaceful process whereby a dependent territory could be guided along the path to self-government, it is incompatible with the notion that a territory, as long as the mandate or trusteeship continued, could have a measure of international person-ality. Sovereignty, as Judge McNair said, was in abeyance, and would only revive "when the inhabitants of the territory obtain recognition as an independent state." And in practical terms, the tendency has been with

---

16. A balance that it is no longer possible to maintain, see below, p. 548.

the less developed of the dependent communities for the mandatory power or the administering power to retain close control over both the economic and political development of the territory concerned. South-West Africa has been administered by South Africa as an integral part of its own territory; New Guinea was joined to the Australian External Territory of Papua in 1949 by Act of the Australian Parliament and together they have been administered as one territory since that date; and only in 1968 did Nauru obtain complete independence. Until the granting of independence and the recognition of statehood, therefore, while a mandate or trusteeship territory has a status established by international law, it is not entitled to be regarded as an international person and an actor on the international plane.

3   INTERNATIONAL ORGANISATIONS

The numerous inter-governmental organisations that exist today vary enormously, both in powers and importance, and in the extent of their membership. The contrast in competence and significance between the United Nations on the one hand, and a body like the International Institute of Refrigeration on the other, could hardly be more striking. The size of the membership of international institutions provides the extremes of near universality, as with United Nations and certain of its specialised agencies at one end of the scale, and of a very small membership, as in the case of the European Communities of the "six" at the other end of the scale. As the subsequent discussion will demonstrate, both their powers and extent of their membership are relevant factors in considering whether these institutions, or some of them, are endowed with international personality.

The concept of international personality in relation to international organisations

From the original statement that *an international person is an entity having the power of independent action on the international plane*, and from the difficulty of applying even such a general definition to the position of non-self-governing states, it will have been realised that the concept of international personality cannot be defined or applied with precision. This lack of precision is equally apparent in its application to the field of international organisations. It is legitimate to argue, as the International Court did in the *Reparations* case,[17] that, because an entity (in that case the United Nations itself) was entitled to certain privileges and immunities and had the power to enter into treaties as an equal party with Member States, it must be considered as possessing international personality: in the Court's own words:

---

17.   I.C.J. Rep. 1949, p. 174.

". . . the Organisation was intended to exercise and enjoy, and is in fact exercising and enjoying, functions and rights which can only be explained on the basis of the possession of a large measure of international personality and the capacity to operate upon an international plane."

It is further permissible to deduce from this "measure of international personality" that the entity has the capacity to bring claims under international law:

". . . the Court has come to the conclusion that the Organisation is an international person . . . it is a subject of international law and capable of possessing international rights and duties, and it has capacity to maintain its rights by bringing international claims."[18]

However, because international legal personality is a variable concept, denoting no more than the capacity to act on the international plane, the Court's conclusion cannot be read as meaning more than that, from the type of functions the United Nations has the competence to undertake, the extent of its personality includes that of bringing international claims in its own name. Although a particular institution may lack some of the indicia of personality, it does not necessarily follow that it cannot be considered as an international "person", for, as the Court pointed out in the *Reparations* case, "the subjects of law in any legal system are not necessarily identical in their nature or in the extent of their rights".[19] In the last resort, while the concept of personality is a useful omnibus expression for referring to the complex of powers and privileges possessed by entities operating under international law, and the definition suggested has been framed to reflect this generalisation, the practical question must always remain, has this particular entity the legal competence to do this particular act?

The difficulty of deciding whether a given entity is endowed with personality is well illustrated by the position of a number of subsidiary organs of the General Assembly. The majority are clearly subsidiary to, and never lose their dependence on, the Assembly. Such treaties as concern them are made in the name of the Organisation, as with the Exchange of Letters between the United Nations Secretary-General and the Egyptian Foreign Minister of February, 1957, which provided for the status of the United Nations Emergency Force in Egypt. However, a small group of these organs have asserted a degree of freedom of operation which is difficult to reconcile with their origins under Article 22 of the Charter. The United Nations Relief and Works Agency, the United Nations International Children's Emergency Fund, and the United Nations Special Fund have all entered into treaty relations in their own name, both with states and with other international organisations, and their privileges and immunities have been provided for in agreements with the states in the territory of which they were about to operate. However,

---

18. *Ibid.*, p. 179.   19. *Ibid.*, p. 178.

unlike U.N.R.W.A., both U.N.I.C.E.F. and the Special Fund have made provision for the settlement of disputes in their treaties, though only in the case of the Special Fund does the standard disputes clause provide for full-scale international arbitration. Even if the status of U.N.R.W.A. and U.N.I.C.E.F. might therefore remain doubtful, the Special Fund had more obviously established its capacity to act independently on the international plane by the time it was merged with the Technical Assistance Programme to form the new U.N. Development Programme.[20]

4   THE INDICIA OF PERSONALITY

Only rarely will the constitution of an international organisation provide an express answer to the question whether or not the organisation is endowed with personality under international law. Outright recognition of personality by treaty has been largely avoided, though, occasionally, as in Article 4 of the Statute of the International Hydrographic Bureau,[21] an institution may be prohibited altogether from operating on the international plane. Normally, therefore, the question whether an institution possesses international personality can only be answered by inference from the type of functions, powers, privileges and immunities, often referred to as the *indicia of personality*, conferred by, or to be implied from, its constitution or agreements it might have entered into with states.

a STATUS UNDER MUNICIPAL LAW

Many constitutions do make provision for the capacity of the organisation under municipal law, either in the form of Article 104 of the Charter:

> "The Organisation shall enjoy in the territory of each of its Members such legal capacity as may be necessary for the exercise of its functions and the fulfilment of its purposes"—

or of Article 39 of the I.L.O. Constitution:

> "The International Labour Organisation shall possess juridical personality and in particular the capacity—
> (a) to contract;
> (b) to acquire and dispose of immovable and movable property;
> (c) to institute legal proceedings."

These provisions are generally coupled with a requirement that the organisation itself, representatives of members attending its meetings, and officials of the organisation, should be entitled to such privileges and immunities under municipal law as are necessary for carrying out their

---

20. See below, p. 594.
21. Article 4 provides:
"(a) The Bureau is a purely consultative agency: it has no authority over the hydrographic offices of Member States. . . .
(b) The Bureau shall not be concerned with matters involving questions of international policy."

respective functions. The attempt has been made to deduce from the grant of immunities the existence of international personality on the ground that such immunities are reserved for bodies which have that personality. However, the conclusion of one such writer that the "granting of such immunities is, to a certain extent, equivalent to a conveyance of international legal personality . . . as well as recognition of that status"[1] must be regarded with caution. The constitution of the International Institute of Refrigeration makes provision for "Legal capacity, privileges and immunities", but these in themselves are not sufficient to establish the Institute's status under international law. In order to establish its claim to a measure of international personality, it is necessary to look at the provisions of its constitution as a whole (the fact that disputes over the interpretation of its constitution are to "be submitted to the International Court of Justice or to an arbitration procedure determined by the General Conference" of the Institute is obviously significant) and to consider the attitude of governments to its claims. If states deal with it as an international person (negotiate with it, enter into agreements with it, etc.), the presumption is that they recognise its separate legal identity. Thus, the absence of any provision relating to capacity and privileges and immunities under municipal law is not fatal to the existence of international personality, providing that other evidence of its existence is available. The constitution of the International Wheat Council contains no reference to its municipal status, but its structure and the tasks entrusted to it, suggest that the Council has the power to operate in its own right both on the international and municipal plane.

b TREATY-MAKING POWER

Undoubtedly the most important attribute of international personality is the treaty-making power. It has already been suggested that the separate identity of the United Nations Special Fund stemmed from its assumed authority to enter into treaty arrangements independently of the General Assembly. Moreover, the multitude of treaties entered into by the United Nations, and by the Specialised Agencies, are illustrative of the wide measure of personality enjoyed by these institutions. In the *Reparations* case, the International Court referred to the treaty-making powers conferred upon the United Nations by the Charter, and, in citing specifically the Convention on Privileges and Immunities, drawn up by the General Assembly in 1946, the Court stated that it was "difficult to see how such a convention could operate except upon the international plane and as between parties possessing international personality."[2]

c INTERNATIONAL CLAIMS

In the *Reparations* case, the right of the United Nations in dispute was its power to present claims on the international plane. The conclusion of

---

1. Weissberg, *International Status of the United Nations*, p. 12.
2. I.C.J. Rep. 1949, at p. 179.

the Court was that, from the powers exercised by the Organisation, and from the privileges and immunities to which it was entitled, it was possible to conclude that the United Nations had a sufficient degree of international personality to be able to bring such claims. But it is possible to imagine the reverse situation, in which an institution is claiming to be entitled to, for example, privileges and immunities in the territory of its members in the absence of an express provision in its constitution, and where one of the main factors supporting its claim to international personality is its power to be a party to international adjudication. A disputes clause providing for the settlement of disputes by arbitration or other international process of adjudication in a treaty to which the organisation is a party would be of particular significance.

d GENERAL POWERS

Although privileges and immunities, a treaty-making power and the right to take part in international adjudication are important indications of the existence of international personality, they should be considered in the wider context of the specific powers conferred on an organisation and the type of duties it is required to perform under its constitution. To refer to the *Reparations* case once more, the Court stated that the United Nations "was intended to exercise and enjoy, and is in fact exercising and enjoying, functions and rights which can only be explained on the basis of the possession of a large measure of international personality and the capacity to operate on the international plane",[2] and when it went on to decide that the organisation did have the power to exercise "a measure of functional protection of its agents"[3] it based its conclusion on the "character of the functions entrusted to the Organisation", particularly the need "to entrust its agents with important missions to be performed in disturbed parts of the world."[4]

e EXPRESS OR IMPLIED RECOGNITION

If the constitution of an organisation grants it sufficiently wide powers to establish its personality on the international plane, it is not open to its members to deny the existence of that personality: their signing and acceptance of the constitution is tantamount to recognition of the independent status of the organisation created by its constitution. But a non-member state will not have thus recognised the status of the organisation. Is the personality of an organisation an objective status effective as against states which are not signatories to its constituent treaty? Another of the issues before the Court in the *Reparations* case was whether the United Nations had the capacity to bring an international claim against a state which was not a member of the Organisation. The Court cautiously upheld the capacity of the United Nations by asserting that:

> "fifty States, representing the vast majority of the members of the international community, had the power, in conformity with international law, to bring into

---

3. *Ibid.*, at p. 184.   4. *Ibid.*, at p. 183.

being an entity possessing objective international personality, and not merely personality recognised by them alone. . . ."[5]

This pronouncement leaves open the position of organisations like the European Economic Community, the Coal and Steel Community or E.U.R.A.T.O.M. for example, which were established by a small number of states. Obviously, it would not be possible for one of their members to deny the international status of the Communities for the "six" are signatories to treaties expressly providing for the personality of the institutions, both under municipal and international law. Similarly, by entering into negotiations with the Communities, or even into treaty relations,[6] a large number of states must be taken to have tacitly accepted the corporate status of the Communities on the international plane. However, there is no clear answer to the question whether one of the Communities has the "objective personality" which would enable it to bring a claim on its own behalf for an international wrong committed against it by a state which has never by any previous act tacitly accepted, and still refuses to acknowledge, its international capacity.

5 THE POSITION OF THE INDIVIDUAL

There is a wealth of juristic writing which has derived international personality for the individual from various treaties for the protection of minorities; from the United Nations Declaration, and the European Convention, on Human Rights; and from the imposition of criminal responsibility on individuals for the breach of rules of international law relating to piracy, the slave trade, or war crimes.

As the introduction to this chapter pointed out, however, the fact that rules of international law apply to individuals does not necessarily mean that individuals are the "persons" of international law unless "international personality" is given a definition sufficiently wide to include them. Closer to the realities of international life is the definition suggested that the attribute of personality should be reserved for those entities, primarily states and certain international organisations, which have an objective, and independent, capacity to operate on the international plane. As Jessup recognized:

> "So long . . . as the international community is composed of states, it is only through an exercise of their will, as expressed through treaty or agreement or as laid down by an international authority deriving its power from states, that a rule of law becomes binding upon an individual. . . . The inescapable fact is that the world is today organised on the basis of the co-existence of states, and that fundamental changes will only take place through state action. . . ."[7]

---

5. *Ibid.*, at p. 185.
6. See, for example, the Agreement of 1954 between the United Kingdom and the European Coal and Steel Community, 258 U.N.T.S. 322.
7. *A Modern Law of Nations*, p. 17.

In order to draw a clear distinction between the personality of a state or of an international institution on the one hand, and the position of the individual on the other, some elaboration is required of the ways in which international law does apply to individuals. Historically, those rules which first developed imposed duties designed to prevent piracy and the slave-trade, and to protect the persons and status of foreign sovereigns and their diplomatic representatives. It was from the existence of rules of this type that certain writers at the end of the nineteenth century classified states as the "subjects", and individuals as the "objects" of international law. Whatever the merits of the "object" theory in its historical context, it was certainly inadequate to explain situations, such as under a number of minority and other treaties after the First World War, where individuals were granted rights directly or indirectly enforceable against foreign states. Typical of a treaty allowing direct action to be taken was the arbitral system created by the minority provisions of the Upper Silesian Convention, Article 5 of which stated that "the question of whether or to what extent an indemnity for the abolition or diminution of vested rights must be paid by the *state* will be settled by the Arbitral Tribunal on the complaint of the *person* enjoying the right."

There is also no reason why a treaty should not grant individuals the right to prosecute a claim against a foreign state in proceedings before municipal tribunals. In the *Jurisdiction of the Courts of Danzig* case,[8] for example, the Permanent Court held that certain Danzig railway officials could bring an action before the Danzig Courts against the Polish State Railways for the recovery of compensation payable under an international agreement binding on Poland and Danzig. The Court pointed out that "the very object of an international agreement, according to the intention of the contracting Parties, may be the adoption by the Parties of some definite rules creating individual rights and obligations and enforceable by the national courts."[9]

The appearance of treaty rules bestowing rights directly on individuals destroyed the logical foundation of the "object" principle, but the result was not the acceptance of individuals as "subjects" of international law. Instead of "objects" they became "beneficiaries" of its rules. However, even in this modified guise, theory fell out of step with reality. In the War Crimes Trials following the Second World War, the principle of individual responsibility for breach of international obligations was given extended application. In rejecting the defendants' contention that it was the German State alone which could be liable for acts contrary to alleged rules of international law, the Nuremberg Tribunal made the following well-known statement:

"That international law imposes duties and liabilities upon individuals as well as upon states has long been recognised. . . . Crimes against international law are

8. (1928) P.C.I.J. Rep., Ser. B, No. 15.
9. *Ibid.*, at pp. 17–18.

committed by men, not by abstract entities, and only by punishing individuals who commit such crimes can the provisions of international law be enforced."[10]

The most notable example of the creation by states of a quasi-judicial process enabling the prosecution of claims directly by individuals against states is the machinery established under the European Convention of Human Rights.[11] The Convention governs the relations between the states parties to it and all persons within the jurisdiction of each state; it is also open to any state to declare that the provisions of the Convention shall apply to "any of the territories for whose international relations it is responsible." Individuals anywhere within the territorial scope of the Convention are granted the right to petition the Commission established by the Convention to look into alleged violations of the rights safeguarded by the Convention. However, it remains doubtful whether this right of petition greatly strengthens the argument that individuals should be regarded as endowed with a measure of international personality. The function of the Commission is essentially that of conciliation, so that even if the allegations made by the petitioner are accepted, the most that the Commission can do is to report its findings together with any proposals it may care to make to the state concerned and to the Committee of Ministers of the Council of Europe. It is entirely a matter for the Commission or the state concerned whether the matter is referred to the European Court of Human Rights: there is no right allowing an individual to initiate proceedings before the court. Any action to be taken on the recommendation of the Commission or following a decision of the court is entirely a matter for the Committee of Ministers.

It will be recalled that, whereas the United Nations, or any organisation with similarly large membership, and having power to act on the international plane, could be said to have objective personality, doubt was expressed as to the status of organisations of restricted membership, except in so far as their capacity had been impliedly acknowledged by non-member states. Similar considerations apply to the position of individuals who have been granted enforceable rights under a number of treaties signed by only a few states. There exists no international instrument—the United Nations Declaration on Human Rights being no more than a general statement of moral purpose and not a vehicle of legal obligation[12]—which grants to individuals a universally accepted status under international law, together with the right to operate on the international plane. But while an international organisation, with a restricted membership may by tacit recognition achieve an objective existence, the position of the individual on the international plane is still at the whim of each state. Even the European Convention of Human Rights allows states parties to

---

10. *Nuremberg Judgment*, p. 41.
11. See further, below, pp. 616–621.
12. The United Nations Convention on Human Rights of December, 1966, has not yet received sufficient ratifications to enter into force.

the Convention a right of denunciation. A withdrawal from an international organisation does not affect the personality of the organisation; but a denunciation of the European Convention is the equivalent of the withdrawal of international rights from all persons within the territory of the state concerned.

CHAPTER FOUR

RECOGNITION

The international community is not a static body. New states come into existence. Revolutions occur and new governments establish themselves. Territorial changes take place. Of these changes the members of the international community have the choice of approving or disapproving. Recognition is the process whereby a state acknowledges its approval of the change that has occurred. But because the tendency is for the approval or non-approval to be based upon political motives and not upon considerations of the legality of the change, recognition must be regarded as primarily a political act. Although political in the sense that it is accorded or withheld for political reasons, it is an act which nevertheless has legal consequences. It is in the first place evidence of the factual situation thus recognised, and, secondly, it has the effect of bringing about certain legal consequences in regularising the relations on the diplomatic level between the recognising state and the entity recognised, and in clarifying the juridical standing of the recognised entity in the courts of the recognising state.

1 THE INTERNATIONAL ASPECTS OF RECOGNITION

A. The act of recognition

Recognition may be effected either expressly, through formal announcement, or the conclusion of a bilateral treaty recognising one of the parties as a state; or by implication, as any act which clearly indicates the intention to recognise may be regarded as recognition.

a EXPRESS RECOGNITION

The formal announcement may take the form of a public statement, the text of which is sent to the party recognised as a state or government, or of a diplomatic note alone. Usually, such a step is taken unilaterally by the recognising state, but examples do exist of recognition being accorded jointly by a group of states, most notably of Estonia and Latvia in 1921 by the Inter-Allied Conference, and the recognition of Albania in 1922 by the Conference of Ambassadors, comprising representatives of Great Britain, France, Italy and Japan. Recognition may also be granted by treaty: indeed, it has been the method usually employed by the United Kingdom in establishing the independence of its colonial or other dependent territories. For example, under the treaty between the Government of the United Kingdom and the Provisional Government of Burma signed on 17th October, 1947, and to come into operation on 4th January, 1948, the Government of the United Kingdom recognised "the Republic of the Union of Burma as a fully independent sovereign state".

b IMPLIED RECOGNITION

Normally, no problem will arise over whether state A has recognised state B or government C, because it will have issued an unequivocal statement granting recognition. Since, however, it is possible for recognition to be implied from the conduct of state A towards state B or government C, "implied recognition" has been accorded a significance in juristic writings out of all proportion to its practical importance. Once it is accepted that "to bring about recognition by implication the act must be an unequivocal one and of such a character as clearly to indicate that recognition was intended or is inescapable"[1] the theory of implied recognition would be seen in its appropriately narrow perspective. In 1928, the United States Minister in China entered into a treaty of commerce with a representative of the new Nationalist Government of China: it was subsequently held by a United States Court of Appeals that the signing of the treaty constituted recognition of the new régime as the government of China.[2] The Court went on to state that, if the treaty alone was not sufficient, the fact that the United States had received an accredited diplomatic representative from the new government was conclusive.

The emphasis on the need for the existence of a clear intention to recognise has been lost sight of in recent years. Writing in 1947, Lauterpacht was able to state with certainty that there was no implied recognition in the fact that a state had become party to a treaty to which an unrecognised state was already a party (or remained a party after an unrecognised state became a party), nor did participation in an international conference to which an unrecognised state was invited amount to recognition.[3] It is becoming increasingly the practice, however, for formal reservations to be made in circumstances in which denial of recognition would formerly have been otiose. When the Berlin Conference of Foreign Ministers in 1954 resolved to hold the Geneva Conference on Korea and Indo-China, a final paragraph stated:

---

1. Hackworth in a Department of State Memorandum, quoted Whiteman, *Digest of International Law*, Vol. 2, p. 48.
2. *Republic of China* v. *Merchants' Fire Ass. Corpn.*, 30 F. (2d) 278 (1929); (1929–30) 5 A.D., Case No. 21.
3. *Recognition in International Law*, p. 405.

"It is understood that neither the invitation to, nor the holding of, the above-mentioned conference shall be deemed to imply diplomatic recognition in any case where it has not already been accorded."

Similarly, though negotiations by a state with an unrecognised entity are by no means exceptional, when, during the Geneva Conference itself, the United States entered into separate negotiations with the Chinese Communists for the release of certain American airmen, the American delegation issued a statement that:

"The U.S. Government has made the decision to authorise informal U.S. participation in this meeting because of its obligation to protect the welfare of its citizens... U.S. participation in these conversations in no way implies U.S. accordance of any measure of diplomatic recognition to the Red Chinese régime."

B. Recognition is accorded for political reasons

a THE RECOGNITION OF STATES

In the previous chapter the concept of statehood was defined in terms that included recognition by other states as an essential factor in the creation of a new state.[4] An entity which otherwise fulfils the factual requirements of territory, population and a stable government will fail to qualify as a state in the absence of recognition of this status by the international community. It was suggested, however, that this constitutive aspect of recognition is more a political fact of international life than it is a fundamental legal principle. As soon as the constitutive nature of recognition is seen in terms of the strict theory that through recognition alone can a state become a legal person, logical problems arise in attempting to reconcile the theory with the practice of states. For example it is not easily reconciled with the fact that, unless recognition is accorded jointly by a large number of states, the timing of the individual acts of recognition will often vary considerably from one state to another. In order to avoid this problem by making it likely that the individual acts of recognition take place more or less contemporaneously, the proposition has been advanced that once the factual characteristics of statehood exist, there is a legal duty to accord recognition to the new state.

"To recognise a community as a State is to declare that it fulfils the conditions of statehood as required by international law. If these conditions are present, existing States are under the duty to grant recognition. In the absence of an international organ competent to ascertain and authoritatively to declare the presence of requirements of full international personality, States already established fulfil that function in their capacity as organs of international law. In thus acting, they administer the law of nations. This rule of law signifies that in granting or withholding recognition States do not claim and are not entitled to serve exclusively the interests of their national policy and convenience regardless of the principles of international law in

4. See above, pp. 77–79.

the matter. Although recognition is thus declaratory of an existing fact, such declaration, made in the impartial fulfilment of a legal duty, is constitutive, as between the recognising State and the community so recognised, of international rights and duties associated with full statehood. Prior to recognition such rights and obligations exist only to the extent to which they have been expressly conceded or legitimately asserted, by reference to compelling rules of humanity and justice, either by the existing members of the international society or by the people claiming recognition."[5]

Although states do make reference to the presence or absence of the factual characteristics of statehood when granting or withholding recognition, in the last resort their decision will normally be based on political expediency. It is true that the Spanish colonies in central and South America in revolt against Spanish domination at the beginning of the nineteenth century were in the process of establishing the characteristics of statehood, but there were convincing political reasons why recognition should have been granted by Great Britain and the United States. Whatever might be the true status of the German Democratic Republic today there are powerful political factors making recognition by the western powers unlikely. The political discretion to grant or withhold recognition was emphasised by Senator Warren Austin in the Security Council in May, 1948, with reference to the recognition by the United States of the nascent state of Israel:

"I should regard it as highly improper for me to admit that any country on earth can question the sovereignty of the United States of America in the exercise of the high political act of recognition of the *de facto* status of a state. Moreover, I would not admit here, by implication or by direct answer, that there exists a tribunal of justice or of any other kind, anywhere, that can pass judgment upon the legality or the validity of that act of my country."[6]

But even if the thesis were accepted that states should recognise as a state an entity that had attained a certain factual status, there would still be situations in which an entity was recognised as a state by some members of the international community, but not by others. The application of a purely factual test would still be influenced by political predilection. To take a simple illustration—entity A breaks away from state B, but there remains unsettled a boundary dispute between them; entity A is immediately recognised as a state by those states which favour its political cause, but supporters of state B refuse recognition on the ground that the boundaries of entity A remain unsettled. If political factors influence recognition in this type of situation, far greater political discretion would be available if recognition were withheld on the ground that the new entity was not capable of entering into relations on its own behalf on the international plane. It was universally believed that Manchukuo, as the creature of Japanese military intervention, did not have the independent

---

5. Lauterpacht, *Recognition in International Law*, p. 6.
6. S.C.O.R., 3rd Year, at p. 16.

capacity to conduct its foreign relations; but what of the German Demo-cratic Republic today? Is it possible for all states to make an impartial, non-political, judgment in such a situation?

b THE RECOGNITION OF GOVERNMENTS

Although the practice of states is far from establishing the existence of a legal duty to recognise an entity which has established the factual characteristics of statehood, it is even more apparent that no such duty exists in relation to the recognition of new governments. The Tinoco régime in Costa Rica between 1917 and 1919 was not recognised by the Allied Powers largely in deference to the wishes of the United States. The Soviet Government which came to power in 1919 was not recognised as the government of Russia by Great Britain until 1921 and by the United States until 1933. The present Communist government of China which established its authority over the whole Chinese mainland in 1949 is still not recognised by the United States.

i *British practice*

Nevertheless, although there may not exist any duty to recognise, there are still general criteria against which a new régime may be tested before recognition is granted; indeed, in more recent years, successive governments of the United Kingdom, largely influenced by the views expressed by Lauterpacht, have attempted to apply what might be termed the *de facto* test of control. In 1951, the then Foreign Secretary, Herbert Morrison, stated in the House of Commons:[7]

> "The conditions under international law for the recognition of a new régime as the *de facto* government of a state are that the new régime has in fact effective control over most of the state's territory and that this control seems likely to continue."

This approach was more fully explained by the then British Ambassador to the United States, Sir Roger Makins, in 1954:[8]

> "If a government is in effective control of the country in question; if it seems to have a reasonable expectancy of permanence; if it can act for a majority of the country's inhabitants; if it is able (though possibly not willing) to carry out its international obligations; if, in short, it can give a convincing answer to the question, 'Who's in charge here?' then we recognise that government."

Consequently, the Kadar régime which came to power in Hungary with the assistance of Russian military intervention following the 1956 up-rising, was by implication accepted as the *de facto* government: British diplomatic representatives in Budapest, and the Hungarian mission in London, remained. When questioned on the attitude of Her Majesty's Government, a government spokesman explained that its policy was, "to

---

7. 485 H.C.D., col. 2410.   8. Quoted, Whiteman, *op. cit.*, Vol. 2, p. 111.

face facts and to acknowledge *de facto* a Government which has effective control of the territory within its jurisdiction, and of the inhabitants within that territory. Such *de facto* recognition does not constitute a judgment on the legality of the Government concerned; still less does it imply approval of it. . . ."[9]

Where the logic of the approach adopted by the United Kingdom would seem to break down is in its attitude towards governments claiming to act on behalf of areas which the United Kingdom is unwilling to recognise as states. North Korea, North Vietnam, and East Germany are Democratic Republics with their own governments exercising legislative and administrative control over defined geographical areas. The United Kingdom does not recognise these entities as states because it does not accept the legality or permanence of the division of Korea, Vietnam and Germany into two separate units. It is unwilling to apply the *de facto* test of the existence of a government apparently because it is thought that even to recognise the authorities concerned as governments would be to support their claim to an independent existence as a state. But is not the fear of being taken to accept the legality of a situation as much a political consideration as any other motive for refraining to recognise a particular government?

ii *United States practice*

United States practice may be distinguished from the approach of the United Kingdom in the following ways.

First, it is clear from the statement quoted from the speech of the United States representative to the Security Council on the attitude of the American Government towards recognition that the United States does not attempt to conceal the value of recognition, or the withholding of recognition, as a diplomatic weapon in the conduct of international relations.

Secondly, the United States claims that, in the absence of overriding political factors, recognition will be accorded if the entity concerned satisfies the *de facto* test, although this test is amplified by a greater emphasis on whether the government has obtained the consent of the governed. Whether a government has obtained the consent of the population of a state may be a relevant factor when considering the degree and effectiveness of its control, but, taken in isolation, it can be used as a means of passing political judgment on any régime which does not accord with the democratic ideal. On the other hand, there have been examples of the United States Government giving support to, and recognising, régimes which are renowned more for their strong anti-Communist policies than for their high-standing in the opinion of the people they govern.[10]

---

9. 204 H.L.D., col. 755 (4th July, 1957).

10. It can hardly be argued that the Nationalist Government of China enjoys much support on the mainland of China, though the United States continues to recognise the Nationalists; nor can it be said that the régimes in the Dominican Republic and, certainly until the elections of 1967, in South Vietnam were any the less dictatorships dependent on the army and United States assistance and not on popular support.

Thirdly, United States practice has repeatedly paid regard to the question of whether a government has shown its readiness to discharge its international obligations. While the United Kingdom looks upon *ability* to fulfil such obligations as a test of a government's capacity to represent the state concerned, the United States has insisted upon the further requirement that the government seeking recognition should also intend to fulfil those obligations. Though the People's Republic of China undoubtedly has the physical power to fulfil its obligations—which satisfies the British test—it has, in the American view, shown a degree of aggressiveness in Korea, in Tibet, and towards India, quite incompatible with any intention to abide by the rules of international law.

Fourthly, because, even in the theory of United States practice, there are likely to exist governments which are not recognised, the State Department has been more inclined than the British Foreign Office to engage in quasi-diplomatic relations with unrecognised governments. As a former Secretary of State said in 1958 of the attitude of the United States to Communist China:[11]

> "There is no doubt we recognise Communist China as a fact, as we deal with Communist China. Indeed, I suspect that the United States has had more continuous serious dealings with Communist China than any other free-world country over the last ten years. We have dealt with it in Korea in terms of the Korean armistice. We . . . dealt with it at Geneva at the Indo-China armistice. We have had talks at the diplomatic level, first at Geneva and now in Warsaw, over the last four years with the Chinese Communists. It's a fact and we deal with it as a fact . . . we do not accept the blind policy of pretending that it doesn't exist."

C. De jure and de facto recognition

The statement that a particular entity has been recognised *de jure* or *de facto* is a convenient shorthand form of saying that it has been recognised as a *de jure* or *de facto* government. In other words, it is its status as a government, and not the recognition, that is *de jure* or *de facto*.

Although the practice of states does establish the existence of both *de jure* and *de facto* recognition, any legal distinctions between the two arise in the municipal law of the recognising state rather than in the sphere of international law. As far as recognition on the international plane is concerned, therefore, all that can be attempted is a summary of the circumstances in which *de jure* and *de facto* recognition have frequently been employed.

De facto recognition of a state seldom arises because until a new state has become sufficiently well established to qualify for *de jure* recognition, the practice of states has favoured either the recognition of the government claiming to act on behalf of the nascent state as a *de facto* authority[12] or no recognition at all.[13] Any differences that may appear from the practice

---

11. Quoted, Whiteman, *op. cit.*, Vol. 2, pp. 104–105.
12. See *The Gagara*, [1919] P. 95.
13. As with the present German Democratic Republic.

of states between *de jure* and *de facto* recognition relate essentially to the recognition of governments.

Recognition, whether it be *de facto* or *de jure*, usually implies that the recognised authority has effective control over a given area, but *de jure* recognition suggests that this control shows evidence of a substantial degree of permanence. Any inquiry into the differences between the two must, therefore, concentrate upon the situations in which *de facto* recognition is selected in preference to *de jure*. Such situations would seem to fall mainly into two categories:

(a) *where a* de facto *authority is exercising the powers of government in an area under the nominal control of the existing* de jure *government of a state;*

The distinction between *de jure* and *de facto* recognition in such circumstances has been described as follows:[14]

> "A *de jure* government is one which—in the opinion of the person using the phrase—ought to possess the powers of sovereignty, though at the time it may be deprived of them. A *de facto* government is one which is really in possession of them, although the possession may be wrongful or precarious."

A typical illustration of such a situation was the recognition *de facto* by Great Britain of the administration set up in Abyssinia in 1936 by the invading Italian armies: it was two years before *de jure* recognition was withdrawn from the Emperor Haile Selassie and accorded to the Italian authorities. Similarly, during the course of the Spanish Civil War, the Republican Government was still regarded as the *de jure* government though increasingly large areas of Spain were occupied by the Nationalist forces of General Franco, whose authority was recognised *de facto* by His Majesty's Government.

(b) *where the* de jure *government has ceased to exist and the recognised* de facto *authority is the only possible government of the state, but in circumstances where* de jure *recognition is withheld because of doubts as to the authority's degree of permanence, or as a sign of disapproval.*

It will be seen from the examples quoted above of the recognition of the Italian régime in Abyssinia and of the Nationalist Government of General Franco in Spain that *de facto* recognition frequently precedes *de jure* recognition. This use of *de facto* recognition as a provisional measure has also been employed in situations where the original *de jure* government has ceased to exist. The period of *de facto* recognition accorded by the United Kingdom to the Soviet Government in Russia was at a time when there was no existing *de jure* government of Russia. And, more recently, following the overthrow of the Egyptian monarchy in 1953, the United Kingdom recognised the new régime tacitly by acknowledging a communication from the Egyptian Ambassador: in the words of a government spokesman in the House of Commons, "Her Majesty's Government are thus *de facto* in relations with the Egyptian Government."[15] The distinc-

---

14. Quoted by Bankes, L.J., in *Luther* v. *Sagor*, [1921] 3 K.B., at p. 543.
15. 517 H.C.D., col. 204 (30th June, 1953). See also 183 H.L.D., cols. 1417–18 (28th October, 1953).

tion between *de facto* and *de jure* recognition is much favoured by the United Kingdom, though it has largely been discarded in contemporary American practice. Whatever public statements might be made about *de facto* recognition connoting lack of permanent stability, in certain situations it has been used by the United Kingdom as a sign of disapproval. The Soviet Government of Russia was recognised *de facto* in 1921, but *de jure* recognition was withheld for a further three years. This delay resulted not only from doubts as to the stability of the régime but also from its obvious refusal to fulfil its international obligations.[16] On the other hand, the United States normally accords simply "recognition", even in the case of recently established "provisional" governments. When Castro succeeded in seizing control of Cuba and installed Dr. Urrutia as President, the United States stated that it was "pleased to recognise the government under the presidency of Dr. . . . Urrutia, as the provisional government of the Republic of Cuba." Genuine disapproval is recorded by withholding recognition altogether, though, as the example of the Communist Government of China shows, the United States will often acknowledge the *de facto* existence of the unrecognised authority.

D. The doctrine of non-recognition

When a state refuses to recognise a new state or government, its actions are usually based on a variety of political motives, but the doctrine of non-recognition only applies when the withholding of recognition is expressly designed as a protest against some international illegality. If, for example, the government of a state is overthrown by force in the form of foreign intervention, or if a new state is created and maintained by foreign troops, a declaration of non-recognition is necessary to withhold from the wrongdoer the benefits arising from acquiescence in, or tacit acceptance of, the new situation. The doctrine is particularly associated with the name of the American Secretary of State, Stimson, who, in connection with the Japanese intervention in China in 1932, made public the following note:

> "In view of the present situation . . . the American Government deemed it to be its duty to notify both the Imperial Japanese Government and the Government of the Chinese Republic that it cannot admit the legality of any situation *de facto* nor does it intend to recognise any treaty or agreement entered into between these Governments . . . which may impair the treaty rights of the United States . . . including those which relate to the sovereignty, the independence, or the territorial and administrative integrity of the Republic of China . . . and that it does not intend to recognise any situation, treaty or agreement which may be brought about by means contrary to the Pact of Paris. . . ."

---

16. Some of the doubts as to the stability of the régime arose from the fact that British and other Allied troops were engaged in hostile operations on the side of Anti-Bolshevik forces in Russia: see the guarded Foreign Office Certificate in *The Annette*, [1919] P. 105.

Despite the attempt by the Assembly of the League of Nations to recommend the doctrine to its Members, non-recognition was applied only haphazardly to territorial changes in the years from 1932 to 1940. The Italian seizure of Abyssinia in 1936 was generally recognised, and the *anschluss* of 1938 whereby Austria was absorbed into Germany was tacitly accepted, though the United States, Britain and other "western" states have consistently to the present day refused to recognise the Soviet annexation of the Baltic Republics in 1940.

A duty to apply the principle of non-recognition was said to stem from the undertaking in the Paris Pact of 1928 to condemn resort to war for the solution of international controversies and, more particularly, from Article 10 of the Covenant of the League which stated that "Members of the League undertake to respect and preserve as against external aggression the territorial integrity and existing political independence of all Members of the League." Although the Charter of the United Nations contains no such undertaking that Members should *preserve* the territorial integrity and existing political independence of other states, Article 2 contains a series of complementary obligations of which paragraph 4 requires that Members should nevertheless refrain from "the threat or use of force against the territorial integrity or political independence of any state". Although recognition of territorial changes in breach of Article 2 (4) would not necessarily be incompatible with a state's obligations under the Charter, the fact that force had been used by another state contrary to the provisions of the Charter would be a strong reason for other states to adopt a policy of non-recognition towards any territorial or other changes brought about thereby.

E. Withdrawal of recognition and conditional recognition

In so far as *de facto* recognition implies some degree of uncertainty as to the future stability of the recognised entity, it may clearly be withdrawn if the status of the state or government is thrown once more into doubt. It may also be argued that *de facto* recognition is in this sense conditional on the continued factual existence of the recognised entity, so that if the entity clearly ceased to exist, the recognition itself ceases to apply.

Although the same basic principles apply in the case of *de jure* recognition, there is marked difference in emphasis. *Prima facie*, *de jure* recognition cannot be withdrawn from a state or government simply because of, for example, internal disorders within the state. Indeed, it is probable that *de jure* sovereignty will remain even after all semblance of authority has vanished. The United States and Britain have consistently refused to recognise the Soviet seizure of the Baltic States of Latvia, Esthonia and Lithuania in 1940 and have continued to accept the diplomatic agents of those states as accredited representatives of a *de jure* sovereign.

Recognition of an annexation or usurpation *de facto* may not be sufficient to destroy the ultimate rights of the *de jure* sovereign. It is certainly the case under English law that nothing short of *de jure* recognition of the successor power will affect the rights of the original sovereign over areas not controlled by the usurping authority. Despite the *de facto* recognition of the authority of General Franco over large areas of Spain during the Civil War, and of the Italian forces over the whole of Abyssina in 1936, it was only with their subsequent *de jure* recognition as the governments of Spain and Abyssinia respectively that the former *de jure* authorities were supplanted. Indeed, it would seem that the English courts would apply this principle so rigorously that a *de facto* government would not be entitled to recover state property, even state documents, deposited in England, although all vestiges of the former *de jure* authority had disappeared.[17]

In a limited sense, therefore, both *de facto* and *de jure* recognition are conditional. *De facto* recognition depends on the continued existence of the criteria of statehood or of governmental capacity, while *de jure* recognition will not survie the *de jure* recognition of a successor power. However, the expression "conditional recognition" has a more specialised meaning: it implies that the granting of recognition is made dependent upon the fulfilment by the recognised state or government of stipulations in addition to the normal requirements. Although frequently to be found as a means of exerting political pressure, particularly during the nineteenth century, it has largely disappeared from contemporary state practice. If the earlier precedents are any reliable guide, the type of condition might vary from the specific demand that a state would meet its debts—as was the case with the British recognition of the government of Mexico in 1861—to the more general request for assurances that the recognised state or government would fulfil its international obligations. Both the United Kingdom and the United States recognised the Provisional Governments of Czechoslovakia and Poland during the 1939–45 war on the understanding that free elections were held after the liberation of the two countries from German occupation. Even more striking was the famous Litvinov Agreement of 1933 when the United States finally recognised the Soviet Government of Russia under a settlement which covered all outstanding differences between the two states. Matters covered included the settlement of financial claims, and an undertaking by the Soviet Government to avoid acts prejudicial to the internal security of the United States.

As a legal concept, however, conditional recognition has no real significance. The reason for this is partly that recognition is normally a unilateral act, in which case the recognised state is clearly not bound to observe conditions to which it has not assented, and partly that many of the assurances required before recognition is granted—that a government will honour its obligations or will sometime in the future hold free

---

17. This would seem to be the implication from Bennett, J.'s decision in *Haile Selassie v. Cable & Wireless, Ltd.* (*No. 2*), [1939] 1 Ch. 182, esp. at pp. 189–190 when commenting upon *Luther v. Sagor*, [1921] 3 K.B. 532; and from *U.S.S.R. v. Onou* (1925), 69 Sol. Jo. 676.

elections—are imposed for political motives and are expressed in political, not legal, terms. It follows that breach of such a condition involves not an automatic termination of recognition, but a choice by the recognising state on the forms of political action open to it. While in the nineteenth century when the recognised government failed to pay its debts, the answer might have been "gunboat diplomacy", the selection today would be rather more restricted—diplomatic protest, breaking off diplomatic relations, but not normally withdrawal of recognition. Even when the recognition formed part of a wider settlement embodied in a formal agreement, as in the Litvinov Agreement, many of the undertakings—such as that of the Soviet Union to refrain from acts likely to cause disorder in the United States—were still primarily formulated in political terms, and alleged breaches of this undertaking left the United States with the choice of political remedies alone.

F. Recognition and the United Nations

Matters relating to recognition arise in two different situations in United Nations practice: the recognition of states may be in issue in applications for admission to membership; and the recognition of governments will often be involved should there be a dispute over credentials—the question of who is entitled to represent a certain member state in the Organisation.

a ADMISSION TO THE UNITED NATIONS AND THE ISSUE OF STATEHOOD

As far as the first situation is concerned, whether an applicant for admission has been recognised as a state will clearly be relevant if any doubts are raised about its status. Arguments in favour of the admission of Israel stressed the fact that more than fifty states had recognised its independence by the time the question was debated in the General Assembly. Two other problems, however, are not so simply answered: does admission to membership in itself constitute recognition of the applicant as a state? Secondly, if a member state has not recognised the applicant, what is the effect of the actual voting on its application for membership?

As Article 4 of the Charter provides that subsequent membership "is open to all other peace-loving states" which fulfil certain conditions, the act of admission is an acknowledgment by the Organisation that, within its field of competence, the new member is a state. Within that field, it would not be open to any member to challenge the status of another member, unless there had been such a fundamental change of circumstances that it could be argued that the other member had ceased to exist as a state altogether. It will be recalled that, under international law, recognition plays two major roles: as far as the recognising state is concerned, recognition only means that it "proposes to treat the new entity as a state", while, for the international community, recognition is evidence of the statehood of the new entity. Admission to membership fulfils a similar function in that, internally, the Organisation proposes to treat the new entity as a state. Similarly, as far as its external effects are concerned, the fact of admission to the United Nations would be of probative value should a tribunal be called upon to decide, in accordance with international law, the status of a particular entity. Once this similarity of function between admission by the United Nations and recognition by states is understood, the debate whether admission is the equivalent of recognition becomes pointless.

Why has there been a dispute as to the nature of the act of admission and its relationship with recognition? There seems to have been a fear expressed by a number of states that the act of admission involves "recognition" not by the Organisation, but by its individual members. As the existence of a state under international law is independent of individual acts of recognition, the view expressed by the majority of members of an international organisation would not appear to affect the attitude to recognition maintained by a state in the minority, except within the sphere of competence of that organisation. In *U.S.S.R.* v. *Luxembourg & Sarr Co.*,[18] a Luxembourg Court reached the conclusion, justifiable in terms of constitutive theory, but not of practical reality, that the admission of the Soviet *State* to membership of the League of Nations, in the voting for which Luxembourg abstained, constituted recognition, binding on Luxembourg, of the Soviet *Government*. If recognition can ever arise out of an application for admission, it can only be by implication from the support given to a particular application. However, as it would not necessarily be improper for a member to vote in favour of an application from an entity which it had yet to recognise, whether recognition could be implied in such circumstances would require supporting evidence of an intention to recognise.

b REPRESENTATION OF MEMBER STATES AND THE RECOGNITION OF GOVERNMENTS

The credentials of a new representative from a state already a member of the Organisation, even following a change of government, are normally accepted without challenge, though occasionally a point is taken over some procedural error in their presentation. It is only rarely that a dispute arises over credentials that really involves the more fundamental issue of representation, i.e. whether the government which the delegate represents is rightly entitled to act on behalf of the member state. A question of representation, therefore, will arise out of the same situation which demands that individual states make some decision on the recognition of a new government.

The problem is seen in its most emotional setting with regard to the position of the Communist Government of China. China, then ruled by the Nationalist Government of Chiang Kai-shek, was one of the original

---

18. (1935–7), A.D., Case No. 33.

members of the United Nations and entitled under the Charter to a permanent seat on the Security Council. The Nationalist Government was
gradually driven from the whole of the mainland of China and by 1949
was confined to the island of Formosa. The Communist régime being
thus firmly established, it was recognised by a number of states, including
the United Kingdom. From the outset the new Chinese Government
showed little respect for foreign-owned property rights, and any hopes of
relations between the United States and Communist China improving
were destroyed by the events of the Korean War. Because, in the opinion
of the American Government, the Chinese Communists have persistently
disregarded their international obligations, the United States has refused
to recognise the Communist régime and has applied the same basic argument, adopted to include the objection, based on Article 4 of the Charter,
that Communist China is not "peace-loving", to prevent Communist
representatives replacing the present representatives of the Nationalist
Government in the various organs of the United Nations.

This connection between representation and recognition was criticised
by a legal memorandum prepared for the Secretary-General in 1950[19] as
being "unfortunate from the practical standpoint, and wrong from the
standpoint of legal theory". The basis of the argument was that since
"recognition of either state or government is an individual act, and
either admission to membership or acceptance of representation in the
Organisation are collective acts, it would appear to be legally inadmissible
to condition the latter acts by a requirement that they be preceded by
individual recognition." Certainly, a number of states, notably Yemen
and Burma, had been admitted to membership when they had been
recognised by only a minority of members. The authors of the memorandum were therefore of opinion that the "unbroken practice" of the
Organisation had established that a member "could properly vote to
accept a representative of a government which it did not recognise", and
that "such a vote did not imply recognition". The solution suggested by
the authors was to apply Article 4 of the Charter by analogy.

> "This Article requires that an applicant for membership must be able and willing
> to carry out the obligations of membership. The obligations of membership can be
> carried out only by governments which in fact possess the power to do so. Where
> a revolutionary government presents itself as representing a state, in rivalry to an
> existing government, the question at issue should be which of these two governments
> in fact is in a position to employ the resources and direct the people of the State in
> fulfilment of the obligations of membership. In essence, this means an enquiry as
> to whether the new government exercises effective authority within the territory
> and is habitually obeyed by the bulk of the population."

The conclusion is unexceptionable, but the reference to Article 4 is
erroneous. Article 4 relates to admission to, not continuation of, membership; it makes admission subject to a degree of political judgment whether

---

19. S/1466; S.C.O.R. 5th Year, Supp. for January–May, 1950, pp. 18–23.

or not a state is willing to carry out the obligations of the Charter, whereas continuation of membership should only be subject to Article 6 which provides that a member state may be expelled from the Organization for persistently violating the principles of the Charter. There is no authority in the Charter for refusing to accept the representatives of an authority which has control of virtually the entire territory and population, and claims to be the effective government, of a member state.[20]

G. The effects of recognition in international law

a RECOGNITION OF STATES

In discussing the position of states as international persons, it was pointed out that for political reasons, and to a limited extent, the recognition of an entity as a state was likely to have a creative or *constitutive* effect. But, for the general purposes of international law, recognition is primarily declaratory of an existing fact. Even in a situation where the fact that states have sufficiently approved of the emergence of a new state as to accord it recognition has been politically of vital importance, and therefore has tended to be constitutive in effects, the acts of recognition by individual states are still only *evidence* of the existence of statehood.[1]

b RECOGNITION OF GOVERNMENTS AND OTHER AUTHORITIES

As far as the position of a new government or of any other governmental authority is concerned, its position under international law springs from its actual control over a certain area of territory, and not from its recognition or non-recognition by the members of the international community.[2] The expression "government or other governmental authority"

---

20. Fitzmaurice considered this refusal to amount to a virtual "disenfranchisement" of a member state, and met the attempt to apply a moral judgment to the issue of Chinese representation with the question: why, if the American objection is a valid one, is it "apparently applicable only to immorally behaved Governments which are both new Governments of a State and have achieved power by revolutionary means, and not to immorally behaved Governments which either, though new Governments, have come into power in the ordinary way by regular constitutional methods, or are not new Governments at all, but the existing Governments of member States?" (1952) 6 Y.B.W.A., p. 47.

1. It would be rare indeed for recognition by a particular state to prove decisive. Perhaps the only situation in which this might be the case would be where a colonial territory declared its independence but recognition was not forthcoming from the international community. Recognition by the former colonial power in such a situation could well be decisive.

2. In *Madzimbamuto* v. *Lardner-Burke* (see below, p. 112), the High Court of Rhodesia drew the distinction between a revolutionary change of government in an existing state and a revolutionary régime attempting to create a new state. In the first situation, "provided that the old order has completely disappeared, the existing judges of the courts are in no difficulty. Their former allegiance to the old order disappears . . . and it is then a simple step to recognise their allegiance to the new order and to continue to function as if they had been appointed under the new order" (a proposition illustrated by the Pakistan case following the annulment of the 1956 Constitution by the President in 1958, *State* v. *Dosso* (1958), 27 I.L.R. 22). In the case of a revolution attempting to create a new state, however, the evidence must show that the revolution had succeeded: it could not be said "that the

is used because most of the problems relating to the recognition of governments have arisen in the context of civil wars. The revolutionary party
in a civil war is in no sense the government of a state, as it is normally
attempting either to establish a separate state (as in the American Civil
War), or to seize power from the existing government of a state (as in
the Spanish Civil War). But, providing that the revolutionaries display
some of the manifestations of political organisation (and are not simply
a band of robbers[3]), they are entitled, irrespective of recognition, to a
qualified status stemming from their actual control over the areas they
occupy. This principle may be stated in the form of two propositions:

1. *In so far as the revolutionaries are attempting to seize power in their own
   state, they may by their acts involve their state in responsibility towards
   other states under international law, and their status is not dependent upon
   recognition.*

In the *Hopkins* case,[4] an arbitral commission had to deal with a claim
on behalf of a U.S. national for the money due on postal orders, which
had been issued by the revolutionary Huerta régime that had at one time
gained control over much of Mexico, but which the *de jure* government
of Mexico on re-establishing itself had refused to honour. The Commission drew a distinction between acts of a "personal nature" ("to this
class belong voluntary undertakings to provide a revolutionary administration with money or arms or munitions and the like"), and those of an
"impersonal nature" ("The sale of postage stamps, the registration of
letters, the acceptance of money orders and telegrams . . . the registration
of births, deaths, and marriages . . . the collection of several types of taxes
go on, and must go on, without being affected by new elections, government crises, dissolutions of parliament and even coups d'état"). As long
as Huerta was in complete control of the entire country, he was the
effective government of Mexico, and all his acts, whether of a "personal"
or "impersonal" nature, were the acts of the Mexican State. Once his
power began ebbing, however, so that he was only one among a number
of contesting factions, only his "impersonal" acts of routine administration could be carried out effectively in the name of the State. In this
particular case, the issue of money orders being an "impersonal" act, the
United States claim against the legitimate government of Mexico succeeded and it was irrelevant that the postal order might have been issued
at a time when Huerta no longer constituted the only government of
Mexico. It was no defence for Mexico to argue that the Huerta régime

---

1965 Constitution is the lawful Constitution (of Rhodesia) or that the present Government
is a lawful Government until such time as the tie of sovereignty vested in Britain has been
finally and successfully severed".

3. See the question posed by Pound, C.J., in *Salimoff* v. *Standard Oil Co.*, 186 N.E. 679
(1933), at p. 682:
    "As a juristic conception, what is Soviet Russia? A band of robbers or a government?"
4. (1926), 4 U.N.R.I.A.A., 41.

had not been recognised by the United States: the absence of recognition was a fact of an evidentiary nature which could not preclude the Commission from looking into the *de facto* existence of the Huerta régime. The Commission referred to a similar case, the *Tinoco* arbitration,[5] between Great Britain and Costa Rica, in which the arbitrator had said:

> "The non-recognition by other nations of a government claiming to be a national personality, is usually appropriate evidence that it has not attained the independence and control entitling it by international law to be classed as such. But when recognition *vel non* of a government is by such nations determined by inquiry, not into its *de facto* sovereignty and complete governmental control, but into its illegitimacy or irregularity of origin, their non-recognition loses something of evidential weight on the issue with which those applying the rules of international law are alone concerned. . . . Such non-recognition for any reason, however, cannot outweigh the evidence before me as to the *de facto* character of Tinoco's government, according to the standard set by international law."

2. *Where a politically organised group are attempting to establish a separate state, although the ultimate success of their venture depends upon the recognition or acceptance of the area under their control as a state, even if that stage is never reached, their acts are not totally ineffective in relation to the territory under their control irrespective of recognition of their de facto authority.*

Despite the difficulty facing the United States Courts after the Civil War that they could hardly regard the Confederate Government as having had any legal existence, in a number of cases they accepted the validity of various acts of the Confederate States. In *U.S.* v. *Insurance Co.'s,*[6] for example, the Supreme Court held that the plaintiff companies, though created by the legislature of Georgia while that state was a member of the Confederacy, could still be considered as corporate persons and entitled to sue under United States legislation. The basis of the decision was stated in the following terms:[7]

> "The State had thrown off its connection with the United States, and the members of the Legislature had repudiated or had not taken the oath by which . . . the Constitution requires the members of the several State Legislatures to be bound. But it does not follow from this that it was not a Legislature, the Acts of which were of force when they were made, and are in force now. If not a Legislature of the State *de jure*, it was at least a Legislature *de facto*. It was the only lawmaking body which had any existence. Its members acted under colour of office, by an election, though not qualified according to the requirements of the Constitution of the United States. Now, while it must be held that all their Acts in hostility to that Constitution . . . have no validity, no good reason can be assigned why all their other enactments, not forbidden by the Constitution, should not have the force which the law generally accords to the action of *de facto* public officers."

The status and powers of a revolutionary, but unrecognised, authority were dramatically placed in issue before the Rhodesian Courts following the unilateral declaration of independence by the British Crown Colony of Southern Rhodesia in November, 1965. In *Madzimbamuto* v. *Lardner-*

---

5. (1923), 1 U.N.R.I.A.A., 369.
6. 89 U.S. 99 (1874).   7. *Ibid.*, at p. 101.

Burke,[8] the Rhodesian Courts had to consider the validity of the detention of the plaintiff under a proclamation and emergency regulations issued by the "Officer Administering the Government" whom the Rhodesian régime had appointed to supersede the Governor of Southern Rhodesia as the Crown's representative under the new constitution of the "independent" Rhodesia. *Prima facie*, the acts of the Administering Officer and of the Rhodesian Government, the members of which had been formally dismissed by the Governor following the declaration of independence, had no constitutional foundation. As Lewis, J., asserted,[9] legal sovereignty over Rhodesia was "still vested in the United Kingdom Parliament and the acquisition of sovereign independence by this country . . . could only have come about legally and constitutionally by the grant of such independence by Her Majesty the Queen through an Act of the United Kingdom Parliament". However, the Court went on to hold that, as there could not be a legal vacuum ("one cannot say that since November 11, 1965, no valid and effective laws whatsoever have been made in this country"), effect must be given to the regulations and orders under which the plaintiffs were detained. The régime, although illegal, was nevertheless "the only effective government of the country and therefore, on the basis of necessity and in order to avoid chaos and a vacuum in the law, this court should give effect to such measures of the effective government, both legislative and administrative, as could lawfully have been taken by the lawful government under the 1961 Constitution for the preservation of peace and good government and the maintenance of law and order."[10]

Nor is there a lack of authority from the decisions of International Tribunals. In the *Levi* claim,[11] the Italian–United States Conciliation Commission was called upon to consider the effect of a provision in the Italian Peace Treaty which laid down that the term "United Nations nationals" included all individuals which "under the laws in force in Italy during the war", had been treated as enemies. The claimants, a Mr. and Mrs. Levi, were Italian Jews who had lived in Turin, but who fled to the United States where they became naturalised in 1946. Their property had been seized under legislation emanating from the Italian

---

8. The decisions of both the General Division and the Appellate Division of the High Court were published separately as an official "Blue Book" by the Government Printer, Salisbury.

See also the Dutch case of *Republic of the South Moluccas* v. *Netherlands New Guinea* (1954), 21 I.L.R. 48. The so-called Republic of the South Moluccas was not recognised even by the Netherlands, although for a short period after 1950 it maintained a status independent from Indonesia.

9. General Division, Judgement of 9th September, 1966: "Blue Book", p. 9.

10. *Ibid.*, pp. 76–77. This decision was affirmed by the Appellate Division. Despite the fact that Rhodesia no longer recognised the final appellate jurisdiction of the Privy Council, an appeal was heard by the Judicial Committee ([1968] 3 All E.R. 561). The detention orders were declared invalid. Though certain of the decrees of an unrecognised government *might* be considered effective by the courts of other states, the Judicial Committee was, legally, a Rhodesian Court. The only question was, therefore, whether it had "joined the revolution". As it obviously had not done so, it could not give effect to legislation emanating from, or to governmental acts performed by, the usurping régime.   11. (1957) 24 I.L.R. 303.

Social Republic which was established under Mussolini by German forces in Northern Italy between 1943 and 1945. This legislation had contained the provision that individuals belonging to the Jewish race were aliens. The Commission had no doubt that the legislation of the Social Republic fell within the wording "laws in force in Italy during the war" contained in the Peace Treaty, so that the United States could present a claim on behalf of the Levis as "United Nations Nationals" within the terms of the Treaty. However, in the course of giving its decision, the Commission commented on the *de facto* status of the Social Republic:

> "For nineteen months, and therefore not transiently, there were, thus, *de facto* two Italys, each claiming to be the lawful one. Each had its territorial base . . . the Italian Social Republic, which cannot be considered as an Agency of the German Reich, had its government . . . which exercised legal powers . . . by means of appropriate agencies; these agencies carried out a legislative, jurisdictional and executive activity; the legislative enactments had the force of law for all citizens subjected to that system, and were enforced, as far as was permitted, by the presence of foreign troops, by the war fought by these troops in the territory of the peninsula. . . ."[12]

c IS RECOGNITION CONSTITUTIVE OF LEGAL RIGHTS?

As far as the objective status of new entities is concerned, recognition, despite some political similarity to the constitutive theory in relation to states, is primarily declatory in effect. However, supporters of the constitutive school have been reluctant to yield this position without further argument. Accepting that a new state or government might "exist" although unrecognised, they have argued that, until it is recognised, the new state is deprived of all rights under international law, and the new government of many of the privileges of acting on behalf of its state. In the words of Oppenheim:[13]

> "International Law does not say that a state is not in existence as long as it is not recognised, but it takes no notice of it before its recognition. Through recognition only and exclusively a state becomes an International Person and a subject of International Law."

The fallacy of this argument can be demonstrated by reference to a fact already considered—that recognition is primarily a political act. By refraining from recognising the existence of a new state, an existing member of the international community is not thus able to free itself from the obligation to respect the territorial sovereignty of that state. Article 9 (Article 12 under the 1967 Protocol of Amendment) of the Charter of the Organisation of American States probably goes beyond existing international law in laying down for members of the Organisation the principle that the "political existence" of a state is "independent of recognition by other states". But once established as a state through acceptance by at least a section of the international community, the entity has "the right to defend its integrity and independence", and it would be no answer for another state if it launched an attack against the territorial integrity or political independence of the nascent state to contend that it had not recognised the new state.

---

12. *Ibid.*, at p. 310.   13. *International Law*, Vol. 1 (2nd ed.), p. 117.

If recognition does not create the general rights of a state under international law, it may be of limited constitutive effect in allowing the establishing of formal diplomatic relations between the recognising and the recognised state. But even this aspect of recognition may be over-emphasised. It is not unkown for diplomatic relations to be broken off between existing states and recognised governments, but this rupture is not usually taken as the equivalent of a withdrawal of recognition. Nor is it possible to ignore completely an unrecognised entity, and even in the absence of a formal exchange of diplomatic representatives contacts may have to be maintained with the unrecognised state or government. For example, although the United Kingdom does not recognise the Chinese Nationalist Government even so far as the authority of that government extends over the island of Formosa, the United Kingdom has regularly maintained consular posts in Formosa, and has from time to time presented diplomatic claims to the Nationalist authorities for damage caused to the property of United Kingdom nationals.[14] This policy of what might be termed "acknowledgment" is to be seen most clearly in United States practice. Consistently, the United States has refused to recognise the People's Republic as the government of China on a variety of grounds— that it came to power by force, that its policies are aggressive and viru- lently anti-American, and that no benefit to the U.S. would arise from recognition, an act that, on the contrary, would only add to the prestige of the Communist régime. But, as the quotation given[15] from a statement made by a former Secretary of State illustrates, the United States has frequently had dealings and other quasi-diplomatic exchanges with the Chinese Communists.

2 RECOGNITION AND MUNICIPAL LAW

a THE POSITION OF THE UNRECOGNISED STATE OR GOVERNMENT

i *In English law*

Recognition is effected by act of the executive and, because of the degree to which the municipal courts of most states treat statements of the executive as binding, it has tended to be constitutive in its effects. As far as English law is concerned, it has generally been accepted since the beginning of the nineteenth century that an unrecognised state or govern- ment has no *locus standi* in the courts.[16] Nor is the unrecognised entity entitled to immunity from the jurisdiction of the English Courts. In *The Annette and the Dora*,[17] it was claimed that the two vessels in dispute were in the possession or service of the Provisional Government of Northern

---

14. See (1957) 6 I. & C.L.Q., pp. 507–8.   15. Above, p. 101.
16. *City of Berne* v. *Bank of England* (1804), 9 Ves. Jun. 347.
17. [1919] P. 105. Though, because of the wording of the Diplomatic Privileges Act, 1964, it is possible for the Foreign Secretary to make a statement, which is "conclusive evidence" of any fact stated therein, that a representative of an unrecognised government has been received as a diplomatic agent by the Crown. See also *Fenton Textile Assoc.* v. *Krassin* (1922), 38 T.L.R. 259.

Russia, but Hill, J., on being informed by the Foreign Office that the government was "merely provisional in nature, and has not been formally recognised either by His Majesty's Government or by the Allied Powers", refused to set aside the two actions.

The English Courts have also taken the view that non-recognition by the Foreign Office is equivalent to a denial of the existence of the state or government concerned, and of any of its laws. In *Luther* v. *Sagor*,[18] Soviet officials had seized timber belonging to the plaintiffs under legislation passed by the recently constituted Soviet Government of Russia. A quantity of the timber was sold to the defendants who shipped it to London. The plaintiffs commenced proceedings in the English Courts seeking a declaration that they were still owners of the timber. At the time of the proceedings at first instance, the Soviet régime had not been recognised as the government of Russia. Roche, J., held that in the absence of recognition he was unable to hold that the Soviet Government had "sovereignty" or was "able by its decree to deprive the plaintiff company of its property."

Before the appeal was heard, the British Government accorded recognition to the Soviet régime, so that the decision of the Court of Appeal is of no authority on the present point,[19] although individual members of the Court did comment that Roche, J., had correctly decided the case on the facts as presented to him at the time of the trial.[20] Nevertheless, his decision did not escape criticism, because the issue of recognition had been allowed to override a basic rule of private international law that "questions as to the transfer or acquisition of property in . . . movables . . . are generally to be decided by the *lex situs*",[1] i.e. the law of the place where the property was situated at the time of the transfer. As the law in force in the area concerned was the law enacted and enforced by the Soviet Government, the recognition or non-recognition of that government should have been irrelevant.

Despite this objection to the conclusion reached in *Luther* v. *Sagor* at first instance, the Court of Appeal in *Carl Zeiss Stiftung* v. *Rayner & Keeler Ltd.*,[2] has recently confirmed Roche, J.,'s view of the law. The

---

18. [1921] 1 K.B. 456. 19. [1921] 3 K.B. 532.

20. E.g. Bankes, L.J., *ibid.*, at p. 540.

1. Westlake, *Private International Law*, 6th ed. (1922), at p. 197.

2. [1965] Ch. 596. Throughout the proceedings in the Court of Appeal and the House of Lords, it appears to have been assumed that earlier authorities were unanimous in denying validity to all acts of an unrecognised government. The present writer does not accept this view (see (1967) 83 L.Q.R., esp. at pp. 103–12), nor it would seem did the Foreign Office and the Board of Trade before the Soviet Government was recognised in 1921 believe that the position had already been determined by the earlier decisions. In the conclusions of an inter-departmental Russian trade committee on the chief obstacles to the resumption of trade with Russia it was noted:

"In connection with legal processes likely to arise as a result of the arrival in this country, as payment for goods imported into Russia, of gold or other commodities requisitioned by the Soviet Government, the Committee points out that, while it is not possible to forecast the attitude likely to be taken by the Courts in this country upon a legal issue of this complicated kind, the refusal of the British Government diplomatically to recognise

issue before the Court of Appeal in the *Carl Zeiss* case was whether the plaintiffs had properly initiated proceedings in the English Courts. The authorisation had been given by an official of the Stiftung who owed his appointment to the Council of Gera which, while it answered the description of the governmental authority responsible for the town and University of Jena (the beneficiaries of the profits of the Stiftung) within the terms of the constitution of the Stiftung, was a creature of the unrecognised German Democratic Republic. The Court of Appeal refused to apply the relevant East German law to determine the status of the Council of Gera and therefore of the validity of the commencement of proceedings in the English Courts. According to Diplock, L. J.,[3] where the English rules of private international law made reference to a foreign system of law, that law would only be regarded as effective in so far as it was "made by or under the authority of those persons who are recognised by the Government of the United Kingdom as being the sovereign government of the place where the thing happens": the English Courts would "not treat the happening as having in England any legal consequences which are claimed to result from a law made by persons who are not recognised as being either the sovereign government of that place or persons authorised by that sovereign government to make laws for that place."

The House of Lords was able to avoid making a final pronouncement on the question by reversing the decision of the Court of Appeal on the ground that Her Majesty's Government did recognise the *de jure* authority of the Soviet Union in East Germany: it was therefore possible to accept the acts of the unrecognised German Democratic Republic as those of a subordinate authority of the Soviet Union.[4] The failure of the House of Lords to reconsider the position of the unrecognised government in English law is hardly to be welcomed. The present attitude of the English Courts has been justified by the argument that the British Government adheres to the Lauterpacht approach to recognition—that once a state or government exists in fact this situation will be recognised. However, as the brief survey of British practice on recognition showed,[5] there is an unsatisfactory divergence between theory and reality, particularly in relation to governmental authorities like East Germany, North Korea or North Vietnam. Although the logical conclusions of the application of the strict doctrine that non-recognition equals non-existence were avoided in its application to East Germany, it is salutary to consider its effects on the acts of other unrecognised governments should they ever be called in question in the English Courts. As Lord Reid explained in his judgment in the *Zeiss* case:[6] it is not disputed that

"we must not only disregard all new laws and decrees made by the German Democratic Republic or its government, but we must also disregard all executive and

---

the Soviet Government is not *ipso facto* enough to prevent an English Court of Law from deciding that the Soviet Government should be treated for all legal purposes as a *de facto* Government. This is an issue which apparently can be decided only in the Courts."
3. [1965] Ch. 596., at p. 656.   4. [1967] 1 A.C. 853; [1966] 2 All E.R. 536.
5. Above, p. 99.   6. [1966] 2 All E.R., at p. 548.

judicial acts done by persons appointed by that government because we must regard their appointments as invalid. The results of that would be far reaching. Trade with the Eastern zone of Germany is not discouraged; but the incorporation of every company in East Germany under any new law made by the German Democratic Republic or by the official act of any official appointed by its government would have to be regarded as a nullity so that any such company could neither sue nor be sued in this country. Any civil marriage under any such new law or owing its validity to the act of any such official would also have to be treated as a nullity so that we should have to regard the children as illegitimate; and the same would apply to divorces and all manner of judicial decisions whether in family or commercial questions. That would affect not only status of persons formerly domiciled in East Germany but also property in this country the devolution of which depended on East German law."

ii *American law*

In the same way as the unrecognised City of Berne was not allowed to sue in the English Courts, the unrecognised R.S.F.S.R. was not allowed to sue in the Courts of New York.[7] On the other hand, an unrecognised government may be entitled to immunity from the jurisdiction of the American Courts if its existence can be proved in the absence of recognition. In *Wulfsohn* v. *R.S.F.S.R.*,[8] it was held that, in citing the Soviet Republic, the plaintiff had conceded its existence: no proof was required as there was clearly "an existing government sovereign within its own territories".

When it comes to the question of whether the acts of an unrecognised government, as opposed to the unrecognised government itself, shall in some way be acknowledged, the American Courts have felt similarly troubled by the possible conflict with the executive policy of non-recognition. If the State Department makes a clear pronouncement on the extent to which the U.S. Government wishes the policy of non-recognition to be applied, the courts will accept the statement as binding. Both *The Maret*[9] and *Latvian State Cargo Lines* v. *McGrath*[10] concerned the effectiveness of decrees promulgated by the Soviet authorities in the Baltic States which had been annexed by the Soviet Union in 1940. The State Department certified that the incorporation of these states by the U.S.S.R. had not been recognised, nor had any "of the so-called 'nationalisation' laws and decrees, nor any of the acts of the Soviet régime . . . been recognised by the Government of the United States." In both cases the Courts refused to disregard this statement of policy: once "the fact of non-recognition of a foreign sovereign and non-recognition of its decrees by our Executive is demonstrated . . . the Courts of this country may not examine the effect of decrees of the unrecognised foreign sovereign and determine rights in property . . . upon the basis of those decrees."[11] In contrast, in *Salimoff* v. *Standard Oil Co.*,[12] the Court was called upon to

---

7.   R.S.F.S.R. v. *Cibrario*, 139 N.E. 259 (1923); (1923–4), 2 A.D., Case No. 17.
8.   138 N.E. 24 (1923); (1923–4), 2 A.D., Case No. 16.
9.   145 F. (2d) 431 (1944); (1943–5), 12 A.D., Case No. 9.
10.   188 F. (2d) 1000 (1951); (1951), 18 I.L.R., Case No. 27.
11.   145 F. (2d), at p. 442.
12.   186 N.E. 679 (1933); (1933–4), A.D., Case No. 8.

consider the effectiveness of Soviet decrees expropriating the plaintiff's
oilfield on a quantity of oil from the oilfield which had been sold to the
defendant company. The New York Court was able to apply the normal
rule of private international law that the transfer of ownership was
governed by the *lex situs*, the law of Soviet Russia, because an elaborate
certificate provided by the State Department, while stating that the U.S.
Government refused to recognise the Soviet régime, explained that the
U.S. Government was nevertheless "cognisant of the fact that the Soviet
régime is exercising control and power in territory of the former Russian
Empire and . . has no disposition to ignore that fact." In answer to the
question "What is Soviet Russia, a band of robbers or a government?"
Pound, J., stated[13] that everyone knew that it was a government—the
State Department, the Courts, the man in the street, and if "it is a government in fact, its decrees have force within its borders and over its
nationals."

But what if there is no explicit direction or implicit invitation in the
State Department Certificate? A possible line of development was provided by a number of decisions whereby the Courts of the United States
upheld acts of the Confederate States which were not directly related to
the conduct of the Civil War. The clearest statement of this approach
occurred in *Texas* v. *White*:[14]

> "It may be said, perhaps with sufficient accuracy, that acts necessary to peace
> and good order among citizens, such, for example, as acts sanctioning and protecting
> marriage and the domestic relations, governing the course of descents, regulating
> the conveyance and transfer of property . . . and providing remedies for injuries to
> person and estate, and other similar acts, which would be valid if emanating from a
> lawful government, must be regarded in general as valid when proceeding from an
> actual, though unlawful, government. . . ."

It will be recalled that the Supreme Court, by applying this principle in
U.S. v. *Insurance Co.'s*,[15] was able to hold that the plaintiff companies,
though created by the unlawful legislature of Georgia while that state
was a member of the Confederacy, could nevertheless be considered as
corporate persons and entitled to sue under Federal legislation.

This suggestion that American Courts might take notice of the acts
of an unrecognised authority has been developed by a number of cases
in the New York Courts. In *Sokoloff* v. *National City Bank*,[16] Judge
Cardozo admitted that juridically "a government that is unrecognised
may be viewed as no government at all, if the power withholding
recognition chooses thus to view it" but added the comment that "juridical
conceptions are seldom, if ever, carried to the limit of this logic", but are
subject to "self-imposed limitations of common sense and fairness".[17] In

---

13.   186 N.E., at p. 682.   14.   74 U.S. 700 (1868), at p. 733.
15.   Above, p. 111.   16.   145 N.E. 917 (1924); (1923–4) 2 A.D., Case No. 19.
17.   145 N.E., at p. 918. For the application of this principle while attempting to maintain the fiction that the court was not applying the law of the unrecognised government: see
Russian Reinsurance Co. v. *Stoddard*, 147 N.E. 703 (1925); (1925–6) 3 A.D., Case No. 40.

other words, the non-recognition of a government should not be equated with non-existence if "common sense and fairness" require that some effect should be given to its legislative and administrative acts. More recently, the Appellate Division has taken a step towards a doctrine better suited to "a time in which governments with established control over territories may be denied recognition for many reasons."[18] In *Upright* v. *Mercury Business Machines*,[19] the plaintiff, an American resident in New York, was the assignee for value of a bill drawn on and accepted by the defendant company. The assignor was Polygraph Export, a "state-controlled enterprise of the so-called German Democratic Republic". The trial judge had accepted the defendant company's argument that, as the German Democratic Republic had not been recognised by the United States Government, it would not itself have been able to maintain an action in the American Courts, and the plaintiff, as assignee, could be in no better position. The Appellate Division, however, held that such a defence could not succeed against an assignee who could show that his assignor had a clearly established position as a *de facto* authority. In the words of Justice Breitel:[20]

> "A foreign government, although not recognised by the political arm of the United States Government, may nevertheless have *de facto* existence which is juridically cognisable. The acts of such a *de facto* government may affect private rights and obligations arising either as a result of activity in, or with persons or corporations within, the territory controlled by such *de facto* government."

iii *Other systems of law*

There is a dearth of authority in other states and even the attempt to make a few generalisations about the position of an unrecognised government under other systems of law might tend to mislead. Nevertheless, it would seem that the more generally accepted view is that an unrecognised government has no *locus standi* in municipal courts. The Supreme Court of Sweden refused to hear the case in *The Soviet Government* v. *Ericsson*[1] expressly on the ground of absence of recognition. As far as actions against an unrecognised government are concerned, there appears to be no reported case, though in *Spanish Government* v. *Campuzano*,[2] the Norwegian Supreme Court rejected the defendant's contention that the Franco Government which he represented, though unrecognised by Norway, was nevertheless entitled to sovereign immunity.

On the effects of the legislative and administrative acts of an unrecognised authority, though the authorities are more numerous there is no consistency between the attitudes of various states. French law has taken the doctrine of non-existence to the logical and extreme conclusion of refusing to recognise Soviet legislation creating new grounds for divorce.[3]

---

18. 213 N.Y.S. (2d), at p. 422.
19. 207 N.Y.S. (2d) 85 (1960); rev. 213 N.Y.S. (2d) 417 (1961).
20. 213 N.Y.S. (2d), at p. 419.   1. (1919–22) 1 A.D., Case No. 30.
2. (1938–40), 9 A.D., Case No. 27; and see *In Re the Estate of Bielinis*, 284 N.Y.S. (2d) 819 (1967).
3. *Chiger* v. *Chiger* (1925–6), 3 A.D., Case No. 18.

However, there is a more general trend to apply the law actually in force in the area concerned, irrespective of the recognition of the government from which such laws emanated. In a series of cases,[4] the Swiss Federal Court ignored the issue of recognition, pointing out that the non-recognition of the Soviet Government by Switzerland was operative on the diplomatic plane, but that a Swiss judge would "take cognisance of the Russian rules of law" so long as they did not "offend against the canons of public policy".[5] Similarly, the Belgian Courts have refused "to ignore completely the fact of the existence of the Soviet Government" and have applied the Soviet divorce legislation of the unrecognised Soviet régime in Latvia.[6]

b THE EFFECTS OF RECOGNITION
i *English law*

Obviously a claim can be brought in municipal courts by an entity recognised by the government of the state concerned, and proceedings against a recognised entity or its representatives can be met by the appropriate plea of sovereign or diplomatic immunity. Indeed, as far as English law is concerned, the House of Lords established in the *Arantzazu Mendi*[7] that a plea of immunity can be raised by an authority recognised as being in *de facto* control of a particular area, even if the proceedings are brought by the *de jure* sovereign.

Problems of particular complexity arise from the fact that recognition is often withheld until some time after the new state or government has begun functioning in that capacity. In *Luther* v. *Sagor*,[8] for example, the Soviet authorities had been carrying out their policies for some time, but as long as they had not been recognised by the British Government, no effect whatsoever was given to their decrees. If recognition simply affected transactions from the date it was granted, the courts of the recognising state would still be obliged to treat legislative acts prior to recognition as nullities. This unsatisfactory consequence is avoided by the principle of retroactivity: recognition dates back to the actual coming into being of the recognised entity. By the time *Luther* v. *Sagor* went to the Court of Appeal,[9] His Majesty's Government had accorded *de facto* recognition to the Soviet régime, and it was held that, whether the recognition was *de facto* or *de jure*, it was still operative from the time the Soviet régime

---

4. *Hausner* v. *International Commercial Bank of Petrograd* (1925–6), 3 A.D., pp. 37–38, in which the Court said:

> "The non-recognition of the Soviet Government has the sole consequence that, in the field of international law, this government has no qualification for representing Russia in Switzerland. . . . But this . . . does not prevent the Russian law from existing and from having its effects."

Schinz v. *High Court of Zurich* (1925–6), 3 A.D., Case No. 23; *Tcherniak* v. *Tcherniak* (1927–8), 4 A.D., Case No. 39.

5. 4 A.D., at p. 63.
6. *Pulenciks* v. *Augustoviskis* (1951), 18 I.L.R., Case No. 20, at p. 49.
7. [1939] A.C. 256.   8. [1921] 1 K.B. 456.
9. [1921] 3 K.B. 532.

seized power: the confiscation of the timber could therefore be recognised, and given effect to, by the English Courts.

A number of cases have come before the English Courts in which two competing authorities have existed within a particular territory, the one recognised as being in *de facto* control of part, the other as being the *de jure* sovereign, of the entire territory. The general rule to be applied in such circumstances is that the *de facto* authority is competent within the limits of the area under its control, while the *de jure* sovereign remains competent to deal with all matters arising outside that area.[10] In *Banco de Bilbao* v. *Sancha*,[11] for example, the Court of Appeal held that the question of which board of directors was legally entitled to represent the plaintiff bank depended upon the law of the place of incorporation. As, at the time when the Republican *de jure* Government passed a constitutionally valid decree moving the corporate seat from Bilbao to Barcelona, Bilbao was already under the control of the forces of General Franco, whose authority in the area was recognised *de facto* by the British Government, the decree was ineffective, a "mere nullity": the direction of the Bank's affairs, therefore, remained in the hands of the Bilbao board. On the other hand, property situated extraterritorially falls within the competence of the *de jure* government. Thus, in *Haile Selassie* v. *Cable & Wireless Ltd.* at first instance[12] it was held that the exiled Emperor of Ethiopia, because he was still regarded as the *de jure* sovereign, was entitled to recover a debt due to the Ethiopian state in proceedings brought in the English Courts, though the whole of Ethiopia (Abyssina) was under the control of the Italian army whose authority was at that time recognised *de facto* by His Majesty's Government.

The normal effect of recognition is to validate the decrees of the previously unrecognised entity or, in the case of *de jure* recognition, to give to the new *de jure* government retroactively the right to enforce its claims extraterritorially. When *Haile Selassie* v. *Cable & Wireless Ltd.* was heard on appeal,[13] *de jure* recognition had been withdrawn from the Emperor, and accorded to the King of Italy, as sovereign of Ethiopia. It followed that it was the Italian authorities who became entitled to recover the debt due in England to the Ethiopian State.

However, the withdrawal of *de jure* recognition and the retroactive effect of the granting of *de jure* recognition to the successor will not affect the validity of transactions already completed by the previous sovereign. In *Gdynia Ameryka Linie* v. *Bogulsawski*,[14] the House of Lords was faced with a chronology of events which began on 28th June, 1945, with the creation of a new Polish government in Lublin. The Minister of Shipping of the London Polish Government-in-Exile, realising that recognition of the new government was imminent, entered into an agreement with seamen of the Polish mercantile marine whereby they were given a choice

---

10. See *The Jupiter* litigation: [1924] P. 236; [1925] P. 69; [1927] P. 122, 250.
11. [1938] 2 K.B. 176. 12. [1939] 1 Ch. 182.
13. [1939] 1 Ch. 194. 14. [1953] A.C. 11.

between returning to Poland when their ship came under the control of the Lublin Government, or of leaving the shipping line and receiving a gratuity. At midnight, 5th–6th July, the British Government withdrew its recognition from the London Government-in-Exile, and granted *de jure* recognition to the new Lublin Government. The appellant shipping line subsequently refused to pay the promised gratuities, and the question was thus raised of the effectiveness of the decrees of the London Government after 28th June, and before midnight 5th-6th July. The Foreign Office statement simply recited the facts giving rise to the recognition of the Lublin Government and concluded that "the question of the retroactive effect of recognition of a government is a question of law for decision by the courts". Their Lordships were unanimous in upholding the validity of the agreement: although the recognition of the Lublin Government might be retroactive in its effects as far as Poland itself was concerned where the government had effective control, it could not be retroactively applied to events over which it had no control, such as the actions taken in Britain prior to midnight 5th–6th July, by the Government-in-Exile. As Viscount Simon commented in a subsequent case before the Privy Council:[15]

> "Primarily . . . retroactivity of recognition operates to validate acts of a *de facto* government which has subsequently become the new *de jure* government, and not to invalidate acts of the previous *de jure* government."

ii *American law*

Once a government is recognised, American law is essentially the same as English law in upholding the right of the government to have its acts accepted as authoritative within its territories, and its right to sovereign immunity for itself and to diplomatic immunity for its agents. Where American law does not appear to be so well settled is in the relationship between *de facto* and *de jure* recognition and the extent to which they are both retroactive in their effects.

In *Luther* v. *Sagor*, the English Court of Appeal was referred to a dictum of the American Supreme Court in *Oetjen* v. *Central Leather Co.*:[16]

> ". . . When a government which originates in revolution or revolt is recognised by the political department of our government as the *de jure* government of the country in which it is established, such recognition is retroactive in effect and validates all the actions and conduct of the government so recognised from the commencement of its existence."

Bankes, L.J., took this statement to mean that while *de jure* recognition was retroactive in its effects, the same was not necessarily true of *de facto* recognition. But there is nothing in the *Oetjen* case to support such a conclusion. The Mexican Government of Carranza was recognised *de*

---

15. *Civil Air Transport Inc.* v. *Central Air Transport Corpn.*, [1953] A.C. 70, at p. 93.
16. 246 U.S. 297 (1918), at pp. 302–303.

facto by the United States in 1915 and *de jure* in 1917. The Supreme Court only referred to the *de jure* recognition in 1917 as relating back to validate acts of the Carranza régime that had taken place in 1913.

The question may be largely academic in that *de facto* recognition as such has largely been discontinued in United States practice. What is more important is the extent to which American Courts might be prepared to allow *de jure* recognition to operate retroactively over matters arising outside the area over which the régime had *de facto* control before it was recognised. In *Kennett* v. *Chambers*,[17] the Supreme Court held invalid an agreement made in Cincinnati, one of the parties to which was a Texan general, acting on behalf of the *de facto*, but unrecognised, Texan military authorities. At that time, Texas was formally acknowledged by the United States as being part of Mexico, and it was not until six months later that its independence was recognised. The question of the possible retroactive effect of the act of recognition by the United States was not discussed. Nevertheless this decision was quoted by a Circuit Court of Appeals in *Lehigh Valley Railway Co.* v. *Russia*,[18] as authority for the proposition that it was only the acts of an unrecognised government "performed in its own territory" that could be "validated by the retroactive effect of recognition": acts performed outside its own territory could not be "validated by recognition". An action had been commenced in the name of the "Imperial Russian Government", but the name of the plaintiff had been changed following the 1917 revolution to the "state of Russia". The United States had recognised the provisional government of Russia created in 1917 as successor to the Tsarist régime, but had not recognised the Soviet take-over of Russia that had occurred before the hearing in the present proceedings. The Railway Company sought to set aside the original proceedings on the ground that the actual government of Russia was in the hands of the Soviet authorities, so that an action pursued by the accredited representative of the still recognised provisional government in the name of the Russian State would not prevent a subsequent action by the Soviet authorities if they were ever recognised. The Court rejected this contention as "fallacious" as the recognition of the Soviet régime would only relate back to events occurring in Russia itself during the period of Soviet control.

However, the statement that recognition can *never* operate retroactively outside the territory under the control of the unrecognised régime is difficult to reconcile with two subsequent cases heard by the Supreme Court in its attempt to grapple with the Litvinov Agreement. By this agreement, the United States agreed to recognise the Soviet Government of Russia in return for a number of undertakings, including the settlement of all outstanding claims between the two countries. As a preliminary step, the Soviet Government assigned to the United States all debts due to the Soviet régime "as the successor to prior Governments of Russia, or

---

17.   56 U.S. 38 (1852).
18.   21 F. (2d) 396 (1927); (1927–8) 4 A.D., Case No. 35.

otherwise". In *U.S.* v. *Belmont*,[19] the Supreme Court had to decide whether the United States was entitled on the strength of the Litvinov Agreement to the assets of a Russian corporation deposited with a New York bank. In order to succeed, the United States had to show that the assets of the corporation were vested in the Soviet Government by virtue of Russian legislation confiscating the assets of the corporation, including assets situated outside Russia. There were two obstacles to the Soviet legislation having this effect: first, the rule of public policy that confiscatory decrees will not be given extraterritorial effect; and secondly, the principle of law that the act of the Soviet régime being originally the act of an unrecognised government could not operate outside the area under its control. It was held on the first point that the doctrine of public policy could not take precedence over rights vested in the United States by virtue of an executive agreement having the same legal force as a treaty made with the approval of the Senate. But, on the second point, the Court could only have upheld the validity of the assignment of the Soviet assets to the United States if the contemporaneous act of recognition of the Soviet régime by the United States had operated retroactively in order to give effect to the Soviet decrees over assets situated extraterritorially. This conclusion would seem to be the one adopted by the Court when it stated that the effect of the recognition of the Soviet Government was "to validate, so far as this country is concerned, all acts of the Soviet Government here involved from the commencement of its existence".[20]

However conclusive this statement may appear, its value as authority is weakened by the fact that the question of the circumstances in which recognition may be retroactive in its effects outside the territory controlled by the recognised government does not seem to have been raised in argument before the Court, nor was the point discussed by the Court itself. Furthermore, from the context in which the statement was made, it may well be that the act of recognition, being part of "an international compact between the two governments", was regarded as having the effect of vesting the assets in the Soviet Government because of its affinity with a treaty which, under the law of the United States, takes precedence over the existing law of the land. In the subsequent decision of the Supreme Court on similar facts in *U.S.* v. *Pink*[1] the supremacy of the executive in foreign affairs was also advanced as a reason for allowing the United States' claim to assets confiscated by the Soviet Government, but the Court did suggest more strongly that the extraterritorial situation of the assets confiscated by the Russian decrees was irrelevant once the Soviet régime was recognised. By refusing to give effect to the Soviet decrees in order first to vest in the Soviet Government the property to be assigned to the United States, the decision of the New York Court was tantamount to disapproval or non-recognition of the nationalisation programme of the Soviet Government: it was therefore contrary to the

---

19. 301 U.S. 324 (1937).   20. *Ibid.*, at p. 330.
1. 315 U.S. 203 (1942).

policy adopted by the United States when it recognised the Soviet Government, and must be reversed.

If the Supreme Court did accept the proposition that recognition of the Soviet régime operated to validate its claims to assets situated externally, it cannot be supposed that the Court intended to reverse the conclusion reached on the facts of the *Lehigh Valley Railway Co.* case. Once a transaction has been completed on the basis that a certain government is recognised by the United States, the recognition of a successor to that government should not destroy the validity of the transaction. However, the basis upon which the *Lehigh* case was decided, that recognition does not operate retroactively over acts of the formerly unrecognised government outside its territory must be treated with caution. The decision could readily have been supported on the ground later adopted by the English Courts that recognition can operate to validate the actions of the formerly unrecognised government, but it cannot invalidate the transactions effected by the former *de jure* government outside the area at the relevant time under the *de facto* control of the formerly unrecognised régime. If this principle could be read into the *Lehigh* case there would remain no conflict between it and the retroactivity rule upon which the Supreme Court relied at least in part in *U.S.* v. *Pink*.

CHAPTER FIVE

STATE TERRITORY

The territory of a state is the foundation of its factual existence and the basis for the exercise of its legal powers. Two different distinctions follow from this proposition. There is a distinction in theory at any rate between the original *corpus* upon which the state's first claim to statehood depended and its title to territory which it might subsequently acquire. The need to draw such a distinction arises from the fact that, whereas a state can clearly acquire territory to add to its existing territory, it can hardly acquire its original territory, for until it does acquire that territory, it fails to fulfil one of the conditions of statehood. The second distinction exists between the main *corpus* of state territory, and the rights that automatically attach to the territory, which might be termed the state's "appurtenant rights" over airspace or maritime territory. In addition, a state might acquire additional territorial rights over dependent territories or by way of servitudes over the territory of other states.

1 THE ACQUISITION OF TERRITORY

A. The acquisition by a state of its original territory

There would seem to be no simple answer to the question of what is the basis of a state's title to its original territory, and it may well be that the answer has in any case changed in the course of time. For the European state *in esse* at the period when international law began to influence the conduct of inter-state relations in the sixteenth century, no legal rule could do otherwise than accept its territorial sovereignty as a pre-existing fact. Before non-European countries were regarded as part of the international community, their right to statehood, to be considered as a subject of rights and duties under international law, depended on their tacit acceptance or express recognition by the narrow circle of the community. Although their territorial rights might be limited by the act of recognition, as with the capitulations which first gave the Turkish Empire access to European society, nevertheless the factual existence of their authority pre-dated their admission to the Family of Nations. This factual existence and authority of an entity which was not a member of the European community seems to have been accepted by the International Court in the *Right of Passage* case.[1] The Court held that Portugal had a limited freedom of access to Portuguese possessions in Indian territory based *inter alia* on a treaty of 1779 made with an Indian prince before the coming of British rule. If the factual existence and authority of a territorial unit outside the European community was not without effect even under the European system of international law, it is possible to regard the recognition or tacit acceptance of a pre-existing entity as a state in the European sense of the term as confirming not only the existence of the state but also the state's title to its territory. In this sense, it is possible to accept Oppenheim's statement that "through recognition . . . a new State becomes . . . a subject of International Law" and that "as soon as recognition is given, the new State's territory is recognised as the territory of a subject of international law, and it matters not how this territory was acquired before . . . recognition."[2]

Similar considerations would seem to apply to the situation where a rebellious colony succeeds in establishing its independence. The *factum* of the previous sovereignty is destroyed by force; but the international status and the creation of the new title to the territory depend upon recognition. On the other hand, where the new state comes into being as a result of an amalgamation of existing states, or of the peaceful emergence of a colonial dependent of an existing state, the events have more in common with succession than with recognition. It is the transfer of sovereignty from one entity to another, not the acknowledgement of an existing, or the creation of a new, title. This transfer is easily recognisable when it is a case of existing states forming a new state because the whole transaction is accomplished on the international plane, but in the case of a colonial possession obtaining independence, it cannot attain statehood until it has been granted sovereignty over the territory concerned. However, whereas an agreement between state A and state B that they should amalgamate to form state X is clearly an internationally binding obligation, there should be no obstacle to allowing a similar status to an agreement between the colonial power and the colonial territory about to be granted independence. Such a conclusion can be reached by accepting either that dependent territories have limited personality, or that the colonial government which is ready to take over at the moment of independence has itself a measure of personality. Although it is difficult to analyse a given situation in precise legal terms, the granting of independence to Burma does illustrate the possibility of a government exercising *de facto* authority over an area which has yet to be transferred to its sovereignty. In February, 1947, Burmese leaders reached agreement with the Attlee government in London for the granting of independence within the year; in the interim, a Provisional Government was to be elected to take over the complete internal administration of the country with an

---

1. I.C.J. Rep., 1960, p. 6.
2. *International Law*, Vol. 1, 2nd ed. (1912), p. 282: 8th ed., p. 544.

equal say in defence and external affairs. The final transfer of power was effected by an agreement of October, 1947, between His Majesty's Government in the United Kingdom and the Provisional Government of Burma which operated both as a grant of territorial sovereignty and as an act of recognition.

B. The modes of acquiring additional territory

With the "expansion of Europe" from the sixteenth century onwards, it was hardly surprising that international law paid particular attention to rules for the acquisition of territory. The traditional modes of accretion, cession, annexation, occupation and prescription, the terminology and characteristics of which were drawn largely from Roman law, were categorised as giving an *original* title, when there was no transfer of ownership from a previous sovereign, or a *derivative* title, where there was such a transfer. However, it was not the most helpful of distinctions because whereas accretion and occupation clearly gave original titles, and cession a derivative title, annexation and acquisitive prescription were only derivative in the sense that territory acquired by these methods had formerly been under the sovereignty of another state, but the application of both modes involved the destruction of the former title, and the creation of a new title. While the title of the acquiring state by cession would depend upon the validity of the title of the previous sovereign, annexation and acquisitive prescription created a new and independent title.

a ACCRETION

Accretion is of little legal interest, as in theory it gives rise to few problems, though it still has obvious practical applications. A state has the exclusive right to additions to its territory by way of silting or other deposits, or to islands forming within its territorial waters.[3] As far as boundary rivers are concerned, the Roman law rules of *alluvio* are applied directly. On non-navigable rivers the middle line continues to be the boundary, so that a newly formed island might well fall partly on one side and partly on the other; but where the river is navigable, the boundary moves with the centre of the navigable channel, so that the island must lie on one side or the other. Should, however, the river undergo a sudden change of course, an *avulsion* as it is called, the boundary remains along the original river bed. In the case of *Louisiana* v. *Mississippi*,[4] the United States Supreme Court applied principles of international law to a boun-

---

3. It is likely that islands forming outside territorial waters, but within close proximity to the territory of a state would also automatically belong to the coastal state: see below, p. 152, where the case of the *Anna* is discussed. If the coastal state is entitled to exclusive rights of exploitation over its continental shelf (below, p. 159), it would seem logical that if that part of the seabed were thrown up to form an island, it would automatically belong to the coastal state.

4. 282 U.S. 458 (1931).

dary dispute between two states of the Union. It held that the gradual erosion of soil from the Mississippi bank and its deposit on the Louisiana bank between 1823 and 1912, passed title to Louisiana, but that the sudden change of course in 1912–13 across the accretion of the previous century did not divest Louisiana of the territory already acquired: the change being an avulsion, the boundary remained what it had been in 1912.

b CESSION

Cession is the most obvious illustration of a derivative title, for if the previous title was defective, the purported cession from the previous sovereign cannot cure the defect. In the *Island of Palmas* case,[5] the United States claim to the island was based in part on the Treaty of Paris of 1898, which transferred all territorial rights which Spain possessed in the region. It was stated by the Arbitrator and acknowledged by the United States that "Spain could not transfer more rights than she herself possessed": the "essential point", therefore, was whether the island at the moment when the Treaty came into force was part of Spanish territory.

State practice would seem to establish that there should normally be both a treaty and an actual transfer of possession in order to effect a valid cession. In the *Iloilo* case,[6] a claim was presented to the British–American Tribunal for damage to the property of British subjects at Iloilo in the Philippines, which occurred on 11th February, 1899. The Treaty of Paris, signed on 10th December, 1898, provided that on the exchange of ratifications, Spain should evacuate the islands in favour of the United States, but Spanish forces were compelled to withdraw by local insurgents on 24th December. On 10th February, American troops captured Iloilo from the insurgents, but on the following day the insurgents succeeded in carrying out their threat of setting fire to the town. The Tribunal held that as the treaty did not take effect until it was ratified on 11th April, the transfer of *de jure* sovereignty to the United States, and the obligations resulting therefrom, did not commence until that date.

The requirement that there should be a transfer of possession is only correct as a general proposition. There would obviously be no need for such a transfer if, as has often happened, the state to which the territory is ceded is already in possession. Similarly, a treaty ceding territory from state A to state B and a treaty ceding the territory from state B to state C could be implemented by state C taking over the territory directly from state A without the need for state B to enter into possession. The Arbitrator in the *Columbia–Venezuela Boundary* dispute[7] referred specifically to the cession of Lombardy by Austria to France in 1860 and to its immediate retrocession by France to Italy, to the cession of Venice to France in 1866 and to its retrocession to Italy, and to several cases of cession under the Treaties of Versailles and St. Germain.

One aspect of cession that has acquired particular contemporary

---

5. (1928), 2 U.N.R.I.A.A., 829.   6. (1925), 4 U.N.R.I.A.A., 158.
7. (1919–22), 1 A.D., Case No. 54.

importance is the relevance of the principle of *self-determination*. It was one of the cornerstones of the policy of American President Wilson towards the reorganisation of Europe after the First World War. According to his view, the "settlement of every question, whether of territory, of sovereignty, of economic arrangement, or of political relationship" should only take place "upon the basis of the free acceptance of that settlement by the people immediately concerned."[8] The new states of central Europe which emerged from the break-up of the Austro–Hungarian Empire were applications of the principle of self-determination. The argument that peoples should be allowed to choose their political future for themselves was the basis of the Saar plebiscite held under the auspices of the League of Nations to decide whether the Saar should become part of France or be reincorporated in Germany. The principle of self-determination became enshrined in Article 55 of the United Nations Charter and is an article of faith for the majority of the members of the Organisation. At its Twelfth Session the General Assembly resolved that—

> "(a) Member States shall, in their relations with one another, give due respect to the right of self-determination;
> (b) Member States having responsibility for the administration of Non-Self-Governing territories shall promote the realisation and facilitate the exercise of this right by the peoples of such territories."

In giving effect to this principle, the United Nations has supervised plebiscites in Togoland and in West Irian. Although it is not possible to regard "self-determination" as imposing a legal obligation on the parties to a treaty of cession, or on a state granting independence to one of its former colonies to pay heed to the wishes of the people of the territory concerned, it is a potent political factor. No account of contemporary international law is complete without reference to it, for if a state does help bring about a territorial change in contravention of the principle, it runs the risk of having recognition withheld from the attempted change, and even of the imposition of international sanctions.

c ANNEXATION AND CESSIONS IMPOSED BY FORCE

Whereas under traditional international law a cession imposed by force would be valid, the development of the twentieth century concept of the illegality of aggressive war would seem to cast doubts on the possibility that such a rule has survived. Indeed, prior to the Covenant of the League of Nations and to the Kellogg–Briand Pact of 1928, a treaty of cession was not even necessary to validate a seizure of territory by force, for international law recognised annexation (or subjugation, or conquest, as it is variously termed) as a means of acquiring territory. The only problem was to distinguish between military occupation and annexation. In order for annexation to be legally effective, the former sovereign had to be

---

8. Quoted Hackworth, *Digest of International Law*, Vol. 1, p. 425.

subjugated so that there were no longer forces in the field to free the occupied territory from the control of the annexing power. Referring to the occupation of a piece of American territory by Great Britain during the war of 1812, Story, J., rightly commented:[9]

> "It could only be by a renunciation in a treaty of peace, or by possession so long and permanent, as should afford conclusive proof, that the territory was altogether abandoned by its sovereign, or had been irretrievably subdued, that it could be considered as incorporated into the dominions of the British Sovereign."

It follows, therefore, quite apart from the question of whether territory could be acquired by aggressive war, that the purported annexations of various areas in Europe by Germany during the Second World War were invalid and therefore ineffective to pass title. As the Nuremberg Tribunal pointed out,[10] "the doctrine of subjugation . . . was never considered to be applicable so long as there was an army in the field attempting to restore the occupied countries to their true owners." Conversely, even when a state had been completely subjugated, there would be no transfer of sovereignty in the absence of an intention to annex. When Germany surrendered unconditionally to the Allied Powers in 1945, an Allied Declaration was issued which provided that the United States, the Soviet Union, the United Kingdom thereby assumed "supreme authority with respect to Germany, but that such assumption . . . of the said authority . . . does not effect the annexation of Germany."

Whatever might have been the position before the Covenant of the League became operative with the signing of the Peace Treaties in 1919–20, the various war crimes tribunals were convinced that Article 10 of the Covenant, together with the undertaking to renounce war as an instrument of national policy in the Kellogg–Briand Pact, and a series of bilateral and multilateral arrangements tending in the same direction, had made annexation in the course of a war of aggression ineffective as a means of transferring title. The Nuremberg Tribunal expressed the view that it was unnecessary to decide whether the "doctrine of subjugation, dependent as it is on military conquest, has any application where the subjugation is the result of aggressive war."[11] This conclusion has been further reinforced by Article 2 (4) of the United Nations Charter which requires that all "Members shall refrain in their international relations from the threat or use of force against the territorial integrity or political independence of any state". And once the proposition is accepted that an annexation based upon the illegal use of force is ineffective, it logically follows that a treaty of cession imposed by the victor on the vanquished is similarly vitiated.[12] However, in so far as it may not be possible for the

---

9. *U.S.* v. *Hayward*, 2 Gall. 485, at p. 501.
10. *Re Goering* (1946), 13 A.D., Case No. 92, at p. 220.
11. *Ibid.*
12. Obviously force used in self-defence (i.e. force legally used) cannot give rise to problems in this context. As Jennings succinctly points out:

international community in its present disordered state to prevent the wrongdoer from retaining the fruits of his wrong, a reconciliation between the new situation and the attitude of international law can only take place through the attitudes of other states; but the relevance of recognition and acquiescence in this context will be discussed later.

d OCCUPATION

In the theory of international law, occupation is a clearly defined concept. It is an original mode of acquisition whereby a state acquires sovereignty over a *terra nullius* (i.e. a piece of territory not under the sovereignty of any state). In practice, occupation might be difficult to distinguish from prescriptive rights to territory, because of the rarity with which it will be possible to show conclusively that a particular area of territory was not subject to the sovereignty of another state at the time when the "occupation" took place. However, the theory of occupation as a mode of acquiring territory in its own right is clear enough: there must be a taking of possession with the intention to occupy as sovereign.

i *The taking of possession*

The taking of possession must give the occupying state control over the territory concerned, but what constitutes the necessary degree of control will vary with the circumstances of the case. This point was well made by the Arbitrator in the *Clipperton Island Arbitration*:[13]

> "It is beyond doubt that . . . besides the *animus occupandi*, the actual, and not the nominal, taking of possession is a necessary condition of occupation. This taking of possession consists in the act, or series of acts, by which the occupying State reduces to its possession the territory in question and takes steps to exercise exclusive authority there. Strictly speaking, and in ordinary cases, that only takes place when the State establishes in the territory itself an organisation capable of making its laws respected. But . . . there may be cases where it is unnecessary to have recourse to this method. Thus, if a territory, by virtue of the fact that it was completely uninhabited, is, from the first moment when the occupying state makes its appearance there, at the absolute and undisputed disposition of that state, from that moment the taking of possession must be considered as accomplished, and the occupation is thereby completed."

In the *Clipperton Arbitration* itself, a geographical survey of this uninhabited island from a short distance offshore, and a landing of a few members of the crew, accomplished only after great difficulty, followed by a declaration of sovereignty published in an Honolulu journal, were held to be sufficient to support the French claim. Furthermore, the Arbitrator obviously had in mind the inaccessible and uninhabited nature of the

---

"Force used in self-defence . . . is undoubtedly lawful. But it must be proportionate to the threat of immediate danger, and when the threat has been averted the plea of self-defence can no longer be available . . . it would be a curious law of self-defence that permitted the defender in the course of his defence to seize and keep the resources and territory of the attacker." *The Acquisition of Territory in International Law*, p. 55.
13. (1931), 6 A.D., Case No. 50, at p. 107.

island in holding that the fact that France "never had the *animus* of abandoning" it prevented "the forfeiture of an acquisition already definitively perfected."

An additional factor, at least latent in this decision, was the absence of any real foundation for a rival claim. Mexico had argued that the island had been one discovered by the Spanish Navy and, under the Bull of Alexander VII, had belonged to Spain, so that from 1836 sovereignty had passed to Mexico as successor state. It was held, however, that there was no evidence that this particular island had been discovered by the Spaniards, nor was proof of such an historic right "supported by any manifestation (by Mexico) of her sovereignty over the island." It was this consideration which influenced the Permanent Court in the *Eastern Greenland* case[14] to decide that Danish sovereignty extended over the entire island, and not simply over the colonised areas. And, as the Court readily acknowledged, this was true of most cases involving claims to territorial sovereignty: all that the tribunal had to do was decide which of the two was the stronger. The unusual feature of the *Eastern Greenland* case was that it was not until 1931 that Norway attempted to claim un-colonised areas of the territory. In the absence of any "competition", Denmark's contention that sovereignty had already been acquired before 1931 succeeded largely by default.

ii *The intention to occupy as sovereign*

The need for an intention to occupy as sovereign is obvious enough: clearly the setting up of a weather station by a state on a headland of an uninhabited island not yet under the sovereignty of any state would not create title if there was no manifestation of the intention to occupy as sovereign. Similarly, a state cannot base its claim on unauthorised acts by its subjects. If, to take the example of the uninhabited island, fishermen of the claimant state had for many years landed there to set lobster pots or to weather out storms, such evidence without any intention to take possession on behalf of the state would have no legal effect. When discussing Norwegian claims in the *Fisheries* case, Judge McNair referred to this well established principle in the following terms:

> ". . . some proof is usually required of the exercise of state jurisdiction . . . the independent activity of private individuals is of little value unless it can be shown that they have acted in pursuance of a licence or some other authority received from their Governments or that in some other way their Governments have asserted jurisdiction through them."[15]

e PRESCRIPTION

Even if a particular land area is under the dominion of one state, it does not follow that the taking possession of that area by another cannot create a new title. Whereas occupation applies to a territory which is a *res nullius*,

---

14. (1933) P.C.I.J. Rep., Ser. A/B, No. 53.   15. I.C.J. Rep., 1951, at p. 184.

prescription applies a similar line of reasoning to territory that did have a
sovereign. A combination of the passage of time and the implied acquiescence of the dispossessed sovereign are the basis of prescriptive rights. The
underlying principle is that a state which has "slept upon its rights" should
not be allowed to revive them against a state that has been in constant and
long continued enjoyment of those rights. But although this basic assumption is obvious enough, it is less clear whether prescription can be defined
in more precise terms.

i *The relevance of protest*

It is not disputed that in theory at any rate prescription arises from the
enjoyment of certain rights, originally belonging to, or being exercised
by, another state, without effective protest on the part of that other state.
The problem is to define what is meant by "effective" protest.

In the *Chamizal Arbitration*,[16] the United States laid claim to an area
of Mexican territory, which had become joined to United States' territory
by the movement of the Rio Grande southwards, *inter alia* on the ground
of undisturbed possession. This argument was rejected because Mexico
had made a number of protests to the United States, and a convention
had been signed in an attempt to settle "the rights of the two nations with
regard to the changes brought about by the action of the waters of the
Rio Grande." In this case, the Tribunal could point not only to diplomatic protests by Mexico, but also to the fact that the diplomatic pressure
had been sufficiently effective to bring from the United States an acknowledgment, in the form of the signing of the convention, that there was a
dispute over the territory which should be formally settled.

If state A is in possession of a tract of territory claimed by state B, it is
doubtful whether diplomatic protests alone are sufficient to preserve the
rights of state B. What seems to be required is something that shows that
state B "means business", and is not simply protesting for "form's sake".
If the dispute is of a particularly serious nature, the severing of diplomatic
relations or the taking of retaliatory measures such as the restricting of
trade with state A might be sufficient. If the possession against which
state B is protesting relates to a period after 1920, it would assist state B
if it had raised the dispute before the League of Nations or the United
Nations. Diplomatic protest could also be reinforced by a *bona fide* suggestion that the dispute should be submitted to arbitration or judicial
settlement. In the *Minquiers and Ecrehos* case,[17] the facts of which are
considered below, the United Kingdom argued that French protests
against British legislation applying to the disputed islands were ineffective
inter alia on the ground that they should have been reinforced by pressure
to have the issue determined by an international tribunal. This view was
largely accepted by Judge Carneiro in his separate opinion:[18] the French
Government should have "proposed arbitration", particularly since both

---

16. Hackworth, *op. cit.*, Vol. 1, p. 441.   17. I.C.J. Rep., 1953, p. 47.
18. *Ibid.*, at pp. 106–8.

states were bound by treaty which provided for the settlement of their legal disputes by the Permanent Court of Arbitration.

ii *The practical application of prescription*

The significance attributed to the absence or inadequacy of protest in the application of prescription demonstrates that international law does not lay down precise rules for the acquisition of prescriptive rights in the way that municipal systems of law lay down such rules. All that international law requires is that the possession must be possession as sovereign (as in the case of occupation, the unauthorised acts of private citizens would hardly constitute possession as sovereign; nor would possession under the terms of an international lease of territory be an adequate basis of prescription), and that it should be sufficiently undisturbed to raise the presumption that it has been acquiesced in. As the arbitrators said in the *Grisbadarna* case,[19] it was a settled principle of international law that "a state of things which actually exists and has existed for a long time should be changed as little as possible."

Although prescription is referred to as a mode of acquiring territory, international jurisprudence does not always clearly distinguish between prescription and other modes, notably occupation and historical consolidation. In practice, because the majority of disputes are resolved between contesting claims based upon the nominal exercise of sovereignty, the dividing line between occupation and prescription may either be impossible to draw, or the attempt to make such a distinction will be no more than a pointless academic exercise. For example, if a territory is nominally under the sovereignty of a state according to the less stringent requirements of control before the nineteenth century, and is subsequently occupied in the name of another state, does the failure to keep pace with the need to exercise greater control constitute an abandonment of an existing title, so that the subsequent acquisition is by occupation, or does the second possession supersede a prior title by prescription?

In the *Minquiers and Ecrehos* case,[20] the International Court was called upon to settle a dispute between France and the United Kingdom as to which state had sovereignty over a number of small islands between the Channel Islands and the Normandy coast. The events with which the dispute dealt commenced with the Norman Conquest of 1066 which brought the Dukes of Normandy to the English throne. The Minquiers and Ecrehos islands, together with the Channel Islands, were part of the Duchy of Normandy, and as such were part of the feudal territories of the French Crown. However, in 1204 the French drove the Anglo-Norman forces out of Continental Normandy and the Court was of opinion that thereafter the island possessions of the Dukes of Normandy were held as part of English territory and not as part of the Norman duchy. In any case, even if the original feudal title had survived the events

---

19.   Scott, Hague Court Reports, Vol. 1, p. 130; (1909), 11 U.N.R.I.A.A. 147.
20.   I.C.J. Rep., 1953, p. 47.

of 1204 and the following years, the French Government would have to show that it had been replaced by another title "valid according to the law of the time of replacement" because the original feudal title "could today produce no legal effect". This was something the French Government was unable to do. On the contrary, most of the acts of sovereignty that could be cited were of local administration by the Jersey authorities—the holding of inquests on corpses found on the islets; the rating of houses constructed on the islets by Jersey fishermen; and the exercise of criminal jurisdiction over events occurring on the islets. The Court was unanimous in its conclusion that the two groups of islets were under British sovereignty, but little explanation was given of the mode by which the United Kingdom acquired this sovereignty.

Initially, the British claim depended upon the uniting of the Duchy of Normandy with the English Crown and the subsequent destruction of the link between Normandy and the English Crown by the dismemberment of the Duchy in 1204; the claim could not be based, therefore, upon the occupation of *terra nullius*. Nor did the French claim depend upon any original acquisition of the islands, because the parties were in substantial agreement on the fact that the Minquiers and Ecrehos had been part of the territories of a feudal vassal of the French king. As the Court stated, the case did not "present the characteristics of a dispute concerning the acquisition of sovereignty over *terra nullius*": what was of "decisive importance" was not any indirect presumption deduced from events of the Middle Ages, but the evidence which related "directly to the possession" of the islands However, although the use of the term "possession" suggests prescription as the basis for the rival claims, it does not appear from the approach adopted by the Court that its analysis was made in terms of prescriptive rights to the islands The Court considered that its task was to "appraise the relative strength" of the claims. The Court based its decision on the facts that the islands had been part of the Channel Islands at the beginning of the thirteenth century, and therefore under the dominion of the English Crown; that in more recent times the British authorities had "exercised state functions" with respect to the islands; and that the French Government had been unable to show any evidence of title.

In adopting this approach of refraining from classifying the method whereby the territory was acquired, the International Court was following a trend that had been apparent in earlier international jurisprudence. In the *Eastern Greenland* case,[1] for example, the Court admitted that in many cases tribunals had been satisfied "with very little in the way of actual exercise of sovereign rights, provided that the other state could not make out a superior claim." In such circumstances, although theory lays down methods of acquiring territory, tribunals are usually concerned with deciding between rival claims neither of which might satisfy such theoretical requirements.

---

1. (1933) P.C.I.J. Rep., Ser. A/B, No. 53.

iii *Prescription and historical consolidation*

Although prescription can be defined in terms wide enough to cover the situations that arise out of long possession in international law, it does suffer to some extent from its analogy with municipal law notions of prescriptive rights. An obvious situation that is not covered by prescription in the municipal law sense is the seizure of the territory of one state by another state. By the principles of most systems of municipal law, a prescriptive title cannot be acquired where the original taking of possession was by force. But where there is little likelihood of the wrong-doer being deprived of the fruits of his crime, and when the apathy of the international community amounts to acquiescence, some method is required whereby the law can keep pace with reality. It is, of course, possible simply to disregard the municipal law analogy to apply prescription to all instances of adverse possession, whether originating in force or not. This is certainly the view expressed by Oppenheim who, after pointing out that international law recognised prescription however unlawful its origin, defined it in the widest terms as "the acquisition of sovereignty over a territory through continuous and undisturbed exercise of sovereignty over it during such a period as is necessary to create under the influence of historical development the general conviction that the present condition of things is in conformity with international order."[2]

However, the suggestion in the use of the expression "under the influence of historical development" is that whatever limitations exist in some cases of adverse possession, there will come a time when there will be created a general conviction that however wrongful the original taking, or whatever protests have been made, the present condition of things should not be disturbed. It is this greater emphasis which suggests that historical consolidation, though perhaps a form of prescription, has greater potency. It does not suffer, therefore, from the restrictions that apply to other modes of acquisition that might be applied in similar situations. This aspect of historical consolidation is implicit in the decision of the International Court in the *Fisheries* case in which the doctrine made its first express, though fleeting, appearance.[3] As De Visscher has said:

> ". . . consolidation differs from acquisitive prescription . . . in the fact that it can apply to territories that could not be proved to have belonged to another State. It differs from occupation in that it can be admitted in relation to certain parts of the sea as well as of land. Finally, it is distinguished from international recognition... by the fact that it can be held to be accomplished . . . by a sufficiently prolonged absence of opposition either, in the case of land, on the part of States interested in disputing possession or, in maritime waters, on the part of the generality of States."[4]

---

2. *Op. cit.*, Vol. 1, 8th ed., p. 576.
3. I.C.J. Rep., 1951, at p. 130. With reference to the Norwegian decrees which had the effect of extending the area of internal waters, the Court commented:
"Since . . . these . . . constitute . . . the application of a well-defined and uniform system, it is indeed this system itself which would reap the benefit of general toleration, the basis of an historical consolidation which would make it enforceable against all states. . . ."
4. *Theory and Reality in Public International Law* (Eng. trans.), pp. 200–201.

To refer again to the situation where territory has been seized by an illegal use of force, whether there will be sufficient hostility to the wrongful act to make sanctions effective and the restoration of the territory to its former sovereign likely will depend upon political circumstances. Even the application of the doctrine of non-recognition may in time be futile to preserve the rights of the former sovereign. Situations can arise in which the use of force, though a breach of international obligations, may engender sufficient sympathy for the underlying cause to make acquiescence likely. In the case of Goa, where Portugal had retained its dependent territories on the Indian sub-continent long after other colonial powers had withdrawn, the use of force was regarded at least with tacit approval by many members of the United Nations, partly motivated by anti-colonialist prejudices, but partly also because there seemed little likelihood of the dispute being settled by peaceful means. As the seizure was not branded as aggression either by the Security Council or by the General Assembly and as there appears no evidence of the doctrine of non-recognition being positively applied as a mark of disapproval, it can be suggested that India has obtained a basis of title which, even if there is no express recognition of the fact, will become consolidated by the acquiescence of the international community over a comparatively short period of time into a fully valid title.

iv *The relevance of contiguity*

Whatever might have been the position in earlier centuries, it has become established in the present century that contiguity alone is not a basis of title. As the arbitrator in the *Island of Palmas* case pointed out, "it is impossible to show the existence of a rule of positive international law that islands situated outside territorial waters should belong to a state from the mere fact that its territory forms the . . . nearest continent or island of considerable size."[5]

Nevertheless, contiguity is a fact which is not ignored by international law. The tendency in the nineteenth century was for states to lay claim to areas of hinterland as contiguous to their coastal settlements in Africa.[6] Although such a principle never became clearly established as a means of creating title, it was probably a latent consideration in the Permanent Court's decision in the *Eastern Greenland* case.[7] The actual areas of the

---

5. 2 U.N.R.I.A.A., at p. 854. Though there may be other reasons, of more recent origin, why an island formed by a raising of the seabed might be claimed by the nearby state, see below, pp. 159 *et seq.*

6. In discussing Britain's disputed sovereignty over the Falkland Islands, Waldock commented, (1948) 25 B.Y.B.I.L., at p. 342:
"The hinterland and contiguity doctrines . . . were much in vogue in the nineteenth century. They were invoked primarily to mark out areas claimed for future occupation. But, by the end of the century, international law had decisively rejected geographical doctrines as distinct legal roots of title and had made effective occupation the sole test of the establishment of title to new lands. Geographical proximity, together with other geographical considerations, is certainly relevant, but as a fact assisting the determination of the limits of an effective occupation, not as an independent source of title."

7. (1933) P.C.I.J. Rep., Ser. A/B, No. 53.

disputed territory settled by Denmark were few, but, in view of the inhospitable nature of the region, the Court was prepared to accept the intention to occupy the more remote areas coupled with the actual possession and settlement of areas of coast-line as establishing Danish sovereignty in a territory to which until a year before the case was heard there had been rival claims.

Contiguity is also the basis of the law concerning territorial waters, the contiguous zone and the continental shelf. Propinquity is also a highly relevant factor in historical claims to areas of the high seas. Where states have for a long period of time exercised rights of sovereignty in such areas adjoining their territorial waters, then, in the absence of effective protest by other states, they acquire a title to continue exercising such rights. The Hudson Bay has long been considered as an historic bay by Canada, so, too, the Delaware and Chesapeake Bays by the United States; while the Soviet Union lays claim to the Arctic waters along her northern coast. In relation to such rights contiguity is a material fact, though not a legal necessity: the basis of title is historical consolidation or perhaps prescription, but not contiguity.

C. The acquisition of territory in polar regions

a THE ARCTIC REGION

The inaccessible and inhospitable polar regions create unique problems in the context of territorial acquisition. Nowhere else are there to be found such large uninhabited areas virtually incapable of "occupation" in any accepted sense of the term. Indeed, in the case of the North Pole, the situation is further complicated by the fact that the region is mostly ice, with what must be considered as high seas capable of being navigated by submarines, and not land, beneath the frozen wastes.

Where there is land, then the *Eastern Greenland* case demonstrates that it may be reduced to the sovereignty of a state by a minimum of settlement and exploitation. Greenland itself is clearly Danish territory, and from the working of minerals on Spitzbergen, it would seem that Norway has made good its title to that island. Canada and the Soviet Union have been particularly concerned to prevent foreign and perhaps hostile settlement, and have called in aid the so-called "sector principle". Where the earth "flattens out" towards the Poles, the contiguity principle can hardly be applied directly and it has been modified to provide the basis for the "sector principle". According to this principle, all land lying within the triangle between the east–west extremities of a state contiguous to the Pole and the Pole itself should be subject to its dominion, unless any particular territory already belongs to another state. Canada, for example, has from the beginning of the century laid claim to all territory except Greenland between its northern land mass and the Pole.

b ANTARCTICA

Because of the different geographical factors involved, primarily the absence of any contiguous land mass to the Antarctic continent, the South Pole has been the subject of less closely defined and justifiable claims. British claims to the Falkland Islands date from the beginning of this century, and although initially perhaps of dubious validity, they have been reinforced by settlement and by the exercise of governmental rights over the inhabitants. In relation to the continental land mass itself, however, the initial basis of British claims (and therefore of the extensive Australian claims) was simply discovery. Rival claims have been made by Chile and Argentina, based principally on the contiguity of the tip of South America to Antarctica. In recent years, scientific exploration has proliferated in the south polar regions, and in an attempt to lessen friction between the claimants so as to allow increased scientific co-operation and exploration, the Antarctic Treaty of 1959 put in abeyance all existing claims to territorial sovereignty as long as the Treaty should remain in force, and provided for the use of the area "for peaceful purposes only". As the Treaty contains no provision for termination, it potentially creates a perpetual régime. Although withdrawal is automatic if a state fails to ratify within two years an amendment agreed upon unanimously by the Contracting Parties, voluntary withdrawal is only possible in a specific case—if an amendment agreed upon by a majority of the Conference, which can be called at the request of any of the Contracting Parties at the end of thirty years from the date of entry into force of the Treaty, has not come into effect within two years. However, perhaps the most interesting aspect of the Treaty is its effects on non-parties. The signatories (Argentina, Australia, Belgium, Chile, France, Japan, New Zealand, Norway, South Africa, Soviet Union, Britain and the United States) include all the states with territorial claims in the area together with others who have invested in scientific exploration of the area. In view of the Parties' expressed intention in Article X of the Treaty "to exert appropriate efforts, consistent with the Charter of the United Nations, to the end that no one engages in any activity in Antarctica contrary to the principles or purposes of the present treaty" the conclusion seems inescapable that the Treaty creates an international régime binding upon the whole of the world community.

2   THE LOSS OF TERRITORY

a   WHERE THE TERRITORY FALLS AUTOMATICALLY UNDER THE
SOVEREIGNTY OF ANOTHER STATE

Loss of territory is not usually a subject that creates legal problems. For the most part it is no more than the antithesis of the appropriate mode of acquisition. A treaty of cession is normally a transfer of rights by one state to another. Prescription, as far as it applies to land territory, necessarily involves the extinction of a previously existing sovereignty.

Recognition of a new state will either accompany a form of peaceful evolution and transfer of sovereignty from the former colonial power or may be necessary because the former sovereignty is destroyed by revolt.

b WHERE THE TERRITORY IS ABANDONED

Although it is sometimes said that dereliction requires both a physical abandonment and an intention to abandon dominion, this rule may well be restricted solely to uninhabited regions. Such a rule was applied in the *Clipperton Island* case and referred to in the *Eastern Greenland* case,[8] but, in less inhospitable territory, it is submitted that dominion will only remain if a physical manifestation of control subsists. Even if discovery had been sufficient to create a valid title in the fifteenth century, the absence of any subsequent manifestation of Spanish sovereignty was held fatal to the American claim in the *Island of Palmas* arbitration.[9]

Peace treaties which provide for the redistribution of various of the vanquished's possessions have often transferred sovereignty to the joint disposal of the victorious powers (as under the Treaty of Peace with Italy in 1947). But the position of Formosa would seem to have more in common with an abandonment or dereliction of sovereignty. By the Cairo Declaration of 1943, confirmed at Potsdam in 1945, one of the Allied aims was stated to be to restore a number of territories, including Formosa (at the time belonging to Japan), to China. Formosa was occupied by Chinese forces at the time of the collapse of Japan, but the Peace Treaty in which Japan renounced sovereignty over the island was not signed until 1951, by which time the mainland of China was effectively controlled by the Communists, Formosa itself being retained by the Nationalists. As the Peace Treaty contained no express disposition of sovereignty over the island the exact status of the territory is in doubt. According to the United Kingdom, Formosa remained under Japanese sovereignty until the Peace Treaty came into force in 1952. At that time the island was being administered by the Chinese Nationalists to whom it had been entrusted in 1945 as military occupants. However, by 1952 the United Kingdom no longer recognised the Nationalists as the Government of China so that their military occupation could not give them sovereignty over the island. On the other hand, the Chinese People's Republic, though recognised as the Government of China by the United Kingdom, was not in occupation of Formosa when Japan renounced all rights to the island, so the Communists too were unable to claim sovereignty over Formosa.[10]

The view of the Chinese Nationalists, which is substantially that of the United States as well, is that the Nationalists are the Government of

---

8. See De Visscher, *Theory and Reality in International Law* (Eng. trans.), pp. 201–203.
9. 2 U.N.R.I.A.A., at p. 854.
10. See the statement by an Under-Secretary of State in the House of Commons on 4th May, 1955: H.C. Deb., Vol. 540, cols. 1870–1.

China so that the effect of the Japanese Peace Treaty was to vest sovereignty over the island in their hands.

On the other hand the Chinese People's Republic has based its claim on the argument that the Cairo Declaration was a legally enforceable instrument. According to the Communist view:

> "When the Chinese Government accepted the surrender of the Japanese armed forces in Taiwan and established sovereignty over the island, Taiwan became, not only *de jure*, but also *de facto*, an inalienable part of Chinese territory. And this has been the situation as regards Taiwan since 1945. Hence, during the five post-war years from 1945 to . . . 1950, no one ever questioned the fact that Taiwan, *de jure* and *de facto*, is an inseparable part of Chinese territory."[11]

It followed that, with the expulsion of the Nationalists from the mainland of China, all sovereign rights, including those over Formosa, passed to the new Communist Government.

As a solution to the Formosa question can only be accomplished by a political settlement, whether by tacit acceptance of a situation developing over a period of time, or by some international *détente*, the better view would seem to be that at the moment, the status of the island is uncertain. Neither the American and Chinese Nationalist view, that the Nationalist Government as the sole Government of all China is the sovereign authority for Formosa as well, nor the Chinese Communist view, is likely to form the basis of such an international arrangement.

3   THE RIGHTS OF A STATE OVER THE TERRITORY OF ITS COLONIAL POSSESSIONS

It will be recalled from an earlier chapter that a state might have powers to regulate the foreign relations of a protectorate, a trusteeship territory or other colonial possession, or even to regard such a non-self-governing community as part of its own territory for legislative and administrative purposes. The exercise of such powers will depend upon a variety of factors, the provisions of the "treaty" which established the protectorate, the terms of the agreement with the United Nations under which a state administers a trusteeship territory, or the constitutional law of the state itself which might, like France or Portugal, treat its overseas colonies as part of the national territory. Such extensive rights are *prima facie* inconsistent with the international personality of the dependent territory, but it does not necessarily follow that sovereignty is vested in the colonial power.

a   MANDATE AND TRUSTEESHIP TERRITORIES

As was stated earlier, the view expressed by Judge McNair in the *Status of South–West Africa* case,[12] that sovereignty had no application to "this new system", the important question being not where sovereignty lay, but "what are the rights and duties of the Mandatory in regard to the

---

11.   S.C.O.R. V, 490th Sess., at p. 34.   12.   I.C.J. Rep., 1950, at p. 150.

area of territory being administered by it", has received general acceptance as representing the law. Despite the fact that in certain cases the administering power has been granted quasi-sovereign rights (Article 4 of the Trusteeship Agreement with Australia relating to the status of New Guinea granted the same powers of "legislation, administration and jurisdiction in and over the Territory as if it were an integral part of Australia"), the territory of the non-self-governing community is held on trust by the administering power and cannot be considered as part of the territory of that power.

b PROTECTORATES AND OTHER COLONIAL TERRITORIES

No such clear answer would seem to be available to the question of whether the territory of other non-self-governing communities can be considered as part of the territory of the colonial power. It will be recalled that protected states (entities which had attained the status of an international person before granting by treaty ultimate control over their affairs to the protecting power) probably retain a measure of personality. Clearly their territory cannot be considered as being under the sovereignty of the protecting state. Similarly, state practice favours the view that sovereignty over a protectorate could only be acquired by annexation, recognition for which today would probably not be forthcoming in view of political pressures against colonialism in any form. Colonies, on the other hand, have usually been considered as under the sovereignty of the colonial power. Even within the British Commonwealth, the dependent territories of which are not "incorporated" as part of the United Kingdom in the way that members of the French community are integrated, matters concerning the internal affairs of these territories are regarded by the United Kingdom as falling within the "domestic jurisdiction" of that state.[13] This claim to sovereignty over colonial possessions is made manifest by the fact that in granting independence to Cyprus (one of the territories with respect to which the plea of domestic jurisdiction had previously been made before the United Nations) the United Kingdom purported to retain sovereignty over certain military base areas. It would seem, therefore, that unless the powers of a state over its colonial territories are restricted by a treaty of protection, or by an international mandate or trusteeship agreement, the territory of a non-self-governing community must be considered subject to the dominion of the colonial power.

4 THE RIGHTS OF A STATE OVER THE TERRITORY OF ANOTHER STATE

Whereas the power of a colonial or other administering authority over a dependent territory concerns the relationship between an international person and an entity the status of which would seem to fall short of

---

13. On the question of domestic jurisdiction, see below, pp. 314–322.

international personality, two other types of territorial right, leases and servitudes, relate to the privileges which may be exercised by one state over the territory of another. Leases and servitudes, like their counterparts in municipal systems of law, are examples of rights *in rem*, or *real* rights, in that they attach to territory and remain enforceable against the territory, even if the territory passes subsequently under the dominion of another state. Although normally created by treaty, they constitute something more than the normal treaty obligation, breach of which only gives rise to a personal remedy for compensation against the state which undertook the obligation.

a LEASES

The lease of territory was an essentially nineteenth-century method of acquiring control of an area subject to the dominion of another state without having recourse to annexation. The most obvious illustrations were the grants made by China in favour of France, Russia, Germany and Britain in 1898, perhaps the best known being the lease of the "New Territories" which Britain attached to, and administered together with, the colony of Hong Kong. The usually accepted view is that such leases amounted to a transfer of sovereignty by the grantor for the period of the lease.

The grant by Panama in favour of the United States in 1903 of the ten-mile strip of territory through which the Panama Canal was constructed differed from the leases of Chinese territory, as the Panama lease was "in perpetuity". The United States received under the Convention all the "rights, power and authority" within the Canal Zone "which the United States would possess and exercise as if it were the sovereign of the territory" concerned.

More recently, military bases have been granted for periods of years by one state in favour of another. The status of such bases is perhaps doubtful and would in any case vary according to the terms of the actual treaty which made the disposition. Thus the bases granted by the United Kingdom to the United States during the Second World War were not of such an exclusive nature as the other leases that have been discussed. By an agreement of March, 1941, the United Kingdom agreed to lease a number of bases to the United States. By the terms of the agreement, the United States was to have "all the rights, power and authority . . . necessary for the establishment, use, operation and defence" of the areas concerned, or for their control. No mention was made of the exercise of such "rights, power and authority" as if the United States were "sovereign of the territory" as in the Convention dealing with the Panama Canal Zone. Nevertheless, throughout this agreement and in the indentures governing each territory, the grants were referred to as leases, and in most cases they were for 99 years. But, and this is a question that is difficult to answer, is it not possible to consider the actual leases as leases in the municipal law sense granted as a result of, and not by means of, an international treaty? If this is the status of the leases, then they are not leases in the international law sense at all. They are binding in the municipal law sense, but they would not create a real right under international law binding upon the territory even after a change of sovereign. All that can be stated with certainty is that some support may be found for this view in that following the granting of independence to the West Indies Federation (in the territory of which a number of the bases are situated), the United States concluded an agreement with the Federation on the future of the bases.

b SERVITUDES

The extent to which the territory of a state may be subject to a right of user by another state, or by a restriction of user binding on the territorial sovereign and enforceable by other states, is an issue which has caused excessive juristic controversy and no little confusion in international practice. The difficulties have stemmed partly from the use of the term "servitudes" (which, with its emotive suggestion of dominance and servience, is diplomatically unsuitable) and partly from the attempt to classify together a number of disparate situations under the one heading.

It is clear that state A can by treaty grant state B rights exercisable on the territory of state A; rights such as the right to fish in territorial waters, or to collect dues on a toll-bridge which crosses into the territory of state A. Such rights are of a personal and contractual nature: they may be abrogated by state A, giving state B a right of action for breach of the treaty obligation, but no right *in rem*. But can state A create a right for the benefit of state B, or for the community of states, which is binding on the territory of state A even if that territory is acquired by state X?

i *Rights benefiting the international community*

When some sort of international status is involved, then clearly restrictions on the territorial sovereign are effective against successors in title. In the *Aaland Islands* dispute,[14] Sweden argued that Finland was bound by the provisions of a convention of 1856 whereby Russia, Finland's predecessor in title, had agreed with France and Britain to the demilitarisation of the islands. In a report to the League of Nations, a committee of jurists stated that the provisions of the 1856 Convention had created "a special international status":

> "It follows that until these provisions are duly replaced by others, every state interested has the right to insist upon compliance with them. It also follows that any state in possession of the Islands must conform to the obligations binding upon it...."

The nature of such restrictions on sovereignty was later summarised by Judge McNair in the *Status of South-West Africa* case, in the following terms:[15]

---

14. L.o.N.J., 1920, Supp. No. 3, p. 3.   15. I.C.J. Rep., 1950, at pp. 153–154.

"From time to time, it happens that a group of great Powers, or a large number of states both great and small, assume a power to create by a multipartite treaty some new international régime or status, which soon acquires a degree of acceptance and durability extending beyond the limits of the actual contracting parties, and giving to it an objective existence. This power is used when some public interest is involved, and its exercise often occurs in the course of the peace settlement at the end of a great war."

The régimes established over the Suez and Panama canals provide good illustrations of "rights *in rem*" benefiting the international community. Both canals are clearly "international waterways", even though in the case of the latter the "constitutive" treaty was in fact two bilateral arrangements, the Hay–Pauncefote Treaty of 1901 between the United States and Britain and the Hay–Varilla Treaty of 1903 between the United States and Panama. The Hay–Pauncefote Treaty and the Suez Canal Convention of 1888 both stated that the canal concerned was to be open in peace and war to all vessels. The termination of the existence of the Canal Zone occupied by British forces and the subsequent "nationalisation" of the assets of the Canal Company by Egypt had no effect on the international status of the canal; nor would a relinquishment of the Panama Canal Zone by the United States in itself affect the status of the canal as an international waterway. The position of the Kiel Canal is less readily analysed. Article 380 of the Treaty of Versailles provided that the canal and its approaches should be maintained "free and open" to the vessels of commerce and war of all nations at peace with Germany on terms of entire equality. The Permanent Court held in the *Wimbledon* case[16] that as a result of this provision the canal had ceased to be a national waterway, passage through which was entirely at the discretion of the riparian state, and had "become an international waterway intended to provide under treaty guarantee easier access to the Baltic for the benefit of all nations of the world." Although the special régime for the canal was denounced by Hitler in 1936, it is not altogether certain whether this action was effective. As the régime created a right *in rem* the abrogation was *prima facie* illegal unless it was acquiesced in by the members of the international community.[17]

ii *Rights benefiting only a single state*

Authority is less readily available when the benefit of a restriction on the territorial sovereignty of a state belongs to a single state and not to the international community. There are numerous situations of this type—mining rights where coal seams cross international frontiers, the right to run an oil pipeline across the territory of a neighbouring state, the right to have an uninterrupted flow of a river the source of which is in another state—but there are few disputes which have given rise to adjudication or other form of judicial settlement. It is important to the

16. (1923) P.C.I.J. Rep., Ser. A, No. 1.
17. See *Kiel Canal Collision Case* (1950), 17 I.L.R., Case No. 34.

beneficiary that it should establish a right *in rem*, for compensation might be an inadequate remedy. Despite doubts cast on the existence of private, as opposed to public, rights of this nature, it would be fatal to any system of law to have to admit that a wrongful act in this field should be without a satisfactory remedy. If state A is dependent upon the waters of a river passing through its territory, it would seem that it has a prescriptive or historic, right to the enjoyment of the river water to the extent that it has normally used that water; and any act by state B on its territory further upstream would not just be an abuse of rights arising from its territorial sovereignty for which compensation would be payable, it would be a breach of a real obligation binding on state B and enforceable by state A.

There is authority for the general proposition that international law recognises and will safeguard a riparian state's right to a necessary minimum flow. In the *Lake Lanoux* case of 1957,[18] an arbitral tribunal held that France was entitled, provided that state returned to Spain by tunnel an amount of water sufficient to satisfy the needs of Spanish agriculture and to provide an adequate emergency reserve, to divert the waters of the lake from the Spanish river Sègre to the French river Aviège. Although the arbitration was possible under the Treaty of Bayonne of 1856 which had been designed to safeguard Spanish rights, it is significant that the French claim was clearly based on general principles of law and not on the Treaty. This had been acknowledged by France as early as 1922 when an official note from the French Prime Minister and Minister of Foreign Affairs had stated that, in cases of alteration in a régime governing the use of waters by more than one state, the state effecting the alteration must subordinate the carrying out of the alteration to the interests of other riparian states. This principle was one of natural law: the Treaty of 1856 added nothing new.

The chief obstacle to the general application of this equitable conclusion would seem to be the *North Atlantic Fisheries* arbitration[19] in which a panel of arbitrators from the Permanent Court of Arbitration had to consider the effect of a treaty of 1818 between the United States and Great Britain which stated that "the inhabitants of the United States shall have, for ever, in common with the subjects of His Britannic Majesty, the liberty to take fish of every kind" from the seas off the Newfoundland coast. The arbitrators held that this provision did not create a servitude which prevented Britain making regulations limiting the fishing rights of all persons, including United States' nationals in the areas concerned. Although the decision has been quoted as negativing any doctrine of servitudes under international law, it is possible to justify the tribunal's conclusion without giving cause for doubting their existence. The tribunal itself seemed to be talking in terms of the "inter-temporal"[20] law when

---

18. 24 I.L.R., 101.   19. (1910), 11 U.N.R.I.A.A., p. 167.

20. According to the principle of the inter-temporal law, "a juridical fact must be appreciated in the light of the law contemporary with it, and not of the law in force at the time when a dispute in regard to it arises or falls to be settled." Thus, in the *Island of Palmas* arbitration from which this statement is taken, the effect of Spanish discovery of the island

referring to the lack of evidence that in 1818 international servitudes were even considered, let alone accepted, by American or British statesmen. Furthermore, by making the contrast between servitudes, which predicate "an express grant of a sovereign right", and the grant of a liberty to fish which was "a purely economic right", the tribunal was by implication accepting the validity of a limited class of servitudes. Admittedly, it might not always be easy to draw the distinction between economic and political rights, and, as a rule, it might not apply to all cases, nevertheless, as a guiding principle, economic concessions, even those in favour of foreign states as opposed to individuals, will not normally give rise to rights *in rem* which are irrevocable by the grantor state.

Another aspect of the *North Atlantic Fisheries* arbitration which may give rise to misunderstanding is the emphasis on an express grant as a prerequisite of a valid servitude. Even if this suggestion was accurate in 1910, it cannot be accepted today. State sovereignty can clearly be extended by prescription or consolidation over neighbouring sea areas as the *Anglo-Norwegian Fisheries* case[1] demonstrates, and as the examples of "historic bays" illustrate. Furthermore, in the *Right of Passage* case,[2] the International Court held that rights of sovereignty could be limited by a similar process. For a century and a quarter there had existed "a constant and uniform practice allowing free passage between Daman and the enclaves" for private persons, civil officials and goods in general, sufficient to establish a right of passage binding on India. As the Court had earlier commented:[3]

> "With regard to Portugal's claim . . . on the basis of local custom, it is objected on behalf of India that no local custom could be established between only two states. It is difficult to see why the number of states between which a local custom may be established on the basis of long practice must necessarily be larger than two. The Court sees no reason why long continued practice between two states accepted by them as regulating their relations should not form the basis of mutual rights and obligations."

The International Court in the *Right of Passage* case certainly approved the existence of rights *in rem*, although it refused to categorise them as "servitudes". "Rights of way" are the most obvious illustrations of rights exercisable by one state over the territory of another, but authority is lacking on whether servitudes benefiting a single state might exist in other situations. The *North Atlantic Fisheries* arbitration demonstrates the

---

had to be "determined by the rules of international law in force in the first half of the 16th century". If the Spanish claim was valid by the international law of that period, the inter-temporal law had yet another application. "The same principle which subjects the act creative of a right to the law in force at the time the right arises, demands that the existence of the right, in other words its continued manifestation, shall follow the conditions required by the evolution of law." Even if discovery did create a valid title in the sixteenth century, it could not continue to provide a valid title under the changed conditions of the nineteenth century when discovery must be followed within a reasonable period by effective occupation of the region claimed. (1928) 2 U.N.R.I.A.A., 829.

1. I.C.J. Rep., 1951, p. 116.   2. I.C.J. Rep., 1960, p. 6.   3. *Ibid.*, at p. 39.

reluctance of tribunals to recognise economic rights over the territory of other states, but it does not follow that economic servitudes cannot exist. Although only the decision of a municipal court, *Aix-la-Chappelle-Maastricht R.R. Co.* v. *Thewis*[4] has been generally regarded with favour amongst writers. The Supreme Court of Cologne had to consider whether Dutch legislation and control were effective over a mine, owned by the Dutch Government, which ran under German territory. By a boundary treaty of 1816 between Prussia and the Netherlands, the Prussian Government was in no way to interfere with or restrict the mining of coàl. The Court held that because certain of the rights of territorial sovereignty had been excluded from their application to the mine, there had arisen a "sort of international servitude" which was binding on Germany as successor to the Prussian State and by which Holland was "entitled to exercise its own legislative authority and police supervision" with respect to an "object situated within the territory of the foreign state". Refined distinctions between different authorities are out of place in attempting to define rules of international law, particularly when the ultimate authority, state practice, provides no real guidance in favour of one view or the other. The most that can be stated is that a servitude in favour of a single state, particularly of an economic nature, will only be upheld by an international tribunal if there is the clearest evidence of the intention to create such a right on the part of the state granting it.

5 MARITIME TERRITORY

The maritime boundaries of a state mark both the extent of a state's territorial jurisdiction, and also the areas within which a state may exercise certain other rights to the exclusion of, or in addition to, the rights of other states. Thus, the base-lines of a state's territorial waters establish the limit of a state's sovereignty over its territory and internal, or national, waters, and provide the starting point for the measurement of the territorial waters of a state. A state may also be entitled to certain jurisdictional rights over a contiguous zone which extends beyond the limit of territorial waters. Finally, the littoral state is entitled to exclusive rights of exploitation over the continental shelf, that is, over the seabed of the shallow waters that extend around the shores of most land masses. In the present chapter, these maritime boundaries will be discussed from their territorial aspect, while the jurisdictional rights they create will be dealt with in a later chapter.

a INTERNAL WATERS

As the extent of internal waters depends upon the base-lines from which territorial waters are measured, the first matter that needs to be considered is the method of determining this line of demarcation.

---

4. (1914) 8 A.J.I.L., p. 858, and p. 907.

Although during the seventeenth century extravagant claims were made to areas of what today would be considered as parts of the high seas, the rule became established that the base-line of territorial waters should follow the low-water mark. Prior to the Hague Conference of 1930 the question "whether the breadth of territorial waters is to be measured from low-water marks following all the sinuosities of the coast, or whether an imaginary line connecting particular salient points of the coast is to be taken as the base-line" was answered by a large majority of states which supplied information to the preparatory committee in favour of the first formula which had "already been adopted in various international conventions". Similarly, the first of the Geneva Conventions on the Law of the Sea of 1958 stated in Article 3, which was undoubtedly declaratory of existing customary international law, that "the normal base-line for measuring the breadth, of the territory sea is the low-water line along the coast". The only difficulties that arise over the application of this rule concern its relation to exceptional indentations of the coast-line, such as gulfs and bays, or to off-shore islands.

i *Bays*

The definition of bays for the purpose of measuring the base-lines of territorial waters has been largely influenced by the fact that the determination of the base-lines has the effect of classifying the waters within the base-lines as internal waters and therefore subject to the territorial jurisdiction of the coastal state. Definitions have tended to emphasise therefore that the bay should be "within the territory" of the coastal state, and that its mouth should not be too wide. At various times, and by various states, one or other of these requirements has been treated as the more important.

In the *North Atlantic Fisheries* arbitration,[5] a majority of the arbitrators held that the width of territorial waters was to be measured "from a straight line drawn across the body of water at the place where it ceases to have the configuration and characteristics of a bay". This decision was not without support from cases heard by municipal courts. In 1875, the Supreme Court of South Australia had to consider whether it had jurisdiction over a murder committed on board a British ship in Gulf St. Vincent between Kangaroo Island and the mainland.[6] Stow, J., held that the test was whether the gulf was "land-locked", and that, as the entrance was blocked by the island it must be land-locked, so that the gulf was within the territorial limits of South Australia. A similar approach was undoubtedly adopted by the English Courts until the executive interfered with the proceedings before the Court of Appeal in the *Fagernes*.[7] A collision had occurred in the Bristol Channel over ten miles from the English coast and a mile or so less than ten miles from the Welsh coast.

---

5. (1910), 11 U.N.R.I.A.A., p. 167.
6. *R. v. Wilson* (unreported): discussed in *International Law in Australia*, p. 265.
7. [1927] P. 311.

Hill, J., held that as the collision had occurred within the "arms" formed by the English and Welsh coasts it had occurred within British territory and was therefore subject to the jurisdiction of the English Courts. Before the Court of Appeal, however, it was stated by the Attorney-General on behalf of the Home Secretary that the place where the collision was alleged to have occurred was not within the territorial sovereignty of the Crown. The Court accepted this statement as conclusive on the issue.

Despite the trend of English decisions towards what might be termed the "configuration" test—that a bay is an area of the sea falling within and to some extent enclosed by land—the British Government has tended to favour the so-called ten-mile rule—that a line could be drawn across the mouth of a bay as long as it did not exceed ten miles in width, or at such point on the indentation nearest the mouth where the width did not exceed ten miles. The rule was recommended by the arbitrators in the *North Atlantic Fisheries* case, and acted upon by the United States and Britain in a treaty of 1912 dealing with the disputed waters. The Hague Codification Conference of 1930 based its discussions on the rule, although there was a general feeling, particularly amongst the maritime powers, that there should be some additional provision in the definition limiting "bays" to areas of water that were greater than the area of the half-circle drawn with the base-line across the mouth of the bay as its diameter. It was probably the uncertainty expressed at the Hague Conference as to the acceptability of the ten-mile rule that led the International Court in the *Anglo-Norwegian Fisheries* case to refuse to acknowledge its existence. The Court pointed out that although the rule had been adopted by a number of states "both in their national law and in their treaties and conventions, and although certain arbitral decisions have applied it as between these states", other states had "adopted a different limit".[8]

The Geneva Convention on the Territorial Sea attempted to include both the requirement that a bay should be something more than an indentation of the coast-line, and that it should not exceed a certain width at its mouth. By Article 7, a bay is defined as "a well-marked indentation whose penetration is in proportion to the width of its mouth", and not a "mere curvature of the coast": an indentation is not to be regarded as a bay "unless its area is as large as, or larger than, that of the semi-circle whose diameter is a line drawn across the mouth of that indentation". While this part of the Article clearly gave expression to the general feeling among states, the paragraph of the Article providing a maximum of twenty-four miles for the straight base-line at, or as near as possible to, the mouth of a bay, was less readily accepted. However, it was included in the final draft of the Convention, which has been ratified by a sufficient number of states to bring it into operation as a treaty obligation between those states, and, in the absence of protest by

8. I.C.J. Rep., 1951, at p. 131.

other states, the rule will rapidly become applicable as against them as a customary rule of international law.[9]

ii *Islands*

Islands, defined by the Convention on the Territorial Sea as naturally formed areas, surrounded by water, which are above water at high tide,[10] are treated in the same way as other land areas for the purposes of delimiting the territorial sea. This principle has a long history. As early as 1805 in the case of the *Anna*,[11] an English Court had to consider whether the capture of prize effected more than three miles from the mainland, but at a less distance from islands formed at the mouth of the River Mississippi, was invalidated as taking place within the jurisdiction of the United States. In decreeing restitution of the *Anna*, Sir William Scott rejected the argument that, as the islands were uninhabited and resorted to only "for shooting and taking birds' nests", they should be considered as a sort of "no-man's-land". It would be unthinkable to consider the prospect of another state occupying, and thus acquiring dominion over, what were in reality "natural appendages of the coast". Such a possibility, he commented, was enough "to expose the fallacy of any arguments that are addressed to show that these islands are not to be considered as part of the territory of America."

Where an area of land is only exposed at low water, it is termed by Article 11 of the Convention a "low-tide elevation". Despite earlier opinions to the effect that such elevations have no territorial water of their own, there was a large measure of agreement at the 1958 Conference that they could be used as a base-line for measuring territorial waters if situated "wholly or partly at a distance not exceeding the breadth of the territorial sea from the mainland or an island", but that if they were not so situated they would have no territorial sea of their own.

iii *Deeply indented coasts, or coasts bordered by an archipelago*

Whereas these traditional rules provide a straight-forward delimitation of the line dividing internal from territorial waters, the *Anglo-Norwegian Fisheries* case[12] introduced a totally new system into international maritime law, the effects of which are still far from clear. By a decree of 1935, mainly confirming earlier proclamations, Norway claimed to draw the base-lines from which to measure its territorial waters along the rock "rampart" (or *skjaergaard*) formed by innumerable islands, and rocks uncovered at low water, and the extremities of a number of mainland promontories, although some sections of the base-line joined points

---

9. Hence the introduction of the twenty-four-mile rule in s. 4 of the British *Territorial Waters Order-in-Council*, 1964, is an important step in establishing it as part of customary international law, unless of course the Order is the subject of effective protest by other states. See also the discussion of the application of Article 6 of the Continental Shelf Convention to non-parties in the *Continental Shelf* cases (1969), 8 I.L.M. 340; and above, pp. 13–15.
10. Article 7 (4).   11. (1805) 5 Ch. Rob. 373.
12. I.C.J. Rep., 1951, p. 116.

fifteen, twenty and even, in one case, more than forty miles apart. Despite the wealth of authority in favour of the traditional rules, which had been applied without difficulty even to rocky and indented coasts as in the case of Nova Scotia and the western coast of Canada north of Vancouver, the Court upheld the Norwegian claim, not only on the ground that Norway had an historic title, but also on the basis of general international law. The low-water base-line was the normal application of the more fundamental principle (a principle, it would seem, entirely of the Court's own creation) that the base-line should follow the "general direction of the coast". What was the general direction of a rugged and deeply indented coastline like the Norwegian depended as much on the islands and rocks offshore as in the delineation of the mainland, for according to the Court:

> "The coast of the mainland does not constitute, as it does in practically all other countries, a clear dividing line between land and sea. . . . Since the mainland is bordered in its western sector by the *skjaergaard*, which constitutes a whole with the mainland, it is the outer line of the *skjaergaard* which must be taken into account in delimiting the belt of Norwegian territorial waters. This solution is dictated by geographic realities."[13]

Among the geographic realities were both the physical configurations of the land, and the economic dependence of the inhabitants of the region on the sea; furthermore—

> "Where a coast is deeply indented and cut into . . . or where it is bordered by an archipelago such as the *skjaergaard* . . . the base-line becomes independent of the low-water mark, and can only be determined by means of a geometric construction. In such circumstances, the line of the low-water mark can no longer be put forward as a rule requiring the coast line to be followed in all its sinuosities; nor can one speak of exceptions, when contemplating so rugged a coast in detail. Such a coast, viewed as a whole, calls for the application of a different method."[14]

Before considering the "different method" propounded by the Court, some comment is necessary on the premise upon which the Court based the need for the adoption of a different method. The statement that where the coast is deeply indented "the base-line becomes independent of the low water mark, and can only be determined by means of a geometric construction" seems to follow from a misunderstanding of the method by which territorial waters are normally measured. The base-line under the traditional rule follows the sinuosities of the coast, but the extent of territorial waters is clearly not a line parallel to the base-line, in fact it is not a "line" which is drawn at all. The question whether a vessel at point X is within or outside territorial waters can be determined by whether it is within the arc of the circle drawn from the nearest land, a radius of which is the width of territorial waters, or, from the ship's point of view, whether a circle centred on its position X, with the same radius, cuts the land at any place. Such an obvious method is easily employed

---

13. *Ibid.*, at pp. 127–8.   14. *Ibid.*, at p. 129.

no matter how indented or island-fringed a coast might be: indeed there would seem to be no practical alternative. Nevertheless, the Court dismissed the "arcs of circles method" as "a new technique in so far as it is a method for delimiting the territorial sea", even though it admitted that the method was "constantly used for determining the position of a point or object at sea".[15]

Having rejected the traditional rule, the Court prescribed a system of straight base-lines, but made no attempt to suggest how they should be drawn. The Court did reiterate in general terms when the system could be adopted, but in some instances these limitations were stated so broadly as to be incapable of precise application. For example, the requirement that the base-lines "must not depart to any appreciable extent from the general direction of the coast" could produce different results depending upon the scale to which the map used had been drawn. The Court also stated that the choice of base-lines must depend upon whether the sea areas thus enclosed "are sufficiently closely linked to the land domain to be subject to the régime of territorial waters". Apart from the obvious difficulty of deciding whether a sea area is "sufficiently linked to the land domain" (in the case of bays, the narrowness of the mouth compared with the extent of the water within the area enclosed establishes such a link), the proposition is inaccurate, because the areas enclosed by the base-lines become subject to the régime of national and not of territorial waters. Finally, the Court's suggestion that "certain economic interests peculiar to a region, the reality and importance of which are clearly evidenced by long usage" should be taken into consideration is tantamount to calling in aid the reasons for its decision in Norway's favour on the ground of historic title to support an unconvincing pronouncement in Norway's favour on the basis of general international law.

In the discussion of the sources of international law, the *Anglo-Norwegian Fisheries* case was given as a striking illustration of "judicial law-making". Although it seemed unrelated to existing rules, it was nevertheless stated by the Court to be no more than "the application of general international law to a specific case". The decision was accepted by the International Law Commission and the principles written into the draft Convention on the Territorial Sea. They were retained in the final draft as signed by the states represented at the 1958 Conference, and have become operative between those states which have ratified the Convention. Much of Article 4 is taken directly from the Court's judgment in the *Fisheries* case, but an exception has been made to meet one particular criticism of the Norwegian system of straight base-lines. Norway had made use of low-tide elevations as fixed points from which to draw base-lines, but it had been forcibly objected that, because of the long distances between these points, at high water it might be impossible for any vessel to calculate accurately either the position of the base-lines or the limit of Norwegian territorial waters. By paragraph (3) of Article 4, base-lines "shall not be drawn to

---

15. *Ibid.*

and from low-tide elevations, unless lighthouses or similar installations which are permanently above sea-level have been built on them."[16]

b TERRITORIAL WATERS

Whereas internal waters are subject to the absolute territorial sovereignty of a state, the position of territorial waters is less clearly defined. Article 1 of the Territorial Sea Convention provides that the "sovereignty of a state extends, beyond its land territory and its internal waters, to a belt of sea adjacent to its coast, described as territorial sea." Although a state has the right to prohibit the ships of other states from fishing, and to prevent the hostile operations of foreign vessels, within its territorial waters, the "sovereignty" is nevertheless subject to a number of exemptions in favour of the ships of foreign states, principally the right of innocent passage.

Although some doubts still exist as to the jurisdictional rights enjoyed by a state over its territorial sea, there has been no measure of agreement at all upon the width of territorial waters. Prior to 1930 it had been generally thought that, with the main exception of the Scandinavian claims to four miles, there would be a sufficient measure of agreement to settle three miles as the limit for territorial waters. Not only did the Hague Codification Conference of 1930 demonstrate the complete lack of agreement, but also two successive Conferences at Geneva in 1958 and 1960 failed to achieve the compromise of a maximum limit of six miles to territorial waters and a further extension up to twelve miles of a fishery zone from which, in time, all foreign fishing vessels would be excluded.

The basic reasons for the failure to agree on the compromise proposals in 1958 and 1960 stemmed from the sharp divisions in the attitudes of various groups of states. As a broad generalisation, the western maritime powers operating large fishing fleets wished to uphold the traditional three-mile limit, and to this was added their security interest, which particularly motivated the United States, in retaining the maximum freedom of movement for their naval forces. The majority of smaller states, however, were anxious to establish the widest limit of territorial waters, to safeguard themselves from both foreign fishing fleets and from foreign naval forces being used as a means of exerting political pressure. While some of these states would have been satisfied with a lesser limit of territorial waters providing they were granted a wider zone of exclusive fishing rights, many of them insisted upon the absolute protection of the widest possible breadth of territorial waters. To some extent the Communist states had divided interests in this conflict, because the Soviet Union had a large fishing fleet operating in foreign waters, but this consideration was outweighed by the security policy of wishing to limit as far as possible

---

16. And see the provisions of the British *Territorial Waters Order-in-Council* of 1964 which enabled the United Kingdom to ratify the *Territorial Sea Convention*.

the effectiveness of United States naval forces by insisting upon the wider limit for territorial waters. Because of the failure to reach agreement, a number of states made it clear that they would not recognise any departure from the three-mile limit which they believed represented existing international law. The United States representative said that "his delegation's offer to agree on a six-mile breadth of territorial sea, provided that agreement could be reached on such a breadth on certain conditions, had been no more than an offer; its non-acceptance therefore left the pre-existing situation unchanged. His country was satisfied with the three-mile rule and would continue to regard it as established international law. Three miles was the sole breadth of territorial sea on which there had ever been anything like common agreement, and was a time tested principle. . . . Unilateral acts by states claiming a greater breadth of territorial sea were not sanctioned by international law, and conflicted with the universally accepted principles of freedom of the seas."[17]

Despite the stand taken by the United States, the United Kingdom and other states favouring the three-mile limit, in view of the number of states which by municipal legislation lay claim to territorial waters of six or twelve miles from the respective base-lines, it is not easy to accept the proposition that the limit of territorial waters remains three miles. It is unlikely that an international tribunal would declare a claim to six or twelve miles *ipso facto* illegal, although it might not be prepared to uphold a wider claim against a state which had consistently adhered to a lesser limit and which had *effectively* protested against the extensions to territorial waters. However, as the earlier discussion on prescription and the role of protest illustrated, it will often be a difficult task for a state to demonstrate the effectiveness of its protests if restricted solely to diplomatic communication.

c THE CONTIGUOUS ZONES

Before the 1958 Conference, there was already evidence of state practice supporting the existence of a contiguous zone, that is, an area of the high seas outside territorial waters within which the littoral state might nevertheless enforce its customs and sanitary regulations. As the International Law Commission stated in its commentary accompanying the 1956 draft articles on the law of the sea:

> "International law accords states the right to exercise preventive or protective control for certain purposes over a belt of the high seas contiguous to their territorial seas. . . . Many states have adopted the principle that in the contiguous zone the coastal state may exercise customs control in order to prevent attempted infringements of its customs and fiscal regulations within its territory or territorial sea, and to punish infringements of those regulations. . . . The Commission considered that it would be impossible to deny to states the exercise of such rights. . . . Although the number of states which claim rights over the contiguous zone for the purpose of applying sanitary regulations is fairly small, the Commission considers that . . . such rights should also be recognised for sanitary regulations."

---

17.   Second U.N. Conference on the Law of the Sea (1960), 14th Plen. Mtg., para. 18.

Article 24 of the Territorial Sea Convention may be taken as in accord with established practice in recognising the right of the coastal state to prevent and punish infringements of its customs and sanitary regulations within twelve miles of the base-line from which the breadth of the territorial sea is measured.

What the International Law Commission refused to recognise was any exclusive right of the coastal state to engage in fishing in the contiguous zone. One of the reasons why the traditional fishing states had resisted claims to twelve miles as the breadth of territorial waters was because they would thereby be excluded from valuable fishing grounds, so it was hardly likely that they would accept a narrower width of territorial waters to which was attached an exclusive right for the coastal state to fish within the contiguous zone. At the 1958 Conference and the second Conference in 1960, the attempt was made to reach a compromise based on a six-mile limit of territorial waters with a further six-mile fishing zone. In 1958, the fishing zone was to be available in perpetuity to those states which had normally fished in those waters for the 5 years prior to the 1st January, 1958. In 1960, the proposal was modified to preserve existing fishing rights for a limited period of 10 years. Both proposals narrowly failed to obtain the necessary two-thirds majority for inclusion in the final Draft of the Convention.

Despite the lack of agreement at Geneva, there has been an increasing trend since 1958 to recognise the primary rights, though not necessarily the exclusive rights, of the coastal state to fish in the waters within twelve miles of the base-lines of its territorial waters. As early as 1959, the United Kingdom entered into an agreement with Denmark which provided for the exclusion of British fishing vessels from a belt of six miles width round the Faroe Islands, and to the regulation by agreement of fishing within the belt between six and twelve miles from the low-water line. This agreement is more significant as the starting point of a new trend than of importance for the development of international law, for it was terminated in 1963 because the two parties were unable to agree on the subsequent regulation of fishing in the outer zone. More significant therefore has been the change in the attitude of the British Government towards fishing off the coast of the United Kingdom. After both the 1958 and 1960 Conferences the United Kingdom reiterated its view that "under existing international law the breadth of the territorial sea of any state is generally limited to three miles and that a coastal state does not enjoy exclusive fishing rights outside its territorial sea". Nevertheless, Britain was a prime mover in the European Fisheries Conference which met in London for two periods between December, 1963, and March, 1964, and has since passed the *Fishery Limits Act* which empowers the government by statutory instrument to bring into operation the provisions of the Draft Fisheries Convention. The régime countenanced by the Convention follows the pattern of the earlier Faroe's agreement, though with certain modifications: a six-mile belt reserved exclusively to the littoral state, and a second belt of six miles is envisaged in which fishing is allowed only to the coastal state and "such other contracting parties, the fishing vessels of which have habitually fished in that belt between 1st January, 1953, and 31st December, 1962", both provisions allowing fishing by signatories should such a right be granted to third states; but the attempt is also made to prevent fishing of "stocks of fish or fishing grounds substantially different" from those which the contracting states have "habitually exploited" within the extended fishing limits of the coastal state.

Amongst other states, not parties to the European Convention, a number of bilateral arrangements have been entered into, of which the most notable are those between Norway and the United Kingdom, Denmark, Sweden and the Soviet Union. The object achieved by Norway was the establishment of a twelve-mile fishery limit from the base-lines of territorial waters in certain designated areas subject to the rights of the other state to fish in the waters stated until 1970. Outside Europe, a Canadian Act of 1964 established an exclusive fishing zone for nine miles outside territorial waters, although, pending consultations, it has not been enforced against the states most likely to be affected. In 1965, New Zealand also passed legislation establishing an exclusive twelve-mile fishing zone, although in the face of Japanese protests, a special Fisheries Agreement was signed between the two states in July, 1967, and, pending ratification, put into effect provisionally. Under the Agreement fishing by Japanese vessels was limited to licensed "bottom fish long-line fishing" in specified areas of the six- to twelve-mile belt up to the end of 1970; otherwise Japanese vessels are not to engage in any fishing at all in the twelve-mile zone. Towards the end of 1966 the United States Congress passed an Act "to establish a contiguous fishery zone beyond the territorial sea of the United States". The zone was established outside territorial waters for nine miles beyond the limit of the territorial waters but was expressly made "subject to the continuation of traditional fishing by foreign states within this zone as may be recognised by the United States".

Although the trend[18] is, therefore, strongly towards the limitation of fishing by foreign vessels within a contiguous zone outside territorial waters, and a move towards the establishment of exclusive rights by the littoral state at least to six miles from the base-lines of territorial waters, state practice has yet to achieve a degree of stability and certainty to create new rules of international law. Until such a stage is reached, the rights of a state to exclude foreign vessels from fishing off its coasts outside its territorial sea must be established by treaty. But in view of the emergence of a zone in which states claim far wider powers over fishing than they are entitled to exercise under Article 24 of the 1958 Convention, it is perhaps more correct to talk in terms of *Contiguous Zones*, rather than *the* Contiguous Zone.[19]

---

18. A number of other states have passed similar legislation, e.g. Australia and Brazil.
19. See below, pp. 243-245, dealing with the jurisdictional aspects of these Zones.

d THE CONTINENTAL SHELF

Only in the last twenty years have technological advances made possible the exploitation of the natural resources contained in the continental shelf, that is, in the areas of land submerged beneath the shallow waters that surround most land masses. The best known, though not in fact the first, of the early claims to the continental shelf came in the Truman Proclamation of 1945. After pointing out that the resources of the continental shelf were frequently but a seaward extension of petroleum and other mineral deposits lying within the territory of the state, and that the effectiveness of measures of exploitation would depend upon co-operation and protection from the shore, the Proclamation stated that: "the Government of the United States regards the natural resources of the subsoil and the sea bed of the continental shelf beneath the high seas but contiguous to the coasts of the United States as appertaining to the United States, subject to its jurisdiction and control" but that "the character as high seas of the waters above the continental shelf and the right to their free and unimpeded navigation are in no way . . . affected". A host of similar claims followed, many in restrained terms, but some asserting exclusive sovereignty over the waters covering the continental shelf. By a process of claim and acquiescence, of claim and protest, and with the assistance of rationalisations attempted by leading writers on international law,[20] the basis of customary law began to crystallise sufficiently for the International Law Commission to prepare a Draft Convention on the Continental Shelf, which was approved by the Geneva Conference of 1958.

The Convention defined the continental shelf as applying "to the seabed and subsoil of the submarine areas adjacent to the coasts but outside the area of the territorial sea, to a depth of 200 metres or, beyond that limit, to where the depth of the superadjacent waters admits of the exploitation of the natural resources of the said areas" and "to the seabed and subsoil of similar submarine areas adjacent to the coasts of islands". Although Article 2 provides that the coastal state exercises "sovereign rights", it is clear from the rest of the paragraph, which limits the rights to the exploration and exploitation of natural resources, that the term "sovereign" is designed to connote a general proprietary control, and not any precise authority based on sovereignty. Thus, while the continental shelf is reserved exclusively for the coastal state, and rights over it cannot be acquired by other states without the consent of the coastal state, the rights of the coastal state "do not affect the legal status of the superadjacent waters as high seas, or that of the airspace above those waters". In exploring and exploiting the seabed, the coastal state must not impede the laying or maintenance of cables or pipelines, nor should there be "unjustifiable interference" with navigation, fishing or conservation of living resources of the sea, nor "interference" with "fundamental" oceanographic or other scientific research. But, whenever installations are

---

20. E.g. (1951) 45 A.J.I.L., 225; (1950) 27 B.Y.B.I.L., 376; and (1950) 36 Tr. Gr. Soc. 115.

erected, the coastal state is entitled to establish safety zones up to a distance of 500 metres around such structures which ships of all nationalities must respect.

The rapid development of means of exploiting particularly the gas and petroleum in the seabed has given a great impetus to a corresponding development in the law relating to the continental shelf. The provisions of the Convention have been adopted by states as a basis for their exploitation of new sources of mineral wealth. However, difficulties are already arising with regard to the application of Article 6 which provides that where the continental shelf is adjacent to or opposite the territory of two or more states, those states should determine the extent of their respective rights by agreement, but, if no agreement can be reached, "unless another boundary is justified by special circumstances" the boundary is to be the median line. When more than two states are involved, as is more usually the case in the North Sea and the Baltic, the application of the median line is uncertain enough without the introduction of a criterion base-upon "special circumstances".

In relation to the North Sea, a number of agreements have been entered into between parties to the Convention based upon the equidistance principle: United Kingdom—Norway of 10 March, 1965; Netherlands—United Kingdom of 6 October, 1965; Denmark—Norway of 8 December, 1965; Denmark—United Kingdom of 3 March, 1966; Netherlands—Denmark of 31 March, 1966. On the other hand, France ratified the Convention subject to a reservation that it would not accept any boundary to its continental shelf determined by the equidistance principle in areas in which, in the French government's opinion, the "special circumstances" referred to in Article 6 existed, those areas being "the Bay of Biscay, the Bay of Granville, and the sea areas of the Straits of Dover and of the North Sea off the French coast".[1]

If one of the states involved is not a party to the Convention, and has not by implication accepted the application of Article 6 to the determination of its continental shelf, what principles of law are there to resolve disputes over the boundaries of its areas of continental shelf? In the *Continental Shelf* cases,[2] the International Court, having held that the Federal Republic of Germany was not bound to accept the application of Article 6 to the delimitation of the boundaries with Denmark and the Netherlands of its continental shelf, went on to consider, as requested by the parties,[3] the principles of international law, outside the Convention, which should govern a delimitation as between adjacent states. The Court's decision was to the effect that the delimitation should take place by agreement "in

---

1. This reservation gave rise to formal objections by the Netherlands, the United Kingdom, the United States and Yugoslavia.
2. (1969) 8 I.L.M. 340.
3. The Special Agreements under which the case was brought before the Court asked the Court to state the principles and rules of international law applicable to the dispute, but reserved to the parties the right to delimit their continental shelf in accordance with those principles by subsequent agreement.

accordance with equitable principles and taking account of all the relevant circumstances".

The Court was not asked to deal with a situation in which there had been a total failure to agree upon a delimitation and in which it was required to make a delimitation binding on the parties. However, it would appear that the factors which are to be taken into account when negotiating an agreed delimitation are equally relevant to a final determination in the absence of such an agreement. The basic proposition put forward by the Court was that any determination should take place "in accordance with equitable principles". It might be that the equidistance method will be in accordance with these principles, "but other methods exist and may be employed, alone or in combination, according to the areas involved".[4] In "certain geographical circumstances which are quite frequently met with, the equidistance method, despite its known advantages, leads unquestionably to inequity", so that some alternative approach must be found. For example, in the case of the German and Dutch coastlines, the concave nature of the former and the convex nature of the latter were "automatically magnified by the equidistance line as regards the consequences for the delimitation of the continental shelf"; so "great an exaggeration of the consequences of a natural geographical feature must be remedied or compensated for, as far as possible".[5]

If equity excludes the use of the equidistance method as the sole method of determination, the law of continental shelf delimitation does not involve any imperative rule but permits resort to various principles or methods, or a combination of them, provided that a reasonable result is achieved. The Court pointed out that there was no legal limit to the considerations which states might take into account in ensuring that they are applying equitable principles, and "more often than not it is the balancing-up of all such considerations that will produce this result rather than reliance on one to the exclusion of all others".[6]

However, the Court did enumerate three particular considerations upon which *inter alia* the parties should rely when reaching an agreed delimitation of their North Sea continental shelf, and it is reasonable to suppose that they would normally be of primary importance in any delimitation. The factors specified were:

"(1) the general configuration of the coasts of the Parties, as well as the presence of any special or unusual features;

(2) so far as known or readily ascertainable, the physical and geological structure, and natural resources, of the continental shelf areas involved;

(3) the element of a reasonable degree of proportionality, which a delimitation carried out in accordance with equitable principles ought to bring about between the extent of the continental shelf areas appertaining to the coastal State and the length of its coast

---

4. (1969), 8 I.L.M. 340 at p. 378.   5. *Ibid.*, at p. 380.   6. *Ibid.*, at p. 381.

measured in the general direction of the coastline, account being taken for this purpose of the effects, actual or prospective, of any other continental shelf delimitations between adjacent states in the same region."[7]

One other point made by the Court was that in the case of the North Sea (and presumably in other geographically similar situations) taking into account geological factors might lead to an overlapping of the areas of continental shelf because a purely geographical test might divide an oil or gas field in such a way as to make separate exploitation impossible, or alternatively advantageous only to the first comer. If such were the case, the Court suggested that joint exploitation was a solution that appeared "particularly appropriate when it is a question of preserving the unity of a deposit".[8]

It may be that this notion of joint rights to exploit a particular area will have greater significance in the future. As technological progress makes exploitation of the resources of the sea-bed possible at even greater depths, some means of delimitation may become necessary between the interests of larger numbers of states at increasing distances out to sea. To avoid friction, and to provide the necessary funds for projects which will obviously be extremely expensive, joint ventures based upon joint ownership of the rights to the seabed might prove the most satisfactory compromise. This object will be taken even further if the policy of communal rights contained in the General Assembly Resolutions on the Reservation of the Sea-Bed and Ocean Floor for Peaceful Purposes of December, 1968, achieves general acceptance. In the first resolution the Assembly created a Committee on the Peaceful Uses of the Sea-Bed and the Ocean Floor beyond the Limits of National Jurisdiction, composed of forty-two states, to "study the elaboration of the legal principles and norms which would promote international co-operation in the exploration and use" of these areas, and to "ensure the exploitation of their resources for the benefit of mankind". And the third resolution requested the Secretary-General of the United Nations "to undertake a study on the question of establishing in due time appropriate international machinery for the promotion of the exploration and exploitation of the resources of this area, and the use of these resources in the interests of mankind, irrespective of the geographical location of states, and taking into special consideration the interests and needs of the developing countries".[9] In other words, beyond the present national rights to the continental shelf, all states will have a joint interest in the resources of the ocean floor which will entitle them to benefit in the proceeds of exploitation even though, in the case of developing states, they may not be able to contribute *pro rata* to the costs of exploration and exploitation.

---

7. (1969), 8 I.L.M. 340, at p. 384.
8. *Ibid.*, at p. 383.
9. The texts of the four resolutions are reproduced in (1969) 8 I.L.M. 201–8.

Hitherto discussion on the "sovereign rights" that the coastal state might exercise over the Continental Shelf has centred on mineral exploitation. In origins, and predominantly, Continental Shelf doctrine was concerned with mineral resources, but it should be kept in mind that the Convention applies to the "natural resources" of the sea-bed and subsoil. And Article 2 (4) defines these natural resources to include "living organisms belonging to sedentary species, that is to say, organisms which, at the harvestable stage, either are immobile on or under the sea-bed or are unable to move except in constant physical contact with the sea-bed or the subsoil". It will be realised that this description is so vague that it produces uncertainty whether certain forms of marine life are or are not covered by the definition. Particular difficulty has been encountered with the classification of crustacea. A dispute between France and Brazil during 1962–3 became so acrimonious that it was referred to as the "Lobster War";[10] and it required an agreement between Japan and the United States of 1964[11] to settle their dispute over the Alaskan King Crab.

---

10. For details, see (1964), 13 I. & C.L.Q. 1453.
11. (1965), 4 I.L.M. 157.

CHAPTER SIX

JURISDICTION—1
TERRITORIAL JURISDICTION
AND EXEMPTIONS FROM ITS
APPLICATION

1 JURISDICTION IN GENERAL

The jurisdictional competence of a state under international law is in many respects ill-defined. Although it is true to say that jurisdiction is primarily "territorial"—a state has jurisdiction over persons and things, and over events occurring, within its territory—there exist both exemptions from the application of the local law within a state's territory, and extensions of its law to certain events occurring outside that territory. In order to establish even the most general rules of international law, all that can be attempted is to examine these exemptions from, and extensions of, a state's competence by reference to the circumstances in which states normally claim to exercise, or consciously refrain from exercising, jurisdiction according to their own municipal law. Only in relation to maritime jurisdiction are a number of decisions by international tribunals available to help clarify the principles of international law, though many of the judgments rely heavily on deductions drawn from municipal legislation and the attitudes of municipal courts.

The task of determining, and then of explaining, the scope of international law in this field is complicated by the fact that the word "jurisdiction" is itself used to denote at least two similar, though nevertheless distinct, notions. In the first place, it may refer simply to the competence of a court of law to try a particular dispute. Thus the statement—

> Under English law, the English courts have jurisdiction over crimes committed on board British ships on the high seas; but not normally over crimes committed abroad, even when the offender is a British subject—

implies that the *offence* is (or is not) one over which the English courts have jurisdiction. On the other hand, jurisdiction may signify the rights of a state to control or interfere with a particular person or object. In the sentence—

> Only in limited circumstances does international law allow a state to exercise jurisdiction over foreign ships passing through its territorial waters or on the high seas—

the jurisdiction is to *apprehend*, and not (at least at this stage) to *try* the wrong-doer.

Nor is this an end to the difficulties. The rules of international law restricting the right of a state to apprehend an offender are much more clearly defined than those governing the offences for which an offender may be tried once he is apprehended. For example, it is established beyond question that it is contrary to international law for one state to commit acts of sovereignty on the territory of another state. The most notable illustrations of this principle are provided by arrests or abductions carried out by agents of, or by private persons with the connivance of, a state. In the most notorious of a series of diplomatic incidents occurring during the 1930s in which German officials were involved in the seizure of individuals from the territory of neighbouring states, one Jacob-Soloman, a former German citizen, was induced into a car in Switzerland and was then driven at high speed across the border. Not only was the barrier on the German side of the frontier conveniently (and unusually for the time of evening) open, but a number of German officials were waiting to effect the arrest as soon as Jacob-Soloman reached German soil. Before the dispute went to arbitration, Germany admitted responsibility, and a joint declaration was issued in which it was stated that "a German functionary had acted in an inadmissible manner".[1]

A more recent illustration was the kidnapping of Adolf Eichmann, a Nazi war criminal, from Argentina and his subsequent handing over to the Israeli authorities. The Security Council of the United Nations, to which Argentina had complained, adopted a resolution which recited that "the violation of the sovereignty of a Member State is incompatible with the Charter", and requested the Israeli Government "to make appropriate reparation in accordance with the Charter of the United Nations and the rules of international law".[2]

There is also authority to suggest that the same rule of international law applies when it is fraud or trickery, and not force, which leads to the prisoner leaving the safety of one state for the territory of another where his arrest is accomplished. In the *Colunje* claim,[3] a Canal Zone officer had gone to Colunje's offices in Panama and had induced him to return to the Canal Zone where he was arrested. In the course of allowing the claim presented against the United States, the American-Panamanian Claims Commission said that it was "evident that the police agent of the Zone by inducing Colunje by false pretences to come with him to the Zone with the intent of arresting him there unduly exercised authority within the jurisdiction of the Republic of Panama".

On the other hand, there is considerable uncertainty as to how far a state might legislate with respect to, and its courts decide issues arising out of, events taking place entirely abroad. It cannot be doubted that there

---

1. See (1935) 29 A.J.I.L., 502; (1936) 30 *ibid.*, 123.
2. Discussed (1961) 55 A.J.I.L., 307, esp. pp. 311–338.
3. (1933), 6 U.N.R.I.A.A. 342; (1933–4) 7 A.D., Case No. 96.

should be some link between either the offence or the offender and the state claiming jurisdiction, but how close that link must be to satisfy the requirements of international law may be difficult to state with accuracy. Although the generality of practice of municipal courts is of some assistance, it must be remembered that many states refrain from claiming jurisdiction in circumstances where there is no rule of international law prohibiting the assumption of jurisdiction, while a few states might positively assert their competence beyond the area recognised by international law as falling within their jurisdiction. Finally, as in many situations international law acknowledges the possibility of concurrent jurisdiction by two or more states, there is the additional complication of conflicting claims in which neither state is willing to give the other precedence, and between which international law may provide no satisfactory solution.

Problems of this type, and the difficulties which might face a court called upon to consider them, are well demonstrated in the case of the *Lotus*.[4] The *Lotus* was a French ship that collided on the high seas with a Turkish vessel, the *Boz-Kourt*, which sank with loss of life. When the *Lotus* reached Constantinople, the French officer of the watch at the time of the collision (together with the Turkish captain) was arrested and charged with manslaughter before a Turkish Court. Turkey refused to accept vehement French protests about the legality of the Turkish action, though it did agree to submit the dispute to the Permanent Court. The principal French argument concerned the burden of proof: it was for the Turkish Government to point to some title to jurisdiction recognised by international law in favour of the Turkish Courts. The contention had much to recommend it: if the incident did not occur within Turkish territory, it should surely have been for Turkey to justify its exercise of jurisdiction under some recognised extension of its competence. However, the Court's rejection of this argument started from what it considered the fundamental principle of state sovereignty: because international law was based on the consent of states, restrictions upon their independence could not be presumed. The foremost restriction imposed by international law was that a state might not exercise its power in any form in the territory of another state. In that sense jurisdiction was territorial: it could not normally be exercised by a state outside its territory. But, the Court continued, it did not follow that international law prohibited a state from exercising jurisdiction in its own territory over acts which had taken place abroad. Far from laying down such a prohibition, international law left a wide measure of discretion to states to decide for themselves how far they should extend the application of their laws and the jurisdiction of their courts to persons, property, and acts outside their territory. In such circumstances, all that was required of a state was that it should not overstep the limits set upon its jurisdiction by international law.

Once that stage was reached, the onus was clearly on the complaining state to demonstrate the existence of a prohibitive rule precluding the

---

4. (1927) P.C.I.J. Rep., Ser. A, No. 10.

defendant state from applying its municipal law to the subject matter of the dispute. However, because of the uncertainty of the rules of international law in this field, the onus was almost impossible to satisfy. France put forward two main contentions:

(1) that international law did not allow a state to take proceedings with regard to offences committed by foreigners abroad; and

(2) that international law recognised the exclusive jurisdiction of the flag state over events occurring on board a ship on the high seas.

As far as the first objection was concerned, the Court reserved its opinion on whether jurisdiction could legitimately be assumed simply on the basis of the nationality of the victim; but it went on to hold that "the offence produced its effects on the Turkish vessel and consequently in a place assimilated to Turkish territory in which the application of Turkish criminal law cannot be challenged, even in regard to offences committed there by foreigners". The second objection was also rejected. The French Government, although able to show that jurisdiction normally followed the flag, was unable to establish that international law recognised the *exclusive* jurisdiction of the flag state over incidents occurring on the high seas. The fact that states usually refrained from exercising jurisdiction over foreigners or over events occurring on a foreign ship was not conclusive proof that there existed a rule of international law that states should never exercise such jurisdiction.[5]

In what circumstances, then, may a state exercise jurisdiction? Territory and population being two of the essential characteristics of statehood, it is natural that territorial supremacy and the bond of nationality should form the basis of a state's jurisdictional competence. Normally jurisdiction will be:

(1) *territorial*, for, as has already been stated, subject to certain exceptions, incidents occurring in, or persons even transiently within, the territory of a state are subject to its legal system; but it can also be

(2) *personal*—a state has the right, even if the right is not always exercised, to extend the application of its laws to nationals, even with respect to events occurring entirely abroad.[6]

However, from time to time claims are advanced to jurisdiction in situations arising outside a state's territory and where the persons responsible are not nationals of the state concerned. Thus, jurisdiction may also be

(3) *universal*—only in the case of piracy is the universal principle, that any state may exercise jurisdiction over a crime committed abroad and whatever the nationality of the perpetrators, generally recognised, though some writers suggest that genocide, perhaps war crimes and slave trading, fall within the same category;[7]

(4) *protective*—there is no rule of international law forbidding the punishment of a foreign national by a state the safety or public order of which

5. For the present position with regard to criminal jurisdiction over events occurring on the high seas, see below, pp. 273–274.
6. For further discussion of personal jurisdiction, see below, pp. 303–307.
7. For piracy, see below, pp. 257–262, slave-trading, pp. 262–263.

has been jeopardised by acts occurring outside its territory;[8] or, more doubtfully,

(5) according to the *passive personality* principle—it is not at all certain whether a state may exercise jurisdiction over a foreigner in respect of an incident taking place abroad simply because injury was caused to one of its own nationals.[9]

2 TERRITORIAL JURISDICTION

The reasons for the close connection between a state's territory and its jurisdictional competence are obvious enough. As one writer[10] explained with regard to the criminal law:

> "There are solid reasons . . . for the general principle that criminal jurisdiction is linked with territory. (1) The State where a crime is committed generally has the strongest interest in punishing it. (2) It is in this State that the offender is likely to be found. (3) Generally, the local forum is the most convenient one, since the witnesses are probably there. (4) Legal systems differ from one another, and it would be vexatious if, say, an Arcadian visiting London had to obey two systems of law, English and Arcadian."

Nevertheless, although as a principle it is clear enough to assert that a state has jurisdiction over incidents occurring, or persons or things situated, within its territory, it is at most a generalisation which forms the basis, though not always the content, of a number of rules of law.

In a sense, all criminal jurisdiction is territorial: it is unusual under most legal systems for a trial to take place in the absence abroad of the accused. However, reference has already been made to the fact that the concept of territorial jurisdiction has a more limited connotation: there must be some closer link than simply the subsequent presence of the offender between the offence itself and the territory of the state claiming jurisdiction. Normally, of course, no problems will arise, for an offence is either committed within the territory of a state, or it is committed outside that territory. But what is the position where the crime, though planned and set in motion in one state, only has its effects in the territory of another state?

The primary rule would seem to be that a crime is committed, and may be tried by the courts of the state, where it is actually completed.[11] There are certainly numerous municipal decisions which support the proposition, but whether it is possible to deduce from them a practice accepted as international law, rather than a rule of convenience, is problematical. In many cases the final outcome will depend primarily on the interpretation of the

---

8. E.g., below, pp. 266–267, 306.   9. See below, pp. 306–307.
10. Glanville Williams, in (1965) 81 L.Q.R., at pp. 276–7. This entire article, in three parts, discloses many interesting lacunae in English criminal jurisdiction over events occurring extraterritorially.
11. Cp. s. 36 of the Single Convention on Narcotic Drugs, 1961.

relevant municipal statute. In *R* v. *Blythe*,[12] for example, the accused, by a letter written from Canada, persuaded a girl under the age of sixteen, living in the United States, to leave her father and join him in Canada. A Canadian Court held that he could not be convicted of the offence of taking a girl under the age of sixteen out of her father's control because the offence had been completed by the girl leaving home, an event which had occurred outside the jurisdiction. On the other hand, in *R.* v. *Mackenzie*,[13] the two accused, in order that one of them should have sexual intercourse with a certain young girl, induced her to leave home in Scotland and to come to England. As the act of intercourse subsequently took place in England, the English Court of Criminal Appeal held that the crime of procuring a girl under twenty-one to have unlawful carnal connection was not completed until the procurer had "gained his . . . object, and carnal knowledge (had) been obtained"; it was the English Courts, therefore, and not the Scottish Courts, which had jurisdiction.

Recognition of the principle that jurisdiction should, if possible, be left to the state in the territory of which a criminal act takes effect is also to be found in a number of extradition cases. If an offender sets in motion a sequence of events culminating in the commission of a crime in another state, the normal practice is for him to be surrendered for trial to the authorities of that other state. In the English case of *R.* v. *Godfrey*,[14] the Divisional Court accepted without comment that the defendant, arrested by the British police on a warrant for his extradition to Switzerland, could properly be charged in that country with the crime of obtaining by false pretences committed, at his instigation, by one of his partners in Switzerland, although he himself had never left England. The same conclusion was reached by a Federal District Court in *U.S. ex. rel. Hatfield* v. *Guay*.[15] The Canadian Government sought the extradition of Hatfield on the ground that he was guilty of obtaining money by false pretences. The prisoner, in a statement made to a British consul in Florida, and later reiterated before a Canadian Commissioner in Boston, had initiated a fraudulent claim to the Canadian Government for damages to his ship, which he alleged had been torpedoed by a German submarine. Although, therefore, the crime had been set in motion entirely within the United States, extradition was granted, the Court commenting that if there was evidence "reasonably tending to establish that Hatfield, through false and fraudulent statements set in motion in the United States, obtained payment of money in Canada, the latter country has jurisdiction of the crime."[16] Yet even these cases do no more than establish that it is the usual, not the *compulsory*, practice for jurisdiction to be left to the state where the crime is finally consummated.

Not only is there no rule of international law that the state where a

---

12. (1895) 1 C.C.C. 263.   13. (1910) 6 Cr. App. R. 64.
14. [1923] 1 K.B. 24; (1919–22) 1 A.D., Case No. 190.
15. 11 F. Supp. 806 (1935); on appeal, 87 F. (2d) 358.
16. 11 F. Supp., at p. 809.

crime is completed has exclusive jurisdiction, but also there would seem to be no restriction on the right of the state where the crime was initiated to exercise jurisdiction. The latter state has a discretion whether to bring such preparatory acts within the ambit of its criminal law. In general, states do not choose to exercise this type of jurisdiction, though there do exist a few situations in which an actual duty is imposed upon a state to punish acts designed to bring about the commission of a crime on the territory of another state. An obvious illustration is the duty of a state to prevent the fitting out on its territory of an hostile expedition against another state. However, there are less dramatic examples, probably the best known being the obligations accepted by the parties to the Geneva Conventions, for the Suppression of Counterfeiting in 1929, and for the Suppression of the Illicit Drug Traffic in 1936. Thus, as a result of the 1929 Convention, the United Kingdom Parliament passed legislation, *inter alia*, to amend the Forgery Act, 1913, and the Coinage Offences Act, 1861, so that it would be as much a crime to counterfeit foreign, as British, coinage.

While there is an obvious and close connection between territory and criminal jurisdiction, civil jurisdiction is less dependent on the territorial principle. Although it is true that in commercial matters and in actions in tort, the mere presence of the defendant will often be sufficient, where personal status is involved the courts of most states insist upon a personal link between the parties and the particular state concerned. Under Anglo-American systems the basic requirement is domicile, though the states of Continental Europe require nationality as the basis of their competence. There is a further distinction between criminal and civil proceedings. A criminal court has jurisdiction if the criminal law of the state is applicable to the circumstances of the case. As the ambit of the criminal law is the test of jurisdiction, there is no room for the secondary issue of "choice of law": the criminal court can only apply the criminal law of its own state. On the other hand, a civil court called upon to adjudicate in a dispute involving a foreign element, once it decides in favour of its jurisdictional competence, can apply the law of the place with which the transaction has the most real connection, or the law of the place where the events giving rise to the litigation occurred, according to the circumstances of the case.

3 EXEMPTIONS FROM TERRITORIAL JURISDICTION

Although, as a general principle, the local law applies universally throughout the territory of a state, it has long been recognised that certain persons, because of their position as representatives of foreign states, are entitled to immunity from the jurisdiction of the local courts. Express recognition of the exemption in favour of diplomatic agents can be found in English practice certainly as early as the sixteenth century; but implicit in the case law was recognition of the underlying principle that immunity was accorded to them in their capacity as representatives of a foreign sovereign. It was the immunity of the sovereign which was the basis of the immunities accorded to his servants, and to public ships operating under his commission. The quasi-diplomatic privileges of state representatives to, and officials of, a number of international organisations, and the exemptions from the local jurisdiction sometimes granted to visiting foreign armed forces, are very much twentieth-century phenomena. However, before dealing first with English law, then with the law of the United States, and finally with the position under other legal systems, some prefatory remarks on the basic principle that no state may exercise jurisdiction over another might help to make the whole subject of immunities more easy to follow.

Until the creation of the new Republics, in France, and more particularly in central and north America, at the end of the eighteenth and the beginning of the nineteenth centuries, sovereignty had always been a personalised concept. Political philosophy talked largely in terms of an individual sovereign, and this approach was reflected in the attitudes of most municipal tribunals to the question of the jurisdictional immunities of foreign states. As a sovereign could not himself be sued before the courts of his own state, it was readily understood that the sovereign of another state was similarly exempt from the processes of the local law. Furthermore, because of the notion of the independence and equality of states, it was unthinkable that one sovereign should be able in any way to exercise jurisdiction over another sovereign. A good illustration of this line of thinking is to be found in the English case of *De Haber* v. *Queen of Portugal*,[17] decided in 1851. The plaintiff had issued a series of writs against the defendant and a number of agents of the Portuguese Government, claiming that sums of money due to him had been wrongfully paid to the Portuguese Government, but the defendant succeeded in having all further proceedings stayed. In the course of his judgment, Lord Campbell, C.J., stated the law in traditional terms: "to cite a foreign potentate in a municipal court . . . is contrary to the law of nations and an insult which he is entitled to resent."[18] Even the Supreme Court of republican United States found it difficult to escape from prevailing contemporary doctrine. In the earlier case of the *Schooner Exchange*[19] in 1812, Marshall, C.J., stated that the absolute nature of territorial jurisdiction would, nevertheless, "not seem to contemplate foreign sovereigns nor their rights as its objects", and that, as one sovereign was "in no respect amenable to another", no sovereign could be taken as having entered foreign territory except "in the confidence that the immunities belonging to his independent station . . . will be extended to him."[20]

A second factor which should be borne in mind is that municipal courts, when deciding a question of immunity, often declare that they are applying a rule of international law. However, although it is generally recognised that one state may not, in principle, be sued in the courts of another state, the application of the rule to the facts of a particular case varies,

---

17. 17 Q.B. 196.   18. *Ibid.*, at p. 207.   19. 7 Cranch 116.
20. *Ibid.*, at p. 137.

sometimes very widely, from one state to another. As we shall see, in most states a distinction is drawn between sovereign acts (acts *jure imperii*), in connection with which a plea of immunity would be upheld, and private acts (acts *jure gestionis*), where such a plea would be rejected; but it is a distinction which produces its own variations even between one state and another purporting to apply the same rule. On the other hand, English law, despite some hesitations, seems to have settled for the principle of absolute immunity: whether the litigation concerned the public or private affairs of a foreign sovereign, or concerned public ships employed for public or purely commercial purposes, it was still the foreign sovereign who was being made a defendant in the action, and that is something which English law would not allow.

4 ENGLISH LAW

A. The immunity of foreign states

a THE PERSONAL IMMUNITY OF THE FOREIGN SOVEREIGN

The immunity of a foreign sovereign from suit in the English Courts was implicit in the early cases on the immunities of diplomatic agents.[1] As representatives of a foreign sovereign they could no more be subject to the jurisdiction of the courts than could the sovereign himself. Nevertheless, it long remained unsettled whether the immunity attached absolutely to the foreign sovereign, or only in relation to his public acts. As late as 1851 it was possible for the Lord Chief Justice to state that "an action cannot be maintained in an English Court against a foreign potentate for anything done or omitted to be done by him in his public capacity as representative of the nation of which he is the head . . . no English Court has jurisdiction to entertain any complaints against him in that capacity."[2] Indeed, for a brief period, it seemed as if the principle would be applied by the English Courts. It formed the basis of the decision in the *Charkieh*[3] in which Sir Robert Phillimore held that, though owned by the Khedive of Egypt, the vessel forfeited its immunity, because it was chartered to a private individual and engaged in carrying cargo as an ordinary merchant ship.

However, this development did not survive the decade. In the *Parlement Belge*,[4] the defendant ship was owned by the King of the Belgians: it was a mail-boat which also carried passengers and some cargo on the Channel crossing. Sir Robert Phillimore followed his own line of reasoning in the *Charkieh*: a public vessel was not entitled to immunity if it engaged in the

---

1. E.g., the statement of Lord Talbot in *Barbuit's Case* (1737), Cas. t. Talb. 281, at p. 282:
   ". . . the privilege of a public minister is to have his person sacred and free from arrests, not on his own account, but on account of those he represents . . . the foundation of this privilege is for the sake of the prince by whom an ambassador is sent. . . ."
2. *De Haber* v. *Queen of Portugal* (1851), 17 Q.B., at p. 207.
3. (1873), L.R. 8 Q.B. 197.   4. (1879), 4 P.D. 129.

carrying of goods and passengers as a commercial venture. His decision was reversed by the Court of Appeal,[5] but the rule adopted to accomplish this result was far wider than was necessary, or even desirable. It would have been possible to have reversed the decision at first instance simply on the ground that the *Parlement Belge* was still primarily operating for public purposes, the carrying of cargo and passengers being secondary to the carrying of mail. However, the principle applied by the Court of Appeal may be stated thus: as a result of the theory of the independence of sovereign states and the comity of nations, one state should decline to exercise its jurisdiction over another state: as the immunity was an immunity from process, it mattered not whether the sovereign's property was a warship or a mail-boat as the proceedings *in rem*, if allowed to continue, would oblige the sovereign to appear to protect his property.

b THE EXTENSION OF SOVEREIGN IMMUNITY TO PROPERTY

Once the emphasis was on the impleading of the foreign sovereign at the expense of the notion of public capacity, or public purposes, the basis of a rule of absolute immunity was established. In relation to property, it no longer appeared to matter for what purpose the property was employed, or even if the foreign sovereign owned the property, as long as he had some interest in it which required protection. As far as ships were concerned, the high-water mark of this development was the decision of the Court of Appeal in the *Porto Alexandre*.[6] This ship had gone aground in the Mersey and had only been refloated with the assistance of three tugs. Unable to obtain payment for their services, the tug owners issued a writ *in rem* against the ship itself. It appeared that the *Porto Alexandre* had been requisitioned by the Portuguese Government, but was being employed entirely in carrying cargoes for private individuals. In upholding a claim to immunity, the three members of the Court had no doubt that the case was covered squarely by the earlier Court of Appeal decision in the *Parlement Belge*.

The judges were not blind to the possible injustice likely to be suffered by the private litigant, but, once the wider principle laid down in the *Parlement Belge* was accepted, it is difficult to suggest how its application to the facts of the *Porto Alexandre* could have been avoided. The House of Lords has yet to make a final pronouncement on the issue, although a majority of its members in the *Cristina*[7] did express doubt as to the correctness of the decision in the *Porto Alexandre*. To take an illustration from the judgment of Lord MacMillan:[8]

"... I should hesitate to lay down that it is part of the law of England that an ordinary foreign trading vessel is immune from civil process within this realm by reason merely of the fact that it is owned by a foreign state.... When the doctrine

---

5. (1880), 5 P.D. 197.   6. [1920] P. 30; (1919–22) 1 A.D., Case No. 100.
7. [1938] A.C. 485; (1938–40), 9 A.D., Case No. 86.
8. *Ibid.*, at p. 498. See also *per* Lord Thankerton, at p. 496, and *per* Lord Maugham, at pp. 519–520.

of the immunity of the person and property of foreign sovereigns from the jurisdiction of the courts of this country was first formulated and accepted it was a concession to the dignity, equality and independence of foreign sovereigns which the comity of nations enjoined. It is only in modern times that sovereign states have so far condescended to lay aside their dignity as to enter the competitive markets of commerce, and it is easy to see that different views may be taken as to whether an immunity conceded in one set of circumstances should to the same extent be enjoyed in totally different circumstances. I recognise that the courts of this country have already . . . gone a long way in extending the doctrine of immunity; but the cases which have gone furthest have not been hitherto considered in this House, and like my noble and learned friend Lord Thankerton I desire to reserve my opinion on the question raised in the case of *The Porto Alexandre*."

Despite the misgivings expressed in the *Cristina*, there are few signs of a change of attitude by the English Courts towards the problems raised by increasing state control especially over foreign trade. Foreign governmental agencies, like the United States Shipping Board[9] and the Soviet news agency, Tass,[10] have been recognised as exempt from suit, but in 1957 in *Baccus S.R.L.* v. *Servicio Nacional del Trigo*[11] the Court of Appeal went a step further. The defendant was a department of the Spanish Ministry of Agriculture, but, according to expert evidence accepted by both parties, it was an independent legal personality. Nevertheless, a majority of the Court upheld its plea of immunity, even though it was in Spanish law a separate company, and the subject matter of the dispute was a commercial transaction—the sale of 26,000 tons of rye by the plaintiffs to the defendant.

Inherent in the rule that a plea of immunity is a bar to further proceedings is the difficulty of settling whether the foreign state has any interest at all in the subject matter of the dispute. If the claim to immunity has the effect of preventing the court considering whether the foreign sovereign is in fact obliged to intervene in the proceedings, there would be a grave danger of injustice to the plaintiff. On the other hand, if the court does investigate the basis of the foreign state's claim to immunity, it can only do so by obliging the foreign sovereign to appear, even though under protest, and to produce at least *prima facie* evidence of title. But by obliging the foreign state to intervene to establish evidence of title, the court is in effect exercising a measure of jurisdiction over the foreign sovereign in a manner contrary to the basic philosophy of the doctrine of sovereign immunity.

Faced with this problem, the English Courts have not always shown consistency in their approach, although more recently the main difficulty has been over the application, rather than the content, of the rule. A useful starting point to the discussion is provided by the litigation arising out of the changes in control and ownership of the *Jupiter*. The plaintiffs, who owned the vessel, had moved their head office and trading fleet from Russia to Marseilles in 1919. The *Jupiter* was laid up at Dartmouth, but

---

9. *Compania Mercantil Argentina* v. *U.S. Shipping Board* (1924), 93 L.J.K.B. 816.
10. *Krajina* v. *Tass Agency*, [1949] 2 All E.R., 274; (1949) 16 A.D., Case No. 37.
11. [1957] 1 Q.B. 438; (1956) 23 I.L.R. 160.

they continued to pay the wages of the crew. In 1924, the master of the vessel handed over control to the Russian Trade Delegation in London, and a fresh registration was issued. As soon as the plaintiffs commenced proceedings to recover the ship, the Russian Government moved to set aside the writ on the ground that the vessel had been nationalised by a decree of 1918. The Court of Appeal held[12] that the proceedings, by their very nature, constituted an attempt to implead the Russian Government, so that the Court had no jurisdiction. Scrutton, L.J., was prepared to go further: once a foreign state applied to have a writ set aside on the ground that the subject matter of the dispute was its property, "without going any further, without investigating whether the claim is good or bad . . . the Court . . . must decline jurisdiction." This wider rule certainly has the virtue of simplicity, and it need not make for injustice, at least in the majority of cases. The drawback is, of course, that there would be no *guarantee* that injustice was being avoided.

If the foreign sovereign is owner, or is in physical control, no problem arises; similarly, if the foreign sovereign transfers its rights to a third party. The *Jupiter* was subsequently transferred by the Russian Government to an Italian company. The plaintiffs' action was then allowed to proceed[13] because it was apparent from the pleadings that the defendant company could only have title at all if the Soviet Government's interest in the ship had terminated. In the words of Atkin, L.J.:[14]

> "The Russian Government do not claim at the moment to be the owners or to have the right of possession, though they do say . . . that they passed their title to the defendants. Under those circumstances it seems to me to be a mere question of fact or of law as to whether or not the defendants, who are not a sovereign state, have in fact got a title to this ship, and no question, therefore, of impleading the foreign sovereign arises."

The wider rule of claiming immunity may well cause injustice in situations involving a dispute as to ownership or possession between the plaintiffs and a sovereign state or someone holding the property on its behalf, where the facts upon which the claims are based are also in dispute. This danger does not arise where the facts are not contested, because the court is able to decide as a matter of law whether the foreign sovereign has been impleaded or not without forcing him to become a party to the proceedings. In *U.S.A. and France* v. *Dollfus Mieg*,[15] for example, the respondent company instituted the action against the Bank of England alleging that certain gold bars held there had been wrongfully seized from the company by the Germans before they were driven from France in 1944. The gold bars had been recovered from the Germans by the Allied Powers and deposited in the Bank of England. The House of Lords upheld the claim made on behalf of the Bank, and of France and the United States,

---

12. [1924] P. 236; (1919–22) 1 A.D., Case No. 100.
13. [1925] P. 69; (1919–22) 1 A.D., Case No. 100. 14. *Ibid.*, at p. 78.
15. [1952] A.C. 582; (1952) 19 I.L.R., Case No. 37. And see also the *Jupiter*, the facts of which are given above.

that to allow the proceedings to continue would be indirectly to implead two foreign sovereign states. As Lord Jowitt pointed out, to decline to apply the doctrine of immunity to a bailment made by or on behalf of the sovereign in which the action was brought against the bailee would lead to the absurd result that goods belonging to a foreign sovereign deposited at a railway station, an hotel or a bank, could be the subject of litigation in the English Courts by the simple course of suing the railway, hotel or bank.

Where the real danger lies, of course, is in the case of bogus claims to property, particularly if the foreign sovereign asserts a proprietary interest but does not disclose sufficient facts upon which a court can determine the validity of its claim to immunity. If the plaintiff's pleadings are inconsistent with the existence of any right to immunity, it must be necessary for the foreign sovereign to adduce at least some evidence in support of its claim. In *Juan Ysmael* v. *Republic of Indonesia*,[16] the Privy Council was called upon to consider the position of a ship which an agent of the plaintiff company had purported to sell to an agent of the Indonesian Government. It was found as a fact that not only did the company's agent have no authority to complete the transaction on the terms provided, but also the Indonesian Government's representative was aware of the lack of authority. As the master of the ship was a servant of, and had remained loyal to, the company, there was no question of the Government having obtained actual physical control of the ship. It was held, therefore, that the writ *in rem* issued against the ship did not indirectly implead the Indonesian Government. The principle underlying the decision was stated by Lord Jowitt in the following terms:[17]

"... a foreign government claiming that its interest in property will be affected by the judgment in an action to which it is not a party, is not bound as a condition of obtaining immunity to prove its title to the interest claimed, but it must produce evidence to satisfy the court that its claim is not merely illusory, nor founded on a title manifestly defective."

In the present case, the knowledge of the Indonesian agent that the company's agent lacked authority to complete the transaction did render the title claimed by the Indonesian Government "manifestly defective".

c WHO IS ENTITLED TO IMMUNITY?

In order for immunity to attach to a particular person or entity, it must be shown that the person is in fact the sovereign, or that the entity is a department or agency of the foreign sovereign. The method of establishing the claim to immunity depends upon whether it is the foreign state or one of its governmental agencies which is being impleaded. The proper course where there is a dispute as to the status of the foreign ruler, government or state, is for the court to seek the guidance of the Secretary of State for Foreign Affairs. In the *Charkieh*,[18] Sir Robert Phillimore went behind

16. [1955] A.C. 72; (1954) 21 I.L.R. 95. 17. *Ibid.*, at pp. 89–90.
18. (1873), L.R. 8 Q.B. 197.

the Foreign Office Certificate and only after an exhaustive examination of the status of Egypt held that the Khedive of Egypt was still subject to Turkish suzerainty; but this approach was rejected categorically by the Court of Appeal in *Mighell* v. *Sultan of Johore*.[19] Since then the words of Lord Esher in that case have been accepted as authoritative: "once there is the authoritative certificate of the Queen through her minister of state as to the status of another sovereign, that in the courts of this country is decisive."[20]

In endorsing this principle in *Duff Development Co.* v. *Kelantan*[1] the House of Lords provided a striking illustration of its application in practice. Kelantan was a Malay state, the ruler of which had agreed to have no political relations with any foreign power except through the Crown and to accept the advice of the Crown's appointed Resident in nearly all internal matters. Despite this clear evidence of Kelantan's subservient status, their Lordships accepted as binding a statement from the Colonial Office that "the Sultan . . . generally speaking exercises without question the usual attributes of sovereignty." Lord Cave explained that if "after this definite statement a different view were taken by a British Court, an undesirable conflict might arise . . . it is the duty of the Court to accept the statement of the Secretary of State thus clearly and positively made as conclusive upon the point."[2]

On the other hand, if it is not the sovereignty of the foreign state which is in doubt, but whether a department or agency of an admitted foreign sovereign is to be identified with the foreign sovereign for the purposes of a claim to immunity, the issue falls to be decided according to principles of English law, although to a limited extent the constitutional law of the foreign state concerned may be relevant to the degree of connection required between the foreign sovereign and the agency claiming immunity. In *Krajina* v. *Tass Agency*,[3] the plaintiff, faced with a plea of immunity contained in a statement by the Russian Ambassador that "the Tass Agency constitutes a department of the Soviet State", sought to distinguish the earlier decision in *Compania Mercantil Argentina* v. *U.S. Shipping Board*[4] on the ground that the Board was only a government department whereas the Agency was a separate legal entity. The Court of Appeal held that, as the statement of the Soviet Ambassador had raised a *prima facie* case of immunity, it was for the plaintiff to prove that the Agency was something more than a government department. As the plaintiff did not adduce sufficient evidence to support his contention, the defendant's claim to immunity was upheld. However, it was apparent that, even if the plaintiff had been able to demonstrate the separate legal existence of the Agency, a majority of the Court were doubtful whether he would have succeeded. This uncertainty did not last for long. Eight years later, in *Baccus S.R.L.* v.

---

19. [1894] 1 Q.B. 149.   20. *Ibid.*, at p. 158.
1. [1924] A.C. 797; (1923–4) 2 A.D., Case No. 65.
2. *Ibid.*, at pp. 808–9.   3. [1949] 2 All E.R. 274.
4. (1924), 93 L.J.K.B. 816.

Servicio Nacional del Trigo,[5] a majority of the Court of Appeal upheld the defendant's claim to immunity on the ground that it was a department of the Spanish State, despite the fact that by Spanish law it had separate legal personality with power to contract on its own behalf. In justifying this conclusion, Jenkins, L.J., commented:[6]

> "In these days, the Government of a sovereign State is not as a rule reposed in one personal sovereign: it is necessarily carried out through a complicated organisation which ordinarily consists of many different ministries and departments. Whether a particular ministry or department or instrument, call it what you will, is to be a corporate body or an unincorporated body seems to me to be purely a matter of governmental machinery."

d WAIVER OF IMMUNITY

An English Court can only exercise jurisdiction over a foreign sovereign if he waives the immunity from suit to which he is entitled. The basic principle is clear enough: if a foreign sovereign comes to the court as plaintiff, or appears without protest as defendant, in an action, he has submitted to the jurisdiction with respect to those proceedings and to all matters incidental to them. Thus, if he appears as plaintiff, he can be obliged to give security for costs,[7] to allow discovery of documents required by the other party,[8] and also to submit to any counter-claim which may be necessary to enable the defendant to defend himself adequately. However, even if the defendant considered he had been libelled by the plaintiff in the course of their dealings, he could not counter-claim for slander in an action commenced by the plaintiff to appoint a trustee of a trust fund,[9] or to recover a debt due from the defendant,[10] for such a counter-claim would not be sufficiently closely connected with his defence to the plaintiff's action. As defendant, he is similarly bound to comply with orders, for example, in relation to discovery, made in the course of the proceedings.

It is clear, however, that the submission must be a genuine act of submission. If the foreign sovereign, or his agent, raises no objection at the outset of a suit commenced against him, it is still open to the sovereign to plead his immunity at a later stage, provided he can show that he had not been aware of the right of immunity he was foregoing by entering a defence to the claim, or by giving security for costs, or other similar act, or that his agent had acted without his knowledge. In the *Jassy*,[11] the defendant vessel was owned and operated by the Roumanian State Railways. It had been seized under a writ *in rem*, and was only released on payment of £1,000 bail by solicitors acting on behalf of the London agents of the Roumanian Government. As soon as the dispute came to the notice of the

---

5. [1957] 1 Q.B. 438; (1956) 23 I.L.R. 160.   6. *Ibid.*, at p. 466.
7. *Republic of Costa Rica* v. *Erlanger* (1876), 3 Ch. D. 62.
8. *Prioleau* v. *United States* (1866), L.R. 2 Eq. 659.
9. *South African Republic* v. *La Compagnie Franco-Belge*, [1897] 2 Ch. 487.
10. *High Commissioner for India* v. *Ghosh*, [1960] 1 Q.B. 134; 28 I.L.R. 150.
11. [1906] P. 270. *The Bulgaria*, [1964] 2 Lloyd's Rep. 524.

Roumanian Government, their chargé d'affaires in England was instructed to intervene. The President held that all further proceedings should be stayed according to the principle laid down in the *Parlement Belge*: the undertaking to put in bail and the appearance entered on the instructions of the London agents had occurred "without the knowledge of the Roumanian Government and under a misapprehension as to the privilege enjoyed by a sovereign state in respect of the immunity of its public vessels from arrest."[12]

Whether the foreign sovereign appears as plaintiff or defendant, he submits not only to the jurisdiction of the court of first instance, but also to all necessary stages of appeal. Illustration of the normal application of this rule is scarcely necessary, although its application to the unusual circumstances that arose in *Sultan of Johore* v. *Abubakar*[13] is worth mentioning. The appellant had obtained a declaration from a court established by the Japanese during their occupation of Singapore that he was entitled absolutely to certain land. The respondent brought this action under the Japanese Judgments and Civil Proceedings Ordinance, 1946, s. 3 (1) of which enabled any party aggrieved by a Japanese decree to apply by originating summons "for an order—(a) that such decree be set aside either wholly or in part; or, (b) that the applicant be at liberty to appeal against such decree". The Judicial Committee of the Privy Council held that, although the method of reopening the issue in the Singapore court was by a new summons, the proceedings were essentially a continuation of the proceedings commenced by the Sultan himself in the Japanese Court, and by commencing those proceedings he had already waived his immunity.

On the other hand, once an action has become *res judicata*, it is not open to the unsuccessful party to obtain an injunction to prevent the foreign sovereign enforcing the court's decision: even if the issues concern the subject matter of the previous litigation, this is a new action, and the proceedings must be stayed if the sovereign pleads his immunity.[14] Similarly, even if a foreign sovereign has waived his immunity and a decision has been given against him, it is not possible for the successful plaintiff to proceed to execute the judgment against the sovereign.

This principle applies to cases where a plaintiff seeks to enforce an arbitration award, and even though, by contract, the foreign sovereign has agreed to accept the jurisdiction of the English Courts. In *Duff Development Co.* v. *Kelantan*,[15] the House of Lords held that a clause in a contract whereby the respondent sovereign agreed to the provisions of the Arbitration Act, 1889, and itself attempted to take advantage of the clause by going to arbitration was not a sufficient waiver by implication of immunity from the jurisdiction of the English Courts. And in *Kahan* v. *Pakistan Federation*,[16] the Court of Appeal refused to hold that a clause expressly stating that the government "agrees to submit for the purpose of this

---

12. *Ibid.*, at p. 273.   13. [1952] A.C. 318; 19 I.L.R., Case No. 38.
14. *Strousberg* v. *Republic of Costa Rica* (1880), 44 L.T. 199.
15. [1924] A.C. 797; (1923–4) 2. A.D., Case No. 65.
16. [1951] 2 K.B. 1003; 18 I.L.R., Case No. 50.

agreement to the jurisdiction of the English Courts" was an effective waiver. The Court stated that it was bound by the *Duff Development* case and by *Mighell* v. *Sultan of Johore*[17] to accept the proposition as "established beyond question" that a "mere agreement by a foreign sovereign to submit to the jurisdiction of the courts of this country is wholly ineffective if the foreign sovereign chooses to resile from it. Nothing short of an actual submission to the jurisdiction—a submission, as it has been termed, in the face of the Court—will suffice."[18]

B. Diplomatic immunities

At common law the immunity of diplomatic staff was a corollary of the immunity of the foreign sovereign. If the sovereign could not be impleaded before the English Courts, neither could his representatives. As a consequence, English law recognised the widest immunities as attaching to the person and property of diplomatic and other staff in the service of a foreign ambassador. Even if a particular immunity was not accorded under the Diplomatic Privileges Act of 1708, the courts took the view that the Act was declaratory of, and only covered part of the area governed by, existing principles of law.

Because of the divergence in the practice of states towards diplomatic privileges and immunities, an international Conference at Vienna in 1961 adopted a Convention on Diplomatic Intercourse and Immunities which became the basis of the British Diplomatic Privileges Act of 1964. This new Act "shall, with respect to the matters dealt with therein, have effect in substitution for any previous enactment or rule of law" (s. 1).

a CATEGORIES OF PERSONS ENTITLED TO PRIVILEGES AND IMMUNITIES

Under the provisions of the Convention enacted as part of English law by Schedule 1 of the Act, persons entitled to various degrees of immunity are divided into a number of separate categories, diplomatic agents and their families, administrative and technical staff and their families, service staff, and private servants.

i *Diplomatic agents and their families*

Diplomatic agents are to enjoy immunity from the jurisdiction of the English Courts in both criminal and civil matters except in three cases:

(a) where the action relates to private immovable property situated in the territory of the receiving state, unless it is held on behalf of the sending state for purposes of the mission;

(b) if the action relates to matters of succession and the agent is involved as executor, administrator, heir or legatee as a private person and not on behalf of the sending state;

(c) where the action concerns any commercial venture undertaken by the agent outside his official functions (Article 31(1)).

This last provision reverses previous authorities, but in the other two

---

17. [1894] 1 Q.B. 149.   18. [1951] 2 K.B., at p. 1012, *per* Jenkins, L.J.

situations the position was less clear. It was obviously desirable that the English Courts should have jurisdiction in such cases, and a number of *dicta* can be found in support of this view, but neither point had been settled. Article 31 also stipulates that a diplomatic agent is not obliged to give evidence as a witness, nor can he be subject to measures of execution except in cases falling under (a), (b) and (c) above, and then only if such measures can be taken without infringing the inviolability of his person or his residence. This rule relating to execution is reinforced by Article 32 (4) which states that waiver of immunity shall not be held to imply waiver of immunity in respect of the execution of the judgment, for which a separate waiver shall be necessary.

The person of a diplomatic agent shall be inviolable (Article 29); so also is his private residence to the same extent as the premises of the mission (Article 30). He is also exempt from social security legislation in force in the receiving state, except insofar as he employs servants who are not exempt in which case he must observe the obligations which the social security provisions of the receiving state impose upon employers (Article 33). A diplomatic agent is also exempt from most forms of taxation whether national or local in the receiving state, but he will be liable to pay such taxes as purchase or sales tax on goods he buys, duty on the transfer of private immovable property not held on behalf of the sending state for purposes of the mission, and tax on income having its source in private investments in commercial undertakings in the receiving state, etc. (Article 34). Personal baggage and articles for the mission and for the personal use of the agent shall be admitted to the receiving state free from all customs duties and charges other than for storage, cartage and similar charges (Article 36). An agent cannot be made liable for personal or public service of any kind (Article 35). However, these various privileges and immunities are restricted by Article 38 (1) in cases where the diplomatic agent is a national of, or is permanently resident in, the receiving state. In such a case, except insofar as additional privileges and immunities may be granted by Order in Council (s. 2(6)), the diplomatic agent shall enjoy only immunity from jurisdiction and inviolability in respect of official acts performed in the exercise of his functions. Under Article 37 (1), "members of the family of a diplomatic agent forming part of his household shall, if they are not nationals of the receiving State, enjoy the privileges and immunities specified in Articles 29 to 36."

ii *Administrative and technical staff and their families*

The definition of such staff contained in Article 1 of the Convention is not particularly helpful as the relevant paragraph states that they are "members of the staff of the mission employed in the administrative and technical service of the mission". The question of what personnel are included in this category is more easily answered by excluding personnel covered by the other categories. Hence, they are staff not having diplomatic rank and not in domestic service; i.e. they comprise typists, clerical assistants, communications officers, etc.

According to Article 37 (2) members of the administrative and technical staff, together with members of their families forming part of their respective households, shall, if they are not nationals of or permanently resident in the receiving state, enjoy the privileges and immunities specified in Articles 29 to 35, except that the immunity from civil and administrative jurisdiction shall not extend to acts performed outside the course of their duties. Neither the Act nor the Convention attempts to define what is meant by "acts performed outside the course of their duties" so that the application of the expression will be a matter for the courts to decide. Finally, Article 37 (2) also provides that administrative and technical staff are entitled to the exemptions from customs duties specified in Article 36 in respect of articles brought into the receiving state at the time such staff first take up their appointment.

If the staff in this category are nationals of, or permanently resident in, the receiving state they shall enjoy privileges and immunities only to the extent admitted by Order in Council (s. 2(6)), though the receiving state must exercise such jurisdiction in a manner that will not interfere unduly with the performance of the functions of the mission (Article 38 (2)).

iii *Service staff*

Service staff are defined as "members of the staff of the mission in the domestic service of the mission". Members of such staff who are not nationals of or permanently resident in the receiving state shall enjoy immunity in respect of acts performed in the course of their duties, and exemption from taxes on the emoluments they receive by reason of their employment and from obligations imposed by social security legislation (Article 37 (3)). The provisions of Article 38 (2) by which privileges and immunities are at the discretion of the receiving state with respect to its own nationals or permanent residents apply to service staff; hence any privileges and immunities that might be granted depend upon an Order in Council under s. 2 (6) of the Act.

iv *Private servants*

Article 37 (4) provides that private servants of members of the mission shall, if they are not nationals of or permanently resident in the receiving state, be exempt from tax on emoluments received by reason of their employment, but in other respects they may enjoy privileges and immunities entirely at the discretion of the receiving state, although the receiving state should exercise jurisdiction in such a manner as not to interfere unduly with the performance of the functions of the mission. The provisions of Article 38 (2) also apply to private servants who are nationals of, or permanently resident in, the receiving state.

While this classification of personnel and their families is very much different from the common law rules which were generally all-embracing, the 1964 Act is largely in line with the common law on a number of other issues.

b EXISTENCE OF DIPLOMATIC STATUS

Under s. 4 of the 1964 Act, if in any proceedings any question arises whether or not any person is entitled to any privilege or immunity under the Act, a certificate issued by or under the authority of the Secretary of State stating any fact relating to that question "shall be conclusive evidence of that fact". The rule that no evidence would be accepted to *contradict* the statements contained in the Secretary of State's certificate has already been considered in relation to a number of other issues. In the context of diplomatic status, the point was settled by the House of Lords in 1928 in the case of *Engelke* v. *Musmann*.[19] The Attorney-General, on behalf of the Foreign Office, notified the Court that the defendant had been appointed as a Consular-Secretary to the German Embassy, and had been accepted in that capacity by the British Government. The Court of Appeal declined to accept this statement as conclusive and sought to have the defendant cross-examined as to his precise status (a person holding a consular appointment would not at that time have been entitled to the same privileges as a diplomatic agent). The House of Lords held that its own previous decision in *Duff Development Co.* v. *Kelantan* on the conclusiveness of the Foreign Office statement in relation to sovereign status applied equally to diplomatic status: "the acceptance and recognition of persons who form the staff of an ambassador are matters which, having regard to the practice in the conduct of foreign affairs, are equally based on the comity of nations and necessarily also within the cognisance of the Crown acting through the Foreign Office."[20] It would seem, therefore, that the power granted to the Secretary of State by the Act is more extensive than that formerly recognised by the courts.[1]

c   POSITION OF DIPLOMATIC AGENTS ACCREDITED TO A THIRD STATE

Article 40 (1) provides that if a diplomatic agent passes through or is in the territory of a third state, which has granted him a passport visa if such visa was necessary, while proceeding to take up or return to his post, or when returning to his own country, the third state shall accord his inviolability and such other immunities as may be required to ensure his transit or return. The same principle applies to members of the diplomat's family. In the case of other staff of the mission (technical, administrative or service staff) and their families, Article 40 (2) simply requires that third states shall not hinder the passage of such persons.

This provision defines in legal terms a principle which is obviously desirable, though it is not one which had been finally pronounced upon by the English Courts. In *New Chile Gold Mining Co.* v. *Blanco*,[2] the defendant was the Venezuelan minister in France. There was much argument between counsel as to whether a writ could be served upon a foreign ambassador, but the Divisional Court preferred to decide in the defendant's favour on the ground that, the subject matter of the dispute being a

---

19. [1928] A.C. 433; (1927-8) 4 A.D., Case No. 245.
20. [1928] A.C., at p. 443, *per* Lord Buckmaster.
1. Para. 27 of the Attorney-General's submissions to their Lordships (*ibid.*, at pp. 436–437) contains an accurate statement of the pre-Act position.
2. (1888), 4 T.L.R. 346.

concession in Venezuela, there was no reason in any case for allowing service of a writ outside the jurisdiction. On the question of the immunity of a minister accredited to another state, Mainsty, J., was emphatically of the view that the court ought not to call upon such a person to leave his post in order to defend an action in this country: it would "interfere vastly with the duties he had to discharge".[3] Huddleston, B., on the other hand, was of opinion that "the privilege of ambassador ought not to be extended beyond ambassadors in our own country".[3]

While it is unlikely that the English Courts would as a matter of discretion allow service of a writ outside the jurisdiction on a foreign diplomatic agent accredited to a third state, Article 40 does not cover every eventuality. Foreign representatives attending conferences in the United Kingdom are covered by other legislation, but what if the foreign diplomat takes a vacation in the United Kingdom? As there is no question of serving the writ outside the jurisdiction, the courts would seem to have no power to prevent the action proceeding.

d TERMINATION OF IMMUNITY

Article 39 (3) and (4) of the Convention, as reproduced in the first schedule of the Act, both deal with the position of the family after the death of a member of a mission, a situation that does not appear to have been considered by the English Courts; but Article 39 (2) substantially reproduces the common law rule on two issues:

(i) when the functions of a person enjoying privileges and immunities have come to an end, such privileges and immunities shall normally cease at the moment when he leaves the country, or on the expiry of a reasonable period in which to do so;

The case of *Musurus Bey* v. *Gadban*[4] illustrates the common law rule. The Court of Appeal had to consider whether recovery of a debt contracted by a foreign ambassador was barred by the Statute of Limitations. The Court held that the limitation period could not run against the creditor while the ambassador was entitled to diplomatic immunity, nor once the ambassador had left the country. It became vital to decide, therefore, whether the ambassador retained his immunity from suit during the two months between the time he relinquished his post and the time he left the country. The Court was of opinion that this issue had already been settled, and it accepted the averment that the ambassador had remained in England only for the purpose of making the necessary preparations for his departure, Davey, L.J., adding[5] that in "handing over the affairs of the embassy to his successor the ex-ambassador is still engaged on his sovereign's business, and must have a reasonable time allowed for that purpose." Although the case deals with the position of an ambassador, the same principle would apply to any other person entitled to diplomatic immunity. The only difference in the case of a subordinate member of a

---

3. *Ibid.*, at p. 349.   4. [1894] 2 Q.B. 352.
5. *Ibid.*, at p. 362. It is clear, therefore, that the immunity is from suit and does not affect the legal liability of the diplomat: *Dickinson* v. *Del Solar*, [1930] 1 K.B. 376; *Empson* v. *Smith*, [1966] 1 Q.B. 426.

mission would be that a reasonable time to hand over to his successor and to arrange for his departure from the country would likely be a shorter period than that allowed to an ambassador or other head of mission.

(ii) but immunity continues even after a person entitled to privileges and immunities has left the country or after a reasonable period has elapsed with respect to acts performed in the exercise of his functions as a member of the mission.

The basis of this rule in English law is that to challenge the acts of a diplomatic agent in his official capacity, even after his diplomatic immunity had ceased, would nevertheless be tantamount to impleading the foreign sovereign on whose behalf the agent acted. This principle is clear where the agent acquired title to property on behalf of the sovereign. In *Rahimtoola* v. *Nizam of Hyderabad*,[6] the members of the House of Lords thought that the fact that the appellant had ceased to be Pakistan's High Commissioner in London was irrelevant because for the respondent to be allowed to continue proceedings against a fund placed in a bank by the appellant would inevitably oblige the State of Pakistan to defend the action. And in *Zoernsch* v. *Waldock*,[7] the Court of Appeal had no hesitation in applying the principle to all acts of a diplomatic agent performed in his official capacity.

e WAIVER OF IMMUNITY

It is for the sending state to waive immunity at its discretion (Article 32 (1)), but s. 2 (3) of the Act provides that waiver by the head of a mission shall be deemed to be a waiver by the state he represents.

But may immunity be waived by a subordinate diplomatic agent, or other person entitled to immunity, on his own account? The position is not altogether clear. If he commences proceedings, a diplomatic agent is precluded by Article 32 (3) from invoking immunity from jurisdiction in respect of any counterclaim directly connected with the principal claim. This principle had already been accepted by the English Courts in relation to sovereign immunity, and had been applied in a case which also involved diplomatic immunity by the Court of Appeal in *High Commissioner for India* v. *Ghosh*.[8] The plaintiffs were the High Commissioner, the State of India and the government of West Bengal. They were suing for the recovery of money lent to the defendant, who sought to counterclaim against the first two plaintiffs for alleged slander by their servants or agents. The Court held that clearly the High Commissioner was entitled to diplomatic immunity and the State of India was entitled to sovereign immunity. By choosing to come before the English Courts, they had waived their immunity to a certain extent: they must be taken to have submitted to the jurisdiction not only for the purpose of having their claim adjudicated on, but also for the purpose of enabling the defendant to defend himself adequately, and his adequate defence might include a demand asserted by way of counterclaim. However, such a counterclaim could only be maintained if it was "sufficiently connected with or allied to

---

6. [1958] A.C. 379; (1957) 24 I.L.R. 175. 7. [1964] 2 All E.R. 256.
8. [1960] 1 Q.B. 134; 28 I.L.R. 150.

the subject-matter of the claim as to make it necessary in the interests of justice that it should be dealt with along with the claim". In this case, it could not be said that a counterclaim for damages for slander had "any material bearing at all" on the subject matter of the plaintiffs' claim to recover money lent.[9]

Although this case dealt with a head of mission, there is nothing in the authorities, nor is there any suggestion in the 1964 Act, to suggest that a subordinate official requires approval from his state or the head of mission before waiving his immunity by taking proceedings in the English Courts. However, the Act does not appear to have altered the existing common law rule that a subordinate member of the staff of a mission cannot, by appearing as defendant in an action, waive an immunity which is primarily that of his state and not his own. In order for the waiver to be effective his appearance must have the approval of his state or of his head of mission.

In *R. v. Madan*,[10] the appellant had been convicted in August, 1960, of obtaining a season ticket by false pretences and of attempting to obtain money by false pretences. He was at the time, and continued to be, employed in the passport office of the Indian High Commission, and was entitled to diplomatic immunity. The solicitor who appeared on behalf of the appellant in the committal proceedings had purported to waive this immunity. In November the Deputy High Commissioner wrote to the Commonwealth Relations Officer stating that although the appellant was entitled to immunity, in order not to impede the course of justice, the High Commissioner was prepared to waive the appellant's immunity. The Court of Criminal Appeal stated that, as this waiver by the High Commissioner could not be retroactive, the validity of the proceedings in which the appellant was convicted depended upon the effectiveness of the waiver purported to be made on his behalf. However, this waiver was clearly not effective. The rule was well established as far as civil jurisdiction was concerned that the immunity was not that of the person but that of the state he represents, and the Court could see no reason in such a case as this for drawing a distinction between the principles of law applicable in the case of civil proceedings and criminal charges. The position at common law that "it is not the person entitled to a privilege who may waive it unless he does so as agent or on behalf of the representative of the country concerned", was in the circumstances of the present case reinforced by the provisions of the Diplomatic Immunities (Commonwealth Countries and Republic of Ireland) Act, 1952, s. 1 (5) of which stated the powers of a chief representative to waive the immunity conferred by the Act on himself, his staff or their families.

f INVIOLABILITY OF THE MISSION, ITS RECORDS AND
    COMMUNICATIONS

The concept of inviolability is the right of the sending state to have its diplomatic premises, its diplomatic personnel, and all official records and

---

9. *Ibid.*, at pp. 140, 141.   10. [1961] 2 Q.B. 1; 33 I.L.R. 368.

communications safeguarded against interference of any sort. The provisions of the Vienna Convention incorporated in the 1964 Act specify a number of applications of this principle, which is not one that has been litigated in the English Courts.

Article 22 (1) states the basic proposition that the premises of the mission shall be inviolable and that agents of the receiving state may not enter the premises without the consent of the head of the mission. Paragraph (2) provides that the receiving state is "under a special duty to take all appropriate steps to protect the premises of the mission against any intrusion or damage and to prevent any disturbance of the peace of the mission or impairment of its dignity." The inviolability of archives and documents is laid down in Article 24.

Under Article 27 (1), the receiving state must permit and protect free communication on the part of the mission for all official purposes. Official correspondence of the mission is declared inviolable (paragraph (2)), and it is stated that the diplomatic bag shall not be opened or detained (paragraph (3)). Article 27 (5) provides that the diplomatic courier shall be "protected by the receiving state in the performance of his functions", and "shall enjoy personal inviolability and shall not be liable to any form of arrest or detention". These obligations apply equally to third states. According to Article 40 (3), official correspondence and other official communications in transit shall be allowed the same freedom and protection by third states as must be provided by the receiving state. Third states shall accord to diplomatic couriers and diplomatic bags in transit the same inviolability and protection as the receiving state is bound to accord.

g RESTRICTION OR EXTENSION OF THE PRIVILEGES AND
   IMMUNITIES PROVIDED FOR IN THE CONVENTION

i *Restriction of privileges and immunities*

Under s. 3 of the 1964 Act, if it appears to the British Government that the privileges and immunities accorded to a British mission or its personnel in the territory of a foreign state are less than those conferred by the Act on the mission of that state or its personnel in the United Kingdom, the Crown might by Order in Council withdraw any of the privileges and immunities from the foreign mission or its personnel as appears proper. This section replaces the Diplomatic Immunities Restriction Act of 1955, but a number of Orders made under the 1955 Act have been kept in force by s. 8 (5) of the 1964 Act.

ii *Extension of privileges and immunities*

Under s. 7 of the 1964 Act, a number of bilateral arrangements providing for an extension of privileges and immunities to persons not included in the Act, or for exemption from customs and other duties in respect of articles not covered by the Act, are safeguarded.

C. Quasi-diplomatic privileges and immunities

In a number of situations some of the privileges and immunities accorded
to diplomatic agents have been granted to other personnel representing
foreign states (consular officers, visiting armed forces) in the territory of
the "receiving" state, and to representatives to, and officials of, a large
number of international organisations.

a CONSULAR OFFICERS

As neither the Diplomatic Privileges Act of 1708, nor the more recent
Act of 1964, apply to consuls, their position is governed by common law
principles, including such rules of international law that are sufficiently
crystallised to be considered as part of the law of England, and by the provisions of ss. 3 and 4 of the Consular Conventions Act, 1949.[11]

Because consuls are not accredited to the receiving state, they are not
entitled to the privileges and immunities accorded to diplomatic agents.
The early English cases establish this principle;[12] and in 1879, when the
Danish Government suggested that the British Government should support a protest to the local authorities in Haiti for the violation of the privileges of foreign consuls in Haiti, the Law Officers had no hesitation in
reporting that "as a general rule, consuls are amenable to the civil and
criminal jurisdiction of the country in which they reside, and their
property and effects are subject to the recourse of execution and process of
the local courts."[13] Indeed, it is hardly surprising that the courts and the
Law Officers held this view. Career consuls were largely unknown, and
the duties of consuls were normally undertaken by members of the trading
community whose commercial activities continued to take up a proportion of their time and energies.

But if a consul is not "as a general rule" immune from the local jurisdiction, is he entitled to immunity with respect to his official acts? As late as
1914 the Foreign Office informed the Colonial Office that the Secretary of
State was "unable to agree with the view which he understands the Crown
Advocate to hold, that if a consular officer acting in his official capacity
and even by the direct instructions of his own Government, does something that violates the law of the country of his residence, he is immune
from the ordinary consequences of such an act", and that he was of opinion
that "while such immunity would doubtless attach to a diplomatic envoy,
it would not apply in the case of a consular officer."[14] However, it would
seem that this view has largely disappeared in British practice. Sec. 3 of the
Consular Conventions Act, 1949, rather avoided the issue by excluding
the operation of "any rule of law·conferring immunity or privilege in
respect of the official acts and documents of consular officers" from any
act done in pursuance of the power conferred on consuls by the Act to

---

11. Text given in British *Digest*, Vol. 8, p. 459.
12. See esp. *Barbuit's Case* (1737), Cas. t. Talb. 281.
13. *British Digest*, Vol. 8, p. 145.   14. *Ibid.*, p. 151.

administer certain estates. While suggesting that some rule does exist, the Act does not suggest the content of the rule, except that it relates to immunity with respect to official acts and documents. But modern consular conventions entered into by the British Government do accept the principle that consular officers shall not be subject to the local jurisdiction in respect of acts performed in their official capacity. As such conventions depend for their efficacy upon the 1949 Act, either the Act established the immunity of consuls from process for acts done in their official capacity, or it is assumed that such a view now represents English law on the issue.

The proposition that a consul does enjoy a limited degree of immunity is certainly accepted in a number of Acts of Parliament, and is obviously reasonable. The Vienna Convention on Consular Relations, which has yet to be ratified by the United Kingdom, provides that criminal proceedings against consular officers shall be conducted in a manner which will hamper the exercise of consular functions as little as possible, and only in the case of a grave crime should he be arrested or detained pending trial (though there is nothing to prevent the courts of the state concerned imposing a sentence of imprisonment on a consular officer) (Article 41). Under Article 43 (1) of the Convention, neither consular officers nor consular employees shall be amenable to the jurisdiction of the judicial or administrative authorities of the receiving state in respect of acts performed in the exercise of consular functions. As with other multilateral "codifying" treaties that have come into force between a limited number of states, the Convention is nevertheless strong evidence of customary international law binding on non-signatories, at least on this particular issue (i.e. of what states recognise to be the accepted, as much as the acceptable, limits of consular immunities); and, as such, is perhaps also some indication of the present state of English law.

b INTERNATIONAL ORGANISATIONS

The immunities relating to international organisations are largely based on international agreements which are considered later; but the rules of English law are set out in an Act of 1950,[15] which deals with the status of the organisations to which it applies, and the privileges and immunities of the officials, and of representatives attending meetings of such organisations.

i *The status of the organisations*

The Act is to apply to any organisation of states or of governments named by Order in Council of which the United Kingdom or its government are members (s. 1 (1)). The Order may not only name the organisation concerned, but may also specify whether the organisation is to enjoy all, or only some, of the immunities and privileges set out in Part I of the Schedule to the Act (s. 1 (2) (a)). The immunities and privileges specified

---

15. International Organisations (Immunities and Privileges) Act.

are immunity from suit and legal process, and inviolability of official archives and premises, together with a number of exemptions from local taxes, rates, customs duties, etc. Orders have been made under s. 1 (1) in relation to the United Nations, the International Court, most of the Specialised Agencies, some of the Commodity Councils, and a number of other organisations.

ii *Representatives on organs of any organisation specified, officers of any such organisation holding high office in the organisation, and persons employed on missions by the organisation*

To the extent specified in the Order, the above classes of persons may be accorded the immunities and privileges set out in Part II of the Schedule. These are the same immunity from suit and legal process as is accorded to an envoy of a foreign sovereign accredited to the Crown, the same inviolability of residence, and like exemption from taxes. In the case of I.M.C.O. which has its headquarters in London, the relevant Order provides that as long as the headquarters remains in the United Kingdom, no citizen of the U.K. and colonies should be entitled to immunities beyond the functional immunities set out in Part III of the Act, even if that person should become Secretary-General of the Organisation or Secretary of the Maritime Safety Committee.

iii *Other officers and servants of the organisation*

Other officers and servants of the organisation may be granted the immunities and privileges stated in Part III of the Schedule, namely exemption from income tax on emoluments received as an officer or servant of the organisation, and the functional immunity from process in respect of things done or omitted to be done in the course of official duties.

iv *The official staff of a representative on any organ of the organisation*

The official staff accompanying a representative entitled to any of the immunities and privileges mentioned in Part II are entitled under Part IV to the same immunities and privileges as the retinue of an envoy of a foreign sovereign accredited to the Crown is accorded.

v *The family of high officials of organisations*

If an officer of any organisation is entitled to immunities and privileges under Part II, Part IV lays down that his spouse and children under twenty-one years of age are entitled to the immunities and privileges accorded to the family of a foreign envoy accredited to the Crown.

vi *Representatives of states attending international conferences*

Sec. 4 of the International Organisations (Immunities and Privileges) Act also extended diplomatic status to representatives of foreign states and their staffs attending international conferences. Similar provisions were made for representatives of Commonwealth countries by an Act of 1961.

D. Foreign armed forces

Contingents of foreign troops stationed on the territory of a state are often regarded as an organ of the state to which they belong. According to this view "a crime committed on foreign territory by members of these forces cannot be punished by the local civil or military authorities, but only by the commanding officer of the forces or by other authorities of their home state in cases where the crime is committed either within the place where the force is stationed or in some place where the criminal was on duty."[16]

If such a rule does exist the status of visiting armed forces would be but an aspect of the principle that a foreign sovereign was immune from the jurisdiction of the local courts. This approach seems to have found favour with Marshall, C.J., in his formulation of the principle of sovereign immunity in the American case of the *Schooner Exchange*,[17] but although it has been widely referred to outside the United States on the general principle, it has not found favour in relation to visiting forces. While the territorial state is normally prepared to allow purely disciplinary matters to be subject to the adjudication of the foreign contingent, any more substantial derogation from the local jurisdiction is usually made the subject of formal agreement.

As far as the United Kingdom is concerned, the most important multilateral treaty relating to visiting forces was the N.A.T.O. Status of Forces Agreement of 1951. To enable the United Kingdom to ratify this Agreement, Parliament passed the Visiting Forces Act, 1952, which also replaced a number of earlier statutes dealing with Commonwealth forces and also with allied forces which were stationed in Britain during the Second World War. The Act is not therefore confined to troops from N.A.T.O. countries, but applies to a number of Commonwealth states, which then included South Africa, and to any other country designated by Order in Council. The Order may also specify limitations, adaptations or modifications of the effect of the Act in relation to any particular country.

As the provisions of the Act may be varied in their application to a particular state, the Act itself lays down the maximum degree of immunity from the local jurisdiction allowable by English law. Under s. 2, the service courts and authorities of a country specified may within the United Kingdom or on board any of Her Majesty's ships or aircraft, exercise over persons subject to their jurisdiction all such powers as are exercisable by them according to the law of the state concerned. Persons subject to their jurisdiction are defined as members of the visiting force, and "all other persons who, being neither citizens of the United Kingdom and Colonies nor ordinary resident in the United Kingdom, are for the time being subject to the service law of that country". As far as criminal

---

16. Oppenheim, *International Law*, Vol. 1, 8th ed., pp. 847–8.
17. (1812), 7 Cranch 116.

matters are concerned, s. 3 provides for the exclusion of trial by United Kingdom Courts of offences committed by a member of a visiting force or a member of a civilian component of such force if:

(a) the alleged offence arose out of and in the course of his duty; or

(b) the alleged offence, being an offence against the person, was committed only against a person or persons having at the time a relevant association with the visiting forces of the country concerned; or

(c) the alleged offence being against property, the whole of the property belonged either to the sending country or to an authority of that country or to a person having the necessary association with the visiting forces of the country concerned.

The section also provides that, even in such a case, a prosecution may take place if the Director of Public Prosecutions (in a case under English law, as opposed to a case under Scottish law, or before a court in Northern Ireland) certifies that the appropriate authority of the sending country has notified him that it is not proposed to deal with the case under the law of that country; but if a member of a visiting force has been tried for an offence, he shall not be tried again for the same crime by a United Kingdom Court (s. 4). Civil jurisdiction by the United Kingdom Courts is not excluded, except in relation to questions of pay on matters of which no proceedings shall be entertained by any United Kingdom Court (s. 6), and where a coroner would otherwise hold an inquest on a deceased person (s. 7).

5 THE LAW OF THE UNITED STATES

A. The immunity of foreign states

For the reasons referred to below, the problems arising out of claims to sovereign immunity have presented themselves to the American Courts in different ways than those dealt with by the English Courts. The American Courts have reached a different conclusion on the interest required of a foreign sovereign before his plea of immunity will be allowed. There has been an increasing tendency to distinguish between the public and the commercial activities of foreign states. And, finally, as will be recalled from Chapter 2, the role of the State Department in deciding issues of immunity is of greater significance than the Foreign Office Certificate which only deals with the status of the foreign entity, not with the acceptability of its title, and other issues of fact.

a THE SOVEREIGN'S TITLE

Far removed from the monarchies of Europe, and unaffected by a colonial empire containing sultans that needed to be placated, the United States Courts were not troubled by the personal immunities of foreign sovereigns, but they were called upon to deal with an increasing number of claims to immunity on behalf of state-owned or operated merchant vessels. Starting from the proposition laid down in the *Schooner Exchange* that "national ships of war, entering the port of a friendly power open for their reception, are to be considered as exempted by the consent of that power from its jurisdiction",[18] and influenced by the trend of the English authorities, the American Courts moved towards the general principle of immunity. As was stated in 1918 in the *Roseric*,[19] the "privilege was based on the idea that the sovereign's property devoted to state purposes is free and exempt from all judicial process" and this principle was "as cogently applicable to an unarmed vessel employed by the sovereign in the public service as to one of his battleships". Any doubts that may have existed on this point were settled by the Supreme Court in the case of the *Pesaro*.[20]

The *Pesaro* was owned and operated by the Italian Government in carrying goods for hire between Italian ports and ports overseas. This action was a libel *in rem* against the ship for an alleged non-delivery of a consignment of artificial silk to New York. The Italian Ambassador appeared on behalf of his government claiming that the vessel, being at the time of her arrest owned and in the possession of the Italian Government, was immune from process in the courts of the United States. The Supreme Court upheld this claim to immunity, stating that the principles laid down in the *Exchange* were "applicable alike to all ships held and used by a government for a public purpose, and that when, for the purpose of advancing the trade of its people or providing revenue for its treasury, a government acquires, mans and operates ships in the carrying trade, they are public ships in the same sense that war ships are." The Court knew of "no international usage which regards the maintenance and advancement of the economic welfare of a people in time of peace as any less a public purpose than the maintenance and training of a naval force."[1]

The *Pesaro* is clear authority for the granting of immunity to the property of a foreign state, provided that it is owned and possessed by that state. But the case does not lay down that there *must* be both ownership and possession, so that it is necessary to consider whether some lesser interest will be sufficient to enable the sovereign to sustain his claim to immunity.

In this context it should be understood that there are differences between the English writ *in rem* which is in effect against all persons interested in the defendant ship (so that whatever his interest, the sovereign would be obliged to intervene in the action if he could not have the proceedings stayed on the ground of immunity), and the libel *in rem* which the American Courts have tended to regard as being directed against those in possession of the vessel, irrespective of ownership. In the *Roseric*,[2] the British Government was held entitled to claim immunity in respect of a vessel which it did not own, but which it had requisitioned and was operating under Admiralty direction. On the other hand, if the foreign state has not

---

18. (1912), 7 Cranch, at pp. 145–146.   19.   254 F. 154, at p. 158.
20.   271 U.S. 562; (1925–6), 3 A.D., Case No. 135.
1.   *Ibid.*, at p. 574.   2.   See above fn. 19.

possession of the property even if it is the owner, a claim to immunity would fail.

In *Mexico* v. *Hoffman*[3] the defendant vessel was owned by the Republic of Mexico, but the District Court had held that, though owned by the Mexican State, the ship was in "the possession, operation and control" of a privately owned and operated Mexican corporation which engaged in the commercial carriage of cargoes for hire. The Supreme Court held that the distinction between ownership and possession was supported by the overwhelming weight of authority, but even more important was the fact that, despite many opportunities of doing so, the United States Government had refrained from recognising the immunity from suit of a vessel owned but not possessed by a foreign government.

b THE PROCEDURE FOR CLAIMING IMMUNITY

The normal procedure for claiming immunity is for the accredited representative of the foreign state concerned to make a request to the State Department that its immunity be recognised. Both the plaintiff and the foreign state are given an opportunity of stating their case before the Legal Adviser recognises or not the claim to immunity.

i *If the claim is allowed*

If the State Department recognises the claim to immunity it informs the Attorney-General who then notifies the court. "If the claim is recognised and allowed by the executive branch of the government, it is then the duty of the courts to release the vessel upon appropriate suggestion by the Attorney-General of the United States, or other officer acting under his direction."[4]

ii *If the claim is not allowed by the State Department*

If the State Department does not allow the claim, it is still open to the foreign state to present the defence of immunity on its own account, usually, of course, through its accredited representative. The fact that a positive statement of immunity by the State Department is conclusive on certain issues of fact, such as the possession of the property by the foreign sovereign, means that, in the absence of a certificate from the Attorney-General, it is for the foreign state to establish such facts to the satisfaction of the court. The circumstances of the *Navemar* are instructive in this context, although they are only indirectly relevant to the issue of sovereign immunity.

The *Navemar* was the subject of litigation brought by its owners. The Spanish Ambassador sought to intervene in the proceedings as claimant on the ground that property in the vessel had vested in the Spanish Republican Government as a result of a Presidential Decree of 1936, and that the vessel was therefore entitled to sovereign immunity. The State Department

---

3. 324 U.S. 30; (1943–5) 12 A.D., Case No. 39.
4. *The Navemar*, 303 U.S. 68, at p. 74 (1938); (1938–40) 9 A.D., Case No. 68. For a recent case in which a State Department "suggestion" that the defendant was *not* entitled to immunity was disregarded: *N.Y. World's Fair* v. *Guinea*, 159 N.Y.L.J. 15 (1968).

declined to instruct the Attorney-General to make representations to the court on behalf of the Spanish Government, but advised the Spanish Ambassador that his government was entitled to appear directly before the court to establish its claim to immunity. Before the District Court, neither evidence of the 1936 decree and endorsements made on the ship's papers of the change of ownership by the Spanish Consul in Buenos Aires, nor a subsequent seizure of the ship by members of the crew, were held sufficient to show that possession of the vessel had been taken on behalf of the Spanish Government. The vessel had not come under Spanish jurisdiction since the decree of 1936, nor had anyone taken possession of the vessel in the name of, and on behalf of, the Spanish Republican Government. The Supreme Court accepted this line of reasoning, but went on to hold that, as the claim of the Spanish Government was that it had a right to intervene, as well as that the vessel should be granted immunity, the District Court, while correct in disallowing the claim to immunity, should nevertheless have allowed the Spanish Government to intervene for the purpose of asserting its ownership and right to possession of the vessel. The order made by the District Court was modified accordingly.

c   THE EFFECT OF THE TATE LETTER

In 1952, the Acting Legal Adviser made public a change of attitude towards sovereign immunity on the part of the State Department in a letter to the Acting Attorney-General. A part of this communication is worth closer examination:

"Finally, the Department feels that the widespread and increasing practice on the part of governments of engaging in commercial activities makes necessary a practice which will enable persons doing business with them to have their rights determined in the courts. For these reasons it will hereafter be the Department's policy to follow the restrictive theory of sovereign immunity in the consideration of requests of foreign governments for a grant of sovereign immunity. It is realised that a shift in policy by the executive cannot control the courts but it is felt that the courts are less likely to allow a plea of sovereign immunity where the executive has declined to do so. There have been indications that at least some Justices of the Supreme Court feel that in this matter courts should follow the branch of the Government charged with responsibility for the conduct of foreign relations."

It is the last part of this extract which is of particular interest. It is not a reference to the conclusive nature of the State Department's recognition of a claim to immunity, but to the possibility that, even in cases where no statement is made to the courts by the Attorney-General, the courts will, while retaining their power to decide issues of fact, reverse their previous stand on the legal principle laid down in the case of the *Pesaro*.[5] In other words, now that the executive branch of government has adopted a restrictive theory of immunity, it is for the courts to apply the same rule.

As the letter itself states, there is authority for the view that the courts will follow the executive's lead. In *Mexico* v. *Hoffman*, the Supreme Court based its decision against the claim to immunity on the ground that the

---

5.   271 U.S. 562; (1925–6) 3 A.D., Case No. 135.

State Department had repeatedly refused to recognise the immunity of vessels owned by, but not in the possession of, foreign governments. In the Court's view it was not for the judiciary to "deny an immunity which our Government has seen fit to allow, or to allow an immunity on new grounds which the Government has not seen fit to recognise."[6] Similar pronouncements are to be found in a number of other cases, but even more emphatic were the views expressed in *National City Bank of N.Y.* v. *China*,[7] a case heard by the Supreme Court subsequent to the Tate Letter. Both the Court and the dissenting opinion favoured following the State Department's attitude towards the law even in cases where no intimation had been given of the decision considered desirable by the executive on the facts. As Justice Reed said in his dissenting opinion, "international relations are pre-eminently a matter of public policy" and "judicial views of supposed public interests are not the touchstone whereby to determine the law": the change from "a generous to a parsimonious application of the principle of sovereign immunity should come from Congress or the Executive."[8]

While there are strong indications that the courts will follow the principles suggested in the Tate Letter, it does not mean that the State Department itself is "bound" to follow its own stated policy. In discussing the effects of notifications by the State Department to the courts, and the policy reasons behind such pronouncements, reference was made to the extraordinary circumstances of the *Bahia de Nipe* case.[9] The *Bahia de Nipe* was a ship, formerly belonging to a Cuban Corporation that had been taken over by the Cuban authorities and operated as a carrier of freight. It was, within the terms of the Tate Letter, a publicly-owned ship engaged in commercial operations. While on a voyage from Cuba, it was taken over by some of the crew and sailed into a United States port. Immediately a number of actions were commenced against the ship by persons claiming title to the ship, and by others having claims against the Cuban Government. The Secretary of State informed the Attorney-General, who presented the communication to the court, that "release of this vessel would avoid further disturbance to our international relations". Despite this obvious inconsistency with the policy laid down in the Tate Letter, the District Court and the Circuit Court of Appeals held that a certificate and grant of immunity must be accepted by the courts without further enquiry. In the words of the District Judge, "no policy with respect to international relations is so fixed that it cannot be varied in the wisdom of the Executive": "flexibility, not uniformity, must be the controlling factor in time of strained international relations."[10]

---

6.   324 U.S. 30, at p. 35.   7.   348 U.S. 356; (1955), 22 I.L.R. 210.
8.   348 U.S. 356, at pp. 370–371. It is not yet clear how the American Courts will distinguish between private and public acts. In the *Victory Transport* case, Judge Smith suggested limited categories of acts to which immunity would attach (336 F. (2d) 354, at p. 360). These categories were referred to with approval in the more recent case of *Ocean Transport* v. *Ivory Coast*, 269 F. Supp. 703, at pp. 705–706 (1967).
9.   *Rich* v. *Naviera Vacuba*, 197 F. Supp. 710; 295 F. (2d) 24 (1961); 32 I.L.R. 127.
10.   197 F. Supp., at p. 724.

Although there is thus no doubt that, whatever conclusion is favoured by the executive certificate, the courts must accept it as binding, once inconsistencies appear in the policy of the State Department, the reason for the courts applying the view of the law held by the executive in situations where no certificate is issued on the facts disappears. It is no longer possible for the courts to apply the principle that it is not for them to "deny an immunity which our government has seen fit to allow", or to allow an immunity on grounds "which the government has not seen fit to recognise" when the practice of the government is patently inconsistent.

d OTHER ASPECTS OF SOVEREIGN IMMUNITY

i *Execution*

The uncertainties that exist in relation to claims of immunity by states in respect of their commercial activities also affect the rules governing the attachment of property in execution of a judgment debt. Even if an action is held to be maintainable against a foreign state, a judgment in his favour will be of no assistance to a plaintiff if the state is unwilling to submit to the proceedings and continues its non-co-operation to the extent of refusing to satisfy the damages awarded.

If the subject-matter of a dispute is the ownership and possession of property, a decision by the court on the merits in favour of the plaintiff precludes the defendant state from raising the defence of immunity with respect to that property. But what if the action is for damages arising out of some alleged tort? The successful claimant is precluded from attaching property belonging to the sovereign against its will, whether or not the sovereign submitted to or resisted the court's jurisdiction in the original claim.

In *Dexter & Carpenter* v. *Kunglig Jarnvagsstyrelsen*,[11] the defendant to an order of attachment was the Swedish Railways Administration which was in no sense a distinct entity from the Swedish Government. It had been held liable on a counterclaim in proceedings which it had itself instituted, but was now attempting to claim immunity from attachment. A Circuit Court of Appeals held that, however regrettable it might be that Sweden could thus escape payment of a valid judgment against it, the weight of international authority favoured the granting of immunity with respect to property of a sovereign against which it was sought to levy execution.

This view of the law has been accepted by the State Department. In *New York and Cuba Mail S.S. Co.* v. *Korea*,[12] the Secretary of State supported a claim by the defendant state that its funds in certain New York banks were immune from attachment, in a communication placed before the court by the Attorney-General. In the view of the State Department, "under international law property of a foreign government is immune from attachment and seizure": furthermore, this principle was in no way affected by the Tate Letter of 1952.

11.　43 F. (2d) 705; (1929–30) 5 A.D., Case No. 70.
12.　132 F. Supp. 684; (1955), 22 I.L.R. 220.

ii *The immunity of state instrumentalities*

Departments of government

The United States Courts have consistently upheld claims to immunity with respect to government departments and agencies with no separate legal personality, e.g. the Mexican Railways in a case of 1925,[13] and the Swedish Railways in *Dexter v. Kunglig Jarnvagsstyrelsen*.[14]

Public corporations

The test that seems to have been favoured by American Courts is that an independent legal personality is not entitled to plead sovereign immunity, whether it is a public corporation owned entirely by the government concerned, or a corporation in which the government holds a majority of shares. In one case a public corporation created by the Swiss Government to import coal was held amenable to the jurisdiction of a Federal Court,[15] and a similar conclusion was reached against an institution created by the French Government to administer potash mines in Alsace.[16] In the course of giving the decision in the second of these cases, the District Judge pointed out that a "suit against a corporation is not a suit against a government merely because it has been incorporated by direction of the government, and is used as a governmental agent, and its stock is owned solely by the government."[17]

Although there is thus no conclusive federal authority by an appellate court on the issue, it is worth noting that these decisions by Federal District Courts have been approved by the appellate division of the New York Courts. In *Ulen v. Bank Gospodarstwa Krajowego*,[18] proceedings were instituted against the defendant bank, which claimed immunity as an instrumentality of the Polish State. Under the bank's charter it was a "state institution", a "distinct legal person possessing the right of autonomous legal representation". Its share capital was to be owned by the State Treasury, and state enterprises, which were to hold at least sixty per cent of the shares, and by municipal authorities and enterprises. Supreme control of the bank was vested in the Minister of Finance. In rejecting the claim to immunity, the court was influenced not only by the federal decisions, but also by a number of cases which had refused instrumentalities of the United States Government immunity in American Courts when it could be shown that they possessed a separate legal existence.

Political units within a state

The only decision by a federal court on the point in *Sullivan v. Sao Paulo*[19] was to the effect that the State of Sao Paulo within the federal

---

13.   *Oliver American Trading Co. v. Mexico*, 5 F. (2d) 659; (1923–4), 2 A.D., Case No. 21.
14.   Above, fn. 11.
15.   *Coale v. Société Co-opérative Suisse des Charbons*, 21 F. (2d) 180; (1919–22), 1 A.D., Case No. 88.
16.   *U.S. v. Deutsches Kalisyndikat Gesellschaft*, 31 F. (2d) 199; (1929–30) A.D., Case No. 71.   17.   31 F. (2d), at pp. 201–2.
18.   24 N.Y.S. (2d) 201; (1938–40) 9 A.D., Case No. 74.
19.   122 F. (2d) 355; (1941–2) 10 A.D., Case No. 50.

state of Brazil was entitled to immunity from suit. This decision is criticized in the recent Restatement[20] on the ground it is contrary to the majority view of the courts of other states.[1] However, it is not unreasonable for the courts to allow a plea of immunity to federal units or other authorities which exercise wide public powers with respect to the administration of justice, local government, public health, etc.

iii *Waiver*

Under the law of the United States, waiver may take place as the result of failing to raise a plea of immunity, or of the sovereign itself initiating proceedings, or of an agreement that the sovereign will accept the jurisdiction of the American Courts.

1 *Failure to object to the jurisdiction*

In order to be effective, an objection to the jurisdiction in the Federal Courts must be made:

(a) before the merits of the dispute are placed in issue by the foreign state.

In *Flota Maritima Browning de Cuba* v. *m.v. Ciudad de la Habana*[2] it was held that the Cuban Government had waived its immunity from suit and from execution in respect of a vessel which had been arrested in proceedings *in rem* when the government generally appeared and filed objections and answers to the libel, but did not raise a plea of immunity until three years after the original libel had been filed. The Circuit Court of Appeals was of opinion that this was a firmly established principle of law.

(b) by the appropriate authorities, i.e. either through the State Department, or through the foreign state's accredited representative.

In *Victory Transport* v. *Comisaria General de Transportes*,[3] a Circuit Court of Appeals held that a plea of immunity supported only by the affidavit of the Spanish Consul in New York was plainly insufficient in the absence of evidence that the Spanish Consul was specially authorised to interpose a claim of sovereign immunity.

2 *Where the foreign sovereign initiates proceedings*

If a foreign state does commence proceedings, there is some authority for the proposition that the defendant in the action may, as under English law, raise a counterclaim, regardless of amount, arising from the same subject matter as the original claim; but, unlike English law, the defendant is entitled to raise any counterclaim at all against the foreign sovereign,

---

20. Second *Restatement*, volume entitled: *Foreign Relations Law of the United States*, pp. 204-5.
1. And in conflict with the New York case, *Schneider* v. *City of Rome*, 83 N.Y.S. (2d) 756; (1948), 15 A.D., Case No. 40.
2. 335 F. (2d) 619 (1964); 35 I.L.R. 122.   3.   336 F. (2d) 354 (1964); 35 I.L.R. 110.

provided that the amount claimed does not exceed the amount involved in the original claim. Although doubts exist as to the first part of the rule relating to counterclaims arising out of the same subject matter, it is clearly established that, as long as the defendant is not seeking "affirmative relief", i.e. seeking some additional remedy against the plaintiff sovereign, the defendant can always raise the plaintiff's indebtedness as a counterclaim up to the limit of the amount being claimed by the plaintiff.

In *National City Bank of N.Y.* v. *China*,[4] the Supreme Court was called upon to decide whether a claim by the Republic of China for the sum of $200,000 deposited with the Bank by a Railway Administration which was an official agency of the Republic of China could be made the subject matter of a counterclaim by the Bank which alleged a debt of $1,634,432 on defaulted Chinese Treasury Notes. The Supreme Court held that provided the amount of the counterclaim was limited to that originally claimed by the Republic of China, the plea of immunity should not be allowed. While it was recognised that "a counterclaim based on the subject matter of a sovereign's suit is allowed to cut into the doctrine of immunity" this principle was only proof that the doctrine was not absolute, but such a limitation in respect of counterclaims "based on the subject matter" was "too indeterminate, indeed too capricious, to mark the bounds of the limitations on the doctrine of sovereign immunity."[5]

3 Waiver by agreement

The United States has entered into a number of *international* agreements which provide for submission to the jurisdiction with respect to trading operations. For example, Article XVIII (3) of an agreement of 1951 with Israel provided:

> "No enterprise of either Party, including corporations, associations, and govern-
> ment agencies and instrumentalities, which is publicly owned or controlled shall, if
> it engages in commercial, manufacturing, processing, shipping or other business
> activities within the territories of the other Party, claim or enjoy, either for itself
> or for its property, immunity therein from taxation, suit, execution of judgment
> or other liability to which privately owned or controlled enterprises are subject
> therein."

If a state with which such an agreement had been made attempted to plead immunity in an American court with respect to its trading operations, it is certain that the State Department would intimate to the court that the immunity of the defendant enterprise had been waived.

There is no conclusive authority on the proposition that immunity can be waived by private agreement, but such indirect evidence that does exist strongly favours this view. In *Victory Transport* v. *Comisaria General*,[6] the Circuit Court had, it is true, already rejected a plea of immunity on the ground that the transaction, an agreement to transport quantities of

---

4. 348 U.S. 356; (1955), 22 I.L.R. 210.   5. 348 U.S., at p. 364.
6. 336 F. (2d) 354 (1964); 35 I.L.R. 110; see also s. 2 of the International Organisations
Immunities Act, below, p. 210.

surplus wheat to Spain, was a commercial operation; but in holding that a provision in the contract agreeing to arbitration in New York implied a consent to the Court's jurisdiction to compel arbitration proceedings, the Court was going some way towards admitting that a bar to jurisdiction can be waived by agreement. The Court referred to earlier authorities in which such an agreement had been held a sufficient jurisdictional basis for a court to order a foreign corporation to submit to arbitration, and the Circuit Court saw "no reason to treat a commercial branch of a foreign sovereign differently from a foreign corporation".[7]

B. Diplomatic immunities

Although the 1961 Vienna Convention on Diplomatic Relations has been ratified by the United States Senate as required by the Constitution, the United States has yet to become bound by the Convention under international law, for it has not deposited an instrument of ratification with the Secretary-General of the United Nations as required by the Convention. The Senate was informed at the time it was asked to ratify the Convention that the executive did not intend to deposit such an instrument until implementing legislation had been passed. Federal and State laws on diplomatic privileges and immunities vary amongst themselves and also differ from the provisions of the Convention, and it was presumably felt that a self-executing treaty of this type would lead to further confusion if applied by the courts in conjunction with existing legislation. However, in view of the likelihood of the various laws being brought into line with the provisions of the Convention, only a brief summary will be given of the existing law on the subject.

a CATEGORIES OF PERSONS ENTITLED TO PRIVILEGES AND IMMUNITIES

The same division will be employed as that adopted in the Convention. Although these categories are not always recognised by existing United States practice, they will serve to illustrate where Federal law differs from the provisions of the Convention.

i Diplomatic agents and their families

By s. 252 of 22 U.S.C., suits against *inter alios* "any ambassador or public minister of any foreign prince or state, authorised and received as such by the President" are prohibited. This provision, together with s. 253 which deals with the punishment of persons suing forth or prosecuting a writ or process against any such ambassador or public minister,[8] was first enacted in 1790 and is very similar to English Diplomatic Privileges Act of

---

7.   336 F. (2d), at p. 363; also *Petrol Shipping Corp.* v. *Greece*, 360 F. (2d) 103 (1966).
8.   The corresponding provision of the English Act of 1708 (s. 3) was in fact a "dead letter".

1708. Like that Act, the 1790 statute was extended by the courts to exempt other diplomatic agents duly "authorised and received" from process. In the well-known case of *Respublica* v. *Longchamps*,[9] the defendant was convicted of an offence against the law of nations for striking the person of the Secretary to the French Legation who was "entitled to all the immunities of a minister"; and in *Dupont* v. *Pichon*,[10] an immunity from process was allowed to a *Chargé d'Affaires*. In more recent times it has been held that immunity extends to the press counsellor of the Legation of the People's Republic of Roumania.[11]

The State Department designates families of accredited diplomatic agents as entitled to immunity, and it would seem that American practice restricts members of the family, as under the Convention, to those who form part of the household, but, unlike the Convention, no distinction is drawn if the family of the diplomat happen to be citizens of the United States. There is no wealth of authority dealing with the status of diplomatic families, but such incidents as have been reported would seem to support immunity in the case of the wife and children of the diplomat. In *Friedberg* v. *Santa Cruz*,[12] a New York Appeal Court was faced with a claim to immunity on behalf of the wife of the Chilean Ambassador to the United Nations. As an ambassador to the United Nations was entitled to the immunities that were accorded to a diplomatic agent accredited to the United States, the success of her plea depended upon whether she would be entitled to immunity as the wife of such an agent. It was held that the wife of a diplomatic agent was entitled to immunity, so that the defendant's plea succeeded. Perhaps the most flagrant incident[13] concerning a child of a diplomatic agent resulted from the running down and killing of a pedestrian in Washington by the son of the Irish Ambassador. Although the son was aged 21, a number of charges, including homicide, were dropped when diplomatic immunity was invoked.

ii *Other staff*

No distinction is drawn between other employees of the mission who are not diplomatic agents in the way that the Vienna Convention distinguishes between administrative and technical staff on the one hand and domestic servants on the other. The American Courts have consistently allowed the widest immunities to all such personnel. In one early case an embassy cook was held entitled to immunity.[14] More recently, in 1948, in *Carrera* v. *Carrera*[15] the plaintiff sought custody of her 15-year-old son, and maintenance for herself and support for him from her husband. When the action was commenced both the plaintiff and her husband were domestic servants in the Czechoslovakian Embassy. A Circuit Court of

---

9. 1 Dall. 111 (1784).   10. 4 Dall. 321 (1805).
11. *Mongillo* v. *Vogel*, 84 F. Supp. 1007; (1949), 16 A.D., Case No. 96.
12. 84 N.Y.S. (2d) 148; (1948), 15 A.D., Case No. 103.
13. Discussed by Clifton E. Wilson in (1965) 14 I. & C.L.Q. 1265, at pp. 1287–8.
14. *U.S.* v. *Lafontaine*, Fed. Cas. 15550 (1831).
15. 174 F. (2d) 496; (1949), 16 A.D., Case No. 99.

Appeals upheld the defendant's claim to immunity on the ground that diplomatic immunity extended not only "to an ambassador, but to his subordinates, family, and servants as well".

b EXISTENCE OF DIPLOMATIC STATUS

The Department of State keeps a record of diplomatic personnel on a Diplomatic List (usually referred to as the "Blue List"), but this list is not conclusive on the status of the person claiming immunity. The proper procedure is for the ambassador or other head of mission, to request the State Department that immunity be granted. A certificate by the Secretary of State that an individual has been accepted as a diplomatic agent is conclusive in any court. As Fuller, C.J., said in *Re Baiz*,[16] "we do not assume to sit in judgment upon the decision of the executive in reference to the public character of a person claiming to be a foreign minister, and therefore have the right to accept the certificate of the State Department that a party is or is not a privileged person, and cannot properly be asked to proceed upon argumentative or collateral proof."

As far as employees or servants of a diplomatic mission are concerned, there seems to be some dispute whether such personnel have to be accepted in that capacity by the State Department and their names published in the "White List". Sec. 252 of the Code prohibits suits against any ambassador or public minister "authorised and received as such by the President, or any domestic or domestic servant of any such minister". In other words, the statute itself suggests that it is only ambassadors and public ministers who have to be authorised and received as such. Under the similar provisions of the 1708 statute in England a servant, though not registered, was entitled to immunity; but both the judiciary and the executive in the United States seem to have reached an opposite conclusion. In *Haley* v. *State*,[17] the appellant contended that as the servant of the Swedish Air Attaché, he was immune from criminal process. The State Department Certificate was to the effect that the appellant was not entitled to immunity because "there had been no official notification to the United States of any diplomatic status, hence he could not be accepted and received as such by the United States." The court accepted the State Department's determination of the appellant's status as conclusive, pointing out that while a number of federal decisions did not "specifically hold" that the immunity for domestic servants was dependent upon registration on the White List, there was a "strong presumption that such is the case".

c DIPLOMATIC AGENTS ACCREDITED TO A THIRD STATE

A diplomatic agent accredited to a third state, who is in transit through the United States, either proceeding to or returning from his diplomatic post, is entitled to the same immunity from suit as is accorded to a diplomatic agent accredited to the United States. This principle was adopted

---

16.   135 U.S. 403, at p. 432 (1890).
17.   88 F. (2d) 312; (1952) 19 I.L.R., Case No. 90.

and applied by a Circuit Court of Appeals in *Bergman* v. *De Sieyes*[18] in upholding a claim to immunity by the French Minister who was on his way to take up his post in Bolivia. In a more recent case, *U.S.* v. *Rosal*,[19] the defendant pleaded that, as Guatemalan Ambassador to Belgium and the Netherlands in transit through the United States to Guatemala, was immune from arrest and prosecution on a narcotics charge. The District Court held that, while a diplomat in transit as the defendant claimed was entitled to immunity, on the evidence it was clear that the defendant was in New York solely on personal, non-diplomatic business, and far from intending to proceed to Guatemala, he was booked on a flight to Paris. His claim to immunity therefore failed.

d TERMINATION OF IMMUNITY

American law on this subject is identical with English law. Hence:

(i) immunity continues until the diplomatic agent leaves the United States, or until a reasonable period for such departure has elapsed.

In *Dupont* v. *Pichon*[20] it was held that the defendant was entitled to be discharged from arrest even though he was no longer French *Chargé d'Affaires* since the arrival of a minister plenipotentiary. It had been stated on behalf of the defendant, and was accepted by the court, that he had been preparing his departure for France, but that he had been held up partly because of official business and partly because of the impossibility of arranging a passage from Philadelphia to Europe.

(ii) but in respect of official acts, a diplomatic agent remains permanently immune from process.

There does not appear to be any American authority directly bearing on this point. In *Dupont* v. *Pichon*, it was argued on the defendant's behalf that the debt for which he had been arrested concerned the issue of bills of exchange in his official capacity as representative of France, so that he would in any case have been entitled to immunity in respect of those acts. The brief report of the court's decision suggests, however, that it relied exclusively on the principle stated above that a diplomatic agent is allowed a reasonable time to arrange his departure before his immunity ceases. The wealth of international practice, accepted as representing the requirements of international law by American commentators, supports the rule that in respect of official functions, the immunity persists even after normal diplomatic privileges have ended. The reason has already been explained in connection with the position under English law. The immunity is primarily that of the state in carrying out its functions. As one writer[1] has explained, "the exemption from local jurisdiction of diplomatic agents pertains exclusively to the private acts of diplomatic agents. Their exemption from local jurisdiction for their official acts has nothing to do with

---

18. 170 F. (2d) 360; (1947) 14 A.D., Case No. 73.
19. 191 F. Supp. 663 (1960), 31 I.L.R. 389.
20. 4 Dall. 321 (1805).
1. Kunz in (1947) 41 A.J.I.L. 828, at p. 838.

diplomatic privileges and immunities; their official acts are 'acts of state' and are legally imputed not to them but to the sending state."

e WAIVER OF IMMUNITY

The position with regard to waiver of immunity under American law is not altogether clear because it is not an issue that has been the subject of litigation. The most that can be attempted, therefore, is to set out the principles that seem to have been acknowledged as representing the law of the United States.

i *Express waiver*

The attitude of the State Department is that, for American diplomats in foreign states, their immunity from the local jurisdiction can only be waived by the United States Government. "Immunity of an American diplomatic officer from local jurisdiction attaches to his office and cannot be waived except with the consent of his government; neither the legation nor a member of a staff is authorised to waive the immunity."[2] This practice would seem to be more restricted than that generally accepted even before the Vienna Convention laid down that waiver by the head of mission should be deemed a waiver by the state itself. The Harvard Draft of 1932, for example, suggested that "waiver may be made only by the government of the sending state if it concerns the privileges and immunities of the chief of mission; in other cases, the . . . waiver may be made either by the government of the sending state or by the chief of mission."[3]

It is doubtful whether the United States would apply its own practice to a purported waiver of immunity by a foreign ambassador on behalf of a member of his mission. In 1939, the Polish Ambassador had waived the immunity of an attaché at the Polish Embassy. In the proceedings,[4] the attaché raised the question whether the waiver of immunity was effective as it had not been given by the Polish Government itself. The matter was referred by the plaintiff's attorney to the State Department who approached the ambassador in order to ascertain the nature of the waiver of immunity. The ambassador replied that the waiver had been granted for and on behalf of the Polish Government. In transmitting a copy of this reply to the plaintiff's attorney, the Department commented that it could not see any reason why the action of an accredited foreign ambassador to the United States in waiving the immunity from process of a member of his staff should have been called in question in this way. If this case is any guide, it would seem that even though the Vienna Convention has not yet been accepted as binding by the United States, the State Department would act upon the general proposition that a foreign head of mission is

---

2. Telegram from the U.S. Acting Secretary of State to the American Legation in Vienna, 12th August, 1925: cited Hackworth, *Digest of International Law*, Vol. IV, p. 544.
3. (1932) 26 A.J.I.L. (Supp.), p. 125 (draft article 26).
4. *Von Kupsa* v. *Budny* (1939), Hackworth, *op. cit.*, pp. 544–5. But cp. *Herman* v. *Apetz*, 224 N.Y.S. 389; (1927–8), 4 A.D., Case No. 244.

presumed to have the authority of his state to waive the immunity of members of his mission before the courts of the United States.

ii *When the diplomat has initiated proceedings*

It will be recalled that, in the context of sovereign immunity, a waiver implied from the initiation of proceedings by the foreign sovereign will extend to any counterclaim, whether connected with the original proceedings or not, unless the value of the counterclaim exceeds the amount of the original claim. But it would seem that no such limit would apply if the counterclaim were restricted to the subject matter of the original claim. It is doubtful whether the waiver in a case of diplomatic immunity is so extensive. Whereas a diplomatic agent can usually initiate proceedings without the approval of the sending state, he himself cannot waive his immunity on his own account. A reasonable interpretation of a waiver arising from the initiating of proceedings by the diplomat would be to limit it to counterclaims arising out of the subject matter of his original claim. This view was apparently adopted by the State Department in 1875 over litigation in the Austrian Courts involving the American Minister in Vienna. The minister had filed a petition against his landlord. Later the landlord commenced a new suit against the Minister which, "though the parties were the same, was a distinct proceeding resting on different grounds from the previous one". The Minister sought the protection of the Austrian Foreign Office, and reported the matter to the Department of State. The Department, while repeating its disapproval of the minister's actions in initiating litigation, were of opinion that he was entitled to raise a plea of immunity in the new suit, if it was "entirely independent of the previous one". The Austrian Foreign Office took the necessary steps to have proceedings in the new suit stayed.[5]

iii *Execution*

There is no doubt that waiver of immunity with respect to the original proceedings is not sufficient to enable execution to issue against the individual entitled to immunity. There must be a fresh waiver by the authority competent to waive the immunity of the particular defendant. Although direct authority on this point is lacking, the rule is well established in relation to sovereign immunity, and the same principle is accepted as applicable equally in the case of diplomatic agents by most commentators.

f INVIOLABILITY OF THE MISSION, ITS RECORDS AND COMMUNICATIONS[1]

It is a generally recognised rule of international law that diplomatic premises are inviolable, that is, that the receiving state should not interfere in incidents occurring on the premises of a foreign mission, unless requested to do so by the head of the mission concerned. This principle was accepted and applied by a Pennsylvanian court in the early case of

---

5. Moore, *Digest of International Law*, Vol. IV, p. 635.

Respublica v. *Longchamps*.[6] One of the charges against the accused was that he had entered the premises of the French Legation and had there threatened the French Secretary. The accused was found guilty and in considering what sentence to impose, the court explained that the first crime in the indictment was "an infraction of the law of nations", which law was, "in its full extent", part of the law of Pennsylvania. The person of a public minister was "sacred and inviolable". But the same reasons which established the inviolability of a minister applied also to "secure the inviolability of his house" which was "to be defended from all outrage": it was "under a peculiar protection of the laws; to invade its freedom is a crime against the state and all other nations."

The inviolability of diplomatic premises is often referred to as the principle of extraterritoriality—that the premises are not part of the territory of the receiving state but are notionally part of the territory of the sending state. While this principle may be a helpful description of the status of diplomatic agents who are immune from the local jurisdiction, it can also be confusing. Although immune from process, a diplomatic agent is nonetheless subject to the laws of the receiving state, even if for the period of his immunity those laws remain unenforceable.[7] Similarly, while diplomatic premises are inviolable, in the sense that the agents of the receiving state should not attempt to enter the premises in order to enforce the local law, events taking place on those premises are nevertheless regulated by the laws of the receiving state.

This view is certainly the one accepted by the United States. In 1925 the State Department refused to extradite Oskar Tomberg to Estonia in respect of an incident that had occurred in the Estonian Legation in London. It was the Department's opinion that the incident had occurred within the territorial jurisdiction of the United Kingdom, not of Estonia.[8] As the Legal Adviser to the State Department stated on a later occasion: "While the United States Government owns the premises occupied by the American Embassy in Paris, it is not believed that a private contract signed in the Embassy would because of this fact be held not to have been executed on French territory. The immunity from local jurisdiction attaching to a diplomatic mission, sometimes referred to as giving the mission extraterritorial status, is not believed to be susceptible of expansion to the extent of giving a private contract signed on the premises occupied by the mission the status of a contract concluded in the country represented by the mission."[9]

The immunity that attaches to a diplomatic agent and to the premises of a diplomatic mission also extends to the archives of the mission and to all diplomatic correspondence. There is a wealth of State Department

---

6. 1 Dall. 111 (1784).
7. See the English case of *Dickinson* v. *Del Solar*, [1930] 1 K.B.; 376 (1929–30) 5 A.D., Case No. 190. Of course, in respect of official acts, the immunity remains even after the termination of diplomatic status and the end of a reasonable period for departure.
8. Hackworth, *op. cit.*, p. 565.
9. Communication from the Legal Adviser to the State Department, *ibid.*

practice in support of this principle of international law. In 1933, for example, the Acting Secretary for State wrote to the United States Ambassador to Peru stating that the diplomatic pouch had been "established for the safe carriage of the official correspondence of this Government" and "on that basis" it had "a recognised status in international law and practice".[10] Similarly, the Foreign Service Regulations[11] lay down that "couriers and bearers of dispatches employed by a diplomatic representative in the service of his government are privileged persons, so far as is necessary for their particular service, whether in the state to which the representative is accredited or in the territory of a third state."

C. Quasi-diplomatic privileges and immunities

a CONSULAR OFFICERS

It is the view of the State Department that international law recognises the inviolability of consular premises and archives. In 1920 the American Consul in Barbados, then part of the British West Indies, reported to the Department that attempts had been made by local authorities to obtain possession of an affidavit relating to a visa application that had been filed in the Consulate. The attempt to serve a writ on the Consul had been reported to the Governor of the colony who refused to interfere. The American Embassy in London was instructed to bring the matter to the attention of the British Government. The Foreign Office expressed regret at the incident and assured the United States Ambassador that the matter would be taken up with the Secretary of State for the Colonies to prevent a recurrence.[12]

In the absence of a treaty regulating consular relations with a particular state, and providing for wider immunities than those recognised by international law, foreign consuls in the United States are immune from neither criminal nor civil process. In *Re Baiz*,[13] the Supreme Court refused a writ of prohibition to prevent a district court exercising jurisdiction over the Guatemalan Consul-General in New York. As the Consul-General was not a diplomatic agent, even though in the absence of the Guatemalan Minister to the United States he was authorised to communicate at an official level with the State Department on behalf of the Republic of Guatemala, he was not entitled to immunity from process in the United States Courts.

However, a consul is entitled to immunity in respect of his official acts, because if a suit is brought in connection with matters falling within his official capacity the effect of the claim is to implead the foreign sovereign he represents. This factor is well brought out by the case of *Lyders* v. *Lund*.[14] The plaintiff alleged that he had been employed as attorney on

---

10. Assistant Secretary of State to the U.S. Ambassador in Peru, *ibid.*, p. 619.
11. Reg. III—1, n. 5, of January, 1941, *ibid.*, p. 621.
12. *Ibid.*, p. 723.   13. 135 U.S. 403 (1890).
14. 32 F. (2d) 308; (1929–30), 5 A.D., Case No. 211.

behalf of the Danish Consulate for fifteen years, and sought an account and a decree for the balance due in respect of expenses and fees for his services. The defendant, the Danish Consul, sought to have the action dismissed as it was against him in his official capacity. Such an action against him was in effect an action against the government he represented. The defendant's motion failed because the court was not satisfied that Denmark regarded actions by private litigants against its consuls as any: thing other than the acts and liabilities of the consul, and, in any case, the proper method of raising a plea of sovereign immunity was by the foreign state or its accredited representative approaching the State Department or appearing formerly before the court. A consul had no power to raise such a plea. However, in the course of giving judgment on the defendant's motion, the district judge distinguished carefully between the official and the unofficial acts of a consul:[15]

> ". . . in actions against the officials of a foreign state not clothed with diplomatic immunity, it can be said that suits based upon official, authorised acts, performed within the scope of their duties on behalf of the foreign state, and for which the foreign state will have to respond directly or indirectly in the event of a judgment, are actions against the foreign state. Acts of such officials, beyond the scope of their authority or in connection with their private business, cannot be regarded as acts of the foreign state, and the official may be sued on account of any such acts."

b INTERNATIONAL ORGANISATIONS

The law of the United States, which has not ratified either the Convention on the Privileges and Immunities of the United Nations or the Convention on the Privileges and Immunities of the Specialised Agencies, is governed by the International Organisations Immunities Act, 1945.

i The status of the organisation

The 1945 Act applies only to those public international organisations "in which the United States participates pursuant to any treaty or under the authority of any Act of Congress authorising such participation or making an appropriation for such participation, and which shall have been designated by the President through appropriate Executive order." Sec. 1 also authorises the President, "in the light of the functions performed by any such international organisation", to "withhold or withdraw" or to "condition or limit" the enjoyment by any such organisation, its officers or employees of any privilege, exemption or immunity provided for in the Act; or in cases of abuse of the privileges, exemptions and immunities, to revoke altogether the designation of the organisation concerned as an organisation entitled to the benefits of the Act.

Sec. 2 of the Act deals with the status of the organisations that have been designated by Executive order: (a) they shall "to the extent consistent with the instrument creating them", possess the capacity (i) to contract, (ii) to acquire and dispose of real and personal property, (iii) to institute legal

---

15. 32 F. (2d), at p. 309.

proceedings; (b) the organisations themselves, their property and assets are to enjoy "the same immunity from suit and every form of judicial process as is enjoyed by foreign governments, except to the extent that such organisations may expressly waive their immunity for the purpose of any proceedings or by the terms of any contract"; (c) their property and assets shall be immune from search, unless such immunity is expressly waived, and from confiscation: their archives are declared inviolable.

The United States is the "host" to a number of international organisations and has by agreement undertaken to extend to the organisation concerned certain privileges and immunities. The most important headquarters' agreement is of course that with the United Nations. The agreement is designed to ensure good relations between the Organisation, the United States, and police and other local authorities in the state of New York. Thus it deals with matters like the application of the local law, the provision of police protection, as well as more general principles relating to the status of the premises of the headquarters district which is stated to be "inviolable" (s. 9 (a)).

ii *Representatives of foreign governments in or to international organisations and officers and employees of such organisations*

The United States Act does not attempt to distinguish between different classes of personnel. Provided that the person concerned has been accepted by the Secretary of State as a representative, officer or employee (sec. 8 (a)), such person "shall be immune from suit and legal process relating to acts performed by them in their official capacity and falling within their functions" unless such immunity has been waived by the foreign government or international organisation concerned (sec. 7 (b)).

Two interesting ussues are raised by those two provisions. Sec. 8 (a) suggests that although representatives of foreign states are representatives *to* the United Nations, and not accredited to the United States, they must nevertheless be accepted by the United States. Does this mean that the United States has the right to refuse unacceptable representatives from a foreign state to an international organisation access to the premises of the organisation in the United States? The answer to this question would appear to be in the affirmative. As far as the United Nations is concerned, the Headquarters Agreement refers to such resident members of the staffs of a principal resident representative "as may be agreed upon between the Secretary-General, the Government of the United States and the Government of the Member concerned".

The second problem is raised by the extent of the immunity accorded by the provision that the immunity relates only to acts performed in an official capacity and falling within the functions of the person concerned. The position is further complicated by the fact that, in relation to the United Nations, various representatives are to be entitled "to the same privileges and immunities" as are accorded by the United States to diplomatic envoys accredited to it (sec. 15).

There have been a number of decisions in the New York courts on the question of the immunities of representatives to and officials of the United Nations, but these cases do not altogether solve the difficulties. The chauffeur who was driving the Secretary-General to an official function was held not entitled to claim immunity with respect to a speeding charge,[16] but a plea of immunity was allowed from the wife of the Counsellor of the Swedish Delegation to the United Nations in a prosecution for unlawful parking.[17] The distinction was that in the second case the claim of immunity had been supported by the Department of State, but no such support had been obtained in the first. In another case[18] it was held that an action for damages for negligent driving against the wife of the Chilean Ambassador to the United Nations should be allowed to proceed partly because the defendant had already pleaded to the merits of the action and partly on the totally unsupportable ground that the defendant, by obtaining a New York State driving licence, must be deemed to have waived immunity in respect of claims and other proceedings arising out of the use of a car!

How to define the extent of immunity relating to acts performed in an official capacity has been considered in two cases in which it was alleged that the accused had been engaging in espionage. In *U.S.* v. *Coplon*,[19] the second accused, one Gubitchev, was a Soviet official who had joined the staff of the Headquarters Planning Office of the United Nations. He refused to plead to the charge, but the court, of its own accord, dealt with the question of whether he was subject to the jurisdiction of the court. It reached the conclusion that Gubitchev could not claim immunity under the International Organisations Immunities Act because espionage could not be considered as an offence falling within the category of acts performed by the accused within his official capacity; nor, even if he could be considered a member of staff of the Russian mission to the United Nations as well as a member of the U.N. Secretariat, was he entitled to immunity under the Headquarters Agreement as his status as a member of the Soviet mission had never been agreed upon with the United States Government as required by that Agreement in respect of all but the principal resident representative of a State to the United Nations.

In the more recent case of *U.S.* v. *Melekh*,[20] the accused was in a similar position to Gubitchev. Espionage could hardly be considered as an act performed by him in his official capacity as chief of the Russian language section in the office of Conference Services of the U.N. Secretariat, so he could not claim immunity under the International Organisations Immunities Act. Nor could he claim full diplomatic immunity under the Headquarters Agreement, s. 15 of which extended such immunities only to a limited number of categories of state representatives to the United Nations. Melekh argued, however, that he was entitled to complete immunity either under Article 105 of the Charter, or because such immun-

16. *Westchester County* v. *Ranollo*, 67 N.Y.S. (2d) 31; (1946), 13 A.D., Case No. 77.
17. *People* v. *Von Otter*, 114 N.Y.S. (2d) 295; (1952), 19 I.L.R., Case No. 89.
18. *Friedberg* v. *Santa Cruz*, 84 N.Y.S. (2d) 148; (1948), 15 A.D., Case No. 103.
19. 88 F. Supp. 915; (1949) 16 A.D., Case No. 102.
20. 190 F. Supp. 67; 193 F. Supp. 586; 32 I.L.R. 308.

ity was a recognised principle of international law. The District Court rejected both contentions. Even if Article 105 (2) of the Charter was self-executing, the "principles and immunities to be enjoyed by representatives of the members of the United Nations and by officials of the United Nations itself are by the very terms of Article 105 qualified and conditioned. Their privileges and immunities are those that 'are necessary for the independent exercise of their functions in connection with the Organisation'. As expressly formulated by the United Nations Charter, the immunity is limited and specifically functional in scope and character. It is not the unlimited and unqualified immunity traditionally given to diplomats." As to the other argument, customary international law recognised the immunity of diplomatic agents, but it was clear that consent or acquiescence of the receiving state was a necessary condition precedent to such immunity. Far from the United States "receiving" the accused, the Soviet Union had only sought permission five years earlier for the accused to proceed to New York to take up a post in the service of the United Nations.

ii *The immunity of members of families*

The 1945 Act limits the immunity of the families of representatives to, and officials of, the international organisations designated to the same exemptions from the laws regulating entry into and departure from the United States as are accorded to the families of officers and employees of foreign governments in similar circumstances (s. 7 (a)). In addition, the Headquarters Agreement, by granting full diplomatic immunities to certain classes of representatives of foreign states to the United Nations, in effect has granted a full immunity from suit to members of their families. In *People* v. *Von Otter*,[1] the court accepted the State Department's certificate that the defendant, the wife of the Counsellor of the Swedish Delegation to the United Nations, was entitled to the privileges and immunities granted to her husband under the Headquarters Agreement.

While the existing legislation does not make provision for immunity from suit for the families of officials of any organisation, nor for the families of representatives of states to any organisation other than the United Nations, the State Department would as a matter of courtesy treat favourably a request for immunity on behalf of the family of an official or representative not covered by the legislation.

D. Foreign armed forces

Unlike the United Kingdom, which has been both a "sending" and a "receiving" state in respect of foreign armed forces, the United States has been primarily a "sending" state. The tendency has been, therefore, for the United States to favour the widest possible exemptions from the local

---

1. 114 N.Y.S. (2d) 295; (1952), 19 I.L.R., Case No. 89.

jurisdiction. Consequently, even in the absence of a treaty or other agreement, United States practice supports the primary, or concurrent, jurisdiction of the sending state in all cases except infractions of the local criminal law which affect the public order of the receiving state.

a   MATTERS OF INTERNAL DISCIPLINE

The United States claims and concedes primary jurisdiction by a military force over offences against its own internal discipline. When the Australian Government asked the American Government whether Australian authorities might exercise disciplinary powers under Australian law over Australian military personnel in the United States, the Department of Defense replied that there was no statutory provision prohibiting the Australian authorities from exercising disciplinary powers: it was the view of the United States Government that the right of a friendly foreign force to exercise disciplinary jurisdiction over its members by means of service courts was implicit in its permitted presence in the United States.[2]

b   JURISDICTION WITH RESPECT TO OFFENCES OTHER THAN DISCIPLINARY MATTERS

As, in the absence of special agreement, consent to the presence of a foreign force does not deprive the receiving state of its rights of territorial jurisdiction, there is potentially a conflict of jurisdiction between the receiving state over acts occurring within its territory and the sending state over acts committed by its personnel. The view has been expressed from time to time in the United States (notably in the proceedings in the Senate on the ratification of the N.A.T.O. Status of Forces Agreement) that under customary international law, and therefore under American law, visiting forces enjoyed absolute immunity from the local courts. Prior to the N.A.T.O. Agreement, there was so much divergence in the practice of states that it is impossible to define the existence of any particular rule of international law on the subject. And the only American authority which has been relied upon in favour of absolute immunity is the well-known dictum in the *Schooner Exchange* that the grant of free passage for foreign troops implies a waiver by the territorial sovereign of "all jurisdiction over the troops during their passage, and permits the foreign general to use that discipline, and to inflict those punishments, which the government of his army may require".[3] But the whole significance of this passage from the judgment of Marshall, C.J., concerns the non-interference with a force which the territorial sovereign has allowed to pass through its territory. It is no authority at all for the proposition that foreign forces stationed for any length of time in the territory of a state are immune from the local jurisdiction.

In so far as state practice, including the acceptance of treaty provisions by a large number of states, is capable of developing or crystallising rules of international law, there is perhaps some likelihood of the N.A.T.O. Status

---

2. (1964) 58 A.J.I.L. 994.   3.   7 Cranch, at p. 140.

of Forces Agreement forming the basis of the creation of customary rules. This Agreement was ratified by the United States in July, 1953, so that it became operative between the United States and other N.A.T.O. members, and the provisions of the agreement have also been adopted by the United States in its relations with Japan, and with Korea.[4]

The outline of the N.A.T.O. agreement has already been considered in relation to English law, but one American case is worth considering as an illustration of the application of the similar provisions in the American-Japanese Protocol of 1953. In *Wilson* v. *Girard*,[5] Girard had been arrested by American military authorities for shooting and killing a Japanese woman with an expended shell from a grenade launcher. Under the Protocol, in cases of concurrent jurisdiction, U.S. military authorities were to have the primary right to exercise jurisdiction over U.S. armed forces or civilian components in relation to (i) offences solely against the property or security of the United States, or offences solely against the person or property of another member of the United States armed forces or a civilian component or of a dependant; or (ii) offences arising out of any act or omission done in the performance of official duty. At the time of the shooting, Girard had been left guarding a machine-gun on a range: the United States contended, therefore, that the incident fell under (ii) above and was subject to the jurisdiction of U.S. military authorities. The Japanese countered by saying that the evidence strongly suggested that Girard had induced the deceased and a Japanese man to come close to him by dropping empty cartridges for them to pick up and had then fired at them. In such circumstances the United States could not claim that Girard had been acting in the performance of official duty so that it was Japan which had the primary right to exercise jurisdiction. Consultations under the machinery created to resolve disagreements arising over the application of the Protocol having failed to satisfy either side, the United States decided to compromise. Under a subsequent paragraph of the Protocol, if "the state having the primary right decides not to exercise jurisdiction, it shall notify the authorities of the other state as soon as practicable. The authorities of the state having the primary right shall give sympathetic consideration to a request from the authorities of the other state for a waiver of its right in cases where that other state considers such waiver to be of particular importance." This hearing before the Supreme Court was an attempt by Girard to prevent the United States authorities from handing him over to the Japanese. The Court held that as a "sovereign nation has exclusive jurisdiction to punish offences against its laws committed within its borders, unless it expressly or impliedly consents to surrender its jurisdiction",[6] the granting by Japan to the United States of jurisdiction to try American military personnel for conduct constituting an offence against the laws of both countries was limited by the terms of the Protocol.

4.　For the similar provisions in treaties among parties to the Warsaw Pact, see below, pp. 225–226.

5.　354 U.S. 524; (1957), 24 I.L.R. 248.　　　　6.　354 U.S., at p. 529.

It was perfectly proper, therefore, and in no way prevented by any constitutional or statutory barrier, for the United States to give sympathetic consideration to a request from the Japanese authorities for the waiver of the American right of jurisdiction and to grant such a request.

c CIVILIAN COMPONENTS

Under the N.A.T.O. Agreement, civilian components of a foreign military force are regarded for jurisdictional purposes as members of the force. The object of Article VII (1) is to provide for concurrent jurisdiction with respect to acts that are offences under the law of the sending state and offences punishable by the law of the receiving state. Paragraph (3) then goes on to grant to the military authorities of the sending state the primary right to exercise jurisdiction in such cases over a member of a force or of a civilian component in relation to certain classes of offence; while other offences are subject to the primary right to exercise jurisdiction of the receiving state.

However, this privileged position of civilian components can no longer apply to such civilian members of United States forces stationed in the territory of other N.A.T.O. members. The basis of the jurisdictional rules of the N.A.T.O. Agreement is that the civilian components are subject to the military law and jurisdiction of the sending state, as well as to the local law. If civilian personnel are not subject to the military law and jurisdiction of the sending state, then they can only be subject to the jurisdiction of the receiving state. As the United States Supreme Court has held, in a series of cases culminating in 1960,[7] that "a civilian, entitled as he is by the Sixth Amendment (to the Constitution) to trial by jury, cannot legally be made liable to the military law and jurisdiction in time of peace",[8] the consequence, as far as the United States is concerned, is that its civilian component can only be tried, if at all, by the courts of the receiving state.

For two main reasons this result of the Supreme Court decisions is regarded as most unsatisfactory in the United States. In the first place, an act by a civilian component of a United States force might not be an offence against the local law at all; or, if it is an offence, the receiving state might regard it as of such minor importance as to be reluctant to prosecute. Yet the act could well be of a much more serious nature from the American viewpoint. Secondly, and this is a factor which weighed heavily with members of both the legislature and the executive in their approach to the N.A.T.O. Agreement, is the suspicion that trials in the courts of some members of N.A T.O. would not measure up to American standards of justice and fairness (the "due process" required of American Courts under the Constitution). The consequence of the Supreme Court decisions in conferring jurisdiction on the courts of the receiving state was to render ineffective

---

7. *Reid* v. *Covert, Kinsella* v. *Krueger*, 354 U.S. 1; (1957), 24 I.L.R. 549: *Kinsella* v. *U.S. ex rel. Singleton*, 361 U.S. 234: *Grisham* v. *Hagan*, 361 U.S. 278: *McElroy* v. *U.S. ex rel. Guagliardo, Wilson* v. *Bohlender*, 361 U.S. 281.

8. A quotation from Winthrop, *Military Law and Precedents*, published in 1896, p. 143, which the Supreme Court cited with approval.

the safeguards of the N.A.T.O. Agreement whereby civilian components would in cases most closely affecting the force be subject to American (military) law and procedures. It is ironic that the reasons for the Supreme Court decisions, that the administration of military justice did not measure up to the standards required by the Constitution, should result in the likelihood that many of the civilians concerned could only be subject to the jurisdiction of non-American Courts, some of which might be regarded by the United States as similarly not satisfying the standards laid down in the American Constitution.

Various possible remedies have been publicly discussed, but short of the unlikely and drastic step of an amendment to the Constitution, the simplest solution would seem to be the incorporation of civilian personnel into the forces so that they would automatically become subject to military law and jurisdiction.

d DEPENDANTS

The position of the families of members of the military force and of families of civilian components is not altogether clear under Article VII of the N.A.T.O. Agreement though the tendency has been for receiving states to allow the sending state the same rights over dependants as the Agreement allows with respect to civilian components. However, whatever doubts exist as to how far their position is assimilated to civilian components as far as concurrent jurisdiction is concerned under this Article, such doubts are irrelevant so far as United States civilians are concerned. The series of Supreme Court decisions already referred to dealt with both civilian dependants and civilian members of United States forces. Civilian dependants, therefore, like civilian components, cannot be subject to United States military law and jurisdiction. Hence, whatever the meaning of Article VII of the N.A.T.O. Agreement, civilian dependants of members of United States forces, or dependants of civilian components of these forces, can only be subject to the exclusive jurisdiction of the receiving state.

As the same objections apply to this unsatisfactory situation as to the case of civilian components, similar suggestions have been made in the United States to enable American military courts to exercise jurisdiction over dependants. It would seem, however, as if nothing short of Constitutional amendment would provide a complete solution to the problem: it would hardly be possible to "conscript" entire families, including children of the age of criminal responsibility, into the armed forces!

6 THE LAW OF OTHER STATES

A. The immunity of foreign states

The basic principle that, because of the sovereign equality of states, the courts of one state cannot exercise jurisdiction over a foreign sovereign, has long been accepted and applied by the municipal courts of states. It is a principle that has been applied with equal consistency by the courts of states with legal systems based on the common law, and of those with legal systems based on the civil law. The words of Ferguson, J.A., in the Appellate Division of the Supreme Court of Ontario that the courts of Canada "will not issue a writ directed to a foreign sovereign state, and therefore a foreign state cannot be sued"[9] find their echo in a number of equally emphatic pronouncements to the same effect by the French Court of Cassation.[10]

Although all states seem to recognise this basic principle, its application in a number of states, particularly of Continental Europe, has been modified to meet the problems raised by foreign states engaging in commercial undertakings. In these European states, a distinction has been drawn between acts *jure imperii* (acts of a sovereign nature), and acts *jure gestionis* (acts which "though public acts in the sense that they are performed by the state, are considered by the courts to be acts of commerce or of administration falling outside their concept of what the sovereign powers of a state comprise"). It must be borne in mind, however, that this distinction is something of a generalisation, and variations in its application can be found in the attitude of the courts between one state and another, and even in the jurisprudence of one particular state.

The state which has perhaps gone furthest in restricting the ambit of pleas of sovereign immunity is Italy. The Italian Courts have consistently applied their normal jurisdictional rules with respect to foreigners over foreign sovereigns or states, unless the defendant concerned could show that he or it was acting in a sovereign capacity. Thus, in 1921 the Court of Cassation held[11] that it had jurisdiction over the former Emperor of Austria in relation to obligations arising from undertakings that had taken place in Italy. As the Italian Courts could exercise jurisdiction over a foreigner with respect to acts, such as entering into a contract, taking place in Italy, it was for the ex-Emperor to demonstrate the public nature of his acts. But by Italian law, entering into a contract in Italy could not be an act of a public nature, for in such a situation the Italian State would certainly be subject to the jurisdiction of the Italian Courts.

The consequence of this attitude on the part of Italian Courts is that some of their decisions deny immunity in situations where the courts of other states would be prepared to accept a plea from the foreign state. In the well-known case of *Government of Roumania* v. *Trutta*,[12] the appellant government claimed immunity with respect to an action arising out of a contract for the supply of leather soles for making boots for use by the Roumanian army. The Court of Cassation rejected the plea. As the contract of sale had been concluded with the national of another state, it did not involve the public power of the Roumanian Government, but was

---

9. *U.S.A.* v. *Motor Trucks*, [1923] 3 D.L.R. 637, at p. 663.
10. E.g. *Spanish Government* v. *Casaux* (1849), *Hanukiew* v. *Minister of Afghanistan* (1933), conveniently dealt with by Hamson in (1950), 27 B.Y.B.I.L. 293, at pp. 300–2.
11. *Nobili* v. *Emperor Charles I of Austria* (1919–22), 1 A.D., Case No. 90.
12. (1925–6), 3 A.D. 179.

essentially an act of its "private personality", and it made no difference that the use of the goods purchased was ultimately a public purpose.

The Belgian Courts have similarly adopted a most restricted view of sovereign acts with the result that they developed an approach much in line with that of the Italian Courts. In the *Liège-Limberg Railway Company* case,[13] the Belgian Courts had to consider a plea of immunity by the Dutch Government, as operator of a state railway system. The Dutch Government had entered into a contract with the Liège-Limberg Railway Company whereby the company, by contributing to the expense of enlarging a station in Holland, became entitled to reimbursement should their joint use of the station be terminated. The Belgian Court of Cassation held that the nature of the contract precluded it from being considered as an act *jure imperii*: the Dutch Government had engaged in a transport enterprise, and had entered into a contract in its capacity as carrier with another railway concern.

A number of other states, while accepting that a distinction does exist between public and private acts have drawn the distinction rather differently. The French view, for example, seems to be that the foreign state is immune from jurisdiction, but that, when engaged in commercial activities, the French Courts may exercise jurisdiction if they can do so over some person or entity other than the foreign state itself. The way was made clear for such a development in a case[14] brought by a Frenchman who was injured by a railway carriage, belonging to the Russian State Railway, which was being carried through the streets of Paris from the exhibition ground where it had been on show. The plaintiff's suit had been successful in a judgment against both the carriers and the Russian Railways, but the plaintiff was obliged to bring further proceedings against the Russian Government to obtain the damages he had been awarded. The Paris Court of Appeal held that while official exhibits at an exposition in a foreign country could be considered as governmental action for which a suit would not be entertained in the French Courts, the same could not be said of arrangements made with private firms that were incidental to the actual exhibition of the various items. However, even in respect of non-governmental acts, no suit would be entertained in an action directed against the foreign state itself. Only if the state were operating through some separate organ or agency could a distinction be drawn between its public personality, and its private or commercial capacity which could be subject to the jurisdiction of the courts.

In summarising the different approaches that had been adopted by other states, the Tate Letter of 1952, which has already been mentioned in the context of United States law and practice, made the following observations:

> "The classical or virtually absolute theory of sovereign immunity has generally been followed by the courts of the United States, the British Commonwealth, Czechoslovakia, Estonia, and probably Poland. The decisions of the courts of

---

13.   Bishop, *International Law*, 2nd ed., p. 562.
14.   *Gamen-Humbert* v. *Russia* (1912), 27 B.Y.B.I.L., at p. 304.

Brazil, Chile, China, Hungary, Japan, Luxembourg, Norway, and Portugal may be deemed to support the classical theory of immunity if one or at most two old decisions anterior to the development of the restrictive theory may be considered sufficient on which to base a conclusion. The position of the Netherlands, Sweden, and Argentina is less clear since although immunity has been granted in recent cases coming before the courts of those countries, the facts were such that immunity would have been granted under either the absolute or restrictive theory. However, constant references by the courts of these three countries to the distinction between public and private acts of the state, even though the distinction was not involved in the result of the case, may indicate an intention to leave the way open for a possible application of the restrictive theory of immunity if and when the occasion presents itself. A trend to the restrictive theory is already evident in the Netherlands where the lower courts have started to apply that theory following a Supreme Court decision to the effect that immunity would have been applicable in the case under consideration under either theory. . . . The newer or restrictive theory of sovereign immunity has always been supported by the courts of Belgium and Italy. It was adopted in turn by the courts of Egypt and of Switzerland. In addition, the courts of France, Austria, and Greece, which were traditionally supporters of the classical theory, reversed their position in the 20's to embrace the restrictive theory. Roumania, Peru, and possibly Denmark also appear to follow this theory. Furthermore, it should be observed that in most of the countries still following the classical theory there is a school of influential writers, favouring the restrictive theory and the views of writers at least in civil law countries, are a major factor in the development of the law."

Because of the variety of attitudes of different states, it is only possible to consider in barest outline the effect of these attitudes on the application of the principle of sovereign immunity to different types of state property, or to different types of state organisation.

a PUBLIC SHIPS

Although the Brussels Convention of 1926, as modified by an Additional Protocol of 1934, was only ratified by a limited number of states, it did provide strong support in favour of immunity being restricted to cases of non-commercial activity. Under Article 1, "seagoing vessels owned or operated by states, cargoes owned by them, and cargoes and passengers carried on Government vessels, and the States owning or operating such vessels, or owning such cargoes, are subject in respect of claims relating to the operation of such vessels or the carriage of such cargoes, to the same rules of liability and to the same obligations as those applicable to private vessels, cargoes and equipments." However, Article 3 (1) laid down, *inter alia*, that this provision should not apply to "ships of war, Government yachts, patrol vessels, hospital ships, auxiliary vessels, supply ships, and other craft owned or operated by a state, and used at the time a cause of action arises exclusively on Governmental and non-commercial service."

In addition to the indirect support the existence of the Convention gave to the move towards a more restricted view of immunity, it did have direct results for those states which ratified it. Germany and the Scandinavian states all favoured the wider principle of sovereign immunity but their ratification of the Convention and the adoption of implementing legislation fundamentally altered their approach towards public vessels, and brought it more into line with that already apparent in Italy and Belgium. The change in attitude of the German Courts may be illustrated by a comparison between the decision in the case of the *Ice King* in 1921[15] that the vessel, although operated by the United States Shipping Board for commercial purposes, was immune from process, and the later decision in the case of the *Visurgis* and the *Siena* in 1938[16] that the German Courts did have jurisdiction over a vessel under a time charter to a foreign government (though, admittedly, the vessel was not under the control of the government for this purpose).

While there has been a strong tendency in the courts of a number of European states to limit the application of sovereign immunity in respect of ships to those operated for non-commercial purposes, the position in common law jurisdictions is largely influenced by the English decisions. In Canada the leading case of *Brown* v. *S.S. Indochine*[17] in 1922 decided that a vessel owned by the French Republic was immune from suit even though it was engaged in a commercial venture. After dealing with the English cases prior to 1922, Maclennan, L.J.A., concluded that they recognised the immunity from seizure of "all government-owned or government-requisitioned ships, whether used for military, political or commercial purposes". The position today would depend largely upon how far the Canadian Courts would take advantage of the doubts expressed by the House of Lords in the *Cristina*[18] to adopt a rule more in keeping with accepted doctrine elsewhere in the world and more particularly in the United States after the Tate Letter. Recently, in *Flota Maritima* v. *Cuba*,[19] the Supreme Court of Canada avoided having to decide the issue. The plaintiff company claimed to be entitled to a number of ships under a lease-purchase agreement with a Cuban Bank. Alleging breaches of the contract by the plaintiff company, the Bank sold the vessels to the Cuban Government. At the time of the hearing the vessels were still lying at Halifax and had yet to be employed by the Cuban Government. They were in fact being fitted out as trading or passenger ships, but until the ships were operated on a commercial venture, the Court held that it did not have to consider whether a restricted view of immunity should be

---

15. (1919–22), 1 A.D., Case No. 102.
16. (1938–40) 9 A.D., Case No. 94. For the application of the Convention by the Swedish Supreme Court, see the case of the *Rigmor* (1941–2), 10 A.D., Case No. 63; and by the Norwegian Courts, see the *Fredrikstad* (1950), 17 I.L.R., Case No. 42, and the *Irania* (1950), 17 I.L.R., p. 168, n. 1.
17. (1922), 21 Ex. C.R. 406; (1919–22), 1 A.D., Case No. 106.
18. See above, pp. 173–174.
19. (1962) 34 D.L.R. (2d) 628. At first instance, 30 D.L.R. (2d) 172, Pottier, D.J.A., held that "having regard to the development of the law on the subject in other nations, and especially in the United States, and to the unsettled position of the law in England, it must be held that in Canada a ship engaged in commerce while owned by a foreign government and in its possession or control is not immune from the jurisdiction of Canadian courts" (headnote).
    On appeal, this decision was reversed by the Exchequer Court [1962] Ex. C.R. 1, Cameron, J., apparently adopting an absolute rule of immunity.

applied. At the time of the action they were owned and in the possession of a foreign state and therefore immune from suit.

b STATE AGENCIES

Obviously the attitude of states towards pleas of immunity by foreign state agencies and corporations is determined largely by their overall approach to the problem of sovereign immunity. The Italian Courts, for example, on a number of occasions[20] rejected claims to immunity from the U.S. Shipping Board. The Board, although a state body, could not be identified with the American Government for undertaking maritime navigation and business as a commercial enterprise did not constitute a sovereign act. Similarly, the Italian Courts have exercised jurisdiction over Sovexportfilm, on the ground that, being an economic entity, it was distinct from the personality of the Soviet State.[1] Although in the *Ice King*[2] the German Courts upheld a plea of immunity on behalf of a vessel engaged in a commercial venture on behalf of the U.S. Shipping Board, the impetus given by the Brussels Convention and changes of attitude elsewhere have led the courts of the Federal Republic to reject the authority of the former Supreme Court on this subject. In the *Danish State Railways* case,[3] a Kiel court held that an action against the Kingdom of Denmark in respect of a bus service operated by the State Railways should be allowed to proceed. The operation of such a service was clearly a commercial activity, and could not be considered as an act of sovereignty.

The existence of a state agency which cannot be proved to form part of the foreign government is of most significance in relation to French law. It will be recalled that, even if the foreign state had engaged in a commercial transaction, its plea to immunity would be upheld unless the action could proceed without naming the foreign state as defendant. If the action involves a shipping agency, or some other governmental organ, the fact that it is engaged in commercial, and therefore basically non-governmental, functions will lead the French Courts to distinguish between the non-governmental capacity of the defendant and the immunity of the state itself and of any organs carrying out governmental functions on its behalf. In *Lakhowsky* v. *Swiss Federal Government*,[4] a court of first instance assumed jurisdiction over a Swiss Government Office which was in charge of obtaining supplies for Switzerland during the First World War on the ground that the transaction at issue was of a commercial nature (it was in fact a contract to charter ships to keep the Swiss chocolate industry supplied with cocoa). An appeal court reversed this decision, holding that, in the circumstances, the object of the transaction was political rather than commercial, but it accepted the principle that a state agency could be sued in respect of commercial activities as, not being governmental

---

20. E.g. *U.S. Shipping Board* v. *Societa Italiana Cementi*, Guirt. It., 1925–1–2.
1. *Floridi* v. *Sovexport film*, Tribunale di Roma, Annali X (1952), p. 115.
2. (1919–22), 1 A.D., Case No. 102.   3. (1953), 20 I.L.R. 178.
4. (1919–22), 1 A.D., Case No. 83.

acts, they must be regarded as the acts of the agency and not of the foreign state.

B. Diplomatic immunities

In view of the Vienna Convention, it is not proposed to deal at length with diplomatic privileges and immunities. The Convention was based on the general consensus of state practice, so that it reflected what was already in whole or in part the law of a number of states. And even in those states the law of which differed from the provisions of the Convention, legislation has been passed to enable many of those states to ratify the Convention. The British Diplomatic Privileges Act of 1964, in giving effect to the Vienna Convention, is therefore as good an illustration as any of what is now generally accepted as the law governing diplomatic privileges and immunities.[5]

C. Quasi-diplomatic privileges and immunities

a CONSULAR OFFICERS

The Vienna Convention on Consular Relations of 1963, which was intended to be complementary to the earlier Diplomatic Convention, received sufficient ratifications to enter into effect in 1967. While the precise position of foreign consuls in states that have not given effect to the Convention will depend upon the municipal courts of the states concerned, it is believed that, even in those states, the 1963 Consular Convention largely reflects existing customary law in relation to consular privileges and immunities. The main difference would seem to be that the Convention is probably more detailed than the existing law of most states that have not ratified it.

Article 31 of the Convention describes what is meant by the inviolability of consular premises. The authorities of the receiving state are prohibited from entering, without the consent of the head of the consular post or of the sending state's diplomatic mission, "that part of the consular premises which is used exclusively for the purpose of the work of the consular post". The consular premises, its furnishings, the property of the post and its means of transport are immune from requisition even for purposes of national defence or public utility unless necessary. If expropriation does become necessary, it should be carried out so far as possible to "avoid impeding the performance of consular functions, and prompt, adequate and effective compensation shall be paid to the sending state". Article 32 deals with the exemption from taxation of consular premises and Article 33 with the inviolability of consular archives and documents "at all times

---

5. For the legislation of other states, see, e.g. Soviet *Law Concerning Diplomatic and Consular Missions* (1966), 5 I.L.M. 801; and the Australian *Diplomatic Privileges and Immunities Act*, 1967.

and wherever they may be". Article 35 deals at length with freedom of communication, but the basic principle is that the "receiving state shall permit and protect freedom of communication on the part of the consular post for all official purposes".

Article 40 provides that the receiving state "shall treat consular officers with due respect and shall take all appropriate steps to prevent any attack on their person, freedom and dignity". The personal inviolability of a consul is more limited than that of a diplomatic agent. Criminal proceedings against a consul can be instituted though they must be conducted "with the respect due to him by reason of his official position"; arrest or detention pending trial is only allowed "in the case of a grave crime and pursuant to a decision by the competent judicial authority"; but committal to prison or other form of restriction on personal freedom is possible "in execution of a judicial decision of final effect" (Article 41). The immunity from jurisdiction of consular officers and employees only extends to "acts performed in the exercise of consular functions", but not where the suit is a civil action "arising out of a contract concluded by a consular officer or a consular employee in which he did not contract expressly or impliedly as an agent of the sending state or by a third party for damage arising from an accident in the receiving state caused by a vehicle, vessel or aircraft" (Article 43).

b INTERNATIONAL ORGANISATIONS

i The status of the organisation

The Convention on the Privileges and Immunities of the United Nations, Article II, s. 2, provides that the Organisation, its property and assets shall enjoy immunity from every form of legal process except in so far as, in a particular case, the immunity has been waived. The Convention on the Privileges and Immunities of the Specialised Agencies and a large number of Headquarters Agreements contain similar provisions. Sec. 3 of the General Convention states that the premises of the Organisation shall be inviolable, and s. 4 that its archives and all its documents shall also be inviolable. There are equivalent provisions in a large variety of constitutions of international institutions and in their Headquarters Agreements.

ii Representatives of member states

Article IV, s. 11, of the General Convention extends a number of what amount to diplomatic privileges and immunities to representatives of member states to the United Nations, notably in respect of documents, communications, immigration restrictions, exchange control restrictions, etc. However, such representatives do not enjoy full immunity from judicial process but only "immunity from personal arrest or detention and from seizure of their personal baggage, and, in respect of words spoken or written and all acts done by them in their capacity as representatives, immunity from legal process of every kind." A similar provision is repeated in the Convention on the Privileges and Immunities of the Specialised Agencies, and has been applied in a number of Headquarters

Agreements (e.g. the Agreement between Canada and I.C.A.O., Article III). On the other hand, many states have extended the privileges and immunities enjoyed by representatives of members of organisations to which they are host to full diplomatic status (for example under the Headquarters Agreement between the United States and the United Nations which has already been considered, and under s. 15 of the Agreement between Switzerland and the I.L.O.).

iii *Officials of the organisation*

Under s. 18 of the General Convention, officials of the United Nations are entitled to exemptions from taxation, national service obligations, immigration restrictions, exchange facilities, etc., and to immunity from legal process "in respect of words spoken or written and all acts performed by them in their official capacity" (s. 18). However, under s. 19, in addition to these privileges and immunities, the Secretary-General and all Assistant Secretaries-General shall be accorded "in respect of themselves, their spouses and minor children, the privileges and immunities, exemptions and facilities accorded to diplomatic envoys, in accordance with international law". A similar set of provisions was included in the Specialised Agencies Convention, except that s. 21, the counterpart of s. 19 in the General Convention, limits the grant of full diplomatic immunity to "the executive head of each specialised agency, including any official acting on his behalf during his absence from duty". However, in the Annexes to the Convention, the operation of s. 21 is extended to the Deputy or Assistant of the head of a number of the larger agencies (as, for example, under paragraph 2 of the I.L.O. Annex and paragraph 3 of the F.A.O. Annex). While these provisions have been largely adopted by states, particularly states which act as host to an organisation or one of its regional Agencies, there are some variations. For example, the U.N.E.S.C.O. Agreement with France, which grants full jurisdictional immunities to senior officials of the Organisation, withholds these immunities from such personnel if they are French nationals, in which case immunity is limited to their official acts. Limitations upon exemptions from the local law in respect of nationals of the host state are to be found in a number of other Headquarters Agreements (for example, under the Agreement between I.C.A.O. and Canada).

D. Foreign armed forces

In the absence of treaty or statutory regulation, the general tendency has been to regard visiting armed forces as subject to the jurisdiction of the local courts, except in so far as the local authorities refrain from acting in relation to purely disciplinary matters.

In *Wright* v. *Cantrell*,[6] the Supreme Court of New South Wales held that an officer in charge of a Transportation Unit of the United States

---

6. 44 S.R (N.S.W.) 45; (1943–5), 12 A.D., Case No. 37.

Army was not entitled to immunity from suit in a civil action. Some degree of exemption might be necessary in order for the force to operate effectively as an independent unit, but the efficiency of its operations could hardly be affected by its personnel being subject to civil claims. This principle was accepted by the High Court of Australia in a later case[7] in which Latham, C.J., pointed out that "in the absence of express agreement the permitted presence of an armed force necessarily implies some degree of exemption from local jurisdiction, because it would be impracticable to have the armed force of a friendly power subject in respect of such matters as discipline and internal administration to the control of the local authorities."

The generalisation that the permitted presence of foreign visiting forces "necessarily implies some degree of exemption" from local jurisdiction is perhaps the furthest one can venture in the absence of express statutory or treaty provision. A majority of the Supreme Court of Canada decided in 1943[8] that in the absence of express provision United States forces, even though they entered Canada at the invitation of the Dominion Government, were subject at least to some extent to the jurisdiction of the Canadian Courts. The uncertainties of the position are well illustrated by the sharp divergences of opinion between the judges. Two were of the opinion that the Canadian Courts had complete jurisdiction over visiting forces, although they did not in fact exercise it "in respect of acts committed within the lines of such forces, or of offences against discipline generally committed by one member of such forces against another member in cases in which the act or offence does not affect the person or property of a Canadian subject." Two judges strongly favoured the view that the United States forces, having entered Canada by invitation, must be allowed complete immunity from prosecution for criminal offences in the Canadian Courts. The fifth member of the Court limited the immunity to offences against the local law committed in camp, except against persons not subject to American military law, or offences wherever committed against other members of the forces, their property, or the property of their government.

As far as express agreements are concerned, it will be recalled that the provisions of the N.A.T.O. Status Agreement apply amongst members of the Organisation, and very similar principles have been accepted by the Japanese Government in its dealings with United States personnel. The Soviet Union has entered into a number of bilateral arrangements with other members of the Warsaw Pact to cover the position of Soviet troops stationed on the territory of those states. In general, the local law is to be applied to criminal acts committed by Soviet forces (including civilians, i.e. Soviet citizens employed in units of the Soviet forces in the state con-

---

7. *Chow Hung Ching* v. *R.* (1949), 77 C.L.R. 449, at p. 461; (1948) 15 A.D., Case No. 46.

8. *Re Exemption of U.S. Forces from Canadian Criminal Law*, [1943] 4 D.L.R. 11; (1943-5) 12 A.D., Case No. 36.

cerned) or their families in the territory of the receiving state, unless the offences are against the Soviet Union, or other members of the forces or their families, or the offence occurs in the discharge of official duties. Provision is also made whereby the two states may request the transfer or acceptance of jurisdiction in individual cases.

CHAPTER SEVEN

JURISDICTION—II
MARITIME AND AIR JURISDICTION

1 MARITIME JURISDICTION

It is a basic principle of maritime law that jurisdiction follows the flag. As a general proposition, a vessel which is rightfully, according to the law of the flag state, flying the flag of that state,[1] carries with it the law of that state. The extent to which the law of the flag applies in criminal and civil matters arising out of incidents on board the ship is essentially a matter for the municipal law of the flag state. International law allows the flag state a complete discretion in the matter. Thus, the common law rule that a British ship carried its own criminal law with it into the waters of a foreign state is not contrary to international law.

As international law permits the flag state to exercise jurisdiction over events on board even when the ship is within foreign waters, the only problems that are the concern of international law are those involving attempts by a state to exercise jurisdiction over foreign vessels. The first major problem is whether international law provides any rules to prevent conflicts arising if a state tries to assume jurisdiction over events happening on board a foreign ship in a port, or within the territorial waters, of the state on the ground that the incident also occurred within its territorial jurisdiction. The second main problem arises in relation to incidents occurring on the high seas: are there any circumstances in which a vessel of one state can interfere with the freedom of passage on the high seas of a ship flying the flag of another state?

However, while the extent to which one state might exercise jurisdiction over vessels flying the flags of other states was the main, if not the sole, concern of the traditional rules of maritime law, and still remains, of course, a major concern, a variety of factors since the Second World War have produced both increasing claims to exclusive use or exploitation of areas of the high seas, and a gradual realisation that unfettered freedom of use and exploitation of the high seas in general by all states is not in the best interests of the international community. On the one hand the freedom of

---

1. The application of the concept of nationality to ships is considered in the following chapter, below, pp. 308–310.

the seas has been encroached upon by the rights of the coastal state to the continental shelf, and by the closing of large areas of sea by individual states as weapon testing grounds. On the other hand, problems of oil-pollution and the over-exploitation of fishing stocks have brought an increasing awareness of the need to control the extent to which states make use of their freedom of the seas.

A. Jurisdiction in coastal waters

a CANALS

Even sea-water canals like the Corinth Canal are not subject to a special régime unless one has been created by treaty as happened with the Suez, Panama and Kiel Canals. The creation of such a régime has the effect of limiting the territorial supremacy of the riparian state to the extent of obliging it to allow freedom of passage through the canal, but its right to exercise jurisdiction over, and apply its own law to, incidents occurring in the canal would seem to remain unimpaired. In the *Kiel Canal Collision* case,[2] the defendants, the owners of one of the vessels involved, argued that, the canal being an international waterway, the collision must be treated as having occurred on the high seas and therefore outside the jurisdiction of the German Courts. In rejecting this contention, the Supreme Court of the British Zone of Germany stated what is clearly the correct principle. "Unless express rules of international law have provided for a more far-reaching limitation of territorial sovereignty, freedom of navigation on international waterways does not by any means imply a limitation of the power of jurisdiction and the field of application of the local system of law." As far as jurisdiction over events taking place entirely on board one particular ship is concerned, the rules would seem to be the same as the principles applicable to ships in port or in other internal waters.

b PORTS AND INTERNAL WATERS
i *Access*

Traditionally, as internal waters were considered part of the territory of the state, they were regarded as being subject to the full territorial sovereignty of the state. It followed that a state could, at its discretion, exclude foreign ships from these waters. In regard to maritime ports dealing with international traffic, however, the disadvantages of the possibility of the mutual exclusion of each other's vessels by states were manifest. In the course of time a large number of bilateral arrangements were entered into for reciprocal access to the maritime ports of the contracting states, and a similar provision was accepted by a larger number of states in the 1923 Convention on the Régime of Maritime Ports. In the light of these developments, it is doubtful whether a coastal state still retains the right

---

2. (1950), 17 I.L.R., Case No. 34.

arbitrarily to exclude the vessels of a foreign state from those of its ports catering for international maritime traffic even in the absence of a treaty with the state concerned. This is certainly the conclusion reached by the tribunal which heard the *Aramco* arbitration.[3]

Aramco, an American company, was the concessionary under a 60-year agreement originally entered into with Saudi Arabia in 1933. The agreement granted to Aramco exclusive rights of exploitation and transportation of the oil produced. By an elaborate arrangement with a number of other companies, Aramco granted to its regular purchasers the right to select their own tankships to load the oil at the various outlets established by Aramco. In 1954, however, the Saudi Arabian Government entered into a contract with Onassis for the creation of a fleet of tankers to operate under the Saudi Arabian flag. Satco, the company formed by Onassis, was to have priority treatment in the carriage of oil to such an extent that the Saudi Arabian Government undertook to compel all present and future concessionary oil companies in Saudi Arabia to ship and carry their oil and its products on board Satco tankers. The Tribunal held that the exclusive rights of transportation granted by the concession applied to distribution of oil overseas and not, as argued by the Saudi Arabian Government, solely to transportation in the areas covered by the concession. However, the Tribunal also held that, quite apart from the concession, a state could not discriminate against foreign ships by excluding them from its ports.

> "It is indisputable that every sovereign State has the right to contol its ports, for they are a part of its maritime communications. It has the international competence, by virtue of its internal independence and of its territorial supremacy, to regulate as it deems best, transportation from its territory, whether by land or by sea. With regard to the development and safeguard of its economic and financial interests particularly, a State has undeniably the right to regulate and to control importation into, and exportation from, its territory of articles of every description; this right of control embraces the right to prohibit the ingress or egress of certain goods, and to levy duties upon imports and exports. . . . However, the territorial sovereignty of the State over its means of maritime communications is not unrestricted. It can only be exercised within the limits of customary international law, of the treaties the State has concluded and of the particular undertakings it has assumed. According to a great principle of public international law, the ports of every State must be open to foreign merchant vessels and can only be closed when the vital interests of the State so require. . . . It follows that the Company, by virtue of the rules of the Law of Nations, is plainly entitled to sell its oil and its products to any purchasers it chooses, under such terms and conditions as are agreed upon with them, and thus to conclude f.o.b. sales, in which tankers are supplied by the buyers. It cannot be impeded by discrimination based on nationality of the ships and resulting in the exclusion, from the loading and transport of oil for export, of customers who wish to carry away the oil on their own tankships or on tankships especially chartered for this purpose."[4]

While the right to exclude foreign vessels from internal waters that do not provide access to international maritime ports is obviously unimpaired by

---

3. (1958), 27 I.L.R. 117.   4. *Ibid.*, at pp. 214–215.

this developing principle of customary international law, the change in the method of delimiting the boundaries of internal waters brought about by the *Fisheries* case,[5] and accepted by Article 4 of the Convention on the Territorial Sea, has necessitated the introduction of another modification in the rules governing exclusion from internal waters. According to Article 5 (2) of the Convention, where the establishment of straight base-lines in accordance with Article 4 "has the effect of enclosing as internal waters areas which previously had been considered as part of the territorial sea or of the high seas", the vessels of foreign states should nevertheless retain a right of innocent passage in those waters.

The definition of innocent passage is considered below, and also the problem of whether warships have the right of innocent passage will be discussed, but, as far as ports are concerned, no right of access can be claimed for warships. The 1923 Convention on the Régime of Maritime Ports which gave impetus to the development of a right of access under customary international law was explicit on this point: the right of access was not to apply "in any way to warships or vessels performing police or administrative functions, or, in general, exercising any kind of public authority. . . ."

ii *Jurisdiction*

The problems that arise once a foreign ship enters the internal waters of a state stem from the fact that it is potentially subject to two jurisdictions. It remains subject to the jurisdiction of the state of the flag of which it is flying; but, unless it is a warship or other public ship operated for a non-commercial purpose, it also comes under the territorial jurisdiction of the coastal state.

1   *In criminal cases*

Unless the vessel is a public ship and entitled to immunity according to the laws of the coastal state, a crime committed on board a foreign ship in port is subject to the jurisdiction both of the local courts and of the courts of the flag state. Are there any guiding principles to avoid constant wranglings over which state should exercise jurisdiction in such cases?

Prima facie, a ship, by entering the internal waters of a foreign state (unless it is in distress and obliged to do so), places itself within the territorial jurisdiction of that state and therefore subject to the operation of its laws and within the competence of its courts. As a matter of comity, "it is not usual for the authorities to intervene and enforce the local jurisdiction, unless their assistance is invoked by, or on behalf of, the local representative of the flag state, or those in control of the ship, or a person directly concerned, or unless the peace or good order of the port is likely to be affected", but in the last resort it is for the authorities of the coastal state to decide whether or not to intervene. This statement[6] represented the view

---

5. I.C.J. Rep. 1951, p. 116, see above, pp. 152–155.
6. Reply of the United Kingdom Government to one of the questions (point 15) submitted to governments by the Preparatory Committee of the League of Nations prior to the Hague Codification Conference of 1930: cited McNair, *International Law Opinions*, Vol. II, p. 194.

of the United Kingdom in 1930, and it is doubtful whether this principle of comity has crystallised into a rule of international law restricting the jurisdictional rights of the coastal state.

In the *Eisler* case,[7] British police boarded a Polish vessel at anchor in internal waters off Southampton to arrest Eisler on a warrant pending the hearing of a request for his extradition by the United States Government. In reply to a protest by the Polish Government that a state's jurisdiction over territorial and internal waters did not entitle it to arrest persons on board a foreign vessel for the purpose of extradition to a third state, the British Government argued that the Polish claim was tantamount to a right of asylum on board a merchant ship, a right "quite contrary to the practice of States" which had been rejected on previous occasions by the Polish Government itself. "The absence of any right to grant asylum on board merchant ships sprang", the reply continued, "from a universally recognised principle of international law that a merchant ship in the ports or roadsteads of another country falls under the jurisdiction of the coastal state."

Although the 1958 Territorial Sea Convention is not primarily concerned with jurisdictional rights in internal waters, Article 19 lays down a number of rules relating to foreign ships in territorial waters which would clearly apply *a fortiori* to vessels in internal waters. Thus, paragraph 5 would seem to support the view of the law represented by the British action in the *Eisler* case. Under this provision the coastal state "may not take any steps on board a foreign ship passing through the territorial sea to arrest any person or to conduct any investigation in connexion with any crime committed before the ship entered the territorial sea, if the ship, proceeding from a foreign port, is only passing through the territorial sea without entering internal waters." In other words, even if the crime was committed before the vessel entered the territorial sea, if the vessel had entered (or, obviously, was still within) internal waters, it is open to the authorities of the coastal state to effect an arrest or conduct an investigation on board the foreign vessel.

As far as crimes committed on board ship during its stay in internal waters are concerned, Article 19 (1) of the Convention lays down that only in specified circumstances can the coastal state exercise jurisdiction over crimes committed on board during passage through territorial waters, but paragraph (2) provides that these limitations "do not affect the right of the coastal state to take any steps authorised by its laws for the purpose of an arrest or investigation on board a foreign ship passing through the territorial sea after leaving internal waters." It would seem that the implication of this paragraph is that international law allows the coastal state a complete discretion whether to exercise jurisdiction over matters occurring on board a foreign vessel while it is in port.

Even if the Convention apparently leaves the coastal state's discretion completely unfettered, a large number of states have entered into consular

---

7. (1949), 26 B.Y.B.I.L. 468.

conventions in which the coastal state has relinquished its jurisdictional claims in favour of the flag state, certainly in matters of internal discipline. In the course of its decision in the *Wildenhus* case,[8] the United States Supreme Court explained that ". . . by comity it came to be generally understood among civilised nations that all matters of discipline and all things done on board which affected only the vessel or those belonging to her, and did not involve the peace or dignity of the country, or the tranquillity of the port, should be left by the local government to be dealt with by the authorities of the nation to which the vessel belonged as the laws of that nation or the interests of its commerce should require. But if crimes are committed on board of a character to disturb the peace and tranquillity of the country to which the vessel has been brought, the offenders have never by comity or usage been entitled to any exemption from the operation of the local laws for their punishment, if the local tribunals see fit to assert their authority. Such being the general public law on this subject, treaties and conventions have been entered into by nations having commercial intercourse, the purpose of which was to settle and define the rights and duties of the contracting parties with respect to each other in these particulars, and thus prevent the inconvenience that might arise from attempts to exercise conflicting jurisdictions." Wildenhus, a Belgian subject, and a member of the crew of the *Noordland*, a Belgian ship moored at the time at Jersey City, stabbed to death another member of the ship's crew in a fracas that took place entirely on board the ship. The Supreme Court held that the crime was clearly one to "disturb tranquillity and public order on shore, or in port" within Article XI of the U.S.–Belgium Consular Convention of 1880. It might not be easy at all times to decide whether a particular offence should be subject to the jurisdiction of the flag state or to that of the territorial sovereign, but "all must concede that felonious homicide is a subject for the local jurisdiction".[9]

More recently, the Supreme Court has referred to "the well-established rule of international law that the law of the flag state ordinarily governs the internal affairs of a ship" in a case dealing with the application of United States legislation to foreign vessels and their crews.[10] However, existing authorities do not seem to substantiate such a proposition. The acceptance of the principle in a large number of conventions dealing with consular jurisdiction is undoubtedly evidence of a widespread practice among states, but it is not conclusive on whether the coastal state should as a matter of comity, or must as a matter of international law, refrain from exercising jurisdiction in matters where the "peace and tranquillity of the port" is not affected. The absence of any provision limiting the territorial state's jurisdiction in cases where a vessel had been in internal waters in the

---

8. 120 U.S. 1, at p. 12 (1887).

9. *Ibid.*, at p. 18. For the attitude of the French Courts to the application of a similar provision in a Franco-American Consular Convention, see the cases of the *Sally* and the *Newton* (1806) and of the *Tempest* (1859) considered by the U.S. Supreme Court in the course of the *Wildenhus* judgment: *ibid.*, at pp. 13–14.

10. *McCulloch* v. *Marineros de Honduras*, 372 U.S. 10, at p. 21 (1963).

Territorial Sea Convention suggests that the rule is one of comity and not of law.

2   In civil cases

There would seem to be no limitation on the exercise of civil jurisdiction over a foreign vessel (not being a vessel entitled to sovereign immunity) in internal waters. The English and American Courts have a wide Admiralty jurisdiction in suits *in rem* arising out of actions for possession, or for damages following a collision, against a foreign ship. That this jurisdiction is not contrary to international law is clear. It has a long and respectable history and is generally accepted by the community of maritime nations. Furthermore, while Article 20 (2) of the Territorial Sea Convention prohibits the coastal state from levying execution against or arresting for the purpose of civil proceedings any ship (save only in respect of obligations arising in the course of its passage through the territorial waters of the coastal state), Article 20 (3) excludes the limitations contained in paragraph (2) from applying to any ship lying in the territorial sea or passing through the territorial sea after leaving internal waters. If civil jurisdiction is not restricted in such circumstances, it would *a fortiori* not be limited when the ship was actually within internal waters.

c   TERRITORIAL WATERS

i   *Access—The right of innocent passage*

Article 1 (1) of the Territorial Sea Convention lays down that the "sovereignty of a state extends, beyond its land territory and its internal waters, to a belt of sea adjacent to its coast, described as the territorial sea"; but paragraph (2) adds that this sovereignty is to be "exercised subject to the provisions of these articles and to other rules of international law".

The principal limitation upon the sovereign powers of the coastal state is the so-called *right of innocent passage*. While a state may exclude foreign ships from its internal waters, with the probable exception of international maritime ports, it has no such power to prevent the passage of foreign ships through its territorial sea, provided that such passage is innocent. "Innocent passage" is essentially a compromise between the freedom of maritime navigation on the high seas and the rights of the territorial sovereign, but it is a principle that has been long established. As one commentator wrote in 1927, "the right of innocent passage requires no supporting argument or citation of authority; it is firmly established in international law".[11]

The concept of innocent passage comprises two aspects: the route actually taken, and the purpose or nature of the voyage.

As far as the route is concerned, Article 14 (2) settled earlier controversies over whether the passage included the part of a voyage from a

---

11.   Jessup, *The Law of Territorial Waters and Maritime Jurisdiction*, p. 120.

port across territorial waters to the high seas, by stating that passage "means navigation through the territorial sea for the purpose either of traversing that sea without entering internal waters, or of proceeding to internal waters, or of making for the high seas from internal waters". And paragraph (3) provides that passage includes "stopping and anchoring, but only in so far as the same are incidental to ordinary navigation or are rendered necessary by *force majeure* or by distress".

The qualification of the innocence of the passage has been the subject of lively discussion. A number of leading jurists who attended the 1958 Conference at Geneva were strongly of the opinion that customary international law and the Territorial Sea Convention itself distinguished between matters relating to the innocence of the passage and those concerning compliance with regulations governing passage through the territorial sea.[12] Thus, Article 14 (4) provides in part that passage is innocent "so long as it is not prejudicial to the peace, good order or security of the coastal state", while Article 17 states that foreign ships "exercising the right of innocent passage shall comply with the laws and regulations enacted by the coastal state in conformity with these articles and other rules of international law and, in particular, with such laws and regulations relating to transport and navigation." For breach of the former provision, the passage ceases to be innocent, and the coastal state may take the "necessary steps" to prevent such passage (Article 16 (1))—i.e. the offending vessel may be excluded from passing through the territorial sea. For breach of Article 17, the offences are governed by the law of the coastal state, though the actual enforcement of its regulations may depend upon the application of Article 19 which is considered below.

While the Convention bears out this analysis in part, a number of provisions do not fit in particularly well with the division between matters relating to the innocence of the passage and those concerning compliance with local regulations. Article 14 (4) itself, having defined the innocent nature of the passage, qualifies the concept further by adding that the passage "shall take place in conformity with these articles and with other rules of international law". And Article 14 (5) cuts across any theory of such a division by laying down that the passage of foreign fishing vessels "shall not be considered innocent if they do not observe such laws and regulations as the coastal state may make and publish in order to prevent these vessels from fishing in the territorial sea". Furthermore, it would seem unlikely that Article 16 (1), in granting the coastal state the right to prevent a passage that was *not* innocent, at the same time limits the right to a power of excluding the offending vessel from the territorial sea. If the passage of a foreign vessel is prejudicial to the peace, good order, or security of the coastal state, the coastal state might as reasonably exercise a power of arrest over the vessel as it would for any breaches of its laws and

---

12. E.g. Fitzmaurice, Conference Records, Vol. III (First Committee), 28th Mtg., para. 25; cp. (1956) Y.B.I.L.C., I, 201, para. 74: Verziji, (1959) 6 Netherlands Tijdschrift 1, at p. 29.

regulations of the type covered by Article 17.[13] It is at least arguable that the test of the innocence of the passage is the motive behind the voyage. If the object of the passage is contrary to the laws of the coastal state, whether a security matter such as listening-in to the military or naval radio communications of the coastal state, or a customs matter like smuggling, the passage is not innocent because its primary purpose is not that of *traversing the territorial sea* within Article 14 (2) of the Convention. All that Article 17 stipulates is that, providing the passage is innocent (i.e. is undertaken for the genuine purpose of passage and not with the ulterior motive of breaking the laws of the coastal state), a passing vessel should abide by local laws and regulations, particularly those relating to transport and navigation. Solely because the passage is innocent, the fact that criminal jurisdiction is only exercisable over a passing vessel in the cases of offences affecting the coastal state under the provisions of Article 19, is no excuse for being careless about the requirements of the local law.

It is clear, therefore, that passage is not innocent—

(1) if it is prejudicial to the peace, good order or security of the coastal state;

This principle is stated in vague terms because states are unwilling to accept a precise definition of their rights over their territorial sea.

(2) if foreign fishing vessels disregard local regulations designed to prevent their fishing in the territorial sea;

It is not fishing alone which may be prohibited. Fishing vessels which disregard regulations designed to prevent their fishing may be excluded from the territorial sea, even though they have not actually engaged in fishing. It would be open to the coastal state to prescribe rules requiring that fishing gear be stowed in a certain manner during passage, but the fact that foreign fishing vessels are entitled to exercise the right of innocent passage implies that the local regulations should not be so onerous as to prevent passage under normal circumstances.

(3) but it is far from clear whether passage that takes place in violation of the provisions of the Convention and of other rules of international law still retains its "innocent" character.

Members of the International Law Commission suggested a number of specific instances for inclusion in the definition of the innocence of passage. They proposed that the interests of the coastal state should be enumerated —health, customs and excise, immigration, etc.—for disregard of which the passage of a foreign ship would cease to be innocent. It is possible to regard the vagueness of the first part of Article 14 (4), particularly the use of the expression "good order", as covering such breaches of the rights of the coastal state, but in any case the remainder of Article 14 (4), and indeed the Convention as a whole, recognises the existence of rules of customary international law in areas not covered by the Convention.

---

13. While the provisions of the Convention exclude public vessels from the jurisdiction of the coastal state it would nevertheless seem possible that, under general international law, for an act flagrantly prejudicial to the security of the coastal state, jurisdiction could even be exercised over a foreign warship.

When the claims of the coastal state to exercise jurisdiction in the territorial sea are examined in more detail below, it will readily be seen that, in the last resort, any foreign ship passing through the territorial sea of a state is subject to that state's territorial jurisdiction. Whether the passage remains innocent or not within the terms of Article 14, the coastal state still retains the ultimate discretion to deal with breaches of its laws occurring within the territorial sea. If it does interfere with the passage of the foreign vessel responsible for such breaches, it may have to justify its conduct in relation to the extent of the infringements of its laws, but it would be a matter of academic nicety whether the passage of the foreign vessel could still be qualified as innocent. The jurisdictional rights of the coastal state under Article 19 are designed to cover situations where there has been a breach of the local law, but the coastal state's jurisdictional rights are not defined in relation to the innocence of the passage at all. It would be small consolation for a foreign ship-owner to learn that the passage had remained innocent if the coastal state had nevertheless rightfully detained the ship and fined the owner heavily for breach of the local laws!

Before leaving the question of access and dealing more specifically with the jurisdictional issues that arise, some comment is necessary on whether innocent passage may be exercised by warships. Innocent passage in Article 14 (1) is defined under a heading reading "Rules applicable to all ships" (although there is a heading entitled "Rules applicable to warships"), and relates to "ships of all states". The only limitations contained in the Convention are set out in Article 14 (6) to the effect that submarines exercising the right are to navigate on the surface and show their flag, and Article 23 which states that if "any warship does not comply with the regulations of the coastal state concerning passage through the territorial sea and disregards any request for compliance which is made to it, the coastal state may require the warship to leave the territorial sea."

However, it will be recalled from an illustration given in Chapter 1 of one of the difficulties of the codification process,[14] that there was considerable support among some states for a restriction being imposed on the right of foreign warships to proceed through the territorial waters of another state. Consequently the International Law Commission, which at its sixth session in 1954 had taken the view that passage should be granted to warships without prior authorisation or notification, felt obliged to amend its recommendations the following year. Consequently, the 1956 draft which was considered by the 1958 Conference provided that the coastal state "may make passage of warships through the territorial sea subject to previous authorisation or notification", though normally "it shall grant innocent passage" subject to the observance of the draft Articles 17 (dealing with the right of the coastal state to protect its security) and 18 (relating to compliance with local laws and regulations, particularly those dealing with navigation). Because of the failure to obtain the necessary

---

14. Above, p. 12.

two-thirds majority, draft Article 24 failed to be adopted, as also did a proposal to adopt the provision without the reference to "authorisation".

Although the Convention as finally adopted apparently allows warships of one state to exercise the right of innocent passage through the territorial waters of another, the position is not altogether clear. A number of Communist states made reservations to the Convention on this point. For example, the Soviet reservation to Article 23 was that it considered that "a coastal state has the right to establish procedures for the authorisation of the passage of foreign warships through its territorial waters". And the Government of Czechoslovakia deemed it necessary to stress that Articles 14 and 23 could not, in view of the failure by the Conference to adopt a special article dealing with the passage of warships, "in any sense be interpreted as establishing a right of innocent passage for warships through the territorial waters". In contrast, the United Kingdom maintains that the absence of such a provision has the effect of retaining, or even re-enforcing, the existing rule that warships have the right of innocent passage.

All that can be suggested by way of conclusion, therefore, is that the present position with regard to warships is uncertain. As a matter of courtesy most states would notify another state of the intended passage of one of its warships through the territorial waters of that other state. Although it is doubtful whether such a courtesy can be considered as establishing a rule of international law, it would obviously be a serious step for one state to send its warships, however peaceably, through the territorial seas of another state without seeking the authority of that state if that state demanded the right to allow only authorised warships through its territorial sea. Even if warships are normally accorded a right of innocent passage, it would be unlikely that the flag state would ignore a regulation made by the coastal state with reference to Article 23 of the Convention requiring conformity with some sort of authorisation or notification procedure.

ii *Jurisdiction*

1 *In criminal cases*

When dealing with the position of a ship in a foreign port, it was stated that the role granting exclusive jurisdiction of the flag state in matters of internal discipline was most likely a principle of comity rather than a rule of law. Even when a ship is exercising a right of innocent passage through territorial waters, it is uncertain how far the law of the coastal state is excluded over incidents occurring on board.

The 1958 Geneva Conference had before it the International Law Commission's draft articles in which it was provided that, except in cases where the effects of a crime extended beyond the vessel, a "coastal state may not take any steps on board a foreign ship passing through the territorial sea to arrest any person or to conduct any investigation". This provision amounted to an absolute prohibition on the exercise of jurisdiction unless the case fell within one of the specified exceptions, and was referred to by the leader of the British delegation to the Conference as accurately reflecting "the generally accepted view under international law as to the circumstances in which criminal jurisdiction could be exercised over passing vessels".[15]

The exceptions specified in the original draft, and adopted in the Convention were to the effect that the coastal state could clearly exercise jurisdiction:

> "(a) If the consequences of the crime extend to the coastal state; or
> (b) If the crime is of a kind to disturb the peace of the country or the good order of the territorial sea; or
> (c) If the assistance of the local authorities has been requested by the captain of the ship or by the consul of the country whose flag the ship flies."

The Committee of the Conference which considered the draft added a fourth exception which was adopted by the whole Conference and included as a new sub-paragraph: the coastal state could also exercise jurisdiction:

> "(d) If it is necessary for the suppression of illicit traffic in narcotic drugs."

However, a further alteration was made to the wording of the provision as a whole. The original recommendation of the International Law Commission was to have mandatory effect: the coastal state *may not* take any steps on board a foreign ship passing through the territorial sea except in the circumstances specified. However, the Committee amended this text to read, "the criminal jurisdiction of the coastal state should, generally, not be exercised on board a foreign ship passing through the territorial sea", subject to the specified exceptions. The alteration had been proposed by the United States because "the declaration in the Commission's text that 'A coastal state may not take any steps . . .' was a departure from the doctrine of international law that the coastal state had unlimited criminal jurisdiction within its territorial sea."[16] In the Plenary Session of the Conference, the word "generally" was omitted, but the retention of the expression "should not" instead of the original draft "may not" clearly emphasises the discretionary nature of the powers of the coastal state. In the exceptions specified it can clearly exercise criminal jurisdiction; and it can also do so in other situations, although the Convention and principles of international comity suggest that it should refrain from exercising jurisdiction.

The provision of the Geneva Convention relates to the exercise of criminal executive jurisdiction to arrest or to investigate; it is silent on the application of the criminal law and jurisdiction to events happening in the territorial sea. Once a person accused of having committed a crime on board a foreign ship in territorial waters is brought before a court of the coastal state, he would seem to have no protection from the application of

---

15. Fitzmaurice, Conference Official Records, Vol. III (First Committee), 38th Mtg., para. 31.
16. Dean, *ibid.*, 28th Mtg., para. 36.

the local law.[17] The British Territorial Waters Jurisdiction Act of 1878. the provisions of which were largely reproduced throughout the territories of the former British Empire, extended the jurisdiction of the English (or the appropriate local) Courts over all indictable offences committed within three miles of the coast, subject to the sole restriction that, where the accused is an alien, proceedings shall not be instituted without the comment of "one of Her Majesty's Principal Secretaries of State". And as far as the United States is concerned, the case of *Cunard Steamship Co.* v. *Mellon*[18] provides ample evidence of the dangers of the concurrent application of two different systems of law. A number of shipping companies sought a ruling from the Supreme Court that the Prohibition Act did not apply to intoxicants normally served on board passenger ships, particularly if serving was suspended during the time these vessels were in American waters. A majority of the judges held, however, that the territory subject to a state's jurisdiction included its territorial waters in addition to its ports, bays and other internal waters, and that, in the absence of any restrictive provision in the Act, it would apply even to the transportation of liquor by foreign ships as part of their normal stores.

In both English and American law, the application of municipal legislation will take precedence over a limiting rule of international law and over any principle of international comity.[19] The only defence available to the person accused in such circumstances would be to argue that the particular statute was not intended to impinge upon the jurisdiction of the flag state. The rejection of this argument in the *Cunard* case led to a series of diplomatic protests by a number of states, including the United Kingdom. But the weakness of the position of the protesting states was the fact that their argument was based upon a rule of comity and not of international law. The British protest admitted that it did not "deny the strictly legal right of the United States or any other country to impose its jurisdiction on all ships, whether national or foreign, within territorial waters. His Majesty's Government themselves claim that right and it is even the case that some of the provisions of the British Merchant Shipping Acts are such that ships visiting in the United Kingdom must comply with them before and after leaving the jurisdiction. These provisions, however, relate solely to the safety and welfare of the ship, crew and passengers. Similar provisions exist in the legislation of the United States and other countries and they are generally recognised as reasonable."[20]

It is unfortunate that the principle of comity has yet to crystallise into a rule of international law that would clearly delimit the jurisdiction of the

17. In fact it would seem to be a rule of the common law that even if an arrest is wrongful according to international law (for example, if it took place on foreign territory), such a consideration is irrelevant to the exercise of jurisdiction by an English or American Court once the accused is physically before the court: *Ex parte Susannah Scott* (1829), 9 B. & C. 446; *Ker* v. *Illinois*, 119 U.S. 436 (1886). See generally (1960) 36 B.Y.B.I.L. 279; and in relation to the *Eichmann* case (1962), 38 B.Y.B.I.L. 181, at pp. 193–202.

18. 262 U.S. 100 (1923).   19. See above at pp. 50–51 and p. 58.

20. U.S. For. Rel., 1923, Vol. 1, p. 133. And see Lord Curzon's statement in the House of Lords on 28th June, 1923: cited Hackworth: *Digest of International Law*, Vol. 1, p. 677.

coastal and the flag state in such circumstances. However, states are reluctant to abandon their rights over their territorial waters, and are not prepared to accept any prohibition in precise terms on their power to legislate for and control passing shipping.

2   *In civil cases*

The position with regard to civil jurisdiction also is not free from uncertainty. Article 20 (1) of the 1958 Convention is probably an accurate statement of the law as far as individuals on board ship are concerned in providing that the "coastal state should not stop or divert a foreign ship passing through the territorial sea for the purposes of exercising civil jurisdiction in relation to a person on board the ship." However, the rest of the Article is more controversial. Paragraph (2) provides that if a vessel is in passage through territorial waters, it may only be arrested or diverted as a result of liabilities arising whilst passing through such waters; only if the vessel stops, or enters internal waters, can a right of arrest be exercised under paragraph (3) as a result of *any* civil proceedings against that vessel.

The rule set out in these last two paragraphs is certainly contrary to the decision of the U.S.–Panama General Claims Commission in the *David*.[1] This ship, belonging to a Panamanian company, had been arrested by American authorities whilst passing through the territorial waters of the Canal Zone in proceedings arising out of a collision between the *David* and another vessel two years earlier. In upholding the validity of the seizure, the Commission commented:[2]

> "The general rule of the extension of sovereignty over the three mile zone is clearly established. Exceptions to the completeness of this sovereignty should be supported by clear authority.... There is no clear ... authority to the effect that ... vessels when passing through territorial waters are exempt from civil arrest. In the absence of such authority, the Commission cannot say that a country may not, under the rules of international law, assert the right to arrest on civil process merchant ships passing through its territorial waters."

This decision has been criticised, and in view of subsequent contrary conventional rules, it is doubtful whether it can now be regarded as good authority. For more than 60 years the English Courts had jurisdiction under s. 688 of the Merchant Shipping Act, 1894, to hear suits *in rem* against foreign vessels within territorial waters if they had caused damage anywhere to British property. With the repeal of this provision by the Administration of Justice Act, 1956, designed to enable the United Kingdom to comply with the provisions of the 1952 Brussels *Convention on the Arrest of Sea-going Ships*, there remained no statutory rule allowing the arrest of a foreign ship in British territorial waters. In this respect, therefore, English law was already in accordance with the provisions adopted at

---

1.   (1933), 6 U.N.R.I.A.A. 382; (1933–4), 7 A.D., Case No. 52.
2.   6 U.N.R.I.A.A., at p. 384.

Geneva in Article 20 of the Territorial Sea Convention, and no further amendment was necessary to enable the United Kingdom to ratify the Convention.

As has already been pointed out, one significant difference between civil and criminal jurisdiction is that, whereas a municipal court, once it takes cognisance of a criminal matter, will apply its own criminal law, if it is faced with a civil suit, it may have to consider a choice of law issue. That is, if the case involves some foreign element, its own municipal rules of private international law might regard some other system of law as being more appropriate to decide the issues involved. For example, under English rules of private international law, the case of *Phillips* v. *Eyre*[3] decided that to be actionable in tort an act must be both unlawful by the law of the place where the act occurred, and "actionable" under English law. In part, at least, a plaintiff's action for an alleged injury occurring outside the territorial jurisdiction of the English Courts will depend upon the application of a system of law other than English law. And in American jurisdictions, i.e. under the law of the American states, the primary reference would be to the law of the place where the alleged wrongful act happened.[4]

There is no doubt that in the case of an incident on the high seas, English and American Courts would apply what they believed to be general principles of maritime law.[5] But what is the appropriate law for events taking place in territorial waters? If two foreign vessels were to collide in the territorial waters of state X, the appropriate law would be that of state X. But if a member of the crew of a ship was injured as the result of some purely internal accident on board while the vessel was passing through the territorial waters of state X, there would seem to be room for doubt whether the law of state X or the law of the flag should apply.

In *Mackinnon* v. *Iberia Shipping Co.*,[6] a member of the crew of a British ship registered in Scotland was killed while engaged in engine room repairs at a time when the vessel was within the territorial waters of the Dominican Republic. The Scottish Court of Session saw the absurdity of events on board a ship proceeding along a coast line and passing through

---

3. (1870), L.R. 6 Q.B. 1. The statement in the text is something of a simplification: see generally Cheshire, *Private International Law*, 7th ed., pp. 240–52.

4. The present trend in the United States is for the choice of law rules to favour the place where the wrong occurred, unless the incident has only a casual connection with that place and has a more obvious connection with the law of the forum. Thus, it is stated in the 1964 edition of Goodrich's *Handbook of the Conflict of Laws* (at p. 165) that, according to the general rule, "the forum will be guided in the determination of the existence and extent of tort liability by the law of the place which is most significantly related to the occurrence or issue before the court." The place that is "most significantly related" to the occurrence is defined (at p. 168) as, in most cases, the place of wrong; but in cases in which the facts are related to several states "one state will normally appear as the most concerned", and if the contacts are "evenly balanced between the forum and another state, the forum law will generally be controlling."

5. *Chartered Mercantile Bank of India* v. *Netherlands India S.N. Co.* (1883), 10 Q.B.D. 521, esp. at p. 537. *The Belgenland*, 114 U.S. 355 (1885).

6. [1954] 2 Lloyd's Rep. 372; 21 I.L.R. 126.

the territorial waters of a number of states coming under successively different legal régimes, and the merit of the argument that in matters internal to the ship the law of the flag alone should apply. However, it was the Court's opinion that the issue was already settled in favour of the view that the law of the place where the incident occurred in such circumstances was the law of the coastal state. It made no difference "whether the vessel was navigating or at anchor, in a roadstead or tied up to a quay, and also, what is equally clear, whether the events founded on as the basis of the delict . . . are wholly internal to the vessel, or partly external to it as in the case of a collision between vessels in territorial waters".[7]

The American Courts, on the other hand, have rejected the application of the law of the coastal state where the effects of the occurrence are limited to the ship itself. In *Lauritzen* v. *Larsen*,[8] the Supreme Court had to consider a suit brought by a Danish seaman against the Danish owner of a Danish ship. The plaintiff had joined the ship's crew in New York, and had been injured while serving on board when the ship was in Cuban internal waters. The Court held that the law of the place where the wrong occurred was only of limited assistance in maritime torts. In this case the law most closely related to the incident was clearly Danish law as the law of the flag.

d STRAITS

Passage through straits will only give rise to special problems if the strait falls entirely within the territorial waters of the state or states bordering on it, or if, though it is wide enough to include an area of high seas through the middle, the deep water channel necessitates larger vessels proceeding through the territorial waters of the states adjacent to the strait. In essence, the problems involve special applications of the principles relating to territorial waters, or, where the strait is narrow enough and bordered by a single state, to national waters.

According to Article 16 (4) of the Territorial Sea Convention, there "shall be no suspension of the innocent passage of foreign ships through straits which are used for international navigation between one part of the high seas and another part of the high seas or the territorial sea of a foreign state". Thus it is clear that for the right of innocent passage to exist, whether through internal or territorial waters, the strait must form part of a route used by international shipping. A flag state cannot assert the rights available to ships passing through an international strait if the strait is not normally used as a shipping lane at all. However, as Lauterpacht has commented in the context of the *Corfu Channel* case, "it is irrelevant that the strait is not a necessary but only an alternative route. . . . It is sufficient that it has been a useful route for international maritime traffic."[9]

The additional qualification in Article 16 (4) that the strait should connect either two areas of high seas, or connect the high seas with the territorial

---

7. [1954] 2 Lloyd's Rep., at p. 375.   8.   345 U.S. 571 (1953).
9. Oppenheim, *International Law*, Vol. 1, 8th ed., at p. 512.

sea of a foreign state has not been accepted without controversy. All states were prepared to accept a definition of a strait based upon the notion that it should connect two areas of high seas, but Arab states in particular contested the application of innocent passage to straits giving access to the high seas only at one end. Their reluctance to accept a wider definition was based on their dispute with Israel over use of the Straits of Tiran. In a simplified form, their argument was that the Straits gave access from the Red Sea to the territorial waters of Egypt and Saudi Arabia in the Gulf of Aquaba so that the straits could not be considered as an international strait through which vessels not of the coastal states had a right of passage under customary international law.

There are two main advantages to the flag state is its relations with the coastal state of being able to show that the waters are part of an international strait.

In the first place, Article 16 (3) allows the coastal state to "suspend temporarily in specified areas of its territorial sea the innocent passage of foreign ships if such suspension is essential for the protection of its security", but, as stated above, paragraph (4) excludes the application of (3) to "straits which are used for international navigation".

Secondly, whatever doubts exist about the right of innocent passage for warships through the territorial sea of another state, this right clearly exists if the territorial sea forms part of an international strait. The authority for this proposition is the decision of the International Court in the *Corfu Channel* case.[10] In October, 1946, two British naval vessels were heavily damaged by mines while asserting a right of passage through the North Corfu Channel. The Court held, *inter alia*, that it was "generally recognised and in accordance with international custom that states in time of peace have a right to send their warships through straits used for international navigation between two parts of the high seas without the previous authorisation of a coastal state, provided that the passage is *innocent*."[11] In this case, the mission did not lose its innocent nature because it was "designed to affirm a right that had been unjustly denied".[12]

e CONTIGUOUS ZONES

The territorial jurisdiction of a state, though not its sovereignty, is given a further artificial extension by the notion of a Contiguous Zone. According to Article 24 (1) of the Territorial Sea Convention, in a "zone of the high seas contiguous to its territorial sea, the coastal state may exercise the control necessary to:

(a) Prevent infringement of its customs, fiscal, immigration or sanitary regulations within its territory or territorial sea;
(b) Punish infringement of the above regulations committed within its territory or territorial sea."

---

10. I.C.J. Rep. 1949, p. 4.   11. *Ibid.*, at p. 28.   12. *Ibid.*, at p. 30.

The Convention does not determine the precise extent of this zone directly, though in effect sets it at twelve miles by laying down in Article 24 (2) that it shall not "extend beyond twelve miles from the base-line from which the breadth of the territorial sea is measured".

During the eighteenth and early nineteenth centuries, a series of Hovering Acts extended British revenue jurisdiction over foreign vessels originally to a distance of two leagues from the coast, later to four, and, during the Napoleonic Wars, to eight leagues. Although this trend was halted, and largely fell into desuetude, during the later part of the nineteenth century, claims to extended jurisdictional rights became common again in the present century. Hackworth[13] cited a number of legislative provisions from France, Egypt, Estonia and the Scandinavian states which allow customs supervision at various distances from the coast-line. However, although in the case of *Croft* v. *Dumphy*[14] in 1933, Lord MacMillan reaffirmed the existence of such a zone, explaining that "whatever be the limits of territorial waters in the international sense, it has long been recognised that for certain purposes, notably those of police, revenue, public health and fisheries, a state may enact laws affecting the seas surrounding its coasts to a distance seaward which exceeds the ordinary limits of its territory", his statement was not in accord with the contemporary practice of states. It was clearly inaccurate with regard to fishing, for only very recently have attempts to restrict fishing by foreign vessels outside the three-mile limit of territorial waters, but within twelve miles of the base-line, whether by means of a special fishing zone, or by the extension of territorial waters themselves, shown signs of more general acceptance. Nor was the existence of a contiguous zone for other purposes beyond dispute. When the United States wished to enforce the Prohibition Act by measures taken outside territorial waters, it proceeded by way of international agreement, the most notable being the Convention signed in 1924 with Great Britain. And in protesting to the American Secretary of State against the wide jurisdictional rights provided for in an Anti-Smuggling Bill being considered by the American Senate in 1935, the British Ambassador asserted the view of His Majesty's Government that under international law a country had no right to interfere with foreign ships outside the limits of territorial waters except insofar as such a right had been granted by treaty.[15]

Whatever doubts there may be with regard to the existence of a contiguous zone prior to the Second World War, it is a concept which has rapidly been accepted. It is interesting to contrast with the 1935 protest by the United Kingdom Government a statement made in the House of Commons by a government spokesman in 1956 that "Her Majesty's Government are prepared to recognise jurisdiction for customs, fiscal and sanitary purposes only, in a contiguous zone bounded by a line not more

---

13.   *Digest*, Vol. 1, pp. 663–4.
14.   [1933] A.C. 156, at p. 162; (1931–2) 6 A.D., Case No. 82.
15.   Whiteman, *Digest of International Law*, Vol. 4, pp. 490–1.

than twelve miles from the coast, in association with territorial waters of not more than three miles' breadth."[16] Article 24 of the 1958 Convention was only spelling out in precise terms the extent of a state's jurisdiction that had already been generally accepted by the international maritime community.

Although the attempt was made at Geneva in 1958 and again in 1960 either to define territorial waters to include a separate "fishing zone" or to include fishing as one of the matters covered by Article 24, there is in fact a striking difference between the extensions of jurisdiction with regard to fisheries envisaged by the Geneva Conference, or subsequently claimed by an increasing number of states, and the type of jurisdiction within the Contiguous Zone allowed under Article 24. The recent claims and agreements by states to exclude foreign fishing vessels from operating within twelve miles of their coasts is a jurisdiction to prescribe rules for the area in question and to enforce those rules. On the other hand, Article 24 makes it clear that jurisdiction in relation to a state's customs, fiscal, immigration or sanitary regulations is essentially "protective" in nature. It is expressly limited to exercising the control necessary to prevent and punish infringements taking place within its territory or territorial sea. The article does not enable a state to make regulations applicable to conduct in the contiguous zone alone and to exercise jurisdiction for breach of those regulations. Until such time as a general consensus is reached amongst states on an extension of territorial waters to twelve miles, the zones between the outward limits of territorial waters and twelve miles from the base-lines from which territorial waters are measured must be considered as part of the high seas subject to whatever accommodations states may make along the lines of Article 24 or in relation to fishing rights.[17]

f CONSTRUCTIVE PRESENCE AND HOT PURSUIT

Before dealing with jurisdiction on the high seas *simpliciter*, it is convenient at this stage to consider two notional extensions of a state's jurisdictional rights within its territorial sea and contiguous zones. Although the concept of constructive presence and the doctrine of hot pursuit allow a state to effect a seizure of a foreign vessel on the high seas, they are logically part of its jurisdiction over events occurring within its marginal seas.

i *Constructive presence*

This concept is basically simple. If a vessel, though anchored or in passage outside territorial waters, uses its own ship's boats to break the laws of the coastal state inside that state's territorial waters, the offending ship may be seized as if it were itself inside those waters. The scope of application of this

---

16.   554 H.C. Deb., col. 64: cited Whiteman, *op. cit.*, vol. 4, p. 493.

17.   Although the area of water, or "zone", is the same for both "protective" and exclusive fishing purposes (i.e. the belt of water between the outer limit of the territorial sea and twelve miles from the baseline of territorial waters), for jurisdictional purposes it is obviously more accurate to refer to "zones" in the plural, and perhaps more helpful to consider both as "contiguous zones" in view of their physical proximity to the coastal state.

principle has been reduced by the provisions of Article 24 of the Territorial Sea Convention which allows the coastal state to exercise control in a contiguous zone to prevent or punish infringements of its customs, fiscal, immigration or sanitary regulations. However, constructive presence might still be of importance if a foreign vessel stationed itself outside the contiguous zone and then sent ashore illegal immigrants in a ship's boat, or if ship's boats were to engage in illegal fishing in the waters of the coastal state while the foreign vessel itself remained outside the fishing zone.

The concept of constructive presence is well illustrated by the incident of the *Araunah*[18] in 1888. This Canadian ship was seized by Russian authorities on the ground that members of the crew had been catching seals from open boats about half a mile off the Russian coast. It was acknowledged by the British Government that even "if the *Araunah* at the time of her seizure was herself outside the three mile territorial limit, the fact that she was, by means of her boats, carrying on fishing within Russian waters without the prescribed licence warranted her seizure and confiscation".

On the other hand, the better view is that the doctrine of constructive presence does not apply to a situation where a foreign vessel, lying outside the waters over which the coastal state is entitled to exercise jurisdictional control, is assisted by boats sent out from the shore. In the case of the *Sito*,[19] a British ship transhipped contraband to an Italian vessel outside the Italian twelve-mile customs zone. The Italian Court of Cassation ordered the release of members of the *Sito*'s crew on the ground that, under international law, a state cannot exercise jurisdiction over a foreign vessel on the high seas, save in the exceptional case of hot pursuit, which could not be established in the case of the *Sito* which had never entered Italian waters.

ii *Hot pursuit*

Under the doctrine of hot pursuit the authorities of a coastal state may pursue a foreign vessel which they have good reason to believe has violated the laws and regulations of the state from the waters over which by international law they are entitled to exercise jurisdictional rights, and may seize the vessel on the high seas. However, while this description defines in general terms the nature of the doctrine, there are a number of aspects of the description which require more detailed examination.

1 *Breach of the local law*

Article 23 (1) of the 1958 Convention on the High Seas requires that the authorities of the coastal state should have "good reasons to believe that the ship has violated the laws and regulations of that state" before exercising the right of hot pursuit. In many cases, a coastal state will "act on suspicion" rather than on conclusive evidence of infringements of its laws by the foreign ship concerned. If suspicions of the coastal authorities prove

---

18. Moore, *Digest of International Law*, Vol. 1, p. 908.
19. Case decided in 1957; reported in English in (1962) *Clunet*, Vol. 89, p. 229. The decision is in accord with Art. 23 (1) of the High Seas Convention; but cp. the wider wording of Art. 23 (3) in this context.

unfounded, Article 23 (7) restates an obvious principle of customary international law that the foreign vessel should be compensated for any loss or damage that it might have suffered. Presumably compensation would also be payable if the foreign vessel suffered "loss or damage" in escaping from an unjustifiable pursuit.

One issue that the Convention does not consider is whether any breach of the local law would be sufficient to justify hot pursuit. Common sense suggests that hot pursuit should be limited to acts of some seriousness, such as smuggling or the deliberate flouting of immigration laws. It would be unthinkable to allow pursuit and capture on the high seas for some trivial error of navigational regulations or documentation procedure. Support for this proposition may perhaps be found in the case of the *I'm Alone*, which is considered below in more detail. This case does suggest that the sinking of a foreign ship for liquor smuggling may be excessive: in other words, the degree of force used should be commensurate with the crime. If this principle can be accepted, it would follow that, in the case of a trivial offence against the local law, any attempt to effect the arrest of a foreign ship on the high seas would be illegal.

2 *From the waters of the coastal state*

Under Article 23 (1) of the Convention, the pursuit "must be commenced when the foreign ship or one of its boats is within the internal waters or the territorial sea or the contiguous zone of the pursuing state", and if the pursuit relates to the presence of the foreign ship within the contiguous zone, it "may only be undertaken if there has been a violation of the rights for the protection of which the zone was established".

3 *The carrying out of the pursuit*

Article 23 of the High Seas Convention lays down a number of principles governing the commencement of the pursuit. Under paragraph (1), it is "not necessary that, at the time when the foreign ship within the territorial sea or the contiguous zone receives the order to stop, the ship giving the order should likewise be within the territorial sea or the contiguous zone". Paragraph (3) provides that hot pursuit is not "deemed to have begun unless the pursuing ship has satisfied itself by such practicable means as may be available that the ship pursued or one of its boats or other craft working as a team and using the ship pursued as a mother ship are within the limits of the territorial sea, or as the case may be within the contiguous zone"; and that the pursuit "may only be commenced after a visual or auditory signal to stop has been given at a distance which enables it to be seen or heard by the foreign ship."

This latter paragraph, however, is not without its problems. First, at the Geneva Conference there was controversy over the methods that could be used for verifying the position of the suspected vessel. The United States was anxious to evolve a formula that would permit the use of the most modern methods of navigation. Although this idea was opposed by both the Soviet Union and the United Kingdom, the latter in particular doubting the reliability of electronic devices in rough weather, the text eventually adopted in this paragraph is wide enough to include all types of navigational aid. The second difficulty does not appear to have troubled the Conference unduly, and that is the stipulated requirement that the pursuing ship should, before the pursuit may be commenced, have given the foreign vessel a visual or auditory signal to stop at a distance which enables it to be seen or heard by that vessel. It is implicit in this provision that no right of hot pursuit may be exercised against a foreign vessel which, as soon as it realises that an unidentified ship is approaching, flees from the "scene of the crime". Such a rule appears unrealistic, and not entirely in keeping with previous practice.

In the *Newton Bay*,[20] a United States Circuit Court of Appeals had to consider whether the seizure of this British vessel by the U.S. coast guard cutter, the *Gresham*, was legitimate in view of the fact that no signal had been given until the *Newton Bay* had reached a position outside the twelve-mile zone established by the United States Tariff Act, and agreed to by the United Kingdom in the 1924 Treaty between the two states.[1] The *Gresham* had seen the *Newton Bay* showing anchor lights about eight and a half miles from the nearest land. As soon as the *Newton Bay* had become aware of the approach of the *Gresham*, it had proceeded on an erratic course into the gathering darkness to shake off the pursuing vessel. Eventually the *Gresham* got close enough to fire blank shots and bring the *Newton Bay* to a stop, but by this time the vessels were thirteen miles from the coast. The Court was of opinion that the absence of a signal to stop by the *Gresham* was irrelevant for two reasons. In the first place, it was impracticable, "for the very good reason" that the *Gresham* was unable always to see or apprehend the *Newton Bay* while it was "dodging in the darkness": as a "practical matter" it would have been "useless to signal by a blast or horn, or by firing shots when the vessel was attempting to escape". Secondly, the action of the *Newton Bay* in attempting to escape was "clear enough evidence" that the master and the crew knew that they were being pursued for breaches of the laws of the United States since the vessel had come to anchor within the twelve-mile limit with a forbidden cargo. Although based upon an American view of the doctrine, the common sense of the Court's ruling has much to commend it. It would be unsatisfactory if a coastal state's acts were considered contrary to international law simply because the offending vessel, fully aware of its own transgressions of the

---

20.   36 F. (2d) 729 (1929).
    1.   There was in fact a discrepancy between the Act which created a twelve-mile juris-dictional zone and the Treaty which allowed the United States to interfere with suspected British vessels within one hour's sailing distance of the coast. In the *Newton Bay* the conse-quences of the difference between a twelve-mile limit and a limit of one hour's sailing distance was not in issue: the court dealt with the case on the basis of the twelve miles laid down in the Act. However, in certain cases, the difference could be vital. In the case of a ship only able to travel ten miles in an hour (*Cook* v. *U.S.* 288 U.S. 102 (1933)) the Supreme Court held that the Treaty, being self-executing, took precedence over the Act and limited the jurisdictional competence of the American Courts: the seizure of the offending vessel eleven and a half miles from the coast was therefore illegal.

local law, made off before the pursuing vessels got within hailing or signalling distance.

The Convention envisages that the right of hot pursuit may be exercised by ships or aircraft, but they must be "warships or military aircraft,
or other ships or aircraft on governmental service specially authorised"
(Article 23 (4)). Some doubts exist whether the pursuit must be undertaken
throughout by the same vessel or vessels. Provided that the pursuit is continuous by one vessel or another, it would not be improper for a warship of
the coastal state joining the pursuit at a later stage to effect the arrest. In its
commentary to the 1956 draft articles, the International Law Commission
stated that the vessel "finally arresting the ship pursued need not necessarily be the same as the one which began the pursuit, provided that it has
joined in the pursuit and has not merely effected an interception."[2] No
provision along these lines appeared in the draft or in the final Convention,
although Article 23 (5)(b) did lay down a special rule for aircraft. "The
aircraft giving the order to stop must itself actively pursue the ship until a
ship or aircraft of the coastal state, summoned by the aircraft, arrives to
take over the pursuit, unless the aircraft is itself able to arrest the ship. It
does not suffice to justify an arrest on the high seas that the ship was merely
sighted by the aircraft as an offender or suspected offender, if it was not
both ordered to stop and pursued by the aircraft itself or other aircraft or
ships which continue the pursuit without interruption."

4   *The seizure*

Article 23 (2) of the Convention is probably declaratory of existing
customary international law in providing that the right of hot pursuit
ceases "as soon as the ship pursued enters the territorial sea of its own
country or of a third state".

The leading authority for the proposition that a seizure is illegal if it
follows entry into the territorial waters of the state the flag of which
the apprehended vessel is flying is the case of the *Itata*.[3] This Chilean
vessel was suspected of being in breach of United States neutrality laws. It
was pursued by American cruisers into Chilean territorial waters before
surrendering. An arbitral tribunal held the capture contrary to international law. Although this decision has been widely cited as an illustration
of the limitations upon the doctrine of hot pursuit, it is doubtful whether
the tribunal considered the doctrine as relevant. It is not entirely certain
whether there had in fact been a breach of United States neutrality laws,
nor whether the actual pursuit by the cruiser commenced in circumstances
to which the doctrine would apply. However, the actual decision by the
tribunal was based on the broader ground that any seizure in the territory
or within the territorial waters of another state is contrary to international
law.

The *Itata* is relevant to the doctrine of hot pursuit in that, once it is

---

2.   Year Book of the I.L.C., 1956, Vol. II, p. 285.
3.   Moore, *Digest*, Vol. 2, p. 985.

established that any seizure in foreign territory is contrary to international law, it is also true to say that a seizure on the basis of hot pursuit in the territorial waters of another state (whether of the state to which the offending vessel belongs, or of a third state) would be contrary to international law. As it would similarly be inconsistent with the sovereignty of that other state for the pursuit to be continued through its territorial waters, the rule laid down in Article 23 (2) is both reasonable and in accord with the practice of states.

The most frequently cited, and at the same time, the least satisfactory, arbitration arising out of the right of hot pursuit was the incident of the *I'm Alone*.[4] This ship, registered in Canada and flying a British flag, had been engaged in smuggling liquor into the United States. It was sighted and pursued by the coast guard cutter *Wolcott*, from a position which the United States alleged was just over eight miles from the coast, but which the Canadian authorities claimed was over fourteen miles distant. Under the 1924 agreement between the United States and Great Britain, the United States was granted the right to exercise jurisdiction over liquor smuggling within one hour's sailing distance from the base-lines of territorial waters. The pursuit was subsequently joined and taken over by another cutter, the *Dexter*, which eventually caught up with the *I'm Alone*. The *Dexter* warned the vessel to stop and, when this call was ignored, fired at, and sank, the *I'm Alone*.

The incident clearly raised a number of issues. Did the right of hot pursuit exist in extension of the rights conferred upon the United States under the treaty? It was plausibly argued on behalf of the United States that, if the treaty created a right of arrest which would have been validly exercised had the *I'm Alone* not fled from the zone created by the treaty, it would render ineffective many of the treaty's provisions if a right of hot pursuit were not automatically assumed to exist for prevention of breaches of those provisions. Could the pursuit be joined and taken over by a vessel of the coastal state other than the one involved at the outset? Provided the pursuit was continuous enough to satisfy the notion of "hot" pursuit, there seemed no major obstacle to such a procedure. And, once the pursuing ship or ships had caught up with the offending vessel in what way could they legitimately effect an arrest? It was on this issue alone that the Commissioners decided the case. Even if a right of hot pursuit did exist (that is, if they accepted the American statement of the facts on the position of the *I'm Alone* at the start of the chase, and the American view of the law on the existence of a right of hot pursuit under the treaty), it could not justify the degree of force used against the *I'm Alone*.

This finding by the Commissioners, however, does not make clear what they would have considered to be a justifiable use of force. They held that the deliberate firing at, and sinking of, the *I'm Alone* could not be justified either under the 1924 Convention or under general international

---

4. (1935), 3 U.N.R.I.A.A. 1609.

law. But they gave no explanation of what powers the pursuing vessel had to arrest the offending vessel if it failed to stop when hailed. It is unrealistic to talk in terms of reasonable force if, *as a last resort*, the pursuer cannot fire at the offending vessel. It is clear that the *Dexter* should at least have interposed a shot across the bows, before aiming to hit the *I'm Alone*. But when faced with a choice between allowing the offender to escape and making the pursuit effective, the pursuer should be able to fire at the vessel it is pursuing. If all else has failed, and so far as accuracy of aim permits, the pursuer would be within its rights to take its warnings to the extent of firing at the offending vessel. However, and this additional factor is one that has already been mentioned, the authorities of the coastal state are acting at their peril. If their suspicions are unfounded, they will be under a duty to make reparation. In deciding to take the final course of firing at the pursued vessel, it would be important for the authorities of the coastal state to reconsider carefully their certainty of the guilt of the pursued vessel, and whether the offence which they believe it has committed justifies its seizure on the high seas.

B. Jurisdiction on the high seas

The fifteenth century saw the culmination of the attempts of a number of states to claim sovereignty over various parts of the high seas. The northern seas, mainly the Baltic, were claimed by Denmark and Sweden, whilst trading in the Mediterranean had for long been the monopoly of the fleets of the Italian municipalities. For several centuries, England had regarded the western approaches, the English Channel and parts of the North Sea as being subject to English control, and all foreign vessels in these waters were expected to salute the English flag. Towards the end of the century, a series of Papal Bulls purported to grant large areas of the newly discovered central America to Spain and Portugal together with a monopoly of trade and the trading routes.

While continuing to demand and to try to enforce English pre-eminence in the shallow seas, successive Tudor monarchs preached the doctrine of freedom of the seas in their relations with Spain and Portugal and later, at the end of her reign, Elizabeth contested Danish claims in the northern seas. Indeed, this contradiction in British policy lasted another two centuries. Britain continued to expect acknowledgment of her maritime supremacy throughout the Stuart period, and, despite increasing opposition from other powers, this claim was not discarded until the beginning of the last century.

However, by the end of the Napoleonic Wars, the doctrine of the freedom of the seas had become firmly established; and the main controversy then centred on a state's jurisdictional rights within the waters immediately adjoining its coast-line. Nevertheless a number of problems relating to the high seas remained unsettled, though only in the present century have these ill-defined issues, together with a number of totally novel situations, assumed any great importance. What, then, are the major controversies of contemporary maritime law?

Among the more obvious, the following must be dealt with: the change from steam to other forms of propulsion, and the increase in world shipping, have brought with them the hazards of oil pollution; areas of the high seas have been declared prohibited to all vessels because of the need of certain states or groups of states to carry out naval manœuvres, or to test nuclear or other weapons; on one occasion the historic right of self-defence has been invoked for the stopping of foreign merchant ships on the high seas—the so-called Cuban Quarantine of 1962; while the whole issue of pacific blockade has been raised by the embargo on tankers carrying oil for Rhodesia imposed under the authority of the Security Council; and, in a politically less vital incident, the year 1961 saw an act of something akin to piracy on the high seas. However, perhaps of the greatest importance has been the gradual realisation by states that the resources of the sea, if left at the mercy of unrestricted exploitation, could eventually be exhausted. An increasing number of states have felt obliged to attempt to establish exclusive fishing rights in a contiguous zone around their shores. But even this step is only a partial answer to the problem. Such rights will be of limited value to the coastal state if measures are not taken to preserve existing stocks of fish from uncontrolled exploitation by fishing fleets operating on the high seas.

a THE STATUS OF THE HIGH SEAS

The second Geneva Convention of 1958, the High Seas Convention, defined the "high seas" as "all parts of the sea that are not included in the territorial sea or the internal waters of a state", thus making it clear that, subject to certain limited rights over contiguous zones and the continental shelf, the coastal state has no powers of restricting the enjoyment by other states of navigation, whether by sea or air, or of fishing, outside its territorial waters. This freedom of the seas is not absolute: Article 2 of the Convention accepts that it must be exercised subject to the provisions of the Convention and to other rules of international law, and with reasonable regard to the interests of other states in their exercise of the freedom of the high seas. As the High Seas Convention itself does not "spell out" in detail how "reasonable regard to the interests of other states" might limit the traditional notion of unrestricted freedom of the high seas, it is necessary to examine the extent to which increasing claims to the use of the high seas by states may have brought about modifications in the relevant rules of international law.

i *Pollution*

1   *Oil pollution*

Article 24 of the High Seas Convention requires states to "draw up regulations to prevent pollution of the seas by the discharge of oil from ships or pipelines or resulting from the exploitation and exploration of the seabed and its subsoil, taking account of existing treaty provisions on the subject." The reason for the general nature of this provision was the fact that there was already in existence a 1954 Convention for the Prevention of Pollution of the Sea by Oil.[5] Although the number of states becoming parties to this Convention increased only gradually, the main defects of the Convention were first that certain vessels were not covered at all (naval auxiliaries, ships under 500 gross tons in weight, and whaling vessels), secondly that the prohibition on the discharge of oil only applied within certain zones delimited in the Convention (mainly 50 miles from land, although the distance was increased to 100 miles for most of the North Sea, and to 150 miles off all but a limited stretch of the Australian coast), and thirdly that the duty to enforce the Convention rested with the flag state, other contracting states only having a right to bring evidence of breaches to the attention of the flag state.

A subsequent Convention of 1962 drawn up under the auspices of I.M.C.O., and designed to prevent the discharge of oil anywhere at sea has had but a limited acceptance by states. However, while the two Conventions were primarily concerned with the discharge of oil as part of the normal processes of sea travel, and in fact, expressly exempted discharge in cases of necessity, the building of so-called "super-tankers" of up to 200,000 gross tons has created a new hazard. If one of these vessels were to run aground and be obliged to discharge its cargo in an attempt to refloat, the consequential oil pollution could be catastrophic.

The dangers were illustrated in the most dramatic manner with the stranding of the Liberian tanker *Torrey Canyon* of 61,000 gross tons off the south-west coast of England in March, 1967. In an attempt to prevent the worst excesses of pollution along the south-west coast of England caused by the oil released from the ship as it broke up, the United Kingdom Government ordered the bombing of the stranded vessel. The justification for the British action is the concept of self-preservation which is a wider application of the right of self-defence. It is universally recognised that a state can act in self-defence in cases of "instant and overwhelming necessity . . . leaving no choice of means, and no moment of deliberation",[6] and there is support for the application of a similar doctrine to situations in which a state is not acting to protect itself from the imminent danger of attack but from some other evil.

In the case of the *Neptune*,[7] an Arbitral Commission had to consider the validity of the seizure of this American vessel, bound for a French port with provisions, by a British frigate. The British Government requisitioned the cargo, allowing a ten per cent profit, which was far below the price that could have been obtained on the open market in London or in France. One of the grounds upon which the British Government justified its action was the great scarcity of food in Britain as a result of the war with France. The Commission rejected this argument on the ground that, as

5. 327 U.N.T.S. 4.
6. The *Caroline* case (1837), Moore, *Digest of International Law*, Vol. 2, at p. 412.
7. Moore, *International Arbitrations*, Vol. 4, p. 3843.

the offering of a bounty on corn helped relieve the shortage a few months later, the necessity of the seizure of the *Neptune's* cargo had not been established. However, the opinion of one of the Commissioners on the existence of a right to act in self-preservation is regarded as correctly stating the law. In his view, the "necessity which can be admitted to supersede all laws and to dissolve the distinctions of property and right must be absolute and irresistible, and we cannot, until all other means of self-preservation shall have been exhausted, justify by the plea of necessity the seizure and application to our own use of that which belongs to others."

Whether the bombing of the stranded *Torrey Canyon* can be justified as a "last resort" in an attempt to prevent the entire cargo of oil being deposited by the sea along the English coast is uncertain, but the issues involved are of the greatest significance. Existing charts of major sea lanes are inadequate in some parts of the world for the needs of giant tankers. The clearance required by these ships is far greater than that envisaged at the time the charts were prepared. The *Torrey Canyon* has brought home to the shipping nations of the world the need to provide more clearly for the rights of the various states involved should another tanker go aground and create a similar threat to the coasts of states in the area.[8]

2   *Pollution by radio-active materials*

The 1958 Geneva Conference had to deal with two possible sources of pollution by radiation: the dumping of radio-active waste, whether from nuclear powered ships or from shore installations using nuclear power; and the radioactive materials left from the testing of nuclear weapons. Understandably, the first source of potential pollution proved more amenable to compromise than did the second. As a result, while under the first part of Article 25 of the High Seas Convention, all states "shall take active measures to prevent pollution of the seas from the dumping of radio-active waste", the second part is drafted in more general terms. States are only required to "*co-operate* . . . in taking measures for the prevention of pollution of the seas or air-space above, resulting from any activities with radio-active materials or other harmful agents."

The claims of states to make exclusive use of large tracts of ocean for nuclear tests are most open to criticism on the question of pollution. States have frequently made use of areas of the high seas for naval manœuvres or as rocket ranges, and reasonable claims to exclusive use for such purposes are generally recognised as reasonable. It will be recalled that Article 2 of the High Seas Convention emphasises that the various "freedoms" of the high seas specified or "recognised by the general

---

8.   The issues raised were immediately taken up by I.M.C.O. which decided to undertake a series of studies of the technical and legal implications of the disaster with a view to a further revision of the Convention on the Prevention of the Pollution of the Sea by Oil: see 6 I.L.M. 652.

principles of international law" must be exercised "with *reasonable* regard to the interests of other states". Provided claims to the use of the high seas are generally accepted and are exercised with reasonable regard to the rights of other states, such claims cannot be categorised as contrary to international law. If the "use" in question is the test of a nuclear weapon, the criteria against which its legality is measured remain the same. Weapon testing is a use which has been accepted by states, so that the vital issue is that of reasonableness. The test will only cease to be reasonable if it causes harm to another state, its property, or its nationals. In view of the second part of Article 25 of the Convention which only requires states to "co-operate" in preventing pollution of the high seas from "activities with radio-active materials", it would seem possible to argue that pollution of the high seas *in itself* would not constitute a failure to pay reasonable regard to the rights of other states.[9]

ii *Conservation*

Unrestricted fishing of the resources of the high seas has produced two major problems. First, the efficient use of long distance fishing fleets by a few developed states is a threat to the very existence of the fishing industries of states which have not the resources to compete on the same scale. And, secondly, the more systematic and efficient fishing becomes, and the greater the demands of a hungry world, the greater are the dangers of exhausting stocks of fish.

To meet the first threat, states have made increasingly persistent claims to exclusive fishing rights in their coastal waters. The majority of claims have been limited to a twelve-mile zone, but a number of South American states have made more extravagant claims to exclusive use of the seas at a hundred or two hundred miles from their coasts. To many states the establishment of a fishing zone had the additional advantage of "conserving" stocks that they did not require for their own use by preventing foreign fleets from catching the fish. However, basically exclusive fishing zones, of whatever size, are an inefficient method of conservation. They may prove valueless if the stocks of fish are exhausted by activities outside the zones, while, if the zones are made extensive enough to conserve stocks, they are likely to prove too much of a limitation on the major fishing fleets which have a role to play in providing food for the world's population.

Isolated attempts were made to investigate particular problems relating to specific fish or to specific areas, but it was the report of a Technical Conference on Conservation at Rome in 1955 which stated clearly the need for a conservation policy and the objects which such a policy should seek to further. Three paragraphs of Part II of the report are worth quoting:

---

9. This is quite apart from any argument based on the principle of self-preservation. If state A is able to carry out large-scale nuclear tests on its own territory, state B would surely have the right to carry out similar tests on the high seas if it was unable to carry out such tests on its own territory, provided it could see in the action of state A a threat to its own security.

"16. Conservation is essential in the development of a rational exploitation of the living resources of the seas. Consequently, conservation measures should be applied when scientific evidence shows that fishing activity adversely affects the magnitude and composition of the resources or that such effects are likely.

"17. The immediate aim of conservation of living marine resources is to conduct fishing activities so as to increase, or at least to maintain, the average sustainable yield of products in desirable form. At the same time, wherever possible, scientifically sound positive measures should be taken to improve the resources.

"18. The principal objective of conservation of the living resources of the seas is to obtain the optimum sustainable yield so as to secure a maximum supply of food and other marine products. When formulating conservation programmes, account should be taken of the special interests of the coastal State in maintaining the productivity of the resources of the high seas near to its coast."[10]

Influenced by the Rome report, the 1958 Geneva Conference adopted an entire Convention devoted to Fishing and Conservation. The object of conservation was defined as obtaining "the optimum sustainable yield" in order to "secure a maximum supply of food and other marine products" (Article 2). While all states have the right for their nationals to engage in fishing on the high seas this right is subject to treaty obligations, including the interests of coastal states as provided for in the Convention, and the conservation provisions of the Convention (Article 1 (1)).

Article 3 lays down that if only one state fishes in a particular area of the high seas, it should itself apply conservation measures. Under Article 4, if nationals of two or more states are engaged in fishing the same stock or stocks of fish, they should negotiate an agreement upon what restrictions should be imposed on their own nationals in the interests of conservation. If, after such an agreement is entered into, nationals of other states start fishing the same stocks, Article 5 requires that such states shall apply the terms of the agreement, "which shall not be discriminatory in form or in fact" to their own nationals.

The first major drawback to the Convention can be seen in relation to Articles 4 and 5. Not only is Article 5 an attempt to impose obligations upon a "non-party" to a conservation agreement, but the Articles provide for reference of a failure to reach agreement or of a failure by a "newcomer" to comply with existing conservation measures to a Special Commission set up under Article 9. Even among states recognising the need to create obligations aimed at conserving the resources of the sea (a sufficient innovation in itself), the idea that fishing régimes could be established without their agreement by a form of compulsory arbitration was unacceptable.

The second main issue upon which disagreement was fundamental was the principle that coastal states had a special interest in the conservation of stocks of fish in the high seas adjacent to their territorial waters. This principle was recognised by Article 6 (1), but the provisions of the Convention designed to give effect to it were a compromise between

---

10. Quoted, Whiteman, *Digest of International Law*, Vol. 4, pp. 1099–1100. The last sentence of para. 18 was only included in the report by a bare majority of one vote.

supporters and opponents of the principle which in the event did not prove entirely satisfactory to either side. A coastal state is entitled to take part on an "equal footing" with other states fishing in such waters in any system of research and regulation for the purposes of conservation (Article 6 (2)). Its only right over and above the rights equally available to non-coastal states is that of adopting unilateral measures of conservation if no agreement is possible within six months of the start of negotiations (Article 7 (1)); *but* such measures shall only be valid against other states *inter alia* if the measures do not discriminate against foreign fishermen (Article 7 (2) (c)).

Although the Convention has received sufficient ratifications to enter into force, it has not been accepted by a number of the major fishing nations. While these states accept in principle the need for conservation, they are not prepared to accept the far-reaching implications of the Convention. In the immediate future, therefore, the major advances in conservation are likely to be by *ad hoc* arrangement[11] rather than by general acceptance of the Convention.

b GROUNDS FOR INTERFERENCE ON THE HIGH SEAS

According to Article 23 of the High Seas Convention, in the absence of any treaty right of intervention, a foreign vessel can only be boarded if there are reasonable grounds for suspecting that the ship is engaged in piracy or the slave trade, or if the ship, though flying a foreign flag, or refusing to show any flag, is of the same nationality as the vessel sending the boarding party.

i *Piracy*

The traditional notion of pirates as a group of men sailing the seven seas on a ship seized from no one knew where in search of plunder, or in the form of the Barbary corsairs operating off the coast of North Africa almost as that country's main source of revenue, may seem far removed from the safety of maritime traffic today. How can piracy have any relevancy to the mid-twentieth century?

The discussions on the various drafts drawn up by the International Law Commission concerning the law of the sea showed wide disagreement on the nature of piratical acts. The definition finally decided upon by the Geneva Conference is set out in Article 15:

> "Piracy consists of any of the following acts:
> (1) Any illegal acts of violence, detention or any act of depredation, committed for private ends by the crew or the passengers of a private ship or a private aircraft, and directed:
> (a) On the high seas, against another ship or aircraft, or against persons or property on board such ship or aircraft;
> (b) Against a ship, aircraft, persons or property in a place outside the jurisdiction of any State;

---

11.   For a brief discussion of specific conventions in the light of recent developments, see Bowett, *Law of the Sea*, pp. 24–32.

(2) Any act of voluntary participation in the operation of a ship or of an aircraft with knowledge of facts making it a pirate ship or aircraft;

(3) Any act of inciting or of intentionally facilitating an act described in sub-paragraph 1 or sub-paragraph 2 of this article."[12]

1 *For private ends.*—According to the Soviet Union and other Communist states, piracy should not be restricted to acts for purely private ends. It should apply equally to all depredations on the high seas, including, in their view, to the acts of the Chinese Nationalists and their American allies in intercepting vessels in the Formosa Strait, forcing them to enter Formosan ports and, on occasions, seizing both them and their cargoes. The explanation given by the Chinese representatives in the United Nations, before the organs of which a number of charges had been made, was that the Formosan authorities had been exercising a legitimate right of self-defence in limiting supplies of strategic materials to the Communist mainland.[13] The suggestions made by the Communist states at the Geneva Conference were designed primarily as a further political protest rather than as a constructive proposal in defining piracy which most of them regarded as an obsolete notion.

In stressing that piracy consists of illegal acts of violence committed for private ends, Article 15 does leave a further area of uncertainty with reagard to the position of insurgents or other groups operating against the existing government of a state. Although decisions of municipal courts, which are primarily concerned with the existence or not of piracy under municipal legislation, must be treated with caution, two cases do give some guidance on what is the correct rule of international law on the subject.

In the case of the *Magellan Pirates*,[14] Chilean insurgents had seized two vessels in a Chilean port and murdered their owners who were on board. Both vessels were later captured by a British ship which claimed bounty under the British Piracy Act of 1850. Leaving aside for the moment the question whether piracy could be committed in port, the significance of the case in the present context is that an English Court held that it was possible for insurgents to be considered as pirates. In the words of Dr. Lushington:[15]

> ". . . it does not follow that, because persons who are rebels or insurgents may commit against the ruling powers of their own country acts of violence, they may not be, as well as insurgents and rebels, pirates also; pirates for other acts committed towards other persons. It does not follow that rebels or insurgents may not commit piratical acts against the subjects of other states, especially if such acts were in no degree connected with the insurrection or rebellion."

A similar conclusion was reached in the American case of the *Ambrose Light*.[16] A Federal District Court had to consider the status of a vessel

---

12. For an English case deciding that under international law piracy includes attempted robbery on the high seas: *Re Piracy Jure Gentium*, [1934] A.C. 586.

13. A claim which, as the discussion on self-defence shows (see below pp. 264–273), must be considered of dubious validity.   14. (1853) 1 Sp. Ecc. & Ad. 81.

15. *Ibid.*, at p. 83.   16. 25 F. 409 (1885).

flying the flag of Columbian insurgents, who had not been recognised in any way by foreign powers. The vessel was engaged in an expedition to blockade the town of Cartagena, held by the lawful Columbian Government, and was under orders to attack any Columbian ship not flying the rebel ensign. Brown, J., held that the seizure of this vessel by the American gunboat *Alliance* was lawful. "Rebels who have never obtained recognition from any other power are clearly not a sovereign state in the eye of international law, and their vessels sent out to commit violence on the high seas are therefore piratical."[17]

Two distinct propositions may be deduced from these cases.

(1) If insurgents are sufficiently established to have a measure of international personality, then their acts will only be deemed piratical in so far as the depredations have no connection with the rebellion.

(2) If the rebel group has no definite identity, then all acts of violence on the high seas are *prima facie* piratical.

Although there is no direct support for drawing such a distinction in the High Seas Convention, there is indirect evidence favouring these two propositions. Article 15 defines piracy in terms not only of acts committed for private ends, but also of acts committed by the passengers or crew of a private ship or private aircraft. Piracy can only be committed by a warship, government ship, or government aircraft if its crew has mutinied and taken control of the ship or aircraft (Article 16). While the public nature of the ship would clearly be a relevant factor in deciding upon the piratical nature of its acts under proposition (1), a warship seized by a rebel group within proposition (2), and committing acts of depredation on the high seas, could be considered a pirate ship and subject to seizure by the warships of any state.

The usefulness of drawing the distinction drawn by the above two propositions may be further illustrated by reference to the incident in 1961 in which Captain Galvao and about seventy men, travelling as passengers on board the Portuguese liner, the *Santa Maria*, seized control of the ship on the high seas. They claimed to act on behalf of the "National Independence Movement" led by General Delgado who had unsuccessfully opposed General Salazar in the Portuguese Presidential elections of 1958 and had later been granted political asylum in Brazil. Although the passengers were treated with every respect, the crew were terrorised, and one member of the crew was killed. In the circumstances, it is difficult to regard the action, despite its political motives, as anything other than an act of piracy. As the "National Independence Movement" was not a *de facto* organisation exercising authority in a particular area of territory, it could not lawfully exercise any rights of seizure against the property of the state or government against which its operations were directed. Initial reaction was that an act of piracy must be punished. Both the United States and the United Kingdom expressed willingness to intercept the *Santa Maria* (admittedly at the request of the Portuguese Government),

---

17. 25 F. 409 (1885), at p. 412.

provided that such action could be taken without danger to the passengers and crew. However, doubts about the status of Galvao in view of his claim to act for political purposes, some public sympathy with an adventure directed against the internationally criticised régime of Dr. Salazar, and the difficulty of stopping the *Santa Maria* without harming passengers and crew, led to an agreed compromise. The United States Government suggested that the *Santa Maria* should make for a South American port under escort. Galvao accepted the suggestion provided the safety of himself and his men was guaranteed. The *Santa Maria* docked in Recife; Galvao and his men were granted political asylum; and the Brazilian Government restored the ship to her rightful owners.

2 *Directed by one ship or aircraft against another.*—One further obstacle to the attempt to classify the *Santa Maria* incident as a case of piracy is the fact that it took place entirely on board one ship. Article 15 of the Convention defines piracy as acts of depredation directed by the crew or passengers of one ship (or of an aircraft) against another ship (or aircraft). This restriction was made by the International Law Commission which stated categorically in its commentary to the 1956 draft that acts "committed on board a ship by the crew or passengers and directed against the ship itself, or against persons or property on the ship, cannot be regarded as acts of piracy". In one sense this attitude is understandable because jurisdiction in a case of "hi-jacking" would remain with the flag state. If the flag state wished to have assistance in bringing those responsible to justice it could presumably enlist the aid of any states willing and able to assist. However, piracy is essentially a "crime against public order"; or, to be more precise, a ground for all states to exercise a power to apprehend in the interest of public order on the oceans. There would seem to be little difference in practical terms between the seizure of a vessel by those on board as part of a prearranged plan and seizure by a band of men who board the vessel on the high seas. And what would be the reaction of the maritime community in the event of the "hi-jacking" of vessels by "passengers" on board becoming a more regular occurrence.[18] Despite the limitation contained in the Convention, there would appear to be no compelling reason to prevent this type of situation being considered as piracy. Insofar as the Convention is based upon the extent to which general agreement could be reached, it is not an exhaustive charter of maritime law. Although a wider definition of piracy might not be universally acceptable, that is no reason for abandoning it altogether.

On the high seas.—It is commonly argued that the reason why piracy is limited to acts on the high seas (or perhaps on land subject to the dominion

---

18. Piracy by one aircraft against another, although included in the Article 15 definition, is unlikely in practice because a seizure could only be effective if the aircraft that is the victim is forced to land, in which case the seizure would almost certainly take place within the territorial jurisdiction of a state. However, "hi-jacking" of aircraft, which has become something of a popular pursuit in recent years, could be accomplished in air space not subject to the territorial jurisdiction of any state (i.e. over the high seas). There seems no good reason for not classifying "hi-jacking" as piracy, whether it be of ships or aircraft.

of no state) is that illegal acts occurring within the territorial waters of a
state enable jurisdiction to be exercised by two states. Thus, according to
one writer:[19]

> "Since, in my view, the essential consequence of an act of piracy is the displace-
> ment of the normal rule that a ship is subject exclusively to the jurisdiction of its
> own state by another rule that the ship in question is subject to the jurisdiction of all
> states, it seems logical and proper to confine piracy to the high seas. Where terri-
> torial waters are concerned, ships are already subject in some measure to the juris-
> diction of the coastal state as well as of the flag state, but there seems no good
> reason to go further than that and authorise the international community as a whole
> to assume jurisdiction over acts that are clearly taking place within national territory."

Admittedly, this aspect of the law relating to piracy may be largely
academic, but if a "pirate" craft were to operate from the high seas against
shipping within the territorial waters of a state which lacked the naval
resources to put an end to these depredations, would the naval forces of a
state, the merchant shipping of which had as yet been unmolested, have
to stand helplessly by until its intervention were requested by the coastal
state or by a state that had suffered damage?

In such a situation, Article 15 of the High Seas Convention is clearly
unsatisfactory, and cannot be regarded as providing an exhaustive definition of piracy. It is submitted that the wider principle propounded in the
English case of the *Magellan Pirates* has much to commend it. It will be
recalled that in that case a group of Chilean rebels seized two vessels while
they were still in port, and murdered a number of people on board. The
rebels then sailed the vessels to the high seas where they were later captured by a British ship. Dr. Lushington refused to hold that murder and
robbery committed in port could never be piracy. The vessels had been
"carried away and navigated by the very same persons who originally
seized them". In his view the possession at sea was a "piratical possession",
a "continuation of the murder and robbery".[20] In other words, where the
offence is sufficiently closely connected with the high seas, either by the
original act, or by subsequent events, then jurisdiction may be exercised
on the high seas by ships of any state.

4 Piracy as a basis of jurisdiction.—Piracy is an example of jurisdiction
according to the *universal* principle. Article 19 of the High Seas Convention recognises that on the high seas, or in any other place outside the
jurisdiction of any state, every state may seize a pirate ship or aircraft and
arrest the persons and seize the property on board. One of the principal
causes of confusion between the international law definition of piracy and
the notion of piracy applied by municipal courts is the fact that piracy is
primarily a basis of jurisdiction under international law. As a basis of jurisdiction, it is a major exception to the normal rule that jurisdiction follows
the flag. Once a pirate vessel has been seized, however, the law to be
applied to punish those guilty of piratical acts is not international law, but
the municipal law of the state the vessels of which have effected the seizure.

---

19. D. H. N. Johnson in (1957) 43 Tr. Gr. Soc. 63, at p. 71.
20. 1 Sp. Ecc. & Ad., at p. 87.

In the words of Article 19 of the Convention, the courts of the state which carried out the seizure "may decide upon the penalties to be imposed".

ii *Slave-trading*

Article 22 of the second Geneva Convention by providing that a ship which is reasonably suspected of engaging in the slave-trade may be boarded on the high seas attempts to assimilate slave-trading to piracy. However, piracy and slave-trading have very different histories and whereas Article 22 is declaratory of existing customary international law as far as piracy is concerned, it is doubtful whether the same can be said of slave-trading.

In 1772, Lord Mansfield gave his famous judgment in the *Somerset* case[1] that no man could be a slave on British soil; and the same rule was applied to British warships not in the territorial waters of another state.[2] In 1824 this *territorial* principle was reinforced by an Act of Parliament based on the *personal* principle. It provided that "British subjects or residents who upon the high seas or in any place where the Admiral has jurisdiction, knowingly and wilfully carry away, convey or trade any person as a slave or confine any person on board a ship for the purpose of his being bought as a slave" shall be guilty of piracy.

However, the law of England, though applicable territorially and personally, could not give British ships the right under international law to interfere with slave-trading by foreign vessels on the high seas. The Congress of Vienna, 1815, had gone no further than to declare the slave trade repugnant to principles of humanity and morality. The British Government, therefore, entered into a series of bilateral arrangements with other states (Portugal, Spain, Sweden and Holland, later with Russia, Austria and Prussia) to secure the right of "visit and search" of vessels suspected of slave-trading. Despite reluctance to allow visit and search of their vessels, conventions were also signed with France (1845) and with the United States (1864 and 1870). The Brussels Conference of 1890, attended by the major European powers and the United States, reached agreement on allowing visit and search of suspected vessels within a limited area of the African coast. Further multilateral agreements followed, in 1926 under the auspices of the League of Nations, and in 1956 under that of the United Nations.

The 1956 Convention was intended largely as a supplement to the 1926 Convention and was aimed at the suppression of "Institutions and Practices Similar to Slavery" (to quote the words of its title). The primary duty imposed remained that laid down in Article 3 of the 1926 Convention, that the states concerned should "adopt all appropriate measures with a view to preventing and suppressing the embarkation, disembarkation and transport of slaves in their territorial waters and upon all vessels flying their respective flags". Article 13 of the High Seas Convention is therefore only declaratory of existing international obligations in requiring every

---

1. Lofft. 1.   2. *Forbes* v. *Cochrane* (1824), 2 B. & C. 448, esp. at p. 467.

state to "adopt effective measures to prevent and punish the transport of slaves in ships authorised to fly its flag, and to prevent the unlawful use of its flag for that purpose", while the second part of the Article providing that any slave "taking refuge on any ship, whatever its flag, shall *ipso facto* be free" had its counterpart in the General Act of Brussels of 1890.

The main innovation in the High Seas Convention is the attempt to assimilate slave-trading with piracy in relation to powers of interference on the high seas. A British proposal designed to effect the assimilation of slave-trading to piracy in the 1956 Convention had not been adopted, so Article 22 of the 1958 Convention clearly extends the powers of states by enabling them to interfere with foreign vessels suspected of engaging in the slave trade. Previous multilateral conventions had imposed on states the duty to prevent slave-trading on ships flying their flag, although a number of bilateral arrangements had allowed foreign warships a limited right of visit and search over suspected vessels. The High Seas Convention was the first occasion upon which a general right had been created.

iii *Verification of the flag*

It is a basic principle of international maritime law that a vessel can only enjoy the freedom of the seas if it is entitled to sail under the flag of a state.

This principle was accepted and applied by the Privy Council in the case of *Naim Molvan* v. *A.-G. for Palestine*,[3] The *Asya* was carrying illegal immigrants to Palestine when it was sighted by a British destroyer on the high seas. The vessel was flying no flag, but later the Turkish flag was hoisted. The destroyer asked for the *Asya*'s destination, but no reply was given. When a boarding party reached the *Asya*, the Turkish flag was lowered and a Zionist flag hoisted in its place. There were no ship's papers, and no other evidence to support the use of the Turkish flag. One of the arguments raised against forfeiture of the vessel was that the destroyer's actions had been contrary to international law. This contention was rejected:

". . . the freedom of the open sea, whatever those words may connote, is a freedom of ships which fly and are entitled to fly the flag of a State which is within the comity of nations. The *Asya* did not satisfy these elementary conditions. No question of comity nor of any breach of international law can arise, if there is no State under whose flag the vessel sails. Their Lordships would accept as a valid statement of the law the following passage from Oppenheim's *International Law*: 'In the interest of order on the open sea a vessel not sailing under the maritime flag of a State enjoys no protection whatever, for the freedom of navigation on the open sea is a freedom for such vessels only as sail under the flag of a State'."[4]

The requirement that a ship should be entitled to fly the flag of a state is not expressly set out in the High Seas Convention, although it is implicit in the provisions of Article 6. By paragraph (1), ships "shall sail under

---

3. [1948] A.C. 351; 15 A.D., Case No. 37.   4. [1948] A.C., at pp. 369-70.

the flag of one state only"; and, under paragraph (2), a "ship which sails under the flag of two or more States, using them according to convenience, may not claim any of the nationalities in question with respect to any other State, and may be assimilated to a ship without nationality".

The generally accepted view is that the "right of any ship to fly a particular flag must obviously be subject to verification by proper authority, and from this it follows that warships have a general right to verify the nationality of any merchant ship which they may meet on the high seas."[5] This "right of approach", as it is called, is "the only qualification [piracy excepted] under customary law of the general principle which forbids any interference in time of peace with ships of another nationality upon the high seas".[6] Once the warship has been shown a flag by the merchant vessel, its power to verify the flag by boarding the vessel is limited. If the merchant vessel is not entitled to any flag, or sails under more than one flag, the boarding of the vessel to verify the flag is justified *ex post facto*. Otherwise the warship acts at its peril.

The better view is that action in such circumstances (which are similar to those of the *Asya* incident considered above) is not affected by the apparently inconsistent provision in Article 22 (2) of the High Seas Convention. Under this paragraph, in cases where the vessel concerned is reasonably suspected of engaging in piracy, or in the slave trade, or where "though flying a foreign flag or refusing to show its flag, the ship is, in reality, of the same nationality as the warship", the warship "may proceed to verify the ship's right to fly its flag", and to this end "it may send a boat under the command of an officer to the suspected ship". The inconsistency is apparent rather than real. Article 22 (2) is concerned with situations in which, provided the warship has reasonable ground for its suspicions, it can board the ship without acting entirely at its peril. Article 22 (3) goes on to provide that if the suspicions prove unfounded, the vessel that has been boarded should be compensated for any loss or damage *unless the vessel has committed some act justifying the suspicions* entertained by the warship.

iv *Action in self-defence and the existence of threats to international peace and security*

It will be recalled that one of the factors which influenced a number of states to press for a twelve-mile limit of territorial waters at Geneva in 1958 and again in 1960 was the belief that the wider the territorial sea the greater the protection to their national security.[7] An alternative suggestion was that security should be included as one of the interests that a state could legislate to protect within a contiguous zone. In the event, the only reference to matters of security in the four Geneva Conventions was the provision in Article 16 (3) of the Territorial Sea Convention that the coastal state should be allowed to "suspend temporarily in specified areas

---

5. Smith, *Law and Custom of the Sea*, p. 64.   6. *Ibid.*
7. See above, pp. 155–156.

of its territorial sea the innocent passage of foreign ships if such suspension is essential for the protection of its security". While the acceptance of Article 24 dealing with the Contiguous Zone in a form which omitted all reference to security might in part be due to the fact that some states were hoping to obtain agreement on a twelve-mile limit to territorial waters, it is reasonable to suppose that other states were influenced by the view expressed by the International Law Commission. In explaining the omission of security from its draft article on the contiguous zone, the Commission suggested that the concept of security was too vague and might well lead to abuse, and that, in the last resort, a state's inherent right of self-defence would provide an adequate safeguard of its legitimate interests.

This reference to self-defence casts an interesting, though only indirect, light on the controversy that exists over the present limits of the right to act in self-defence. The main difficulty is seen as the wording of Article 51 of the United Nations Charter which commences by stating that nothing contained therein "shall impair the inherent right of individual or collective self-defence if *an armed attack* occurs against a Member of the United Nations". The view has been expressed that Article 51 has restricted the right of a state to employ force in self-defence to cases where an armed attack has occurred against it.[8] However, all that Article 51 is stating is that nothing contained in the Charter restricts the pre-1945 rights of a state to meet force with force. In other words, where international law recognised a wider right to use force in self-defence prior to 1945, that same right still exists, subject to modifications introduced by the Charter. These modifications relate to the procedures for settlement available to the parties to a dispute and the powers of settlement granted to the Security Council under Chapters VI and VII of the Charter and to the General Assembly under Chapter IV. But it is clear that if these procedures do not prove adequate, a residual power to act in self-defence must remain even where no actual armed attack has taken place.

In referring to the "security jurisdiction" of a state within a contiguous zone, it can hardly be supposed that the International Law Commission was referring to cases of an armed attack. The whole logic of the reference to the inherent right of self-defence was in the context of a jurisdiction to deal with acts constituting a threat to security, but nevertheless falling short of an armed attack It is clear, therefore, that the Commission's view must have been that Article 51 does not restrict self-defence to cases of armed attack alone. Indeed, the remainder of Article 51 bears out such a view. The first sentence of Article 51 is to the effect that nothing in the Charter should impair the inherent right of self-defence in cases of an armed attack until the Security Council takes the measures necessary to

---

8. By Lauterpacht in Oppenheim's *International Law*, Vol. II, 7th ed., p. 156; Jessup, *A Modern Law of Nations*, pp. 165–6; Kelsen, *Law of the United Nations*, pp. 269, 797–8; Stone, *Legal Controls of International Conflict*, p. 244. The concept of self-defence is considered further, below, pp. 671–687.

maintain international peace and security. This is entirely in keeping with the interpretation suggested that in cases where there has been no armed attack, the "protective" measures should follow, and not precede, a failure of the "community processes" provided by the Charter. Similarly, the second sentence of Article 51 lays down that measures "taken by Members in the exercise of *this* right of self-defence (as opposed to any other right of self-defence that they might be entitled to exercise) shall be immediately reported to the Security Council and shall not in any way affect the authority and responsibility of the Security Council under the present Charter to take at any time such action as it deems necessary in order to maintain or restore international peace and security."

So far it has been suggested that a state has a right to act in self-defence under Article 51 in the interests of its own security or self-preservation either as a last resort if the Charter procedures for settlement have failed, or if there is an armed attack against the state. But it is clear that, for a number of reasons (the fact that the Charter provisions do not provide sufficiently expeditious procedures, or that the situation to be faced is so unusual and novel that the Charter provides no adequate remedy), a right of self-defence exists in circumstances where there has not been a failure of the "community processes", nor yet an armed attack. The main prescriptions against the use of force in the Charter are those contained in Article 2, paragraphs (3) and (4). Paragraph (3) lays down that all members of the Organisation shall settle their disputes by peaceful means, while paragraph (4) provides that all members "shall refrain in their international relations from the threat or use of force against the territorial integrity or political independence of any State, or in any other manner inconsistent with the Purposes of the United Nations". It is not inconsistent with the Purposes of the United Nations to resort to force in self-defence. The Committee of the San Francisco Conference which drafted Article 2 (4) made this point clear in reporting to the Conference that the "use of arms in legitimate self-defence remains admitted and unimpaired".[9] And once the stage is reached where a state feels obliged to use force in its own defence, it may be validly argued that it is no longer within its power to abide by its obligation under Article 2 (3).

In the context of jurisdiction on the high seas, one writer has commented that, while it has been "generally recognised that a state may exercise its authority on the high seas in exceptional circumstances where this is necessary to forestall a real threat to its territorial integrity and general security", there has been no agreement "on the precise nature of the circumstances which enable this protective jurisdiction to be exercised or on the forms of prevention to which the state may have recourse in the exercise of its right of self-defence."[10] Extreme examples do not create problems. A state which is clearly the target of an invasion fleet on the high seas need not wait until the force enters its territorial waters before

---

9. U.N.C.I.O. Docs. Vol. VI, pp. 400, 459.
10. Bowett, *Self-defence in International Law*, p. 66.

taking measures against the ships involved. Similarly, a ship that is about to be attacked, or that is being attacked, on the high seas has the right to retaliate. But are there circumstances which justify a state exercising more normal rights of jurisdiction over a foreign ship on the high seas on the grounds of self-defence?

The incident which is most often cited in this context concerned the ship *Virginius*.[11] It was an American vessel which had come into the possession of Cuban insurgents. When seized by a Spanish warship, the *Virginius* was carrying a large quantity of arms and ammunition, together with numerous passengers who were clearly intending to take part in the rebellion against Spain. In addition to confiscating the arms and ammunition, the Spanish authorities executed the would-be insurgents, some of whom were British and American subjects. While the United States protested the seizure of the *Virginius* as well as the execution of American citizens, the British protest acknowledged the right of the Spanish to seize the ship, but contended that, once the imminent threat of interference in the rebellion was removed, self-defence could not justify any subsequent action against the passengers from the vessel. The majority of writers have accepted the subsequent compensation paid by Spain to Britain as establishing the incident as authority for the proposition that self-defence may be a basis for exercising a power of arrest over foreign vessels, including foreign warships, on the high seas.

The whole issue of the application of a plea of self-defence to action taken against foreign shipping on the high seas was brought into dramatic prominence by the Cuba missile crisis of 1962. The background to the crisis is well known. The seizure of power in Cuba by Communist-inspired revolutionaries led by Castro and the subsequent attempt by Castro to extend the revolution to other Republics of central America brought the policies of the Cuban régime into conflict with the United States and with the majority of the members of the Organisation of American States. The Cuban Government was expelled from the O.A.S. and an economic boycott was instituted. An invasion of Cuba by Cuban exiles with the connivance of the United States Government failed, but there was strong public pressure in the United States to mount a full-scale operation with the intention of overthrowing Castro. Castro took advantage of offers of large supplies of arms from Communist states, and the same Punta del Este meeting of January, 1962, that excluded the Castro régime from the O.A.S. characterised the arms supplies from "extra-continental Communist powers" as "incompatible with the principles and objectives of the inter-American system".[12] In September, 1962, President Kennedy announced that "the Soviets have provided the Cuban Government with a number of anti-aircraft missiles" and several torpedo-boats carrying ship-to-ship guided missiles. The President made it clear in public statements during the first half of September that the introduction

---

11. Moore, *Digest of International Law*, Vol. 2, p. 895 (1874).
12. See Whiteman, *Digest of International Law*, Vol. 5, p. 440.

of long range ground-to-ground missiles which could be used for offensive purposes would be regarded in a totally different light.[13] On 22nd
October the President reported that "unmistakable evidence has established the fact that a series of offensive missile sites is now in preparation"
on Cuban territory, and to "halt this offensive build-up", he announced "a
strict quarantine on all offensive military equipment under shipment to
Cuba": *all* ships bound for Cuba would, "if found to contain cargoes of
offensive weapons, be turned back."[14]

At the same time the United States called for emergency meetings of
both the Security Council and of the Council of the O.A.S. The following
day—23rd October—the O.A.S. resolved to "recommend that the member states, in accordance with Articles 6 and 8 of the Inter-American Treaty
of Reciprocal Assistance, take all measures, individually and collectively,
including the use of armed force, which they may deem necessary to
ensure that the Government of Cuba cannot continue to receive from the
Sino-Soviet powers military material and related supplies which may
threaten the peace and security of the Continent and to prevent the missiles
in Cuba with offensive capability from ever becoming an active threat to
the peace and security of the Continent." It was also resolved to "inform
the Security Council of this resolution in accordance with Article 54 of the
Charter of the United Nations."[15]

On 24th October, the quarantine was put into effect, initially solely by
United States naval forces, but with the subsequent co-operation of vessels
from Argentina, the Dominican Republic and Venezuela. Shippers were
allowed to obtain advance authority to take agreed cargoes through the
quarantine area by a "Clearcert" system. Other vessels were approached
and inspected from alongside; some were boarded and their cargoes
examined. A special procedure was introduced for the identification of
submarines in the quarantine area, requiring them to surface on a given
signal by a pattern of harmless explosive sound signals. The quarantine
remained in operation until the United States was satisfied that the agreement reached between itself and the Soviet Union on the dismantling of
the Cuban missile sites by the Soviet Union in return for an American undertaking not to invade Cuba, had been implemented by the Soviet Union.

It need hardly be stated that the legality of the quarantine has been a
matter of controversy. Was it a valid operation in self-defence, or necessary to maintain international peace and security as the United States has
contended? Or was it an act of "piracy" and an "unprecedented aggressive" act[16] as alleged by the Soviet Union? And, in the context of our
discussion, what is its relevance with regard to the freedom of the seas?

---

13. *Ibid.*, p. 441.   14. *Ibid.*, pp. 443–4.   15. *Ibid.*, p. 445.
16. These terms were not intended to have legal significance, but rather to characterise
in emotive terms the alleged illegality of the quarantine. It will be recalled that the Soviet
Union attempted unsuccessfully to have similar measures of the Chinese nationalists in
stopping strategic materials bound for the Chinese mainland characterised as piracy at the
1958 Geneva Conference on the Law of the Sea, above, p. 258. Though such measures
may be illegal, they are certainly not piratical.

1 *Pacific blockade*

The use of the term "quarantine" was adopted by the President in order to avoid the action being characterised as a "blockade". While a naval "blockade" could be imposed against all shipping trading with a particular port or state under the laws of war, the scope of so-called "pacific blockade" under traditional international law was doubtful, if indeed it had survived the obligations of the Charter to settle disputes by peaceful means. In general terms, a pacific blockade could be used as a means of coercion against a state which had broken its international obligations towards the blockading state or states, and had refused or failed to settle the dispute peaceably. Thus, in 1902, Britain, Germany and Italy had established a blockade against Venezuela for a failure by that state to honour its debts. At that time, the United States, while acknowledging that the right of pacific blockade could be asserted against ships of the blockading powers, and against ships of the state that was being blockaded, protested in the strongest terms that it could not be used as an excuse to interfere with the freedom of the high seas in relation to other states.

2 *Self-defence*

Once the proposition is accepted that self-defence is avilable as a basis for action in the absence of an actual armed attack, it is clear that some form of interference with the freedom of passage of foreign vessels on the high seas may be justifiable. It was suggested that the main restriction upon this right in cases not involving an armed attack was the need to rely upon the procedures for settlement provided for in the Charter. But where the party against which the action is taken would obtain an undeniable "procedural advantage" before the "community methods" would have time to operate, self-defence would seem an adequate reason for taking "interim measures of self-protection". A potential aggressor might well be able to retain the advantages of a quick build-up of materials (as in the Cuba situation) by obstructive tactics in the United Nations. Only prompt action by the state or states thus threatened to prevent the build-up would prevent such an advantage being gained.

However, the difficulty of accepting this argument in relation to the Cuban Quarantine is whether the United States was entitled to rely upon self-defence at all. While the missiles to which exception was ultimately taken were capable of delivering destructive warheads over most of the United States, long range ground-to-ground missiles were a basic aspect of *American* defence strategy. As commentators have pointed out, American missile sites in Turkey were as proximate to the Soviet Union as the Cuban sites were to the United States. Furthermore, all states have a right to provide for their own defence in the manner they think best, and if the United States believed that the missiles constituted a direct threat against itself, the blame lay not entirely with Cuba. The "invasion" of Cuba by exiles in April, 1961, and the vociferous public threats against Cuba in the

KIL

United States gave support to the Cuban argument that Cuba needed sophisticated modern weapons for its defence. Even President Kennedy was obliged to attempt to belittle this argument. At a news conference on 13th September, 1962, the President said that "unilateral military intervention on the part of the United States cannot currently be either required or justified, and it is regrettable that loose talk about such action in this country might serve to give a thin colour of legitimacy to the Communist pretence that such a threat exists."[17] In such circumstances, it is difficult to accept the American contention that it was their naval quarantine which was necessitated on the grounds of self-defence.

3   Collective self-defence

The inter-American system established by the Rio Treaty is partly a mutual defence alliance. In taking its stand against the setting up of long-range missile sites in Cuba, the United States categorised their presence as a threat to the peace of the Continent, and based its action on the need to defend "our own security and . . . the entire Western Hemisphere".[18] Similarly, the O.A.S. resolution of the 23rd October, 1962, recommended the taking of "all measures, individually and collectively, including the use of armed force" that might be deemed necessary to prevent the continued supply of military materials to Cuba that might "threaten the peace and security of the Continent".[19] Clearly, the United States and the other American Republics regarded their actions as justifiable on the grounds of collective as well as of individual self-defence.

Although doubts have been cast upon whether international law recognises collective self-defence as anything more than the right of two states to join together to repel an act of aggression against them both, such a view seems to disregard the practice of states during the inter-war years when mutual defence treaties were much in vogue, the obvious meaning of Article 51 in reserving the inherent right of self-defence, individual or collective, and the resurgent popularity of treaties of collective self-defence after 1945. In an attempt to define self-defence in strictly legal terms, the view has been expressed that collective self-defence requires that the states involved should have some close "personal" interest in their mutual security.[20] If no such interest is involved one state cannot go unasked to the aid of another which is the victim of aggression entitling it to act in self-defence. But such a definition does not appear to have any great practical significance because it is largely an academic question in most situations whether states A, B and C act collectively to suppress aggression against A, or whether A requests B and C to assist it repel aggression. As far as the Cuban Quarantine is concerned, the collective nature of the action can readily be justified by the fact that the threat from Cuban missiles was equally directed against them all, or, alternatively, that

---

17.   Whiteman, *op. cit.*, p. 441.
18.   Statement of President Kennedy, *ibid.*, p. 443.   19.   Text, *ibid.*, p. 445.
20.   Stone, *op. cit.*, p. 245; Bowett, *op. cit.*, pp. 216–7.

states in the same geographical region have an obvious interest in each other's security.

The collective self-defence argument, however, would seem to be faced with the same obstacle as the United States' contention that it was acting on the basis of its own right of self-defence. The major threats, so Cuba would be entitled to argue, were those made, and even attempted to be carried out, of invading Cuba. In the circumstances, Cuba's missile system was justifiable in the interests of its own self-preservation. The aspect of Cuban policy which had created most distrust was the attempt by Castro to "export" his revolution to other parts of central America. But, it will be recalled, President Kennedy in his news conference of 13th September, 1962, expressly disavowed that the United States had any reason or excuse for invading Cuba.[1] If the United States had no justification to act against Cuba, but had already been involved in such an illegal action only a year before; and if frequent public pronouncements were being made of the need to invade Cuba, the plea of self-defence would justify Cuba's accept-ance of Russian missiles, rather than United States' prevention of their being installed in Cuba.

4 Concerted action for the maintenance of international peace and security

Action by, or under the auspices of the United Nations, or under any regional arrangements as defined in Chapter VIII of the United Nations Charter, for the maintenance of international peace and security is con-sidered in detail in a later chapter.[2] However, it is clear that the Security Council has a wide power to take measures affecting the freedom of the seas in the interests of maintaining or restoring international peace and security. Under Article 42, for example, it may take such action as is neces-sary, including "demonstrations, blockade, and other operations by air, sea or land forces".

The only illustration of a direct interference by the Security Council with freedom of navigation was the resolution of April, 1966, directed against oil supplies to Rhodesia. In November, 1965, the Rhodesian Government had declared itself independent from Britain. Neither the United Kingdom nor any other state recognised Rhodesia's independence. In order to oblige the Rhodesian régime to accept progress towards genuine majority rule by all classes of society the United Kingdom imposed a trade boycott. In order to make this boycott more effective, Britain eventually requested the Security Council to prohibit trade with Rhodesia in a large range of commodities, but, before this was done, Britain sought the assistance of the Council in attempting to prevent the flow of oil to Rhodesia through pipelines from the Portuguese port of Beira. In a resolution of 9th April, 1966,[3] the Council "determined" that

---

1. See above, p. 270 fn. 17. The limit to the right of self-defence against Cuban revolu-tionaries crossing to the mainland of central America would presumably be a "quarantine" upon such movements.

2. Below, p. 588.   3. S/RES/221 (1966).

the situation resulting from the passage of tankers carrying oil for Rhodesia
to Beira constituted a "threat to the peace". The resolution called upon all
states to "ensure the diversion of any of their vessels reasonably believed to
be carrying oil destined for Rhodesia", and upon the United Kingdom to
prevent "by the use of force if necessary" the arrival at Beira of such
vessels. Acting under this authority, the United Kingdom has maintained
surveillance of the approaches of Beira with a view to turning back any
tanker that appears to be carrying oil destined ultimately for Rhodesia.

While it is clear that enforcement action by, or under the authority of,
the Security Council, as defined by Chapter VII of the Charter, may
include some form of naval blockade or quarantine,[4] the position of
regional agencies in this respect is limited by the provisions of Articles
53 (1) and 54 of the Charter. Under Article 53 (1) the Security Council
"shall, where appropriate, utilise such regional arrangements or agencies
for enforcement action under its authority", but "no enforcement action
shall be taken under regional arrangements, or by regional agencies without the authorisation of the Security Council" (with certain exceptions
which are now no longer relevant). And Article 54 provides that the
Security Council "shall at all times be kept fully informed of activities
undertaken or in contemplation under regional arrangements or by
regional agencies for the maintenance of international peace and security."

The distinction between the two provisions would logically appear to
be that action relating to the maintenance of international peace and
security falling short of enforcement action can be undertaken by a
regional organisation provided that the Security Council is kept informed.
Action amounting to enforcement action can only be undertaken under
the authority of the Council, which clearly implies a prior authorisation.
Thus, while Articles 53 and 54 extend the powers of a regional organisation, enabling it to go beyond the limits of self-defence, these provisions
also circumscribe the type of action open to such organisations.

The legality of the Cuban Quarantine as an action necessary for the
maintenance of international peace and security must therefore depend
upon whether or not it amounted to enforcement action. As the action
amounted to a forcible interference with shipping on the high seas with
the intention of preventing trade with Cuba in certain types of military
equipment, it is difficult to deny that it was just the type of enforcement
action envisaged by Article 53 of the Charter quoted above. In the face of
this obstacle to the justification of American and O.A.S. action under
Chapter VIII of the U.N. Charter, the suggestion has been made that
Article 53 (1) of the Charter is obsolete and has been superseded entirely by
Article 54. The basis of this argument is considered briefly in a later

---

4. Article 42 of the Charter enables the Security Council to take "such action by air,
sea, or land forces as may be necessary to maintain or restore international peace and
security" and adds that such action may "include demonstrations, blockade, and other
operations by air, sea, or land forces of Members of the United Nations." However, it is
doubtful whether the Council can act under this provision unless forces are made available
to it by agreement with Member states as envisaged by Article 43: see below, p. 568.

chapter,[5] but it cannot be said to have received much support outside the O.A.S., nor can it be said that a privileged position has been conceded to the O.A.S. in this context.

In the final analysis, it can be said that international law does recognise a limited right for states to interfere with foreign vessels on the high seas:

(1) in the exercise of the right of self-defence whether individual or collective, though only in exceptional circumstances; and

(2) under the authority of the Security Council acting in accordance with Chapter VII of the United Nations Charter.

While an operation *like* the Cuban Quarantine could be justified under either of the above alternatives, in the actual circumstances of the 1962 crisis the action must be considered of doubtful validity. On the other hand, measures by a regional agency designed to maintain international peace and security under Article 54 of the Charter could not justify an action on the scale of the Quarantine against freedom of movement on the high seas. To validate such a claim would require rewriting the Charter to exclude the operation of Article 53 (1) or to alter significantly its obvious meaning. Admittedly the Charter, like any treaty, may be revised by the practice of the parties to it, but this cannot be achieved by a minority of contracting powers without the acquiescence of the others.

c THE JURISDICTION OF MUNICIPAL COURTS OVER EVENTS OCCURRING ON THE HIGH SEAS

In circumstances involving interference with a foreign vessel on the high seas, international law determines the limits of the right of interference, and may require that municipal law impose penalties upon the vessel that is in breach of some rule of international law. For example, the definition of piracy lays down generally the extent of the right of seizure, but the punishment of the pirate vessel and its crew is left to the municipal law of the state the ship of which effects the seizure. In the case of a ship seized because it has no claim to sail under a recognised flag, international law allows a right of seizure, but issues such as the power to claim forfeiture of the ship are left to municipal courts.

However, the main concern of this section is to deal with the rules of international law that deal with the right of municipal courts to try cases arising out of incidents occurring on the high seas. If an incident occurs on board ship which has no effect beyond that ship, then the primary rule is that jurisdiction follows the flag, but this principle may not be exclusive, and, if the incident involves ships flying the flags of different states (e.g. in the case of a collision), an additional dimension is added to the problem.

i *Criminal jurisdiction*

If a crime is committed on board ship, the situation is similar to that of a crime committed in the territory of the flag state. The courts of the flag state (i.e. the "territorial sovereign") have jurisdiction, though it would

---

5. Below, pp. 588–591.

not be contrary to international law if the courts of the state of which the accused was a national were to exercise jurisdiction.[6]

While the fiction that a ship is a "floating piece of territory" is harmless enough in cases involving one ship, or perhaps two ships flying the same flag, it can be dangerously misleading in situations arising out of a collision between ships flying different flags. It will be recalled that the *Lotus* case[7] concerned a collision between a French and a Turkish ship. The French officer of the watch at the time of the collision was charged before a Turkish Court in respect of the deaths of a number of those on board the Turkish ship. The French view was that criminal jurisdiction could be claimed either on the ground that the accused was a Turkish national or on the basis of the flag the ship was flying. As the accused was a French national, serving on board a French ship, the Turkish Courts had no claim to exercise jurisdiction in a criminal matter. The Permanent Court, by a majority of one, held that the practice of states relied upon by France in favour of the exclusive jurisdiction of the flag state did not demonstrate a conviction by non-flag states that they were refraining from exercising jurisdiction because they were obliged to as a matter of legal obligation;[8] and that, as the effects of the crime had taken place on Turkish territory (i.e. on board a Turkish ship), the Turkish Courts had jurisdiction.

While, as we have seen, the territorial principle of jurisdiction may be said to apply to crimes perpetrated abroad but taking affect within the jurisdiction,[9] this principle is not logically conclusive on the validity of claims to criminal jurisdiction over events happening at sea. The decision in the *Lotus* case produced particularly hostile reaction in the maritime community, and attempts have been made to reverse the effects of the decision. In 1952 the Brussels Convention for the Unification of Certain Rules relating to Penal Jurisdiction in Matters of Collisions or other Incidents of Navigation laid down the basic proposition that "criminal or disciplinary proceedings may be instituted only before the judicial or administrative authorities of the state of which the ship was flying the flag at the time of the collision or other incident of navigation" (Article 1), but that this should not affect the right of the state that issued a mariner's certificate of competence to take action with respect to that certificate, or of a state to try its nationals for crimes committed on board a vessel flying the flag of another state (Article 3). With minor alterations of drafting these provisions were reproduced in Article 11 of the High Seas Convention, and have substantially reversed the effects of the *Lotus* decision.

ii *Civil jurisdiction*

The English Court of Admiralty, and its American counterpart, traditionally claimed the widest jurisdiction over the civil issues arising out of

---

6. For a discussion of jurisdiction based on the personality principle, see below, pp. 288–313.

7. (1927) P.C.I.J. Rep., Ser. A. No. 10.

8. See above, pp. 166–167.   9. See above, pp. 168–169.

a maritime collision. Providing that there was some basis of jurisdiction in the sense that the defendant or his ship came within the territorial competence of the English Courts, jurisdiction could be exercised even over foreign vessels, and over an incident occurring in foreign waters.

Because of variations in the practice of states, the attempt was made at Brussels in 1952 to standardise maritime practices in a convention dealing with civil jurisdiction. Although the parties to litigation may agree to submit a dispute to a particular court (Article 2), Article 1 restricts the right of the plaintiff to choose the venue for proceedings to:

"(a) either before the Court where the defendant has his habitual residence or a place of business;
(b) or before the Court of the place where arrest has been effected by the defendant ship or of any other ship belonging to the defendant which can be lawfully arrested, or where arrest could have been effected and bail or other security has been furnished;[10]
(c) or before the Court of the place of collision when the collision has occurred within the limits of a port or in inland waters."

However, although the United Kingdom has ratified the Convention, in view of the limited number of ratifications and accessions, the overall effect of the Convention in producing recognised rules of international law relating to jurisdiction in civil proceedings must be regarded as minimal.

2 JURISDICTION IN AIR SPACE AND OUTER SPACE

A. Air space

In the early days of flying a variety of theories were advanced on the subject of freedom of air navigation and rights of overflight. The 1914–18 war, however, brought home to all states the significance of aerial transport and the potential dangers of aircraft to their security. Any doubts that might have existed were resolved by the forthright nature of Article 1 of the Paris Convention of 1919. The High Contracting Parties recognised that every state had "complete and exclusive sovereignty over the air space above its territory", including its territorial waters. This basic principle was reaffirmed by Articles 1 and 2 of the Chicago Convention 1944.

Although jurisdiction in air space is stated to be based upon the "complete and exclusive sovereignty" of the territorial state, this sovereignty is by no means unqualified. It is obviously qualified in one sense by the extent of air space above the territory of a state, which is limited by astronomical fact if not by legal prescription. This qualification is dealt with later in connection with jurisdictional rights in space, but, for the moment, it is important to realise that there must be a limit on the outward extent

---

10. For limitations on the powers of arrest of a coastal state, see above, pp. 230–233; 237–251.

of sovereignty over airspace. It is also qualified in another sense by the degree to which overflight is allowed, in the absence of special agreement, by the Chicago Convention itself. And, in practice, states themselves have restricted their power to exclude foreign aircraft from the air space above their territory by agreements designed to obtain reciprocal rights in the conduct of air transport operations. Finally, there may exist rules of a customary nature, and not based upon international convention, qualifying the right of the territorial state to exercise to the full its sovereign powers.

a QUALIFICATIONS LAID DOWN BY THE CHICAGO CONVENTION

The exclusive sovereignty concept of Article 1 is reinforced in the Chicago Convention by Article 6 which lays down that "no scheduled international air service may be operated over or into the territory of a contracting state, except with the special permission or other authorisation of that state, and in accordance with the terms of such permission or authorisation". However, under Article 5, "aircraft of other contracting states, being aircraft not engaged in scheduled international air services, shall have the right, subject to the observance of the terms of this Convention, to make flights into or in transit non-stop across its territory and to make stops for non-traffic purposes without the necessity of obtaining prior permission, and subject to the right of the state flown over to require landing".

The significance of Article 5 obviously depends upon two facts: the interpretation placed upon "scheduled international air service"; and the extent to which provisions of the Chicago Convention may be said to represent existing rules of international law.

i *Scheduled international air services*

It is clear that Article 5 was intended to apply to a fairly wide field of operations because it goes on to state that aircraft "engaged in the carriage of passengers, cargo, or mail for remuneration or hire on other than scheduled international air services shall also . . . have the privilege of taking on or discharging passengers, cargo, or mail, subject to the right of any state where embarkation or discharge takes place to impose such regulations, conditions or limitations as it may consider desirable".[11] The theory that Article 5 should have a wide application is borne out by the interpretation placed upon it by the I.C.A.O. Council in its 1952 definition of a "scheduled international air service". According to the Council such a service comprised "a series of flights" possessing the following characteristics:

(a) it must pass through the air space of more than one state;
(b) it must be performed by aircraft in the transport of passengers, mail or cargo for remuneration, in such a manner that the flight is open to use by members of the public; and

---

11. Subject to Article 7 which enables any contracting state to refuse permission to any aircraft of other states to carry "internal" traffic (or cabotage as it is called), that is passengers and goods bound for another point in the territory of the same state.

(c) it must be operated in order to serve traffic between the same two or more points, either according to a published time table or with flights so regular or frequent that they constitute a recognisable systematic series.

This definition has in fact been largely superseded by events. The development of non-scheduled "charter" services posed an obvious economic threat to the regular airlines, many of which are government operated or controlled. Despite the obvious meaning of Articles 5 and 6 of the Chicago Convention and the I.C.A.O. Council's 1952 interpretation, members of the organisation have consistently refused to allow charter flights to operate over their territory without prior permission, a permission which some states have withheld altogether.[12] As the opportunities for private aviation are limited, the effect of state practice has been to establish Article 6 as the primary rule and to relegate Article 5 to the position of an insignificant exception.

ii *The Chicago Convention as general international law*

Both the 1919 Convention of Paris and the 1944 Chicago Convention recognised the exclusive sovereignty not of contracting states alone, but of *all states*. In other words, the Conventions purported to be stating an already existing rule of customary international law with regard to rights to air space. In contrast, the *limitations* on the exclusive sovereignty of the territorial state contained in the Paris Convention[13] and in Article 5 of the Chicago Convention were restricted in their application to states parties to each Convention. This would seem to suggest that exclusive sovereignty is the right of all states and that it might be limited only with their agreement. States not parties to the Chicago Convention would, therefore, be free to claim the benefit of Article 1 (as representing general international law), but to reject any restriction flowing from Article 5 on the ground that this provision creates a purely contractual obligation between parties to the Convention. Such an analysis gains support from the extended application of Article 6 of the Convention at the expense of Article 5 by members of the I.C.A.O. The universally accepted rule is exclusive sovereignty over air space, and restrictions upon this right must be clearly established.

b QUALIFICATIONS CREATED BY OTHER MULTILATERAL AGREEMENTS

In drawing up the Convention, the delegates of the Chicago Conference were unable to reach a sufficient measure of agreement on the extent to which states would guarantee reciprocal rights of overflight or of trans-

---

12. A number of European states, including the United Kingdom, have "gone it alone" and made provision for charter flights between their territories under the Paris Multilateral Agreement on the Commercial Rights of Non-Scheduled Air Services, 1956.

13. Article 2, for example, provided that "each *contracting* state undertakes, in time of peace, to accord freedom of innocent passage above its territory to the aircraft of the other contracting states provided that the conditions laid down in the present Convention are observed."

portation of passengers and cargo. The Conference therefore adopted two additional conventions of different scope providing alternative bases for future agreement. The two conventions are usually referred to as the "Two Freedoms" Agreement (or sometimes the "Transit" Agreement) and the "Five Freedoms" Agreement (or "Transport" Agreement).

Before considering these Agreements in more detail it is necessary to analyse more closely what is meant by the so-called "freedoms of the air" which provide the basic classification of international air traffic.

i *First and Second Freedoms*

The first two "Freedoms" are solely *transit rights*. They give the state granted the freedom no commercial rights on the territory of the grantor state. The "First Freedom" is simply the right to fly and to carry traffic non-stop over that territory. The majority of transatlantic flights take advantage of first freedom rights over the Irish Republic. The "Second Freedom" is the right to fly and carry traffic over the territory of the grantor state and to make one or more stops for non-traffic purposes (e.g. refuelling or maintenance).

ii *Third and Fourth Freedoms*

The other three freedoms are *traffic rights* in that they involve permission to carry passengers or cargo to or from the territory of the grantor state. Third and Fourth Freedom rights are readily granted, invariably in conjunction. The "Third Freedom" is the right to carry traffic from the territory of the flag state (i.e. of the state granted the right) to the territory of the grantor state. The "Fourth Freedom" is the right to carry traffic from the territory of the grantor state to the territory of the flag state which has been granted the right.

iii *Fifth Freedom*

The "Fifth Freedom" is the right to carry traffic between the grantor state and the territory of another state. As fifth freedom rights are more extensive, they are less readily made available. However, it is recognised that airlines operating on long haul routes could not do so economically without fifth freedom traffic. It has therefore been necessary for states to open their own third and fourth freedom rights to other states in return for similar concessions from those states.

It will be realised that this "Fifth Freedom" can in fact cover three different types of traffic. To take the grant of fifth freedom rights by India to Australia as an example, the traffic carried by Qantas to or from India under this agreement could:

(1) originate from or be destined for a place anterior to Australia (e.g. New Zealand). This is termed the *anterior-point fifth freedom*.
(2) originate from or be destined for an intermediate point (e.g. Singapore). This is termed the *intermediate-point fifth freedom*.
(3) originate from or be destined for a point beyond India (e.g. Italy). This is termed the *beyond-point fifth freedom*.

It should be noticed that the *route* is always traced *from* the territory of the flag state *to* the territory of the grantor state, so that even when a Qantas flight is operating the return journey from India to New Zealand, New Zealand remains an anterior point on the route. Of course, whether in fact Qantas can pick up or discharge in New Zealand, Singapore or Italy traffic emanating from or destined to India will also depend upon the grant of fifth freedom rights to Australia by those three states.

iv *Other freedoms*

The need to define these various aspects of the fifth freedom stems partly from the fact that the grantor state might only be prepared to allow the flag state to operate an anterior-point service. In other words, the more refined the distinctions between one type of fifth freedom right and another become, the more restrictive is the policy they reflect. Even the classification of fifth freedom rights outlined above has not proved adequate to cover all contingencies. The need has been felt to introduce the notion of a "Sixth Freedom" to cover the situation that can arise when a state attempts to take advantage of its third and fourth freedom rights with two states to create what is in effect an unauthorised fifth freedom through flight. For example, if Italy had not been granted the right to fly, or had been granted only a limited frequency, on the United Kingdom–Australia route through Rome, could it create a service, or add to its existing frequency, by scheduling two ostensibly separate third and fourth freedom services between United Kingdom and Italy, and between Italy and Australia?

Occasionally the expression "Seventh Freedom" is used to cover the unusual situation of a carrier operating entirely outside the territory of the flag state a service between two other states; and "Eighth Freedom" to refer to the right, known as *cabotage*, to carry traffic from one point to another within the territory of the grantor state.

1 *The "Two Freedoms" Agreement*

As its name implies, this Agreement provides for the grant of First and Second Freedom transit rights to all other contracting states (Article 1 (1)). The territorial state is entitled to impose designated routes for transit flights (Article 1 (4)). It can also require airlines taking advantage of the right to land granted to their own state to provide "reasonable commercial service" at airports they are allowed to use (Article 1 (3)), and impose charges for the use of such airports (Article 1 (4)). One interesting feature of the agreement is the right of the territorial state to revoke permission it has granted "to an air transport enterprise of another state in any case when it is not satisfied that substantial ownership and effective control is vested in nationals of a contracting state" (Article 1 (5)).[14] In other words, it does

---

14. Article 1 (5) also allows revocation in case of "failure of such air transport enterprise to comply with the laws of the state over which it operates, or to perform its obligations under this agreement."

not matter if there is no real connection between a state and an airline operating as one of its enterprises, providing that the airline concerned has such a connection with another contracting state.

2   The *"Five Freedoms"* Agreement

This Agreement largely follows the form of the "Two Freedoms" Agreement, except that, of course, it provides for the reciprocal grant among contracting states of all five freedoms (Article 1 (1)). At the outset the Transport Agreement was signed by as many as twenty states, but it soon became apparent that the wide scope of the "Fifth Freedom" had economic repercussions that had not been envisaged. In 1944, for example, the United States was the champion of unrestricted competition in air transport, but United States airlines rapidly realised that the advantages of such a policy were likely to be shortlived. As the European states began to recover from the ravages of war and to provide competition for U.S. operators, it was the European states that benefited most from a "slice of the American Cake", which was much larger than the potential traffic emanating from western Europe.[15]

The initial support for the "Five Freedoms" Agreement rapidly waned, and with the withdrawal of the United States in 1947 it ceased to contribute significantly to international civil aviation. By entering into a multilateral convention of this type, a state would be giving away a valuable economic bargaining counter. A party to such an agreement could not discriminate between one state and another in deciding what policy to adopt. For example, state X might be prepared to allow state Y the widest reciprocal transport rights, but be reluctant to grant similar rights to state Z. Implementation of such a policy would not be possible if the states were parties to the "Five Freedoms" Agreement.

c   BILATERAL AGREEMENTS

Because of the failure of the experiment based upon the "Five Freedoms" Agreement, the trend has been for states to develop their air transport by bilateral arrangement. Most European states preferred what are called "pre-determination agreements" in which the capacity of the route to be operated and the services the route would justify were "pre-determined" by the contracting parties. However, the United States regarded pre-determination of capacity as inconsistent with the liberal development of international air transport. Of major importance to the history of international civil aviation since 1944, therefore, was the

---

15. This problem has continued to vex the American Government and American interests. The United States provides a far greater percentage of passengers than it does of passenger seats. The reason for this disparity is obvious enough. Let us suppose that 5,000 U.S. passengers wish to visit the United Kingdom during any given period, and 1,000 British passengers wish to visit the United States. All international transport agreements recognise the equal rights of the carriers from both the state of departure and the state of destination. Hence both the designated American and British airlines are entitled to halve the traffic between them. In economic terms B.O.A.C. will be carrying 2,000 or more dollar-paying American passengers.

attempted synthesis of the opposing views at the 1946 Bermuda Conference between the United States and the United Kingdom.

The Agreement that the two states reached at the Conference has provided a formula upon which a majority of states have based their bilateral arrangements, the United States itself being a party to more than forty "Bermuda type" agreements. The effect of such agreements is to grant to the designated airline or airlines of the contracting states the "Two Freedoms" and, subject to certain reservations, the Third, Fourth and Fifth Freedoms. The routes to be operated are specified in separate annexes to the agreement in question. The Final Act of the Bermuda Conference also expressed "the understanding of both governments that services provided by a designated air carrier under the Agreement . . . shall retain as their primary objective the provision of capacity adequate to the traffic demands between the country of which such air carrier is a national and the countries of ultimate destination of the traffic. The right to embark or disembark on such services international traffic destined for and coming from third countries at a point or points on the routes specified in the annex to the Agreement shall be applied in accordance with the general principles of orderly development to which both governments subscribe and shall be subject to the general principle that capacity shall be related:

(a) to traffic requirements between the country of origin and the countries of destination,
(b) to the requirement of through airline operation; and
(c) to the traffic requirements of the area through which the airline passes after taking account of local and regional services".

A similar provision is standard to Agreements of the Bermuda type.

It is worth noticing that although these agreements grant reciprocal transit rights, they have not replaced the "Two Freedoms" Agreement which still plays a significant part in the wording of the international air transport system. The reason for this is obvious enough. An agreement between states A and C to operate a weekly four flight frequency each in both directions might be hampered if it were necessary to fly around state B, the territory of which lies on the direct route between the contracting states. However, providing all three states are parties to the "Two Freedoms" Agreement there would be no problem. This situation in fact occurs on the transatlantic route between the United Kingdom and the United States, the airlines of which states take advantage of the transit rights accorded by the Irish Republic under the "Two Freedoms" Agreement. To take another example, when Qantas wished to commence operating a second frequency between Australia and Mexico, it was faced with the problem that the Commonwealth Government had no entitlement to additional third, fourth, or fifth freedom traffic with Tahiti, the normal Pacific "stepping-stone". As France and Australia were both parties to the "Two Freedoms" Agreement, Qantas was able to take advantage of the right to land at Tahiti for non-traffic purposes granted by the agreement in respect of French territory.

In addition to defining the routes available to the designated airlines, Bermuda-type agreements also applied the principle that fares and freight charges should (subject to the approval of the contracting parties) be fixed by the International Air Transport Association. The provisions intended to give effect to this policy often varied between one agreement and another (even agreements entered into by the United Kingdom were not standard in this respect), but a wide degree of uniformity has been achieved through the I.A.T.A.

I.A.T.A. is not a governmental organisation; it consists of airlines operating international services. Although membership is in no sense compulsory, some ninety airlines have joined the Association. The reason for the strength of its membership is obvious enough. I.A.T.A. members participate in the process of tariff-fixing and adjusting. I.A.T.A.'s powers in this field depend not only upon its own constitution, but are reinforced by the provisions of a multitude of bilateral air transport agreements. If their own states have agreed to accept in principle the rates established by I.A.T.A., naturally enough the airlines wish to take advantage of a right to help establish those rates. This close liaison between the airlines, I.A.T.A. and states is emphasised by the rate-fixing process. A new rate or the adjustment of an existing rate can only be effected with the unanimous agreement of the I.A.T.A. Traffic Conference upon which all members are represented. The rate thus established must then be approved by the governments of the member airlines. A failure by a government to accept a new rate would have the undesirable effect of creating an "open rate" situation, bringing an undesirable "free for all" among airlines. Furthermore, in the majority of cases such a failure would also be a breach by the state concerned of one or of a number of the bilateral arrangements creating its transport rights in foreign air space. States would usually prefer to accept a tariff alteration of which they disapproved rather than jeopardise the right of their airlines to operate a particular route.[16]

d CUSTOMARY INTERNATIONAL LAW

It has already been suggested that both the Paris Convention of 1919 and the Chicago Convention of 1944 were based upon the premise that the absolute and exclusive sovereignty of states over their air space was a pre-existing rule of customary international law, while any limitations upon that sovereignty contained in those Conventions were only binding upon contracting states. The right of a commercial airline to operate in the air space of a foreign state depends, therefore, upon some treaty

---

16. In 1963 the I.A.T.A. approved an increase in transatlantic fares. The U.S. Civil Aviation Board refused to agree to the increase. When the new rates went into effect, Pan American and T.W.A. continued to charge the lower rates. Thereupon several European states, notably the United Kingdom, threatened to impound any Pan American or T.W.A. aircraft landing on their territory. Upon the advice of the State Department the C.A.B. reversed its previous decision and Pan American and T.W.A. raised their fares on routes to those states threatening the drastic action against them. A compromise rate was subsequently agreed to and went into effect in July, 1963.

provision granting such a right to the airline's flag state. But what is the position of an aircraft which has made an unauthorised entry into foreign air space?

i *Civil aircraft in distress among parties to the Chicago Convention*

The Chicago Convention itself deals with one possible reason for an intrusion. Under Article 25, each contracting state "undertakes to provide such measures of assistance to aircraft in distress in its territory as it may find practicable, and to permit, subject to control by its own authorities, the owners of the aircraft or authorities of the state in which the aircraft is registered to provide such measures of assistance as may be necessitated by the circumstances". Although this provision is stated in the most general terms, it is clear that amongst parties to the Convention the absolute and exclusive sovereignty of the territorial state does not give a state the power to deal with intruding civil aircraft in distress at its unfettered discretion. It could not, for example, instruct its military aircraft to shoot down the intruder.

While this may be the position under Article 25, it is obvious that, even among parties to the Convention, cases of intrusion might arise to which the provision does not apply, while other situations may occur which involve a state or states not parties to the Convention at all.

ii *An unauthorised civil flight over the territory of a party to the Convention*

It is unlikely that there should be a deliberate infringement of the air space of another state party to the Chicago Convention by a civil aircraft unless the motives were criminal (e.g. smuggling or espionage). In view of Article 4 of the Convention which lays down that each contracting state "agrees not to use civil aviation for any purpose inconsistent with the aims of this Convention", it is difficult to imagine protests being made by the state of registration if the territorial state resorts to force against deliberate intruders.

Even in the case of aircraft equipped with modern aids, errors in navigation, and consequent unauthorised but inadvertent incursions into foreign air space, can occur. Straying aircraft are not necessarily in distress so that their position falls outside Article 25 of the Convention. The practice of parties to the Convention in such circumstances was summarised by the Israel Government in its written pleadings to the International Court in the *Aerial Incident* case as follows:

> "When a State party to the Chicago Convention in time of peace encounters instances of an infringement of its air space, such as the intrusion of international scheduled air services contrary to Article 6, or intrusion of any aircraft into a duly established prohibited area contrary to Article 9 of the Convention, it normally reacts in one or both of two ways. In the first place, if this is physically possible, it indicates to the aircraft in the appropriate manner, and without causing an undue degree of physical danger to the aircraft and its occupants, that it is performing some unauthorised act. In taking this action that State may also, always exercising due care, require the intruder either to bring the intrusion to an end (i.e. to return to its

authorised position, within or without the air space of the State in question), or to submit itself to examination after landing, at a place, in the territory of the State in question, duly, properly and effectively indicated to it in the appropriate manner. In the second place, and subsequently, it may deal with the infringement of its sovereignty by making the appropriate démarche through the diplomatic channel."[17]

It would certainly be an unsatisfactory situation if parties to the Convention, though obliged to accord certain rights to civil aircraft in distress of other contracting states, could take any action they pleased, including the use of force, against the civil aircraft of other parties that might have strayed into its air space.

iii *Civil aircraft straying into the air space of a state not party to the Convention*

On purely humanitarian grounds, there should be no reason for distinguishing between the position of a territorial state that is, and one that is not, a party to the Convention. Nevertheless, if a state has not accepted any conventional limitations upon the "exclusive sovereignty" it is entitled to exercise in its air space, it is difficult to point to any principle preventing it from treating intruding aircraft as it wishes.

The tragic consequences of military action being taken against a civil airliner in such circumstances can be seen in the *Aerial Incident* case.[18] An Israeli airliner, on a journey from London to Lod via Paris and Vienna, strayed from the flight plan allocated to it between Yugoslavia and Greece with the result that it entered Bulgarian air space. Bulgarian fighter aircraft, sent to investigate the intrusion, attacked and destroyed the airliner. The Bulgarian authorities, while admitting that their aircraft might have acted hastily in not ensuring that the airliner was made aware that they wished it to land for purposes of investigation, denied responsibility for an incident arising out of the violation of Bulgaria's territorial sovereignty.

Although references were made in the separate written submissions of the applicant states (Israel, and the United Kingdom and the United States, nationals of both of which states had been killed in the disaster) to the general duty upon all states to assist aircraft in distress, it was clear from the evidence that the airliner had not been in distress and had in fact been flying in clear weather conditions. Nevertheless, this principle must be relevant to the question of liability. If there is a general duty (and not one limited to parties to the Chicago Convention) to assist aircraft in distress, it would be absurd to suggest that an aircraft, not in distress, which had strayed into the air space of a state, could be put in jeopardy as the result of an attack by military aircraft. Furthermore, it was emphasised by the three states that the remedy for an infraction of a state's sovereignty by the straying of a civil airliner could never be to shoot it down, an act out of all proportion to the wrong. Reference was made to the *Corfu Channel* case[19] in which

---

17. *Pleadings*, at pp. 86–87.
18. Details of the case are to be found in the volume of *Pleadings*.
19. I.C.J. Rep. 1949, p. 4.

the International Court had based its decision partly upon "elementary considerations of humanity even more exacting in peace than in war", and to a decision of the Mexico–U.S. Claims Commission of 1928[20] in which the Commission had laid down that an unauthorised incursion into U.S. territory could not be met with force "unless the importance of preventing or repressing the delinquency by firing is in reasonable proportion to the danger arising from it to the lives of the culprits and other persons in their neighbourhood".

In the event, the Court held that it was not competent to hear a claim against Bulgaria because of the absence of a declaration which was still in force, by that state accepting the compulsory jurisdiction of the Court.[1] Although the Court was thus not able to pronounce upon the merits o the case, such parallels as it is possible to draw from similar situations with regard to the aspects of territorial sovereignty do suggest that the three applicant states' claims were legitimate. In so far as national legislation can be a basis of rules of international law,[2] some states recognise that straying aircraft should either be requested to land while others only require that the aircraft should be escorted from their air space. The legislation of no state provides for the immediate destruction of civil aircraft that have made an unauthorised entry of airspace. A state's rights over its air space, even if termed "absolute and exclusive", can be no greater than its rights over the rest of the national territory. Deliberate killing of trespassers should be no more allowed in the air than on land.

iv *The position of military aircraft*

If a military aircraft is engaged in operations over or against the territorial state, it is clear that the use of force against the offender would be legitimate. Similarly, if a military aircraft, engaged in operations near the border of a state, strays into the territory of that state, it does so at its own risk. On a number of occasions United States aircraft have been shot down either when engaged in espionage activities over the Soviet Union (the well-known "U-2" incident of May, 1960[3]) or having entered Chinese air space following operations over North Vietnam. The United States Government does not seem to have taken the view that the actions of the Soviet Union or of Communist China were contrary to international law.

A number of incidents have occurred involving military aircraft, often unarmed, that have inadvertently (at least, so it was alleged) strayed into foreign air space. In 1952 a Swedish aircraft was shot down by a Soviet aircraft over part of the Baltic Sea claimed by Russia to be within its territorial waters. Apart from any dispute over the extent of these waters, there was also a fundamental disagreement over the rights of the territorial state. The Soviet Union in this and other incidents has contended that it has the right to insist that the offending aircraft land at a Soviet airport for investigation. If the aircraft fails to comply with a request to land it can be

---

20. *Garcia* v. *U.S.*, 4 U.N.R.I.A.A. 119.   1. See below, pp. 511–523.
2. See above, p. 20.   3. See the discussion in (1960) 54 A.J.I.L. 836.

attacked. The view of Sweden, and of the United States when involved in subsequent similar incidents, was that the territorial state has the right to "warn off" straying foreign aircraft, but has no right to demand that they should land.[4]

It is doubtful whether the United States view can be considered as a rule of international law. A number of states claim that an intruding aircraft can be called upon to land and fired upon if it ignores signals to do so.[5] If directives are given to aircraft flying in the vicinity of such states to leave air space and not to obey orders to land if they should stray, incidents are inevitable. Military aircraft are in a category apart from civil airliners. If they travel near the territory of a potentially hostile state (in the idealogical sense) their motives if they enter that territory by accident are likely to be misconstrued. Even the concession that they should first be called upon to land before an attack is made seems a concession to humanity and the comity of states rather than to legal principle.

B. Jurisdiction in space

a THE BOUNDARY OF AIR SPACE

The final limitation upon the exclusive sovereignty of states over their air space is that the upward extent of air space is no longer regarded as indeterminate. The launching of satellites into orbit round the earth and the absence of protest by states over the territory of which these orbits are projected have led to a substantial alteration in the concept of air space.

No precise delimitation has yet been made of the boundary between "air space" and "space", although it must lie somewhere between the highest point at which an aircraft can fly and the lowest point at which satellites can orbit without burning up in the thicker parts of the earth's atmosphere. Hitherto this general proposition has not required greater precision, although there may come a time when states wish to "operate" rockets and satellites through the territorial air space of other states. As long ago as 1959 a government spokesman said in the House of Lords that "Her Majesty's Government consider that sovereignty over space above national territory cannot extend indefinitely upwards. It cannot, however, be said that international law has yet determined the exact limit to be placed on the extension of sovereignty upwards. . . . There are still too many unsolved problems in this field to justify the adoption of any sweeping legal propositions in whatever direction they tend."[6]

---

4. Details of a number of incidents are given in (1953) 47 A.J.I.L. 559.
5. In many of the incidents claims were made that a signal to land had been ignored. The difficulty of making understandable signals in supersonic aircraft is apparent enough, particularly when the evidence available suggests that no recognised system of signalling was employed. In the *Aerial Incident* case (*Pleadings*, p. 94) Israel referred to Annex 2 of the I.C.A.O. Convention laying down a system of signals indicating that an aircraft is flying in the vicinity of a restricted, prohibited or danger area, but no such signals were employed by the Bulgarian fighters, or in any of the other incidents.
6. Viscount Hailsham, Parl. Deb. (H. of L.), 1958-9, Vol. 216, col. 975.

b THE LEGAL REGIME OF SPACE

In 1961 by Resolution 1721, the General Assembly of the United Nations unanimously commended to states two principles: that international law, including the U.N. Charter, applied to "outer space and celestial bodies", and that outer space and celestial bodies were "free for exploration and use by all states in conformity with international law and are not subject to national appropriation". Indeed, from the earliest days of orbital flight states have repeatedly asserted their beliefs in the communal enjoyment of the benefits of space exploration. Both the United States and the Soviet Union have reiterated their adherence to the principles of the 1961 Assembly resolution as representing existing international law.

This substantial measure of agreement enabled the Committee on the Peaceful Uses of Outer Space to draw up under the auspices of the United Nations a draft treaty which the General Assembly commended to member states in December, 1966. Article II of the Treaty restates the already accepted principle that "Outer space, including the moon and other celestial bodies, is not subject to national appropriation by claim of sovereignty, by means of use or occupation, or by any other means." Space exploration is to be carried out "for the benefit and in the interests of all countries" (Article I): all activities are to be carried "in accordance with international law" (Article III); and parties to the Treaty undertake not to place in orbit round the earth, or install in space, weapons of mass destruction, and to use the moon and other celestial bodies exclusively for peaceful purposes (Article IV).

On the question of jurisdiction, however, the Treaty is obviously defective. Article VIII applies the concept of "national character" by providing that jurisdiction and control over satellites and other objects launched into space is vested in the state of registry while the projectile is in outer space or on a celestial body. But what happens when it is possible to establish space stations along the lines of the various Antarctic bases, on the moon? Does the state creating a station of this type acquire sufficient physical possession of the base area to claim jurisdiction on the ground of a quasi-territorial principle? Such issues are for the future to settle; the Treaty itself is but the barest outline of the legal framework that will be necessary once space travel and exploration are an established feature of international life.

CHAPTER EIGHT

JURISDICTION—III
OTHER ASPECTS OF JURISDICTION

While the first of the chapters dealing with jurisdiction contained a central theme—that is, territorial jurisdiction and the main exemptions from its application to persons within the territory of a state—and the previous chapter was concerned with maritime and aerial jurisdiction, there remain a number of isolated topics relating to jurisdiction which must be considered in the present chapter. In the first place, it is necessary to examine the concept of nationality in the context of jurisdiction according to the "personal" principle. Then it is proposed to deal with "domestic jurisdiction"—the notion that a state has certain basic jurisdictional rights untrammelled by international obligations. Finally, some comment is required on extradition—the process for returning fugitive criminals to the state where the crime was committed—and the theory of political asylum.

I NATIONALITY AND PERSONAL JURISDICTION

A. Nationality

As a general proposition, international law does not limit the right of a state to extend its nationality to whomsoever it pleases, although international law may not prevent other states from refusing to recognise a grant of nationality in certain circumstances. In other words, for internal purposes (the right to vote or to participate in social benefit schemes, etc.) a state may bestow its nationality with complete freedom, but for the grant of nationality to be effective against other states it must conform to certain general principles recognised by international law as the basis of the bond of nationality.

This point was made very forcibly by the International Court in the *Nottebohm* case,[1] in which Liechtenstein attempted to exercise a right of diplomatic protection with respect to a person who had been naturalised as a Liechtenstein citizen after a period of residence in that state of barely

---

1. I.C.J. Rep. 1955, p. 4.

a few weeks, against Guatemala where that person had lived and built up a business over a period of years. The Court first explained the basic proposition that it was for Liechtenstein, "as for every Sovereign State, to settle by its own legislation the rules relating to the acquisition of its nationality, and to confer that nationality by naturalisation granted by its own organs in accordance with that legislation",[2] and then pointed out that the issue it had to consider was not one that was the concern of the legal system of Liechtenstein alone. "To exercise protection, to apply to the Court, is to place oneself on the plane of international law. It is international law which determines whether a state is entitled to exercise protection and to seise the Court" of a dispute.[3] The reason for this apparent conflict, the Court explained, was that "the diversity of demographic conditions has thus far made it impossible for any general agreement to be reached on the rules relating to nationality, although the latter by its very nature affects international relations. It has been considered that the best way of making such rules accord with the varying demographic conditions in different countries is to leave the fixing of such rules to the competence of each state. On the other hand, a state cannot claim that the rules it has thus laid down are entitled to recognition by another state unless it has acted in conformity with this general aim of making the legal bond of nationality accord with the individual's genuine connection with the state which assumes the defence of its citizens by means of protection as against other states."[4]

While the existence of such a genuine link between a state and someone whom it claims to be its national is primarily of importance in the context of the rule of nationality of claims with regard to diplomatic protection, it is obviously a factor which must be borne in mind in relation to the external effects of a state's nationality laws whenever they might come in conflict with the rights of other states. To take an extreme situation which nevertheless illustrates a potential area of conflict, if state A and state B were bound by treaty to adhere in their municipal legislation to the principle that foreign nationals, even if also nationals of the conscripting state, could not be called up into the armed forces, it would not be open to state B, which disapproved of a military build-up by state A, to pass legislation "naturalising" all nationals of state A as nationals of state B, and then claim that the call up of such persons was a breach of state A's obligations under the treaty. Similarly, a state could not free itself from its obligation to extradite a fugitive offender by hurriedly bestowing its nationality upon the individual concerned in order to take advantage of a term in the extradition treaty with the requesting state allowing the parties to withhold surrender of their own nationals.[5]

The International Court in the *Nottebohm* case talked in terms of a genuine link between the individual and the state claiming him as its

---

2. I.C.J. Rep. 1955, at p. 20.   3. *Ibid.*, at pp. 20–21.   4. *Ibid.*, at p. 23.
5. For the extradition of nationals, see below at pp. 334–335, 345–346.

national. However, for a grant of nationality to be entitled to international recognition it would seem likely that it must at least coincide in manner or conditions with the circumstances in which states in general bestow their nationality. It is clearly necessary, therefore, to examine the circumstances in which nationality can normally be acquired.

B. Acquisition of Nationality

a NATIONALITY ACQUIRED BY BIRTH

The nationality laws of every state provide for the acquisition of its nationality by birth. The manner in which nationality is thus granted, may be divided into two basic principles—the *jus sanguinis*, i.e. by descent, by being born of parents who are nationals; and the *jus soli*, by being born in the territory of the state itself. In most states, the nationality laws are based primarily on one or on the other principle, though provision is also made in certain exceptional cases for acquisition of nationality according to the alternative principle. For example, as will be discussed later, both the United Kingdom and the United States, although their nationality laws are based on the *jus soli*, allow the children of their nationals, although born abroad, to acquire their nationality in certain circumstances.

i *Jus sanguinis*

It is a reasonable enough rule that a state should be entitled to bestow its nationality upon children born of parents who are themselves nationals. In practice, municipal legislation tends to adopt the nationality of the father as decisive in the case of a legitimate child[6] (partly at least because marriage does not in all states automatically bestow the husband's nationality on the wife). It should be realised that the consequence of such an absolute rule of descent is that a person might be entitled to a particular nationality although for generations no member of the family has resided in the state concerned. This situation can arise under the nationality laws of most European states, which base their legislation on the *jus sanguinis* concept. For example, under Article 17 (1) of the French Nationality Law of October, 1945, a person is French who is the "legitimate child of a French father". Similar provisions are to be found in the laws of most European States,[7] and in a large number of states outside Europe (particularly those in South-East Asia and North Africa that at one time formed part of the French overseas empire).[8]

---

6. Many nationality laws accept that an illegitimate child will usually take the nationality of its mother: e.g. 8 U.S.C., Sect. 1409 (c); Art. 1 of the Swiss Federal Nationality Law of 1952; Art. 1 (3) of the Swedish Citizenship Act of 1950, etc.

7. E.g. s. 4 of the German Nationality Act, 1913; Art. 1 of the Greek Nationality Law of 1955; Art. 1 of the Swiss Law of 1952, etc. The texts of the nationality laws of many states are to be found in the U.N. Legislative Series publications *Laws Concerning Nationality* (1954) and the 1959 *Supplement* to that volume.

8. E.g. Laos, Cambodia, Tunisia, etc.

On the other hand, in common law jurisdictions, which take as their basis the *jus soli*, acceptance of the *jus sanguinis* has only been partial, and limitations have been placed on the acquisition of nationality by descent. Under the British Nationality Act, 1948, for example, although citizenship by descent is automatic in all cases where the father was born in the United Kingdom and Colonies, citizenship by descent is only possible to a child whose father acquired citizenship by descent in a limited number of cases. In all cases but one, these exceptions deal with situations where the father had at the time of the birth some other connection with the United Kingdom (for example, being in the service of the Crown).[9] However, the Act also allows the child of a father who is a citizen of the United Kingdom and Colonies by descent to be registered within twelve months of the birth.[10] The United States Immigration and Nationality Act, 1952, is similar in that it provides for a number of situations in which a person born outside the United States is automatically an American citizen, but in each case some connection is required with the United States other than the American nationality of one or other, or both, of the parents.[11]

ii *Jus soli*

Under the British Nationality Act, s. 4, the basic principle is that "every person born within the United Kingdom and Colonies . . . shall be a citizen of the United Kingdom and Colonies by birth." The main exception to the application of the *jus soli* is that it does not apply if the father "possesses such immunity from suit and legal process as is accorded to an envoy of a foreign sovereign power accredited to His Majesty, and is not a citizen of the United Kingdom and Colonies". This exception is drafted in general terms to include persons who, though not diplomatic agents, are granted a similar "immunity from suit and legal process" as, for example, representatives to or officials of an international organisation. A similar result is achieved by the United States Act of 1952 which lays down that "a person born in the United States, and subject to the jurisdiction thereof" shall be a national and citizen of the United States at birth (8 U.S.C., sect. 1401 (a) (1)).

The *jus soli* provides the basic principle in the Nationality Laws of the states of the British Commonwealth, and of a number of former members, like Ireland and South Africa. There are also several states of South America which apply the *jus soli* in preference to the *jus sanguinis*. The Argentine Nationality, Citizenship and Naturalisation Act of 1954 provides in Article 1 that every person born in Argentine territory shall be an Argentinian, except in the case of a "child of an alien officer of the foreign service of another state" (Article 2), while the *jus sanguinis* is only applied if the child of an Argentine father or mother becomes domiciled in the Argentine for an uninterrupted period of twelve months before reaching

---

9. S. 5 (1) (c).   10. S. 5 (1) (b).
11. 8 U.S.C., Sect. 1401 (a) (3), (4), (5) & (7).

the age of 18, or if the father or mother is an officer in the Argentine foreign service, or if the law of the country where the birth occurred does not confer nationality on the child. Under the Paraguay Constitution of 1940, s. 38, a person is a Paraguayan national if he was born in Paraguayan territory, but if born abroad of Paraguayan parents, one of them must have been at the time of the birth in the service of the Republic, and if only one parent was a Paraguayan, there is an additional residential requirement.

Even in states that apply the *jus sanguinis* as the primary rule, the *jus soli* is also adopted in certain situations. The degree to which the *jus soli* is used to "supplement" the *jus sanguinis* varies considerably between one state and another. In Spain, for example, Article 17 (1) of the Civil Code, which declares that a person born in Spanish territory is a Spanish national, is limited in Article 18 by the provision that the benefit of Article 17 (1) "shall not extend" to a child born of alien parents unless the prescribed declaration is made in which they "opt on behalf of the child for Spanish nationality and denounce any other nationality". French nationality is bestowed automatically on a legitimate child born in France of a father who was also born there (Article 23 (1) of the Nationality Code), and, subject to a right of repudiation within the six months preceding his majority, on a legitimate child born in France of a mother who was also born in France (Article 24 (1)). These provisions do not apply, however, to children born in France of diplomatic agents or career consuls of foreign nationality (Article 33).

b NATIONALITY SUBSEQUENTLY ACQUIRED

(i) *Marriage*

A majority of states at one time had nationality legislation, based upon the concept that the wife was in some way subject to the *potestas* of her husband, to the effect that a foreign woman marrying a national automatically acquired his nationality and that a woman who was a national marrying a foreigner lost her nationality on marriage. The German Nationality Act of 1913, for example, laid down in s. 6 that a woman who married a German citizen acquired the citizenship of the husband by virtue of the marriage, and in s. 17 (6) that a woman would cease to be a citizen on marrying an alien. As far as Britain was concerned, the Naturalisation Act, 1870, had first laid down that a woman British subject marrying an alien should be deemed an alien, so that s. 10 (1) of the British Nationality and Status of Aliens Act, 1914, was declaratory of existing law in stating the general principle that "the wife of a British subject shall be deemed to be a British subject, and the wife of an alien shall be deemed to be an alien".

With the increasing emancipation of women in the western hemisphere, there was agitation to have these relics of female subservience removed. In addition, there was the more obvious practical problem that, if a wife did *not* acquire the nationality of her foreign husband (as could happen under the laws of some states), she might well become stateless by the operation of the laws of her own state governing loss of nationality. It was the practical problem which was dealt with first. Article 8 of the Hague Convention Relating to the Conflict of Nationality Laws, 1930, laid down that if the national law of the wife "causes her to lose her nationality on marriage with a foreigner, this consequence shall be conditional on her acquiring the nationality of the husband". In the United Kingdom, in order to bring the 1914 Act into line with the Convention, an Act of 1933 amended s. 10 (2) of the earlier Act to provide that where a woman has "married an alien, and was at the time of her marriage a British subject, she shall not, by reason only of her marriage, be deemed to have ceased to be a British subject unless, by reason of her marriage, she acquired the nationality of her husband". The British Nationality Act, 1948, has made significant alterations in the law relating to loss of nationality which will be discussed below. As far as women are concerned, on marriage to a foreigner, they retain their citizenship of the United Kingdom and Colonies, although, if they also acquire their husband's nationality, they may make a declaration renouncing this citizenship of the U.K. and Colonies (s. 19). The Act also alters the position of foreign women married (at any time) to citizens of the U.K. and Colonies. Under s. 6 (2), such a woman is entitled as of right to be registered as a citizen of the U.K. and Colonies.[12]

This change in attitude towards the position of married women is reflected in the legislation of other states. In the Federal German Republic, for example, the 1949 Constitution enunciated the principle of the equality of the sexes (Article 3 (2)), and that any legislative provision in conflict with the principle of equality should remain in force, subject to prior amendment, until 31st March, 1953, at the latest. As no amendment was made by that date, the discriminating provisions of the 1913 Nationality Act ceased to operate. The result was far from satisfactory because the repeal of s. 6 meant that no woman marrying a German citizen could acquire her husband's German nationality. To fill this gap, the Federal parliament passed an Act of 1957 which enabled an alien woman marrying a German to claim naturalisation, or, if the marriage was contracted before a German registrar, to acquire German nationality automatically by lodging with the registrar, at the time of the marriage, a declaration that she wished to become a German national.

The present legal position in the United States based upon the Act of 1952, is that marriage by any alien to a United States citizen, man or woman, enables the foreign spouse to be naturalised upon compliance with all the requirements of the naturalisation laws except that, instead of the more stringent residential requirements, the applicant need only have resided continuously in the United States for at least 3 years immediately preceding the filing of the petition, providing *inter alia* that during the 3 years immediately preceding the filing of the petition he or she has been living in marital union with the citizen spouse and has been

---

12. See also s. 1 of the British Nationality Act, 1965.

physically present in the United States for at least half that period (8 U.S.C., Sect. 1430 (a)). Marriage by a United States citizen to a foreigner does not in itself deprive the U.S. citizen of his or her status unless, as a consequence of the marriage, the citizen applies for and is granted naturalisation in the foreign state.[13]

ii *Naturalisation*

Naturalisation is the method adopted for admitting foreign nationals voluntarily to citizenship. The legislation of most states is extremely detailed, so that the most that can be attempted is an outline of the relevant British and American law together with a few references to the law of other states. However, it is possible to suggest a number of common features. For example, the naturalisation provisions in the legislation include requirements of good character, knowledge of the national language, residence, government service, etc., though, from the international standpoint, the most important are obviously those like residence or governmental service which establish the connection between the state and the applicant.

Most states require that the applicant should normally have a residence qualification. Under the British Nationality Act, 1948, the period is 12 months immediately preceding the application and not less than 4 years out of the 7 years prior to the twelve months (Article 10 (1); 2nd Sched., paras. 1 & 2). Under the United States Act of 1952, the usual period is 5 years residence, which must include half that time of actual physical presence in the United States (8 U.S.C., Sect. 1427). The Austrian Citizenship Act of 1949, Article 5 (3), requires that an applicant shall have been resident for at least 4 years; in Chile the period of continuous residence is 5 years (Decree of 1925, Art. 2); as also in Czechoslovakia (Act of 1943, Art. 3 (1) (b)); the Greek law of 1856, as amended, prescribes a period of 2 years if the applicant is of Greek ethnic origin, otherwise 3 years, *after* a declaration of intent to acquire nationality (Art. 15); and so on. The periods may vary, but they do at least create some link between the granting state and the applicant.

Under both the British and the American legislation, the period of residence may be shortened if the applicant has some other connection with the United Kingdom or the United States as the case may be. Service under the Crown on behalf of the United Kingdom government is taken into account, and the Secretary of State may also take into consideration periods of service under the government of a Commonwealth country. As far as the American legislation is concerned, service in the U.S. forces or employment under contract with the U.S. Government or on behalf of a U.S. firm or corporation abroad may be counted, provided, having

---

13. 8 U.S.C. Sect. 1481 deals only with loss of nationality by voluntary act. Consequently where a U.S. citizen *automatically* acquires a foreign nationality by marriage to a foreigner, that citizen does not lose U.S. citizenship: see, for example, *Rueff* v. *Brownell*, 116 F. Supp. 298 (1953).

been admitted for permanent residence, the applicant has fulfilled an initial period of physical presence in the United States.

The legislation of a number of states recognises that there may be links between the applicant and the state itself which are sufficiently close to give the applicant a *right* to citizenship. With the change in attitude towards the effect of marriage on nationality, the trend has been to allow the wife to acquire her husband's nationality as of right if she so wishes. This is certainly the case under the British Nationality Act which entitles "a woman who has been married to a citizen of the United Kingdom and Colonies . . . to be registered as a citizen of the United Kingdom and Colonies" (s. 6 (2)).[14] The position in the Federal German Republic is slightly different in that an alien woman marrying a German may "claim naturalisation", although, if the marriage is contracted before a German registrar, she may acquire German nationality by deposit with the registrar at the time of the marriage of a declaration that she wishes to become a German national.

Registration under the British Nationality Act of 1948 was not, however, limited to women married to citizens of the U.K. and Colonies. Because of the common nationality of British subjects shared with the independent Dominions and the Colonies before the 1948 Act came into force, part of the agreed plan upon which the Act and similar legislation throughout the Dominions was based was that a single transfer of citizenship *inter se* should be freely available. Hence s. 6 (1) of the British Act provided that a citizen of any Commonwealth country (or of Eire) was entitled to be registered as a citizen of the U.K. and Colonies if he satisfied the Secretary of State that he was ordinarily resident in the United Kingdom and had been so resident throughout the previous twelve months or was in the service of the United Kingdom Government.[15] With the passage of time a number of Commonwealth countries have enacted nationality legislation significantly different from that envisaged by the 1948 Plan.[16] And the United Kingdom Government itself has substantially altered s. 6 (1) by requiring a 5 year residential qualification.[17]

A more common type of exemption from the normal processes of naturalisation is an overall discretion allowing the appropriate government minister or department to naturalise any alien if such action is in the public

---

14. For the problems of interpreting this provision, see Parry, *Nationality and Citizenship Laws of the Commonwealth*, pp. 258–262; see also s. 1 of the British Nationality Act, 1965, which extends the registration procedure to women marrying British subjects without citizenship.

15. Which includes service in the Government of Northern Ireland, or any Colony, protectorate or trust territory administered by the United Kingdom: s. 32 (1).

16. E.g. the Malayan Constitution of 1957 makes no provision for the registration of citizens of the United Kingdom or of any other Commonwealth country as Malayan citizens; in 1959 New Zealand amended s. 8 (1) of its Nationality Act which allowed registration as of right to provide for a Ministerial discretion and for more stringent requirements: *British Nationality and New Zealand Citizenship Amendment Act*, s. 4 (1). Other Commonwealth states (e.g. Ghana and Nigeria) have legislation requiring a 5 year residential qualification similar to that later adopted in the United Kingdom.

17. *Commonwealth Immigrants Act*, 1962, s. 12 (2).

interest. For example, Article 5 (3) of the Austrian Act allows waiver of the 5 year qualifiying period if the Federal Government indicates that to grant citizenship would be in the interests of the state: Article 3 (2) of the Czechoslovakian Act allows waiver "in special cases" of the residential requirement. Article 6 of the Swedish Citizenship Act of 1950 enables the King in Council to confer Swedish citizenship upon an alien who fulfils certain conditions including a 7 year Swedish domicile, but goes on to provide that naturalisation may be granted even though these conditions are not fulfilled "if it is found to be of advantage to Sweden that the applicant should be granted Swedish citizenship". If naturalisation "in special cases" is granted in states having legislation of this type there is the obvious danger that there might not be a close connection between the applicant and the granting state.

The procedures for naturalisation in most states are essentially of an administrative nature. The executive retains a power to exclude, except in a limited number of instances where a right to obtain nationality may be available by formal application or registration alone because of the close link between the applicant and the granting state. However, to these administrative procedures the law of the United States provides an unusual and major exception. In the United States naturalisation is by a purely judicial process.[18] Because of this fact, the provisions of the 1952 Immigration and Nationality Act are more detailed than those of the British Act of 1948. There being no administrative discretion to exclude "undesirables" (other than the strict immigration procedures to which aliens are subjected on initial entry to the United States), the grounds upon which naturalisation may be refused are spelt out at great length. For example, in addition to specifying the need that the petitioner should be and remain a person of good moral character, attached to the principles of the Constitution, and well disposed to the good order and happiness of the United States (8 U.S.C., Sect. 1427 (a) (3)), the Act states that no person shall be naturalised who advocates anarchy or is an anarchist, or is a member of the Communist Party or any other totalitarian party, or advocates or who is a member of a party that advocates the overthrow by force or violence or other unconstitutional means of the United States government, etc. (Sect. 1424).

iii *Other means of acquiring nationality*

   1   *Collective naturalisation*

Collective naturalisation is the term often used for the process whereby the inhabitants of an area, which is incorporated into the territory of a state and therefore comes under its sovereignty, acquire the nationality of that state.

If the transfer of territory is effected by force contrary to international law, non-recognition of the territorial change would involve non-recognition

---

18. "Exclusive jurisdiction", in naturalisation proceedings is bestowed on Federal District Courts and upon all state courts of record: 8 U.S.C. 1421 (a).

of any change of nationality claimed by the annexing state to have occurred as a result of the transfer. But the more important question is whether, assuming the validity of the title acquired by the new sovereign, international law allows the successor state an unfettered discretion to grant or withhold its citizenship from the inhabitants of the acquired territory.

One writer has described the practice of states as "sporadic and *ad hoc*", but from such evidence of state practice that was available deduced the following principles:[19]

> "1. Subject to any relevant international agreements, the question of the acquisition of nationality by virtue of incorporation of territory is regulated by the municipal legislation of the state to whom the territory is transferred in sovereignty.
> 2. Such legislation must be based upon the principle of connexion between individuals and the territory concerned.
> 3. Such legislation can normally affect only the nationality of aliens who were nationals of the state to whom the territory formerly belonged, since no greater connexion is created, by virtue only of the territorial transfer, between the nationals of third states and the annexing state than between those nationals and the latter's predecessor in title.
> 4. A distinction exists between cases where the predecessor in title has become totally extinct and cases where there is a partial annexation or cession of its territory, or secession from it, whilst the predecessor state continues to exist, albeit in a truncated form, or with the addition of fresh territory in compensation. Where the predecessor state becomes totally extinct the possibility does not exist of retaining its nationality, and its former nationals must, in most cases, either become nationals of the successor state (or successor states where there is partition or fragmentation) or stateless."

Because of the possibility that the inhabitants of a territory might be deprived of their previous nationality and not acquire the nationality of the new territory, the International Law Commission included a common article to deal with such a situation in two conventions it drafted in 1954 on the subject of statelessness. Under this article it was provided that treaties dealing with transfers of territory "shall include provisions for ensuring that, subject to the exercise of the right of option, inhabitants of these territories shall not become stateless" and that, "in the absence of such provisions, states to which territory is transferred, or which otherwise acquire territory, or new states formed on territory previously belonging to another state or states shall confer their nationality upon the inhabitants of such territory unless such persons retain their former nationality by option or otherwise or unless they have or acquire another nationality". While the members of the Commission did not suggest that this common article was based on existing customary international law, they did feel that the notion of acquisition of the new sovereign's nationality, subject to a right of option, had "acquired a degree of recognition" in the practice of states.[20] Eventually a conference was called under

---

19. Jones, *British Nationality Law*, p. 18.
20. See the I.L.C. Report reproduced in the docs. section of (1954) 48 A.J.I.L., at p. 60.

the auspices of the United Nations to consider the question of statelessness, and the convention adopted by the conference did include a provision largely reproducing the common article of the Commission's drafts. Although the new convention has received few ratifications, its existence is an encouragement to states to accept a common approach to matters of nationality in general, and to issues like the consequences of a change of sovereignty, upon which there already exists a measure of agreement, in particular.

The practice of the United Kingdom and of the United States has been largely influenced by the territorial nature of the common law. It was early recognised under English law that the inhabitants of territory annexed by the Crown acquired the status of a British subject. This rule certainly applied to persons who were nationals by birth and intended to remain resident in the territory, but it was not clear how far the application of the rule extended to persons with a less obvious connection (e.g. nationals who, though domiciled in the territory, were resident abroad). In practice, the position was usually settled by treaty or Order in Council. S. 11 of the British Nationality Act does no more than provide that if any territory "becomes a part of the United Kingdom and Colonies, His Majesty may by Order in Council specify the persons who shall be citizens of the United Kingdom and Colonies by reason of their connection with that territory".

The principle that the inhabitants of an acquired area may become, if they choose to remain in the area concerned, citizens of the new sovereign has also been adopted by the United States. In the case of the cession of Florida by Spain to the United States in 1819, the treaty of cession provided that the inhabitants of Florida "shall be incorporated in the Union of the United States as soon as may be consistent with the principles of the Federal Constitution, and admitted to the enjoyment of the privileges, rights and immunities of the citizens of the United States". The effect of this cession was considered by the Supreme Court in the case of the *356 Bales of Cotton*.[1] The Court held that, because of the self-executing nature of the treaty, it was unnecessary to consider the effect of the transfer of sovereignty to the United States on the nationality of inhabitants of Florida in the absence of express provision. However, the Court did state that the relations of the inhabitants "with their former sovereign are dissolved, and new relations are created between them and the government which has acquired the territory"; and then added that the "same act which transfers their country, transfers the allegiance of those *who remain in it.*" Thus it was held in another case[2] that a British subject, in New York at the time of the revolt of the American Colonies, had by withdrawing to the dominions of the British Crown elected not to acquire United States citizenship following the severance of the link between the Colonies and the Crown.

---

1. 1 Pet. 511 (1825).   2. *Inglis v. Sailor's Snug Harbor*, 3 Pet. 99.

2 *Change of status: adoption and legitimation*

The laws of most states accept that a change in the family of an individual, whether by adoption or by legitimation, will have the effect of altering his nationality if the adoptive parents or the father acquired by legitimation have a different nationality from his own.

Under the British Nationality Act, s. 23 (1), a person born out of wedlock and legitimated by the subsequent marriage of his parents shall be treated "for the purpose of determining whether he is a citizen of the United Kingdom and Colonies" as if he had been born legitimate. As far as adoption is concerned, successive Adoption Acts have laid down that where an adoption order is made in respect of an infant who is not a citizen of the United Kingdom and Colonies, then, if the adopter, or in the case of a joint adoption, the male adopter, is a citizen of the United Kingdom and Colonies, the infant shall be a citizen of the United Kingdom and Colonies as from the date of the order.

United States law is similar in relation to legitimation. By 8 U.S.C. sect. 1409 (a) the normal rules for acquiring nationality at birth under sect. 1401 "shall apply as of the date of birth to a child born out of wedlock . . . if the paternity of such child is established while such child is under the age of twenty-one years by legitimation." This rule is wider than that contained in the British Act which restricts legitimation for the purposes of acquiring citizenship of the United Kingdom and Colonies to legitimation by the subsequent marriage of the parents. Sect. 1409 envisages any alternative method of legitimation by establishment of paternity recognised by the law of the father's domicile. So, if a United States citizen acquires a domicile in a place by the law of which natural children may be legitimated by the father's acknowledgment of the children, acknowledgment by that citizen of the children of an alien mother to whom he was not married will be effective to bestow United States citizenship upon them.

On the other hand, adoption of an alien by a United States citizen does not automatically bestow citizenship on the person adopted. Subject to certain age restrictions, sect. 1434 enables the adoptive parent or parents to present a naturalisation petition on behalf of the child. In order for the petition to succeed the child must fulfil the general requirements for naturalisation except that the period of residence is reduced to two years, while the required length of physical presence is set at one year. If the child is of "tender years he may be presumed to be of good moral character, attached to the principles of the Constitution, and well disposed to the good order and happiness of the United States."

C. Loss of nationality

For the sake of completeness, some comment is necessary on the means whereby nationality can be lost. Basically, there is a distinction between voluntary and involuntary loss, but these categories do not adequately describe the situation where an individual as a result of a voluntary act (e.g. accepting a post in the service of a foreign government) loses his nationality, a consequence which he may or may not wish. It is proposed, therefore, to classify situations in which nationality may be lost according to the legislation of a number of states under three headings: voluntary renunciation; loss by operation of law; and involuntary loss.

a VOLUNTARY RENUNCIATION

Loss, as opposed to deprivation, of nationality under the British Nationality Act is *only* possible by a formal act of renunciation (s. 19 (1)). In many other states, loss may occur in a number of ways, including renunciation. To a limited extent, renunciation is possible under French law, which gives certain children entitled to French nationality by birth the right to renounce it on attaining their majority.[3] The law of the United States allows formal renunciation before a diplomatic or consular officer of the United States in a foreign state, or before such officer as the Attorney-General may prescribe in the United States (8 U.S.C., sect. 1481 (a) 6 & 7).

b LOSS BY OPERATION OF LAW

It has already been explained that this classification has something in common with renunciation in that it is usually based upon voluntary conduct by the individual, although the loss of nationality is only a consequence of the conduct. It has been adopted in the laws of a majority of states. The type of conduct covered is the acquisition of a new nationality, taking an oath of allegiance to another state, desertion from the armed forces of which the individual is a national, etc. Under the Brazilian Act of 1949, Article 22, a Brazilian shall lose his nationality if, *inter alia*, he acquires another nationality by voluntary naturalisation, or accepts from any foreign government any commission, employment or pension without permission of the President of the Republic. The French law of 1945 lays down a number of ways in which French nationality can be lost: voluntary acquisition of a foreign nationality (Article 87); acting as if a national of a foreign state (Article 96); taking employment in the service of a foreign state or a foreign army (Article 97). Congress has legislated that United States nationality may be lost by obtaining naturalisation in a foreign state; taking an oath or making an affirmation or other formal declaration of allegiance to a foreign state; serving in the armed forces of a foreign state without prior authorisation from the Secretary of State and the Secretary of Defence; acquiring foreign nationality as a result of service under the government of a foreign state; or taking an oath of allegiance because of accepting service with a foreign government; voting in an election in a foreign state; deserting from U.S. forces in time of war; etc. (Sect. 1481 (a)); or, if also entitled to the nationality of another state, by voluntarily seeking or claiming the

---

3.   Arts. 20 and 24 of the Nationality Code; see also Art. 91.

benefits of nationality of any other state and then continuously residing for three years in the foreign state of which he is a national (Sect. 1482), unless of course such residence results from service on behalf of the U.S. government, etc., as defined by Sects. 1485 and 1486. However, the Supreme Court has in a series of decisions declared a number of these provisions unconstitutional. For example, it has been held that leaving the United States in time of war to evade military training could not be a ground for expatriation without the provision of judicial safeguards; that 3 years residence in the territory of a foreign state of which a U.S. naturalised citizen was formerly a national or in which the place of his birth is situated denies equality to naturalised citizens as compared with natural born citizens; and that it was inconsistent with the Fourteenth Amendment that the state should be able to deprive a citizen of his citizenship for voting in a foreign election.[4] In its approach to the question of expatriation the Supreme Court has rather "taken the bit between its teeth", but the rationalisation of this series of decisions is still not altogether clear. In the most recent case, *Afroyim* v. *Rusk*, a bare majority seemed to favour the wide principle that a citizen should not be deprived of his citizenship without his consent, though what constitutes "consent" for the purposes of this rule is left for future determination.

c INVOLUNTARY LOSS

The loss of nationality is particularly serious when it renders the individual stateless. In most cases of voluntary loss or loss by operation of law the individual has sought a connection with a foreign state, and situations where this connection is not a basis for claiming a new nationality have been reduced by international agreement, most notably in the case of marriage. However, compulsory expatriation against the will of an individual is essentially a political problem. Large numbers of Jews lost their German nationality in the Hitler era. Refugees from Communist persecutions in the years following the Second World War were deprived of their nationality.[5] International law being primarily a system of law concerning the relations of states and other entities operating on the international plane, such mass "expatriations", however immoral, gave no international remedy to these unfortunate persons nor did any state have a legal right of complaint against their former homeland. Their future depended, or will

---

4. In *Kennedy* v. *Mendoza-Martinez*, 372 U.S. 144 (1963); *Schneider* v. *Rusk*, 377 U.S. 163 (1964); and *Afroyim* v. *Rusk*, 87 S. Ct. 1660 (1967) respectively. *Schneider* v. *Rusk* is dealt with further below.

5. E.g. Art. 17.1 (2) of the Hungarian Nationality Act of 1948 provided that the Government may "on a proposal made by the Minister of Interior deprive of his Hungarian nationality a person who . . . on going abroad contravenes or evades the statutory provisions relating to departure from the country". Art. 17.3 goes on to provide that the property of such a person "shall be confiscated".

Art. 12 of the Polish Nationality Act of 1951 laid down that a Polish national who is resident abroad may be deprived of Polish nationality *inter alia* if he has "failed in his duty of loyalty to the Polish State", "acted against the vital interests of the People's Poland", "left the territory of the Polish State unlawfully", or "refused to return to Poland at the summons of the competent authority".

depend, entirely upon the good will of those states prepared to allow them entry and, subsequently, a new national identity.[6]

Cases of individual deprivation of citizenship are most common in municipal laws relating to naturalised persons. Most states have rules providing for the revocation of naturalisation in cases where the naturalisation was obtained by fraud or misrepresentation (e.g. s. 20 (2) of the British Nationality Act which applies to both naturalised and "registered" citizens at the discretion of the Secretary of State: 8 U.S.C., Sect. 1451 (a) by court proceedings). In addition many states impose more stringent requirements for the retention of nationality by naturalised persons than in the case of natural born subjects.

This is particularly true of the British Nationality Act, under which natural born subjects or subjects duly "registered" can only lose their U.K. citizenship by voluntary renunciation, while naturalised citizens can be deprived of their citizenship on the grounds specified in s. 20 (3) & (4). The grounds mentioned are showing disloyalty or disaffection towards the Crown; assisting the enemy in wartime; being sentenced anywhere to a prison sentence of not less than twelve months within 5 years of naturalisation; and being resident for 7 years in a foreign country without being in the service of the Crown or of an international organisation of which any part of the Crown's dominions was a member, or without registering annually at a British Consulate of his intention to retain citizenship of the U.K. and Colonies.

Because of the wide scope of the rules of American law dealing with the expatriation of natural born or naturalised nationals alike, Sect. 1484 relating to the loss of nationality by naturalised subjects alone was of limited application. It dealt only with foreign residence. Thus, it was enacted that a naturalised subject would lose his United States nationality if he lived in the territory of the state of which he was formerly a national or where he was born for a period of 3 years (unless such period of residence was discounted on the grounds laid down in Sect. 1485), or in the territory of any other foreign state for a period of 5 years (discounting any such time covered by Sects. 1485 and 1486). The legality of this provision was successfully challenged in the case of *Schneider* v. *Rusk*.[7] The appellant, a German national by birth, had later acquired United States citizenship, but then married a German national and went to live in Germany. The Solicitor-General pointed to the special problems engendered when

---

6. Problems of a different kind arise when a state attempts to limit the rights of its citizens, as opposed to depriving them of citizenship, e.g. the refusal of a right of entry to certain classes of citizen. In such circumstances, there would seem to be an obligation owed by the state of nationality to other states to allow entry if no other state is willing to receive them, and the state of residence insists upon its power to deport. While this obligation would not necessarily give the individual national a right of redress under the municipal law of the state of nationality (this question would depend upon the existence of relevant constitutional safeguards: the Parliament of the United Kingdom, which has no constitution as such, would be unfettered in this respect), it would entitle the state of residence or other deporting state to complain on the international level.

7. 377 U.S. 163 (1964).

naturalised citizens returned to the country of their former nationality, particularly the likelihood of a weakening of ties with the United States. In seeking to regulate such situations, Congress was only attempting to do what was considered quite proper in many other states which had adopted similar legislation. Nevertheless, a majority of the Supreme Court held the provision unconstitutional because it discriminated against naturalised citizens.[8]

D. Nationality and jurisdiction

States being the primary possessors of rights and duties under international law, it follows that any rights to which individuals may be entitled are derived from the state of which they are nationals.[9] In the case of diplomatic protection, a state can only present a claim on behalf of its own nationals.[10] As far as personal jurisdiction is concerned the bond of nationality is recognised as its basis, and under international law as it stands today it may be said that, subject to limited exceptions created by treaty, no state has a right to object to the way in which another state treats its own nationals.

a THE EXTENT OF JURISDICTION BASED ON NATIONALITY

i *Civil jurisdiction*

According to generally accepted principles of private international law, the courts of most states will decide issues of personal status and allied matters (marriage, divorce, devolution of property upon death, etc.), by applying the "personal" law of the parties.[11] In states with a legal system based upon the common law this personal law will be the law of the domicile (the place where the individual concerned has, or had at the appropriate time, his permanent home);[12] but in civil law systems the personal law will be that of the state of nationality.

ii *Criminal jurisdiction*

Most civil law systems claim a wide jurisdiction to punish crimes committed by their nationals, even on the territory of a foreign state. Although a state cannot enforce its laws within the territory of another state, its citizens remain bound not to disregard those laws, and the national state may in the last resort compel observance of its laws by punishing a person who has broken them should he return within its jurisdiction. On the other hand, the punishment of crimes committed extraterritorially on the basis of nationality is unusual in common law

---

8.　377 U.S. 163, at p. 168–169.　　9.　See above, pp. 91–94.
10.　See below, p. 403.
11.　See Ehrenzweig, *Conflict of Laws*, p. 372; and Dicey, *Conflict of Laws*, 7th ed., Chap. 10.
12.　Dicey, *op. cit.*, p. 85; Goodrich, *Conflict of Laws*, 4th ed., pp. 32–38.

jurisdiction. British statutes have made notable exceptions in the case of murder and bigamy.[13]

b CONFLICTS OF JURISDICTION

Conflicts of jurisdiction are possible in a number of related situations: where the laws of the national state and the laws of the territorial sovereign prescribe entirely different rules of conduct, or where the individual concerned is a dual national, or has close connections with more than one state.

i *Conflicts between "national" law and "territorial" law*

Although it is undoubtedly true that a state's right to exercise jurisdiction over its nationals with respect to events occurring entirely abroad is not unlimited, the practical application of this principle is not readily illustrated. Thus, while it may well be that "a state is prevented from requiring such acts from its citizens abroad as are forbidden to them by the Municipal Law of the land in which they reside, and from ordering them not to commit such acts as they are bound to commit according to the Municipal Law of the land in which they reside"[14], the cases in which such a contention has been raised have been heard by the municipal courts of the national state. While the existence of such a principle has been recognised, the courts have taken the view that it was not applicable in the circumstances of the particular case.

For example, in *Chandler* v. *U.S.*,[15] the appellant had been convicted of treason against the United States in that, during the years 1941 to 1945, he had broadcast Nazi propaganda in German radio programmes directed at listeners in the United States. It was argued on behalf of Chandler, *inter alia*, that, being resident in Germany, he was subject primarily to German law. A Circuit Court of Appeals quoted the words of the trial judge as a correct charge to the jury. The judge had stated that the defendant "while domiciled in the German Reich, owed a qualified allegiance to it; he was obligated to obey its laws and he was equally amenable to punishment with citizens of that country if he did not do so. At the same time", however, the defendant, "while residing in Germany . . . owed to his government, full, complete and true allegiance." The Appeal Court added that this was not a case where the accused had been under legal compulsion to carry out the acts charged in the indictment: his conduct had been entirely voluntary in seeking employment with the German radio.[16]

ii *Conflicts of nationality*

It is arguable that international law would regard as improper the exercise by a state of criminal jurisdiction over an individual having that

13. See generally, Glanville Williams in (1965), 81 L.Q.R. 395–408.
14. Oppenheim, *International Law*, Vol. 1, 8th ed., p. 296.
15. 171 F. (2d) 921 (1948).   16. *Ibid.*, at p. 944.

state's nationality in circumstances where his conduct was lawful or even prescribed by the law of another state the nationality of which he also possessed and with which he had a much closer connection. In relation to diplomatic protection the principle of a dominant nationality is firmly established,[17] and the "genuine link" principle enunciated by the International Court in the *Nottebohm* case would seem to be equally applicable to the concept of nationality as a basis of jurisdiction.[18]

Mindful of the possible objection to exercising jurisdiction in a case[19] of treason in which the individual charged was also a Japanese national, the Supreme Court of the United States was careful to emphasise two factors: that the accused had claimed advantages of Japanese citizenship was not inconsistent with his U.S. citizenship (indeed he had obtained an American passport to return to the United States in 1946); and that his conduct in brutally ill-treating United States prisoners of war had gone far beyond what was required of him by Japanese law.

iii *Where jurisdiction is exercised on the basis of a connection other than nationality*

In the situations that have been considered so far, the state had been exercising jurisdiction over its own nationals, although in each case the individual concerned also possessed a residential link with another state. However, it is clear that the basis of jurisdiction on a charge of treason under Anglo-American law is not nationality but allegiance. It is true that a national owes allegiance, but it is not true that the only persons owing allegiance are nationals. It has long been a rule of the common law that an alien within the territories of the Crown owes a temporary allegiance to the Crown. In the same way that a British subject could not expatriate himself in time of war and thus free himself from the duty of allegiance,[20] it was also held that an alien resident in territory of the Crown was not absolved from the duty of allegiance by the enemy occupation of that territory.[1]

It is thus possible for an individual to owe a duty of obedience to more than two systems of law. He may be a national of one state, owing temporary allegiance to another state, and yet be subject to the control of a third state. This situation arose in a most striking form in the case of *Joyce* v. *D.P.P.*[2] Joyce had been born in the United States in 1906 at a time when his father, formerly a British subject, had already acquired United States citizenship by naturalisation. Joyce was therefore a natural born citizen of the United States. However, at the age of three Joyce was brought to England. From 1933 onwards he was a holder of a British passport which he obtained by declaring that he was a British subject by birth, having been born in Ireland. In August, 1939, he left England on

---

17. See below, p. 404.   18. See above, p. 289.
19. *Kawakita* v. *U.S.*, 343 U.S. 717 (1952).
20. *R.* v. *Lynch*, [1903] 1 K.B. 444: see now, *British Nationality Act*, 1948, s. 19 (1).
1. *DeJager* v. *A.G. of Natal*, [1907] A.C. 326; cp. *Carlisle* v. *U.S.*, 16 Wall. 147 (1876).
2. [1946] A.C. 347.

a British passport which had just been renewed, and in September, a short period after the outbreak of war, he accepted a post as a radio announcer in the English service of Berlin radio, a post which he held until 1945. Not only was Joyce not a British subject, but he also claimed to have acquired German nationality in 1940. The House of Lords held, however, that Joyce, by going abroad under the protection of a British passport, owed a correlative duty of allegiance to the Crown. As he had broken that duty of allegiance, he was guilty of treason against the Crown.

In the course of the case, it was strongly argued that the English Courts did not have jurisdiction to try an alien for a crime committed abroad. In answer to this contention Lord Jowitt, L.C., declared that no "principle of comity demands that a state should ignore the crime of treason committed against it outside its territory" adding that, on the contrary, "a proper regard for its own security requires that all those who commit that crime, whether they commit it within or without the realm should be amenable to its laws". The fact that the appellant was an alien became irrelevant once it was established, as was clearly the case, that an alien could commit, and that the appellant had committed, a treasonable act.[3]

While it is undoubtedly true that a state is entitled to exercise a "protective" jurisdiction with respect to the acts of aliens outside its territory which adversely effect the state or its interests,[4] it could not, for this reason, reasonably punish all persons who had engaged in a war against it. However, once an alien can be shown to have a sufficiently close connection with a state, either by nationality or residence, it is arguable that "international law will attach no importance to the principle of territoriality of crime and will not deny to a state the right to exercise jurisdiction over an alien with regard to acts committed abroad."[5] On the facts of the Joyce case, his lengthy residence in England, coupled with his repeated assertions that he was a British subject and entitled to a British passport, are reasons enough for asserting jurisdiction over acts committed by him against the Crown. Neither the state of which he was born a national (the United States), nor the country where his acts were performed (Germany), could complain that their rights had in any way been infringed.

iv *Nationality of the victim*

Hitherto discussion has centred on the extent to which a state can exercise jurisdiction in cases involving the activities of its nationals or of persons owing allegiance outside its territory. But what is the position with regard to an act which has no connection with a state except that the victim is its national?

The *cause célèbre* on this subject was the *Cutting* case.[6] Cutting, a U.S.

---

3. *Ibid.*, at p. 372.
4. E.g. see the Harvard Research *Jurisdiction in Respect of Crime*, comment on Art. 7 (1935), 29 A.J.I.L. Supp., pp. 543–61.
5. Lauterpacht, in (1947) 9 C.L.J., at p. 344.
6. Moore, *Digest*, Vol. 2, p. 228 (1886).

citizen, had published defamatory statements amounting to a criminal offence against a Mexican national under Mexican law, even though publication had taken place in Texas. Cutting was fined and convicted of the offence, *inter alia*, on the ground that Mexico was entitled to exercise jurisdiction on the basis of the *passive personality* theory. It was this view which was strongly challenged by the United States and after prolonged diplomatic exchanges Cutting was released, the reason given by the Mexican authorities, however, being the withdrawal of the offended party from the action.

This basis of jurisdiction was also raised before the Permanent Court in the *Lotus* case.[7] It will be recalled that France challenged the right of the Turkish Courts to exercise jurisdiction over a French officer who had been on board a French ship at the time of a collision with a Turkish vessel. The Turkish criminal code enabled jurisdiction to be exercised in circumstances where a Turkish national was injured. The Court avoided deciding whether this aspect of Turkish law was contrary to international law by holding that the crime took effect on Turkish territory, i.e. on board the Turkish ship, so that jurisdiction could rightfully be claimed on the basis of the territorial principle. In addition to the obvious reluctance of the Court to rely upon the passive personality principle, Judge Moore, in a dissenting opinion, criticised the principle in the strongest terms. The Turkish claim to exercise jurisdiction on the sole basis of the nationality of the victim was "at variance not only with the principle of the exclusive jurisdiction of a state over its own territory, but also with the equally well-settled principle that a person visiting a foreign country, far from radiating for his protection the jurisdiction of his own country, falls under the dominion of the local law and, except so far as his government may diplomatically intervene in case of a denial of justice, must look to that law for his protection."[8]

It is a basic proposition of criminal jurisprudence that the criminality of the act should depend upon the nature of the accused's act. It should also be true that jurisdiction should depend upon the system or system of law to which the accused is obviously subject, usually the territorial law and his own national law. It would seem as illogical to make jurisdiction depend upon the purely fortuitous fact of the victim's nationality as it would be to vary the criminality of the accused's conduct with the status or other attributes of the victim.[9]

E. The quasi-nationality of ships, aircraft and corporations

For purposes of jurisdiction and of diplomatic protection it has been necessary to attribute a national character to such things as ships and air-

---

7. P.C.I.J. Rep., Ser. A, No. 10 (1927).   8. *Ibid.*, p. 93.
9. That the passive personality principle is still applied by some States is apparent from its inclusion in the grounds upon which jurisdiction might be claimed in the Tokyo Convention on Crimes Aboard Aircraft of 1963: see below, pp. 311–312.

craft, and to entities like corporations created under systems of municipal law.

a SHIPS

As with the nationality of individuals, the basic doctrine has always been that it is for each state to decide for itself the grounds upon which it will grant registration, and therefore the right to fly its flag, to a ship. This principle was implicit in state practice, at least until recent years, and was accepted unreservedly by all writers on the subject. The only restriction on this right was the fact that a state could not confer its "nationality" on a vessel already entitled to fly the flag of another state (except of course in consequence of a change of registration). That these principles are still of primary importance is emphasised by the first part of Article 5 (1) of the High Seas Convention of 1958 which lays down that each state "shall fix the conditions for the grant of its nationality to ships, for the registration of ships in its territory, and for the right to fly its flag"; and by the requirement of Article 6 (1) that ships "shall sail under the flag of one state only".

However, in addition to the traditional doctrine, the Convention attempted to impose a requirement that attribution of national character must depend upon the existence of a "genuine link" between ships and the state "whose flag they are entitled to fly"; "in particular, the state must effectively exercise its jurisdiction and control in administrative, technical and social matters over ships flying its flag". While it is obviously necessary, in the interests of maritime safety and "public order" on the high seas, that a state should be able to exercise the necessary controls over ships flying its flag to ensure these basic requirements, the principle that there should be criteria additional to registration in the determination of "nationality" was both novel and likely to introduce a factor of uncertainty into what had hitherto been an aspect of state jurisdiction upon which the law was basically clear.

As the previous chapter dealing with maritime jurisdiction demonstrated, it was a fundamental doctrine that jurisdiction followed the flag. A ship properly flying the flag of a recognised state *according to the law of that state* was entitled to a certain status on the high seas, and was subject primarily to the jurisdiction of that state. Does it follow from Article 5 of the Convention that a state which has not a "genuine link" (whatever the expression might mean) is not entitled to exercise the jurisdiction formerly available to it as the flag state under traditional customary international law?

Before it is possible to estimate how far this new requirement for registration of ships has altered existing law some attempt must be made to explain the appearance in the Convention of the reference to a "genuine link". It will have been realised, of course, that the expression is taken from the International Court's judgment in the *Nottebohm* case. It was incorporated into the 1956 draft articles by the International Law Commission. In presenting the draft articles to the General Assembly, the

United Nations Secretariat explained the Commission's attitude in a manner which demonstrated its own uncertainty on the matter. The Secretariat cautiously stated that it was "possible that some of the principles laid down by the Court may be relevant to the question of the nationality of ships".[10]

There is, however, an obvious danger in reaching a conclusion based upon a too ready acceptance of the analogy between the nationality of individuals and the national character of ships. The *Nottebohm* judgment dealt with the special problems arising out of the attempts by states to present diplomatic claims on behalf of those of their nationals who were also nationals of another, usually the respondent, state. To resolve such a conflict it was clearly necessary to look to the social, family and economic ties which might connect the individual more closely with one state rather than the other. The Court applied similar principles to resolve a conflict between a state claiming that an individual had acquired its nationality, and a state in the territory of which the individual concerned had spent most of his life. In order to exercise diplomatic protection on behalf of an individual, there should exist a genuine link between that person and the state exercising protection. If there is not such a link the respondent state need not recognise the right of the complainant state to present the claim.

In relation to ships, the use of the word "nationality" has only been a convenient shorthand term for the fact of registration and the entitlement to fly a particular flag. It is, however, a *national character* and not *nationality* in the sense in which the term is used in relation to individuals. Whereas the attribution of nationality to individuals has as its chief international consequence the right of a state to exercise diplomatic protection, the most important result of the granting of national character to a ship is the right of the state to exercise jurisdiction over the ship and all that takes place on board. Problems of dual nationality do not arise because maritime law only recognises the status of ships entitled to sail under one flag. It will be recalled that Article 6 (2) of the Convention lays down that a "ship which sails under the flags of two or more states, using them according to convenience, may not claim any of the nationalities in question with respect to any other state, and may be assimilated to a ship without nationality". In fact, in the course of the International Law Commission's discussions it was clear that the paramount significance of the jurisdictional question was recognised, and that it was at least as important that the flag state should be able to exercise effective control over the vessel as that it should be able to show the existence of a "genuine link".[11] It is perhaps significant that Article 5 (1) of the Convention defines the "genuine link" to mean "in particular" the requirement that a state "must

---

10. G.A.O.R. 11th Sess., Agenda Item 53, Annexes, p. 29 (1956–7).
11. In its comments on the 1956 Draft, the Commission stated, (1957) 51 A.J.I.L., p. 154: "The jurisdiction of the State over ships, and the control it should exercise . . ., can only be effective where there exists in fact a relationship between the State and the ship other than mere navigation or the mere grant of a certificate of registry."

effectively exercise its jurisdiction and control over ships flying its flag".

It is obvious that a ship can hardly have the same associations with a country as those enjoyed by an individual. However, the laws of many states do require that vessels to which they grant registration should be owned by their nationals or by companies incorporated in their territory. As this is by no means a universal practice, and indeed a large percentage of the world's shipping is registered with states of which the owners are not nationals (notably those states, like Liberia, Honduras and Panama, providing so-called "flags of convenience"), it is hardly possible, or even wise to attempt, to legislate for the maritime community by the introduction of a vague and totally unnecessary concept of a "genuine link". As will be discussed in a later chapter, the right to present a claim for the destruction of a ship in circumstances giving rise to international responsibility would lie with the state suffering damage by loss of one of *its* ships, whatever the nationality of the owners.[12]

The attempt to introduce a test of national character of which registration was no longer the sole criterion was undoubtedly due to the attitude of the traditional maritime states towards most states allowing shipowners to use their flags as "flags of convenience". The large shipping fleets registered in Liberia, Honduras and Panama were not owned by nationals of these states, but were attracted by the considerably lower costs of registration and operation under such flags compared with similar charges in the traditional maritime states. The basic objection to the use of "flags of convenience" has been, therefore, economic, and has nothing to do with the legal issues of registration and national character. It is unfortunate that, in an attempt to bring political pressure against these states, the High Seas Convention should have included a reference to the need for a "genuine link" between a state and the ships it registers. In view of the uncertainties in the meaning and in the effects of its inclusion, however, the use of the phrase would appear to be more a symptom of a current controversy than of immediate legal significance.

b AIRCRAFT

Whatever doubts have been created in relation to ships, the 1944 Chicago Convention on International Civil Aviation laid down that aircraft have the nationality of the state in which they are registered (Article 17)[13] and that they cannot be validly registered in more than one state (Article 18).

As far as jurisdiction is concerned, both the English and the American Courts have been faced by the difficulty that their jurisdiction is primarily territorial so that any extension to cover crimes committed on board aircraft had to be accomplished by statute. In England the position has not been helped by the obscure wording of s. 62 (1) of the Civil Aviation

---

12. See below, pp. 400–412.
13. For the question of jurisdiction in airspace, see above, pp. 275–286.

Act, 1949. "Any offence whatever committed on a British aircraft shall, for the purposes of conferring jurisdiction, be deemed to have been committed in any place where the offender may for the time being be." If one takes the effect of "for the purposes of conferring jurisdiction" literally it means no more than that the English Courts can proceed to try an accused if he is within the jurisdiction at the time they come to hear the case. Such a provision would obviously be unnecessary, as, if a person has committed a crime known to English law, he can always be tried by the English Courts provided he has been apprehended and brought before them. To make sense of the provision it is necessary to read it as conferring not only jurisdiction but also the right to apply the English criminal law to the event as if the offence had been "committed in any place where the offender may for the time being be" (i.e. in England where the trial is taking place). This is certainly the conclusion reached by Lord Parker, C.J., in *R. v. Naylor*,[14] though it must be admitted that if it is the correct view it is a pity that Parliament did not employ clearer words to express its wishes. The U.S. Congress attacked the problem piecemeal. In 1952, it extended the jurisdiction of the Courts to aircraft, owned wholly or in part by the U.S. or any of its citizens, while in flight over the high seas or over waters within U.S. jurisdiction (18 U.S.C. Sect. 7 (5)). In 1956, it dealt with the sabotage of aircraft (18 U.S.C. Sect. 31–35). And, in 1961, a wide ranging series of amendments to the Federal Aviation Act extended the jurisdiction of Federal Courts to cover *inter alia* the various crimes dealt with in the 1952 legislation if committed on board "an aircraft in flight in air commerce", an expression which is given the widest interpretation in the Act (49 U.S.C. 1301 (4)) and covers aircraft with no U.S. ownership connection.[15]

In an attempt to regulate jurisdiction over aircraft by international agreement, a Conference was held at Tokyo in 1963 under the auspices of the International Civil Aviation Organisation to draft a Convention on Offences and Certain Other Acts Committed on board Aircraft. The Convention is not yet in force and it suffers from a number of unfortunate defects. It lays down the basic principle that the state of registration is "competent to exercise jurisdiction over offences and acts committed on board" (Article 3 (1)), and also requires that contracting states "shall take such measures as may be necessary to establish its jurisdiction as the state of registration over offences committed on board (Article 3 (2)). But it also provides for an ill-defined degree of concurrent jurisdiction on the part of a number of other states. Article 4 lays down that a contracting state other than the state of registration "may not interfere with an aircraft in flight in order to exercise its criminal jurisdiction over an offence committed on board" except in a number of specified cases. In other

---

14. [1962] 2 Q.B. 527; but cp. *R. v. Martin*, [1956] 2 Q.B. 272.
15. The first legislation was prompted by *U.S. v. Cordova*, 89 F. Supp. 298 (1950); the second by *Graham v. Colorado*, 302 F. (2d) 737 (1956); and the third by a series of "hijacking" incidents, although of course the legislation went far beyond what was necessary to combat that crime.

words, in any of the cases specified there should be a right to interfere with an aircraft in flight. Such a rule is extraordinary enough in itself, but it becomes even more surprising when the cases specified in Article 4 are examined. A state may interfere with an aircraft in flight:

(a) where the offence has effect on its territory;

(b) if the offence has been committed *by* or *against* a *national* or a *permanent* resident of the state;

(c) if the offence is against the security of the state;

(d) if the offence consists of a breach of the flight or navigational regulations in force in the state;

(e) if the exercise of jurisdiction is necessary to enable the state to fulfil its obligations under any multilateral agreement.

It is small wonder that the Convention has not received sufficient ratifications to bring it into force. The majority of states are reluctant to allow any other state even limited rights of interference with aircraft having their registration. The extensive powers envisaged by the Convention are therefore totally unrealistic.

The Convention does not deal directly with the right of states other than the state of registration to extend their criminal law to events happening on board an aircraft. In fact, providing that states claim to act in accordance with jurisdictional principles acknowledged by international law, there is no reason why they should not enforce their law over events occurring on board a foreign aircraft. The problem of Article 4 of the Convention is that in providing far wider *bases* of jurisdiction than those generally accepted, it may encourage states to extend the field of application of their criminal law. It has already been stated that jurisdiction on the basis of the nationality of the victim (passive personality principle) is a matter of controversy.[16] The Convention provides support for jurisdiction based not only upon the victim's nationality, but also upon his permanent place of residence!

c CORPORATIONS

The main problems relating to the national character of corporations arise in the context of the nationality of claims rule which is considered in the chapter on state responsibility.[17] For the purposes of this rule the test of "nationality" is that of the place of original incorporation. Although this test has a close affinity to Anglo-American jurisprudence, it has the advantage of coinciding in fact, though not in name, with the test usually applied in civil law countries. For example, the emphasis under French

---

16. See above, p. 306. Another objection to the Tokyo Convention was that, far from settling problems relating to aerial jurisdiction, Article 4 left them unanswered. In a comment on the Convention, the Italian Government asked what was the good of convening an international conference if the agreement was merely to embody existing disagreement. The result of the efforts of the Conference were entirely negative. "We are just where we were before. And the reason for that is that the drafting committee failed to take into account the true reason for, and the essential purpose of, the Convention."

17. See below, pp. 413–426.

law is on the *siège social*, or seat of management of the company, but it is also true that a company must be incorporated in the place where that *siège social* is situated.

Because of the significance attached particularly by English municipal law to the legal personality of corporations as distinct from the individual shareholders, there has been a tendency to adopt a similar approach to the issues of the nationality of companies on the international plane. Thus the existence of a corporation and the rights and duties established by its constituent documents (called, in the case of a limited company incorporated under English law, its memorandum and articles of association, although corporations may also be set up by Royal Charter or Act of Parliament) are the creation of the legal system of the place of incorporation. That system alone governs the continued existence of the corporation, and its eventual dissolution. In this limited sense, the national character of the corporation and jurisdiction over it, i.e. the basis of selecting the appropriate rules of municipal law, are coincidental.

The separation between the identity of the corporation and the individual shareholders which is so typical of English law has also had its impact upon the "nationality of claims" rule. Fundamentally, the nationality of a corporation for the purpose of the exercise of diplomatic protection is that of the state of incorporation. In certain circumstances international law may recognise the rights of shareholders, but any such claims will not be on behalf of the company, but on behalf of the shareholders, and in order to protect their rights. There is no question of the corporation being considered as possessing an additional or latent nationality of the shareholders, or of a proportion of them.[18]

One situation in which international law would appear to recognise this "lifting of the corporate veil" is in connection with the customary rule that in time of war a state is entitled to expropriate enemy property, or is entitled to declare illegal all transactions entered into with an enemy national or corporation. But here again much of the evidence supporting the application of the rule in practice is to be found in decisions of the English Courts. According to these cases, the fact that a company is incorporated in England is no guarantee that its profits will not be of benefit to the enemy. Such a company may be treated as having enemy character "if its agents or the persons in de facto control of its affairs, whether authorised or not, are resident in an enemy country, or, wherever resident, are adhering to the enemy or taking instructions from or acting under the control of enemies", and in assessing "whether the company's agents, or the persons in de facto control of its affairs, are in fact adhering to, taking instructions from or acting under the control of enemies" the "enemy character of individual shareholders and their conduct" may be a very material factor.[19]

---

18. See below, p. 417.
19. Per Lord Parker of Waddington in *Daimler & Co., Ltd.* v. *Continental Tyre & Rubber Co. (Great Britain), Ltd.*, [1916] 2 A.C. 307, at p: 345.

2 DOMESTIC JURISDICTION

A. Domestic jurisdiction within the framework of international law

The traditional notion of "domestic jurisdiction" was based upon the theory that certain matters were within the exclusive competence of states and could not be made the subject of international obligations. It was an aspect of the sovereignty of states that its policies in such matters were unfettered by any principles of international law. Among these matters were included tariffs, the granting of nationality, the admission of aliens, and the treatment of a state's nationals inside its own territory.

With the quickening development of international law in the present century, and its extension to regulate new fields of state conduct, it became increasingly uncertain whether the traditional view of the role of "domestic jurisdiction" could be maintained. Article 15 (8) of the Covenant of the League of Nations (which provided that if a dispute was claimed by one of the parties, and was found by the League Council, to arise out of a matter which *by international law* was solely within the domestic jurisdiction of that party, the Council should so report, and should make no recommendation on the matter) reflected a growing reluctance to accept the potentially inhibiting effect of traditional doctrine. The attitude of the Covenant was that the criterion of what matters fell within the reserved domain was not to be the existence of a specific list based upon past attitudes of states, but the standards of international law.

The significance of this change in attitude was emphasised by the Advisory Opinion given by the Permanent Court in the *Tunis–Morocco Nationality Decrees* case.[20] The decrees in question had the effect of conferring French nationality (and a resulting liability to military service) on a large number of second generation residents of Tunis and Morocco, some of whom were British subjects. The British Government objected to the application of the decrees to British subjects, and, the French Government having refused arbitration, referred the dispute to the Council of the League. When the French Government invoked Article 15 (8), the Council sought an advisory opinion from the Permanent Court on the question whether the application of the decrees to British subjects resident in Tunis and Morocco was, or was not, "by international law, solely a matter of domestic jurisdiction". In rejecting the French claim, the Court made the observation that the question "whether a certain matter is or is not within the domestic jurisdiction of a state is an essentially relative question: it depends upon the development of international relations." In the existing state of international law questions of nationality were "in principle within this reserved domain", but it

---

20. P.C.I.J. Rep., Ser. B., No. 4 (1923).

could well happen that "in a matter which, like that of nationality, is not, in principle, regulated by international law, the right of a state to use its discretion is nevertheless restricted by obligations which it may have undertaken towards other states. In such a case, jurisdiction which, in principle, belongs solely to the state, is limited by rules of international law."

The relativity of the concept of domestic jurisdiction may be further illustrated by reference to the *Nottebohm* case.[1] It will be recalled that Nottebohm, a German national, had been naturalised as a Liechtenstein subject in 1939 after the briefest residence in that country, but had lived for most of his life in Guatemala. Nottebohm had been arrested and subsequently expelled from Guatemala and had his property seized as an enemy national when Guatemala joined the war against Germany in 1943. Guatemala objected to the jurisdiction of the International Court on the ground that Liechtenstein was not competent to submit a claim on behalf of an individual with whom it had no genuine bond of nationality. In upholding this objection, the Court expounded upon the relationship between nationality and domestic jurisdiction. It was for Liechtenstein, as for every sovereign state, to settle for itself the rules relating to the acquisition of its nationality. Nationality had "its most immediate, its most far-reaching and, for most people, its only effects within the legal system of the state conferring it." Nationality served above all to determine that the person upon whom it was conferred enjoyed its rights and was bound by the obligations which the law of that state granted to or imposed upon its nationals. This was implicit in the wider concept that questions of nationality fall within the domestic jurisdiction of a state. Although the naturalisation of Nottebohm was an act performed by Liechtenstein in the exercise of its domestic jurisdiction, what was in issue was whether this act had the external effect of enabling Liechtenstein to exercise diplomatic protection over Nottebohm. But to exercise protection, to apply to the Court, was to place the matter on the plane of international law. Liechtenstein could not claim, solely on the ground that the issues of nationality fall *prima facie* within a state's domestic jurisdiction, that the rules it had laid down were entitled to recognition by Guatemala, unless it could show that it had acted in conformity with the general aim of making the legal bond of nationality accord with the individual's genuine connection with Liechtenstein. It was clear from the record of the facts that Nottebohm had no such connection.

B. Domestic jurisdiction and the competence of international tribunals

Although the relationship between the notion of domestic jurisdiction and the competence of international tribunals is considered further below in connection with the jurisdiction of the International Court, for the

---

1. I.C.J. Rep. 1955, p. 4.

sake of completeness some comment is necessary at this stage on the influence the notion has exerted over the practice of international tribunals.

If the concept of domestic jurisdiction is given its traditional meaning of a category of matters exclusively subject to the jurisdiction of a state, it is obvious enough that it would have a limiting effect on the potential jurisdiction of an international tribunal. Interpreted in this sense it was complementary to the notion that certain inter-state disputes concerned the honour or vital interests of a state and were therefore non-justiciable. The advent of the possibility of compulsory jurisdiction under the optional clause of the Statute of the Permanent Court was in harmony with the attitude towards domestic jurisdiction demonstrated by Article 15 (8) of the Covenant. In theory at any rate, if a dispute concerned a matter of international law it was justiciable, and if it concerned a matter of international law it could not be subject to the exclusive domestic jurisdiction of a state. As a consequence, the Permanent Court tested objections to its competence on the ground that a particular issue fell within the respondent state's domestic jurisdiction by means of a provisional finding on whether factors existed which might establish the international nature of the subject-matter of the dispute. In the *Tunis–Morocco* case, the existence of a number of treaties relating to British rights in these French territories was a sufficient basis for a provisional finding that the Council had competence in the dispute. Whether or not it in fact was competent depended upon the ultimate decision on the merits of the case; i.e. on whether the various treaties restricted the French right to legislate for British subjects resident in the two territories. In other words, if the British Government had a valid claim, the matter was not subject to French jurisdiction and the Council was competent; but if it could not establish its claim, the matter was subject to French domestic jurisdiction, and the Council was not competent to hear the dispute.[2]

As the competence of the League extended beyond purely legal disputes, the existence of a domestic jurisdiction limitation defined in terms of international law did have some meaning in the context of Article 15 of the Covenant. However, the same could not be said of the attempt to adapt a domestic jurisdiction reservation into declarations under the Optional Clause whereby states accepted the compulsory jurisdiction of the Permanent Court, and of the present International Court.[3]

---

2. The issue was also raised before the International Court in the *Peace Treaties* case (discussed below). For the views of the U.S. and U.K. Governments expressed in that case, see *Pleadings*, at pp. 153–5 and 322–8.

3. Exclusion of disputes which by international law fall exclusively within the jurisdiction of the state accepting the jurisdiction of the Court are to be found in the declarations made by Australia, Cambodia, Canada, Malta, New Zealand, Pakistan, and the United Kingdom.

Similar reservations have been made by France, Gambia, and Kenya.

India, and Israel have adopted the term "essentially" from Art. 2 (7) of the Charter.

States which have attempted to reserve to themselves the right to decide whether a matter is within their domestic jurisdiction are Liberia, Malawi, Mexico, Sudan, U.S.A. A similar reservation was included in the French declaration of acceptance that was withdrawn in

As the Court's jurisdiction was, and is, limited exclusively to legal disputes concerning the interpretation of a treaty, any question of international law, the existence of any fact which, if established, would constitute a breach of an international obligation, and the nature or extent of the reparation to be made for the breach of an international obligation, it is patently obvious that it could not, and cannot, deal with a case which by international law falls within the domestic jurisdiction of a state,[4] because such a case would not involve any question of international law. If it did involve a question of international law, it could not be subject to the domestic jurisdiction of a state.

But what would be the position if a state were to accept the jurisdiction of the Court subject to a reservation of matters within its domestic jurisdiction without defining the standard against which this concept is to be tested? Unless it is possible to argue that there exists a reserved domain which remains exclusively subject to the domestic jurisdiction of a state, it would be unlikely that the absence of an express reference to the international law standard would alter the attitude of the Court. Although the majority of cases in which the concept of domestic jurisdiction has been in issue[5] have concerned reservations defining it in terms of international law, the approach adopted by the Court has been so uniform as to make it unlikely that the absence of express definition would make any difference.

This surmise gains considerable support from the *Peace Treaties* case[6] in which the General Assembly requested the International Court to give an advisory opinion *inter alia* on the duties of the former enemy states, Bulgaria, Hungary and Roumania, and on the powers of the Secretary-General of the United Nations, in relation to the procedure for the settlement of disputes arising out of the Peace Treaties with those states. One of the arguments put forward against the exercise of jurisdiction by the Court was that the General Assembly had no power to make such a request with regard to alleged breaches of the human rights provisions of the Treaties, because matters relating to human rights were essentially within a state's domestic jurisdiction and therefore outside the competence of the Assembly and of the Court as limited by Article 2 (7) of the Charter. Although Article 2 (7) is considered in more detail in the following section, its relevance in the present discussion is that it contains no reference to matters which, *by international law*, are within a state's jurisdiction. Despite the absence of a reference to the international law standard, the

---

1959. The United Kingdom declaration of 1957, which was modified in 1958 and replaced in 1963, excluded disputes "relating to any question which, in the opinion of the Government of the United Kingdom, affects the national security of the United Kingdom or of any of its dependent territories".

4. Except perhaps by treaty or other agreement: art. 36 (2) of the Statute of the Court deals only with the Court's compulsory jurisdiction.

5. E.g. *Nationality Decrees in Tunis and Morocco*; *Peace Treaties*; and *Anglo-Iranian Oil Company* cases. For the last named case see the discussion in Rajan, *The United Nations and Domestic Jurisdiction*, pp. 325–335.

6. I.C.J. Rep. 1950, p. 65.

Court rejected the argument in words which strongly echo its earlier pronouncements. The interpretation of the terms of a treaty could not be "considered as a question essentially within the domestic jurisdiction of a state. It is a question of international law which, by its very nature, lies within the competence of the Court."[7]

If a state wishes to restrict the competence of the Court by a domestic jurisdiction reservation it would seem that it is not possible to do so unless it can in some way substitute a criterion other than the international law standard for the determination of the category of matters within its domestic jurisdiction. A specific list might be at the same time too precise and too restricting. There may be occasions upon which a state wishes to subject matters of nationality or immigration or economic policy to the Court. In an attempt to obtain a maximum degree of flexibility and protection of its own interests, the United States included in its acceptance of the Court's compulsory jurisdiction a reservation with respect to "matters which are essentially within the domestic jurisdiction of the United States of America as determined by the United States of America." The validity of a reservation which purports to withdraw from the Court its right under its statute (Article 36 (6)) to decide the extent of its jurisdiction is considered in the discussion of the International Court in a later chapter. The strength of the objections to the United States "automatic reservation", as it is often termed, from international lawyers both within and outside the United States stems in part from the feeling that such a reservation is an attempt to "turn the clock back". It had already been established in international jurisprudence that the extent of a tribunal's jurisdiction, including the question whether a matter was subject to a state's domestic jurisdiction or regulated by international law, was an issue for the tribunal itself to decide in accordance with the standards and rules established by international law.

C. Domestic jurisdiction under Article 2 (7) of the U.N. Charter

The Dumbarton Oaks proposals contained a paragraph 7 along traditional lines that other paragraphs of Chapter VIII Section A, dealing with the powers of the Security Council for the pacific settlement of disputes, should not apply to "situations or disputes arising out of matters which by international law are solely within the domestic jurisdiction of the state concerned." When this particular proposal was considered by the sponsoring powers,[8] they radically revised its wording and altered its position in the Charter. As a consequence, it appeared as one of the basic principles laid down in Article 2 in accordance with which the *Organisation and its Members* "shall act" (and no longer only as a limitation on the council as under Article 15 (8) of the Covenant of the League of Nations

---

7. *Ibid.*, at p. 70.   8. United Kingdom, United States, U.S.S.R. and China.

or the Security Council as envisaged by the Dumbarton Oaks formula);
and in a novel form—

"Nothing contained in the present Charter shall authorise the United Nations
to intervene in matters which are essentially within the domestic jurisdiction of any
state or shall require the members to submit such matters to settlement under the
present Charter; but this principle shall not prejudice the application of enforcement
measures under Chapter VII."

Three problems in particular are raised by this provision and by the
practice of United Nations organs in applying it: two concern issues of
interpretation of Article 2 (7) itself—the significance of the terms "intervene" and "essentially"; and the third relates to the meaning attributed
to "domestic jurisdiction" against the wider background of international
law.

a INTERVENTION BY U.N. ORGANS

Two principal views have been advanced as to the meaning of "intervene" in Article 2 (7). In the first place it is suggested that the term should
be given its "popular" meaning of "interfere"; but in opposition to this
view it has been argued that "intervene" should be given a technical
meaning based on the notion of "intervention"—*forcible* interference in
the internal affairs of another state. In view of the obvious ambiguity of
the expression, it is permissible to consider the records of the San Francisco
Conference, the implications for Article 2 (7) of the alternative readings,
and the subsequent practice of the United Nations in the approach of its
organs to the provision.

As far as the San Francisco Conference is concerned, it would seem that
the delegates themselves had no clear idea of what "intervene" really
meant: support can be found for both interpretations. As for the sense of
Article 2 (7), to apply "intervene" as connoting an act of (forcible) intervention would be to render the provision meaningless. United Nations
organs have no power to take forcible action directed against the conduct
and policies of a state unless that conduct and those policies constitute a
threat to the peace, a breach of the peace and act of aggression enabling
the Security Council to take enforcement action under Chapter VII.[9] But
Article 2 (7) expressly does not apply to the one situation in which "intervention"
in this sense is possible.

However, if it is necessary to interpret "intervene" as "interfere" and
as applying only to action not amounting to forcible interference, that is
not an end to the difficulties. Such an interpretation is potentially
extremely wide. Is it to "intervene" in a matter of domestic jurisdiction
for a U.N. organ to place a matter on its agenda, or to investigate the
facts of a situation? Organs of the United Nations have consistently taken
the view that, like judicial tribunals, they have an inherent power to
decide their own competence, and have held that preliminary discussion

---

9. See below, pp. 563 *et seq.*

or even investigation of the facts of a situation is necessary in order to determine whether a matter *is* essentially within the domestic jurisdiction of a state. But once a matter is "investigated" and the facts ascertained, is the passing of a resolution dealing with a particular dispute or situation prohibited by Article 2 (7)?

It is at this point that the ambiguities of the provision become apparent. If the notion suggested by the use of "intervene" is to apply to anything, it must apply to resolutions of United Nations organs, or at least to resolutions of certain types. If Article 2 (7) were to apply to all resolutions of U.N. organs dealing with the policies of member states it would have a stultifying effect on United Nations action. In the practice of the United Nations there is nothing to suggest that such a view has gained much favour with member states. If, on the other hand, Article 2 (7) were to apply only to certain types of resolution, the difficulty arises of how to distinguish between one type of resolution and another.

A number of writers[10] have suggested that it would be a breach of the limitation contained in Article 2 (7) for a U.N. organ to address a resolution directly to a state, requiring it to alter its domestic policies. It is certainly true to say that the more directly a resolution seems to involve matters of domestic jurisdiction, the greater the emphasis that has been placed by member states upon features of the situation justifying U.N. discussion and recommendation. In other words, the argument of whether the discussion and recommendation constitutes "intervening" has been avoided by concentrating on the aspects of the situation which take it out of the sphere of domestic jurisdiction. Before considering these various features and aspects of situations which have been put forward in support of United Nations action, however, a brief comment is necessary on the significance of the use of the term "essentially" in this context.

b MATTERS "ESSENTIALLY" WITHIN A STATE'S JURISDICTION

It will be recalled that Article 15 (8) of the Covenant of the League of Nations referred to matters "solely" within the domestic jurisdiction of a party to a dispute. The opinion of the Permanent Court in the *Tunis–Morocco Nationality Decrees* case to the effect that the question "whether a certain matter is or is not *solely* within the domestic jurisdiction of a state is an essentially relative question" is not conclusive on the issue of whether a matter is "essentially" within the domestic jurisdiction of a state. Whether or not a matter is solely within the reserved domain may be estimated with accuracy by deciding whether or not international law is applicable to the case. If it is applicable, the matter cannot be *solely* within the reserved domain. On the other hand, while the absence of relevant rules of international law may be decisive in proving that a matter is within domestic jurisdiction, the existence of such rules is not conclusive that the essence of a matter does not lie within the domestic

---

10. Wright, *International Law and the United Nations*, p. 386; Preuss (1949), 74 H.R. at pp. 605–19; Ross, *Constitution of the United Nations*, at pp. 125–7.

jurisdiction of a state. It would seem possible to argue that, although international law may be relevant to a situation, the "essence" of the matter nevertheless lies within the reserved domain.

In a sense, such an argument harks back to the pre-Covenant notion of categories of issues beyond the competence of international law, that there are certain matters essentially the concern of a state, and not subject to interference by its neighbours, or anyone else affected by its activities. Even though the use of "essentially" instead of "solely" does suggest that Article 2 (7) was intended to have a broader application on this point than Article 15 (8), and this view has been advanced in the debates of U.N. organs, no such distinction has been drawn in the practice of these organs. The conclusion invariably reached has been the standard attitude that a situation cannot fall within the reserved domain if it concerns a matter of international obligation.[11]

c THE PRESENCE OF FACTORS JUSTIFYING U.N. ACTION

The concept of domestic jurisdiction under the League was based on the test of the absence of international obligation. Even though the policies of a state might have international repercussions, they were nevertheless entirely its own concern unless they involved a possible breach of its international obligations. Strictly interpreted, Article 2 (7) of the Charter should have made no difference to this approach because it expressly states that nothing in the Charter shall authorise the United Nations to intervene in matters of domestic jurisdiction. In other words, while developments in international law might affect or cut down the ambit of domestic jurisdiction, the Charter itself was not to have this effect. Despite this obvious meaning of Article 2 (7), U.N. Organs have developed a concept of "international concern" based upon their jurisdiction in matters falling short of an actual breach of the peace, but constituting a potential future threat to the peace.

Upon this basis, resolutions have been passed dealing specifically with internal forms of government, a question traditionally and indisputably within the domestic jurisdiction of a state. The first attempt concerned the Franco régime in Spain. In 1946, the General Assembly adopted a resolution recommending the breaking of diplomatic relations with Spain. In more recent years a series of resolutions have been adopted aimed at altering the structure and membership of governments in South Africa and Angola. The arguments put forward in favour of U.N. competence and against the application of Article 2 (7) have related to the international nature of the problem—that white minority régimes constitute a threat to international peace and security; that the failure of the governments of these states to provide an outlet for the principle of self-determination is a matter of international concern, and so on.

Although the attempt is still made to define Article 2 (7) in legal terms even in the light of U.N. practice, the conclusion seems inescapable that

---

11. See the discussion of the *Peace Treaties* case, above, p. 317.

it is largely disregarded as an inconvenient potential limitation on U.N. action. It may well be, of course, that it was drafted in such general and imprecise terms to placate those states, notably the United States, which viewed with suspicion the wide powers of the General Assembly and of ECOSOC in economic and social matters, but in the hope that it would not be applied as a restrictive influence on the work of the organisation in those fields. If this was indeed the intention of many of those who drafted the Charter, their hopes have been largely fulfilled.

3 EXTRADITION

A. Introduction

It follows from the basic proposition that one state may not commit an act of sovereignty upon the territory of another state that a convicted or alleged criminal who makes good his escape from the state where the crime was committed to the territory of another state is immune from seizure by the authorities of the former state. However, it would obviously be an unsatisfactory state of affairs if all that a criminal had to do to escape punishment was to escape from the territorial jurisdiction of the state the laws of which he had broken. As a former English Lord Chief Justice said, the law of extradition was "founded upon the broad principle that it is to the interest of civilised communities that crimes, acknowledged to be such, should not go unpunished, and it is part of the comity of nations that one state should afford to another every assistance towards bringing persons guilty of such crimes to justice."[12] Extradition, therefore, is the surrender by one state to another of an alleged or convicted criminal in respect of a crime over which the latter state has *territorial* competence to exercise jurisdiction.[13]

a THE DUTY TO EXTRADITE

There exists no duty to extradite under customary international law. In order to provide for reciprocal rights to claim the extradition of fugitives from justice states have entered into a multitude of bilateral treaties to secure such rights. It is well established under both English law and the law of the United States not only that there is no duty to surrender in the absence of a treaty with the requesting state, but also that the executive in both countries has no *authority* to extradite in the absence of such a treaty.[14] As the Supreme Court said in a leading case, "inter-

---

12. Per Lord Russell in *Re Arton (No. 1)*, [1896] 1 Q.B. 108, at p. 111.

13. S. 26 of the British Extradition Act, 1870, defines a "fugitive criminal" as "any person accused or convicted of an extradition crime committed *within the jurisdiction of any foreign state* who is in or is suspected of being in some part of Her Majesty's dominions". A number of extradition cases dealing with the territoriality of the alleged crimes were considered above, pp. 168–169.

14. For the need under English law for an Order in Council, see below.

national law recognise[s] no right to extradition apart from treaty. While a government may, if agreeable to its own constitution and laws, voluntary exercise the power to surrender a fugitive from justice to the country from which he has fled, and it has been said that it is under a moral duty to do so, . . . the legal right to demand his extradition and the correlative duty to surrender him to the demanding country exist only when created by treaty."[15]

b MUNICIPAL LAW AND EXTRADITION

Because the nature of the various treaties dealing with extradition and the actual procedures for extradition depend primarily upon the municipal law of the states parties to a treaty or involved in the request for surrender of a fugitive, the subject of extradition is best explained and more readily understood in its "municipal" context.

B. English law

a EXTRADITION WITH FOREIGN STATES

Extradition to foreign states is governed by the Extradition Act, 1870 (as opposed to extradition to member states of the British Commonwealth which is covered by other legislation). The Act only applies in relation to a foreign state with which "an arrangement has been made" for the surrender of fugitive criminals and when Her Majesty has by Order in Council directed that the Act shall apply "in the case of such foreign state" (s. 2).

i *Procedure*

Under s. 7, a "requisition for the surrender of a fugitive criminal of any foreign state, who is in or suspected of being in the United Kingdom, shall be made to a Secretary of State by some person recognised by the Secretary of State as a diplomatic representative of that foreign state. A Secretary of State may, by order under his hand and seal, signify to a police magistrate that such requisition has been made, and require him to issue his warrant for the apprehension of the fugitive criminal." It is also possible for a police magistrate or justice of the peace to issue a warrant "on such information or complaint and such evidence or after such proceedings as would in the opinion of the person issuing the warrant justify the issue of a warrant if the crime had been committed or the criminal convicted in that part of the United Kingdom in which he exercises jurisdiction"; but a full report must then be sent to the Secretary of State, "who may if he thinks fit order the warrant to be cancelled" (s. 8).

At the hearing of the case before the magistrate, all that the requesting state need do is to make out a *prima facie* case against the prisoner (as if in

---

15. *Factor v. Laubenheimer*, 290 U.S. 276, at p. 287 (1933).

the preliminary proceedings before a magistrate on a charge of an indictable offence), or to show that he is the person already convicted of an offence under the law of the requesting state. In such a proceeding it is clearly open to the prisoner to argue that there is not sufficient evidence to establish even a *prima facie* case against him, that he is not the person who was convicted, or that the crime was not committed on the territory of the requesting state,[16] etc. S. 9 of the Act also enables the magistrate to receive "any evidence which may be tendered to show that the crime of which the prisoner is accused or alleged to have been convicted is an offence of a political character or is not an extradition crime". If the magistrate commits the fugitive to prison pending extradition, he is required to inform him that he will not be surrendered until after the expiration of fifteen days within which he may apply for a writ of habeas corpus. Only after the expiry of the fifteen days, or, if a writ of habeas corpus is issued, after the decision of the court upon the return of the writ, shall it be lawful for the Secretary of State to surrender the fugitive (s. 11).

The proceedings on the writ of habeas corpus, which are before the Divisional Court, are only partly a form of appeal. The prisoner is entitled to argue that his confinement is unlawful because the alleged crime is unsupported by the evidence, or is not an offence covered by the Extradition Act, or is of a political character, but the Divisional Court is not a Court of Appeal on questions of fact. The Court is only entitled to see whether, on the evidence before the magistrate, he had authority and jurisdiction to commit: it cannot question the magistrate's discretion in order to decide whether it had been exercised properly.[17]

ii *What constitutes an extraditable crime*

In order to satisfy the Act, the crime for which the surrender is demanded must satisfy the following requirements:

> (1) (a) it must be specified in the treaty with the requesting state;
>   (b) it must be a crime against the law of that state;
>   (c) it must be included in the list of crimes set out in the first schedule of the Act;
>   (d) it must be a crime according to English law;[18] and

---

16. *R.* v. *Lavaudier* (1881), 15 Cox C.C. 329; cp. *R.* v. *Nillins* (1884), 53 L.J. M.C. 157 & *R.* v. *Godfrey*, [1923] 1 K.B. 24. And see *Schtraks* v. *Government of Israel*, [1964] A.C. 556.

17. See Lord Russell's comments in *Re Galwey*, [1896] 1 Q.B. 230, at p. 236 and *Re Arton, ibid.*, 509 at pp. 517–18; per Kelly, C.B., in *Ex p. Huguet* (1873), 29 L.T. 41, at p. 43; and per Bigham, J., in *Ex p. Siletti* (1902), 18 T.L.R. 771, at pp. 772–773.

18. Per Lord Russell, C.J., in *Re Arton (No. 2)*, [1896] 1 Q.B. 509, at p. 513. Although in most instances dealing with municipal law it is possible to read Scottish law instead of English law, the Extradition Act defines an extradition crime as "a crime which, if committed in England or within English jurisdiction, would be one of the crimes described in the first schedule to this Act" (s. 26). Thus it would seem possible for a person to be arrested in Scotland in respect of activities not criminal by Scottish law, though criminal by English law, and then surrendered as a result of proceedings before a police magistrate at Bow Street: see the case of *Blierbach*, quoted in [1957] Public Law, pp. 117–18. This possibility is accepted readily enough in other states incorporating separate law units, see below, p. 342.

(2) it must not be an offence of a political character.

It can be seen that the requirements in (1) are essentially different from (2) in that they deal with the criminality of the fugitive's acts, while (2) is only in issue once their criminal nature is established. As (a), (b), (c) and (d) tend to overlap in particular cases, it is proposed to deal with them together before going on to consider the political character of the offence as a bar to extradition.

1 *The criminality of the offence*

To an extent the four requirements (a)–(d) are obvious enough. Although an offence might be listed in the Act, the British Government may have omitted it from the treaty negotiated with the requesting state. Not only must the offence be one set down in the Act, therefore, it must also be included in the relevant treaty. Clearly a fugitive could not be extradited if his acts were not criminal according to the law of the requesting state: he would in no sense be a fugitive criminal if that were the case. It is also established that, even if the activities of the fugitive are criminal by the law of the requesting state, and, according to that law, constitute a crime included in the treaty and covered by the British Act, these activities must also be criminal under English law. In *Ex parte Sjoland & Metzler*,[19] the Divisional Court held that the fugitives could not be extradited to Norway on a charge of obtaining by false pretences contrary to the Norwegian Penal Code because their conduct did not amount to such an offence according to English law.

This requirement that the fugitive's conduct must coincide with the interpretation placed upon the accused's conduct by English law is expressly stated in the Extradition Act itself which defines "extradition crime" to mean "a crime which, if committed in England or within English jurisdiction, would be one of the crimes described in the first section to this Act" (s. 26). The significance of this provision may perhaps be illustrated by the *Eisler* case.[20] Eisler had been convicted under a United States Federal statute which made it an offence "knowingly to make any false statement in an application for permission to depart or enter the United States with intent to induce or secure the granting of such permission". The United States – United Kingdom Extradition Treaty covered perjury, and it was argued on behalf of the United States Government that the facts which had given rise to the conviction could equally well have given rise to a conviction for perjury under American law. It was clear, therefore, that Eisler had not been convicted of perjury, but the United States authorities were faced with the additional

---

19. [1912] 3 K.B. 568. The two fugitives had induced a third party to play the "three card game" by the deception that they were strangers, it thus appearing that one of them was winning by correctly guessing a particular card. This practice was held not to be contrary to s. 17 of the Gaming Act, 1845, and so could not support under English law a charge of obtaining by false pretences the money subsequently won from the third party.
20. Unreported: see (1950) 35 Cornell L.Q. 424.

problem that even if Eisler could have been convicted of perjury on the same facts in the United States, his actions could not amount to perjury under English law. The definition of perjury contained in the 1911 Perjury Act only extended to sworn statements made in the course of or for the purposes of a judicial proceeding, including "a proceeding before any court, tribunal, or person having by law power to hear, receive and examine evidence on oath" (s. 1). S. 2 of the Act dealt with "kindred offences" not amounting to perjury, which included wilfully swearing a false oath otherwise than in a judicial proceeding. It was on this ground that Eisler's counsel pressed for his release. However, even if the magistrate had been prepared to take a liberal view of the terms of the treaty along the lines suggested by counsel for the United States, Eisler's conduct did not amount to the extradition crime of perjury within the English Extradition Act. The magistrate refused to order Eisler's surrender to the United States and Eisler was released from custody.

It can be seen from this case that the argument that the English Courts should place a liberal interpretation on the extraditable offences listed in the relevant treaty is unlikely to succeed. The courts are bound by statute to look at the offences named in the treaty from the standpoint of English law. This does not mean, however, that there must be an exact correspondence between the crime charged under the law of the requesting state and the equivalent offence under English law. All that is required is that the crime charged and the offence which would have covered the accused's conduct had the events taken place in England should both be covered by the extradition treaty.

In *Re Arton (No. 2)*,[1] the Divisional Court had to consider the case of a fugitive whose extradition was requested by France to stand trial on a charge *inter alia* of *faux on écritures de commerce* within Art. 147 of the Penal Code. The nearest equivalent to *faux* in English law was forgery, but the term *faux* covered a much wider range of dishonest conduct. Arton's activities did not amount to forgery under English law, but they did constitute the offence of falsification of accounts which was covered by s. 83 of the Larceny Act, 1861, as extended by the Falsification of Accounts Act, 1875. The Court held that Arton's conduct constituted an extraditable offence both by English and French law, and that, even though the offences were not identical, they were both covered by the extradition treaty between the two states. Arton could, therefore, be properly surrendered to the French authorities.

2   The political character of the offence

Under s. 3 (1) of the 1870 Act, a fugitive criminal "shall not be surrendered if the offence in respect of which his surrender is demanded is one of a political character, or if he proves to the satisfaction of the police magistrate or the court before whom he is brought on habeas corpus, or to the Secretary of State, that the requisition for his surrender

---

1. [1896] 1 Q.B. 509.

has in fact been made with a view to try or punish him for an offence of a political character". The Act itself, though in keeping with contemporary practice in matters of extradition of political refugees, made no attempt to define a "political offence" and the task of developing such a definition has devolved upon the courts.

In *Re Castioni*,[2] the prisoner had been arrested on a warrant for his extradition to Switzerland. In the course of an uprising in which a number of citizens of the Canton of Tigno had seized weapons and had captured the municipal palace, the prisoner had shot a member of the Canton Council in the course of seizing the palace. In holding that the prisoner should be discharged from custody because of the undoubted political nature of the murder he was alleged to have committed, the Divisional Court did not profess to lay down anything akin to an exhaustive definition. Denman, J., suggested that in order to avoid extradition "for such an act as murder . . . it must at least be shown that the act is done in furtherance of, done with the intention of assistance, as a sort of overt act in the course of acting in a political matter, a political rising, or a dispute between two parties in the state as to which is to have the government in its hands."[3] Hawkins, J., was content to adopt the wide interpretation suggested by Stephen, J., in his History of the Criminal Law that the phrase should mean that "fugitive criminals are not to be surrendered for extradition crimes if those crimes were incidental to and formed part of the political disturbances".[4]

The difficulties of such a widely framed definition became apparent four years later in *Re Meunier*[5] in which extradition was sought of a prisoner who had committed two anarchist bomb outrages in France, one of which occurred at a military barracks. The Divisional Court held that the bomb incident could not be considered as a political offence. In the words of Cave, J., "in order to constitute an offence of a political character, there must be two or more parties in the state, each seeking to impose the government of their own choice on the other, and that, if the offence is committed by one side or the other in pursuance of that object, it is a political offence, otherwise not." In this case there were not two such parties: the party with whom the accused was identified, that is, the anarchists, was the "enemy of all governments".[6]

The theory that a "political offence" was bound up with the notion of inter-party strife within a state was very much a product of nineteenth-century philosophy and history. It was not until 1954, however, that an English Court was called upon to face squarely the problem of a political offence by a small group of individuals having no particular design to overthrow the government of their country. In *Ex parte Kolczynski*[7] a group of Polish seamen seized control of the trawler on which they were

---

2. [1891] 1 Q.B. 149. 3. *Ibid.*, at p. 156. 4. *Ibid.*, at p. 166.
5. [1894] 2 Q.B. 415. 6. *Ibid.*, at p. 419.
7. [1955] 1 Q.B. 540. For an earlier attempt to establish that a prisoner would be punished for possessing political secrets though tried on a series of fraud charges: *Re Arton (No. 1)*, [1896] 1 Q.B. 108.

serving, and sailed the vessel to an English port where they sought "political asylum". They alleged that they had been under close surveillance throughout the voyage from a party secretary, one of whom was assigned to each trawler, but particularly after news came through that Kolczynski's brother had escaped to England. It was claimed on behalf of the seamen that their seizure of the trawler was in itself a political offence as they had taken this step in order to escape from political persecution. Furthermore, although the request for extradition had been made for the offence of revolt against the master of a ship on the high seas, if they were returned to Poland, they would be tried or punished for the more serious offence, amounting to treason under Polish law, of escaping to a capitalist country. Lord Goddard, C.J., with whom Devlin, J., agreed, accepted the first argument: the seizure of the vessel was itself an offence of a political character. The evidence showed that the applicants "while at sea found that a political officer was overhearing and recording their conversations and keeping observation upon them for the purpose of preparing a case against them on account of their political opinions, presumably in order that they might be punished for holding or, at least, expressing them. A resultant prosecution would thus have been a political prosecution. The revolt of the crew was to prevent themselves being prosecuted for a political offence and in my opinion, therefore, the offence [i.e. the seizure of the ship] had a political character."[8] Cassels, J., however, preferred to accept the second contention urged on behalf of the seamen: that although their extradition was requested for an apparently non-political offence, they would, if returned to Poland, be tried or punished for the treasonable offence of escaping to the "west". The members of the Court were all aware that their approach to the notion of a political offence was not entirely in keeping with the views expressed in the earlier cases. But as Cassels, J., pointed out, the words "offence of a political character" "must always be considered according to the circumstances existing at the time when they have to be considered. The present time is very different from 1891, when *Castioni*'s case was decided. It was not then treason for a citizen to leave his country and start a fresh life in another. . . . Now a state of totalitarianism prevails in some parts of the world and it is a crime for citizens in such places to take steps to leave. In this case the members of the crew of a small trawler engaged in fishing were under political supervision and they revolted by the only means open to them . . . . and if they were surrendered there could be no doubt that, while they would be tried for the particular offence mentioned, they would be punished as for a political crime."[9]

More recently the House of Lords has been called upon to consider the nature of a "political offence" in *Ex parte Schtraks*.[10] The government of Israel sought extradition of the fugitive to face charges of perjury and child stealing. The child in question had been left with his grandfather

---

8. *Ibid.*, at p. 550.   9. *Ibid.*, at p. 549.
10. [1963] 1 Q.B. 55 (D. Ct.); *affd. sub. nom. Schtraks v. Government of Israel*, [1964] A.C. 556 (H.L.).

for a period of a year, but the grandfather had refused to return the boy to his parents because he wished to continue supervising the boy's religious education. Schtraks was a son of the grandfather and uncle to the boy, and had assisted the grandfather in keeping the child from the parents. He argued that politics and religion were closely related in Israel and that at the time of his alleged offences there had been a well-attended political meeting supporting the grandfather's actions.

Their Lordships were unanimously of the opinion that even though it could be said that the alleged offences were "committed in the political context, and that the action of the grandfather and the appellant received considerable political support",[11] the offences arose primarily out of a family quarrel, and were essentially offences against the ordinary criminal law and not of a political character. However, Lords Reid and Radcliffe in particular entered into a more detailed discussion of the nature of a political offence.

Lord Reid pointed out that, to mid-Victorian eyes, the typical political refugee was the insurgent against the tyranny of certain Continental governments, but although such views may have given rise to s. 3 (1) of the Act of 1870, its scope was not limited to such cases. For example, it should not be limited to cases of open insurrection. "An underground resistance movement may be attempting to overthrow a government and it could hardly be that an offence committed the day before open disturbances broke out would be treated as non-political while a precisely similar offence committed two days later would be of a political character. And I do not see why the section should be limited to attempts to overthrow a government. The use of force, or it may be other means, to compel a sovereign to change his advisers, or to compel a government to change its policy may be just as political in character as the use of force to achieve a revolution. And I do not see why it should be necessary that the refugee's party should have been trying to achieve power in the state. It would be enough if they were trying to make the government concede some measure of freedom but not attempting to supplant it."[12]

Lord Radcliffe accepted that an uprising or other struggle for power within a state was unnecessary, otherwise the decision in the *Kolczynski* case could not have been reached. The idea of "political offence" was not "altogether remote from that of 'political asylum'"; consequently it was "easy to regard as a political offence an offence committed by someone in furtherance of his design to escape from a political régime which he has found intolerable". The idea lying behind the phrase "offence of a political character" was that the fugitive should be "at odds with the state that applies for his extradition on some issue connected with the political control or government of the country". The idea indicated that the requesting state was after the fugitive "for reasons other than the enforcement of the criminal law in its ordinary, what I may call its common or international, aspect."[13]

---

11. [1964] A.C., at p. 582, per Lord Reid.   12. *Ibid.*, at p. 583.
13. *Ibid.*, at p. 591.

Despite these judicial utterances, it cannot be said that the notion of a political offence within the context of s. 3 (1) has been made any clearer. The absence of any attempt at precise definition stems not only from the fact that such a definition might hamper the courts in dealing with specific cases but also from the practical difficulty in framing a satisfactory definition. This difficulty is illustrated by the reactions of their Lordships to the *Kolczynski* case. Lords Jenkins and Evershed expressed no opinion, although the latter accepted the proposition that the interpretation of the notion of a crime of a political character depended upon attention being paid to the historical circumstances in which the 1870 Act had been passed.[14] Lord Hodson stated a preference for adhering as closely as possible to the guidance he found in *Re Castioni*, but added that cases might arise, like *Kolczynski*, "where special considerations have to be taken into account", pointing out that in "some modern states politics and justice may be inextricably mixed, and it is not always easy to say what amounts to a revolt against the government."[15]

What is clear from limited statements made by Lords Evershed and Hodson is that fundamentally they adhered to the requirement of some form of political struggle. A similar trend is apparent from the more lengthy opinions expressed on this point by Lords Reid and Radcliffe. Lord Radcliffe, while accepting the *Kolczynski* decision, asserted that the grounds upon which it was reached were stated "too generally to offer much useful guidance for other cases in future". In commenting upon the cases of *Castioni* and *Meunier*, his Lordship suggested that it was still necessary to maintain the idea of the connection of a political offence "with an uprising, a disturbance, an insurrection, a civil war or struggle for power". Having said this, however, Lord Radcliffe extended the connection almost to the point where it disappeared by adding that it would not be departed from "by taking a liberal view as to what is meant by disturbance or these other words, provided that the idea of political opposition as between fugitive and requesting state is not lost sight of".[16] And perhaps Lord Reid had a similar notion in mind when he said that an attempt to compel a sovereign to change his advisers, or a government its policies, might be as political in character as a revolution: it should not even be necessary that the refugee's party had been trying to achieve power, as it would be enough if they were attempting to make the government concede some measure of freedom.[17]

Despite the attempts by their Lordships to restate the law in the terms of *Castioni* and *Meunier*, it is clear that the international political scene has undergone such radical changes since 1870 that a useful concept of offences of a political character is not attainable in the language of those cases. In some countries "ordinary" criminal offences and offences against the state are not readily distinguishable. An individual could well be persecuted for his political views even though he belonged to no defined

---

14. *Ibid.*, at p. 598.   15. *Ibid.*, at p. 612.   16. *Ibid.*, at p. 591.
17. *Ibid.*, at p. 583.

"party" or group. If he were to commit an offence in escaping to England, he might well be extradited under English law as it now stands. *Kolczynski*'s case at least made an attempt to adopt the 1870 Act to modern conditions: in *Schtraks*, their Lordships seemed more concerned with constricting the law within terms familiar to the political thinking of the Victorian era.

Whatever difficulties exist in relation to the overall definition of political offence, there has been no divergence of opinion on the need for a connection between the fugitive's political activities and the actual crime he is alleged to have committed. From the outset it was accepted that a fugitive could not escape extradition if his crime was committed primarily for personal motives, even if the offence occurred in the course of a political disturbance. In *Castioni*, for example, the members of the court accepted that, even though the killing of the Council member had been unnecessary to the achievement of the fugitive's ends and the objects of the movement he supported, and was therefore to be deplored, it had nevertheless occurred in the course of a political disturbance: in the absence of any personal motive leading the fugitive to kill the victim, this fact was sufficient to classify the offence as "political" within the meaning of the 1870 Act. In the words of Lord Reid in the *Schtraks* case, "not every person who commits an offence in the course of a political struggle is entitled to protection. If a person takes advantage of his position as an insurgent to murder a man against whom he has a grudge I would not think that that could be called a political offence. So it appears to me that the motive and purpose of the accused in committing the offence must be relevant and may be decisive. It is one thing to commit an offence for the purpose of promoting a political cause and quite a different thing to commit the same offence for an ordinary criminal purpose."[18]

It will be recalled that the 1870 Act allows not only the courts to look into the political nature of the offence but also the Secretary of State who may similarly decide to discharge the fugitive. It is clear that executive practice in this field is strongly against interference by the Secretary of State except in the most extreme circumstances.[19] However, the powers of the Secretary of State to interfere are not limited to cases giving rise to disputes over "political offences". If the original order for apprehension of the fugitive is not given by the Secretary of State, s. 8 of the Act gives him a power to order the cancellation of any warrant issued without such an order. The Home Office Memorandum on Extradition Practice of 1913[20] had this to say on the Secretary of State's powers: "Such a step is naturally very rare. The power was given as a precaution against extradition proceedings being begun frivolously or hastily, or without the full authority of the Government of the country from which the fugitive has come . . . the Secretary of State can discharge in any case in which

---

18. [1964] A.C., at p. 583, per Lord Reid.
19. See the cases cited in *British Digest of International Law*, Vol. 6, pp. 673–677.
20. Quoted *ibid.*, p. 537.

the foreign Government would not have applied for extradition, or in which he would not have acted on such an application. . . ." The Memorandum then went on to consider two cases.

In the first, one *Mueller* was arrested on the application of the French Government. His defence was that he was a naturalised British subject so that he could not therefore be surrendered under the relevant treaty. Enquiries were made and it was discovered that he had indeed been naturalised, although his naturalisation had been obtained by fraud. As at the time there was no means of revoking the naturalisation, it was apparent that the extradition proceedings must fail. Rather than insist upon the matter being formally considered and pronounced upon by the magistrate, it was decided that, as the Secretary of State knew from the records of his own Department that the prisoner could not lawfully be extradited, he should order the prisoner's release at once.

In the second case, that of *Marie Silbereisen*, the medical officer of the prison where the fugitive was detained pending extradition to Germany reported that her health was so poor that her removal would involve the greatest risk. The Home Office asked the Foreign Office to inform the German Government of the position and to say that, subject to any observations they might wish to offer, the Secretary of State intended to exercise his power of discharging the prisoner. The German Government raised no objections, but asked that the fugitive might be kept under surveillance with a view to rearrest if her condition improved. She was in fact later rearrested and extradited: discharge by the Secretary of State was held no bar to the recommencement of proceedings arising out of the same activities.

iii *The fugitive when surrendered should only be tried in respect of the offence for which his extradition was requested*

This principle, often referred to as the *principle of speciality*, is laid down, as far as extradition from the United Kingdom is concerned, in s. 3 (2) of the 1870 Act. It provides that a "fugitive criminal shall not be surrendered to a foreign state unless provision is made by the law of that state, or by arrangement, that the fugitive criminal shall not, until he has been restored or had the opportunity of returning to Her Majesty's dominions, be detained or tried in that foreign state for any offence committed prior to his surrender other than the extradition crime proved by the facts on which the surrender is grounded". In cases where the extradition of a fugitive is obtained by the British Government from a foreign state, s. 19 applies a similar rule: "such person shall not, until he has been restored or had the opportunity of returning to such foreign state, be triable or tried for any offence committed prior to the surrender in any part of Her Majesty's dominions other than such of the said crimes as may be proved by the facts on which the surrender is grounded".

Although these provisions are similar, there is nevertheless a significant difference in wording between s. 19 and s. 3 (2). Under the former there is no need for an English Court to allow a surrendered fugitive to return to the foreign state from which he was extradited if the crimes for which he is tried may be proved by the facts on which the surrender was grounded. In *R. v. Corrigan*,[1] the appellant had been extradited from France on a charge of obtaining by false pretences. He was convicted by an English Court on a charge of fraudulent conversion upon the same facts that had been the basis of the original claim for extradition. The Court of Criminal Appeal held that the English Courts had jurisdiction over the appellant within the terms of s. 19.

On the other hand, s. 3 (2) lays down that the law of the requesting state or the arrangement made with that state must guarantee that the surrendered fugitive should not be tried for any offence other than *the* extradition crime proved by the facts on which the surrender is grounded. The difference in wording would seem to suggest, therefore, that a fugitive surrendered by the United Kingdom should *not* be tried on an alternative charge in circumstances similar to those that arose in *R. v. Corrigan*. While this might have been the intention of the legislators in 1870, it is obviously a more difficult matter to insist upon its application in practice. Soon after the passing of the Act, disputes arose between Britain and the United States because the existing extradition treaty between the two countries (of 1842), contained no express guarantee that the fugitive would not be tried on other charges than those for which extradition was obtained. Despite the fact that the United States itself only allowed surrender to a foreign state on the basis that the principle of speciality was adhered to, a number of American Courts took the view that a surrendered criminal could not plead the absence of speciality as a defence to other charges.

After much negotiation, the 1842 Treaty was supplemented by a Convention of 1889 which provided *inter alia* (Article II (4)) that no person "surrendered by or to either of the High Contracting Parties shall be triable or be tried for any crime or offence committed prior to his extradition, other than the offence for which he was surrendered, until he shall have had an opportunity of returning to the country from which he was surrendered". Ironically, the necessity for such a provision had been removed by the decision of the Supreme Court in *U.S. v. Rauscher*[2] that, under the 1842 Treaty, it was clearly implied that the requesting state could not exercise jurisdiction with respect to a charge other than that for which the accused was extradited. As the Treaty was self-executing, Rauscher was entitled to be released. This decision and the wording of the 1889 Convention have largely cleared up the difficulties between the United Kingdom and the United States,[3] but in relation to other states a number of problems might still arise. Can a fugitive be tried for any other offence? Should such other offence be limited to one arising out of the evidence submitted in support of the request for extradition? Must it also be limited to offences included in the treaty? While con-

---

1. [1931] 1 K.B. 527.   2. 119 U.S. 407 (1886).
3. Though not entirely, see the cases cited in *British Digest*, Vol. 6, pp. 610–620.
MIL

tinuing its objections to attempts to try returned fugitives for other crimes, the Foreign Office has been reluctant to press for the release of offenders convicted of other crimes contained in the relevant treaty and arising out of the same facts in view of the wording of s. 19, and of its application by the English Courts.

A cognate problem is whether it is the fugitive criminal or the surrendering state which has the right to complain if the criminal is tried on other charges. This problem is particularly acute where the requesting state alleges that the fugitive has agreed to be tried on other charges. In the case of Emile Arton, whose extradition was allowed on a number of charges arising out of accounts that he had falsified, he was subsequently tried not only on the extradition charges, but also for the offence of corrupting public officials. The French Minister in London notified the Foreign Office that Arton had himself voluntarily renounced the protection of the Treaty and had requested to be tried on the other charge. The Law Officers to whom the matter was referred were emphatically of the opinion that the action of the French authorities was most improper: "as a matter of principle an individual cannot waive the stipulations of a Treaty. The obligation under the Treaty is on the part of the French Republic to Her Majesty's Government, and it is for Her Majesty's Government to decide whether in view of Arton's wishes they will consent to his trial upon other charges".[4]

iv *Extradition of nationals*

Although the Extradition Act creates no special rule for the surrender of nationals, a number of factors have led to the inclusion of provisions dealing with nationals in a large number of treaties entered into by the United Kingdom. It will be recalled that many states, particularly those of Continental Europe, claim the right to exercise criminal jurisdiction over their nationals even though the offence is committed abroad. Some of these states are obliged by their municipal law to insist upon non-surrender of nationals in their extradition treaties with other states. The United Kingdom has not been altogether adverse to accepting a limitation with respect to nationals, because there has from time to time been pressure based on the fear that British subjects might not enjoy all the safeguards of judicial process in some foreign states. However, the main reason why this practice was not encouraged by the British Government was the obvious difficulty that English criminal jurisdiction is based primarily on the territorial principle. In the great majority of cases a crime committed by a British subject abroad was not subject to the jurisdiction of the English Courts. If a British subject could not be extradited in such circumstances the result would be that he could not be tried at all. This possibility may be illustrated by reference to a communication from H.M. Postmaster-General to the Treasury in November, 1887.[5] The occasion of his remarks was the latest in a series of thefts of registered mails in

---

4. *Ibid.*, pp. 631–5.   5. *Ibid.*, p. 689.

international transit on the mainland of Continental Europe. In his opinion, it could be "taken as certain that the robberies were planned in England by two, if not three, different gangs—by British subjects, and that this country was selected as the base of operations chiefly because of the practical immunity afforded by its laws, which make it impossible, on the one hand, to punish in England a crime committed on a foreign territory, and, on the other hand, for the British Government to deliver up one of its subjects committing such a crime to be tried by a foreign Power, however strong the evidence of his criminality".

To avoid such difficulties as far as possible, the British Government renegotiated a number of treaties in order to allow the requested state a discretion whether or not to surrender its own nationals. It was realised that in the case of a request by Britain to France or Belgium, for example, extradition would always be refused, but it did avoid the situation where the United Kingdom could become a refuge to its own nationals who had committed crimes abroad, for which they could not be tried and punished in England.[6]

b EXTRADITION WITH COMMONWEALTH COUNTRIES

Because of the unity of the former British Empire, extradition between the various territories of the Empire was governed by the much simpler procedures and less strict conditions of the Fugitive Offenders Act, 1881. The Act provided for the surrender of fugitives charged with any offence punishable with imprisonment for twelve months and upwards. There was no requirement of "double criminality", that the crime should be known to the laws of the requested as well as of the requesting state; nor was there any provision preventing trial on charges other than those for which the surrender was obtained. In fact, the whole process had as much in common with the system of backing warrants between different counties in England as it has with extradition.

For obvious reasons, an Act governing the surrender of fugitives between different parts of the British Empire in 1881 has little relevance to the relations between the separate states of the British Commonwealth today. Perhaps this change is most clearly illustrated in the context of political offences. An individual could not be surrendered to a foreign state for a political offence under the 1870 Extradition Act, but the fact that the offence was of a political nature was irrelevant if the request was from a Commonwealth state under the Fugitive Offenders Act. In the light of the wide divergence of political views and attitudes held by member states of the Commonwealth, the 1881 Act had become increasingly obsolete with the granting of independence to a large number of new African and Asian states.

The need for revision of the process of extradition (or "rendition" as it is often termed) among Commonwealth countries had been the subject of desultory discussions over a period of some years. The case which

---

6. *Re Galwey*, [1896] 1 Q.B. 230.

perhaps more than any stressed the need for immediate reform was that of *Zacharia* v. *Republic of Cyprus*.[7] The respondent state applied for the rendition of the appellant on a number of charges including murder. Prior to the granting of independence to Cyprus, the appellant had assisted the British security forces against the paramilitary E.O.K.A. movement which was attempting by the use of force to obtain independence for Cyprus. He was therefore regarded by E.O.K.A. as a traitor, and various attempts had been made on his life. For his own safety he had been flown to England by the Cyprus Government in January, 1961. The only serious limitation upon the right of the requesting state to obtain the surrender of the fugitive offender was s. 10, which provided *inter alia* that where it appeared to a superior court that "by reason of the application for the return of a fugitive not being made in good faith in the interests of justice or otherwise, it would . . . be unjust or oppressive or too severe a punishment to return the fugitive either at all or until the expiration of a certain period, such court may discharge the fugitive either absolutely or on bail, or order that he shall not be returned until after the expiration of the period named in the order or may make such order . . . as to the courts seems just". The House of Lords held unanimously that the fact that the offence for which rendition was sought was of a political character was not a relevant consideration in applying s. 10. Not only was no mention made of political offences, but treason, the most serious of political crimes, was expressly included within the range of offences for which surrender should be allowed by s. 9. Furthermore, s. 10 could not be said to apply in the appellant's case because there was no evidence of a lack of good faith on the part of the Cyprus Government which had contended that the appellant's activities with the British security forces had been used as a cover for criminal activities as a gang leader.

Because of the emphasis placed by their Lordships on the criterion of good faith, the absence of which on the part of the requesting state would be difficult to establish and proof of which the courts might be reluctant to accept, the effect of the *Zacharia* decision was largely to nullify s. 10 as a means of escape from the obsolescent distinction between the Fugitive Offenders Act and the Extradition Act. Eventually, a conference was held in London in April, 1966, at which Commonwealth representatives agreed upon changes in the system of extradition to be applied among member states of the Commonwealth. The 1966 Agreement was put into effect as far as the United Kingdom was concerned by the Fugitive Offenders Act, 1967.

The system introduced under the new Act[8] has much in common with the existing procedures under the 1870 Extradition Act. Proceedings for the return of a fugitive offender require an "authority to proceed" from

---

7. [1963] A.C. 634. See also *Ex parte Enahoro*, [1963] 2 Q.B. 455.
8. The Act applies different rules to "United Kingdom dependencies", but the effect is basically to retain a system similar to that of the 1881 Act with regard to the surrender of fugitives between those territories and the United Kingdom.

the Secretary of State, although a magistrate may issue a provisional warrant without this authority, such a warrant being cancellable by the Secretary of State. The offences covered by the Act are referred to in s.3 and designated specifically in the First Schedule. S. 4 applies similar restrictions upon the return of fugitive offenders to those contained in the 1870 Act, although they are expressed in more detail in a more modern form. Under s. 5 (1), for example, no person shall be returned to a Commonwealth country "if it appears to the Secretary of State, to the Court of Committal or to the High Court . . .

(a) that the offence of which that person is accused or was convicted is an offence of a political character;[9]
(b) that the request for his return (though purporting to be made on account of a relevant offence) is in fact made for the purpose of persecuting or punishing him on account of his race, religion, nationality or political opinion; or
(c) that he might, if returned, be prejudiced at his trial or punished, detained or restricted in his personal liberty by reason of his race, religion, nationality or political opinions."

S. 5 (3) lays down that a person may not be returned to any Commonwealth country "unless provision is made by the law of that country, or by an arrangement made with that country,[10] for securing that he will not, unless he has first been restored or had an opportunity of returning to the United Kingdom, be dealt with in that country for or in respect of any offence committed before his return . . . other than—

(a) the offence in respect of which his return . . . is requested;
(b) any lesser offence proved by the facts proved before the Court of Committal; or
(c) any other offence being a relevant offence in respect of which the Secretary of State may consent to his being so dealt with."

c DEPORTATION AS DISGUISED EXTRADITION

Unless its rights are limited by treaty, a state has virtually unrestricted powers to exclude foreign nationals from entering its territory, and an ill-defined power to order them to leave once they have entered. The procedure of ejecting aliens is termed "deportation", and it is usually immaterial to the deporting state where the expelled alien goes once he has left its territory. This contrasts with extradition in which the expulsion is primarily in the interests of the requesting state and is, therefore, directly *to* the requesting state.

Providing the deportee is treated in a manner conforming to the minimum standards of civilised conduct required by international law, the process of deportation, including the destination of the deportee, is at the

---

9.   An offence against the life or person of the Head of the Commonwealth is excluded as not being an offence of a political character (s. 4 (5)).
10.   Which may be either for the particular case or of a more general nature (s. 4 (4)).

discretion of the deporting state. If the state makes use of deportation as a means of enabling it to extradite fugitive criminals which for some reason it is unable to surrender by normal extradition procedures (e.g. because there is no extradition treaty with the "requesting" state, or because the offence is not covered by the treaty, or is of a political character), there is no rule of international law forbidding such conduct, although such conduct may be contrary to the municipal law of the state concerned.

As far as English law is concerned, there have been a number of incidents and cases in which deportation has been used to return a person sought by the authorities of another state to the territory of that state. The most celebrated of the older cases concerned the *Duke of Chateau Thierry*,[11] whose return to France was required by the French authorities in order that the Duke should be conscripted into the French forces during the First World War. The Home Secretary had made an order under the Aliens Restriction Act, 1914, and Art. 12 (1) of the Aliens Restriction (Consolidation) Order, 1916, that the Duke should be deported from the United Kingdom. Although the order did not specify the destination, it was admitted by the Attorney-General that the intention was to place the Duke on a vessel bound for France. The Court of Appeal held that the 1914 Act and the 1916 Order did not give the Secretary of State the power to order the deportation of an alien to any particular place, but, providing the order was good on the face of it (as the order in this case was), there was nothing to stop the executive from achieving the same result by placing the deportee on a ship sailing for the desired destination.

The advantages of this power to the executive are obvious enough. If it is desired to surrender an alien to a requesting state in circumstances where no power exists to extradite, all that the Home Secretary has to do is issue a deportation order and place the individual concerned on an aircraft or ship bound for the appropriate state. One drawback of the exception in favour of political offenders in the Extradition Act, and now in the 1967 Fugitive Offenders Act, is the fact that the fugitive might have escaped from a "friendly" state and hold views as inimical to the well-being of the United Kingdom as of the state from which he has escaped. Extradition being impossible, a residual power to deport, with the right to select the actual route of exit, is a useful political safeguard. But how can such a procedure be reconciled with the spirit and letter of the careful safeguards against the surrender of political fugitives set down in the Extradition Act and in the recent Fugitive Offenders Act?

The problem was highlighted by the *Soblen* case in 1962.[12] Soblen, a naturalised U.S. citizen, had been convicted of passing defence secrets to the Soviet Union and sentenced to life imprisonment by a U.S. Court. He was on bail at the time the Supreme Court finally rejected his appeal

---

11. [1917] 1 K.B. 922.
12. The case provoked a number of articles in legal periodicals. For a detailed survey of the circumstances of the case, see (1963) 12 I. & C.L.Q. 414.

that his conviction should be quashed. Making use of his brother's Israeli passport, he escaped to Israel. He was expelled by the Israeli authorities and was flown on board a specially chartered flight in the custody of a U.S. marshal to Athens where he was transferred to an El Al commercial flight. The aircraft was due to call at London on the way to New York. Before it reached London, Soblen inflicted a number of wounds on himself, so that when the aircraft landed he had to be taken immediately to hospital. Notice of refusal of permission to land was served on the U.S. marshal, on the airline, and, when he had recovered sufficiently, on Soblen himself. There was, therefore, no legal barrier to the deportation of Soblen back to the United States by the simple expedient of placing him once more on board the same aircraft that had been held up in London and was due to leave for New York. An attempt to challenge the legality of this procedure in the courts failed.[13] However, news of the surreptitious removal of Soblen from its territory was by that time becoming generally known in Israel, and such was the public outcry that the Israeli Government forbade the airline to fly Soblen to the United States. Apparently determined to return Soblen to the United States, the British Home Secretary issued an order under Articles 20 and 21 of the Aliens Order, 1953, authorising any immigration officer to place Soblen "on board a ship or aircraft which is about to leave the United Kingdom" and authorising the Governor of Brixton Prison "to detain him until arrangements are completed for so placing him on board". It was also stated to the Press that it was the Home Secretary's intention to give instructions for Soblen to be placed on an aircraft proceeding to the United States.

At this stage a second attempt was made to invoke the protection of the courts. Of the various arguments put forward on behalf of Soblen, the fourth is the main concern of the present discussion. It was contended that the motives of the Home Secretary in using an ostensibly valid deportation order in order to secure extradition of Soblen in breach of the safeguards of the 1870 Act rendered the order *ultra vires*. The members of the Court of Appeal[14] seemed to regard themselves free to consider the situation unhampered by the earlier decision on the 1914 Order in the *Duke of Chateau Thierry* case. Unlike the earlier case, the Court of Appeal in *Soblen* treated the good faith of the Home Secretary as highly relevant. Indeed, Lord Denning went so far as to state that if "the purpose of the Home Secretary in this case was to surrender the applicant as a fugitive criminal to the United States of America because they had asked for him, then it would be unlawful" because "the offence for which the applicant was convicted in the United States is not an extraditable offence". Soblen's difficulty, a difficulty which proved insurmountable, was to show bad faith on the part of the Home Secretary. The attempt to obtain production of all written communications addressed to H.M. Government from the United States was defeated by a claim of Crown

---

13. [1963] 1 Q.B. 829.   14. [1963] 2 Q.B. 837.

privilege.[15] As Lord Denning pointed out, while deportation disguised as extradition was unlawful, "if the Home Secretary's purpose was to deport him to his own country because the Home Secretary considered his presence here to be not conducive to the public good, then the Home Secretary's action is lawful". In the absence of evidence of bad faith, it was not possible to show that the Home Secretary was not acting for the public good.

The *Soblen* affair was widely criticised—both the actions of the Home Secretary, and the apparent haste of the courts to get the matter off their hands (why did the Court of Appeal not give Soblen the benefit of a reserved judgment; why was not legal aid allowed for an appeal to the House of Lords?) It raises the obviously important issue that, if the power of deportation is misused, the elaborate precautions built into the process of extradition can be largely circumvented. But does it necessarily follow that the use of deportation to "extradite" a political offender to a friendly state or ally is inevitably an evil? Deportation of a dangerous spy *to* a friendly state may be as conducive to the public good as the deportation of a dangerous criminal to make sure he does not operate in the United Kingdom. While the law relating to extradition and deportation and the distinction between the two may need clarifying, it should not necessarily involve an absolute prohibition on executive discretion to avoid the restriction on the extradition of political offenders if their surrender is genuinely in the public interest.

C. The law of the United States

a EXTRADITION

i Procedure

The surrender of fugitive offenders is a Federal matter, although state courts are also granted the power to issue warrants for their apprehension. The procedure laid down by 18 U.S.C., Sect. 3184, is not dissimilar to that provided for in the British Act of 1870. Under Sect. 3184, whenever there is an extradition treaty with a foreign government, any U.S. justice or judge, or authorised commissioner, or any judge of a state court of record, may "upon complaint made under oath, charging any person found within his jurisdiction, with having committed within the jurisdiction of any such foreign government any of the crimes provided for by such treaty . . . issue his warrant for the apprehension of the person so charged that he may be brought before such justice, judge, or commissioner, to the end that the evidence of criminality may be heard and considered. If, on such hearing, he deems the evidence sufficient to sustain the charge under the provisions of the . . . treaty . . ., he shall certify the same, together with a copy of all the testimony taken before him, to the

---

15. Under the ruling principle laid down in *Duncan* v. *Cammell Laird*, [1942] A.C. 624; but see now *Conway* v. *Rimmer*, [1968] A.C. 910.

Secretary of State, that a warrant may issue upon the requisition of the proper authorities of such foreign government for the surrender of such person, according to the stipulations of the treaty . . .; and he shall issue his warrant for the commitment of such person so charged to the proper jail, there to remain until such surrender shall be made."

As under English law, all that is required of the requesting state is to make out a *prima facie* case against the fugitive: it does not have to demonstrate that the fugitive actually committed the crime. In *Collins* v. *Loisel*,[16] the British authorities introduced evidence which tended to show that Collins had obtained a pearl button from jewellers as a result of a number of representations to the effect that he was a wealthy man, a retired officer, a partner in an internationally known Glasgow firm, and entitled to draw a draft of £1,700 on a London bank; the evidence also tended to prove that Collins knew the falsehood of these representations. Collins argued, *inter alia*, that such evidence would not be sufficient to establish the crime of false pretences. According to the Supreme Court, this contention was irrelevant. "It was not the function of the committing magistrate to determine whether Collins was guilty, but merely whether there was competent legal evidence which, according to the law of Louisiana, would justify his apprehension and commitment for trial if the crime had been committed in that state."[17] There were clearly grounds upon which Collins could be tried for obtaining by false pretences, even if it was possible that he might be found not guilty on some technical ground.

As it is the task of the magistrate or judge to issue the warrant for arrest of the fugitive pending extradition, and review by way of habeas corpus is not an appeal, the powers of the court of review (normally a Circuit Court of Appeals) are limited. The Supreme Court has repeatedly stated that findings of fact cannot be questioned: all that an applicant can argue is that the committing judge had no jurisdiction, usually on the ground that the crime was not covered by the relevant treaty, or, in extreme cases, because there was simply no evidence or manifestly insufficient evidence upon which the judge could act. The fact that the fugitive might have a valid defence to the charge is no bar to his extradition once a *prima facie* case is made out, and it is not for the court of review, any more than it is for the committing judge, actually to try the case.[18]

ii *What constitutes an extraditable crime*

1 *The crime of which the fugitive is accused or has been convicted must be specified in the treaty with the requesting state*

The crimes that can be included in an extradition treaty are not specified in any United States Statute, Sect. 3184 referring simply to "any of the crimes provided for by such treaty". It will be recalled that the English Courts tended to approach strictly the problem of identifying the crime

---

16. 259 U.S. 309 (1922).   17. *Ibid.*, at pp. 314–15.
18. *Collins* v. *Loisel* (above); *Ex parte Zentner*, 188 F. 344 (1911).

for which the fugitive was to be tried under the law of the requesting state with the equivalent offence under English law. In many respects, this attitude, even though inevitable in view of the wording of the Extradition Act, is unfortunate when taken to the extremes illustrated by the *Eisler* case.[19]

On the other hand, American Courts have been able to adopt a more flexible approach unhampered by precise statutory provisions. The *Eisler* case was widely criticised in the United States because it provided such a sharp contrast with the American case of *Factor* v. *Laubenheimer*.[20] The applicant's extradition was sought by the British authorities for having received money, knowing the same to have been fraudulently obtained. This crime was amongst those added to the list of extradition crimes by the Convention of 1889, which supplemented the earlier 1842 Treaty. Although such conduct was criminal under the laws of a majority of American states, it did not constitute an offence under the law of Illinois. The Supreme Court held that, although some of the offences specified in the Treaty and the Convention had to be criminal by the law of the place where the fugitive was found, a number of others, including the charge in this case, were not covered by this limitation. Not only did this appear from the wording of the Treaty, but it was reinforced by subsequent diplomatic correspondence on the subject. Finally, the Court expressed itself in favour of a liberal construction of extradition treaties, particularly when dealing with technical differences between similar types of offences.[1]

2   *The offence must be of a non-political character*

There is no statutory provision regulating extradition for political offences, although political offences are normally excluded by the terms of the treaties entered into by the United States. If a fugitive claims that the offence for which his surrender is requested is of a political character, the issue is first considered by the committing judge. If he finds in favour of the fugitive, the fugitive is released, and that is an end of the matter. If the judge holds that the offence is not of a political character, this decision may be reviewed on an application for habeas corpus. If this application is unsuccessful, the Secretary of State has a final discretion whether to review the findings of the committing judge, including the political nature of the offence.

While this procedure is generally followed, it must be realised that extradition treaties entered into by the United States are not uniform. The extent of the judicial power depends in part, therefore, on the actual wording of the treaty with the requesting state. In *Re Ezeta*,[2] for example, the District Judge had to consider the effect of a provision in the treaty with Salvador that "the provisions of this treaty shall not apply to any crime or offence of a political character". It was his opinion that such a prohibition extended "to the action of the committing magistrate", and

---

19.   Above, p. 325.   20.   290 U.S. 276 (1933).   1.   *Ibid.*, at p. 303.
2.   62 F. 972 (1894).

terminated "his jurisdiction when the political character of the crime or offence is established. In other words, he has no authority to certify such a case to the executive department for any action whatever".[3] It was suggested, on the other hand, that the effect of terms similar to those contained in the Treaty between the United Kingdom and the United States of 1889 where a fugitive should not be surrendered, "if the offence in respect of which his surrender is demanded be one of a political character", would be to withdraw the issue from the courts altogether and place the obligation of complying with the treaty on the Secretary of State in whose hands the ultimate discretion to surrender rested.[4] While this suggestion may not be completely accurate, it does demonstrate the possibility that different treaty provisions might produce a different relationship between the judiciary and the executive. Whatever might be the precise effect of the treaty between Britain and the United States, it does not limit the *jurisdiction* of the American Courts in the way that the Salvador treaty restricted it. Even if the crime for which surrender was requested by the United Kingdom was of a political character, it is the surrender that is prohibited: the offence itself does not fall outside the treaty.

Even when the courts have decided that the offence for which surrender is requested is not of a political nature, the Secretary of State has a power to review their finding quite apart from any allegations of bad faith on the part of the requesting state. In 1908 the Russian Government requested the extradition of one *Rudewitz*,[5] who sought to establish that the crimes with which he was charged were political offences. The Commissioner who heard the proceedings found against the accused and transmitted the record of the hearing to the Secretary of State. It appeared that the fugitive had been a member of a "Social Democratic Labour Party", members of which at a local meeting had recommended the burning of certain premises and the killing of three persons. In the circumstances, the Secretary of State declined to surrender Rudewitz. The murder and arson were clearly political in nature, while additional acts of robbery committed in the course of the other offences must be considered incidental to those offences unless evidence could be produced separately identifying the fugitive with the robbery. No such evidence had been forthcoming.

It is only in recent years that the United States' Courts have paid much attention to the question of defining a "political offence". Although there were a number of cases in which it was necessary to decide whether or not a particular offence was political, there was little discussion of what constituted a political offence.[6] In *Karadzole* v. *Artukovic*[7] in 1957 it is

---

3. 62 F. 972 (1894), at p. 997.
4. *Ibid*. In other words, it was possible that the correct procedure for a magistrate (under the Treaty with Britain) would be to commit a fugitive criminal, even in respect of a political offence, but to recommend to the Secretary of State that the criminal should be released and not surrendered.
5. Hackworth, *Digest of International Law*, Vol. 4, p. 49.
6. E.g. *Ornelas* v. *Ruiz*, 161 U.S. 502 (1896).
7. 247 F. (2d) 198 (1957). See also *Re Ezeta* (above); *Ramos* v. *Diaz*, 179 F. Supp. 459 (1959) and *Re Gonzalez*, 217 F. Supp. 717 (1963).

interesting to note that the Circuit Judge referred at length to the English cases and judgments in which the question of definition was tackled. And, on a subsequent rehearing of the case,[8] a U.S. Commissioner ventured to comment that "political character" or political offence had not been satisfactorily defined. "Generally speaking it is an offence against the government itself or incident to political uprisings. It is not a political offense because the crime was committed by a politician. The crime must be incidental to and form part of political disturbances. It must be in furtherance of one side or another of a bona fide struggle for political power."

Although it is usually for the courts and not for the executive to make the primary determination of the political nature of an offence, in one situation the judicial view is that the matter is for the political arm of government to decide. This situation arises if the fugitive attempts to argue that, although the offence for which his extradition is sought is not in itself political or of a political character, the reasons why the requesting state is anxious to enforce its ordinary criminal law are political. In *Re Lincoln*[9] the accused asked for the proceedings to be adjourned in order to give him an opportunity to produce evidence to show that he was being extradited for political reasons. Under the treaty, the British authorities could only try the fugitive for the extradition crimes (forgery and obtaining by false pretences), but he alleged that the charges had not been brought against him until political considerations, arising out of anti-British publications of his in the United States, had led the British Government to wish to punish him in order to interfere with his future public pronouncements. The District Court refused to allow the adjournment. It was not "part of the Court proceedings nor of the hearing upon the charge of crime to exercise discretion as to whether the criminal charge is a cloak for political action, nor whether the request is made in good faith. Such matters should be left to the Department of State. The government of the United States, through the Secretary of State, should determine whether the foreign government is in fact able to exercise its civil powers, and whether diplomatic and treaty relations are being carried out and respected in such a way that it is safe to surrender an alleged criminal under a treaty."[10]

iii *The principle of speciality*

Under 18 U.S.C. Sect. 3186, the Secretary of State may authorise the surrender of a person committed under Sect. 3184 "to be tried for the offense of which charged". In other words, the Secretary of State can only surrender a fugitive to stand trial for the offence or offences with which he is charged by the requesting state.

There is no express statutory provision dealing with a person surrendered by a foreign state for trial in the United States. The position is

---

8.   *U.S.* v. *Artukovic*, 170 F. Supp. 383 (1959), at p. 392.   9.   228 F. 70 (1915).
10.   *Ibid.*, at p. 74.

therefore governed by the terms of the relevant treaty. In *U.S.* v. *Rauscher*,[11] the fugitive had been extradited from Britain to the United States to be tried for a murder committed on board an American vessel on the high seas. Presumably because there was no evidence to establish the murder charge, Rauscher was indicted for unlawfully assaulting and inflicting cruel and unusual punishment on the victim. The Supreme Court held that the courts were bound to give effect to the terms of the treaty with Britain which spoke in terms of evidence of criminality in relation to a specific crime or crimes. It was not possible therefore to proceed with any charge against the accused other than that for which his surrender had been requested. And it made no difference if the offence charged arose out of the same evidence as that upon which surrender had been allowed.[12]

iv *Extradition of nationals*

The policy of the United States on this issue is similar to that of the United Kingdom. As the criminal law of most American states is based upon the territorial principle, there are few charges that can be brought in American Courts against a United States citizen in relation to an incident occurring abroad. However, despite its reluctance to exempt nationals from the normal processes of extradition, the United States Government has been obliged in many of its treaties to accept such an exemption.

As a consequence of these treaties, a United States citizen committing crimes abroad may succeed in obtaining a degree of immunity by making good his escape to the United States. In *Valentine* v. *U.S., ex rel. Neidecker*,[13] the French authorities sought the extradition of two United States citizens to stand trial for offences committed in France. Under Article V of the Franco-American Treaty of 1909 neither state was "bound to deliver up its own citizens" under the terms of the agreement. It was argued that while the United States was not bound to surrender its nationals, it had a discretionary power to do so under this provision. This contention was rejected by the Supreme Court. In a number of treaties with other states the discretion had been expressly conferred.[14] The absence of such a discretion in the Treaty with France must have been intentional. In the absence of such a power, the United States Government could not surrender the fugitives to the French authorities.

It is interesting that in 1923 the French and American Governments had discussed the posibility of revising the 1909 Convention to avoid the

---

11. 119 U.S. 407 (1886).
12. The reason for this ruling, that otherwise a state could obtain the surrender of a fugitive wanted for a lesser crime by alleging a more serious crime for which extradition was possible, is acceptable where the alternative charge is not an extraditable offence, but there would seem to be no good reason for holding that a conviction on a lesser charge was not possible where the charge arose out of the same facts alleged in support of the request for extradition and when the lesser offence was also covered by the relevant treaty. See above, p. 333.
13. 299 U.S. 5 (1936); cp. *R.* v. *Galwey*, above, p. 335.
14. E.g. under the treaties of 1886 with Japan and of 1899 with Mexico.

situation where United States citizens committing crimes in France and fleeing to America could escape punishment.[15] The French suggestion was that while the United States should surrender all fugitives covered by the treaty, including nationals, France should surrender all fugitives, except nationals. In rejecting this proposal, the United States pointed out that there were obvious difficulties, particularly the absence of witnesses, in the way of trying crimes committed abroad, even in those states which claimed jurisdiction over their nationals. In the American view, a far more satisfactory remedy was for the French Government to alter its laws to enable it to enter into a treaty with the United States providing for the mutual surrender of all fugitives, including their respective nationals.

b DEPORTATION AS DISGUISED EXTRADITION

The United States has frequently made use of its powers to exclude or expel aliens as an alternative to extradition. These procedures have been employed not only in situations where the offence or the offender was not covered by treaty, or where there was no treaty, but also as a less troublesome method of dealing with an alien whose case would have fallen within the relevant treaty.

Under 8 U.S.C. Sect. 1227, any "alien arriving in the United States, who is excluded under this chapter [under Sect. 1128 an alien shall be excluded from the United States if he has been 'convicted of a crime involving moral turpitude (other than a purely political offense) . . . or . . . who admits having committed such a crime'], shall be immediately deported to the country whence he came . . . unless the Attorney-General . . . in his discretion, concludes that immediate deportation is not practicable or proper." Exclusion can be employed instead of extradition only in limited circumstances under this provision. Obviously it is only possible in the case of an alien; it can only be used to return a person to the state from which he came; and it can only be employed if the alien has been *convicted* of an offence of a particular type, or if he *admits* that he committed such an offence.

Sect. 1251 (a) provides for the deportation of various categories of aliens, including those "excludable" by the law existing at the time of entry. Although under Sect. 1252 (b) deportation proceedings are unnecessary if an alien voluntarily departs from the United States, this alternative is only open to him at the Attorney-General's discretion. The overriding principle is laid down in Sect. 1253 (a) which gives the ultimate discretion in the choice of destination to the Attorney-General. Thus, although the usual procedure is for the Attorney-General to direct deportation of the alien to the destination of the alien's choice, if that state is willing to accept him, this procedure need not be adopted if the Attorney-General "in his discretion, concludes that deportation to such country would be prejudicial to the interests of the United States." In the last resort, however, the executive discretion is virtually unfettered, because Sect.

---

15. Hackworth, *loc. cit.*, pp. 58–59.

1253 (a) allows deportation to any one of a number of alternatives (the country from which the alien last entered the United States, country of birth, to any country of residence, etc.) and then states finally "if deportation to any of the foregoing places or countries is impracticable, inadvisable, or impossible, then to any country which is willing to accept such alien into its territory". Although an alien once he has entered the United States may seek protection from the courts, his right to challenge a deportation order is severely limited by the nature and extent of the Attorney-General's discretion.

It can be seen that, subject to a number of obvious limitations, deportation and exclusion are readily available alternatives to extradition. In practice, the United States Government has tended to regard their use as an exceptional, though nevertheless useful, means of surrendering fugitive offenders. Because of the long land frontiers with its two friendly neighbours, Mexico and Canada, deportation has provided a simple method of transferring offenders that have escaped from those states into the custody of the appropriate authorities with a minimum of publicity. Although occasional protests have been made at the use of deportation as a means of avoiding the formality of extradition, its general acceptance may be illustrated by the tone of the following comment by a former legal adviser to the Department of State:[16]

> "The immigration laws of the United States provide for the exclusion or deportation of aliens who have been convicted of or who admit the commission of certain classes of crimes in foreign countries. These laws are separate and distinct from the laws and treaties relating to extradition. They are not enacted for the benefit of foreign governments or for the purpose of bringing fugitives to justice; rather, they are for the protection of the United States. However, requests are sometimes made by governments for the deportation by other governments of fugitives from justice, and occasionally steps are taken—especially in the absence of an extradition treaty— to deport such persons."

D. An international law of extradition?

From the survey of English law, and of the law of the United States, it is clear that extradition law and procedures are primarily matters of municipal law, and that extradition treaties alone are sources of international obligation. Nor do the laws of other states differ greatly from the position in Britain or the United States. In some states, it is true, a request for extradition may be granted even in the absence of a treaty with the requesting state, but such surrenders depend upon the municipal law of the state concerned and not upon any differing view of the existence of a mandatory rule of international law requiring the surrender.

When a request is made to the state in the territory of which the fugitive has taken refuge, it is the courts and the executive of the requested state

---

16. Hackworth, *loc. cit.*, p. 30.

which have the duty to decide whether to surrender the individual concerned. While their decision is almost certainly conclusive under the law
of the requested state, must the requesting state accept their determination
whatever the circumstances? It would seem reasonable to suppose that, the
obligation of the two states being governed by a treaty giving rise to
rights and duties on the international plane, a failure to surrender in
accordance with the terms of the treaty would constitute a breach of the
requested state's international obligations.

While there are examples of one state protesting diplomatically at the
decision of another state to refuse its request for the extradition of a
particular fugitive, it is not an issue which has arisen with sufficient
seriousness to lead to large-scale controversy or to international adjudication. However, if such a dispute did come before an international tribunal
it is most likely that the tribunal would attempt to measure the conduct
of the requested state against some international standards.

Even if one accepted the notion of an international standard, it is still
a matter of some difficulty to suggest in what circumstances it might
apply. The refusal to extradite its own national when there is no exemption in favour of nationals in the relevant treaty is a straightforward
matter of applying the treaty, subject to any argument that might be
raised to the effect that such an exemption should be implied into the
treaty. But what if there is an exemption in favour of nationals, but the
requesting state refuses to accept the requested state's contention that the
fugitive is its national? In the unlikely event of a state abusing its power
of granting nationality to render fugitive offenders immune from surrender or trial abroad, an international tribunal could apply generally
recognised international criteria in deciding such a dispute.

A number of incidents have occurred of surrendered fugitives being
tried contrary to the terms of the relevant treaty for offences other than
those for which their surrender was requested. Diplomatic protests have
usually resulted in an attempt by the requesting state to placate the requested state, or to justify its conduct in terms of the acquiescence of the
accused[17] or the similarity of the charges.

Perhaps the most likely source of friction is the definition of political
offences, or offences of a political character. If a dispute over a refusal to
surrender were submitted to adjudication, it is unlikely that the tribunal
would take the view that the qualification of the offence was entirely a
matter for the requested state. But according to what standard would it
judge the conduct of the requested state? How would it define its international standard? To an extent the previous attitudes of the courts and
the executive of the requested state would be relevant. If the disputed
determination was in line with previous cases, it would hardly be open
to the other state to protest; if it was clearly at variance with those cases, it
would be strong evidence of a breach of the requested state's obligations
under the terms of the treaty. In the absence of any evidence of past

17. See above, p. 334.

attitudes, it may well be that the tribunal could look at cases from the courts of other states to estimate whether there is any general approach to the definition of political offences.

It would perhaps be clearer if this proposition were illustrated by reference to the facts of an actual case. In *Re Ktir*,[18] the Swiss Federal Supreme Court had to consider a request for extradition from France. Ktir, a French-Algerian, had killed a fellow countryman. Both men had been members of the Algerian Front for National Liberation (the F.L.N.). The victim had been in French custody but had later been released. Ktir's superiors in the F.L.N. suspected the victim of "treason" against the cause. They therefore instructed Ktir and three others to kill the victim. Ktir and his companions carried out their instructions. In the actual case, the court did authorise Ktir's extradition, but what ground of complaint would the French Government have had if the request had been refused?

The Swiss Supreme Court itself analysed its own previous decisions as establishing the following principles:

> "Political crimes are acts which, although they are in themselves common crimes, acquire a predominantly political character by reason of the circumstances under which they were committed, in particular, by reason of their motives and their aim. Such crimes, so-called relative political crimes, presuppose that the act, inspired by political passion, was committed in the framework of a fight to gain power or in order to break away from a power suppressing all opposition, and that the act is in direct and close relation to the political aim envisioned. In addition, the injury done must be proportionate with the result sought; in other words, the interests at stake must be sufficiently important, if not to justify, at least to excuse the impairment which the act has caused to certain private legal values. Where murder is concerned, this relationship exists only where the killing is the only means to safeguard the higher interests involved and to attain the political aim sought."

An international tribunal would have to decide whether other states had accepted previous decisions by the Swiss Courts as satisfying Swiss treaty obligations, and whether Ktir's case fell within or outside the principles previously adhered to. If there were no previous authorities, the tribunal would have the more difficult task of examining the practice of states in general to decide what is normally meant by a political offence. Clearly Ktir's actions were connected with a political movement or uprising which operated in France as well as in Algeria, but were they not also political in the sense of furthering the political purposes of the F.L.N. by eliminating a suspected traitor? And even if the offence was also an act of revenge, it was in no sense an act of private revenge.[19]

The test employed by the Swiss Courts to determine the political nature of an offence is more restricted when the charge is one of murder. A failure to surrender Ktir might have been a breach of its treaty obligations in the light of previous Swiss authorities, providing it was possible to regard Swiss practice as expressing what the parties intended by the terms

---

18. (1961): a translated report is given in 56 A.J.I.L. 224–7.
19. Cp. the words of Hawkins, J., in *Re Castioni*, [1891] 1 Q.B., at p. 165.

of their treaty. If there had been no previous cases before the Swiss Courts establishing evidence of what one of the parties at least understood by the treaty, a refusal to surrender Ktir would have found support in the practice of a number of states towards political offenders.

4 ASYLUM

The popular notion of asylum is usually in the context of "political asylum", in which an alien seeks permission to be allowed entry to, or permission to remain in, a state because he would face political persecution if he were forced to return to his own state. In the absence of an extradition treaty there is no obligation upon a state to return offenders to the state from which they have escaped, and if the individual is in no sense an offender, or if his crime is of a political nature, the territorial state is under no obligation to surrender at all, extradition treaty notwithstanding. It follows that a decision to allow an alien to enter and to remain in a state is only the normal application of its rights as territorial sovereign to exercise exclusive or primary jurisdiction over persons within its territory. The use of the term "asylum" in such circumstances would be too general to be of legal significance or value.

Where the term "asylum" has a legal meaning is in situations in which the principle of extraterritoriality provides a basis for exemption from the jurisdiction of the territorial sovereign, i.e. in diplomatic premises or on warships. "The term 'asylum', or, more correctly, 'exterritorial asylum', is usually employed to describe those cases in which a state declines to surrender a person demanded who is not upon its own physical territory but is upon one of its public ships lying in foreign territorial waters or upon its diplomatic (or, rarely, consular) premises within foreign territory."[20]

a DIPLOMATIC ASYLUM

Although there is much uncertainty about the existence of the right of diplomatic asylum, a number of principles seem to find support in state practice:

(1) Outside Latin-America, there is no general right of asylum.

(2) However, it follows from the inviolability of diplomatic premises (under Article 20 (1) of the Vienna Convention, agents of the receiving state may not enter them without the consent of the head of mission) that if a refugee is allowed to remain in the Embassy, the correct procedure for the territorial state is to take up the matter with the foreign state concerned, not to break into the premises. It is the British view that temporary shelter may be provided to foreign nationals whose lives are in immediate danger (e.g. if pursued by a violent mob).[1]

---

20. McNair in (1951) 28 B.Y.B.I.L. 172.
    1. See the instructions from the Foreign Secretary to H.M. Minister in Port-au-Prince of 13th June, 1913: *British Digest*, Vol. 7, p. 922.

(3) As a matter of agreement between the host and the sending state, consular or diplomatic premises may be granted the right to provide asylum. In the 1860's the government of Haiti apparently allowed foreign consuls to grant asylum freely. In a report of 12th March, 1866, one of the Law Officers of the Crown explained that this was "an exceptional privilege not in accordance with the general law of nations. The present government of Haiti appear to desire the continuance of this privilege, because it spares the government the necessity of inflicting capital punishment on political offenders, which they are obliged to decree, but do not wish to execute." It was his opinion that the privilege ought, as soon as conditions in Haiti returned to normal, to be abandoned as it was a potential source of conflict with the local authorities.[2]

A recent example of diplomatic asylum arising out of an *ad hoc* arrangement was the refuge granted after the unsuccessful Hungarian uprising of 1956 to Cardinal Minszenty in the United States Embassy in Budapest. Any punitive action against the Cardinal would have brought opprobrium on the Hungarian authorities. As long as he remained in the Embassy the Hungarian authorities let it be known that they would take no steps to seize him. The most satisfactory conclusion from the point of view of both the Hungarian and American Governments would have been for the Cardinal to have left Hungary altogether, but this step the Cardinal refused to take.

(4) A right of diplomatic asylum does exist among a number of Latin-American states, although its precise limits are ill-defined. This right depends primarily upon treaty provisions, and it is doubtful whether there exist any customary rules elaborating the framework established by conventional obligations.

In the *Asylum* case,[3] Haya de la Torre, who, it was alleged, had led an unsuccessful revolution against the Peruvian Government, sought refuge in the Colombian Embassy in Lima, the Peruvian capital. The two major issues in dispute, which were subsequently submitted to the International Court, were the Colombian claims (a) that, as the state granting asylum, it was entitled to determine the political nature of the offence and that such a determination would be binding on Peru, the territorial state; and (b) that Peru was obliged to guarantee the safe conduct of the refugee in order to enable him to leave the country.

The main evidences relied upon in support of claim (a) were (i) the Havana Convention on Asylum; and (ii) the Montevideo Convention on Political Asylum of 1933. The Court pointed out that the former did not explicitly grant to the asylum state the right to qualify the offence: indeed the later Montevideo Convention was clearly designed to rectify the omission of this power. A competence to make such a qualification was "of an exceptional character", involving "a derogation from the equal rights of qualification which, in the absence of any contrary rule,

2. McNair, *International Law Opinions*, Vol. 2, p. 75.
3. I.C.J. Rep. 1950, p. 266.

must be attributed to each of the states concerned", and thus aggravating "the derogation from territorial sovereignty constituted by the exercise of asylum".[4] As to the Montevideo Convention, which did include a power for the state granting asylum also to qualify the offence, this Agreement had not been ratified by Peru and consequently could not be invoked against that state. Nor was it possible to argue that the Convention represented "American international law". Far from being able to show that Peru had acquiesced in the development of a rule allowing a binding qualification of the offence by the asylum state, the evidence presented to the Court disclosed "so much uncertainty and contradiction, so much fluctuation and discrepancy in the exercise of diplomatic asylum and in the official views expressed on various occasions" that it was not possible "to discern in all this any constant and uniform usage, accepted as law, with regard to the alleged rule of unilateral and definitive qualification of the offence."[5] In other words, Peru could hardly have acquiesced in the development of a rule which the Court did not believe existed except as a treaty obligation between the contracting states.

As to claim (b), the Havana Convention to which the two states were parties, allowed the territorial state to require that the refugee be sent out of its territory within the shortest time possible, or the asylum state to require the guarantees necessary for the departure of the refugee. However, the application of this provision of the Convention depended upon the validity of the original grant of asylum under the other terms of the Convention. It was the view of the Peruvian Government that the asylum had been wrongfully granted and Peru therefore called upon the Court to declare that the grant of asylum had been made in breach of the Convention.

Under Article 1 (1), asylum could not be granted to persons accused or condemned for "common crimes". In the circumstances it was impossible to show that Haya de la Torre had been involved in anything other than a political offence. However, Article 2 (2) limited the grant of asylum to "urgent cases and for the period of time strictly indispensable for the person who has sought asylum to ensure in some other way his safety". It was on this issue that the Court held the second Colombian claim failed. Haya de la Torre had been at large for three months after his arrest was ordered. It was therefore difficult to contend that his case was urgent as he had been well able to provide for his own safety during that period.

At a subsequent hearing,[6] the parties asked the Court to interpret its decision, with particular reference to what was required of Colombia in order to comply with that decision. All that the Court was able to do was to point out the deficiencies in the Havana Convention. If asylum were granted to a person accused of or condemned for a common crime, there was a duty to surrender to the local authorities, but no such provision existed in relation to a person granted asylum from arrest for a political

---

4. *Ibid.*, pp. 274–5.   5. *Ibid.*, p. 277.
6. *Haya de la Torre* case, I.C.J. Rep. 1951, p. 71.

crime. This omission the Court was prepared to consider as having been made deliberately. As the Court had pointed out in its earlier judgment "asylum as practised in Latin-America is an institution which, to a very great extent, owes its development to extra-legal factors. The good-neighbour relations between the republics, the different political interests of the governments, have favoured the mutual recognition of asylum apart from any clearly defined juridical system. Even if the Havana Convention, in particular, represents an indisputable reaction against certain abuses in practice, it in no way tends to limit the practice of asylum as it may arise from agreements between interested governments inspired by mutual feelings of toleration and goodwill."[7]

The Court's conclusion that, asylum being based upon "extra-legal factors", the only applicable legal rules were those laid down by the Convention and accepted as binding by the disputing states left the dispute over Haya de la Torre at an impasse. The only means suggested by the Court to resolve their dispute was for the parties to reach an agreed solution. In the event, Haya de la Torre spent five years in the Colombian Embassy before Peru finally agreed to allow him a safe-conduct to leave Peruvian territory.

It is not an easy question to decide whether a legal right of asylum exists that is peculiar to Latin-America. Dissatisfaction with the court's decision in the *Asylum* case led to the convening of a conference at Caracas in 1954 which drew up an Inter-American Convention on Diplomatic Asylum. The underlying philosophy of the Convention is to establish the controlling rights of the asylum granting state to categorise the nature of the offences for which the fugitive's arrest is sought, and to decide upon the urgency of the circumstances required before asylum can be validly granted. The Convention has not been widely ratified and the United States refrained from even signing the original draft on the ground that it did not recognise any general right of diplomatic asylum. Nevertheless, it would seem that the majority of states of Latin-America recognise that the inviolability of diplomatic premises extends to cover an immunity from arrest for a fugitive granted asylum in such premises. Once asylum has been granted, it is then for the states involved to reach an accommodation providing for the termination of the asylum. In the course of his dissenting opinion in the *Asylum* case, Judge Alvarez, speaking with the authoritative and experienced voice of his Latin-American background, explained the position in the following terms:

"In view of the fact that asylum is utilised when the political order within a country is disturbed, and inasmuch as the situation resulting from this disorder may vary considerably, there is no customary American international law of asylum properly speaking; the existence of such a law would suppose that the action taken by the Latin States of the New World was uniform, which is not at all the case: governments change their attitude according to circumstances and political convenience.

---

7. I.C.J. Rep. 1950, p. 286.

But if there is no customary Latin-American international law on asylum, there are certain practices or methods in applying asylum which are followed by the States of Latin America. These may be summarised as follows:

1. Asylum is granted only in cases of political offence and not to common criminals.

2. Asylum is granted in accordance with the laws and usages of the State of refuge, and it is for the latter to appreciate whether the offence committed by the refugee is a political offence or a common crime.

3. The territorial State may request the departure of the refugee from its territory and the State of refuge may then require the former State to deliver a safe-conduct enabling the refugee to leave the country safely.

4. The State which granted asylum sometimes, with the same end in view, requests that a safe-conduct be issued to the refugee."[8]

b ON WARSHIPS[9]

Because of the similarity of the rule that diplomatic premises are inviolable with the principle of the immunity of foreign warships and of other public vessels, it has been claimed that there exists an analogous right of asylum on board such ships. To a large extent diplomatic practice has tended to assimilate the position of warships with the status of diplomatic premises in this respect. For example, both the United Kingdom and the United States, while reluctantly accepting that asylum might be granted temporarily in diplomatic premises on humanitarian grounds or by special arrangement with the territorial state, have with similar hesitation allowed their warships to become a temporary haven in exceptional circumstances for fugitives from political persecution.

In the Admiralty instructions to H.M. naval officers of 1863, it was stated that H.M. ships, "while lying in the ports of a foreign country, are not to receive on board persons (although they may be British subjects) seeking refuge for the purpose of evading the laws of the foreign country to which they may have become amenable" but that during "political disturbances or popular tumults, refuge may be afforded to persons flying from imminent personal danger".[10] These principles are still the basis of Queen's Regulations and Admiralty Instructions.

The attitude of the United States is similar. In reply to an enquiry by the Acting Secretary for the Navy in 1913, the Secretary of State explained[11] that it was "as a general rule against the policy of this Government to grant asylum in its ships to the citizens of foreign countries engaged in political activity. . . . Temporary shelter to such persons, when they are seeking to leave their country, has sometimes been conceded on grounds of humanity, but even this is done with great circumspection lest advantage be taken of it to further the political fortunes of individuals with the

---

8. *Ibid.*, p. 295.
9. The extent to which the right extends to public vessels other than warships is doubtful, particularly in view of the gradual erosion of the immunities accorded to such vessels; see above, pp. 195–197, 216–222.
10. *British Digest*, Vol. 7, p. 387.
11. Hackworth, *Digest*, Vol. 2, p. 640.

result of involving us in the domestic politics of foreign countries." Thus U.S. Navy Regulations make specific reference to the possibility of granting asylum on grounds of humanity particularly to political refugees in countries where revolutions are commonplace and the governments unstable.

CHAPTER NINE

TREATIES

I   THE FORMALITIES OF A TREATY

A. What is a treaty?

The expression "treaty" is used as a generic term to cover a multitude of international agreements often referred to by a confusing variety of names. Some treaties are called treaties, but others are termed conventions or protocols, declarations, charters, covenants, or pacts; sometimes a treaty is referred to as an agreement, but on other occasions as a *modus vivendi*, an exchange of notes, or a memorandum of agreement. Whatever expression is used, however, to qualify as a "treaty", the agreement concerned must have certain characteristics:

(i) it should be in writing;
(ii) it must be an agreement between entities with international personality;
(iii) it must be governed by international law; and
(iv) it must create a legal obligation.

a THE AGREEMENT SHOULD BE IN WRITING

It cannot be asserted with confidence that international law *requires* a treaty to be in written form, though as a matter of practice it invariably is put into writing. Apart from obvious problems of proof, a purely verbal "understanding" suggests a reluctance on the part of the parties to enter into a formally binding arrangement. Furthermore, as Article 102 of the United Nations Charter requires registration with, and publication by, the Secretary-General of all treaties entered into by Members of the Organisation, a verbal agreement would clearly not qualify as a "treaty" in the sense of the term as employed in that provision of the Charter.

The most recent draft by the International Law Commission on the Law of Treaties[20] restricts the use of the term to "international agreements

---

20.   At the time of writing only the final I.L.C. draft and commentary were available (for a convenient text, see (1967) 61 A.J.I.L. 285). This Chapter, therefore, is based on the I.L.C.'s draft, although references have been included at the proof stage to the text of the Vienna Convention.

in written form", but the commentary points out that it was not intended to deny "the legal force of oral agreements under international law".[1] The reason for the uncertainty with regard to verbal agreements stems from the well-known Ihlen Declaration in the *Eastern Greenland* case.[2] The Danish Government made it known to the Norwegian Government through the Danish Minister in Norway that Denmark would not raise objections to Norway's claim to Spitzbergen with the obvious intention of securing a similar undertaking from the Norwegian Government with respect to Denmark's claim to Greenland. The Minister pointed out that in return for a cession of the Danish West Indies to the United States, the United States was prepared to declare that it would not object to the Danish Government extending its political and economic interests to the whole of Greenland. The Danish Government was "confident" that the Norwegian Government "would not make any difficulties in the settlement of this question". The Norwegian reply, communicated to the Danish Minister by the Norwegian Foreign Minister, Ihlen, was to the effect that the Norwegian Government would not make any such difficulties. In the context of Denmark's attitude at the Peace Conference (held in the same year as the Ihlen Declaration was made) that the Danish Government would not "oppose the wishes of Norway" with regard to the settlement of the Spitzbergen question, the Court was prepared to accept Denmark's view that the two "assurances" were "interdependent". Even if the Ihlen declaration could not be considered as recognition of Denmark's claims, it nevertheless created an obligation binding upon Norway to refrain from contesting Danish sovereignty over Greenland.

The difficulty raised by the Ihlen Declaration is whether it can be classified as an international agreement, or whether it was effective as a form of estoppel. The emphasis placed by the court upon the contemporaneous acceptance by Denmark of Norway's claims over Spitzbergen might suggest some sort of consensual arrangement, but the words actually used by the court to justify its conclusion hardly explain the juridical nature of the Declaration.

> "The Court considers it beyond all dispute that a reply of this nature given by the Minister for Foreign Affairs on behalf of his Government in response to a request by the diplomatic representative of a foreign Power, in regard to a question falling within his province, is binding upon the country to which the Minister belongs."[3]

However, if there is a trend to limit treaties to written agreements, it might be more helpful to regard the Ihlen Declaration as giving rise to an estoppel. A statement by an authorised agent of a state would clearly be binding upon that state if acted upon by another state. The consensual nature of the Declaration may be explained by the fact that Denmark was relying upon it in framing its policies with regard to Greenland and in relation to Norway's claim to Spitzbergen.

---

1. V.C. Arts 2 (1) (a), 3.   2. (1933) P.C.I.J. Rep., Ser. A/B, No. 53.
3. *Ibid.*, at p. 71. For the nature of estoppel in international law, see above, pp. 30–31.

b A TREATY MUST BE BETWEEN PARTIES ENDOWED WITH
INTERNATIONAL PERSONALITY

As the discussion of international personality demonstrated, the state is
the typical subject of international law, and international personality in
other cases is applicable to entities having rights and duties on the international plane similar to those possessed by states. Of these rights and
duties, the treaty-making power is one of the most important. Although
an international person might exist that has no power of entering into
treaties, it is certain that any entity having a treaty-making power must be
endowed with international personality.

i *Non-self-governing states*

It will be recalled that, in the case of colonial territories their international status depends upon the constitutional structure whereby they are
governed and, in the case of protectorates, upon the terms of the agreement under which the protecting power administers the territory. It may
be that the non-self-governing community has a limited power to enter
into treaty arrangements with other states, but this will depend entirely
upon the circumstances of the particular case.[4]

ii *International organisations*

The power of an international organisation to enter into a treaty can
either be expressly granted by the constitution of the organisation concerned (as with the power of the United Nations to enter into relationship
agreements with the various Specialised Agencies under Articles 57 and 63
of the Charter, or of the Council of Europe to enter into a special agreement with France as the "host state" under Article 40 of the Council's
Statute); or it may be implied by "necessary intendment" from the constitution and the duties the constitution imposes upon the organisation to
carry out (as, most notably, with the treaties of technical assistance under
which the United Nations and the Specialised Agencies carry out their
functions in the field of economic development).

The main question relating to the treaty-making power of an international organisation that is not expressly granted is, of course, whether an
organisation has the implied power to enter into a treaty of a particular
type. It is conceivable that the organisation concerned might not be
endowed with international personality at all, so that its act would be
ineffective on the international plane (although the alleged "treaty" could
be effective as a contract governed by some other system of law, a possibility discussed below). Or it is possible that the organisation, while
endowed with international personality, might not have the power to
enter into a treaty of the type in question. If the organisation, though undoubtedly endowed with international personality, does not possess the
necessary power to enter into the particular treaty, the position is less
certain. In strict theory, the act of the organisation should be ineffective

---

4. See pp. 79–86.

and the treaty void. An organisation cannot act in total disregard of the limitations placed upon it in its constitution. As the International Court pointed out in the *Expenses* case,[5] the purposes of the United Nations were broad indeed, but neither those purposes nor the powers conferred to effectuate them were unlimited. However, in practice the line between an act which is within the powers of an organisation and one which falls outside those powers might be difficult to draw. Not only is there a presumption that if an organisation takes action which "warrants the assertion that it was appropriate for the fulfilment" of one of the aims and purposes of the organisation, its action is not *ultra vires*, but in many potentially doubtful cases the legality of the action is not challenged either by members of the organisation or by states affected by or parties to the treaty.

iii *Individuals or corporations created under municipal law*

It is possible for a state to enter into a contract with a corporation or an individual, but such an agreement will not be a treaty cognisable as such on the international plane. In the *Anglo-Iranian Oil Company* case,[6] the United Kingdom, in an attempt to persuade the International Court that it had jurisdiction over the dispute under the terms of the Iranian declaration accepting the compulsory jurisdiction of the Court, alleged that a concessionary agreement between the Iranian Government and the Oil Company of 1933 was in the nature of an international as well as of a private law obligation. The argument was based on the fact that the concession had been negotiated in order to settle a dispute between Iran and the United Kingdom which had been before the Council of the League of Nations. The matter had been taken off the Council's agenda at the request of the parties when they agreed that the Company should renegotiate the original concession with the Iranian Government. When a new agreement was reached and ratified by the Iranian Government, it was reported to the Council that the dispute between the two states was "now finally settled". The Court held that these proceedings, which formed the background to the granting of the 1933 concession, could not give the concession the double character suggested by the United Kingdom. The United Kingdom was not a party to the contract, which regulated the conduct between the Iranian Government and the Company, not between the Iranian Government and the United Kingdom. Even though the concession had been granted through the good offices of the Council of the League, the only undertaking given by Iran on the international plane was to negotiate with the Company, a promise which Iran "fully executed".

c THE AGREEMENT MUST BE GOVERNED BY INTERNATIONAL LAW

Even if an agreement is between two entities endowed with international personality and possessing treaty-making capacity, it does not follow that the agreement is necessarily a treaty. In the majority of cases such agreements will be treaties in that they will operate on the inter-

---

5. I.C.J. Rep. 1962, at p. 168.   6. I.C.J. Rep. 1952, p. 93.

national plane, and will be governed in their interpretation and effect by international law. However, it would seem that certain inter-state agreements can be subject to a particular system of municipal law, either by express provision or by implication from the nature of the transaction. As the notion of states subjecting certain types of agreement to a system of municipal law is only of recent origin, it is not surprising that the number of clear illustrations of this happening in practice are few. However, a number of loan agreements made by the International Bank for Reconstruction and Development, a Specialised Agency of the United Nations endowed with international personality, with individual states did contain a clause to the effect that the agreement and the bonds issued thereunder were to be "interpreted in accordance with the law of the State of New York". If international persons can expressly subject a transaction to a system of municipal law, there would seem to be no reason why a tribunal should not imply the reference to municipal law from the nature of the transaction itself and the conduct of the parties.

d THE AGREEMENT MUST INTEND TO CREATE A LEGAL OBLIGATION

In the first report by the International Law Commission on the Law of Treaties in 1953, treaties were defined as agreements between states, including organisations of states, which were "intended to create legal rights and obligations" for the parties. An intention to create legal relations would seem to have been considered as a requirement separate from the need for the agreement to operate on the international, as opposed to the municipal, plane. The most recent draft by the Commission has omitted any reference to the intention to create legal relations, but gives no convincing reason for doing so.

There are examples even in recent history of joint declarations by states which express agreement on their future policies but which impose no legal obligation on any of the states to pursue those policies. The joint declaration made by Roosevelt and Churchill in 1941, usually known as the Atlantic Charter, was no more than a statement of "common principles" in the policies of the United States and Britain upon which the two states based "their hopes for a better future for the world". Similarly, the United Nations Declaration of Human Rights adopted by the General Assembly in 1948 was agreed to by member states on the understanding that it did not create legal duties for them. It would seem, therefore, that any definition of a treaty as the term is invariably used should include a reference to the need that the agreement should be made with the intention of creating legal obligations for some at least of the parties.

B. The making of treaties

a ADOPTION OF THE TREATY

After the processes of consultation and negotiation, treaties are normally adopted by the unanimous consent of the parties. This principle may be modified when the treaty is drawn up by an international conference. The rule employed by general conferences of the type which was called at Geneva in 1958 to consider the International Law Commission's draft conventions on the Law of the Sea is that the text of the treaty will be adopted by the vote of two-thirds of the states participating in the conference. It is obvious, however, that the voting rule is subject to the agreement of states participating in the conference, and they may wish in a particular case to adopt some other form of procedure for the adoption of the draft treaty. The unanimity rule will also be modified if the treaty is drawn up by one of the organs of an international institution. In such cases the rule to be applied will depend upon the voting formula set down in the constitution of the institution concerned.

b AUTHENTICATION OF THE TREATY

The authentication of the text of the treaty in the form which the parties may later ratify may be done in a number of ways of which initialling or signing are the most obvious. The method to be used is a matter for the parties to agree amongst themselves. In the case of treaties adopted by international organisations, the question of an authentic text is usually left to the officials of the organisation itself, while international conferences often follow the practice of embodying the text of the treaty in their Final Act.

c SIGNING AS SIGNIFYING CONSENT TO BE BOUND

The signing of a treaty may be no more than an authentication of its text, but, if the parties so agree, the signature of their representatives will signify their consent to be bound. A large number of treaties are expressly made operative upon signature. Treaties entered into by exchange of letters are effective upon the receipt by one party of the acceptance of the other party, and the validity of such treaties is dependent upon the signatures of the representatives who signed the communications. In other cases, it might be clear from the terms of the treaty that signatures of the parties will have the immediate effect of creating a binding obligation. The most obvious illustrations of this type of situation are Minutes or Memoranda of Agreement. It is usual for the signed Minute or Memorandum to state that the parties *have* already agreed upon the terms set out therein so that the document operates immediately upon signature. There are also numerous examples of treaties which, though they are to enter into force upon "approval" or "ratification", are nevertheless to be applied provisionally from the date of signature.

d RATIFICATION

If a treaty can be made effective by the signatures of the representatives of the various parties, why should there be the need for states to insist upon subsequent formal ratification? If the treaty relates to issues of great importance, a state, while being prepared to take part in the drawing up of the treaty, may require a further breathing space in which to consider its implications or in which perhaps to prepare public opinion for the obligation the state is about to undertake. On the other hand, in many states, treaties can only be ratified according to their own municipal law by certain constitutional processes, so that, whatever the political significance of the treaty, the negotiators will require time in which to submit the treaty to the appropriate state organ or organs for approval.

In the great majority of cases treaties will expressly stipulate whether ratification, or approval as it is often termed, is necessary, or by what other act the treaty is to come into force. As the International Law Commission has recently pointed out, "total silence on the subject is exceptional". Because it is only the less formal agreements that are likely to omit such a provision, it would seem to be the better view, and certainly one that is in accordance with the practice of the United Kingdom, that a treaty will only require ratification if ratification is clearly contemplated by the contracting states, and only rarely in the absence of express provision requiring ratification will it be possible to show that ratification is contemplated by the parties.

The act of ratification under international law is the formal act whereby one state declares its acceptance of the terms of the treaty and undertakes to observe them. In the case of bilateral treaties it is the usual practice of states to exchange instruments of ratification, though in the case of a treaty with more than two parties the practice is for the text of the treaty to be held by one party and for all ratifications to be deposited with that state, whose task it is to notify all signatories upon the receipt of ratifications. In the case of multilateral "law-making" treaties, like the Law of the Sea Conventions of 1958, the Secretary-General of the United Nations will often fulfil the functions of depositary for ratifications.

While ratification thus has a clear meaning under international law, much confusion is caused by the use of the same term in dealing with the formalities required by the municipal law of individual states. Thus, according to English law, "ratification" is effected by, that is, in the name of, the Crown, but in many states, as will be recalled from the discussion in Chapter II, the constitution lays down special procedures for the making of treaties. In the majority of cases, international law is only concerned with the act on the international plane (signature or ratification) whereby the treaty comes into force, and not with the question whether a state has complied with the provisions of its constitutional law.

e ACCESSION

Accession, or adherence or adhesion, as it is sometimes termed, is the means whereby a state may become a party to a treaty which it has not signed. A state may only accede to a treaty with the agreement of the parties to the treaty. Their agreement might have been given in advance by the provisions of the treaty. For example, in a number of multilateral "law-making" treaties, like the Geneva Conventions of 1958 or the Narcotic Drugs Convention of 1961, accession is possible by any state which is a member of the United Nations or of any of the Specialised

Agencies. Alternatively, the agreement of the parties might be given sub-sequently, either in accordance with the limitations contained in the treaty, or with the unanimous consent of the parties if the treaty contains no such provision. The most obvious illustrations of methods whereby parties subsequently agree to accept the accession of other states are to be found in the field of international organisations, the constitutional treaties of which lay down specific procedures for the admission of new members which thereby become parties to the treaty concerned.[7]

f RESERVATIONS AND THEIR EFFECT ON A STATE'S ACCEPTANCE OF THE TREATY

A reservation is a formal notification made at the time of signature, or of ratification, or of subsequent adherence, by one party to a treaty to the other parties, that the state making the reservation, while accepting the majority of the provisions of the treaty, does not consider itself bound by the provision or provisions in relation to which it reserves its acceptance.

As the object of a state in making a reservation is to alter its obligations with regard to other parties, the traditional view, based on a strict applica-tion of the principle of consent as the basis of all international obligations, was always to regard reservations as ineffective unless they were accepted or acquiesced in by all the other parties. In the case of a bilateral treaty or other treaty with only a few parties, no real difficulty arose in deciding whether a reservation had been accepted by the other parties (in any case, of course, reservations in such treaties were a rarity). But with the increase in the number of multilateral treaties, often drafted and agreed to in order to provide subsequent rules of conduct for members of the international community, reservations became more frequent and, short of concluding that reserving states were in most cases not parties to the treaty at all, the difficulty of assessing their affect on the legal position between the reserving states and other parties became almost impossible to analyse. Never-theless, the practice of the League of Nations, and later of the Secretary-General of the United Nations, at least until 1950, was based upon the traditional view of the law which had been accepted by a Sub-Committee of the League's Codification Committee in 1927. According to the Sub-Committee's Report,[8] for a reservation to be effective it was "essential" that it should be "accepted by all contracting parties, as would have been the case if it had been put forward in the course of the negotiations": if it was not accepted, the reservation was "null and void".

With the increasing number of multilateral conventions and the reluc-tance of states to refrain from becoming parties, particularly to conventions drafted through the auspices of the United Nations or the Specialised Agencies, it was perhaps inevitable that some change of attitude towards reservations would take place. The opportunity for such a development

---

7. See below, pp. 537–541.
8. Set out in full in McNair, *Law of Treaties*, pp. 173–7.

was given by the Genocide Convention to certain provisions of which a number of states had made reservations. The effects of the reservations were submitted, in the form of a series of questions, to the International Court of Justice for an advisory opinion.[9] Question I was designed to ask whether the reserving state could be regarded as being a party to the Convention if the reservation was objected to by one or more of the other parties to the Convention. The Court stated the basis and content of the traditional rule, but then suggested that the nature of the Genocide Convention, which envisaged a "wide degree of participation" by states, necessitated a more flexible approach. However, one of the most important reasons for adopting a more flexible approach was stated in such a way as to make it applicable to most types of multilateral treaty. The Court pointed out that although the Genocide Convention had finally been approved unanimously, it was in fact the product of a series of majority votes. The majority principle, "while facilitating the conclusion of multilateral conventions, may also make it necessary for certain states to make reservations". But the Court justified this need by reference to the practice of states in "recent years" of appending a "great number of reservations" to multilateral conventions.

This tendency of the Court to start by referring to the particular circumstances of the Genocide Convention and then to state its conclusions on the law in more general terms appears throughout its judgment. The result was inevitable: the conclusions became statements of rules of international law applicable to multilateral conventions in general. For example, the Court stated a number of propositions in answer to the first question on the position of a reserving state in relation to parties refusing to accept the reservation.

> "The object and purpose of the Convention . . . limit both the freedom of making reservations and that of objecting to them. It follows that it is the compatibility of a reservation with the object and purpose of the Convention that must furnish the criterion for the attitude of a state in making the reservation . . . as well as for the appraisal by a state in objecting to the reservation. . . . Any other view would lead either to the acceptance of reservations which frustrate the purposes which the contracting parties had in mind, or to recognition that the parties to the Convention have the power of excluding from it the author of a reservation, even a minor one, which may be quite compatible with those purposes."[10]

The general nature of the Court's opinion is even more apparent in relation to its answers to Questions II and III. To take the example of its reply to Question II which asked the effect of a reservation as between the reserving state and (a) the parties which object to the reservation, and (b) those which accept it. The Court commented in terms of the traditional view that no state could be bound by a reservation to which it had not consented, but added that any danger arising from the implications of a reservation between the state making it and a party objecting to it would

---

9. I.C.J. Rep. 1951, p. 15.   10. *Ibid.*, at p. 24.

be mitigated "by the common duty of the contracting states to be guided in their judgment by the compatibility or incompatibility of the reservation with the object and purpose of the Convention".[11]

As might be imagined from the dual nature of the Court's pronouncements—the initial emphasis on the circumstances of the Genocide Convention coupled with statements of a more general nature on the subject of reservations—the Advisory Opinion, while emphasising the need for a more flexible approach, and also suggesting the basis of such an approach, did not make for certainty in the law. The resulting uncertainty can be seen in the work of the International Law Commission. The Commission eventually modified its stated preference for the traditional view in 1953, although in its Report of that year, the Commission did not feel justified in drafting a precise alternative. And both the 1966 Report and the Vienna Convention tread most warily on the subject of reservations and reflect the lack of agreement amongst states in their attitudes towards reservations. In the circumstances, the most that can be attempted is to suggest what is the present law in the light of such state practice as does show a sufficient degree of certainty.

In the first place, a state cannot make a reservation at all if there is an express provision in the treaty prohibiting reservations. Nor can a state make a reservation to a particular provision of a treaty if the treaty expressly provides that the operation of certain provisions including the particular provision cannot be excluded by reservation. The practice of specifying in the treaty which provisions are of such importance that a reservation would be incompatible with the purposes of the treaty is only giving expression to the International Court's view that reservations of a minor nature can be valid, while those of a major nature must be regarded as ineffective. However, reservations can be of a "major nature" for two different reasons. They may be so because they relate to fundamental provisions of the treaty, or because they are of such a general nature that they are not compatible with the spirit of the treaty. The International Law Commission has accepted that there is more than one way in which a reservation may be inconsistent with the spirit of the treaty by recommending that, in cases where a treaty makes no provision with regard to reservations, a state may formulate a reservation unless it is "incompatible with the object and purpose of the treaty".[12]

Once it is established that a state has the right to make a reservation to certain provisions of a treaty it will then be necessary to decide the effect of the reservation on that state's legal position *vis-à-vis* other parties to the treaty. It is possible for a state or a number of states to obtain the consent of other parties to reservations in advance. Thus, where a treaty expressly or clearly by implication authorises the making of certain reservations, the better view would seem to be that such reservations will not require subsequent acceptance by the other parties in order to be effective. However, the most difficult cases will concern reservations where no provision is

---

11. I.C.J. Rep. 1951, pp. 26–27.   12. 1966 Draft, Article 16 (c); V.C. Article 19 (c).

Nil

made in the treaty itself. As the Court stated in the *Reservations* case,[13] it could not be inferred from the absence of an article providing for reservations that the contracting states were prohibited from making reservations. The very nature of the process of drafting multilateral treaties by the majority vote of an international conference raises the inference that reservations are admissible. The making of a reservation will normally, therefore, be at least *prima facie* legal. At this point the validity, or effectiveness, of the reservation, together with the ratification or adherence to which it is attached, will depend upon the reaction of the other parties to the treaty towards the reservation. Acceptance by another state of a reservation makes the entire ratification effective in so far as it relates to that other state, and a failure by a state to object within a reasonable time to a reservation will be treated as an acceptance. If a state does object to a reservation, this may have the effect either of rendering the entire ratification ineffective in relation to the objecting state, or, if the objecting state signifies its willingness to be bound, of bringing the rest of the treaty into operation between itself and the reserving state.[14]

The beneficial result of the more flexible approach is obvious enough. A large number of states will become parties to the majority of the provisions of a multilateral treaty. But, in relation to provisions of the treaty to which a number of states have formulated reservations, often in differing terms, to which in turn, a number of states have raised objections on a variety of grounds, the actual rule applicable will vary considerably. States A, B, C, D, and E may be bound by the original treaty provision. State X's reservation and ratification may have been rejected altogether by A so that, between A and X, none of the provisions of the treaty are operative. State B may have objected to the reservation but accepted X's ratification of the rest of the treaty. States C and D may also only have objected to the reservation, but for a different reason than that given by B. State E may have accepted the reservation. State X's position thus varies with regard to A, to B, to C and D, and to E over the actual obligations imposed by the treaty, and this "fragmentisation" of the treaty obligation will increase as notice is taken of the attitudes of other states. State Y may have objected to X's reservation, but have made a reservation of its own to the particular provision. States A, B, C, D and E will have their own individual or joint reactions to Y's reservation, and so on. Although such divergencies may be regarded as a disadvantage, the problems can be overemphasised. If one takes the example of the so-called law-making treaties dealt with in the context of sources of law, the basic question for an international tribunal to decide is usually whether a particular rule is binding upon the contesting states. Whether the rule is a customary rule, or contained in a multilateral convention, the tribunal is still dealing with the application of the rule to the parties to the dispute. The complications of whether other states have dissented from a rule of customary law, or objected to a reservation made by one of the contesting states to the treaty

---

13.   I.C.J. Rep. 1951, at p. 22.   14.   V.C. Articles 20 (4), (5); 21.

will not normally be relevant. However difficult it may be to state the rule in general terms or to show how widely it is applicable and how far it is modified in regard to certain states, the statement of the rule applicable to two specific states is rarely so hard a task.

2 THE VALIDITY AND OPERATION OF TREATIES

A. Internal limitations upon the powers of a representative to bind the state under international law

Whether a representative has the necessary power to bind a state is a matter of international law, but international law does not disregard entirely limitations placed upon the powers of a representative, either by the government he represents, or by the constitutional law of the state.

a LIMITATIONS UPON THE POWERS GRANTED TO THE REPRESENTATIVE

Heads of State and Heads of Government are universally recognised as having full competence to negotiate and to enter into treaties on behalf of their respective states. The I.L.C. and the Vienna Conference considered that this unrestricted competence is shared by the Foreign Minister of a state. This is certainly the legal position of the Secretary of State in both the United States and the United Kingdom, but is there such a rule of international law? The Permanent Court, commenting on the Ihlen Declaration in the course of its judgment in the *Eastern Greenland* case,[15] stated that it was "beyond all dispute" that a statement of that nature given by a Foreign Minister in reply to a request by the diplomatic agent of a foreign power, "in regard to a question falling within his province", was binding upon the state to which the Minister belonged. Although this pronouncement by the Court was in relation to a situation which it was not prepared to categorise as a treaty, the statement is undoubtedly equally applicable to the subject of treaty negotiation. The only difficulty that arises from the wording of the Court's statement is the use of the expression "in regard to a question falling within his province". However, while informal statements by a Foreign Minister might relate to a province other than external affairs (e.g. trade or economic policy), the negotiation and conclusion of a treaty must fall within his province.

According to the International Law Commission, heads of diplomatic missions are recognised as having the power necessary to adopt the text of a treaty between their own state and the state to which they are accredited. This view is reinforced by Article 3 (1) of the 1961 Convention on Diplomatic Relations which expressly states that one of the functions of a diplomatic mission is "negotiating with the Government of the receiving State", and by Article 7 (2) (b) of the Treaties Convention. Although

---

15. (1933) P.C.I.J. Rep., Ser. A/B, No. 53.

ambassadors and other heads of mission do frequently enter into treaty relations on behalf of states, most usually by an exchange of letters with the Foreign Minister of the state to which they are accredited, they would require specific authority to do so from the state they represent. Representatives accredited by states to international conferences or to an international organisation have a similar power to take part on behalf of their own state in the adoption of the text of the treaty in the conference or organisation.

In all other cases, a representative can only act on behalf of a state if he has the appropriate "full powers". "Full powers" is the "technical" term for the formal document by which the competent state authority designates a particular person as the representative of the state for the purposes of the matter in hand. Despite the implication of the expression "full powers", the "full powers" only exist with regard to the matters stipulated in the document. Thus, the "full powers" will often include the negotiation and adoption of a treaty, but will not extend to the expressing of the consent of the state represented to be bound by the treaty. In such a situation, the acts of a representative in excess of the powers granted by his "full powers" will be ineffective unless they are subsequently ratified by the state he represents.

b LIMITATIONS IMPOSED BY THE CONSTITUTION OF A STATE PREVENTING ANY REPRESENTATIVE ENTERING INTO A TREATY OBLIGATION WITHOUT PRIOR AUTHORITY OF A PARTICULAR STATE ORGAN

Many states have constitutional provisions which prevent their government from entering into any treaty at all, or into certain types of treaty, without the consent of the legislature or some organ of the legislature. What is the position if a competent representative (i.e. a head of state, a head of government, or a foreign minister, or a representative given "full powers" to bind the state) appears to have committed the state internationally by accepting the obligations of a treaty when it is subsequently alleged that the representative, or the government he represented, had failed to fulfil the requirements of the constitutional law of the state concerned for the signing or ratifying of the treaty?

The problem may be illustrated by reference to the Constitution of the United States. If the Constitution had stated that no treaty *or other international agreement of any sort* may be entered into except by the President with the Advice and Consent of two-thirds of the Senate, it would normally be possible for another state to discover without difficulty whether that Advice and Consent had been obtained. If the President was purporting to bind the United States without that Advice and Consent, other parties to the treaty would at least be in a position to ascertain whether the United States was a party to the treaty according to the law of the United States. However, it will be recalled from the discussion in Chapter II[16] that

---

16. Pp. 62–63.

the American Constitution was not so specific on the legal requirements. Treaties, it is true, require the Advice and Consent of two-thirds of the members of the Senate present at the time, but there is no regulation of other types of international agreements. As was explained, the Supreme Court has accepted the constitutional validity of "executive agreements", which are valid treaties under international law, but which may be entered into by the President without the Advice and Consent of the Senate. Must a state about to enter into a treaty with the United States satisfy itself not only on whether the Senate has approved the treaty but also, if it has not been so approved, on whether it is of the class of treaty which does not require Senatorial approval?

It would place all states in an unsatisfactory position if they had to satisfy themselves that a formal act of acceptance of a treaty by another state had complied with the requirements of that state's internal law, particularly when the question whether such requirements have been satisfied will often involve difficult problems of constitutional interpretation. It is submitted, therefore, that in all but the most extreme and blatant cases of non-conformity with national law, an act by a representative either having or presumed to have full powers, denoting the consent of a state, will have the effect of binding the state. This principle has the support of both the I.L.C. and the Vienna Conference. The Treaties Convention itself provides that a state may not invoke the fact that its consent to be bound by a treaty has been expressed in violation of its internal law as invalidating its consent "unless that violation was manifest, and concerned a rule of its internal law of fundamental importance".[17]

B. The doctrine of international public policy *(jus cogens)*

Most municipal systems of law contain rules, based upon notions of public policy, that certain acts are invalidated by a failure to conform to the underlying principles upon which the legal order is based. It is a subject of controversy whether the international legal order is sufficiently developed to support similar notions of public policy. It is generally accepted that the United Nations Charter lays down certain rules, conflict with which would render a treaty invalid, but such a situation is expressly covered by a provision in the Charter itself. What is less clear is whether there exist principles of customary law which are in some sense fundamental to the international legal order.

According to Article 103 of the Charter, in the event of a conflict between the obligations of Members of the United Nations under the Charter and their obligations under any other international agreement, "their obligations under the present Charter shall prevail". The intention of this provision is to supersede any previously executed treaties that are inconsistent with the Charter, and for the future to place a limitation upon the treaty-making capacity of Members of the Organisation. In

---

17. Article 46, expanding slightly on I.L.C. Draft, Article 43.

view of the near universality of membership, problems arising with regard to treaties involving non-members are likely to be more of theoretical interest than of practical importance, nevertheless they cannot be completely ignored.

The obligations laid down by the Charter, and referred to in Article 103, may be divided into a number of different categories. On the one hand, there are obligations arising out of the constitutional structure of the Organisation, either directly as in Article 28 which lays down that the Security Council "shall be so organised as to be able to function continuously" and that for this purpose each member of the Council shall be "represented at all times at the seat of the Organisation", or indirectly as the result of the vote of a competent organ imposing obligations upon the members concerned, as under Article 17 whereby the expenses of the Organisation "shall be borne by the Members as apportioned by General Assembly". Obligations of this nature would seldom be the subject matter of an international treaty, least of all a treaty involving non-members of the Organisation. On the other hand, Article 2 of the Charter does state a number of principles in accordance with which the Organisation and its Members are to act. Are these the obligations referred to in Article 103? With the exception of paragraph 4, even this interpretation appears unlikely, because the other paragraphs would seem to be cast in terms too general to be considered as bases of legal obligation. For example, paragraph 3 states that all Members shall settle their disputes "by peaceful means in such a manner that international peace and security, and justice, are not endangered". This provision does not in any sense oblige Members to submit their disputes to a particular form of peaceful settlement, or indeed to settle their disputes at all. And insofar as it implies that disputes should not be settled by force, the situation is more adequately covered by paragraph 4 which stipulates that all Members "shall refrain in their international relations from the threat or use of force against the territorial integrity or political independence of any state, or in any other manner inconsistent with the Purposes of the United Nations".

If there is a doctrine of international public policy it would exist primarily in relation to Article 2 (4) of the Charter. The reference to the Purposes of the United Nations makes it a prohibition in the widest terms against the use or threat of force, because the first purpose of the Organisation as stated in Article 1 (1) is the maintenance of "international peace and security" and "to that end" the taking of "effective collective measures for the prevention and removal of threats to the peace, and for the suppression of acts of aggression or other breaches of the peace". The significance of Article 2 (4) is not so much for its binding effect upon members of the Organisation, but for its reaffirmation of the principles of customary international law based upon Kellogg–Briand Pact of 1928[18]

---

18. Under Article 1 the "High Contracting Parties solemnly declare(d) . . . that they condemn recourse to war for the solution of international controversies, and renounce it as an instrument of national policy".

and enunciated by the Nuremberg Tribunal.[19] It is a restatement of customary law and a declaration of the basis of the international legal order. Any treaty, therefore, that has been entered into by a state under the threat or use of force against its territorial integrity or political independence, or in any other way inconsistent with the Purposes of the United Nations is void. And so, too, would be any treaty which involves in its operation any act likely to constitute a threat to the peace, a breach of the peace, or an act of aggression.[20]

It is not easy to lay down any precise guide to whether the notion of an international public policy can be extended to cover situations not directly involving international peace and security. The Vienna Conference attempted to deal with the situation with an all-embracing formula. A treaty is void if it conflicts with "a peremptory norm of general international law"; i.e., "a norm accepted and recognised by the international community . . . as a norm from which no derogation is permitted".[21] The I.L.C. commented that such a "category" of norms was virtually indefinable in general terms, although states would probably be able to agree in specific cases that treaties which encouraged the slave trade, or genocide, the trafficking in drugs, or perhaps piracy, would be rendered illegal by a provision of this type.

C. Other factors affecting the validity or effectiveness of treaties

a FRAUD OR ERROR AS VITIATING CONSENT

There are a number of situations which are met with rarely in international practice where the relevant rule is clear. A state would not be bound by a treaty if the terms and final acceptance had been brought about by the corruption or coercion of its representative.[1] Similarly, the International Law Commission included the fraudulent conduct of a contracting party as a reason for another party to avoid the treaty.[2] As a statement of principle it is acceptable enough, although it is difficult to imagine situations in which such a rule might apply.

Error is dealt with in more detail by the Commission, although even in this context the absence of any conclusive state practice made formulation of a rule difficult.[3] Both the Permanent Court and the International Court have had occasion to consider pleas of error on the part of one of the states

---

19. The German major war criminals were tried by the Tribunal on a number of charges, of which the first two counts concerned the planning, preparation, initiation and waging of wars of aggression. The Tribunal referred to the 1928 Pact and to a number of subsequent international undertakings and then said:

"All these expressions of opinion, and others that could be cited, so solemnly made, reinforce the construction which the Tribunal placed upon the Pact . . . that resort to a war of aggression is not merely illegal, but is criminal."

20. Or, as V.C. Article 52 provides: "A treaty is void if its conclusion has been procured by the threat or use of force in violation of the principles of international law embodied in the Charter of the United Nations."   21. V.C. Article 53.

1. V.C. Articles 50 and 51.   2. Article 46; V.C. Article 49.
3. Article 45; V.C. Article 48.   4. I.C.J. Rep. 1962, at p. 26.

before the Court, but in both cases the plea was rejected. In the *Temple* case,[4] there had been no error in the treaty which had established the border in dispute between Cambodia and Thailand: the error had been in the subsequent acceptance of the delimitation of the boundary contained in a map which was later discovered to have misapplied the terms of the treaty. Such an error could not be of assistance as the party relying on it had either "contributed by its own conduct to the error, or could have avoided it, or . . . the circumstances were such as to put that party on notice of a possible error".

But, even if an error is not contributed to by the party seeking to rely upon it, is it every error that operates to negative consent? The *Mavrommatis* case[5] concerned a concession agreement which, the United Kingdom alleged, would not have been granted if the Turkish authorities had realised that Mavrommatis was not a Turkish subject. The Court expressed the opinion that, since Mavrommatis' identity had never been in any doubt, the error related only to his attributes, and annulment of the concessions could only be based upon the existence of a condition of the grant that Mavrommatis was a Turkish subject. The Court held that the nationality of Mavrommatis was not a condition of the granting of the concessions and in no way, therefore, invalidated the agreement. This judgment of the Court in relation to a concession agreement would seem to be equally applicable to a treaty. In the words of the International Law Commission, "a state may invoke an error in a treaty as invalidating its consent to be bound by the treaty if the error relates to a fact or situation which was assumed by that state to exist at the time when the treaty was concluded and formed an essential basis of its consent to be bound by the treaty". Only if the error is some sense essential or fundamental to the obligation that a state believed it had undertaken will it be a reason for invalidating the treaty.

b FAILURE TO REGISTER AND THE EFFECTIVENESS OF TREATIES

Under customary international law, if a treaty has been validly made between two subjects of international law it is operative between them and fully effective in accordance with its terms. However, Article 102 of the United Nations Charter requires the registration of "every treaty and every international agreement entered into by any Member of the United Nations" with the Secretariat of the Organisation whose duty it is to "publish" the treaty or agreement. If the treaty or agreement is not registered, no party may "invoke that treaty or agreement before any organ of the United Nations".

The act of registration has raised a number of problems about the status of certain agreements because of the view of members of the Organisation not parties to the agreement, that one or other of the parties did not possess international personality. Objections were raised, particularly by the United States, to the registration of agreements entered into with the

---

5. (1927) P.C.I.J. Rep., Ser. A, No. 2.

People's Republic of China, and by the United Kingdom and the United States to the registration of agreements made with the North Korean authorities and with the German Democratic Republic. However, both the United Kingdom and the United States accepted a statement issued by the Secretariat that "registration of an instrument submitted by a Member state does not imply a judgment by the Secretariat on the nature of the instrument, the status of the party, or any similar question"; more specifically, registration "does not confer on the instrument the status of a treaty or an international agreement if it does not already have that status, and does not confer on a party a status which it would not otherwise have."[6] It is thus clear that the act of registration cannot validate and make effective as a treaty on the international plane any agreement which fails to fulfil the requirements of a treaty laid down by international law.

Failure to register, on the other hand, in no sense invalidates a treaty. On the contrary the United Nations Treaty Series contains many examples of agreements which had been in force for a number of years before registration took place. Article 102 only lays down that absence of registration will act as a bar to the setting up of the treaty if any dispute upon which the treaty has a bearing comes before any organ of the United Nations. This bar would presumably apply to disputes before the International Court as much as to matters debated by the political organs. In the terminology of English law, the principle goes to the enforceability of the treaty provisions in a certain form, and does not affect the validity of the agreement and its effectiveness to create legal obligations for the parties.

3 THE INTERPRETATION OF TREATIES

Questions of interpretation frequently come before municipal courts. What is the meaning of a particular statutory provision, or of a term in a written contract? The meaning may have been clear to the persons who drafted the wording used, but it may not be at all clear to the person who was not aware of what it was intended to mean. Or it may have been clear enough in the majority of cases, but in the specific and unusual situation that has arisen, the statute or contract might provide no obvious solution to the difficulty. If possibilities exist for obscure draftmanship, or misunderstandings occur, when the parties involved in a dispute both speak and write the language in which the statute or contract is drafted, how much greater the likelihood of error when, in the case of multilateral treaties, many of the parties are dealing with a language other than their own.

The problems are mitigated by a number of factors. In the first place, international treaties seldom require the precise detail of a municipal statute: most are drafted in general terms. Secondly, the uncertain question of whether an individual is in breach of an obscure provision in a statute or a contract will usually be the subject of litigation requiring a final

---

6. ST/LEG/SER.A/105. The statement is given in an abbreviated form in all volumes of the U.N.T.S. from 212.

determination by a court of law: in the international community judicial settlement is the exception rather than the rule, so that many disputes over the interpretation of a treaty are the subject of political compromise as to the "meaning" of the relevant term. In the field of international institutions, interpretation of the constitutional treaty of an organisation by its political organs will often be much freer and less restrictive than a rigid legal analysis by a judicial body. Thirdly, although the problem of language can never be altogether resolved, the use of equally authoritative texts in more than one language will enable representatives of a state in which neither or none of the languages are spoken to make use of the tongue which is the most familiar. The United Nations Charter laid down that all five languages in which it was drawn up (Chinese, French, Russian, English and Spanish) were to be equally authoritative, although the use of so many languages is exceptional, and was obviously decided upon to emphasise the universal concept of the Organisation.

A. The general principles of treaty interpretation

a THE WORDS USED SHOULD BE GIVEN THEIR NATURAL AND ORDINARY MEANING

The starting-point of any approach to the interpretation of a particular provision, whether it be contained in a municipal law statute or in an international treaty, must be the words actually used. First and foremost, the intention of the parties is to be deduced from the way in which they have expressed their intentions. If the words used are clear and unambiguous, then a judicial tribunal will give effect to the treaty in the sense required by the clear and unambiguous wording, unless some "valid ground" can be shown "for interpreting the provision otherwise". In the *Competence of the General Assembly* case,[7] the International Court was asked whether the Assembly could decide to admit a state to the United Nations when the Security Council had made no recommendation on the matter. According to Article 4 (2) of the Charter, the admission of a state to the Organisation "will be effected by a decision of the General Assembly upon the recommendation of the Security Council". Although the Court went on to consider other reasons supporting its view that the Assembly did not have such a competence in the absence of a favourable recommendation of the Security Council, the basis for its decision was the fact that Article 4 (2) had a clear and obvious meaning which the Court was bound to apply.

> "The Court considers it necessary to say that the first duty of a tribunal which is called upon to interpret and apply the provisions of a treaty, is to endeavour to give effect to them in their natural and ordinary meaning in the context in which they occur. If the relevant words in their natural and ordinary meaning make sense in their context, that is an end of the matter.... When the Court can give effect to a provision of a treaty by giving to the words used in it their natural and ordinary meaning, it may not interpret the words by seeking to give them some other

---

7. I.C.J. Rep. 1950, p. 4.

meaning. In the present case the Court finds no difficulty in ascertaining the natural and ordinary meaning of the words in question and no difficulty in giving effect to them."[8]

b EXCEPTIONS TO THE APPLICATION OF THE "NATURAL AND ORDINARY MEANING" PRINCIPLE

In the course of its opinion in the *Competence* case, the International Court referred briefly to three exceptions to the application of the "natural and ordinary meaning" principle. The meaning must be "natural and ordinary" in the context in which the words occur; the "natural and ordinary" meaning must be unambiguous; and it must not lead to an unreasonable or absurd result.

i *Context*

It is obvious enough that a particular word takes its meaning from its context. The use of a word or phrase in one situation will require a different interpretation from the use of the same word or phrase in a different context. In the case of a treaty, the obvious meaning of a word or phrase in isolation might be demonstrably inaccurate when the word or phrase is taken in the context of the treaty as a whole, or of part of the treaty. Two cases heard by the Permanent Court provide useful illustrations of the importance of interpreting the words of a treaty in the context in which they appear.

In 1922, the Court was asked whether the International Labour Organisation had competence to draft regulations dealing with agricultural workers.[9] A number of provisions of the I.L.O. constitution referred to the powers of the Organisation in relation to industry, but was the term "industry" limited to manufacturing industry? In the case of the provision requiring that the Governing Body of the I.L.O. should include representatives from a number of states of "chief industrial importance", it is most likely that the article was intended to have a restricted meaning. The Court, however, held that the Treaty must be read as a whole, and that the use of the term "industry" or "industrial" should not be given the restricted meaning to limit the competence of the Organisation simply because the term might appear to have that meaning, and might in certain provisions actually have that meaning.

In 1932 the Court was called upon to decide whether the Free Zones of Upper Savoy and Gex, created in favour of Switzerland on French territory by the peace settlement of 1815 and later instruments, had been terminated by Article 435 (2) of the Treaty of Versailles.[10] The part of paragraph (2) upon which France relied stated that the contracting states agreed that "the stipulations of the treaties of 1815 and of the other supplementary acts concerning the free zones of Upper Savoy and the Gex District are no longer consistent with present conditions." The customs

---

8. *I.C.J.* Rep. 1950, at p. 8.   9. P.C.I.J. Rep., Ser. B, No. 2.
10. P.C.I.J. Rep., Ser. A/B, No. 46.

free zones were thus terminated in the French view, and paragraph (2) went on to state that it was for France and Switzerland to reach agreement upon the future status of the territories. Such an interpretation the Court was not willing to accept. Paragraph (2) could not be read in isolation from Article 435 (1). Paragraph (1) also noted that the régime of the free zones was "no longer consistent with present conditions", and for that reason the contracting states took "note of the agreement reached between the French Government and the Swiss Government for the abrogation of the stipulations relating to" the areas in dispute. In other words, the parties to the Treaty of Versailles accepted in principle the need to reconsider the status of the free zones, but recognised that the abrogation of the régime governing the zones was dependent upon the agreement reached between France and Switzerland. However, this agreement, although it had been agreed in draft form at the time of the Treaty of Versailles, was later not ratified by Switzerland. Despite the impression given by the wording of Article 435 (2) standing by itself, the customs free zones of Savoy and Gex, though "no longer consistent with present conditions", still existed because paragraph (1) made it clear that the abrogation was to be brought about by another instrument, an instrument which had never come into force.

ii *Ambiguity or unreasonableness*

If the "natural and ordinary" meaning produces ambiguity or unreasonableness, the tribunal called upon to interpret the particular instrument may rely upon a number of factual evidences, or upon a number of legal presumptions, of what the parties intended. Among the factual evidences may be included the situation that the treaty was intended to remedy or to provide for, which in turn may be evidenced by the preparatory work involved in the drafting of the treaty, or the subsequent practice of the parties regarding the interpretation of the treaty. Among the legal presumptions, there may be circumstances in which the traditional principle that restrictions upon the sovereignty of states will not be presumed may be in conflict with the principle of effectiveness, i.e., that the treaty should be interpreted in order to make it effective.

There are frequent illustrations in international jurisprudence of a tribunal excluding preparatory work on the ground that the relevant provision was clear and unambiguous. In the *Lotus* case,[11] for example, the · Permanent Court recalled what it had said "in some of its preceding judgments and opinions, namely, that there is no occasion to have regard to preparatory work if the text of a convention is sufficiently clear in itself". Similarly, in the *Competence of the General Assembly* case considered above, the Court refused to take any notice of the strong support in favour of the contrary view evidenced in the San Francisco Conference records on the ground that the Charter provision was unambiguous.

There are examples of situations in which factual evidences are used to reinforce the tribunal's view of the ordinary meaning of a treaty. In a

---

11. (1927) P.C.I.J. Rep., Ser. A, No. 10, at p. 16.

case[12] of 1927, the Permanent Court, having stated the principle that preparatory work could not be referred to if the text of the treaty was sufficiently clear in itself, pointed out that, if doubt still existed as to the true meaning of the words used, the preparatory work fully confirmed the conclusion reached by the Court. Similarly, the subsequent practice of states may reinforce, but not contradict, the wording of a treaty. In the *Competence of the I.L.O.* case that has already been mentioned, the Permanent Court referred to the fact that agriculture had been repeatedly discussed and dealt with in one form or another by the Organisation, and suggested that "this might suffice to turn the scale in favour of the inclusion of agriculture, if there were any ambiguity".[13] A more recent case was that concerning the *Status of South-West Africa*,[14] in which the International Court had to decide whether South Africa was still bound by the terms of its mandate over South-West Africa. The Court referred to a number of declarations made to the United Nations by the South African Government and then stated:[15]

> "These declarations constitute recognition by the Union Government of the continuance of its obligations under the Mandate and not a mere indication of the future conduct of that Government. Interpretations placed upon legal instruments by the parties to them, though not conclusive as to their meaning, have considerable probative value when they contain recognition by a party of its own obligations under an instrument. In this case the declarations of the Union of South Africa support the conclusions already reached by the Court."

The *Peace Treaties* case[16] provides a good illustration of the natural and ordinary meaning being applied despite a plea that the treaties should be made "effective". The Peace Treaties with Bulgaria, Hungary, and Roumania contained a number of provisions guaranteeing human rights in each of these states. Disputes arising out of breaches of the provisions were to be submitted to a tribunal comprising three members, one to be chosen by the state alleged to be in breach of the relevant Treaty, one by the Allied Powers that had taken part in the war against Germany, and the third to be agreed upon by the two members already chosen, or, failing such agreement, to be nominated by the Secretary-General of the United Nations. When the former enemy states refused even to co-operate in the setting up of the tribunals, the International Court was asked *inter alia* whether, in the event of one party declining to nominate its member of the tribunal, the Secretary-General could nevertheless nominate the third member, and whether a tribunal comprising only two members, one being the nominee of the Secretary-General, could carry out the functions laid down in the Treaties. The Court answered both questions in the negative. "The principle of interpretation . . . often referred to as the rule of effectiveness cannot justify the Court in attributing to the provisions for

---

12. *European Commission of the Danube* case, P.C.I.J. Rep., Ser. B, No. 14.
13. P.C.I.J. Rep., Ser. B, No. 2, at pp. 39 and 41.
14. I.C.J. Rep. 1950, p. 128.   15. *Ibid.*, at pp. 135–6.
16. I.C.J. Rep. 1950, p. 221.

the settlement of disputes in the Peace Treaties a meaning which . . . would be contrary to their letter and spirit."[17]

A judicial tribunal will have a more positive role in the interpretation of the general powers bestowed upon an international organisation by its constitutive treaty. Whereas in dealing with specific provisions, the International Court has been reluctant to look beyond the obvious meaning of the words used (as in the *Competence of the General Assembly* case[18]), in situations where the Court has been called upon to consider whether the powers granted to an organisation can be extended beyond the specific provisions of the organisation's constitution by implication from the powers expressly granted, the Court has tended to rely much more on the effectiveness principle. In such a situation, there is no question of being limited by the natural and ordinary wording of the words used, because the relevant treaty contains no words covering the situation: in a sense, therefore, the treaty is ambiguous. In the *Reparations* case,[19] the Court was asked *inter alia* whether the United Nations had the capacity to present an international claim on behalf of an agent of the Organisation, or his dependants, against the state responsible for the death of, or injury to, the agent. There was no such power expressly granted by the Charter, but the Court upheld the capacity of the United Nations by reference to the duties that the Organisation entrusted to its agents. As they were often dispatched on missions to dangerous and unsettled parts of the world, it was essential for the effective operation of Article 100 of the Charter, which establishes the international nature of the United Nations Secretariat, that agents of the Organisation should be able to rely upon the diplomatic protection of the Organisation, and should not have to rely upon the states of which they are nationals.

B. Interpretation of the constitutions of international institutions by their political organs

Each organisation is competent to interpret its own constitution, and it will normally only be in cases of serious disagreement among the members of the organisation that issues of interpretation will be submitted to a judicial tribunal. While this does not mean that international organisations will disregard the terms of their constitution, it does mean that they can approach the working of the constitution in a more flexible way. Providing there is general agreement among the members, usages can be adopted which do not conform to the strict letter of the treaty which created the organisation. In time, such a usage may solidify into a rule of law modifying the terms of the treaty, but until that point is reached there would be a divergence between the conclusion adopted by a judicial tribunal, and that acted upon by the organ itself, in the interpretation of the relevant

---

17. *Ibid.*, at p. 229.   18.   I.C.J. Rep. 1950, p. 4.
19. I.C.J. Rep. 1949, p. 174.

text. Article 27 of the Charter of the United Nations requires that decisions of the Security Council on non-procedural matters be made by a certain majority including the concurring votes of the permanent members. Clearly an abstention by a permanent member is not a concurring vote, and no judicial tribunal would accept it as such, yet it is the well established practice, which may well be considered as having modified the terms of the Charter, that a decision of the Council is effective notwithstanding the abstention of a permanent member.[20]

An interesting contrast between possible legal formalism and political expediency arose out of the interpretation of Article 387 of the Treaty of Versailles which seemed to link membership of the I.L.O. to membership of the League of Nations. In the *Free City of Danzig and the I.L.O.* case[1] the Permanent Court avoided committing itself on the issue, although it did accept the possibility that the parties to the Treaty intended to limit membership of the I.L.O. to states already members of the League. Hudson, the legal adviser to the first I.L. Conference in 1919, had given an official opinion to that effect, and Judge Anzilotti, although dissenting from the Court in the *Danzig* case, stated that it was "permissible" to conclude that membership of the I.L.O. was merely the "corollary" of membership of the League.[2] However, as the League never attained the universality of membership that had been intended, the possible restricting effect of Article 387 upon membership of the I.L.O. was quietly disregarded. Most notably, the United States of America which never joined the League, became a member of the I.L.O.

C. Most favoured nation clauses

A most favoured nation clause is a provision in a treaty which automatically grants to one contracting state the most favourable position granted by the other to any third state. The expression "a most favoured nation clause" is used to cover a variety of provisions, sometimes conditional, sometimes absolute in their terms. As there is no such thing as a standard "most favoured nation clause", the effect of the clause used will primarily be a matter of interpretation, and all that can be attempted by way of description is a few generalisations.

The most favoured nation clause belongs essentially to the commercial treaty. As a matter of interpretation, it will only apply to commercial matters unless, expressly or by implication, the treaty has a more extended application. In *National Provincial Bank* v. *Dollfus*,[3] the Bank argued *inter alia* that Article 14 of the French Civil Code, which provided that "aliens who are not resident in France could be summoned before the French Courts for obligations contracted abroad towards a French national", did

---

20. See below, pp. 545–546 and pp. 622–625.
1. (1930), P.C.I.J. Rep., Ser. B, No. 18.   2. *Ibid.*, at p. 18.
3. (1947), 14 A.D., Case No. 79.

not apply to British subjects as they enjoyed most favoured nation treatment by virtue of the Franco-British Convention of 1882 and two agreements of 1929. Under the Franco-Belgian Treaty of 1899, French subjects in Belgium and Belgian subjects in France were to be subject in civil and commercial matters to the same rules of jurisdiction as nationals. The Court of Appeal in Paris rejected the Bank's argument on this point. The Court applied the generally accepted view that a most favoured nation clause only applied in relation to the matters laid down in the treaty containing the clause. The matters laid down in the 1882 Convention neither expressly nor impliedly included matters of jurisdiction and procedure; while the 1929 agreements dealt specifically with the laws on leases.

It has long been the British view that a most favoured nation clause in a commercial treaty was not conditional upon the granting of reciprocal rights by the benefited state. For example, if an agreement between state A and state B provided for most favoured nation treatment, the creation of more favourable tariffs in favour of state C by state A would automatically bestow the same rights upon B, even though state A would gain no benefit from the application of most favoured nation treatment. Since 1923, this has also been the view of the United States, which in that year completely reversed its previous policy. In practice the significance of most favoured nation clauses in relation to trade has been greatly reduced by the existence of the General Agreement on Tariffs and Trade (G.A.T.T.) which was signed in 1948 as an instrument to reduce trade barriers and to settle trade disputes. Reciprocity is the basis of G.A.T.T.[4]

4 AMENDMENT AND TERMINATION OF TREATIES

A. Amendment

a BY FORMAL AGREEMENT

The normal method of amending a treaty is by the unanimous agreement of the parties. However, where a treaty has a large number of parties, it may not be possible to obtain unanimous agreement to a proposed amendment. In such a situation, a number of the parties might formally agree to modify the effects of the treaty amongst themselves, while continuing to be bound by the treaty in their relations with other parties. Although an agreement among a limited number of parties is usually referred to as a "modification" of the original treaty, the effects of such an agreement are little different from the situation where the majority of parties agree to a new treaty covering the whole field of an earlier treaty.[5] The earlier treaty is still effective between states that have not accepted the new treaty and between those states and parties to the new treaty. From the point of view of legal consequences, therefore, formal amendment

---

4. See below, p. 608.
5. As happened in the case of the 1961 Narcotics Convention.

and formal modification can be dealt with together. There is, however, a difference in practice in relation to the procedure for amendment. A group of states may agree amongst themselves to the modification of a treaty in its application to their mutual relations. Such an arrangement is not necessarily the direct concern of the other parties to the treaty in that those parties do not have to take part in the process. If a treaty is to be amended, on the other hand, it is essential that all parties should participate in the formalities. Many treaties contain their own specific procedure to meet this need. The section on procedure relates exclusively to amendment, although some of what is said about the effect of amendments relates equally to formal modifications.

i *Procedure*

Article 109 of the U.N. Charter sets out the method whereby a General Conference of member states can be called "for the purpose of reviewing" the Charter. Other international organisations, notably the Specialised Agencies, give the power to draft amendments to the Conference or Assembly of the institution concerned. It is then a matter for the Conference or Assembly to establish its own procedures for amendment, i.e. whether to hold a special session, how to allow members to participate in the drafting process, etc. Other multilateral treaties provide for possible revision at the end of specified periods. Thus, the Geneva Conventions on the Law of the Sea contain similar provisions to the effect that after the expiry of five years from the entry into force of the Convention, any party can request the revision of the Convention by a notification in writing to the U.N. Secretary-General. It is for the General Assembly to decide what steps, if any, to take with regard to such a request. Others provide for revision at any time; as with the Antarctic Treaty which "may be modified or amended at any time by unanimous agreement of the Contracting Parties", although this Treaty also provides for a possible review of the operation of the treaty at the end of thirty years.

So various are the types of provision contained in multilateral treaties for their revision that the International Law Commission was faced with a problem when it had to draft a rule representative of state practice in cases where the treaty contained no reference to amendment. The most that the Commission could suggest, therefore, was that proposals "to amend a multilateral treaty as between all the parties must be notified to every party" and that all parties had the right to take part in the "decision as to the action to be taken" on such proposals, and in the "negotiation and conclusion of any agreement for the amendment of the treaty".[6]

ii *Effects of Amendments*

In general, an amendment will only bind parties that have agreed to it. Between states that have not agreed to the amendment, and states that have agreed, the terms of the original treaty remain operative. It is believed that

---

6. Draft Article 36 (2); largely reproduced in V.C. Article 40.

the various conventions on the conduct of warfare and the treatment of prisoners of war contain provisions which correctly represent the legal position. Such conventions supersede earlier conventions between the same parties on the same subject-matter, but as between states parties to the earlier conventions which do not become parties to the new conventions, and between those states and parties to the new conventions, the earlier conventions are to remain in force.[7] This same principle applies where by a subsequent agreement a limited number of parties to the original multilateral convention have agreed to modify their legal position *inter se*. The subsequent treaty cannot modify their rights and duties under the original convention with regard to states not becoming parties to the new treaty.

The field of international organisations has introduced with increasing frequency various types of what are termed "legislative" amendment procedures. Whereas normally a state is not bound by amendments to a treaty unless it agrees to them, the constitutions of a number of international organisations contain provisions under which members give their consent in advance to accept amendments agreed upon by a majority. Article 108 of the U.N. Charter lays down that amendments come into force "for all Members" when they have been adopted by two-thirds of the members of the General Assembly and ratified "in accordance with their respective constitutional process" by two-thirds of the Members of the organisation "including all the permanent members of the Security Council". Similar provisions are to be found in the constitutions of the I.A.E.A. (Article 18), I.L.O. (Article 36), U.N.E.S.C.O. (Article 13) and W.H.O. (Article 73).

b BY SUBSEQUENT PRACTICE

The practice of the parties to a treaty is authoritative evidence of the meaning attributed to its provisions by the parties. But evidence of such practice will not be admissible as to the interpretation of the treaty if it conflicts with the wording used. However, a consistent practice, if it establishes "the common consent of the parties" to be bound by a different rule from that laid down in the treaty, will have the effect of modifying the treaty.

It may often be a difficult problem of construction whether the parties were adopting a more convenient practice without intending to modify the treaty, or whether they were consenting to the creation of a new rule. The practice of not allowing abstentions by permanent members to prevent the adoption of non-procedural resolutions by the Security

---

7. Article 135 of the 1949 Geneva Convention relating to prisoners of war states: "In the relations between the Powers which are bound by the Hague Convention relative to the Laws and Customs of War on Land, whether that of 29th July, 1899, or that of 18th October, 1907, and which are parties to the present Convention, this last Convention shall be complementary to Chapter II of the Regulations annexed to the above-mentioned Conventions of the Hague."

Council is clearly inconsistent with the provisions of Article 27 of the Charter. Yet it is a practice that has been consistently applied by the Council for more than twenty years. It is true that members of the Council have from time to time, particularly at the outset, stated that they did not consider the ruling that the resolution was passed in spite of an abstention by a permanent member established a precedent that must always be followed. Nevertheless, the practice has been so uniform, and has been adopted over such important issues—the creation of the U.N. Forces in the Congo, and in Cyprus—that it is difficult to avoid the conclusion that the precise wording of Article 27 has been modified in a way that even a judicial tribunal would accept as effective.

The practice of organs of international organisations in relation to their constitutions might not, perhaps, be considered the most satisfactory illustration of informal modification, because the organ can in no sense be considered a party to the treaty which created it. Nevertheless, the fact that the organisation is comprised of states parties to the constitutional treaty makes a distinction between the practice of the organisation and the practice of states rather unreal. If members of the organisation (states) contribute to a practice modifying the terms of the constitution, or acquiesce in the practice adopted, there is no reason why the normal principles of the effect of consistent practice evidencing the common consent of the parties should not be applied.

Outside the field of international organisations, illustration of modifications by practice are not so well documented, although the principle is generally accepted, as two examples will demonstrate.

The first concerned the Italian Peace Treaty of 1947, which was signed and ratified by nearly twenty states. It provided for the setting up of a Free Territory of Trieste, but this proved impracticable mainly because of disagreements amongst the permanent members of the Security Council. Four of the signatories, Italy, the United Kingdom, the United States and Yugoslavia, therefore arranged for the territory to be administered, half by Yugoslavia, and half by Italy, subject to special guarantees for the inhabitants. This arrangement was acted upon by Yugoslavia and Italy and was not objected to by other states, thus substantially modifying in practice the actual terms of the Peace Treaty.

The second illustration is provided by a recent arbitral decision,[8] arising out of a dispute between France and the United States as to the air routes that the latter state was entitled to use under an Air Transport Services Agreement of 1946 between the two states. In reaching its conclusions, which were on the whole favourable to the American claim, the tribunal referred to the importance of the conduct of the parties not only as "a means useful for interpreting the Agreement", but also as "a possible source of subsequent modification" of the rights that the parties could properly claim under the treaty.[9]

---

8. (1964) 3 I.L.M. 668.   9. *Ibid.*, at p. 713.

B. Termination

a IN ACCORDANCE WITH THE TERMS OF THE TREATY

Most treaties contain clauses limiting the duration of the treaty, either by specific reference to a date, or by reference to a particular event, or by providing specifically for a right to withdraw from the treaty. However, the variety of clauses used is very great, and the most that can be attempted is to give illustrations of those adopted most frequently.

i *For a specified period*

A number of treaties contain clauses that the treaty is to remain in force for five, or ten years, or some other specified period. The 1960 agreement between Australia and the United States relating to Space Vehicle Tracking and Communications provided that "subject to the availability of funds" it was to remain in force "for a period of ten years".

ii *For a minimum period with a right to withdraw at the end of the period*

Several important international conventions, as well as other agreements, stipulate a minimum period during which the treaty is to remain in force, and allow for withdrawal, often subject to a further period of notice, after the expiry of the minimum period. The Convention for the Safety of Life at Sea of 1948 and the Convention for the Prevention of Pollution of the Sea by Oil of 1954 both contain a clause to the effect that a state may denounce the Convention, by giving notice of at least one year, at any time after the expiry of five years from the date on which the Convention comes into force with regard to the denouncing state.

iii *For a specific purpose*

There are examples of a number of treaties which are intended to provide for the holding of a conference or some such matter that do not contain any provision as to termination, simply because they are in one sense "terminated" once the event has occurred.[10] On the other hand, treaties providing assistance, particularly financial, for a specific project, do not depend upon the completion of the project, but upon the term set on the period of the loan. The standard form of contract entered into by the International Bank includes a "closing date";[11] in specific cases, there might also be provisions safeguarding the Bank against excessive rises in the cost of the particular project, or faulty workmanship in its construction.

---

10. E.g. an agreement by a number of states, or by the United Nations or one of the specialised agencies, with a particular state, that the state would act as host to an international conference.

11. E.g. the guarantee agreement with Brazil of June, 1959, Article VIII, Section 8.01, 377 U.N.T.S. 112.

iv *Withdrawal at any time*

Many treaties allow the parties to denounce the treaty at any time, either with or without the need for a period of notice. For example, the standard agreement between the U.N. Special Fund and states members of the United Nations concerning assistance from the Fund stated that the agreement could be terminated by either party "by written notice to the other" and that it should terminate "sixty days after receipt of such notice".[12]

v *Withdrawal only possible in certain circumstances*

Because of the variety of provisions, examples can be found of treaties which expressly allow withdrawal only in certain specified circumstances. The Nuclear Test Ban Treaty of 1963 enables a party to denounce the Treaty by giving three months' notice of withdrawal "if it decides that extraordinary events, related to the subject matter of this Treaty, have jeopardised the supreme interests of its country".

b TERMINATION OR WITHDRAWAL BY THE AGREEMENT OF ALL THE PARTIES

Whatever terms may be included in a treaty, the treaty may be brought to an end by the agreement of the parties; and similarly a state may withdraw from the treaty, if it wishes, with the consent of the other parties. The agreement of the parties might be express, or it might be implied. The obvious illustration of the implied termination of a treaty is if the parties enter into a similar treaty on the same subject matter. In the *Mavrommatis* case,[13] the Permanent Court was asked by Britain to declare that a protocol to the Treaty of Lausanne had the effect of withdrawing from the Court jurisdiction which it would otherwise have had in accordance with the terms of the earlier Mandate agreement under which Britain administered Palestine. The Court refused to put this interpretation on the protocol, but made it quite clear that "in cases of doubt, the Protocol, being a special and more recent agreement, should prevail."[14]

c REDUCTION OF THE PARTIES TO A MULTILATERAL TREATY BELOW THE NUMBER NECESSARY FOR ITS ENTRY INTO FORCE

If the parties to a multilateral treaty stipulate that it should only enter into force once a certain number of states have ratified it, there is no reason why, in the absence of specific provision, the treaty should terminate if, at a subsequent time, the number of parties falls below the number necessary to bring the treaty into force. Some treaties do contain provisions covering the number of parties necessary to keep them in force, and the number required is usually the same as the number necessary to bring the treaty into operation in the first place. In the Convention on the Nationality of

---

12. E.g. the agreement with Panama of March, 1961, Article X (3), 396 U.N.T.S. 3, and the agreement with Saudi Arabia, *ibid.*, p. 27.
13. (1924) P.C.I.J. Rep., Ser. A, No. 2.   14. *Ibid.*, at p. 31.

Married Women of February, 1957, Article 6 (2) laid down that the Convention was to come into force on the ninetieth day after the sixth instrument of ratification had been deposited. By Article 9 (1), any party can denounce the treaty at any time: such denunciation to take effect one year after receipt of a written communication to that effect by the Secretary-General of the United Nations, and, by paragraph (2) of the same Article, the Convention ceases to be in force from the date when the denunciation, which reduces the number of parties to less than six, becomes effective.

d DENUNCIATION OF A TREATY WHICH IS SILENT ON THE MATTER

It is a basic tenet of international law that treaties are binding (*pacta sunt servanda*). It follows that, in principle, it is not possible for a state to denounce a treaty simply because it wishes to be rid of the obligations imposed by the treaty, unless the treaty, expressly or by implication, contains a right of unilateral termination. The question of withdrawal was much debated at Geneva in 1958 in relation to the Conventions on the Law of the Sea, in none of which was a clause allowing denunciation inserted. However, such state practice as exists supports the binding nature of treaties, although usually only indirectly. States, when they purport to denounce a treaty without being able to rely upon a specific provision allowing them to withdraw, usually give legal reasons for their actions, whether or not there is substance to the reasons alleged. The most obvious excuses are that the other party or other parties have broken the terms of the treaty already; or that the treaty is no longer consistent with present day circumstances, or has fallen into disuse. In other words, the denouncing party recognises the applicability of the notion *pacta sunt servanda* in general, but explains why the treaty is no longer binding in the particular situation that has arisen. It should be remembered, of course, that a unilateral denunciation of a treaty, even though ineffective in itself, may become effective because of the acquiescence of other parties to the Convention.

A useful illustration of the various aspects of unilateral withdrawal is to be found in Hitler's denunciation of the Treaty of Versailles in 1936. The reason given for the German action was not that treaties in general could be disregarded at will, but that the Treaty of Versailles was a *diktat*, a peace treaty not negotiated with Germany but dictated to Germany by the victorious Allies, and therefore not binding upon Germany. If it were a rule of international law that a peace treaty could be set aside because it was negotiated from a position of strength by the victorious powers, then no peace treaty would have legal validity. The excuse given by Hitler has no substance in law, but what is the effect of an illegal denunciation? The Dutch Courts on a number of occasions had to deal with provisions of the Versailles Treaty relating to navigation on the Rhine.[15] Their view was that these provisions, although suspended during the Second World War,

---

15. See (1919–42) 11 A.D., Case No. 124; (1946) 13 A.D. Case No. 22; and (1954) 21 I.L.R. 276.

became operative once more in 1945, and were unaffected by the purported German denunciation of 1936. On the other hand, in 1950, a German Court, [16] when considering the application of German law to a collision occurring in the Kiel Canal, suggested that the internationalisation of the Canal brought about by the Treaty of Versailles might have been terminated by the 1936 denunciation, as this denunciation had not been met by any "serious resistance" on the part of signatories of the Treaty. It may be that the denunciation of the Treaty, though illegal and therefore ineffective in most respects, might have brought about certain limited consequences (e.g. with respect to the Kiel Canal) if it can be shown that the other parties acquiesced in the abrogation of only some of the provisions of the Treaty.

e BREACH OF A TREATY BY ANOTHER PARTY

The termination of a treaty because it has been broken by the other party appears a simple enough rule to apply. In the practice of states, however, it has too often been used as an excuse for withdrawing from a treaty that a particular state has found inconvenient. As a consequence, state practice, while accepting the existence of the rule, provides little satisfactory evidence as to its application; and international jurists have attempted to remedy this deficiency in state practice by limiting the scope of the rule in theory.

Because of the uncertainty of the rule, the International Law Commission drafted a provision in the most general terms. A state could only withdraw from a bilateral treaty if the breach by the other party has been "material", and by a material breach was meant the "violation of a provision essential to the accomplishment of the object or purpose of the treaty".[17] It is obvious that a party cannot choose to avoid all its obligations under a treaty if the other party has failed to honour some minor provision of the treaty. And it would also seem correct in principle that a major breach by one state should give the other party the right to withdraw if it wished.

Support for this view of the law is to be found in the *Tacna-Arica* arbitration of 1922 between Chile and Peru.[18] Article 3 of the Treaty of Ancon 1883, provided that the provinces of Tacna and Arica, which constituted part of Peru, should remain in the possession of Chile for 10 years from the date of ratification of the Treaty. At the end of the period a plebiscite was to have been held to decide whether the provinces were to come permanently under Chilean control, or to continue to constitute part of Peru. Chile remained willing to carry out the plebiscite under the terms of Article 3 of the Treaty, but Peru, fearing that the passage of time would result in an adverse decision by the inhabitants of the provinces, contended that the colonisation of the provinces by Chile and the discrimination against Peruvians by the closing of their schools and the

---

16. *Kiel Canal Collision* case (1950), 17 I.L.R., Case No. 34.
17. 1966 Draft, Article 57; V.C. Article 60.   18. 2 U.N.R.I.A.A. 921.

seizure of their property constituted a breach of the Treaty which rendered it no longer operative. The Arbitrator rejected their argument. For abuses of administration to give Peru the right to terminate the Treaty, that state would have to establish "such serious conditions as the consequence of administrative wrongs as would operate to frustrate the purpose of the agreement". In the opinion of the Arbitrator, "a situation of such gravity" had not been shown to have existed.[19]

While the principle that a state may withdraw from a treaty that has been broken by the other party may not be too difficult to apply to a bilateral treaty, what is the position with regard to a multilateral treaty? It is believed that the International Law Commission's recent draft correctly states the position. If one state has been in breach of a treaty, and that breach is sufficiently serious, the other parties can by unanimous agreement terminate the agreement either in respect of their relations with the defaulting state or as between all the parties. It would also be open to an individual state to declare that it no longer accepted the treaty as binding in its relations with the defaulting state, although it is perhaps uncertain whether such a state must show that it has been specially affected by the actions of the defaulting state.[20]

f CHANGE OF CIRCUMSTANCES

The contention that a particular treaty is no longer consistent with present-day circumstances may often be raised in an international community which reflects frequent changes in the balance of power and in the relations between states. Such an argument is basically political, and to accept it unreservedly as a reason for terminating all treaties would be to reduce the international legal order to chaos. Nevertheless, there must be a stage at which a change in the order of things will bring about an ending of a treaty.

i Where the treaty becomes impossible to perform

It is possible to envisage a limited number of circumstances in which a treaty is literally impossible to perform by one of the contracting states. The examples given by the International Law Commission are the submergence of an island, the drying up of a river or the destruction of a dam or hydro-electric installation indispensable for the execution of a treaty.

A different problem is posed by the situation where the treaty may become impossible to perform by one of the parties, but not by some third state. If there were a right of navigation along a river running through the territory of state A in favour of state B, the subsequent acquisition of the whole of the territory of state A by state X (thereby bringing about the extinction of the personality of state A), or the acquisition of the part of the territory through which the river runs by state X, would create problems which relate to state succession. Although the treaty would no longer

---

19.   *Ibid.*, at p. 944.
20.   The Vienna Conference added a new paragraph (Article 60 (5)) to the I.L.C. draft. Suspension and termination are not to be available for breach of a treaty of a humanitarian character in respect of provisions relating to the protection of the human person.

be binding on state A (either because state A no longer existed, or was no longer able to perform the treaty), it is possible that the obligations would pass to state X.[21]

ii *Other fundamental changes of circumstance*

As the changes in circumstances usually invoked by a party are of a political character, there are obvious political solutions to the problem. The parties could well agree to the termination of the agreement, and this need to review obsolete treaties was expressly recognised by Article 19 of the Covenant of the League of Nations which stated that the League Assembly might "from time to time advise the reconsideration" by Members of the League of treaties that had become "inapplicable". And, if it was not possible to reach express agreement, it would be possible for the parties quietly to allow the treaties to "lapse". Although it is probable that desuetude alone does not terminate a treaty, when coupled with evidence of the parties' intention that they should no longer be bound by it, disregard of its provisions would certainly be sufficient. In 1924 the British Government gave notice to a number of other states of its intention to terminate certain obsolete treaties concerning the abolition of the slave trade. Two of the treaties in fact contained clauses enabling a party to denounce, but the denunciations of the rest of the agreements were accepted by the other parties without objection. Even if the treaties had not lapsed, the denunciation by the British Government would have been effective to terminate them, and even less forceful evidence (such as a statement that the treaties were no longer in existence) would have been sufficient. It is submitted that a protest sufficient to prevent an estoppel would not in itself be adequate to safeguard the treaty: the protesting state would at least have to show cause why the treaty was still in existence.

The situation which causes the greatest difficulty is the attempt by one party to plead change of circumstances (*rebus sic stantibus*) as an excuse for no longer being bound by a treaty that cannot be said to have lapsed and which the other party still wishes to observe. The International Law Commission accepted that the doctrine of *rebus sic stantibus* did exist but was careful to suggest that its application should be limited to a "fundamental change of circumstances", which had been unforeseen by the parties at the time the treaty was concluded. However, to qualify as a "fundamental change of circumstances", the existence of the circumstances had to constitute "an essential basis of the consent of the parties to be bound by the treaty" and the effect of the change had to "radically" transform "the scope of obligations still to be performed under the treaty".[1]

The reason for the cautious approach of the International Law Commission to the doctrine is that international tribunals have avoided applying it. Even in the *Free Zones* case,[2] in which the parties to the Treaty of

---

21. See below, pp. 390–393.
1. 1966 Draft Article 59; V.C. Article 62 (1) is substantially the same.
2. (1932), P.C.I.J. Rep., Ser. A/B, No. 46.

Versailles had recognised that the 1815 and subsequent instruments were no longer consistent with present-day circumstances, the Permanent Court held that the facts did not justify the application of the doctrine. The Court added further doubt to the existence of the doctrine by expressly refusing to consider as unnecessary "any of the questions of principle which arise in connection with the theory of the lapse of treaties by reason of change of circumstances, such as the extent to which the theory can be regarded as constituting a rule of international law, the occasions on which and the method by which effect can be given to the theory, if recognised, and the question whether it would apply to treaties establishing rights such as that which Switzerland derived from the treaties of 1815 and 1816."[3]

Because the basis of the doctrine is political change bringing about legal consequences, it might have been expected that the plea of change of circumstances would more frequently be invoked before, and would receive a more favourable response from, the political organs of the United Nations. In fact, this has not been the case. In 1947, for example, Egypt requested the Security Council to bring about the evacuation of British troops from Egyptian territory and to terminate the British administration of the Sudan. The presence of British troops in Egypt was provided for by a treaty between the two states of 1936. Although Egypt disavowed that it was relying on the doctrine of *rebus sic stantibus* as the basis of its argument, the grounds put forward in support of the Egyptian argument certainly seemed in keeping with a plea of change of circumstances. It was suggested that the Treaty of 1936 had been "negotiated under conditions that no longer existed", that the Treaty had been a safeguard against invasion of Egypt in the event of war and that, as the war was over, the Treaty had "outlived its purpose". The United Kingdom representative commented on the limited and controversial application of a plea of *rebus sic stantibus*, and concluded that even if the doctrine existed it could not apply to the situation in Egypt and the Sudan. In the event, the Security Council was unable to agree upon a resolution and the matter was adjourned.[4]

It is thus clear that, even if one accepts, as did the Vienna Conference, the view that the doctrine of *rebus sic stantibus* exists, its application in practice to absolve a party from a treaty which the other party still considers binding is likely to be rare. Indeed, it is difficult to envisage changes in circumstances that would be sufficiently fundamental to bring the doctrine into play, unless one includes impossibility of performance.

5 STATE SUCCESSION AND THE APPLICATION OF TREATIES

A. In General

Traditional doctrine never succeeded in establishing a satisfactory compromise between Roman law theories of succession, based upon the

---

3. *Ibid.*, at pp. 156–158.   4. See generally (1949) 43 A.J.I.L. 762.

premise that all obligations devolved upon the heir, and the "clean-slate" principle, put forward by the United States on obtaining independence from Great Britain to explain why the former colonies were not bound by treaties to which Britain was a party. It can readily be seen that the inheritance of a deceased's estate is scarcely the most useful analogy to problems of state succession which seldom arise out of the complete extinction of one state and its replacement by a new state. Nor does the clean-state theory explain why (as state practice, or at least the weight of it, suggests) many "local" treaties (i.e. treaties dealing with specific areas) should remain in force even though the territory of which the area dealt with in the treaty forms a part is transferred to another state, or even is part of the territory upon which a new state is created.

The approach generally adopted to these "local" treaties has been to decide whether, as a matter of interpretation, they are applicable to the changed situation. For example, following the cession of Alaska by Russia to the United States in 1867 it became necessary to decide what effect the transfer had on navigational rights granted under a treaty of 1825 by Russia to British subjects in perpetuity over rivers flowing from Canada, through Alaska, to the Pacific. In 1898 the United States was preparing to regulate navigation on the rivers in question in a manner contrary *inter alia* to the treaty of 1825. The question of whether British subjects retained their right of freedom of navigation was submitted to the Law Officers of the Crown who replied that "the rights confirmed by the Treaty of 1825 were not . . . affected by the cession to the United States, inasmuch as Russia could cede only what she had."[5]

However, the consequence of adopting this approach is primarily to decide whether the obligations *can* pass, not whether they in fact do. In order to decide the second question, it may be necessary to rely upon some additional principle. In the Alaska example just given, the Law Officers based their advice to the British Government upon the rule that a transfer of territory by cession can only pass to the new sovereign the rights possessed by the former sovereign.

In an earlier chapter, the distinction was drawn between the majority of treaties that are purely contractual in nature, creating rights and obligations for the parties alone, and those few treaties of a special type that create rights *in rem*, binding upon the territory itself and therefore upon any successor in title.[6] Whether a treaty falls into this second category will depend primarily upon a construction of its form in the light of the circumstances giving rise to it. The fact that the treaty refers to a specific area is obviously important (the obligations *can* pass to a successor), but it is not conclusive. In the Alaskan case, the Law Officers were obviously influenced by the *nature* of the rights granted by the 1825 treaty.

But even if one accepts interpretation as a basis for deciding questions

---

5. Discussed in O'Connell, *State Succession in Municipal Law and International Law*, Vol. II, pp. 235–237.
6. For a discussion of treaties creating third party rights, see above pp. 13–15.

of succession to treaty obligations, it cannot provide a complete answer to the many problems facing a new state which has been created out of a former colonial territory. Many treaties made by the colonial powers might have direct relevance to the territory, and, on the interpretative approach, be binding on it. Some of these treaties might be acceptable enough; but others would no doubt be resented in the belief that they served the interests of the former colonial power, or were entered into with scant regard for the interests of the territory and its inhabitants. Among treaties causing particular resentment have been those creating economic régimes or military servitudes mutually beneficial to a number of colonial powers;[7] and treaties establishing boundaries which largely or totally disregard geographical and ethnical divisions.

Practical difficulties between the nascent state and the former colonial power have largely been avoided by specific agreement as part of a wider arrangement designed to deal with all the alterations necessary to meet the changed situation when independence is achieved. The International Law Association's Committee on State Succession noticed a number of general trends in the approach of new states to the question of succession to treaties.[8]

> "(1) The successor State assumes all responsibilities arising from treaties between the predecessor and third parties, as was the method adopted by Nigeria regarding treaty obligations assumed by Great Britain in respect of the former colony;
> (2) The successor undertakes to maintain all treaties during a trial period while they are being studied. At the end of this period it announces which will be maintained while all others lapse. This system was adopted by Malawi in 1964;[9]
> (3) The successor announces its intention to abide by customary law, but seeks to avoid any general commitment in the treaty field and does not commit itself to renounce or ratify old treaties in any determined period of time. This was the method adopted by Zambia;
> (4) A general declaration of succession to treaties is issued."

It is not easy to determine from these trends what stage the law has reached. Two principles would seem to be recognised, at least implicitly. In the first place, it is necessary that some degree of continuity should be achieved, in the short term at any rate. In this period both the new state and third parties will have time to consider their future treaty relations. The new state will be able to establish its own identity and policies by a process of accommodation without being too hampered by the legacies of its colonial past; but at the same time the rights of third states are not immediately prejudiced.

The second principle which seems latent in the various declarations made by new states regarding treaties made by the former colonial power is that, in the last resort, a new state has a discretion whether to accept or

---

7. For example, Tanzania's reactions to the agreement in which Britain granted to Belgium a perpetual lease over dock facilities at Dar-es-Salaam and Kigoma: discussed O'Connell, *op. cit.*, pp. 241–3.
8. I.L.A., 52nd Report (1966), p. 557.
9. Following the examples of Tanzania, Uganda, Kenya and Burundi.

reject any such treaties. It need hardly be said that such a view is potentially destructive of legal order in the international community. Fortunately the political pressures towards some degree of conformity are sufficiently strong to prevent a general refusal to compromise by a new state, a possible consequence of which might be the state's ostracism by the world community.[10] Nevertheless, even if a complete refusal to accept potentially binding obligations is unlikely, the mere fact that new states base their approach to the "re-negotiation" of treaties upon the premise that they have the ultimate right of rejection will inevitably affect the customary international law on the subject. Once there is general acceptance of the principle that other states should negotiate in good faith with a new state the reasonable adjustment of their treaty relations, pre-existing rules of customary law are likely to be regarded as guides rather than as binding obligations with the ultimate consequence that their status as rules of law is denied altogether.

B. Succession and the U.N. Charter

The issue most frequently met with in United Nations practice has been the effect of the granting of independence by a member of the Organisation to one of its dependent territories. The most obvious solution, and the one in fact adopted, was that the membership of the colonial power should continue unimpaired, and the newly independent state should seek admission to membership in the normal way in accordance with Article 4 of the Charter.

However, the precedent which provided the basis for this approach was not strictly speaking on all fours with the normal independence situation. Before the date set for the independence of India and for its separation into the states of India and Pakistan, the question of membership in the U.N. was posed to the Secretariat's legal office by the Secretary-General. The answer given to the Secretary-General was based upon the premise that the situation was "one in which a part of an existing state breaks off and becomes a new state. On this analysis", the opinion continued, "there is no change in the international status of India; it continues as a state with all treaty rights and obligations, and consequently, with all the rights and obligations of membership in the United Nations. The territory which breaks off, Pakistan, will be a new state; it will not have the treaty rights and obligations of the old state, and it will not, of course, have membership in the United Nations."[11]

Largely as a matter of convenience, the Security Council and the

---

10. As happened in the cases of the Soviet Union after 1917 and of the People's Republic of China after 1949. Both entities regarded themselves as régimes of such a totally different character from their predecessors that they were the equivalent of new States. As such, they claimed exemption from international obligations assumed by the pre-revolutionary governments.

11. G.A.O.R., 17th Sess., Suppl. no. 9, para. 72.

General Assembly decided to treat India as the existing member and to admit Pakistan forthwith to membership. When Pakistan deposited its instrument of acceptance of the obligations of the Charter, its representative to the U.N. added a declaration maintaining the Pakistan view that it was as much a successor of British India, which had been an original member of both the League of Nations and the United Nations, as was the new India.[12]

There is much to be said for distinguishing between a situation where the separation of a part of a state to form a new state leaves the "personality" of the original state intact, and where the original personality is itself divided. In the former case, most commonly met when a colonial territory attains independence, the personality of the colonial power remains unimpaired, and it retains its treaty rights and obligations, including membership of international organisations; the newly created state will, in most cases, not be bound by pre-existing treaties, and normally, therefore, will have to seek admission to international organisations. On the other hand, the splitting of one state into two (or more) states creates a situation in which it is logically possible to regard either *both* states or *neither* of them as successors to the previous personality. For example, the parties to the peace treaties at the end of the First World War seemed to regard the two new states of Austria and Hungary as the direct successors of the former Austro-Hungarian Empire; but no one regarded Czechoslovakia, which was also created out of territory of the Empire, as being bound by its treaty obligations. The extent to which there might be a succession in cases of "dismemberment" would seem to depend upon the degree of continuity between the new states and the former administration.

In the case of India and Pakistan, both states should have been entitled to regard themselves as successors of British India, and, problems arising from the provisions of the Charter aside, equally entitled to membership in the United Nations. The reason why the Security Council and General Assembly proceeded to elect Pakistan to membership was to avoid lengthy controversy on whether it was possible, under the Charter, to allow the membership of one state to be split in two. Because of the indecisive nature of the discussion, the Legal Committee of the General Assembly was asked to report on the legal issues involved. The Committee's report[13] emphasised that "when a new State is created, whatever may be the territory and the population which it comprises and whether or not they formed part of a State Member of the United Nations, it cannot under the system of the Charter claim the status of a Member of the United Nations unless it has been formally admitted as such in conformity with the provisions of the Charter."

What this report did not solve was whether the pre-existing member should retain its place in the Organisation whatever changes occurred. If a

---

12. *Ibid.*, 2nd Sess., 92nd pl. p. 311.
13. *Ibid.*, 2nd Sess., 1st Committee, p. 582, Annex 14g.

state in the position of Pakistan had to be admitted to membership, why should not the new state of India have similarly been required to go through the procedures laid down in Article 4? As has already been stated, the procedure adopted was a convenient compromise, and convenience has remained the most notable feature of the U.N.'s approach to problems of membership resulting from the break up of an existing member or of an applicant for membership.

In 1961, for example, the Organisation had to consider what action to take on the dissolution of the United Arab Republic. The Republic had been formed in 1958 by the Union of Syria and Egypt. On that occasion, with the minimum of formality, the Republic had been substituted for the two former states within the U.N. framework. Following dissolution, the process was reversed. The General Assembly raised no objection to the communication sent by the Syrian Government in which it was "recalled that the Syrian Republic was an original member of the United Nations under Article 3 of the Charter and continued its membership in the form of joint association with Egypt. . . . [I]n resuming the former status as an independent state", the communication continued, "the Syrian Arab Republic has the honour to request that the United Nations take note of the resumed membership in the United Nations of the Syrian Arab Republic."[14]

---

14 U.N. Doc. A/4914, 9 Oct., 1961.

CHAPTER TEN

INTERNATIONAL CLAIMS—I
STATE RESPONSIBILITY

1 STATE RESPONSIBILITY IN GENERAL

Claims by one state (or other entity having international personality) against another have two principal aspects. First, there are the rules of law which determine whether a state is in breach of its international obligations towards another state (the principles of state responsibility). Secondly, there are the rules of law and the practices of states which provide the means whereby disputes over responsibility may be settled (the settlement of disputes).

In the course of this chapter, it is proposed to deal with the rules of law which govern the responsibility of states. However, it should be borne in mind that the application of these rules is often varied to meet the exigencies of inter-state relations. The strict application of rules of law is normally to be found within the framework of a relatively sophisticated judicial system. As the following chapter on the settlement of disputes will demonstrate, the cornerstone of such a system—compulsory judicial determination of disputes—is lacking from the present international order. As a consequence, the great majority of incidents to which the rules of state responsibility might apply are the subject of negotiation and settlement at the diplomatic level, either individually, or as part of a general settlement of a large number of outstanding claims between two states.

It is only rarely that an incident will be the subject of litigation between states before an arbitral tribunal or the International Court. The reasons for the rarity with which judicial settlement is used are obvious enough. In many cases the incident will be too trivial to be the subject matter of formal procedures of settlement. And the more important a dispute is considered, the less likely will the states involved be prepared to risk an adverse outcome by entrusting the dispute to impartial adjudication. Arbitration is most likely to be adopted where a special tribunal has been established to decide disputes of a particular class. Occasionally a multilateral treaty will provide for an arbitral tribunal to settle all disputes arising out of its terms (as with a number of peace treaties). Or alternatively, two states might create a tribunal to deal with all outstanding claims between them (the best known example probably being the American-Mexican Claims Commission). Isolated cases of arbitration or judicial settlement are most likely to occur between states which for political reasons are anxious to demonstrate their good faith (as, for example, in the *Anglo-Norwegian Fisheries* case[1]). Often, however, a state which has accepted in advance an obligation to resort to judicial settlement, finds the submission of a particular dispute to the International Court by the other party as an undesirable development and will, as a consequence, put forward all possible arguments in an attempt to demonstrate that the circumstances of the case do not fall within the Court's jurisdiction as defined by the parties' declarations of acceptance.[2]

International law is only concerned with the wrongful acts of one international person against another on the international plane. It is not concerned with the injury suffered by individuals except in so far as such injury entitles a state or international organisation to present a claim on their behalf against the entity responsible. Although international responsibility concerns the rights of international organisations as well as the rights of states, for the moment the discussion will deal with the rights and obligations of states: the way in which the rules of state responsibility have been adapted to claims by and against international organisations will be considered in a later chapter.[3] Obvious examples of wrongful acts by one state against another would be the invasion of its territory, the sinking or seizing of a ship flying its flag in time of peace, the shooting down of one of its aircraft, the arrest of its ambassador, or the breach of a treaty obligation owed to that other state. All such cases involve a *direct* international wrong against the other state for which the first state is responsible.

On the other hand, there are a large number of situations in which (1) the injury suffered by the claimant state is indirect, or in which (2) the responsibility of the respondent state will only arise indirectly, or in which (3) both the injury and the responsibility are indirect.

As far as (1) is concerned, a typical situation would be the wrongful seizure of the property of a national of state B by the officials of state A. The complicity of state A is created by the involvement of its officials. The incident thus constitutes a *prima facie* breach of international law, and if it goes unremedied by state A when the injured individual has recourse to the remedies available under the legal system of state A, that state's responsibility to state B is established. While state A was directly involved from the outset, however, the rights of state B were indirect: the claim was not because of any direct injury to itself, but because of a wrong committed against its national.

In situation (2) the injury to state B is direct, but the responsibility of state A under international law will only arise if a lack of due care on the part of state A can be shown. Illustrations of this type of situation usually concern the acts of individuals causing direct injury to the property of the claimant state. A crowd of demonstrators protesting against the policies of state B gets out of control and burns down the embassy of state B. A shipbuilding company in state A constructs a vessel which is subsequently

---

1. I.C.J. Rep. 1951, p. 116. 2. See below, pp. 494–513. 3. Below, pp. 626–628.
OIL

fitted out as a warship and used by rebels against the government of state B. In both cases state B has suffered direct damage, but state A will only be responsible under international law if it can be inculpated in what happened by a failure to take due care to prevent what occurred.

Situation (3) is in a sense a combination of situations (1) and (2), except that the failure of state A to provide a means of redress (as in situation (1)) creates both is own responsibility and the right of state B to present the claim. In such a situation, a national of state B is injured by private individuals in state A. The police force in state A is so inefficient that those responsible are never brought to trial; or the courts are so corrupt that the national of state B can obtain no redress. The deficiences in the administration of justice in state A give rise to what is known as a "denial of justice". It is for this denial of justice that state A is indirectly responsible (loosely speaking) for the injury suffered by the national of state B.

The distinction between the three categories of what might be termed indirect state responsibility relates primarily to the type of evidence that must be adduced by the claimant state to show that the injury is one which by international law gives rise to the responsibility of the defendant state. In situation (1), the claimant state must first show that the defendant state's conduct (i.e. the conduct of its officials) constituted a wrongful interference with alien property according to international law. In situation (2) the claimant state must normally show a lack of due care on the part of the defendant state in preventing the incident which caused damage to the property of the claimant state. In situation (3) the claimant state must show that the administration of justice falls short of the minimum standards required by international law or that there has otherwise been a denial of justice.

In all cases there is a notion of fault, that the defendant state is in some sense to blame for what has occurred. The whole concept of a "denial of justice" is that, through the shortcomings of the defendant state, justice has not been done to the injured national of another state. There has been much doctrinal discussion of fault as an element in state responsibility, though in practice it is a generalisation for various types of conduct that fail to meet the requirements of a state's international obligations. In the three situations discussed above, the "type of fault" was different in each case. Indeed, the more widely one investigates the circumstances in which states have been held in breach of their international obligations, the more general, and therefore less helpful, must the notion of fault become. To take the most frequently quoted example of the application of "fault" in a case concerning a direct wrong by one state against another, the *Corfu Channel* case,[4] the International Court was called upon to consider, *inter alia*, the responsibility of Albania for the damage caused to two British ships by mines laid in Albanian territorial waters within the Corfu Channel. It could not be shown that Albanian ships had laid the mines, nor was the Court prepared to hold that it could "be concluded from

---

4. I.C.J. Rep. 1949, p. 4.

the mere fact of the control exercised by a state over its territory and waters that that state necessarily knew, or ought to have known, of any unlawful act perpetrated therein, nor yet that it necessarily knew, or should have known the authors".[5] However, on the evidence, the Court held that Albania should have been aware of the presence of the minefield within its territorial waters, and was therefore under a duty to warn shipping of the dangers of passage through the Corfu Channel.

While some degree of fault was present in the situations so far discussed and, in fact, was essential to the existence of responsibility, it would be misleading to conclude that all instances of international responsibility depended upon the "fault" of the defendant state. International law lays down certain obligations for breach of which a state is responsible. The definition of these obligations and the manner in which they will be broken will often include different types of blameworthy conduct. But there are situations in which the obligation is defined in terms which exclude the notion of fault altogether. A state may be in breach of its treaty obligations through no "fault" of its own. In some situations the actions of the defendant state will be judged not by the carelessness or failure to take care of its officials, but by circumstances of which they are totally unaware, and could not have been aware until after they acted. For example, in cases of visit and search on the high seas, whether by treaty or under customary international law, the warship exercising the right will be acting at its peril. Under Article 22, the High Seas Convention of 1958 enables a warship to board a foreign merchant vessel on suspicion that the vessel is engaged in piracy or the slave trade, or, although flying the flag of another state, the vessel is in fact of the same nationality as the warship. However, if the search shows that the warship's suspicions were unfounded, the Article provides that compensation should be paid for any loss or damage that may have been occasioned by the boarding of the foreign vessel.

2 DIRECT INTERNATIONAL WRONGS

Examples of direct wrongful acts by one state against another are legion. Most of the rules of international law discussed in this book would, if broken, give rise to a cause of complaint against the offending state by states affected by its actions. All that can be attempted in the present context, however, is to give some illustrations of situations in which states have been in breach of their obligations owed directly to other states.

a BREACH OF TREATY

It is obvious enough that if a treaty between states A and B is broken by state B, state A has suffered a direct wrong: state B has broken an

---

5. *Ibid.*, at p. 18.

obligation to state A. In a well known passage from its judgment on the preliminary objections in the *Chorzow Factory* case,[6] the Permanent Court stated that it was "a principle of international law that the breach of an engagement involves an obligation to make reparation", and that reparation was therefore "the indispensable complement of a failure to apply a convention".

b FAILURE TO RESPECT THE TERRITORIAL RIGHTS OF OTHER STATES

A state may fail to respect the territorial rights of another state in a number of ways. The Nuremberg Tribunal held that the waging of aggressive war was an international crime, and this principle has been reinforced by the provision of Article 2 (4) of the United Nations Charter which requires that all members of the Organisation shall refrain from the threat or use of force against the territorial integrity or political independence of any state.[7] On a less spectacular scale, the violation of foreign territory might take the form of illegal flights in the airspace of another state (as with the U-2 incident of 1960);[8] or of the unlawful arrest of a wanted criminal on the territory of another state (as with the seizure of Eichman in Argentina by individuals acting with the connivance of the Israeli Government).[9]

c DAMAGE TO STATE PROPERTY

It is clear that if a state is the direct cause, whether through its own unlawful activities or through inactivity when there was a duty to act, of damage to the property of a foreign state, it is under an obligation to pay reparation for the damage so caused. Examples of conduct which, it was claimed, fell within this principle include the Aerial Incident of March 1953 in which a Czech fighter was alleged to have shot down a U.S. fighter over the American Zone of Germany,[10] and the Aerial Incident of 27th July, 1955, in which Bulgarian fighters attacked and destroyed an airliner belonging to the Israeli State airline;[11] the sacking of the British Mission in Peking in 1967; the attack upon an American naval vessel by Israeli ships in the Eastern Mediterranean, also in 1967.

Among disputes which were judicially determined have been the *Naulilaa* incident, and the *Corfu Channel* case. In the former,[12] German troops crossed from German South-West Africa into Portuguese Angola and there destroyed a number of forts and border posts. At that stage in the development of international law it was permissible for a state to use force in reprisal for some prior illegal employment of force by another state. An arbital tribunal held that even if the alleged illegality by Portugal could be established (which was not the case on the evidence submitted to the Tribunal), it could not justify the excessive force used by the German

---

6. P.C.I.J. Rep., Ser. A, No. 9, p. 21.
7. For an arbitration on the former law dealing with reprisals and the excessive use of force, see the *Naulilaa* case (1920) 2 U.N.R.I.A.A. 1013; and below, pp. 678–680.
8. See above, p. 285.   9. See above, p. 165.   10. I.C.J. *Pleadings*.
11. I.C.J. *Pleadings*.   12. See above, fn. 7.

authorities. The alleged reprisal was no justification for the widespread damage caused to property of the Portuguese State.

In the latter case,[13] it will be recalled, the United Kingdom claimed before the International Court that Albania was responsible for the damage caused to two British warships by mines while a number of ships of the Royal Navy were proceeding through the North Corfu Channel. The Court held Albania liable for the damage because Albanian coastal authorities must have seen the activities of whoever was responsible for laying the mines in the Channel and were under a duty to warn shipping using the Channel of the danger.

d INSULT TO THE STATE

It is obvious enough that the deliberate restriction upon the movements, or expulsion, of a diplomatic representative of one state by another without reasonable cause, or acts generally termed "insults to the flag", constitute international wrongs for which the state responsible should make suitable reparation. Although wrongful activities of this type may seem juridically of little significance, in practice the notion of "insult to the flag" can play an important part in the justification of the award of damages in certain situations.

In the *Corfu Channel* case, the damage to the two British ships constituted the basis for an award of compensation because the ships were warships, i.e. they belonged to the British Government. If the damage had been caused to a merchant vessel the basis for the assessment of the compensation would still have been the same (what would constitute compensation for the damage caused to the ships?). It would have been immaterial to an international tribunal whether the payment represented compensation to the United Kingdom for damage caused to a vessel sailing under the British flag, or compensation to the United Kingdom on behalf of United Kingdom nationals (i.e. the owners of the ship) suffering injury as a consequence of damage to their property. But what would be the position if the ship, though sailing under the flag of one state, was owned by the citizens of another state? As will be seen shortly,[14] a state can only take up a claim on behalf of an injured individual if that individual is its national. As the state is thus barred from taking up a claim on behalf of the owners of the ship, the nature of the direct claim for damage to a ship flying its flag will be crucial.

This issue was raised by the case of the *I'm Alone*.[15] The vessel, although registered in Canada, was "de facto owned, controlled, and at the critical times managed, and her movements directed and her cargo dealt with and disposed of, by a group of persons acting in concert who were entirely, or nearly so, citizens of the United States". The arbitration commissioners held that, for this reason, no compensation should be paid for the loss of the ship or of its cargo as a consequence of its destruction by the actions of

---

13. I.C.J. Rep. 1949, p. 4. See also above, pp. 398–399.
14. Below, pp. 403–413.   15. (1933–5) 3 U.N.R.I.A.A. 1609.

a U.S. coast-guard cutter that were contrary to international law.[16] Nevertheless, the Commissioners went on to decide that, as the sinking of the *I'm Alone* by U.S. coastguards was an unlawful act, the United States ought formally to apologise to the Canadian Government and to pay damages in respect of the wrong.[17] But what was to be the extent of the reparation in view of the fact that a claim for the loss of the ship and its cargo was not maintainable? Should not an "insult to the flag", in the absence of damage to state property, be the subject of apology, an under-taking to punish those responsible, and at the most nominal damages?[18] Without explaining the basis of their assessment, the Commissioners awarded the sum of $25,000. It is not altogether clear, therefore, whether these damages were of a punitive nature (the sinking of a vessel flying the flag of another state on the high seas is after all a serious matter), or whether they were in the nature of "costs" for the expenses incurred by the complainant state in preparing the case and submitting it to the Commissioners.

In most cases a public apology and an undertaking to punish those responsible would most certainly be adequate amends for direct state wrongs of the type being examined. Unless there has been material' damage to state property, the award of damages to another state on its own account should be made only in exceptional circumstances. In the cases of the *Carthage* and the *Manouba*,[19] France presented claims against Italy for the temporary seizure of two French vessels. While upholding in part the French claims for damages in respect of the losses by private parties interested in the ships and their voyages, the tribunal rejected the French claims for one franc nominal damages in respect of each offence against the French flag. It stated that the independent establishment of the breach by a state of its obligations in itself constituted a serious penalty. In these cases, the penalty was made heavier by the award of damages in respect of material loss. As a general rule such a penalty would be sufficient and the introduction of a further pecuniary penalty appeared superfluous. Only in exceptional circumstances, which clearly did not exist in either case, might such an additional penalty be called for.

3   INDIRECT INTERNATIONAL WRONGS

It was suggested that international wrongs that have for the purposes of the present discussion been termed "indirect" may be classified into three separate categories, depending upon the circumstances that give rise to them. These indirect wrongs arise (a) where nationals of state A cause

---

16.   For details of the facts of the sinking, see above, pp. 250–251.

17.   Quite apart from damages on behalf of the captain and members of the crew: see below, pp. 460–461.

18.   As in the French claim in the *Carthage* and *Manouba* cases, 11 U.N.R.I.A.A. pp. 451 and 465 respectively: English texts in (1913) 7 A.J.I.L., pp. 623 and 629.

19.   Though see further below, pp. 460–461, 468.

injury to nationals of state B, who are later unable to obtain justice from
the courts or authorities of state A; (b) where the officials or organs of state
A directly injure by their acts or omissions a national of state B; or (c) when
acts of individuals in state A cause damage to the property of state B in
circumstances where state A should have prevented the damage. Although
these separate situations are similar in that they often raise some of the
legal issues, they are not identical. Situation (c) in particular will be dealt
with separately at the end, but the discussion of (a) and (b) will of necessity
require comparisons to be drawn, because between them the similarities
are greatest. However, before considering them it is first necessary to
consider the nationality of claims rule which, unless the defendant state is
willing to waive compliance with it, applies to all cases involving injury to
the person or property of a foreign national.

A. Nationality of claims

a INDIVIDUALS

The right of a state to make representations about the treatment of individuals in the territory of another state may not depend exclusively upon the
question of nationality. Diplomatic protests against violations of international law would seem to be legitimate providing that the protesting
state has some "standing" to make the protest. Normally, this *locus standi*
will depend upon the bond of nationality, but other facts may create a
sufficient "interest": for example, the international community as a
whole may have a sufficient interest in the observance of basic human
rights for individual members of the community of states to protest
against what they believe to be non-observance of those rights, and this
may be the case even if the conduct to which objection is made is not
demonstrably a breach of international law.

However, for a state to make specific representation concerning injuries
to an individual or to a group of individuals, or damage to their property,
it must be able to show that these individuals are in fact its nationals. But
the so-called *rule* of nationality of claims goes even further. Although cases
do exist of claims being accepted by states responsible for injuries to
foreign nationals which do not satisfy the strict requirements of the rule,
the acceptance of such claims was clearly the result of a concession granted
by the "respondent" state.[20] In the absence of such a concession, either to
meet a special case, or by agreement between the states concerned, international law requires that the victim is a national of the plaintiff state "at

---

20. E.g. *Landreau* claims (1919–22), 1 A.D. Case No. 125; *Lusitania* case (1925–6)
3 A.D. Case No. 175. There would, however, appear to be a major exception to the
nationality of claims rule in the case of alien seamen serving on board a ship flying the
flag of the claimant state. In the *I'm Alone* case (above, p. 401) damages were also awarded in
respect of the injuries to the master and the crew of the vessel, including a French seaman
who was drowned when the vessel sank.

the moment when the damage was caused and retains its nationality until the claim is decided".[1]

This principle of the continuity of nationality is well illustrated by the *Stevenson* claim[2] before the British-Venezuelan Commission in 1904. By the time the claim was presented, Stevenson himself was dead so that the claim was in effect on behalf of the heirs to his estate. The Umpire held that Stevenson's widow had Venezuelan nationality, as did the ten of their children who had been born in Venezuela. The claim was only entitled to succeed with respect to the two children who, having been born outside Venezuela and on British territory, had British nationality.

From the earlier account of nationality in the context of jurisdictional conflicts[3] it will be realised that similar difficulties arise where an individual upon whose behalf a state wishes to present a claim has connections with a state other than the claimant state. A number of situations would seem possible. The individual concerned might also have the nationality of the respondent state; or he might also have the nationality of a third state not involved in the proceedings. Alternatively, the individual might have close connections with the respondent state which outweigh the connections he has with his national state; or the close connections might be with a third state.

i *Where the individual also has the nationality of the respondent state*

International tribunals, when called upon to consider this situation, have uniformly applied the test of "dominant nationality".

In the *Canevaro* claim,[4] an arbitral tribunal was asked to decide whether the Peruvian Government was bound to pay £43,140 plus interest to the three Canevaro brothers as present holders of certain drafts drawn by the Peruvian Government to the order of José Canevaro & Sons. The question was raised whether the claim on behalf of one of the brothers could be considered as an Italian claim. The brother was a Peruvian national by Peruvian law because he was born in Peru; and an Italian national by Italian law because he was born of an Italian father. However, the tribunal held that as he had "on several occasions acted as a Peruvian citizen, both by running as a candidate for the Senate, where none are admitted except Peruvian citizens . . . and also especially by accepting the office of Consul General of the Netherlands, after having secured the authorisation of the Peruvian Government and the Peruvian Congress", whatever his status as an Italian national might have been in Italy, the Peruvian government was entitled to consider him a Peruvian citizen and to deny his status as an Italian claimant.

This process of ascribing a dominant nationality in such circumstances was described by the International Court in the *Nottebohm* case with

---

1. Hague Codification Conference, Preparatory Committee, Basis of Discussion No. 28.
2. 9 U.N.R.I.A.A. 494.   3. Above, pp. 293–312.
4. (1912), 11 U.N.R.I.A.A. 397; English text in 6 A.J.I.L. 746.

approval. "International arbitrators", the Court said, "have given their preference to the real and effective nationality, that which accorded with the facts, that based on stronger factual ties between the person concerned and one of the states whose nationality is involved. Different factors are taken into consideration, and their importance will vary from one case to the next: the habitual residence of the individual concerned is an important factor, but there are other factors such as the centre of his interests, his family ties, his participation in public life, attachment shown by him for a given country and inculcated in his children, etc."[5]

A few months after the Court handed down its decision in the *Nottebohm* case, the Italian-United States Conciliation Commission was called upon in the *Mergé* claim[6] to consider the concept of dominant nationality in relation to the Italian Peace Treaty of 1947 which provided for the payment of compensation to "United Nations nationals". As the Treaty simply defined such persons as "nationals of any of the United Nations", and made no special provisions for persons entitled to the nationality of both the claimant state and the defendant state (i.e. Italy), the Commission felt that it must "turn to the general principles of international law". After a survey of earlier judicial decisions, including the extract from the *Nottebohm* judgment given above, and the writings of jurists, the Commission laid down a number of principles to serve as guides for settling future claims before the Commission. The Commission gave the following examples of dominant U.S. nationality: children born in the United States of an Italian father when the children have habitually lived there; Italians who, having acquired U.S. nationality by naturalisation and having thus lost their Italian nationality, later re-acquire it by Italian law by staying in Italy for more than two years though without the intention of residing there permanently;[7] American women married to Italian nationals where the family has had habitual residence in the United States and the interests and the permanent professional life of the head of the family were established in the United States;[8] a widow who at the termination of her marriage transfers her residence from Italy to the United States, although "whether or not the new residence is of an habitual nature must be evaluated, case by case, bearing in mind also the widow's conduct, especially with regard to the raising of her children, for the purpose of deciding which is the prevalent nationality".[9]

ii *Where the individual has the nationality of a third state as well as of the claimant state*

Difficulty could only arise if it appeared that the individual on whose behalf a claim was being presented had the effective nationality of a third state. Such pronouncements that have been made by international

---

5. I.C.J. Rep. 1955, at p. 22.   6. (1955), 22 I.L.R. 443.
7. See the *Zangrilli* claim (1957), 24 I.L.R. 454; and the *Cestra* claim, *ibid*.
8. The *Mergé* claim itself concerned an American woman who had married an Italian national; see also, *Spaulding* claim (1957), 24 I.L.R. 452 and cp. *Puccini* claim, *ibid*., pp. 454–5.
9. 22 I.L.R. at p. 456; and see the *Ruspoli* claim, 24 I.L.R. 457.

tribunals seem to treat the extent of the connection with the third state as immaterial. In the *Salem* case[10] between the United States and Egypt, once the tribunal was satisfied that Salem had Persian nationality as his second nationality and not that of Egypt (the respondent state), it held that this fact constituted no bar to the presentation of the claim on his behalf by the United States. In the words of the tribunal, "the Egyptian Government cannot set forth against the United States the eventual continuation of the Persian nationality of George Salem; the rule of international law being that in a case of dual nationality a third power is not entitled to contest the claim of one of the two powers whose national is interested in the case by referring to the nationality of the other power."[11]

The award in the *Salem* case was given in 1932 at a time when the nationality of claims rule was only just becoming clearly defined,[12] and lacked the sort of refinements which are now required by the judgment of the International Court in the *Nottebohm* case. In the course of that judgment, it was pointed out that on a number of occasions (though not of course relating to diplomatic protection) courts of third states, where two different nationalities have been invoked before them, have had to determine whether a given foreign nationality was one which they ought to recognise.[13] Why should not an international tribunal draw such a distinction in relation to diplomatic protection?

The basic theoretical principle (though one from which a number of practical consequences follow) is that "in taking up the case of one of its nationals, by resorting to diplomatic action or international judicial proceedings on his behalf, a state is in reality asserting its own right, the right to ensure in the person of its nationals respect for the rules of international law."[14] Despite this emphasis on the right of the claimant state, it is nevertheless true that the loss to be compensated if the claim is successful is the loss of the individual national. While it is unreasonable that a person having the dominant nationality of the respondent state should be in a more favourable position than other nationals having no second nationality, it is not so unreasonable that an individual having dual nationality but no national ties with the respondent state should seek the protection of the state more able to obtain redress for the injury, contrary to international law, that he has suffered.

If one takes 1900 as a very imprecise dividing line, it can at least be stated with certainty that before that date a state could not take up a claim on behalf of one of its nationals having the nationality of the respondent

---

10. (1932), 2 U.N.R.I.A.A. 1161.   11. *Ibid.*, at p. 1188.

12. Although the *Canevaro* case dates from 1912, doubts as to the status of the nationality of claims rule were expressed in a case between U.S. and Germany (1919–22) 1 A.D. Case No. 125; and in the *Salem* case itself it was pointed out that the principle of "effective nationality" had yet to be recognised in the practice of some states: 2 U.N.R.I.A.A. at p. 1187. Furthermore, British practice still adopts the traditional view, although the Foreign Claims Commission has on occasion allowed claims in such circumstances: see Lillich, *International Claims: Postwar British Practice*, pp. 31–33.

13. I.C.J. Rep. 1955, at p. 22.

14. *Panevezys-Saldutiskis Rly. Co.* case, P.C.I.J. Rep., Ser. A/B, No. 76, at p. 16.

state, but that it could do so against any state other than the state of the other nationality.[15] Although there has been a trend since 1930 towards allowing claims in the former situation where the individual has the dominant nationality of the claimant state, no such trend is discernible towards limiting claims by the state of "non-dominant" nationality in the latter case. Indeed, the Italian-United States Conciliation Commission accepted without comment the principle that a respondent state could not raise the second dominant nationality of a third state in claims presented by the United States. "United States nationals who did not possess Italian nationality but the nationality of a third state can be considered 'United Nations nationals' under the Treaty, even if their prevalent nationality was the nationality of the third state."[16]

iii *Where the individual has close ties with, but not the nationality of, the respondent state*

Once the general notion of a dominant nationality is accepted, it is logically but a small step to take to reach the proposition that even if the individual has not taken, or is not entitled to, the nationality of the respondent state, nevertheless, if he has ties with that state which are closer than those with the state of his nationality, a claim presented by the latter should not be admissible. However, while the logical proximity of the two principles may be apparent, it is not altogether clear to what extent *international law* has recognised that the second proposition necessarily follows from the first.

In the *Nottebohm* case,[17] the International Court held that Liechtenstein was not entitled to exercise diplomatic protection and present a claim to the court on behalf of Nottebohm with whom it had only the most tenuous connection (naturalisation after a brief period of physical presence) against Guatemala where Nottebohm had spent most of his life. On the facts alone, the case can only be authority for the proposition that a state claiming an individual as its national by naturalisation must, in order to obtain recognition of that claim as a basis for the exercise of a right of diplomatic protection, be able to show a genuine link, or at least a closer link than with the respondent state, between itself and the individual. This restriction on the legal principle upon which the decision was based is further evidenced by the tenor of a number of passages in the Court's judgment. For example, the Court pointed to the "practice of certain states which refrain from exercising protection in favour of a naturalised person when the latter has in fact, by his prolonged absence, severed his links with what is no longer for him anything but his nominal country" as manifesting "the view of these states that, in order to be capable of being invoked against another state, nationality [by naturalisation?] must

---

15. British *Digest*, Vol. 5, pp. 382 and 384.
16. *Mergé* claim (1955), 22 I.L.R. at p. 456. See also the *Flegenheimer* claim, 25 I.L.R. at pp. 148–150, where it was made clear that the Commission regarded the principle of general application and not simply arising out of the meaning of "United Nations nationals" under the 1947 Peace Treaty.   17. I.C.J. Rep. 1955, p. 4.

correspond with the factual situation".[18] And later in its judgment the Court returned to the specific issue of naturalisation. "Naturalisation", the Court said, "is not to be taken lightly. To seek and to obtain it is not something that happens frequently in the life of a human being. It involves his breaking of a bond of allegiance and his establishment of a new bond of allegiance. . . . In order to appraise its international effect, it is impossible to disregard the circumstances in which it was conferred, the serious character which attaches to it, the real and effective, and not merely the verbal preference of the individual seeking it for the country which grants it to him."[19]

It will be remembered that, in an earlier chapter,[20] the naturalisation provisions of a number of states were discussed. It was pointed out that although most of them provided for periods of residence that might well be sufficient to establish a genuine link between the individual and the state granting nationality, many also allowed the waiver of the residential qualification in certain circumstances.[1] It would seem therefore that periods of three or five years residence are so common in the nationality legislation of states that such residence would in most cases establish a sufficient link with the naturalising state.

A similar approach can also be adopted to the question left unanswered by the Nottebohm decision, i.e., whether there is the need for a genuine link between an individual and the state which claims that he was entitled to its nationality at birth. As has already been discussed,[2] nationality at birth may be acquired either according to the *jus soli* or according to the *jus sanguinis*. The only cases of doubt would seem to arise in situations where a person claims a nationality because his father had that nationality, although the family had for some generations lived abroad. It would seem unlikely that the state where the family are resident should have to recognise their nationality, even in cases where they did not acquire the nationality of the state of residence.

But what of the person who is born in a state, or born of a father born in, and a national of that state, who lives most of his life abroad? The traditional British view was that foreign residence, even foreign domicile in the strict sense adopted by English private international law,[3] was no bar to diplomatic protection being exercised *vis-à-vis* the state of residence. However, it must be admitted that the Umpire in the British-American Claims Commission of 1853 took the contrary view,[4] and in 1869 the Queen's Advocate reported that a British subject might have "so incor-

---

18. I.C.J. Rep. 1955, at p. 22.   19. *Ibid.*, at p. 24.   20. Above, pp. 294–297.
  1. This is, in fact, what occurred in the case of Nottebohm. Liechtenstein law required a three-year residential qualification, although this requirement could be waived in special circumstances. Nottebohm's application for naturalisation was granted without the necessary residence although the copy of his application produced in court showed that he had made no formal mention of any circumstances in support of his request for immediate naturalisation.   2. Above, pp. 290–302.
  3. See *Winans* v. *A.-G.*, [1904] A.C. 287; *Bowie* (or *Ramsay*) v. *Liverpool Royal Infirmary*, [1930] A.C. 588.
  4. British *Digest*, Vol. 5, pp. 318–319.

porated himself with a foreign country by domicil, that for commercial purposes he may properly be refused British protection in that country."[5]

The point was not directly in issue in the *Nottebohm* case because Liechtenstein was claiming to exercise diplomatic protection on the basis of Nottebohm's naturalisation. Nevertheless, it is apparent that, while some of the Court's pronouncements deal only with the international recognition of nationality conferred by naturalisation,[6] other passages in its judgment are of more general application. In the opinion of the Court, "nationality is a legal bond having as its basis a social fact of attachment, a genuine connection of existence, interests and sentiments, together with the existence of reciprocal rights and duties. It may be said to constitute the juridical expression of the fact that the individual upon whom it is conferred, either directly by the law or as the result of an act of the authorities, is in fact more closely connected with the population of the state conferring it than with that of any other state. Conferred by a state, it only entitles that state to exercise protection *vis-à-vis* another state, if it constitutes a translation into juridical terms of the individual's connection with the state which has made him its national."[7]

It must be admitted that this passage is framed so widely that it could exclude from protection any person who lives outside his national state without exhibiting a connection with that state by visits, or business or family interests. However, if one can accept the premise that normal grounds for acquiring nationality at birth are *prima facie* sufficient to allow the national state to exercise protection, it is possible to strike some sort of balance between them and factors which might rebut this presumption (e.g. complete identification with a foreign way of life and an absence of interest in, or actual hostility towards, the national state). Similarly, as the basis of nationality becomes less close (e.g. where the individual is the second generation born abroad[8]), so the factors tending to rebut the presumption would need to be less obvious (e.g. permanent foreign residence might in itself be sufficient).

iv *Where the close connection other than nationality is with a third state*

If the authorities that were considered under heading ii where the individual was a national of a third state are any guide, as logically they might appear to be, it would seem that the long residence of an individual in a third state should be irrelevant to a claim presented on his behalf by the national state against the state alleged to be responsible for the injury. However, with the increasing emphasis being paid to the "genuine link" as an aspect of diplomatic protection, the existence of a close connection

---

5. *Ibid.*, p. 322.   6. See above.
7. I.C.J. Rep. 1955, at p. 23.
8. Of course such a factor would be of less significance in a former colony, for example, where members of the family had been born in what had been at the time "national territory".

with a third state might now be considered as of greater significance than a national tie with a third state.

The existence of a close connection with a third state has troubled international tribunals for more than a century. A brief reference has already been made to the British-American Claims Commission of 1853. In the *Laurent* claim, the Commissioners were called upon to decide whether Britain could present a claim against the United States in respect of certain British subjects, domiciled in, but not nationals of, Mexico. In deciding that the claims were not admissible, the Umpire held that by their long residence abroad the persons concerned, though still British subjects for the purposes of English law, could no longer be considered British subjects by international law. While the series of decisions to this effect by the Commission was not justified by the contemporary practice of states,[9] these decisions do demonstrate that even in the middle of the last century there existed doubts whether the conferment of nationality by itself was a satisfactory basis for diplomatic protection in all circumstances.

As has been stated already, the words used in the *Nottebohm* judgment suggest that the state exercising diplomatic protection must show not only that the individual is its national but that the individual is in fact more closely connected with itself than with *any other state*. If these words are taken at face value their meaning is obvious: the existence of a closer link with another state would be fatal to claims presented by the national state.

The danger of reading too much into the *Nottebohm* case was emphasised by the Italian-United States Conciliation Commission in the *Flegenheimer* claim.[10] It was argued by the Italian Government that even if Flegenheimer was entitled to United States nationality, and was not still a German citizen, his American citizenship was not his effective nationality. The Commission emphasised the limited scope of the *Nottebohm* decision: the question which the Court had to decide was "whether the nationality conferred on Nottebohm can be relied upon as against Guatemala in justification of the proceedings instituted before the court."[11] Where there existed a "genuine" single nationality, the connection by residence or otherwise of the individual with another state was irrelevant, particularly if the residence was in a state other than the respondent state.

Whatever defects there may have been in the notion of nationality as a basis for diplomatic protection, the "genuine link" principle if given extended application, would create unnecessary confusion in an area of law which previously had been settled. The remedy would cause more trouble than the defects.[12] Limited to situations where an individual has close ties with the respondent state the principle can help eradicate certain anomalies. For example, it is perhaps unsatisfactory that more or less permanent foreign residents should be in a better position than nationals. And it is

---

9. See the criticisms by the British Commissioner, British *Digest*, Vol. 5, pp. 320-2.
10. 25 I.L.R. 91, at pp. 148-50.   11. I.C.J. Rep. 1955, p. 17.
12. Furthermore, the effect of applying it widely would be to deprive some individuals of diplomatic protection entirely, unless, of course, it were recognised that a genuine link in the absence of nationality should be a basis of protection!

illogical that a state which bestows nationality upon permanent foreign residents and their descendants should be in a more favourable legal position *vis-à-vis* the national state than a state which bestows its nationality less liberally.

v *Nationality by estoppel*

It will be recalled from the discussion of estoppel in Chapter 1[13] that an estoppel can operate to prevent a state from contesting the truth of an assertion which it had previously made. This principle is based upon notions of equity, the question being whether it would be equitable for a state in its dealings with another state to alter its position and to raise a contention totally inconsistent with its previous stand.

The application of the principle in the context of the nationality of claims rule may be conveniently considered from three aspects.

First, and this stems from the basic notion of estoppel, it only applies to prevent a state raising an *inconsistent* argument. Thus, if the dispute is whether state A is entitled to pursue a claim against state B on behalf of an individual whom state B claims to be one of its nationals, the fact that the government of state B seized that individual's property as belonging to an alien would estop state B from claiming the individual as its national. Similarly, if there is a dispute whether the individual is a national of the claimant state at all, activities directed against the individual because of his nationality would raise an estoppel, but activities directed against him as an alien would not be sufficient to preclude the respondent state from later denying his nationality. In the *Hendry* claim[14] the Mexico/United States General Claims Commission rejected the Mexican contention that Hendry was not a United States national *inter alia* on the ground that his dismissal from the service of the Mexican government having been effected solely because of his American nationality, Mexico was estopped from denying his nationality before the Commission.

Secondly, there is authority for the proposition that the actions of the respondent state in treating the individual as a national of the claimant state must be in some way connected with the subject matter of the dispute, though it would perhaps be more helpful to state that the actions of the respondent state must be definite and unequivocal.[15] It may not be sufficient, for example, for the claimant state to show that the individual entered the territory of the respondent state on a passport issued by the claimant state, and, when registering as an alien resident, gave his nationality as that of, and was entered in the records as a national of, the claimant state. In the *Nottebohm* case, the International Court held that such circumstances were not enough to support the argument that Guatemala had

---

13. Above, pp. 30–31.
14. 4 U.N.R.I.A.A. 616; the circumstances out of which the claim arose being similar to those of the *Kelley* claim, *ibid.*, 608.
15. Although the conduct is here stated as being that of the respondent state, it should be realised that the conduct of the claimant state could equally well preclude the claimant state from asserting that the individual concerned was its national.

recognised Nottebohm's Liechtenstein nationality. "All of these acts", the Court said, "have reference to the control of aliens in Guatemala and not to the exercise of diplomatic protection. When Nottebohm thus presented himself before the Guatemala authorities, the latter had before them a private individual: there did not thus come into being any relationship between governments. There was nothing in all this to show that Guatemala then recognised that the naturalisation conferred upon Nottebohm gave Liechtenstein any title to the exercise of protection."[16]

The Court was faced with a problem because it is most likely to follow from the fact that an alien has lived in a state for a long period of time without acquiring the nationality of that state, that he will have been treated as an alien by being subjected to all the restrictions placed on aliens under the laws of that state. To the extent that the principle of the "genuine link" may be based upon residence, the raising of an estoppel from the fact that while so resident the individual concerned has been treated as an alien, or more particularly as a national of the claimant state, is likely to have a contradictory effect. The Court's way out of this dilemma was to suggest that acts by one state dealing with the control of aliens were irrelevant to the issue of diplomatic protection by another state because the acts in question did not bring about any relationship between the states.

The Court's reference to the need for the conduct to bring about a relationship is unfortunate because it is inconsistent with generally accepted notions of estoppel. In the cases of dual nationality referred to earlier it is clear that long residence of a person in one of the states of whom he was a national would prevent a claim being presented on his behalf by the other national state. However, if the state of residence had, even though only under its laws relating to the control of aliens, treated the individual as an alien, that state would scarcely be allowed subsequently to argue that the individual was in fact its national, despite the absence of a connection between the two states arising out of the conduct of the respondent state. The conduct was not only inconsistent with the subsequent assertions of the respondent state, it was definitely and unequivocally inconsistent.

In the *Nottebohm* case, the holding of the passport, the entry in official Guatemalan records as a Liechstein national, were not definitive and unequivocal. It must be remembered that Nottebohm was naturalised according to Liechtenstein law in 1939, but he had been resident in Guatemala since 1905. To the Guatemalan authorities he was still an alien; for purely administrative purposes it made no difference to them whether he was a German national or a citizen of Liechtenstein. As soon as it became important for the Guatemalan authorities to decide Nottebohm's nationality when Guatemala entered the war against Germany in 1943, it is significant that they chose to treat him as a German alien enemy.[17]

---

16. I.C.J. Rep. 1955, at p. 18.
17. Long residence and continuous treatment of a foreign resident as having a certain nationality might well give rise to an estoppel: see *Maunder* claim, British *Digest*, Vol. 5, p. 368.

Thirdly, it is fundamental to the notion of estoppel that the conduct must be by the party alleged to be estopped, i.e. the state concerned. As it is the loss of the right of the state to advance a particular argument, the activities of the individual alone are not conclusive. In the *Flegenheimer* claim,[18] the Italian Government contended that Flegenheimer's apparent nationality had been German because he had made use of a German passport in dealings with the Italian authorities. The Commission held that an individual could not by his conduct create an "apparent" nationality to which he was not entitled: there was no such thing in international law as an "apparent" nationality. This argument by the Italian Government was something of a hybrid between the notion of the "dominant" nationality in cases of dual nationality and the notion of estoppel. It could not be a case of a dominant nationality because the Germans had deprived Flegenheimer of his German nationality; it could not be a case of estoppel, because the United States had in no way held out Flegenheimer as a German national. His use of a German passport had nothing to do with the United States Government.

b CORPORATIONS AND THEIR SHAREHOLDERS

It has already been suggested that *prima facie* a corporation has the "nationality" of the state in which it is incorporated. However, as this nationality denotes only a similarity with the rules governing the allocation of nationality to individuals, it is perhaps less misleading to refer to corporations as possessing a "national character" rather than a nationality. Nevertheless, the term nationality is used with great frequency at government level in referring to the national character of corporations; but it should not for this reason be allowed to obscure the distinctions between the nationality of individuals and the nationality of corporations. The fact of being born in a state, or born of a father who is the national of a state, denotes some connection with a state, but the creation of a company under the laws of a state need denote no substantial or real connection at all. The fact of incorporation alone would therefore seem to be an inadequate basis for the exercise of diplomatic protection. The consequences of applying incorporation as the test to the exclusion of all other criteria would be on the one hand to enable a state to intervene on behalf of corporations owned partly or entirely by foreign nationals; and on the other to enable a state to treat arbitrarily entities established under its own laws even though owned largely by aliens.

i *Protection of corporations created under the laws of the claimant state*

Because a corporation *prima facie* has the national character of the state of incorporation, incorporation alone has been relied upon by states claiming on behalf of corporations the property of which has been seized by the respondent state. Nevertheless, the trend in state practice has been to

---

18. Above, p. 410.

require, in addition to registration, some degree of national control of, or beneficial ownership of shares in, the company concerned. In this context reference can be made to both American and British practice.

Although claims on behalf of United States companies were rare before the present century, it seemed to be well settled in the American view that "a government may intervene on behalf of a company incorporated under its laws, or under the laws of a constituent state or province. In such case the act of incorporation is considered as clothing the artificial person thereby created with the nationality of its creator, without regard to the citizenship of the individuals by whom the securities of the company may be owned."[19] Nevertheless, as a matter of "long standing practice", although the State Department accepted that "claims of American corporations, regardless of the nationality of the owners of the shares, could be filed with . . . Claims Commissions" the Department did "refrain from pressing diplomatically the claims of American corporations in which there was no substantial American interest".[20] In other words, where the beneficial ownership was entirely or mainly in foreign hands, the United States would exercise its discretion against interfering diplomatically on behalf of a corporation incorporated in any of the states of the Union, even though in law it might be entitled to recover reparation for any losses suffered by the corporation.

The attitude of the British Foreign Office is similar. In 1896, a company, Enrique Cortes & Co., incorporated in England, but the principal members and entire shareholders of which were Colombian citizens, enquired whether, in case of disorder in Colombia, the company could seek the protection of the British Government. The matter was referred to the Law Officers who reported that in their opinion "the principle ought not to be recognised that foreigners, by registering themselves here as a Limited Company, are entitled to claim from Her Majesty's Government the protection accorded to British subjects in foreign countries". In each case, the circumstances should be looked at: no "hard and fast line" could be laid down "as to the amount of British interest which would entitle a company to British protection". In this case the enquirers should, however, be informed that the British Government would not be prepared to protect their commercial operations or property: their activities must be carried on entirely on their own responsibility.[1]

While it is thus clear that neither the American nor the British Governments would take up a claim on behalf of a company incorporated under its laws, but owned and operated entirely by foreign nationals, the question does arise whether, if a claim were presented to an international tribunal, the absence of any connection other than incorporation would

---

19. Moore, *Digest*, Vol. 6, p. 641.
20. Hackworth, *Digest*, Vol. 5, p. 839. The U.S. Foreign Claims Settlement Commission will usually require a fifty per cent holding by U.S. nationals before considering the payment of compensation to the corporation: see below, p. 420.
1. British *Digest*, Vol. 5, p. 514: see also the Inter-Departmental Committee Report of 1913, *ibid.*, p. 527, esp. at pp. 529–30.

defeat the claim. The view of the State Department as quoted above was that by international law, such a claim would be successful. In a number of isolated cases before various arbitral tribunals, a state did succeed in pressing claims on behalf of companies incorporated under its laws, despite the fact that beneficial ownership was vested in non-nationals. In the *Burrowes Rapid Transit Company* case,[2] the Mexico/U.S.A. General Claims Commission held that the question as to whether the claim came within its jurisdiction did not depend on the nationality of Greenstreet (the Company's receiver) or of the creditors: Greenstreet was only a representative of an insolvent corporation, and the nationality of the creditors was just as irrelevant as was that of the stockholders in case of a solvent company. As the Transit Company had been incorporated under the laws of Delaware, one of the states of the U.S.A., from the point of view of international law, the claim had been properly presented by the United States Government.

It should be borne in mind, however, that both this decision and the State Department communication referred to above date from the mid-1920s, and it would appear necessary to reconsider this view in the light of the *Nottebohm* case. If the International Court is prepared to interpose a requirement that there should be a genuine link between an individual and any nationality he may have acquired, it seems at least likely that an international tribunal today would require a similar link between a corporation and a state attempting to take up a claim on its behalf. As has already been shown, even in the practice of the United Kingdom and the United States there has been a reluctance to pursue claims on behalf of companies without some connection with the claimant state other than incorporation under its laws.

An inter-departmental committee, set up by the British Foreign Secretary in 1913 and comprising representatives of the Foreign Office and of the Board of Trade, produced an interim report in the same year that elaborated on the criteria which should be taken into account in deciding whether or not to provide diplomatic protection for companies registered in Britain.[3] In the Committee's opinion the basic test should be where the seat of control was situated. Companies the seat of control of which was within British territory should receive protection. However, the Committee did not believe that companies controlled from outside should be ignored. Providing there were sufficient *bona fide* directors (i.e. directors taking an active part in the affairs of the company) having British nationality and residence, even those companies should receive protection. In the Committee's view "membership of the board of a company constitutes a more satisfactory test than the nationality of the shareholders, or the amount of the share capital registered in the name of the shareholders of any particular nationality, because of the ease with which shares can be registered in the name of another person".

---

2. 4 U.N.R.I.A.A., 462.
3. British *Digest*, Vol. 5, p. 527, esp. at pp. 529–30.

The possible significance of control as a factor in establishing the right of a state to intervene on behalf of a company incorporated under its laws is apparent even in some of the cases where incorporation seems to have been preferred to the nationality of the shareholders. In the claim presented on behalf of the *Agency of Canadian Car and Foundry Company, Ltd.*,[4] a corporation created under New York law, before the U.S./Germany Mixed Claims Commission, the German Government argued that the claim was inadmissible because the entire stock in the Agency was owned by a parent Canadian company. The opinion of the American Commissioner set out a series of facts upon which the United States based its right to present the claim, the *first* of which was that the Agency had always had its offices in New York City. It was also stated that a sizeable (about a third) proportion of the shares in the parent company were held by U.S. citizens, a proportion that had risen to approximately half at the time the claim was heard. However, the question who should be considered a U.S. national within the meaning of the agreement establishing the Commission had already been decided by the Umpire: "the existence or non-existence of American nationality at a particular time must be determined by the law of the United States". Under American law it was well settled that "regardless of the place of residence or citizenship of the incorporators or shareholders, the sovereignty by which a corporation was created, or under whose laws it was organised, determines its national character". But even if the authorities cited by the German Agent supported his contention that a state could not present a claim on behalf of a corporation controlled from abroad, the United States' claim in the present case would still be admissible. Although there might be "some form of *remote* control in the parent company, the *direct effective* control of the claimant company was in the New York corporation. . . . Certainly the activities and property of the claimant company were fully impressed with American nationality".

With the advent of the genuine link as the basis of nationality for the purposes of diplomatic protection, it may be that incorporation alone is no longer sufficient, but it is uncertain what emphasis should be placed on the alternative criteria (nationality of shareholders; the place from which control is exercised; the nationality of the individual directors who run the company, etc.). The nationality of individuals for the purposes of diplomatic protection will depend upon a balance of connecting factors (business interests; family ties; mode of living, etc.) in a particular case. Similarly with corporations, the nationality of shareholders may be of more importance than the place from which control is exercised in one case, but not in another: the factors which demonstrate the link between the state and the corporation created under its laws will vary with the circumstances.

---

4 Hackworth, *Digest*, Vol. 5, p. 833.

ii *Claims on behalf of shareholders in foreign corporations*

It follows from the proposition that the basic requirement of diplomatic protection is the incorporation of the company under the law of the claimant state that a state cannot intervene on behalf of a foreign corporation solely on the ground that a percentage of the shareholders are its nationals. It does not necessarily follow, however, that a state is altogether powerless to exercise its right of diplomatic protection over its nationals simply as shareholders, although its right to do so may be limited.

The problem is of particular importance where the state alleged to be responsible for the loss is also the state where the company was incorporated. The reasons why this should be so are obvious enough. In the first place, where the company was incorporated under the law of a third state, it is possible that the third state will itself be able to recover in respect of the company's losses. Secondly, in a number of instances states have granted concessions to foreign nationals on condition that they operate through a company incorporated under the law of the state making the grant. As very often this procedure is required in order to curtail or in an attempt to defeat altogether the rights of foreign states to protect their nationals, it becomes crucial to examine the practice of states to discover how far claims on behalf of shareholders may be admissible.

In the *Delagoa Bay Railway Company* case,[5] an American citizen had acquired a concession to build a railway in a Portuguese colony providing he formed a company under Portuguese law to carry out the project. The American assigned his concession to the company in return for the great majority of shares in the company. In order to comply with the requirements of British financiers who were prepared to support this venture, the American transferred his entire interest in the Portuguese company to a new company, the Delagoa Bay Company, created under English law. The American was then assigned the entire stock in the English company. While the railway was in the course of construction, a dispute arose between the Portuguese company and the Portuguese authorities over the terminus of one end of the line. Despite representations by the British and American governments, the Portuguese Government rescinded the concession, and took possession of the railway so far completed. The British representative in Lisbon was instructed to inform the Portuguese Foreign Minister *inter alia* that, in the British view, the Portuguese action was "wrongful, and to have violated the clear rights and injured the interests of the British company" and that as the Portuguese company was "practically defunct" the British company had "no remedy except through the intervention of its own government". This line was followed by a subsequent American protest which stated that "the Portuguese company being without remedy, and having now practically ceased to exist, the only recourse of those whose property has been confiscated is the intervention of their respective governments". Eventually the Portuguese

---

5   British *Digest*, Vol. 5, p. 535.

Government agreed to pay an amount of compensation to be decided upon by the Swiss Federal Council: the subsequent award was duly paid by Portugal.

The significance of this case is that it marked a departure from earlier refusals by both British and American Governments to take up claims on behalf of shareholders in foreign companies. The earlier view had been based entirely upon the common law attitude towards the separate legal personality of corporations. The *Delagoa Bay* case was a recognition that the corporate personality of a company should not enable a foreign state to destroy the economy of a company while leaving it by municipal law at least as a still existing entity.

The importance of this consideration is further emphasised by the dispute between the United States and the United Kingdom over the destruction of the installations of the *Romano-Americana Company*, a subsidiary of the Standard Oil Company.[6] Romano-Americana had been incorporated under Roumanian law. In 1916, the Allied Powers, which at that time did not include the United States, prevailed upon the Roumanian Government to destroy the company's installations to prevent them falling into enemy hands. The United Kingdom and the other Allied Powers undertook to indemnify the Roumanian Government against loss resulting from this action. Although the demolition was carried out under the supervision of a British officer, the United Kingdom argued that it had been authorised by the Roumanian Government who must bear responsibility for what had occurred. Ultimately the United States sought compensation from Roumania, but, for present purposes, the important question was the reply of the United Kingdom to the United States on the issue of diplomatic intervention on behalf of shareholders:

"His Majesty's Government readily admit that many cases might be cited in which a Government has used its good offices in the interests of its own nationals who are stockholders in a foreign corporation; but it will be found upon examination that the cases in which the right of a Government to intervene on behalf of the shareholders of such a corporation, for the purpose of establishing a claim against another Government, has been admitted, are few in number and exhibit certain marked characteristics, none of which are present in the case now under consideration.

Cases of this kind fall, generally speaking, into two classes: (1) where the actions of the Government against whom the claim is made has, in law or in fact, put an end to the Company's existence, or by confiscating its property, has compelled it to suspend operations; (2) where by special agreement between the two Governments a right to claim compensation has been accorded to the shareholders. From the second class of case it is plain that no principle of international law can be deduced. The first class, so far from being an exception to the general rule, is in fact an example of its application; for it is not until a company has ceased to have an active existence or has gone into liquidation that the interest of its shareholders ceases to be merely the right to share in the company's profits and becomes a right to share in its actual surplus assets."[7]

---

6. Hackworth, *Digest*, Vol. 5, p. 840.   7. *Ibid.*, p. 843.

While there is thus support for the admissibility of claims on behalf of individual shareholders in foreign companies, and there are also a number of pronouncements particularly by the United Kingdom of the circumstances in which such claims may be advanced, it must be admitted that from such limited evidence it is hardly possible to derive any clear rule of international law to that effect. The position is made even more obscure by the inconsistency in the practice of the United States and the United Kingdom in the various "global agreements" they have negotiated since the Second World War with a number of other states (mainly Communist States in Europe) as a means of settling all outstanding claims. While agreements negotiated by the United States generally accept the principle that a shareholder in a foreign corporation, the assets of which have been nationalised, is entitled to compensation,[8] agreements negotiated by the United Kingdom have referred only to property owned "directly or indirectly" by British nationals.[9] And in dealing with provisions in this form, the Foreign Claims Commission, established by the Foreign Compensation Act, 1950, has been guided entirely by the detailed provisions of the Order in Council issued to determine the method by which the compensation paid under each settlement is to be distributed. The result has been to give an artificial and widely differing interpretation to "property owned directly or indirectly" depending upon which Order is being applied; the most that can be said is that claims on behalf of shareholders are not inadmissible solely on the ground of the foreign national character of the corporation concerned.

iii *Claims on behalf of shareholders in companies incorporated in, but having no substantial link with, the claimant state*

Despite the earlier discussions within the Foreign Office on the question of whether incorporation alone within British territory should be a basis for diplomatic protection, British practice in relation to the settlement of foreign claims by "global agreement" after the Second World War has uniformly accepted incorporation irrespective of beneficial ownership as the test of "nationality". While this has not precluded altogether the distribution of funds by the Foreign Claims Commission to United Kingdom nationals holding shares in foreign corporations on the ground that their claims were admissible, it has meant that no problems are created by minority British interests in companies incorporated under the laws of the United Kingdom or of its overseas colonies.

However, as it is in keeping with the concept of a genuine link between the state and the "person" it seeks to protect on the diplomatic plane that there should exist companies on behalf of which the state of incorporation is unable to intervene, it would appear desirable that some principles

---

8. See Lillich and Christenson, *International Claims: Their Preparation and Presentation*, pp. 15–20.
9. See Lillich, *International Claims: Postwar British Practice*, pp. 36–52.

should provide for a minority shareholding in such circumstances. The United States Foreign Claims Settlement Commission can consider claims by shareholders in any "nonnational" corporation. By a "nonnational" corporation is meant either a foreign corporation or an American corporation the beneficial American interest in which is less than fifty per cent. In other words, although a claim on behalf of an American corporation is inadmissible where the American shareholding is less than fifty per cent, individual American shareholders in such a corporation may nevertheless present claims.[10]

The practice of municipal Claims Commissions of this type will be of some value in assessing the present rules of international law in so far as their decisions might constitute particular applications of more general principles for which stronger evidence of state practice exists. However, in the final analysis, state practice has largely been *ad hoc,* and it is to be hoped that some at least of the uncertainties in the law as it now stands will shortly be resolved by the International Court. In the *Barcelona Traction* case, the Belgian government is seeking reparation on behalf of a number of Belgian shareholders in a company incorporated in Canada. In addition to having to establish that the activities of the Spanish state affecting the company are wrongful according to international law, the Belgian government must also show that Belgium has a right to present a claim on behalf of its nationals who are shareholders in that company.

B. The bases of responsibility for indirect wrongs

a DENIAL OF JUSTICE

It is obvious enough that every injury suffered by an alien in foreign territory is not an international wrong. The American in Paris who is beaten up by local hooligans is not for that reason alone entitled to have a diplomatic claim presented on his behalf against the French Government by the State Department. The injury is a wrongful act according to French law: international law is in no way concerned with the incident.

The matter can only come on to the international plane if the French authorities can be in some way inculpated in what occurred. This may be the case if the French authorities had connived at or failed to take adequate measures to prevent such incidents against foreigners (a possibility which is dealt with later); or if, following the incident, the French authorities fail to make an adequate attempt to apprehend those responsible, or if the French courts fail to do justice either in criminal proceedings, or in a civil claim for damages brought by the victim against his assailants. It is with

---

10. In some cases minority shareholders might be without remedy on the ground that the United States would not intervene at all if there was not a substantial interest in a nonnational corporation: see Lillich and Christenson, *op. cit.,* pp. 18–20.

the subsequent failure to do justice that we are concerned. It is this denial of justice which will bring the matter on to the international plane.

What, then, in more precise terms is meant by a denial of justice? It is clear from what has already been stated that it involves any failure to take adequate steps to apprehend and punish offenders, redress injuries etc. Article 9 of the Harvard Draft on the Responsibility of States[11] described a denial of justice as a "denial, unwarranted delay or obstruction of access to courts, gross deficiency in the administration of judicial or remedial process, failure to provide those guarantees which are generally considered indispensable to the proper administration of justice, or a manifestly unjust judgment". The expression, "generally considered indispensable" is a less emphatic alternative to "according to the standards set by international law". Although those who drew up the Research Draft deliberately phrased Article 9 in general terms, and criticisms have been made as to the erratic application of the concept of denial of justice in this respect, it can only be justified as a basis of international responsibility if it is defined in terms of an international law standard.

This international law standard would seem to be based upon two propositions:

1. If the standards of the local administration of justice are higher than those of the minimum standards required by international law, the alien will be entitled to the benefits of the higher standards either on the ground that he should not be the subject of discrimination, or because international law will insist on the observance of those standards irrespective of discrimination.

2. It is, however, no defence to show that an alien has been treated no worse than nationals of the respondent state if the standard of treatment is lower than the minimum standard required by international law.

While a variety of treaties have guaranteed equality of treatment to and among aliens,[12] non-discrimination has yet to receive general acceptance as a rule of customary international law, although it does apply to certain types of state conduct. It would apply to seizure of foreign property, but probably not to a refusal by a state to allow aliens to acquire certain types of property (a number of states still retain rules preventing aliens acquiring ownership of land within their territory) and certainly not to discrimination in matters of immigration. In the context of the present discussion, it *would* fall short of the standards of non-discrimination required by customary international law for a state to grant to nationals procedural advantages in the administration of justice not accorded to aliens, irrespective of whether the advantages exceeded the minimum standards of international law.

The *Faulkner* claim[13] before the Mexico/United States Claims Commission shows the importance of compliance with the local law as the first

---

11. (1929) 23 A.J.I.L. Supp., p. 173.
12. See the discussion of such treaties in the *Oscar Chin* case, P.C.I.J. Rep., Ser. A/B, No. 63; *Minority Schools* case, P.C.I.J. Rep., Ser. A, No. 15.
13. 4 U.N.R.I.A.A. 67.

step in establishing responsibility, before considering whether the conduct, though complying with the local law, falls short of an acceptable standard. Two of Faulkner's complaints were that he had been transferred from one prison to another in a way repugnant to his self-respect, and that, while in detention, his hotel valise had been opened and searched. The Commission held that these allegations could not in themselves "furnish a separate basis for complaints". They were incidental to the treatment of which, if proved, he could justifiably complain, but, providing they were consistent with Mexican law, they could not "in themselves contain anything contrary to international rules and duties."

In practice, of course, the cases where an alien is able to show that the high standards of the local procedures have not been complied with *because* he is an alien will be rare. Most cases of deliberate discrimination against aliens involve conduct falling short of the minimum standards set by international law. However, it may be that the alien does not have to show that he has been discriminated against because he is an alien (although his case will be that much stronger if he can). The failure of the authorities to . allow him all the advantages of the local law may in itself be evidence upon which his own government can base a claim.

While this analysis may be supportable in theory, there is also support for the view that in practice the minimum standard set by international law is itself a variable concept. It must vary to take into account the special measures a state will take in time of emergency (for example, if it is involved in a war) or that a government will take in cases of rebellion or civil disorder. It should also take into account the difficulties of administering justice in less-developed or less stable regions of the world. There have been occasions on which these problems have been recognised. In the *Faulkner* claim mentioned above, and in other international claims, tribunals have accepted that the absence of proper records by the respondent state of the measures taken against a particular alien may be excused if the loss was caused by the activities of rebels. However, while the difficulty of controlling the activities of revolutionaries or bands of marauders has been recognised in principle, many of the associated problems of life in such conditions have been ignored. Hasty police action in some cases, inertia in others; the virtual autonomy of local police and judicial authorities resulting from an absence of adequate communications with the regional or central capital; an attitude that human life is cheap; such factors make the criteria of the professionally trained international lawyer from Europe or from the United States seem divorced from reality. The many extraordinary cases involving injury to American nationals or their property heard by the Mexican/U.S. Claims Commission were not extraordinary occurrences in the context of life in Mexico at the time. The Mexican argument in a number of these claims was that if foreigners came to work in Mexico they must accept life as they found it, and should not be entitled to more favourable treatment than that meted out to Mexican nationals. Almost as often as it was raised, this defence was rejected.

In a number of cases, of which the *Roberts* claim is perhaps the best known,[14] the Commission held Mexico responsible for cruel and inhumane treatment to prisoners. Although these cases are thus primarily examples of wrongs by state authorities against foreign nationals the main features of which will be considered later, they do provide excellent illustrations of the notion of an international law standard extraneous to the idea of equality of treatment between nationals and aliens. It was alleged that Roberts was kept along with as many as thirty or forty other men in "a room thirty-five feet long and twenty feet wide with stone walls, earthen floor, straw roof, a single window, a single door and no sanitary accommodations": that the prisoners had no washing facilities; that they were given no opportunity to take exercise; and that the food given them was "scarce, unclean, and of the coarsest kind." The Mexican Government did not deny these allegations but argued that Roberts had been accorded the same treatment as that given to everyone else. In upholding the American claim on this point the Commission commented that facts "with respect to equality of treatment of aliens and nationals may be important in determining the merits of a complaint of mistreatment of an alien. But such equality is not the ultimate test of the propriety of the acts of authorities in the light of international law. That test is, broadly speaking, whether aliens are treated in accordance with ordinary standards of civilisation."

While this was an extreme example which should not be countenanced by any penal system, there were less obvious cases of maltreatment in which claims were allowed. Faulkner claimed that he was kept for five days in verminous and repulsive filth. After making allowances for "some apparent exaggerations in the claimant's presentation of facts", the Commission held that he had been "in this house of detention for some five days under conditions that were, for an educated man, intolerable." But is this not applying too high a standard to a country where, at the time, conditions *were* primitive? And in the *Swinney* claim,[15] Mexico was held responsible for the killing of an American citizen. The American was engaged in a trapping expedition on a branch of the Rio Grande which formed the boundary between Mexico and the United States. That part of the river was under close supervision by the Mexican authorities because of smuggling activities and because it was used as a crossing place for revolutionaries. The Commission held that, whatever suspicions the Mexican officers may have had, their action in shooting at Swinney had been precipitous. "Human life in these parts, on both sides, seems not to be appraised so highly as international standards prescribe". The absence of

---

14. 4 U.N.R.I.A.A. 77, at p. 80; see also *Faulkner, ibid.*, 67 at p. 70; *Strother* (an associate of Roberts) *ibid.*, p, 262, etc. Of course, cases of false imprisonment, maltreatment while under arrest by state officials, etc., are logically *prima facie* breaches of international law and should therefore be subject to the local remedies rule (see below, pp. 444–446) but they have traditionally been classified as examples of denials of justice and no question of local remedies has been raised in relation to them.

15. *Ibid.*, p. 98; see also *Garcia* claim by Mexico against the United States, *ibid.*, p. 119.

bad faith in judicial procedures and of barbarity in the treatment of accused persons are specific instances of what an international law standard can reasonably require, but it is hardly for international law to require a change in the way of life of a nation in order to meet its obligations to aliens. An alien by entering a foreign state does not submit himself to judicial or administrative bad faith or barbarity, but he should take the way of life of the inhabitants as he finds it.

The distinction between the way of life on the one hand and judicial and penal administration on the other may be difficult to draw, but it is a distinction that should be made if the international law standard is not to be an arbitrary yard-stick to impose unreasonably high standards on states that have not highly developed police, communications, and prison systems. If many of the inhabitants of a state live in squalid conditions, why should the prisons of that state be of a very much higher standard? Or if a gun fight is the likely result of an attempt to arrest a suspected smuggler or revolutionary, how far is it reasonable to require a police or customs officer to delay firing to discover whether the suspect will himself open fire? While international law should set a standard, it is a standard which should take into account local conditions, and not be a reflection of the standards of fully developed communities.

With this criticism of the notion of an international law standard in mind, some comment is necessary on the application of the standard to situations involving injury to aliens by nationals of the respondent state. The obligation to do justice in the case will not be broken if justice is not done through deficiencies in its administration, unless those deficiences are so glaring as to give rise to a presumption of bad faith.

In the case of *Neer*,[16] a claim was presented on behalf of the widow and daughter of an American citizen who had been shot down by a group of armed men while working in Mexico. The Commission accepted that the local authorities could and should have acted in a more vigorous and effective way, particularly on the day following the incident. Indeed the agent of the State Attorney General and the State Governor, who proposed that the local judge should be removed from office, were obviously of the same opinion. However, in the view of the Commission, Mexico could not be held responsible; there was "a long way between holding that a more active and more efficient course of procedure might have been pursued on the one hand, and holding that this record presents such a lack of diligence and of intelligent investigation as constitutes an international delinquency, on the other hand." Without attempting to lay down a precise formula, it was possible to hold that the treatment of an alien, in order to constitute such a delinquency, "should amount to an outrage, to bad faith, to wilful neglect of duty, or to an insufficiency of governmental action as far short of international standards that every reasonable and impartial man would readily recognise its insufficiency. Whether the insufficiency proceeds from deficient execution of an intelligent law or from the fact that the laws of

---

16.   4 U.N.R.I.A.A. 60.

the country do not empower the authorities to measure up to international standards is immaterial."

This case may be contrasted with the *Janes* claim[17] arising out of a not dissimilar incident. However, the killing of Janes was the work of one man, a former employee of Janes' company named Pedro Carbajal, and took place in view of several witnesses. The local police Comisario, although informed of Janes' death within five minutes of the crime, delayed for half an hour in assembling a posse, and then insisted upon a further delay while horses were provided for his men by the mining company. The posse failed to apprehend Carbajal, although the latter had been on foot and remained for a week after the shooting within six miles of the nearby town. Later, when Carbajal moved to a place some seventy-five miles away, his whereabouts was communicated to the authorities in that area, but they also made no move to apprehend him. Later a reward was offered by the mining company, and a detachment of troops was sent to the town where Carbajal was reported to have been, but by then Carbajal had moved on. He was never arrested. The Commission were unanimous in holding that "there was clearly such a failure on the part of the Mexican authorities to take prompt and efficient action to apprehend the slayer as to warrant an award of indemnity."

b WHERE THE ORIGINAL INJURY IS CAUSED BY THE STATE

Where the involvement of the respondent state is brought about by the wrongful act itself, it is permissible to talk in terms of a *prima facie* breach of international law. The state of the injured national has the right to intervene on the diplomatic level to insist that the respondent state remedy the wrong it has already committed. In other words, the incident is already a matter of *international concern* because the respondent state was involved in what happened from the outset, even though the respondent state will only be *responsible* for the injury once it fails to provide adequate redress through "local remedies". This situation should be clearly distinguished from a case of "denial of justice" where it is only the subsequent failure to punish the private offender or to provide other means of legal redress to the injured alien which brings the issue on to the international plane at all.

Wrongful interference by a state, its organs or officials with the rights of a foreign national may occur in a variety of ways, but the separation of cases into those arising out of breaches of contractual obligations on the one hand, and those relating to tortious acts on the other would seem to be necessary in view of the different principles of international law involved. One basic reason for this divergence is the attitude of many municipal systems of law towards claims by private individuals against the state

---

17. *Ibid.*, p. 82.

itself. Until comparatively recent times, a state could not be sued in its own courts for the tortious acts of its officials, and this immunity usually attached to the officials themselves as long as they were acting in the course of their employment. A tortious act by an official of one state against the national of another state was therefore not justiciable in the courts of the former, so that *prima facie* the case could be the subject of international representations by the latter. Although today remedies are available in many states against wrongful acts by government officials, the underlying philosophy persists. The wrongful act is considered as a *prima facie* breach of an international obligation, although, if the respondent state can show that there exists a local remedy available to the injured alien, it will not be responsible for that breach.

Breaches of a contract between a state and alien were not treated according to the same principles. In the first place, municipal systems more readily provided processes for settling disputes of a contractual nature between their own state and a foreign national. Even where the courts themselves had no jurisdiction, arbitration under the terms of the contract provided a ready means of redress. As a consequence, cases of breach of contract by a state were largely assimilated to wrongs committed by private individuals. "Generally speaking the Department of State does not intervene in cases involving breaches of contract between a foreign state and a national of the United States in the absence of a showing of a denial of justice. However, it may use its informal good offices in appropriate cases in an effort to bring about an adjustment of differences. The practice of declining to intervene formally prior to a showing of denial of justice is based on the proposition that the Government of the United States is not a collection agency and cannot assume the role of endeavouring to enforce contractual undertakings freely entered into by its nationals with foreign states."[18]

i *Breaches of contractual obligations having an international character*

There have been contract situations, however, in which responsibility appears to have been based more on a direct breach by a state of its international obligations than upon a denial of justice. While it is possible to detail these situations, it is a less easy task to classify them. The most that can be attempted is to consider the factors which may give contracts of this type their international character.

1 *Legislative interference*

In resorting to its legislative power to alter the law which governs the rights and obligations of itself and the foreign national who is the other party to the contract, a state is acting in a capacity other than that of a defaulting contractor. It is *prima facie* taking the matter out of the field of

---

18. Hackworth, *Digest*, Vol. 5, p. 611.

private rights, ascertainable, if necessary, by litigation, and creating an issue of an international character. This distinction between a state breaking a contract, and a state legislating to abolish or alter its contractual obligations may be illustrated by a comparison between two cases.

In the first, the *Serbian Loans* case,[19] the Permanent Court was asked to consider a dispute between France and Serbia concerning the interpretation of a gold clause in the terms governing a loan under which a number of French bondholders advanced money to the Serbian Government. At the most, if the French argument that the clause established a gold value for payments of interest protecting the bondholders from currency depreciation was correct, the actions of the Serbian Government constituted a breach of contract. It was in no sense a question of international law, and, in normal circumstances, could only become so as the result of a denial of justice. Without discovering whether the Serbian courts would deny a claim against the Serbian Government in such circumstances, the bondholders appealed to the French Government which took up their cause. It was the conflict of views between the two governments which raised an issue on the international plane, and therefore within the Court's jurisdiction. It was common ground, the Court stated, that the Serbian Government had not rejected the intervention of the French Government (e.g. on the ground that it was premature), but had continued to rely upon its previous argument that it had carried out its obligations under the loan contracts. As this view was not shared by the French Government, there existed from that time a difference of opinion which, though "fundamentally identical" with the controversy already existing between the Serbian Government and its creditors, was nevertheless "distinct therefrom". It was the difference of opinion between the governments, and not the dispute between the Serbian Government and the French bondholders over the interpretation of their contract, which was of an international character and fell within the Court's jurisdiction.[20]

In contrast, in the case of *Certain Norwegian Loans*,[1] the dispute between the Norwegian Government and the French bondholders centred on the effect of Norwegian legislation which, if it had the consequences alleged, prevented the respondent state from honouring what in the French view were gold value clauses in the loan contracts. Although the International Court did not decide upon the merits of the dispute as it upheld one of the preliminary objections raised by Norway to its jurisdiction, individual judges did either specifically, or indirectly, deal with the "internationalisation" of the contract.

Judge Read considered the position at the outset "reasonably clear". When the French bondholder bought a Norwegian bond, the transaction came solely within the plane of national law. It was a matter in which the Court was incompetent to adjudicate, as there would have been no rules of international law applicable to the transaction. However, with the

---

19. (1929), P.C.I.J. Rep., Ser. A, No. 20.   20. *Ibid.*, p. 18.
1. I.C.J. Rep. 1957, p. 9.

passing of the Norwegian legislation and the suspension of payments in gold, the question was raised of "whether Norway could, in conformity with the principles of international law, by legislative action unilaterally modify the substance of the contracts".[2] The dispute was therefore "internationalised" by the same action that involved the "breach" of the alleged contractual obligation. And once it became internationalised, i.e. amounted to a *prima facie* breach of international law, the only remaining obstacle to international proceedings was the duty to exhaust local remedies.[3]

A similar view was expressed by Judge Lauterpacht, who was careful to limit the province of the local remedies rule to cases in which the international character of the dispute was already established, and to avoid confusing the rule with the need in other cases to show a denial of justice to establish the international nature of the wrong. He pointed out that the relevance of the many questions of international law raised by the Norwegian legislation could not "properly be denied by reference to the fact that unless and until Norwegian courts have spoken it is not certain that there has been a violation of international law by Norway. The crucial point is that, assuming that Norwegian law operates in a manner injurious to French bondholders, there are various questions of international law involved. To introduce in this context the question of exhaustion of local remedies is to make the issue revolve in a circle. The exhaustion of local remedies cannot in itself bring within the province of international law a dispute which is otherwise outside its sphere. The failure to exhaust legal remedies may constitute a bar to the jurisdiction of the Court; it does not affect the intrinsically international character of a dispute."[4]

2 *Where the contract is itself "internationalised"*

Normally, a contract entered into by a state with a foreign national will be subject to the law of the debtor state. This was the case with the Serbian loans. As the Permanent Court pointed out, they had been contracted by the Serbian State under special laws which were intended to govern the transactions and were set out on all the bonds issued. In addition, the bonds were not clearly identifiable with any other legal system, as, being bearer bonds, they were freely transferable and as also payment of interest was available in a number of foreign cities.[5] It is likely that a similar result would have been achieved under principles of English private international law which, in general, recognises that where a government raises a loan in a number of different states,[6] or under special statutory powers creating a charge on the revenues or property of the state,[7] the transaction will be governed by the law of the debtor state.

---

2. I.C.J. Rep. 1957, at pp. 87–88.
3. For the views expressed on the local remedies issue in the *Norwegian Loans* case, see below, pp. 449–450.
4. *Ibid.*, at p. 38.   5. P.C.I.J. Rep. Ser. A, No. 20, p. 42.
6. *Bonython* v. *Commonwealth of Australia*, [1951] A.C. 201.
7. *Mount Albert B.C.* v. *Australasian Temperance etc. Society*, [1938] A.C. 224; *Bonython* v. *Commonwealth of Australia* (above).

It is, of course, possible that a state will enter into a contract that is subject to some foreign system of law, either expressly or by implication. The House of Lords has held that while the fact that a state is a party to a contract is a factor of great significance in determining the proper law, it is not conclusive. It may still be possible to infer from the circumstances as a whole that the contract is governed by some other legal system.[8]

The fact that a contract entered into by a state with a foreign national is governed by the law of another state will largely remove the contract from interference by the legislative competence of the contracting state, but it will not in itself give a breach of the contract an international character. Before there could be a breach of an international obligation, there would still have to be a denial of justice by the debtor state, which in such a situation might well be a claim of immunity from the jurisdiction of the courts of the state the law of which governs the transaction.

The view has been put forward, however, that certain contracts of a quasi-public nature (a term which is deliberately imprecise) between a state and a foreign individual or corporation are "internationalised" by the fact that they are governed not by any system of municipal law but by general principles of (international) law. This possibility has obvious attractions. The contracting state may be unwilling to subject itself to a foreign system of municipal law while the other party might not wish to risk the vicissitudes that possible political changes might bring about in the law of the contracting state *vis-à-vis* its obligations to foreign nationals.[9] And if the parties can make a choice of law in this way, there is no reason why a judicial tribunal should not infer such a choice from the circumstances of the case.

Support for the proposition that contracts between states and non-international persons can be subject to international law or, at least, to some extra-municipal legal system is available in a number of well known commercial arbitrations involving concessions granted to oil companies.

In the *Abu Dhabi* arbitration,[10] the Umpire was required to decide whether an oil concession granted by the Sheikh of Abu Dhabi in 1939 covered oil rights to which Abu Dhabi might be entitled over the sea bed off its coast. In discussing the problem of the law governing the concession agreement, the Umpire accepted that if any municipal system were applicable it would be that of Abu Dhabi. However, it would have been "fanciful to suggest that in this very primitive region there is any settled body of legal principles applicable to the construction of modern commercial instruments." Nor could it be said that English law was intended to apply, because the agreement itself spoke of the intentions of the parties to act in a spirit of good will and integrity and to interpret the agreement in a reasonable manner. Such references the Umpire took to prescribe "the

---

8. *R.* v. *International Trustee for Protection of Bondholders Akt.*, [1937] A.C. 500.
9. Or, alternatively, where the law of the contracting state is not sufficiently developed to provide rules capable of dealing with the complexities of the situation; see immediately below.
10. (1951) 18 I.L.R. 144.

application of principles rooted in the good sense and common practice of the generality of civilised nations—a sort of modern law of nature."[11]

Two main theories have been advanced in order to identify this "modern law of nature". First, there are those who maintain that this is a new system of law altogether, an international commercial law based upon general principles of law synthesised from municipal systems. Such a system provides a choice of law that can reconcile the conflicting interests of the state on the one hand and the foreign individual or corporation on the other. According to this view, there is no problem arising from the fact that international law only governs the relations between entities having international personality, because this system of law is not international law in its "true" sense at all. Breach of the contract by the state concerned is not a breach of international law giving rise to a claim on the international plane, but a breach according to the proper law of the contract in the same way as a breach according to some municipal legal system would be such a breach.

The second theory is that it is possible for a contract, only one of the parties to which is endowed with international personality, to be governed by public international law. Such a contract would certainly give the individual some protection from having his rights destroyed by legislative action on the part of the contracting state. And it would seem that in theory at least breach of a contract governed by "international law" would amount to a breach of an international obligation. Only in such a case would it be possible to say that the contract is itself "internationalised".

There is some support for this alternative theory in the *Lena Goldfields* arbitration,[12] where the tribunal had to consider the law governing a concession granted by the Soviet Union to a British company. Under the concession agreement it was provided that the parties should base their relations "on the principle of goodwill and goodfaith as well as on reasonable interpretation of the terms of the Agreement." A majority of the members of the tribunal (the Soviet Government had withdrawn its arbitrator) accepted the argument of the complainant company that in regard to performance of the contract inside the Soviet Union, Russian law was applicable, but that for other purposes "the general principles of law such as those recognised by Article 38 of the Statute of the Permanent Court of International Justice . . . should be regarded as 'the proper law of the contract'."

What is not altogether clear is whether this reference to "general principles of law *such* as those recognised by Article 38" is to international law at all. The use of the word "such" may suggest that the general principles are "similar" to those referred to in Article 38, but that they are not for that reason automatically to be considered as "international law". The chief reason, put forward by the Lena company and accepted by the

---

11. (1951) 18 I.L.R. 144, at p. 149; see also *Ruler of Qatar v. International Marine Oil Co.* (1953), 20 I.L.R. 534.
12. (1929–30), 5 A.D. Case No. 258.

tribunal, for the application of general principles to matters "external" to the Soviet Union was that many of the terms of the contract "contemplated the application of international rather than merely national principles of law." But even this statement is not the same as saying that the terms contemplated the application of international law. International principles of law could just as well be taken as referring to principles of law with a general or near universal currency. While this decision may give support to the second theory, it can readily be reconciled with the notion of an alternative system of law exterior to municipal systems but not forming part of international law.

Such an interpretation was adopted by the tribunal which decided the *Aramco* arbitration.[13] Under the arbitration agreement between Saudi Arabia and the Arabian American Oil Company (Aramco), the arbitration tribunal was required to decide a dispute over their concession agreement in accordance with Saudi Arabian law in so far as matters within the jurisdiction of Saudi Arabia were concerned, and in accordance with the law deemed by the tribunal to be applicable in so far as matters beyond the jurisdiction of Saudi Arabia were concerned. The tribunal stated that this provision was in conformity with the rules of private international law adopted in most civilised states, and that in deciding the precise legal system to be applied in matters falling beyond the jurisdiction of Saudi Arabia the tribunal would be guided by those rules. It decided that, in accordance with "the most progressive teachings" in this field, it should apply "the law which corresponded best to the nature of the legal relationship between the Parties". As the concession was not an agreement between two states, but between a state and a private American Corporation, it could not be governed by public international law.[14] The concession itself and the subsequent arbitration agreement established that aspects of the concession fell outside the province of Saudi Arabian law. The tribunal rejected the law of any American state as an alternative because an application of the principle of sovereign immunity might prevent an American court exercising jurisdiction.[15] The tribunal's conclusion was that the concession agreement itself constituted "the fundamental law" of

---

13. (1958) 27 I.L.R. 117.

14. Yet, in apparent contradiction, the Tribunal held that the arbitration itself (by which it presumably meant the procedural and jurisdictional rules) could only be governed by international law on the grounds that the parties had expressed their common intention that it should not be governed by the law of Saudi Arabia, and that there was no basis for applying the American law of the other party. But if general principles of law could be called in aid to supplement the concession agreement between the parties, surely the arbitration agreement was similarly the "fundamental law" of the arbitration and subject to interpretation and application in the light of those general principles?

15. This is hardly a *conclusive* reason for rejecting the law of an American state. Such reason was accepted as conclusive by the English Court of Appeal, following earlier authorities, in *R. v. International Trustee for Protection of Bondholders Akt.*, [1937] A.C. at pp. 509-511, but rejected by the House of Lords in the same case. In the words of Lord Atkin, at p. 531:

"It cannot be disputed that a Government may expressly agree to be bound by a foreign law. It seems to me equally indisputable that without any expressed intention the inference that a Government so intended may be necessarily inferred from the circumstances."

the parties and in so far as doubts might remain as to the content or meaning of the agreement, it was "necessary to resort to the general principles of law and to apply them in order to interpret and even to supplement the respective rights and obligations of the Parties".

The award in the *Aramco* arbitration strongly supports the view that contracts of a concessionary type not governed by the municipal law of the grantor state are subject to general principles of law and not to international law. Not only was international law expressly rejected as an alternative to some system of municipal law on the ground that the parties were not both endowed with international personality, but also the *Lena Goldfields* arbitration was referred to as supporting the selection of general principles of law on the same basis as the award in the *Abu Dhabi* case. Although the issue may not be conclusively settled that these general principles, though often similar in content to those referred to in Article 38 (1) (c) of the Statute of the International Court, are not international law as such, but a new system of legal rules in the field of international commercial transactions, principle and authority clearly favour such a conclusion.

Once the principle is accepted that the proper law in such cases is not public international law, it is clear that breach of a commercial contract subject to general principles as its "proper law" is not *ipso facto* a breach of international law. An award against a state by a tribunal in an international commercial arbitration between the state and a foreign national is not tantamount to a finding that the state has broken its international obligations. The matter would only assume an international character if the state refused to offer an opportunity for a competent tribunal to hear the merits of the dispute, or, if it did submit to adjudication, it failed to carry out an award adverse to its interests. As long as the contract is a transaction between a state and a foreign national only, a breach of its terms by the state falls within the sphere of a system of law other than public international law.

3 Internationalisation of a contract by a collateral understanding or treaty arrangement between States

Where a treaty specifically lays down that a particular contract between one of the states party to the treaty and nationals of the other state which is a party to the treaty shall be performed or that rights under the contract shall be recognised, it is clear that a breach of the contract by the state concerned is also a breach of an international obligation owed to the other state. Similarly, it would also constitute a breach of an international obligation by the defaulting state if the indirect effect of the treaty was to reinforce the rights of a foreign national under the contract.[16] The result of creating a parallel treaty obligation to secure performance of a contract necessarily gives the combined contractual/treaty obligation an international character.

---

16. See the *Martini* case, reported in English in 25 A.J.I.L. 554.

This "internationalisation" by treaty or other international arrangement has long been recognised. In 1861, for example, the British Government was asked to intervene on behalf of British holders of Mexican bonds. The normal attitude of the British Government to such requests was that if British nationals were prepared to risk their assets in this way, they had no cause for complaint if the state concerned was unable to meet its debts. In this case, however, a British representative had negotiated an arrangement whereby a percentage of the customs duties of two Mexican ports should be assigned to satisfy the bondholders claims, and this arrangement had subsequently been confirmed and extended. The reply of the Foreign Secretary was therefore that "to the extent provided for in these arrangements" the claims of the bondholders had "acquired the character of an international obligation".[17]

It may be that, in order to establish the international character of a contract in this way, the undertaking or arrangement need not amount to a binding treaty. A statement by an official within the province of his functions to a representative of the claimant state similar to the Ihlen declaration[18] would probably be sufficient; or even when a contract is entered into to resolve an international dispute as in the *Anglo-Iranian Oil Company* case.[19] The position is, however, far from clear.

4 *Where the breach of contract takes the form of an act of confiscation*

Where the effect of the activities of the foreign state in breaking the contract is such as to destroy a property right already vested in the foreign national, international law looks at the alleged wrong from the point of view of the tortious act against property rather than from the contractual standpoint. For this reason, the issues raised will be discussed later along with other aspects of expropriation of foreign owned property, but at this stage some comment is necessary on those characteristics of a situation which classify it as "tortious" rather than contractual in nature.

The underlying distinction depends upon the creation of a right to property.[20] If the contract creates a property right in a particular "thing", a breach of that contract which has the effect of destroying the property right is, for practical purposes, an act of confiscation; a breach which does not affect such a right is not tortious in character.

In the *Shufeldt* claim[1] presented by the United States against Guatemala by Special Agreement, the arbitrator appointed under the Agreement had to consider the responsibility of Guatemala for a decree of the Legislative Assembly declaring null and void *ab initio* a contract, the benefit of which was assigned to Shufeldt, whereby he was entitled to extract chicle from a defined area of public lands for a specified period. The significance of the case lies in the fact that the parties were clearly agreed that the contract

---

17. Lord John Russell to Sir C. L. Wyke, British minister in Mexico, Moore, *Digest*, Vol. 6, p. 719.
18. Above, p. 357. 19. Above, p. 359.
20. This principle is an aspect of the notion of "acquired rights", see below, pp. 468–470.
1. 2 U.N.R.I.A.A. 1083.

itself, if it was valid, created rights of property. The decree certainly brought the contract to an end, but it could not deprive the beneficiary under the contract of his right to compensation for loss of the interest in property he had acquired under the contract. The "confiscation" of the proprietary right was sufficient to classify the activity of the respondent state as a *prima facie* breach of international law.

While the distinction between purely contractual breaches and those involving property rights may be clear enough in theory, in practice a number of borderline situations may give rise to difficulty. For example, is a debt due from the respondent state to an alien a property right or solely a contractual right? A number of cases heard by claims commissions have taken the view that postal money orders, though evidencing the indebtedness of a state, constitute property rights to the issued value of the orders.[2] Does it make any difference if the indebtedness arises out of a loan contract?

As has already been pointed out, state practice has tended towards the principle of diplomatic non-intervention in the case of alleged breaches by states of loan contracts under which they have raised funds from foreign nationals. Some additional factor has been considered necessary before the issue has been regarded as "internationalised". In other words, the loan itself does not create a property right in the amount of the debt. A refusal or failure to pay principal or interest is not in itself an act of confiscation.

ii *Tortious acts as* prima facie *breaches of international law*

1 *Activities of officials imputable to the state*

Hitherto the discussion in this Chapter has been based on the assumption that it is obvious in any given case whether or not it is the "state" which has acted in a particular way. In most cases it *will* be obvious that the state is the actor; the legislature is clearly a state organ; a government department; a local court or magistrate; a police official; all these and similar entities and individuals constitute the state. The state can only act through them.

Whatever may be the consequences of an *ultra vires* act under the municipal law of the state concerned, it would seem that the notion of the scope of an official's duties has but limited significance under international law. Once a state, through the activities of its organs or representatives, has committed a wrongful act against the person or property of a foreign national within its territory, then the practice of states supports the proposition that *prima facie* such an act constitutes a breach of international law. The reasons why this is so, whereas a similar act by an individual or group of individuals does not constitute such a breach, are first that the state is itself involved *ex hypothesi* in the former case, and secondly that under most municipal systems remedies in tort against the state and its officials were a comparatively late development. In respect of a tortious act by a state, therefore, the only remedy available to an injured alien was

2. E.g. *Hopkins* claim, 4 U.N.R.I.A.A. 41; *Cook* claim, *ibid.*, 213.

likely to be through the diplomatic intervention of his own state.

However, the principle of *ultra vires* acts was not entirely without its influence on international law. Under many municipal systems, the principle that an individual had no remedy against state officials was mitigated in cases where the official concerned had acted outside the scope of his authority. In such a situation the errant official was unable to shelter behind the act of state principle. The effect on international law was to establish the general proposition that, in the absence of a denial of justice in failing to punish or otherwise give a remedy against the defaulting official, there was no *prima facie* breach of international law by the state concerned in a case where one of its officials had caused injury to an alien as a consequence of activities altogether outside the scope of his authority.

Here, as in relation to the notion of a denial of justice, the test is not that of the municipal law of the respondent state, but that of the standard set by international law. The question that should be asked is whether, according to international law, the activities of the official concerned can be *imputed* to the state. This international standard accepted that an act within the scope of an official's authority under the law of the respondent state was imputable to the state for the very practical reason that such a situation caused no problems. The important role of the test of imputability is in cases where it is alleged that, by the law of the respondent state, the official acted outside his authority. In such circumstances it would seem that the state concerned will *prima facie* be liable for the wrongful activities of its officials which, by the standards set by international law, fall within the apparent scope of their authority. There is a wealth of authority from the jurisprudence of international arbitral tribunals supporting such a proposition.

In two cases (the *Jessie*[3] and the *Wanderer*[4]), the United States was held responsible for the exercise of the right of visit and search by its revenue officers over British ships on the high seas. Although the officers concerned had acted in good faith, they had misinterpreted the powers bestowed upon them by agreement between the two states and by Act of Congress. Their actions were, therefore, outside the scope of their actual authority, but the Tribunal was emphatic that any state was responsible for errors in judgment of its officials purporting to act within the scope of their duties.[5]

However, it is clear that it is not only in cases of errors of judgment that responsibility might lie. Even if the official concerned acts in a totally reprehensible manner, the same approach is adopted.

In the *Maal* claim,[6] the local police at the port of La Guaira had arrested a Netherlands subject and ordered him to re-embark. This conduct by the Venezuelan authorities, even if caused by the totally unfounded suspicion that he was in league with Venezuelan revolutionaries, was not a ground

---

3. 6 U.N.R.I.A.A. 57.   4. *Ibid.*, 68.
5. See also the *Union Bridge Company* case, *ibid.*, 138.
6. 10 U.N.R.I.A.A. 730.

for complaint because a state has a discretion whether or not to admit aliens to its territory. However, such a suspicion could provide no excuse for having Maal stripped in public. The umpire acquitted "the high authorities" of the Venezuelan Government "from any other purpose or thought than the mere exclusion of one regarded as dangerous to the welfare of the Government, but the acts of their subordinates in the line of their authority, however odious their acts may be, the Government must stand sponsor for".

In the case of *Quintanilla*,[7] the United States was held responsible for the death of a Mexican national whose body was discovered by a roadside soon after he had been taken into custody by a deputy sheriff and three other men. As Quintanilla had been taken into custody by a state official, the state had to account for what happened to him. Whether the deputy sheriff or someone else had deliberately killed him, the state could not absolve itself from responsibility by ignoring what happened.

Many of the cases in which responsibility arises, not from any original injury, but from a denial of justice, involve acts by officials, often in disregard of the constitutional provisions governing the exercise of their powers. In the *Roberts* case,[8] for example, the Mexican Constitution of 1917 provided that a person accused of a crime had to be brought to judgment within four months of arrest in the case of an offence the maximum penalty for which did not exceed two years imprisonment, and within twelve months if the maximum penalty was greater. Roberts was arrested on 12th May, 1922, proceedings were instituted on 17th May, but he had not been brought to trial on 16th December, 1923, the date when he was finally released. The Mexican Government did not, however, raise the unlawful nature of the activities of its officials under its own law as a possible defence, presumably because such a defence would obviously have been futile.

The contention has been advanced that a distinction should be drawn between high ranking officials and minor officials. Thus Article 7 of the 1929 Harvard Research Draft on the Responsibility of States[9] stated that whereas a State was responsible for the wrongful acts or omissions of one of its high authorities within the scope of the office or function of such authority, it was only responsible for the wrongful acts or omissions of one of its subordinate officials or employees within the scope of his office or function if there had been a denial of justice or a failure to discipline the officer or employee concerned.

Although perhaps it is possible to "interpret" the various arbitral awards to fit such a view, it is doubtful whether the exercise is worthwhile. Apart from any other considerations, it creates the unnecessary difficulty of having to distinguish between various grades of officialdom. The principle that a state is *prima facie* responsible for the wrongful acts of its officials within the general scope of their authority irrespective of rank avoids the

---

7. 4 U.N.R.I.A.A. 101.   8. *Ibid.*, 77.
9. Text in 23 A.J.I.L. Supp. 157.

difficulty and is more readily reconciled with the various arbitral awards.

An interesting case in this context was that brought by the United States on behalf of *Massey*[10] whose husband had been murdered in Mexico by a Mexican named Saenz. Saenz was later arrested, but escaped from prison when, it was alleged, the assistant jail-keeper allowed him to leave unhindered. The Mexican Government argued that it could not be liable for a denial of justice stemming from the misconduct of a minor official in violation of Mexican law and of his own duty. Commissioner Nielsen referred to the conflicting views that then existed with regard to responsibility for the acts of minor officials and to the practical difficulties that would obviously arise from distinguishing between minor and other grades of officials. He suggested that, irrespective of such a distinction, the most important factors to be taken into account were "the character of the acts alleged to have resulted in injury to persons or to property, or the nature of functions performed whenever a question is raised as to their proper discharge". It followed as "a sound general principle that, whenever misconduct on the part of any such persons, whatever may be their particular status or rank under domestic law, results in the failure of a nation to perform its obligations under international law, the nation must bear the responsibility for the wrongful acts of its servants". The denial of justice which was found to have occurred in this case was based both on the conduct of the jail-keeper and on the subsequent failure of the authorities to re-apprehend Saenz, but it is clear that the status of the officials involved was treated as irrelevant by a majority, if not all three members of the Commission.

2 *Acts altogether outside the scope of an official's authority*

The activities of an official which, even by the standards set by international law, fall outside the scope of his authority are in most cases considered in the same light as those of private individuals. In the *Cibich* claim,[11] the United States presented a claim on behalf of one of its nationals who had been arrested for drunkenness. The local police chief had taken from him a sum of about 950 pesos for safe-keeping. During the night the money was stolen by a gang of liberated prisoners and defecting policemen. As the policemen were no longer attempting to act in that capacity, their presence in the gang made no difference to the case. The Mexican government could not be responsible, as the evidence did not disclose a want of reasonable care on the part of the local police authorities in relation to the loss of the money.

Normally, therefore, the unauthorised acts and omissions of state officials will only give rise to responsibility if the state failed to take adequate measures to prevent the injury to the persons or property of aliens or if there is a subsequent failure to remedy the situation (i.e. a denial of justice). The most obvious illustrations of the former situation would be

---

10.   4 U.N.R.I.A.A. 155.
11.   *Ibid.*, 57. See also the *Mallen* claim, *ibid.*, 173.

where the authorities of the respondent state failed to prevent riots directed against foreign nationals,[12] or where the police allowed riots to continue which incidentally caused damage to the property of foreign nationals.[13]

It has been suggested, however, that in exceptional cases tribunals have been willing to hold a state liable where its officials have acted without any vestige of authority on the grounds that the state has failed in its duty to appoint reliable or competent persons to positions of authority or that, to put it in another form, the persons employed have abused the governmental powers entrusted to them.

In the *Caire* claim,[14] a French national was asked to obtain a large amount of money by a major in the Mexican army. Caire attempted unsuccessfully to obtain the money. He was thereupon arrested by the major and a number of soldiers, tortured, and finally executed. Mexico argued in its defence that the activities of the soldiers was so far outside the scope of their authority that the Mexican state could not be held responsible. This contention was rejected, but the reason for the decision in favour of France has been variously explained.

It is possible to use the case as support for the view that a state can be liable irrespective of the imputability of its agent's acts if they, in committing the wrongful act, had made use of the powers and means put at their disposal in their official capacity.[15] This has been put forward as one basis for the decision but its significance depends in part at least on the extent to which other cases support this view.

A case cited in this connection is the *Youmans* claim.[16] A group of three United States nationals was being attacked by a Mexican mob. Troops sent to protect them joined in the attack, which resulted in the death of the Americans. The Mexican government contended that as the soldiers had acted in complete disregard of their instructions, Mexico could not be held responsible for the deaths. The Commission, while recognising that a state might not be responsible in certain cases for malicious acts by officials in their private capacity, held that a state would almost invariably be responsible for wrongful acts committed by soldiers under the command of an officer. In this case the soldiers, as in the *Caire* claim, had been under the immediate supervision and in the presence of the officer in charge of them.

Although the *Youmans* decision did relate to a situation which, on the facts, it is possible to classify as a misuse of governmental authority, the Commission primarily dealt with the issue of whether or not the activities had been within, or outside, the scope of authority of the soldiers concerned. As the Commission pointed out, soldiers (or other officials)

12. *Sarropoulos* v. *Bulgarian State* (1927–8), 4 A.D. Case No. 173. See also *Zafiro* claim, 6 U.N.R.I.A.A. 160.

13 *Karpinsky* v. *Egyptian Government* (1923–4), 2 A.D. Case No. 93.

14. 5 U.N.R.I.A.A. 516.

15. See, e.g. Meron in (1957) 33 B.Y.B.I.L. 85, at p. 110.

16. 4 U.N.R.I.A.A. 110.

"inflicting personal injuries or committing wanton destruction or looting always act in disobedience of some rules laid down by superior authority. There could be no liability whatever for such misdeeds if the view were taken that any acts committed by soldiers in contravention of instructions must always be considered as personal acts". Providing the test applied by international law for determining the scope of the officials' apparent authority is a wide one (and the cases that have been discussed suggest that this is so), there is no need for an additional basis of responsibility. The misuse by officials of the powers entrusted to them by the state will always fall within the scope of their apparent authority as determined by international law. An official can hardly use his power and position as an official if he is not acting as an official, even though he may be employing his powers entirely for his own ends.

In the *Mallén* claim,[18] for example, the Deputy Constable of El-Paso, Texas, twice assaulted the local Mexican consul for whom he had a "profound aversion". On the first occasion the Constable had met Mallén casually in the street, had sworn at him, threatening to kill him, and had then slapped his face. On the second occasion, the Constable had seen Mallén on board a tram, which was proceeding from the Mexican side of the border into El-Paso. He had boarded the tram, waited until it crossed the border, savagely attacked Mallén, and, when the tram reached the vicinity of the police station, demanded that it stop so that he could remove Mallén to jail. On the occasion of the first assault, the Constable had clearly not acted as a Constable, so that responsibility could only arise out of a subsequent denial of justice, which was held not to have occurred. For the purposes of the second assault, however, it was clear that the Constable had taken advantage of his official position to pursue a private vendetta. However unreasonable his conduct, he had, according to the standards set by international law, been acting within his apparent authority.

It would seem that it is more in keeping with other authorities to accept the *Caire* case as having been decided on the ground of apparent authority. Such a view is clearly tenable. The president of the Commission, it must be admitted, placed too great an emphasis on the importance of the position under municipal law that "an act of an incompetent official is not an act of the state". He was therefore obliged to take a round-about route in his reasoning to establish an international law standard. He pointed out that for the purposes of international life, dealings would become too difficult, complicated and uncertain if foreign states were obliged to take into account the legal provisions of municipal law regulating the competences of officials within the state. It was therefore evident that the international responsibility of the state had a purely objective character. For this "objective responsibility" to apply in cases of officials acting outside their authority, it was necessary that they should have acted at least apparently (in the municipal law sense) as competent officials, or that

---

17. 4 U.N.R.I.A.A. 173.

(they could be considered as acting within this competence in the international law sense because) they had made use of powers available to them in their official capacity. The two parts of the above statement in brackets do not appear in the judgment, but they are clearly in keeping with the terms of Commissioner's pronouncements taken as a whole. Read with the passages bracketed included, it is clear that the decision is fully in keeping with the other authorities discussed.

The fact that an official has acted maliciously is relevant to the issue of whether or not he is acting as an official or as a private individual. It is a fact which, if advanced, tends to show that he is acting personally. If he has made use of official powers or his official position, however, this is a factor which rebuts any argument that, because of his personal motives, he was not acting as an official. In the *Caire* case the motives of personal gain were offset by the fact that the soldiers had made use of their powers as soldiers in threatening and finally executing the foreign national.[18]

Whatever doubts may exist in general in relation to the activities of soldiers acting illegally, international law has never imposed liability on a state in cases where troops or other groups are in open rebellion against the government of a state in circumstances outside the government's control.

In the *Home Missionary Society* case,[19] the United States presented a claim against Great Britain for the destruction of the Society's property and murder of its personnel in riots that occurred in the British Protectorate of Sierra Leone. The arbitral tribunal held that it was "a well-established principle of international law that no government can be held responsible for the act of rebellious bodies of men committed in violation of its authority, where it is itself guilty of no breach of good faith, or of no negligence in suppressing insurrection". In this case there had been no failure on the part of the British authorities to take all possible steps to safeguard persons and property in what was, at that time, a "perilous" and "barbaric" country.

3 Nationalisation of foreign owned property situated within a state

Reference has already been made to contracts which create property rights, and to the fact that a breach of the contract which has the effect of interfering with those rights, involves also a *prima facie* breach of an international obligation. However, interference with foreign property rights has assumed such importance in the field of international relations particularly since the end of the Second World War, that a more detailed examination is necessary of the principles of international law applicable to such situations.

Injury to foreign nationals or damage to their property by the organs or

---

18. The incompetence of an official might of course make unlawful an act which otherwise would not be wrongful as far as the respondent state is concerned: see *Malcoussi* v. *Egyptian Government* (1923–4), 2 A.D. Case No. 92.

19. (1920), 6 U.N.R.I.A.A. 42. Though a state may be liable for the activities of an authority which succeeded for a time in establishing itself in power: see above, pp. 109–113.

officials of a state have always been considered a basis for diplomatic intervention on the ground that such activities constitute a *prima facie* breach of international law. There may be little difference to the alien whether his property is destroyed as a result of the acts of state officials, or arbitrarily seized without payment by the state concerned. And there would seem to be no good reasons why the same principles of international law should not be applied in both types of situation.

However, even prior to the Second World War, it was apparent that international law was developing a number of special rules for dealing with the acquisition of foreign property by the state.

1. Discrimination against an individual alien or aliens in general was contrary to international law irrespective of the question whether compensation had been paid.
2. There was also support for the principle that seizure of foreign property, even if compensation was offered, was contrary to international law if the seizure was not part of a programme of public utility.
3. In cases where nationalisation was permissible, prompt, adequate and effective compensation had to be paid.

That it was possible for an expropriation to be contrary to international law even though compensation for property taken was paid may be illustrated by reference to the *Chorzow Factory* case.[20] It had been provided by the Upper Silesia Convention of 1922 that, on the transfer of sovereignty of certain territories from Germany to Poland after the First World War, existing property rights were to be maintained except that the Polish Government was granted a right of expropriation under conditions laid down in the Convention with respect all property belonging to German nationals in Upper Silesia.

In the *Polish Upper Silesia* case,[1] the Permanent Court had held that the expropriation of the Chorzow Factory was not justified under the Convention. In the subsequent proceedings the Court pointed to the significant difference between an expropriation without justification under international law, and one that, though justifiable, was not accompanied by satisfactory compensation. In the latter case, the wrongful act could be remedied by the payment of the appropriate compensation with interest from the date of the nationalisation. In the former situation, however, the amount of reparation was not limited to the value of the property but should also include a sum representing the fact that no right to take over the property existed at all.[2]

The widespread nationalisations which followed the Second World War, and the emergence of new states in Africa and Asia resentful of the economic interests retained by the former colonial powers, has produced a

---

20. (1928) P.C.I.J. Rep., Ser. A, No. 17.
1. (1926) *ibid.*, No. 7.   2. No. 17, at p. 47.

totally different climate of international opinion. The resulting attitude may best be illustrated by reference to the General Assembly resolution of December 1962,[3] known as the Declaration on Permanent Sovereignty over Natural Resources, which referred to the "inalienable right" of states to dispose of this natural wealth and resources in accordance with their national interests. Although the Declaration did not suggest that the nationalising state was entitled to disregard foreign rights of ownership (the Declaration itself refers to the payment of appropriate compensation), it marked a significant step towards the acceptance of the proposition that expropriation is the right of every state.

Since 1945, "western" states (who comprise the main "capital exporters") have continued to categorise acts of nationalisation in traditional terms. In the British submissions to the International Court in the *Anglo-Iranian Oil Company* case it was stated that it was "contrary to international law for a state to subject a concession, granted to a foreign company, to a measure of nationalisation or expropriation, if such measure operates exclusively, or in a discriminatory manner, against the foreign company, and it is not shown by the expropriating government that the measure was justified in order to protect the vital interests of the state—the desire of the state to realise greater profits from the concession not being, as a matter of international law, a sufficient ground to justify the expropriation".[4] The British memorial then went on to argue that even if the nationalisation was not for that reason unlawful, it became unlawful unless provision was made for the payment of compensation which was adequate, prompt and effective: in this case, the terms of compensation laid down in the Iranian Oil Nationalisation Act were plainly inadequate.

During 1958, a large number of Dutch owned enterprises operating in Indonesia were placed under the control of the Indonesian Government. In December of that year the process of nationalisation was taken a step further by the passing of legislation authorising a complete transfer of ownership in such cases to the Indonesian State. Although compensation was to be paid at a rate to be decided upon by a special committee, the initial protests by the Dutch Government were on the grounds (a) that the actions of the Indonesian Authorities were discriminatory, and (b) that, far from being for a public purpose, they were part of a political campaign directed against the continued Dutch presence in West Irian.

In 1960, the Castro régime in Cuba passed a Nationalisation Law authorising the President and the Prime Minister "to order jointly by means of resolutions, whenever they may deem it convenient in defence of the national interest, the nationalisation of the properties or concerns belonging to natural or juridical persons nationals of the United States of America or the concern in which said persons have a majority interest". A committee of experts was to be appointed to evaluate the expropriated properties, but the compensation decided upon was to be paid in special 30-year Cuban bonds secured by payment into a fund of the proceeds of

---

3. G.A. Res. 1803 (XVII).   4. I.C.J. *Pleadings*, p. 100.

sales of Cuban sugar to the United States over a stipulated minimum. Interest was payable on the bonds only if it was paid as a charge against the fund. If sales of sugar to the United States proved insufficient to create a fund large enough to support interest payments, the obligation to make such payments was to be deemed to have been discharged.[5] The United States protested vehemently against the legislation on the ground that it was "in essence discriminatory, arbitrary and confiscatory".[6]

Despite these strongly worded pronouncements suggesting that, irrespective of the question of compensation, other grounds exist which might render an act of expropriation contrary to international law, it is doubtful how much significance can be attached to them. The arguments that the taking was not for a public purpose, or was discriminatory, were employed in situations where the protesting state also alleged that there was inadequate compensation. It is hardly likely that a state would wish to denounce acts of expropriation against its nationals if the compensation was adequate.

Where such arguments might be most relevant is in the context of what is "adequate compensation". In the majority of settlements reached over the past twenty years, whether global[7] or specific,[8] the amount of compensation agreed upon has been but a small fraction of the value of the property seized. Writers have tended to deduce from these illustrations broad generalisations about changes in the notion of the adequacy of compensation. While it may be possible to make a number of tentative deductions from the attitude of states, the evidence of state practice is hardly convincing proof of such changes. In all cases, the "claimant" state has been prepared to settle for something rather than risk obtaining nothing. Furthermore, whatever else may be true, it cannot be denied that the starting point in the negotiations of a settlement will always be, on one side at any rate, the estimated value of the property lost, and the ultimate distribution of sums paid under the settlement will usually be made by the "claimant" state on a pro rata basis. If an international judicial tribunal had jurisdiction over a particular claim of this type it is not easy to estimate what principles it would apply, though it is likely that it would be guided to some extent by the following considerations:

1. A state has the right to take over assets situated with its territory;[9]

---

5. The compensation was geared to sales of sugar to the United States because the nationalisation programme was stated to be in retaliation for United States' restrictions on imports of Cuban sugar.

6. 43 Dept. of State Bulletin 171. See also the decisions of the Federal District Court (193 F. Supp. 375) and the Court of Appeals (307 F 2d 845) in the *Sabbatino* case, discussed above, pp. 64–66.

7. For example, the agreements entered into by the United Kingdom with Yugoslavia (1948), Czechoslovakia (1949), Bulgaria (1955), Hungary (1956), Egypt (1959), Roumania (1960).

8. For example, the agreements settling the Anglo-Iranian Oil Company dispute and dealing with the Nationalisation of the Suez Canal.

9. Though this does not mean that other states need recognise the legality of a seizure which they deem to be contrary to international law.

2. If compensation is adequate, the taking is not contrary to international law;

3. Compensation in cases where the taking was for a public purpose and was genuinely non-discriminatory will be "adequate" even if falling short of the value of the assets seized providing that it is reasonable in the economic and political[10] circumstances;

4. Where the tribunal is satisfied that the taking was intended to discriminate etc. full compensation should be paid: it is most unlikely that, in present day circumstances, a tribunal would apply the pre-1939 principle that damages should be awarded over and above an amount sufficient to compensate for the actual loss.

c WRONGFUL ACTS BY INDIVIDUALS WITHIN THE TERRITORY OF A STATE AGAINST A FOREIGN STATE

Although it is not uncommon for the property of a foreign government or its agents to suffer injury on the territory of a state as a result of the activities of the local populace, it does not raise problems in the same form or as acutely as other cases of "indirect" wrongs. For one reason, the injury being suffered by a foreign state which cannot be required to submit to the jurisdiction of the courts of a foreign state, there is no need for the claimant state to have exhausted local remedies before proceeding on the international plane.

The application of the normal rules relating to responsibility would make the territorial state liable for damage or injury only if (1) it failed to take adequate precautions to prevent such an occurrence; or (2) if it failed to take adequate steps to punish those responsible.

In relation to diplomatic and consular premises, the attitude of most states has been to regard this duty of protection as absolute. As a consequence, even though an isolated bomb attack on the Soviet Embassy in Washington could not have been foreseen, payment for the damage was immediately proffered; similarly an anti-Vietnam war demonstration outside the American Embassy in London or the American Consulate in Melbourne which results in damage to the premises will result in compensation being paid however diligently the local police performed their duties in trying to prevent damage.

Where a foreign government has interests of a commercial nature and property used in connection with such interests is damaged, in principle the normal rules of state responsibility would be applicable. However, in many such cases it is possible that, in the interests of good relations between the states concerned, the territorial state will offer ex gratia compensation irrespective of any fault on the part of its officials.

---

10. Expropriation in retaliation for economic or other measures taken against the expropriating state by the claimant state *may* be legitimate. In the case of the United States' restrictions on sugar imports from Cuba, the American view was that such restrictions were in no sense illegal because a state is, treaty obligations apart, entitled to obtain goods from wherever it wishes: the Cuban nationalisations on the other hand were patently illegal.

C. Exhaustion of local remedies

a APPLICATION OF THE RULE

It is a well-established principle of international law that a state cannot succeed in a claim on behalf of its national before an international tribunal unless all the remedies available under the local law have been tried and found wanting.[11] However, while this general proposition is undoubtedly correct, not all the problems arising from the application of the rule, and from the reasons behind it, are capable of being resolved by reference to such a proposition.

In the first place it is clear that *the rule does not apply in cases of direct injury to the complainant state itself.*

As compliance with the rule is a pre-requisite to a claim by a state on behalf of its national, it does not by definition apply to claims by a state on account of *direct* injuries to itself. In cases where a foreign embassy has been damaged (one of the most frequent examples of direct damage), there is no question of the state suffering the injury being obliged to seek redress in the courts of the territorial state. In the *Aerial Incident* case, the Israeli agent before the International Court said in the course of presenting Israel's claim that he could "recall no precedent in which a government complaining of actions performed by another government *jure imperii* has been referred to the courts of the respondent state as a preliminary condition to the obtaining of international satisfaction": the claim was "for a declaration of Bulgarian responsibility under international law" and it was submitted that no domestic court was "competent to make such a declaration" which could alone lead to the satisfaction of Israel's international claim.[12]

Secondly, *the rule does not apply where the injured alien has no connection with the respondent state.*

The exhaustion of local remedies rule is in many ways a "conflicts" rule to avoid both a conflict of jurisdiction between municipal and international tribunals, and a conflict of law between municipal and international law. By entering the territory of a foreign state, an individual is presumed to subject himself to the jurisdiction of the local courts and to the application of the local law. But the notion of a connection between an individual and a foreign state is probably wider than that of residence alone. In the *Norwegian Loans* case, the French bondholders were not connected by residence with Norway, yet it was accepted by both Judges Lauterpacht and Read that the applicability or non-applicability of the local remedies rule did not depend upon that factor.

But what of the situation where the only connection between the individual and the foreign state is the action causing injury? An ambassador or other diplomatic agent causes injury to a national of the receiving state on the territory of that state. The diplomat is entitled to immunity in the courts of the receiving state. Does the injured individual have to

---

11. *Internhandel* case, I.C.J. Rep. 1959, at p. 27. 12. I.C.J. *Pleadings*, p. 530.

go to the expense of instituting proceedings in the courts of the sending state? In such a situation the remedy would in no sense be "local", and it is submitted that a failure to take such proceedings would not be a bar to a diplomatic claim presented by the receiving state on behalf of its national.

A more difficult case would arise if the wrongful act of the respondent state resulted in the otherwise fortuitous presence of the injured individual within its territory. An example would be if the authorities of a state were to arrange for the forcible abduction of a foreign national outside its territory and for bringing him within the territory.

In the *Aerial Incident* case, it will be recalled that an Israeli airliner had strayed into Bulgarian airspace where it was shot down by Bulgarian fighter aircraft. One of the arguments put forward by Bulgaria against the International Court's power to hear the action was that Israel had failed to exhaust local remedies. The main Israeli contention was that, as the incident had been a direct inter-state wrong, the local remedies rule did not apply. But in any case, it was argued, there was no link of any kind between the victims and the Bulgarian state, so that even if the claim could be regarded as one on behalf of Israeli nationals, there was no need to exhaust local remedies when the only connection with Bulgaria was brought about by the illegal acts of the Bulgarian authorities. All the cases involving an exhaustion of local remedies were by implication based upon the existence of some connection between the individual and the respondent state.[13] While there is no direct authority in support of the exclusion of the local remedies rule where there is only an involuntary or fortuitous connection between the injured individual and the respondent state, it is a principle which accords with the underlying philosophy that an alien by visiting a state, or by conducting business with a state, accepts both its laws and the administration of its justice, so that it is to those laws and that administration that he must look if anything goes wrong.

Nor does the rule apply in cases where there has been a denial of justice but it does apply in cases where the state has already committed a prima facie *breach of international law by itself causing injury to a foreign national.*

While the doctrine of the equality and sovereignty of states is the basis of the reason why, in cases of direct injury, the complainant state does not have to exhaust local remedies, this same doctrine is said to underlie the reason for the existence of the local remedies rule in cases of diplomatic protection. The state in whose territory the injury to an alien occurs should be given the opportunity of doing justice in its own way. It would be an interference with the sovereignty of that state to deny it that opportunity by requiring it to submit immediately to international adjudication.

Described in this way, it is immediately apparent that the local remedies rule applies only to situations in which there has already been a breach of international law by the territorial state. If there has been no breach of international law, but only a breach of the local law, there is no question

---

13. *Ibid.*, pp. 531–532.

of international responsibility arising unless the local judicial system fails in its international law duty to do justice in the case. Confusion is often caused by the tendency in both circumstances to refer to the need to exhaust local remedies. Although it is the absence of a "local remedy" in the broadest sense which predicates international responsibility by giving rise to a denial of justice in a simple case of injury caused by a national of the territorial state to an alien, it has already been demonstrated that a "denial of justice" is a concept of far wider application. If the police of the territorial state cause injury or hardship to a foreign national by subjecting him to cruel and inhumane treatment, it may be a "denial of justice", but it does not arise from the inadequacy of the local remedies. If the denial of justice arose from the failings of the local judicial system there would be no practical purpose served in requiring the injured alien to seek redress in the courts which had already denied him justice. Although no such consideration applies when the denial of justice is caused through wrongful administrative action in the course of legal process (as in the police example given above), nevertheless the principle has become accepted that the local remedies need not subsequently be exhausted in a case of denial of justice, whatever form that denial might take. For this reason it is essential to clarity of thought and discussion to use the expression "exhaustion of local remedies" as pre-requisite to international responsibility only in cases which fall within situations categorised in this chapter as amounting to *prima facie* breaches of international law.

b THE CONTENT OF THE RULE

i *What is meant by "local remedies"?*

Normally, if one talks in terms of "remedies", the inference is that of judicial redress through recourse to the courts. Undoubtedly this is the normal interpretation to be placed upon the word when used in the context of the "exhaustion of local remedies". It would be absurd to suggest that, if he was unable to obtain redress under the local law, the injured alien should be required to seek audience with members of the government of the territorial state, or to launch a political campaign, in the hope of getting the law altered.

However, it may be narrowing the notion of local remedies too much if it were restricted to remedies available through the courts. Writers have on the whole tended to refer to proceedings of a judicial nature, though more recently both the International Law Commission in its 1961 draft[14] and a Harvard Research Draft[15] of the same year have suggested definitions designed to include all administrative or judicial remedies or proceedings available under the local law. There would seem to be no reason why an injured alien should not be required to avail himself of an established procedure for remedying his particular injury even if it takes a non-judicial

---

14. Y.B.I.L.C. 1961, Vol. 2, p. 48 (Article 18).
15. See 55 A.J.I.L., p. 577 (Article 19).

form. For example, if his injury resulted from the loss of mining rights, an established procedure for stating a case for review by a government official might be as effective as a purely judicial remedy. The test in either case should be the likelihood of the "remedy" being effective.

ii *The remedy must not be obviously futile*

The basic proposition is that it would be unreasonable to impose upon an injured alien the obligation of seeking redress in the courts of the respondent state if there was little likelihood of such a claim succeeding.

1 *Deficiences in the judicial and administrative system*

If conditions within a state are such that the remedial processes available are corrupt or inefficient and unreliable, a foreign national would not have to submit his claim to those processes. The fact that there has already been a denial of justice in its broadest sense (including imprisonment for an overlong time, or in barbarous conditions; a failure to arrest the person known to be responsible for the alien's injury, as well as a failure to give a remedy in damages for some tortious act) excuses the alien from any duty of obtaining reparation before a tribunal of the state responsible. This exception appears to have become established through a combination of two factors. In the first place, as has already been mentioned,[16] the wrongful act being that of the state, it was unlikely until comparatively recently that the state could be made defendant in an action in its own courts. Secondly, if the alien has already suffered a denial of justice at the hands of the courts of a state, the likelihood is perhaps that he would fare no better in attempting to have their earlier failings reviewed.

This second factor is part of the wider principle that a claimant "is not required to exhaust justice . . . when there is no justice to exhaust".[17] This principle was applied in the case of *Robert E. Brown*[18] by the Great Britain/ United States Arbitral Tribunal created under an agreement of 1910. Brown, an American citizen, had applied for licences to prospect for gold in an area of the South African Republic. Under the law of the Republic he had been entitled to have the licences granted, but the law was suspended by the Executive Council. He commenced proceedings before the courts of the Republic alleging that the suspension of the law had been *ultra vires* so that at the time of the application he had clearly been entitled to the licences. He obtained judgment that he had been wrongly refused the licences on the ground that the act of the Executive Council had been unconstitutional; but as the areas, licences for which he had applied, had long since been allocated the Court granted leave for Brown to proceed with a motion presenting an alternative claim for damages, rather than having to institute new proceedings. Before the alternative claim was heard the Chief Justice was dismissed, and a law was introduced directing that the judiciary were to apply resolutions of the Volksraad (the lower

---

16. Above, pp. 434–435.
18. 6 U.N.R.I.A.A. 120.

17. Cited in Moore, *Digest*, Vol. 6, p. 677.

chamber of Parliament), the provisions of the Constitution notwithstanding, and declaring that the judiciary "shall not have the competency and has never had it, either by the Constitution or by any other law to arrogate to itself the so-called testing right" (i.e. of "testing" the constitutional validity of legislation). Despite the earlier ruling by the Chief Justice, the newly constituted Court refused Brown the right to claim damages by way of motion, and held that a claim for damages must be in effect a retrial of the case. As the Chief Justice had been dismissed and the judiciary directed to apply legislation irrespective of its constitutionality, a new trial seemed certain to produce a less favourable result from Brown's point of view. Although the Tribunal held that Great Britain, which had annexed the South African Republic, was not liable for the wrongful acts of the Republic, the Tribunal expressly stated that if the claim had been against the Republic (i.e. if there had been no annexation), it would have succeeded. The futility of further proceedings by Brown had been fully demonstrated: there was no justice to exhaust.

2 *Where the laws of the respondent state are the basis of the breach of duty*

If a state breaks a contract with a foreign national, the individual may have a remedy under the law of the state concerned. However, if the state enacts legislation which makes it impossible to perform that contract, or if no action is available against the state for its wrongful acts, there will be no local remedies to exhaust. It is for the complainant state to show that there are no effective remedies to which recourse can be had, and no such proof is required if there exists legislation which apparently deprives the individual claimant of a remedy. However, it would still be open to the respondent state to establish that, notwithstanding such legislation, its courts are nevertheless able to look behind the apparent effect of the legislation.[19] If this possibility could be established, then of course local remedies would not have been exhausted.

In the *Norwegian Loans* case,[20] the French Government claimed that a number of international loans issued by two Norwegian banks on behalf of the Norwegian state were redeemable by the payment of their gold value and not their original face value. In answer to this application to the International Court, the Norwegian Government raised a number of objections to the Court's jurisdiction,[1] including the contention that the bondholders had failed to exhaust local remedies. By Norwegian legislation, convertibility of Norwegian currency into gold had become illegal for several periods between 1914 and 1931 since when convertibility had remained prohibited. By a law of 1923, repayments of debts payable in gold could be postponed for as long as convertibility was prohibited if the creditor refused to be paid in Norwegian notes on the basis of their

---

19. See Judge Lauterpacht's Separate Opinion in the *Norwegian Loans* case, I.C.J. Rep. 1957, at p. 39.
20. *Ibid.*, p. 9.   1. See further, below pp. 499–500.

nominal gold value. In the French view, the combined effect of this legislation was to make recourse to the Norwegian courts pointless. The Court held that two of the Norwegian objections to the Court's jurisdiction were well founded, and did not therefore consider the objection based upon the non-exhaustion of local remedies. However, Judges Lauterpacht and Read in separate opinion did deal with the local remedies issue, although they reached opposite conclusions.

Judge Lauterpacht seemed to apply the rule with undue strictness. In his view it was not at all certain that no remedy was possible under Norwegian law. "There has been a tendency in the practice of courts of many states to regard international law, in some way, as forming part of national law or as entering legitimately into the national conception of *ordre public*. Although the Norwegian Government has admitted that in no case can a Norwegian court overrule Norwegian legislation on the ground that it is contrary to international law, it has asserted that it is possible that a Norwegian court may consider international law to form part of the law of the Kingdom to the extent that it ought, if possible, to interpret the Norwegian legislation in question so as not to impute to it the intention or the effect of violating international law".[2] In the light of the lack of uniformity in the approach of municipal tribunals, even within the same state, to matters of currency and international loans, it was not possible to forecast with assurance the result of an action in the Norwegian courts.

Judge Read, on the other hand, was prepared to accept the French excuse for the failure to institute proceedings before the Norwegian Courts. It was difficult to see how Norway could demand the exhaustion of local remedies as it had consistently argued that the matter was governed by the law of 1923. Even if the individual bondholder could have persuaded the courts that the terms of the loan included a gold value clause, the Norwegian Government itself was acting on the basis that, whatever had been the original position, it had been altered by the law of 1923. In such circumstances, the French argument that recourse to the local courts would be "obviously futile" was reinforced by the proposition that the local remedies rule had no application where the rights of the foreign national had been impaired by the direct intervention of the respondent Government or Parliament. "If there ever was a case in which the respondent Government and Parliament had intervened to impair the rights of non-resident aliens, it is in the present instance".[3] Unless Norway could show that it was possible to challenge governmental activities authorised by the legislature in the Norwegian courts the plea of non-exhaustion of local remedies must fail.

The proposition that the local remedies rule does not apply where the rights of an alien have been directly affected by the activities of the respondent executive or legislature is obviously subject to qualification in states where a possible right of redress before the courts is available against such

---

2. I.C.J. Rep. 1957, pp. 40–41.   3. I.C.J. Rep. 1957, at p. 98.

actions. In the *Interhandel* case,[4] the Swiss Government had instituted proceedings before the International Court against the United States. The United States Government had, during the course of the Second World War, seized the assets of the General Aniline Company, which was incorporated in the United States, under the Trading with the Enemy Act. In the American view the ultimate control of General Aniline was in the hands of I. G. Farben, a German company, although the control was exercised through a Swiss corporation known as Interhandel. The Swiss contention was that any link between I. G. Farben and Interhandel had been severed by 1940, i.e. before the United States entered the War, so that the foreign interest in General Aniline was Swiss and not German. Under the Washington Accord of 1946, the United States Government undertook to unblock all Swiss assets, but continued to hold that the General Aniline assets, being beneficially German, were not covered by the agreement. The Swiss Government and Interhandel did bring proceedings in the courts of the United States, and when these had apparently proved abortive, Switzerland made this application to the International Court. By the time the preliminary objections to the Court's jurisdiction were heard, however, the Supreme Court of the United States granted a writ of *certiorari* allowing Interhandel the right to proceed under the Trading with the Enemy Act, the Company's right to do which had hitherto been denied.

In an attempt to meet the United States' objection to the admissibility of the claim that local remedies obviously had not been exhausted, the Swiss argued, *inter alia*, that the rule did not apply when, as in this case, the activities complained of were those of the foreign government itself, and not of a subordinate authority. This contention the Court rejected: it "must attach decisive importance to the fact that the laws of the United States make available to interested persons who consider that they have been deprived of their rights by measures taken in pursuance of the Trading with the Enemy Act, adequate remedies for the defence of their rights against the Executive."[5] In other words, although the fact that the activities alleged to have caused the injury are those of the foreign government or parliament, this only raises a presumption that there may not be remedies available. But it is a presumption that can readily be rebutted by the respondent state, if it is able to show that its actions may be subject to review in its own courts.

3 The process of appeals

It is obvious enough that, *prima facie* at least, a remedy is not exhausted unless the whole process of appeals is resorted to. Until the highest appellate tribunal determines the issue, the remedies are not exhausted. However, this requirement is subject to the same exception as the rule itself: there is no need to pursue a fruitless course of appeals. "Just as the concept of 'exhaustion' in the ensemble is not absolute, neither is this particular

---

4. I.C.J. Rep. 1959, p. 6.   5. *Ibid.*, at p. 27.

aspect of the rule. It is not a mechanical device requiring the claimant to pursue aimless appeals against adverse decisions. The rule requiring local remedies to be invoked and exhausted would be a meaningless thing were it interpreted as applying to every means of recourse whether it promised hope of redress or not. . . . A 'remedy' which offers no hope of effective redress is not worthy of the name and does not fall within the ambit of the rule".[6]

In the *Finnish Ships* arbitration,[7] Finland claimed that the United Kingdom was responsible for having failed to pay for the hire of thirteen ships owned by Finnish nationals and for the loss of three of those ships as the result of enemy action. The claim of the shipowners had been rejected by the British Government, and it was later rejected by the Admiralty Transport Arbitration Board which had been set up under the Indemnity Act, 1920, to deal with claims against the British Government for compensation for the use or loss of ships requisitioned by the British Government during the 1914–18 war. The Board held that the ships had been requisitioned by the Russian, and not by the British Government, which had employed the vessels under charter from the Russian authorities. Under the Act an appeal lay on matters of law to the Court of Appeal and the House of Lords, but the Finnish Government argued that from the finding of fact that the vessels had been requisitioned by the Russian Government there could be no appeal. In the view of the arbitrator, the British contention that local remedies had not been exhausted depended upon, (a) whether an appeal was possible from this finding, and (b) whether, if an appeal was possible, the points of law to be considered by the higher courts would be sufficient to obtain a reversal of the decision of the Admiralty Board. It was true that the decision that the ships had been requisitioned by the Russian Government was based upon issues of law which would have been appealable. But it would not have been possible, even if the contentions of the Finnish Government as to the law were accepted, for an appelate tribunal to reverse that decision because it had been established as a fact that the actual taking of the vessels had been by the Russian authorities. The remedies available under English law had therefore been exhausted because there was no point in pursuing a fruitless course of appeals.

An interesting question in relation to local remedies arises if the individual claimant fails to take full advantage of the remedies available to him under the local law. Suppose, for example, his case is not well presented; or a witness is not called whose evidence might have been vital to the success of the case. If the situation is one involving an initial wrongful act by a private individual against a foreign national, the respondent state would only have committed an international delinquency as a consequence of a denial of justice. The failure of the alien to present his claim effectively would be inconsistent with any idea of fault, measured against an inter-

---

6. Freeman, *The International Responsibility of States for Denial of Justice*, pp. 423–4.
7. 3 U.N.R.I.A.A. 1484.

national standard, on the part of the respondent state. But such a situation has nothing to do with the local remedies rule, which only applies where there has been a *prima facie* breach of international law. Once there has been activity by the respondent state involving such a breach, then the local remedies rule exists to allow the respondent state to remedy the situation in its own way, by its own procedure. Should a failure by the individual on whose behalf the international claim is made to present his case in the local courts in the most advantageous way bar recourse to an international tribunal?

In the *Ambatielos* case,[8] a claim was presented by the Greek Government against the United Kingdom in a dispute arising out of a contract for the purchase of a number of ships by Ambatielos from the British Government. The British Government had given credit on the sale but had retained a mortgage over the vessels. In proceedings to enforce the mortgage, Ambatielos was allowed to raise an undertaking by the British Government that the vessels would be delivered on specified dates as a defence. However, as the British Government refused to allow discovery of documents, mainly internal correspondence relating to the negotiations, under the plea of Crown privilege, Ambatielos was unable to prove that such an undertaking had been given. On appeal, he asked leave to call a new witness, a Major Laing, with whom most of the negotiations had been carried on. The Court of Appeal held that it could not allow a party to produce a new witness who could readily have been called in the court of first instance. Ambatielos made no effort to pursue his defence by way of appeal to the House of Lords. Had he exhausted local remedies?

A majority of the arbitrators held that the failure of Ambatielos to take full advantage of his opportunities at first instance constituted a failure to exhaust the remedies available to him in those proceedings. In accordance with the ruling in the *Finnish Ships* case, it had to be assumed that Major Laing's evidence was essential to Ambatielos' case. It could have been adduced, but was not in fact adduced. Furthermore, it was not possible for the Greek Government to argue that the remedies had been exhausted because a further appeal would have been pointless. "It would be wrong to hold that a party who, by failing to exhaust his opportunities in the court of first instance, has caused an appeal to become futile should be allowed to rely on this fact in order to rid himself of the rule of exhaustion of local remedies".[9]

It can be seen that this decision is based upon a misconception of the local remedies rule. The failure of the foreign national to take full advantage of the procedural facilities available under the local law would clearly be a defence to a claim that he had been *denied* justice in the local courts. If the Greek case had been based upon an alleged denial of justice arising from the plea of Crown privilege to withhold documents necessary to Ambatielos' defence in the proceedings in the English courts, it would have been a telling point against the claim that he had not taken advantage

---

8. 12 U.N.R.I.A.A. 85.   9. *Ibid.*, at p. 122.

of his right to call Major Laing as a witness. However, as the allegation was that the British Government had already acted in a manner constituting a *prima facie* breach of international law (i.e. had *itself* committed an act which if not remedied would involve international responsibility), the onus was clearly on the British Government to show either that its actions were legitimate according to the requirements of international law or that, as a preliminary issue, Ambatielos had not given the British Government the opportunity of remedying the alleged wrong if it wished to do so.

The onus being on the British Government to remedy the alleged wrong or show why it did not have to do so, it could not answer a *bona fide* attempt to exhaust local remedies by the argument that the failure to call a certain witness prevented the proceedings constituting a sufficient recourse to the remedies available under English law. To an extent the Commission did recognise that the definition of local remedies to include "the use of the procedural facilities which municipal law makes available to litigants" could be taken too literally to "imply that the fact of having neglected to make use of some means of procedure—even one which is not important to . . . the action—would suffice to allow a defendant state to claim that local remedies have not been exhausted, and that, therefore, an international action cannot be brought." However, the Commission felt that it must accept the view of the claimant of the value of the evidence of the uncalled witness. As it had been alleged on behalf of Ambatielos that the evidence of Major Laing had been vital to the case, it could not be said that it was a failure to take advantage of an unimportant procedural facility.

The error of this reasoning also stems from the initial failure of the majority of the Commission to appreciate the role of the local remedies rule. As it is to give an opportunity for a state which, it is alleged, has already committed a wrongful act against a foreign national to redress the injury, the non-exhaustion of local remedies must arise from the refusal of the injured alien to rely upon those remedies or his misuse of those remedies (i.e. he must in some way have wilfully or negligently denied the respondent state its opportunity to redress his grievance). Ambatielos had refrained from calling Major Laing because it was believed that Major Laing's testimony would not support his case. It was only subsequently that Ambatielos and his advisers became aware that testimony that the Major might give would support his case. It could hardly be said in the circumstances that Ambatielos had wilfully or carelessly denied the English courts an opportunity of remedying the harm he alleged he had suffered.

c THE CALVO CLAUSE AND THE LOCAL REMEDIES RULE

During the nineteenth century the tendency of European powers to intervene in the affairs of the states of South and Central America was greatly resented by the states concerned. The excuse for such interventions was usually to safeguard, or to redress damage to, the interests of foreign nationals. Calvo propounded the doctrine that European powers should not intervene on such grounds either militarily or diplomatically, and that claims for damage or injury should be presented by the foreign nationals themselves in the local courts. Although his views had little effect on the policies of the European powers, they did lead to the insertion of clauses in contracts entered into by a number of American states with foreign nationals whereby the latter undertook, *inter alia*, to submit disputes to the local law and courts and to waive or renounce their rights under international law to diplomatic protection.

These "Calvo clauses" took a variety of forms, but a single illustration is worth considering. In the *North American Dredging Company* case,[10] the United States submitted to the Mexico/U.S. General Claims Commission a claim arising out of alleged breaches by the Mexican authorities of a contract in which the Company had undertaken to dredge the Mexican port of Salina Cruz. One of the terms of the contract provided:

> "The contractor and all persons who, as employees or in any other capacity, may be engaged in the execution of the work under this contract either directly or indirectly, shall be considered as Mexicans in all matters, within the Republic of Mexico, concerning the execution of such work and the fulfilment of this contract. They shall not claim, nor shall they have, with regard to the interests and the business connected with this contract, any other rights or means to enforce the same than those granted by the laws of the Republic to Mexicans, nor shall they enjoy any other rights than those established in favour of Mexicans. They are consequently deprived of any rights as aliens, and under no conditions shall the intervention of foreign diplomatic agents be permitted, in any matter related to this contract."

The basic philosophy behind state claims on behalf of injured nationals has been reiterated on many occasions by international tribunals. The classic statement of the philosophy was probably that pronounced by the Permanent Court in the *Mavrommatis* case.[11] "By taking up the case of one of its subjects . . . a state is in reality asserting its own right—its right to ensure, in the person of its subjects, respect for the rules of international law." In keeping with this tenet, international tribunals have refused to hold that a "Calvo clause" can restrict the right of a state to intervene on behalf of its nationals. In the *North American Dredging Company* case, the Commission held that, by agreeing to such a clause, an individual could not "deprive the government of his nation of its undoubted right of applying international remedies to violations of international law committed to his damage. Such government frequently has a larger interest in maintaining the principles of international law than in recovering damage for one of its citizens in a particular case, and manifestly such citizen can not by contract tie in this respect the hands of his Government."

It should also follow that a private contract cannot affect the relations of the parties under international law. But the decisions on this issue are less

---

10. (1926) 4 U.N.R.I.A.A. 26.
11. P.C.I.J. Rep., Ser. A, No. 2, p. 12. See also the *Panevezys-Saldutiskis* case, P.C.I.J. Rep., Ser. A/B, No. 76, p. 16.

clear. In the case under consideration, the Tribunal took the view that the Calvo clause in question "must be upheld unless it is repugnant to a recognised rule of international law." Although the part of the clause purporting to eliminate the right of diplomatic intervention was void because it could not have that effect, there was no rule of international law "striking down" the contract as a whole, or the rest of the Calvo clause. The Tribunal accepted as the "obvious purpose" of such a contract the prevention of abuses of the right of protection, not the destruction of the right; and the drawing of "a reasonable and practical line between Mexico's sovereign right of jurisdiction within its own territory, on the one hand, and the sovereign right of protection of the government of an alien whose person or property is within such territory, on the other hand." Under the Treaty which set up the Tribunal and regulated its jurisdiction, no claim was to be "disallowed or rejected . . . by the application of the general principle of international law that the legal remedies must be exhausted as a condition precedent to the validity or allowance of any claim." However, the total failure of the claimant company in this case to make use of the remedies available under Mexican law had no connection with the local remedies rule. The Calvo clause did not take away the undoubted right of the company to apply to its own Government for protection if the resort to the Mexican courts resulted in a denial of justice; but the claim on the international plane would not be that the contract had been violated but that the claimant had been denied justice. The claim therefore failed.

While the decision was undoubtedly correct, it would seem that there was no reason for the Tribunal to rely upon the Calvo clause at all. Indeed, it did appear to recognise that a breach of an ordinary contract would become subject to international law only if there was an ensuing denial of justice. Why then did the Tribunal purport to rely upon the provisions of the contract in reaching its decision, and what is the effect of the decision?

The reason for the Commission relying upon the Calvo clause stems from the fact that there has always tended to be confusion between the deficiencies of remedies which constitute a denial of justice and the exhaustion of local remedies rule. The tendency of European governments to interfere in South American affairs on the slightest pretext even as late in time as the first part of the present century had the effect of blurring the distinction between breaches of contract which should have been subject to the municipal law of the state concerned, and acts against the person or property of foreign nationals amounting to *prima facie* breaches of international law. In view of the uncertainty that still existed in 1926 when the *North American Dredging Company* case was heard it is hardly surprising that the Commission adopted the proposition that if an alien agrees to submit disputes arising out of the contract to the local courts he should be obliged to do so before his own state was entitled to take up his claim on the international level.

The answer to the second question follows from the answer to the first.

With the emergence of a more precise line of demarcation between the denial of justice situation and the application of the local remedies rule, it can be seen that by drawing this line international law itself is capable of dealing with the problems the Calvo clause was designed to meet. In the *North American Dredging Company* case the Commission gave its opinion of the effect of such a clause as follows:[12]

"Where a claim is based on an alleged violation of any rule or principle of international law, the Commission will take jurisdiction notwithstanding the existence of such a clause in a contract. . . . . But where a claimant has expressly agreed . . . that in all matters pertaining to the execution, fulfilment, and intepretation of the contract he will have resort to local tribunals, remedies and authorities and then wilfully ignores them by applying in such matters to his Government, he will be held bound by his contract and the Commission will not take jurisdiction of such claim."

And similar pronouncements are to be found in other arbitral awards.[13] However, it is now clearly established that a state is not entitled to intervene diplomatically to press a claim on behalf of its national (though it can of course offer its good offices to assist its national in the local courts, etc.) unless there has been a denial of justice or unless the breach of contract itself is of a type to establish a *prima facie* breach of international law.[14]

If a Calvo clause is to retain any significance, it must be something more than a "choice of law" rule in the private international law sense. Can it be said that such a clause has the effect of bringing all breaches of contract, even for example if they involve interference with property rights, within the denial of justice situation? Under the normal rules of international law, a breach of a concession contract involving a sequestration of the concession itself would constitute a *prima facie* breach of international law. The practice of states recognises the right of diplomatic intervention. The success of a claim before a judicial tribunal would depend upon the waiver or satisfaction of the local remedies rule, but the international nature of the claim is established. For a Calvo clause to bring the matter back onto the municipal plane would be to do precisely what the *North American Dredging Company* case laid down was impossible: alter the rights of the parties under international law.

It has also been suggested that the/effect of a Calvo clause is to make exhaustion of local remedies, or application to the local courts in order to establish a denial of justice in cases of breaches only of municipal law, necessary even though the remedies available are, or are likely to be, futile. Not only is such a suggestion also in contradiction to the rights of the parties as regulated by international law, but it is also inequitably burdensome on any claimant. The conclusion is inescapable that a Calvo

---

12. 4 U.N.R.I.A.A. at p. 33.
13. *Woodruff,* 9 U.N.R.I.A.A. 213, at p. 223; *Rudloff, ibid.,* 244, at pp. 251–2; *Turnbull, ibid.,* 261, at pp. 304–5.　　　　　　　14. See above, pp. 426–434.

clause no longer has any useful role in contracts between states and foreign nationals.

4 REMEDIES

A. Damages

In most cases heard before international tribunals the appropriate remedy is an award of damages. In assessing such an award tribunals were at one time clearly influenced by general principles of (municipal) law, but there has developed such a wealth of "precedent" for the guidance of later arbitrators that it is now possible to look to these authorities for definitive statements of principle governing the calculation of damages. The basic notion was expressed by the Permanent Court as follows:[15]

> "The essential principle contained in the actual notion of an illegal act—a principle which seems to be established by international practice and in particular by the decisions of arbitral tribunals—is that reparation must, as far as possible, wipe out all the consequences of the illegal act and re-establish the situation which would, in all probability, have existed if that act had not been committed."

Before dealing with specific principles that apply to the calculation of the amount of damages, it should be borne in mind that such an award will only be made in cases where the wrongful conduct which is attributable to the respondent state has actually *caused* the damage. The respondent state will not have to pay compensation in respect of losses which are too remotely connected with its conduct.

In the *Naulilaa* and *Maziua* claims,[16] Portugal sought compensation from Germany in respect of a series of reprisal raids undertaken by German forces against Portuguese forts and other installations in Portugal's African territories. While holding that the German actions were contrary to international law, the Tribunal nevertheless refused to hold Germany responsible for the damage caused by the native uprising and subsequent campaigns of passive resistance set off or encouraged by the German attacks.

Similarly, claims have been rejected for prolongation of a war[17] and increased maritime insurance rates;[18] when presented on behalf of insurance companies obliged to pay on the premature death of persons killed through the illegal acts of the respondent state;[19] for damage to the engine of a neutral ship through exceeding the safety limit of steam pressure in order to escape from a belligerent submarine.[20]

---

15. *Chorzow Factory* case (1928), P.C.I.J. Rep. Ser. A, No. 17, p. 47.
16. (1928), 2 U.N.R.I.A.A. 1013.   17. *Alabama* arbitration, Moore, *Int. Arb.*, Vol. 4, p. 4057.
18. *Alabama* arbitration (above); *Garland Steamship Corporation* case (1924), 7 U.N.R.I.A.A. 73.
19. *Provident Life Insurance Co.* case (1924), 7 U.N.R.I.A.A., at pp. 112–113.
20. *Winthrop C. Neilson* (s.s. *Nohegan*) case, *ibid.* 308.

Damages arising from loss of credit[1] or profits are recoverable. In the *Chorzow Factory* case,[2] the Permanent Court arranged for an expert enquiry into the affairs of the undertaking with a view to estimating *inter alia* the profits if any that would have accrued during the period between the unlawful confiscation of the factory by Poland and the date of the present judgment. The Court expressed caution at the method that should be employed in making such an estimate. It pointed out that the cost of upkeep of the factory and even the cost of improvement and normal development of the installations was "bound to absorb in a large measure the profits, real or supposed, of the undertaking. Up to a certain point, therefore, any profit may be left out of account, for it will be included in the real or supposed value of the undertaking at the present moment. If, however, the reply given by the experts . . . should show that after making good the deficits for the years during which the factory was working at a loss, and after due provision for the cost of upkeep and normal improvement during the following years, there remains a margin of profit, the amount of such profit should be added to the compensation to be awarded." But the Court rejected as "contingent and indeterminate damage" claims with respect to losses caused to the former owners of the factory by the fact that, without the facilities at the factory, they were less able to conduct experiments, perfect processes and make fresh discoveries.[3]

An award of damages can also include a requirement that interest should be paid. In most cases in which interest has been awarded, the obligation to pay was commenced on the date of taking in the case of property, but such an award is inclined to be in lieu of a loss of profits.[4] In cases of personal injury,[5] or where the measure of damages is at the discretion of the court, interest, if awarded at all, would be payable from the date of judgment.

a REPARATION IN THE CASE OF DIRECT STATE WRONGS

The award of damages in such a case would seem to depend upon two principles. Primarily, as in all cases, the award is to compensate for damage or injury suffered. Whether the damage is to the property of the state or to its nationals, the measure of damages should relate to the actual loss.

In the *Corfu Channel* case, the United Kingdom claim was classified under two heads: the material damage to the two British naval vessels which had struck mines in the course of their passage through the Channel, and the cost of pensions and awards, and of medical treatment in respect of personnel on board the two vessels who had been killed or injured in the

---

1. *Fabiani* claim (1896), Whiteman, *Damages in International Law*, 1785, at p. 1788; *May* claim (1900), *ibid.*, 1821.
2. (1928) P.C.I.J. Rep., Ser. A, No. 17, pp. 52–53.
3. *Ibid.*, p. 57: the Court stated that such damage in accordance with the jurisprudence of arbitral tribunals could not be taken into account. See *Hickson* claim, (1924), 7 U.N.R.I.A.A. 266.
4. *Illinois Central R.R. Co.* case (1926), 4 U.N.R.I.A.A. 134.
5. *Spanish Zone of Morocco* case (1925), 2 U.N.R.I.A.A. 617.

explosions. The International Court had no doubts as to the propriety of these claims once Albania's responsibility had been established.[6] The claims were thus based upon the actual loss to the claimant government. In such a case it would not matter what nationality an injured individual possessed as long as the government suffered loss (i.e. in having to pay a pension or medical expenses) as a result of the incident.

This situation should be carefully distinguished from claims *on behalf of* injured individuals or their dependents, in which of course the question of nationality becomes vital. In the *Aerial Incident* case, Israel alleged that Bulgaria should bear responsibility for the shooting down of an Israeli airliner which had strayed into Bulgarian airspace.[7] The International Court held that it did not have jurisdiction over the dispute.[8] However, it is interesting to note that claims were submitted against Bulgaria, not only by Israel, but by all states nationals of which had been killed in the incident. There was no question of Israel claiming on behalf of *all* persons who had been killed.

The significance of nationality in this context may be further emphasized by the findings of the Commissioner in the case of the *I'm Alone*.[9] It will be recalled that the Canadian claim was in respect of the sinking of a British ship, registered in Canada, by a U.S. coastguard cutter. The American contention that, as the ship had been engaged in smuggling liquor into the United States, the coastguards were entitled to take such action, was rejected. On the question of damages, the Commissioners held that as the *I'm Alone*, although a British ship, was "*de facto* owned, controlled, and at the critical times, managed, and her movements directed and her cargo dealt with and disposed of, by a group of persons . . . entirely or nearly so, citizens of the United States, . . . no compensation ought to be paid in respect of the loss of the ship or the cargo." The non-national character of this part of the claim was thus held to be fatal to its success.[10]

The second principle applicable in cases of direct international wrongs is that damages may be awarded as redress for the insult to the national honour of the claimant state. Although this principle is sometimes referred to as a matter of "punitive damages" the expression is misleading. The greater the affront to the national honour, the more substantial should be the "amends" required of the respondent state. There is no reason why the amends should not be given a money value in the form of damages. In the case of the *I'm Alone*, the Commissioners, probably acting on the promptings of the U.S. Government that they should "interpret their function as that of authoritative advisers to the two Governments" and should make recommendations to either Government with respect to any phase of the

---

6. I.C.J. Rep. 1949, p. 244.   7. See above, p. 446.
8. See below, p. 511.
9. (1933–5) 3 U.N.R.I.A.A. 1609.
10. Claims were allowed in respect of members of the crew of the *I'm Alone*. In so far as these claims were non-national in character (the only seaman who died in the incident was French) this is best explained on the ground that the flag state can always claim on behalf of members of the crew irrespective of nationality.

controversy, suggested that the United States ought formally to acknowledge the illegality of the act of its coastguards, and to apologise therefor;
and further that the United States should "as a material amendment" pay
the sum of $25,000.

b WHERE THE CLAIMS ARE ON BEHALF OF NATIONALS

The theory of state responsibility is that a state is presenting its own
claim. "By taking up the case of one of its subjects and by resorting to
diplomatic action or international judicial proceedings on his behalf, a
state is in reality asserting its own right, its right to ensure, in the person
of its subjects, respect for the rules of international law."[11] What therefore
is the measure of damages in cases of diplomatic protection?

International tribunals have found no difficulty in reconciling the theory
of responsibility with the actuality of damage. Thus the Permanent Court
was able to analyse the position as follows:[12]

> "The reparation due by one state to another does not . . . change its character by
> reason of the fact that it takes the form of an indemnity for the calculation of which
> the damage suffered by a private person is taken as the measure. The rules of law
> governing the reparation are the rules of international law in force between the two
> states concerned, and not the law governing relations between the state which has
> committed a wrongful act and the individual who has suffered damage. Rights or
> interests of an individual the violation of which rights causes damage are always in a
> different plane to rights belonging to a state, which rights may also be infringed by
> the same act. The damage suffered by an individual is never therefore identical with
> that which will be suffered by a state; it can only afford a convenient scale for the
> calculation of the reparation due to the state."

In calculating the amount of compensation to be awarded in respect of the
injuries to the individual national, international tribunals have been
guided by a number of factors which are best outlined briefly in relation
to the type of damage or injury involved.

i *Wrongful acts against property*

In the case of claims arising out of interference with property, the
amount of the award will depend not only upon the value of the property
but also upon the degree of interference.

In the *Union Bridge Company* case,[13] material belonging to a national
of the United States was removed by a British official from Port Elizabeth
and dispatched to Bloemfontein 400 miles away. This action was in itself
treated as a wrongful interference with neutral property. The conduct of
the official fell to be considered "not by reference to nice distinctions
between trover, trespass and action on the case, but by reference to
that broad and well-recognised principle of international law which gives
what, in all the circumstances, is fair compensation for the wrong suffered."

---

11. *Mavrommatis* case, P.C.I.J. Rep., Ser. A, No. 2, p. 12.
12. *Chorzow Factory* case, P.C.I.J. Rep., Ser. A, No. 17, p. 28.
13. (1924), 6 U.N.R.I.A.A. 138.

It is thus apparent that the extent of the award will depend upon what happens to the property concerned. If the property is subsequently returned, this factor will affect the measure of damages, but not the responsibility. In the *Schuber* claim,[14] the claimants had entered into an agreement with the government of Panama to carry mail, and officials and troops, at reduced rates, in return for free entry to, and use of, Panamanian ports. A vessel employed by the claimants was seized by insurgents; and, before being restored to them, it was operated for a while by the Panamanian Government. Under the amnesty granted to the insurgents, the government assumed responsibility for the vessel. The Umpire had no hesitation in awarding what he considered a fair price per day for the use that the insurgents and the government had obtained from the vessel.

The principle of damages as compensation is most obviously to be seen in the context of damage to property, or permanent loss of property whether through destruction or expropriation. If the respondent state is unable or unwilling to make restitution, it has as an alternative the option of paying the value of the property "at the time of indemnification, which value is designed to take the place of restitution".[15]

ii *Wrongful acts against the person*

The bases of calculation in cases of wrongful activities against the person of a foreign national are less easily defined. The difference in theory between the international wrong and the "value" of the loss to the individual or persons claiming through him is even more striking than in the case of damage to property. Many of the claims presented in respect of personal wrongs are only matters of international concern because of a subsequent denial of justice. Whereas it is reasonable enough that compensation for the actual injury caused should be paid to the injured individual or to his family in the case of a fatal injury, if it was caused directly by the activities of state officials, a similar principle would not seem appropriate where the wrongful conduct consisted solely of a failure to punish those responsible for causing the injury or death.

Perhaps the most important arbitration which dealt with this issue was the *Janes* claim.[16] It will be recalled that the claim was presented on behalf of the family of Janes who had been murdered by a vengeful ex-employee of the mine in Mexico of which Janes had been Superintendent. The attack had taken place in broad daylight in front of witnesses. Although there was no doubt about the identity of the assailant, the Mexican authorities were so dilatory in their efforts to apprehend him that he was never brought to justice. Was the United States entitled to recover an

---

14. (1871), Moore, *Int. Arb.*, Vol. 2, p. 1421: cp. *Spanish Zone of Morocco* case (1925) 2 U.N.R.I.A.A. 617, where government "use" of property increased the value of the property.

15. *Chorzow Factory* case, P.C.I.J. Rep., Ser. A, No. 17, p. 48: cp. the special circumstances of the *Union Bridge Company* award, 6 U.N.R.I.A.A. 138, at p. 142.

16. (1926) 4 U.N.R.I.A.A. 82; see above, p. 425.

amount of compensation equivalent to the estimated loss of Janes to his family as a wage-earner, husband and father?

The Tribunal was referred to a number of awards[17] where compensation for a subsequent failure to punish was based upon the "very consequences of the individual's misdemeanour". The reason for the awards was apparently that the failure to punish was tantamount to some sort of approval of what had occurred, especially in cases where the government had permitted the guilty parties to escape or had remitted the punishment by granting a pardon or amnesty. In the view of the Commissioners this notion of presumed complicity might be appropriate where a government knew of an intended crime but refrained from preventing it, but it could hardly apply to cases of non-punishment. In such a situation the "international delinquency is . . . separate from the private delinquency. . . . The culprit is liable for having killed or murdered an American national; the Government is liable for not having measured up to its duty of diligently prosecuting and properly punishing the offender. The culprit has transgressed the penal code of his country; the State, so far from having transgressed its own penal code (which perhaps not even is applicable to it), has transgressed a provision of international law. . . . The damage caused by the culprit is the damage caused to Janes' relatives by Janes' death; the damage caused by the Government's negligence is the damage resulting from the non-punishment of the murderer."

Having clearly established the different basis for the computation of damages in cases of non-punishment, the Commission then proceeded to discuss its application in practice. Admittedly it was a more difficult and uncertain calculation than in the case of direct damage, but not more so than in other denial of justice situations—illegal detention; barbarous treatment in jail; non-punishment of an attack on one's reputation or honour, etc. The extent of the compensation should take into account not only the individual grief of the claimants, but a "reasonable and substantial redress should be made for the mistrust and lack of safety, resulting from the Government's attitude." Finally, the Commission referred to the advantage, stemming from the severance of the government's dereliction of duty from the individual's crime, that a tribunal could take into account "several shades of denial of justice, more serious ones and light ones (no prosecution at all; prosecution and release; prosecution and light punishment; prosecution, punishment and pardon)" whereas the alternative system provided one result only, full compensation for the actual injury suffered irrespective of cause.

In cases not involving a denial of justice, i.e., where the injury suffered by the foreign national arises directly from the activities of officials of the foreign state, the measure of damages is that of the actual injuries caused. In cases of non-fatal injury, compensation may be awarded in respect of the degree of disablement or inconvenience, medical expenses, loss of earnings,

---

17. *Ruden* claim, Moore, *Int. Arb.*, 1653; *Cotesworth & Powell* claim, *ibid.*, 2053; *Bovallins* and *Hedlund* cases, 10 U.N.R.I.A.A. 768.

etc. When the injury is fatal, the calculation is based upon the extent of the financial loss of the dependants and the degree of suffering caused to them.

In the *Di Caro* case,[18] the Italian Government presented a claim against Venezuela *inter alia* for the shooting of the claimant's husband by a detachment of Venezuelan troops. Following a disagreement over the sum to be awarded, the Umpire (Ralston) explained his reasons for dis-agreeing with the limited amount which the Venezuelan Commissioner would have been prepared to award. In the first place, despite the view of the Venezuelan Commissioner that the deceased was only a labourer, the evidence tended to show that he was a shopkeeper and bought and sold coffee and other commodities in considerable quantities. His earning power was thus clearly greater than the 3 bolivas a day he would earn as a labourer. The Umpire did not disagree with the proposition that, as the deceased had been 64 years of age, his life expectancy could not have exceeded six more years: it was "fair and proper" to estimate earning power, expectation of life, and also to "bear in mind his station in life with a view to determining the extent of comforts and amenities of which the wife has been the loser". However, it would be a serious error to restrict the award to such items, and to ignore "the deprivation of personal com-panionship and cherished associations consequent upon the loss of a husband or wife unexpectedly taken away."

c PUNITIVE DAMAGES

As has already been stated, there is a tendency to regard damages other than those awarded for actual loss as being of a penal or punitive nature. Such a view, if it contains any truth at all, is only tenable in a limited range of circumstances.

Awards in cases of a denial of justice or where a foreign national has been subjected to degrading treatment without injury by state officials depend largely upon the degree of misconduct by the respondent state. But the reason why this is so is that the measure of damages is the degree of shock, outrage, suffering, inflicted upon the claimants by the wrongful acts; and these claimants are likely to be affected in proportion to the degree of misconduct.

In the *Maal* claim,[19] presented by the Netherlands against Venezuela, the Tribunal awarded $500 solely in respect of the indignity to Maal who was unnecessarily stripped in public by Venezuelan police.

In the *Roberts* claim[20] the overall award in favour of the United States was $8,000 and part of this sum was in respect of the illegal imprisonment of Roberts by the Mexican authorities for a period of seven months. However, Roberts had been kept in prison for a total of nineteen months, and a substantial part of this award was undoubtedly in respect of the

---

18. (1903), 10 U.N.R.I.A.A. 597. And see also the *Lusitania* claims, 7 U.N.R.I.A.A., esp. at pp. 34–38.
19. See above, p. 435.   20. 4 U.N.R.I.A.A. 77, and see above, p. 423.

cruel and inhumane treatment meted out to him throughout that time.[1]
He, along with thirty or forty other men, had been confined in a room 35
feet by 20 feet. There was no sanitation of any description available. The
prisoners were afforded no opportunity to take physical exercise, and the
food was "of the coarsest kind".

The amount of the award in each case reflected the degree of misconduct by the authorities of the respondent state, but the reason for this was
clearly the effect of such treatment upon the individual claimant. Support
for this contention is provided in the *Maal* case. In the course of giving his
reasons for the award, the Umpire commented that Maal came to Venezuela "as a gentleman, and whether we are to consider him as a gentleman
or simply as a man his right to his own person and to his own undisturbed
sensibilities is one of the first rights of freedom". It was for infringement
of these rights that the claim was allowed.

But is it possible to claim damages, unrelated to any loss or suffering by
a claimant, and designed to punish or make an example of the respondent
state? On occasions the State Department has certainly provided proof that
the United States believes that such an award is possible.

In 1924 a U.S. consular official was brutally attacked in Tehran in broad
daylight. He made his escape but was pursued and later killed. The circumstances strongly suggested that the police and military had made no effort
to protect him. In a communication to the Persian Government, the
American Ambassador explained that the U.S. Government did not wish
"to require punitive damages" but it was "insistent that full reparation
should be made". The Persian Government expressed its "deepest regret";
it paid $110,000 for the cost of an escort to the quayside and of tranship-
ment of the body back to the United States by a U.S. naval vessel, and
$60,000 for the benefit of the widow.[2]

While no claim was made for punitive damages in that case, the United
States believed that it had a right to do so. In the abortive proceedings
instituted against Bulgaria before the International Court principally by
Israel, but also by the United States and the United Kingdom, in the *Aerial
Incident* case,[3] the United States' claim included a sum which can only be
explained as an attempt to obtain punitive damages. The tenor of the
American argument does suggest in part that the sum of $100,000 should
be paid, over and above the amount claimed on behalf of the U.S.
nationals killed when the EL-AL airliner was shot down, as amends for a
direct inter-state wrong. The authorities cited in support, the *I'm Alone*
and the *Imbrie* case, were certainly cases involving damage or injury to
the state (an insult to the flag in the former case, and the killing of a state

---

1. The claim as presented was for loss of earnings at $350 per month (for nineteen
months); $1,000 for legal fees in securing his release from prison; and $10,000 for the
wrongful treatment. It may be surmised that as the illegal imprisonment was only for the
period after the expiry of the time within which Roberts should have been brought to trial, the
award for loss of earnings amounted to $2,450; assuming the claim for $1,000 was allowed
in toto, the award for the inhumane treatment thus amounted to $4,550.
2. *Imbrie* case, Whiteman, *Damages*, Vol. 1, p. 732.
3. I.C.J. Pleadings, *Aerial Incident of 27 July, 1953*, pp. 246-8.

official in the latter). However, in the *Aerial Incident* case, the direct state wrong was perpetrated against Israel, the state of registration of the aircraft, and not against the United States. And when one examines the reasons for this additional claim it is apparent that it was of a punitive nature. In the view of the United States, the Bulgarian authorities should be punished for the wanton killing of the airliner's passengers, and for subsequently resiling from an undertaking given generally to compensate and atone for the destruction of the airliner and the persons on board. In the words of the United States memorial to the Court, in view of the "limitations on tort and criminal powers of this Court, an additional judgment for $100,000 to the United States Government on account of the elements of fraud, deceit, and wilful and premeditated killing of American nationals would be proper, in addition to the awards of monetary damages for the account of the next of kin of the American passengers."

The better view is, nevertheless, that punitive, vindictive or exemplary damages (or whatever other epithet is used to describe such damages) are not an established means of redress under international law. The United States pressed strongly for exemplary damages in the *Lusitania* claims[4] against Germany on behalf of U.S. nationals killed when the British ship of that name was torpedoed by a German submarine. The Commission concluded that it was not necessary for it to go so far as to hold that exemplary damages could not be awarded "in *any* case by *any* international arbitral tribunal", because for its own purposes it was bound by the treaty which created it and gave it jurisdiction—and that treaty granted the Commission no power to award such damages. However, the Commission clearly stated that, in its opinion, international law did not recognise the award of punitive damages. "That one injured is, under the rules of international law, entitled to be compensated for an injury inflicted resulting in mental suffering, injury to his feelings, humiliation, shame, degradation, loss of social position or injury to his credit or to his reputation, there can be no doubt, and such compensation should be commensurate to the injury. Such damages are very real, and the mere fact that they are difficult to measure or estimate by money standards makes them none the less real and affords no reason why the injured person should not be compensated therefor as compensatory damages, *but not as a penalty*. . . . The industry of counsel has failed to point us to any money award by an international arbitral tribunal where exemplary, punitive, or vindictive damages have been assessed against one sovereign nation in favour of another presenting a claim in behalf of its nationals."

B. Other remedies

The remedy in a successful claim will depend largely upon the powers available to the tribunal before which the case is heard. These powers

---

.4. 7 U.N.R.I.A.A. 32, esp. at pp. 38–44.

may be limited in two ways, by the agreement creating the tribunal, and by the agreement or application submitting the claim to its jurisdiction. Particularly in claims arising out of an alleged direct breach of obligation by one state against another, the likelihood is that a more appropriate remedy would be sought than an award of damages.

a DECLARATION

If there is a disagreement between two states over the extent of their obligations, whether under treaty or customary international law, a declaration by an international tribunal of the true legal position will often be sufficient. This course is frequently adopted in disputes over territorial rights. Although the term "declare" is not always used, the phraseology is now well settled. The parties agree that the tribunal shall "determine" the extent, or the existence, of the rights in question. Thus, Article 1 of the arbitration agreement between the Netherlands and the United States of 23rd January, 1925, read in part: "The sole duty of the Arbitrator shall be to determine whether the Island of Palmas . . . in its entirety forms a part of territory belonging to the United States of America or of Netherlands territory."[5] Similarly by a Special Agreement between the United Kingdom and France, ratified by the two states in 1951, the International Court was "requested to determine whether the sovereignty over the islets and rocks . . . of the Minquiers and Ecrehos groups respectively belongs to the United Kingdom or the French Republic."[6]

As far as such cases before the Court are concerned the actual proceedings are usually in the form of an application by a state requesting the Court to "declare" in its favour. In the *Minquiers and Ecrehos* case, the Court, on behalf of the United Kingdom, was asked to "declare" that the United Kingdom was "entitled under international law to full and undivided sovereignty" of the islets and rocks in the two groups, and a similar request was made by France. The United Kingdom application to the Court in the *Fisheries* case[7] sought an award of damages in respect of earlier interference with vessels flying the British flag, and a declaration of the principles of law applicable to the determination of the base lines of territorial waters, by reference to which the Norwegian government was entitled to delimit a fisheries zone.

b RESTITUTION

It is doubtful whether there is any right to restitution under customary international law except perhaps in relation to territory. It is clear that a decision in favour of a state claiming title in preference to another state actually in possession of the disputed territory creates a duty to restore the area concerned to the rightful sovereign.

---

5. *Island of Palmas* arbitration, 2 U.N.R.I.A.A. 831.
6. I.C.J. Rep. 1953, p. 47.   7. I.C.J. Rep. 1951, p. 116.

However, this duty can hardly be termed a "remedy", because the remedy is the declaration of the legal position by the tribunal. Although the point may be largely a matter of wording, it is probably more correct to say that an international tribunal has no power to *decree* restitution unless that power is expressly granted by agreement between the parties, either for the purposes of a particular case, or generally. For example, a number of peace treaties after the Second World War (with Hungary, with Italy, and with Roumania) imposed a duty to restore property seized by former enemy states from territories under their occupation.

c SATISFACTION

In some cases, although there has been no direct damage or injury to the claimant state, but a violation of its rights, the attempt has been made by that state to obtain a judgment in its favour from an international tribunal. By leaving the matter to the tribunal in this way, the claimant state can be said to be seeking "satisfaction". In the *Corfu Channel* case,[8] it will be recalled, the United Kingdom, following the damage to its naval vessels by mines, mounted a large scale mine-sweeping operation in parts of the Channel within Albanian territorial waters. This operation the International Court held to be a violation of Albania's territorial sovereignty. As Albania was not seeking damages, the Court held that a declaration to this effect was "in itself appropriate satisfaction".[9]

While historically the notion of satisfaction was much wider in that one state might demand "satisfaction" in a particularly humiliating form—flag saluting or other extreme forms of apology—it plays no significant role in international law as a judicial remedy.[10] As a gesture of conciliation, an apology or an undertaking to punish those responsible will be deemed sufficient amends for the wrongful acts of the respondent state.[11]

5 STATE SUCCESSION AND INTERNATIONAL RESPONSIBILITY

a THE DOCTRINE OF ACQUIRED RIGHTS

In the context of treaty obligations, some comment was made on the concept of state succession based upon Roman law notions of universal succession of an heir to the property of the deceased. Where this principle of "universal succession" was clearly most relevant was for the purpose of determining private rights at the moment immediately after the transfer of sovereignty. Although the laws of the new sovereign might be different from those of the former sovereign, they would operate only on the legal

---

8. I.C.J. Rep. 1949, p. 4.   9. *Ibid.*, at p. 35.
10. As also with the award of "nominal" damages: *Carthage* case (1913) 11 U.N.R.I.A.A. 457.
11. Hence the Commissioners' *recommendation* (it was not binding as part of the award) that the Unites States, *inter alia*, "ought formally to acknowledge" the illegality of the sinking of the *I'm Alone*, and apologise to His Majesty's Canadian Government.

system as it existed at the moment of transfer. To give one simple illustration, let us suppose that under the laws of the former sovereign a grant of a mining lease to a foreign national is effective without the permission of the Ministry of Mines; but under the laws of the new sovereign no such lease is effective without such permission. A mining lease granted to an alien before the transfer of sovereignty without permission is valid and effective to create a "vested" or "acquired" right which remains in force under the new legal order. Any attempt to interfere with that right (e.g. by cancelling it on the ground that permission had not been given by the Ministry) would be tantamount to an expropriation of alien property within the normal rules of state responsibility.

Such a view has a substantial weight of opinion and authority to support it. The United States Supreme Court was called upon to consider a number of private claims arising out of alleged grants by the authorities of the previous sovereign of land subsequently incorporated into the Union. In the case of *U.S.* v. *Percheman*,[12] the Court had to consider the validity of a claim to land which the appellee alleged had been granted to him by the former Spanish governor of Florida before Florida was ceded to the United States in the treaty of 1819. In giving the opinion of the Court, Marshall C.J. made the following classic statement of principle:[13]

> ". . . it is very unusual, even in cases of conquest, for the conqueror to do more than to displace the sovereign and assume dominion over the country. The modern usage of nations, which has become law, would be violated; that sense of justice and of right which is acknowledged and felt by the whole civilised world would be outraged, if private property should be generally confiscated, and private rights annulled. The people change their allegiance; their relation to their ancient sovereign is dissolved; but their relation to each other, and their rights of property, remain undisturbed."

And in a number of municipal decisions during the inter-war years, the issue was not whether "acquired" rights survived a change of sovereignty, but what sort of interests could be classified as acquired rights.[14]

On the international level, the Permanent Court was asked to give an advisory opinion on the rights of certain settlers of German origin to land transferred from Germany to Poland under the Treaty of Versailles.[15] The interests were of two kinds: leases granted over former German state properties; and a type of rental/purchase arrangement (Rentengutsverträge) whereby the transfer of legal ownership only took place on payment of the final instalment of rental, each instalment of which represented part of the balance of the purchase price. The Court saw no reason

---

12. 7 Pet. 51 (1830).   13. *Ibid.*, at pp. 86–87.

14. E.g. *Matys* v. *Nipanicz* (1919–22) 1 A.D. Case No. 48; *Procurator-General* v. *S.* (1929–30), 5 A.D. Case No. 366.

15. (1923) P.C.I.J. Rep., Ser. B, No. 6. See also *Jablonsky* v. *German Reich* (1935–7), 8 A.D. Case No. 42.

for distinguishing between either type of interest. The holders of Renten-gutsverträge had rights enforceable under German law against the vendor of the property. No one denied that German law had continued without interruption to operate in the territory transferred by the Treaty. It could hardly be maintained that, although the law survived, private rights acquired under it had perished. Such a contention was based upon no principle and was contrary to amost universal opinion and practice. Even those who contested the existence in international law of a general prin-ciple of state succession did not go so far as to maintain that private rights, including those acquired from the state as the owner of the property, were invalid as against the successor sovereign.

As a succession to obligations depended upon the existence of an acquired right, it followed that a successor state was not responsible for "tortious" acts or a denial of justice committed by the previous sove-reign. The leading authority on this point was the *Robert E. Brown* claim[16] which has already been dealt with in relation to a denial of justice. It will be recalled that Brown had been thwarted in attempts to have his mining claims recognised by the government of the South African Republics, which had even gone to the extent of interfering with the judiciary. The tribunal had no doubt that a claim by the United States against the Repub-lics, had they continued to exist, would have succeeded. But the United Kingdom, which had annexed the two Republics, was not in any way responsible for what had occurred. It was "simply a pending claim for damages against certain officials and had never become a liquidated debt of the former state": "properly speaking", there was no "question of state succession here involved."

b PRESENT APPLICATION OF THE DOCTRINE

While the *German Settlers* case adopted what was, by 1923, accepted by a preponderance of state practice, there was nevertheless a strong under-current of opinion hostile to the reception of the doctrine of acquired rights. This hostility took the form of two main legal arguments: (i) that contractual rights, including concessions, depended upon the con-tinued existence of the contracting state, or at least of the sovereignty of the contracting state over the area covered by the concession; and (ii) that rights created by the former sovereign as part of a political programme could be disregarded.

i *Contractual rights*

As the *Robert E. Brown* claim established that there was no succession in cases of unliquidated claims against a former sovereign (i.e. in cases of tortious acts), a rejection of the principles of succession in cases of contrac-tual rights would have reduced the doctrine of acquired rights to insigni-ficance. Yet this view was held by the Transvaal Commission which was created by the British government to advise on the attitude to be adopted

---

16. (1923), 6 U.N.R.I.A.A. 120; see also *Redward and Others* (Hawaiian claims) *ibid.*, 157.

towards the many concessions granted by the government of the Transvaal before annexation by Britain.[17] The Commission asserted that "a state which has annexed another is not legally bound by any contracts made by the state which has ceased to exist".[18] Although the "best modern opinion" favoured the view that, "as a general rule, the obligations of the annexed state towards private persons should be respected", the Commission doubted "whether the duties of an annexing state towards those claiming under concessions or contracts granted or made by the annexed state have been defined with such precision in authoritative statement, or acted upon with such uniformity in civilized practice, as to warrant their being termed rules of international law."

Although the Commission then proceeded to lay down a number of principles that had guided them in allowing claims in respect of a number of concessions, these claims were treated as being based upon moral, not legal, considerations. This attitude was reflected in the view taken of a claim presented diplomatically by the Netherlands government on behalf of the Netherlands South African Railway Company. The Commission had decided that compensation was inappropriate as the company had, through its operations, contributed to the prolongation of the war. The Netherlands government succeeded in obtaining an ex gratia payment from the British Government, though it was accompanied by strenuous denials of legal responsibility.[19]

ii *Rights created for political purposes*

It is understandable enough that a successor state should not be prepared to recognise the rights granted by the former sovereign if the purpose of the grants was to further some political programme. In the *German Settlers* case,[20] it will be remembered, the Permanent Court was asked to consider whether land rights granted to former German nationals in an area ceded by Germany to Poland under the Treaty of Versailles could be arbitrarily abrogated by the Polish authorities. It was clear that the land grants had been part of a deliberate policy of German settlement of an area populated by a majority of Poles. The Court considered the political nature of the scheme as irrelevant: the "fact that there was a political purpose behind the colonisation scheme cannot affect the private rights acquired".[1] As the Court later commented,[2] "the political motive originally connected with the Rentengutsverträge does not in any way deprive them of their character as contracts".

Nevertheless, as the Court then went on to state that "the few clauses which they (the Rentengutsverträge) contain of a distinctively political

17. Cd. 623 of 1901: see Smith, *Great Britain and the Law of Nations*, Vol. 1, p. 355 *et seq.*
18. The Commission also stated that they were "unable to perceive any sound distinction between a case where a state acquires part of another by cession, and a case where it acquires the whole by annexation."
19. Pitt Cobbett, *Leading Cases on International Law*, Vol. 1, 4th ed., p. 354.
20. (1923) P.C.I.J. Rep., Ser. B, No. 6.
1. *Ibid.*, at p. 33.   2. At p. 39.

character become inoperative without interfering in the least with the normal execution of their essential clauses", the decision is not conclusive on the point. In fact, the implication that one must draw from this pronouncement is that the political nature of such a scheme can render it inoperative *vis-à-vis* the successor if provisions of a political nature form an essential or "non-severable" part of the contract creating the interest. If this is indeed the meaning of the Court's statement, it is an attempt to create an unworkable principle of law. Either political motives should be relevant or they should not; it is excessively legalistic to make the application of the rule depend upon the wording of the contract in question. Such a rule might be workable in a municipal system based upon ready access to the courts: it is totally unsuitable to the international sphere where adjustment, not adjudication, is the normal process for settling disputes and claims.

What has, in retrospect, made such a legalistic formulation of the law even less relevant has been the dramatic change in attitudes towards problems of succession brought about by the rapid growth in the number of new states since the second world war. The majority of these states have resented the economic influence retained after independence by the former colonial power. Often this influence has had as its more obvious manifestations the continued operation of business enterprises created during the period of dependency. Expropriation of assets by the new sovereign in such circumstances is primarily a matter of responsibility and not succession, but what if the assets include contractual or concessionary rights granted by the previous sovereign?

Contemporary Communist theory, which has widespread support among the new states of Africa and Asia, rejects universal succession in three cases: "first, when a new state appears as the result of separation from another; second, when a state emerges from the status of dependency by succession from a metropolitan country in assertion of the right of self-determination; and third, when a new type of state appears as the result of social revolution."[3] In such circumstances, the new state should not be bound by obligations not in its political and economic interests.

While this view in an extreme form might, if applied, create anarchy in international trading relations, the reasons behind it are sufficiently important to be worthy of consideration in formulating the current principles of state succession. The Russian Revolution was violent, both internally and as far as external reaction was concerned. The philosophy of the Revolution was of a new world order, and in keeping with that philosophy Soviet Russia regarded itself as a new state, unhampered by the property and other obligations of the Tsarist régime. To this situation, the normal rules of continuity of states whereby one *government* of a state is liable for the acts of former *governments* provided a stereotyped, but inappropriate, answer. But it did not necessarily follow that the Soviets

---

3.   Lukashuk of the U.S.S.R., addressing the International Law Association, 52nd Report (1966), p. 562.

were entitled to reject *all* claims to compensation from foreign interests.

The climate of 1920 was inappropriate for political compromise. There grew up, therefore, two totally different concepts of law and society; that traditionally observed outside the Soviet Union, and that developed in the writings of Soviet apologists of the Revolution. The emergence of the Soviet Union as a world power, and the expansion of the Communist system to states outside Russia, together with the creation of the many new states of Africa and Asia, has altered profoundly the climate of opinion in the international community towards state responsibility and problems of state succession. The traditional rules still exist, although their application in specific cases will depend largely upon the agreement of the states concerned. And as the spirit of compromise affects the application of the rules, it will also affect their content. In relation to contractual and con-cessionary rights, the likelihood is that the differences between the rules of responsibility and of succession will disappear and that these separate "branches" of the law under traditional rules will coalesce. Compensation should be payable, but the amount should depend partly on the value of the rights expropriated, but primarily on the economic and political circumstances of the particular case.

CHAPTER ELEVEN

INTERNATIONAL CLAIMS—II
THE ADJUDICATION OF
INTERNATIONAL DISPUTES

By far the majority of international claims or disputes are dealt with through diplomatic channels, through negotiation between the states concerned, or with the help of the good offices or mediation of a third state. With these diplomatic procedures this book will not deal. Although legal arguments are frequently employed by Foreign Offices in conducting their negotiations, the procedures themselves have no defined legal form. There are no rules of law, though there will be principles of diplomatic protocol, governing the application of such procedures. It is only in relatively sophisticated procedures, whether adjudicative before an international tribunal, or deliberative before the political organs of an international institution, that legal considerations can influence the application of the particular process. Adjudicative procedures will be dealt with in the present chapter: deliberative procedures will be dealt with later.[1]

1 LEGAL AND POLITICAL DISPUTES: THE CONCEPT OF JUSTICIABILITY

Before discussing in detail the procedures of arbitration and judicial settlement available for the adjudication of international claims, some comment is necessary on the notion of "justiciability". It has long been held, or at least argued, that certain disputes could not be judicially determined because they were not "justiciable" or not "legal" (the terms "justiciable" or "legal" on the one hand and "non-justiciable" and "political" on the other being used interchangeably). The expression has been used, and variously defined, as if it was capable of precise ascertainment. For example, in a number of treaties states have undertaken to submit disputes arising out of the treaty, or sometimes even all their disputes, to arbitration, but excluded from the undertaking what have variously been described as "non-justiciable" or "political" disputes.

---

1. Particularly in Chapter 13.

This limitation was usually framed in terms which excluded from third-party adjudication matters affecting the independence, vital interests, or national honour of the contracting states. Being part of a treaty creating a legal obligation to submit disputes to arbitration, it must be supposed that the parties regarded the limitation as having a legal application. It would be inconsistent with the notion of legal obligation if the exemption were drawn in terms incapable of analysis in legal terms. Nevertheless it must be doubted whether expressions such as "vital interests" and "national honour" can be ascertained by reference to any objective standard. What is vital to the interests of a state or what affects its national honour are essentially questions that only the state itself can answer.[2]

Not only is it difficult to define "justiciable" in any such sense as a legal concept, but it is also doubtful whether justiciability is definable in legal terms at all. In layman's terms, "justiciable" as applied to a dispute suggests that the dispute is capable of being resolved by the application of legal principles and procedures. But such an interpretation is hardly adequate because it would make meaningless the distinction between justiciable (or legal) disputes on the one hand, and non-justiciable (or political) disputes on the other. This *reductio ad absurdum* was demonstrated by Lauterpacht, who commented that while "it is not difficult to establish the proposition that all disputes between states are of a political nature, inasmuch as they involve more or less important interests of states, it is equally easy to show that all international disputes are, irrespective of their gravity, disputes of a legal character in the sense that, so long as the rule of law is recognised, they are capable of an answer by the application of legal rules."[3] However, if one meaning of "justiciable" (or "legal") produces a demonstrably inadequate explanation, is there any alternative definition which would give more satisfactory results?

In the conduct of international relations a state might have a variety of reasons for wishing or not wishing to submit a dispute to judicial settlement. The decision to seek such a settlement is a political decision. It might be taken by one state because its wish to harmonise relations with another state, or to prevent a disruption, outweighs the subject-matter of the dispute, or the risk of an adverse verdict. In some circumstances a state might wish to display its sincerity in advocating judicial settlement as a means of settling international disputes. Similarly with the decision not to "go to court": a state might pursue a deliberate policy of opposing judicial settlement, or of non-co-operation with another state or group of states. The examples that could be given are many, but these few illustrations do demonstrate the difficulty, probably the impossibility, of defining the concept of justiciability in legal terms. A state will regard a dispute as justiciable or not according to purely subjective criteria.

---

2. Compare the so-called "automatic" reservation to declarations accepting the jurisdiction of the International Court, below, pp. 501–506.
3. *Function of Law in the International Community*, pp. 157–8.

So far in the discussion the expressions "justiciable" and "legal" have been treated as synonymous. Indeed, in many contexts the expressions are used interchangeably. However, in one specific context it would seem necessary to distinguish between what a state may regard as justiciable and a dispute that is legal. The Statute of the International Court lays down that states parties to the Statute may declare in advance their acceptance of the Court's jurisdiction in "all *legal* disputes" concerning questions of international law (Art. 36 (2)), and that the Court may give an advisory opinion on "any legal question" (Art. 65 (1)), though there is no such limitation upon the Court's conventional jurisdiction. States can by treaty bestow upon the Court the power to determine non-legal disputes. And it is arguable that, even where the basis of the Court's jurisdiction is advance acceptance by the declarations under Article 36 (2), if the parties specifically agree that the Court should, in accordance with Article 38 (2), decide the case *ex aequo et bono*, the non-legal nature of the issues involved would not prevent the Court exercising jurisdiction.[4]

If "legal" as employed in the Statute were equated with "justiciable" in the variety of meanings that expression has assumed, the whole concept of judicial settlement by advance acceptance of the Court's jurisdiction would be jeopardised. But what, then, is meant by a "legal dispute" or "legal question"?

A dispute is clearly not legal though it may be "about" international law, if it is centred not upon the legal "position" (which is clear and not contested by the parties) but upon whether or not that position should be altered or disregarded. The illustration was given at the very start of this book of the Goa dispute between India and Portugal. The major issue was not the validity of Portugal's legal title but whether the law should continue to recognise, i.e. whether it was politically acceptable in present day circumstances, that sovereignty should be retained by one colonial power in an area from which other colonial powers had withdrawn. While it is perhaps possible to consider the changes brought about in the law by a process of evolution as themselves "legal" issues, a fundamental change of the type demanded by India could only be accomplished by political action. There may also be situations in which the issue raised cannot be resolved by the application of judicial techniques. Although interpretation of a treaty is *prima facie* a function within the competence of an international tribunal, the terms of the particular treaty may raise matters requiring political rather than legal "judgments". For example, it is hardly a legal issue if a tribunal were asked specifically whether a particular applicant for admission to membership in the United Nations were "peace-loving" or "willing to carry out its obligations under the Charter"; and it is not converted into a legal issue by the fact that it involves an

---

4. This was certainly the theory in relation to arbitral tribunals (see below, pp. 483–484); but the position of the Court is doubtful in view of the attitude adopted by the Permanent Court in the *Free Zones* case (below, p. 477). Although the Special Agreement purported to bestow upon the Court the widest powers, the Court refused to exercise some of them on the ground that to do so would be inconsistent with its judicial nature.

interpretation of a treaty provision, namely Article 4 of the Charter.

On a number of occasions the Permanent Court was asked to consider issues that were not of a legal character.

In the *Free Zones* case,[5] the Court was asked whether a certain tariff régime was abrogated by the Treaty of Versailles. If it was decided that the régime was abrogated, the Court was empowered to settle all matters outstanding in relation to the carrying out of the relevant provision of the Treaty; but should "the judgment contemplate the import of goods free or at reduced rates through the Federal Customs barrier or through the French Customs barrier, regulations of such importation shall only be made with the consent of the two parties." The Court held that to make its decision subject to the subsequent approval of the parties was "incompatible with the Statute, and with its position as a Court of Justice". But in any case to submit an issue to the Court that might require it to decide on tariff rates or exemptions was "outside the sphere in which a Court of Justice, concerned with the application of rules of law, can help in the solution of disputes between two states."

In contrast, in the *Customs Union* case,[6] the Council of the League of Nations asked the Permanent Court for an advisory opinion on whether a proposed customs régime between Germany and Austria was contrary to Austria's treaty obligations. Under Article 88 of the Treaty of Saint-Germain, Austria undertook "in the absence of the consent of the said Council to abstain from any act which might directly or indirectly or by any means whatever compromise her independence". And by the Geneva Protocol of 1924, Austria undertook *inter alia* not to "violate her economic independence by granting to any state a special régime or exclusive advantages calculated to threaten this independence". The Court held that the régime was calculated to threaten the economic independence of Austria and was, therefore, incompatible with Austria's obligations under the Protocol. But how was it possible to estimate whether the proposed union was calculated to threaten Austria's independence; or was an act which might "indirectly or by any means whatever compromise her independence" within Article 88 of the Treaty? The answers to such questions could only be given by a process of political prediction.[7] Whether a given event deprives a state of its independence might be a legal question. But whether a given event affects, or is likely to endanger, or is calculated to threaten, the independence of a state is not a legal question and consequently does not fall within the competence of a judicial tribunal at all.

Of course this conclusion does not imply that a judicial tribunal should not take into account the political and economic background in defining the content of a particular rule of law. Law cannot exist in isolation

---

5. (1929), P.C.I.J. Rep., Ser. A/B, No. 46. And see also the *Haya de la Torre* case, I.C.J. Rep. 1951, at pp. 78–79.
6. (1931), P.C.I.J. Rep., Ser. A/B, No. 41.
7. The essentially political nature of the task entrusted to the Court is apparent throughout Judge Anzilotti's Separate Opinion in this case.

from the needs of the community it governs. And in the international community most of all, the very existence and future development of its legal framework is dependent upon reconciling the various political forces and pressures within the community. There is, however, a fundamental difference between answering a question which is essentially political, and answering a legal question in the light of political factors. The former is outside the judicial function and competence (a fact recognised by the Statute of the International Court); the latter is permissible even though its propriety is doubted by many states.[8]

2 ARBITRATION

a THE DEVELOPMENT OF ARBITRATION

The essential element of arbitration, as opposed to good offices and mediation, is that it necessarily implies the duty of the parties to abide by the award that is made. The factor that most distinguishes it from judicial proceedings before the International Court is the right retained by the parties to choose some at least of the arbitrators, or to agree between themselves on the sole arbitrator.

In general terms, good offices may be described as the activities of a third state in bringing about negotiations between the parties to a dispute. Mediation is the process whereby the third state or party assists in the settlement of the dispute. As the U.N. Mediator in Palestine in 1948 reported, mediation "is a consequence of the tender of good offices, and the primary task of the Mediator is to initiate proposals calculated to harmonise conflicting interests and claims".[9] In practice, of course, it is seldom possible to break down the diplomatic procedures employed by a third party or parties in a particular dispute into such watertight compartments. However, "good offices" and "mediation" are useful descriptive terms as long as they are not regarded as "terms of art". But their greatest value lies in the fact that they connote processes having "exclusively the character of advice"; they never have binding force.[10]

Arbitration developed from a combination of negotiation and mediation. Many early arbitrations were conducted by panels of equal numbers from each side with no means of resolving the likely deadlock, and the arbitrators to such proceedings saw themselves primarily as diplomatic negotiators. While the "award" made by such panels was regarded as binding, it was very much a negotiated compromise and not an adjudication. It was only with the addition to the panel of an impartial "umpire", thus enabling an award to be made despite a total lack of agreement among the national members of the panel, that arbitration assumed its own separate characteristics. And, of course, once the possibility of an

---

8. For the possibility of the Court declining to give an Advisory Opinion because of the political factors involved in a legal question referred to it, see below, pp. 524–526.
9. Cited Sohn, *Cases on World Law*, p. 433.
10. Hague Conventions on the Peaceful Settlement of Disputes, 1895 and 1907, Art. 6.

award against the wishes of a party was recognised, the whole concept of arbitration was changed. There was a fundamental difference between a binding award negotiated by, and subject to the wishes of, the parties, and a binding award over which, in the last resort, they had no control.

In view of the fundamental change from diplomatic compromise to adjudication it is hardly surprising that the new concept of arbitration was slow to develop. Despite the example of the Jay Treaty of 1794 whereby Britain and the United States agreed to settle by arbitration issues outstanding after the War of Independence,[11] the 1815 settlement of Europe was supervised by the Concert of Europe, the system of meetings between the Great Powers which was intended to keep peace and resolve disputes between them. However, with the second half of the nineteenth century, arbitration became a more fashionable means of settling issues of a minor nature, often issues which remained after some major dispute had been resolved by agreement. There were no settled procedures for establishing the tribunal, and the difficulty of reaching agreement upon basic procedural requirements was often resolved by choosing a head of a third state as arbitrator (as in the case of the *Bulama Island* case between Britain and Portugal which was submitted to the United States President[12]), or by setting up a Commission by a treaty setting out its powers so far as the parties could agree and hoping that problems not covered by the treaty would resolve themselves (as with the Commission set up in 1869 to adjudicate on British claims arising out of the anarchical conditions that had preceded the creation of Venezuela in 1863[13]).

Much in the same way as the Jay Treaty of 1794 revitalised arbitration as a process for the settlement of disputes, the *Alabama* award of 1872[14] demonstrated its potential as a means of settling even the most acrimonious and serious issues between states. By submitting their dispute over the payment of compensation to the United States for the losses caused to American shipping by the depredations of Confederate cruisers built in British ship-yards, the two states were able to resolve a controversy which had appeared insoluble, without loss of face by one side or the other, by normal diplomatic methods. The success of the arbitration provided the impetus which led ultimately to the Hague Conventions of 1899 and 1907 on the Peaceful Settlement of Disputes, the earlier of which provided for the creation of the Permanent Court of Arbitration.

b THE PERMANENT COURT OF ARBITRATION AND PROCEDURES FOR THE APPOINTMENT OF ARBITRATORS

The Permanent Court of Arbitration is in no sense a court. It is in reality a large panel of international lawyers of the highest moral reputation

---

11. The two issues concerned: (1) a part of the Canadian border; (2) debts owed to British subjects by debtors who had become U.S. citizens as a result of the war. A third issue covered by the Treaty concerned claims by U.S. citizens arising out of British activities against U.S. ships during the current Anglo-French War.

12. Discussed in Simpson and Fox, *International Arbitration*, p. 7

13. *Ibid.*, pp. 6–7.   14. Moore. *Int. Arb.*, p. 495.

nominated by states parties to the Conventions. The theory was that Members of the panel were to be available to states wishing to select arbitrators. The most permanent aspect of the Court is its Bureau, comprising a Secretary-General and a small staff. There is also, in name at least, an Administrative Council, comprising the Foreign Minister of the Netherlands as President and the heads of the diplomatic missions at the Hague of states parties to the Convention.

Arbitrators selected from the Court heard thirteen cases before the outbreak of the First World War, but with the creation of the Permanent Court of International Justice in 1920, calls on the Court of Arbitration dwindled. Since 1932, it must be admitted, the chief significance of the nominations to the Court has been their role in the appointment of judges to the Permanent Court of International Justice and to the present International Court of Justice.[15]

The two Hague Conventions did provide a basic procedural code for the conduct of international arbitrations. But it cannot be said that they provided a settled formula for the *appointment* of arbitrators. Article XLV of the 1907 Convention provided:

> "Each party appoints two Arbitrators, of whom one only can be its national or chosen from among the persons selected by it as members of the Permanent Court. These Arbitrators together choose an Umpire.
>
> "If the votes are equally divided, the choice of the Umpire is entrusted to a third Power, selected by the parties by common accord.
>
> "If an agreement is not arrived at on this subject, each party selects a different Power, and the choice of the Umpire is made in concert by the Powers thus selected.
>
> "If, within two months' time, these two Powers cannot come to an agreement, each of them presents two candidates taken from the list of members of the Permanent Court, exclusive of the members selected by the parties and not being nationals of either of them. Drawing lots determines which of the candidates thus presented shall be Umpire."

Despite this example, states continued to employ a variety of other methods. The *Clipperton Island* case was the award of a head of state (the King of Italy);[16] the *Tinoco* arbitration was the decision of the Chief Justice of the United States;[17] the *Island of Palmas* case was heard by a single arbitrator from the Permanent Court of Arbitration (Max Huber).[18] A majority of claims commissions have comprised two Commissioners, one appointed by each party, and an umpire or president to resolve issues upon which the Commissioners disagreed.[19] In many instances this formula is the least satisfactory. A single arbitrator is at least free from the pressures of colleagues who are inclined to reinforce the arguments presented by their own government, while the proposed tribunal of five

---

15. See below, pp. 484–485. 16. (1931), 2 U.N.R.I.A.A. 1105.
17. (1923), 1 U.N.R.I.A.A. 369. 18. (1928) 2 U.N.R.I.A.A. 829.
19. E.g. the Venezuelan Arbitrations of 1903 reported in 9 and 10 U.N.R.I.A.A.; or the *Lusitania* and other claims between U.S. and Germany in 7 and 8 U.N.R.I.A.A.

under the 1907 Convention had the merit of including a majority of non-national arbitrators.[20]

The procedure for the appointment of arbitrators in most international agreements was dependent on the good faith of the parties. In the majority of cases the states were dealing with existing disputes so that there was no question of resiling from an undertaking to arbitrate subsequent disputes. Where states did undertake to settle future disputes by arbitration (as under the General Act of Geneva, 1928), it was obviously necessary to provide for the appointment of arbitrators if one of the parties attempted to thwart the process by refusing to appoint to the tribunal. The General Act did not resolve the problem of total non-co-operation, but it was left to events following the Second World War to bring home most forcibly the deficiency in existing agreements to arbitrate.

The Peace Treaties between the Allies (calling themselves the United Nations) and the former enemy states of Bulgaria, Hungary and Roumania, contained a number of human rights provisions. Disputes over whether the rights had been granted or were being respected in the three states were to be submitted to arbitration. The tribunals envisaged by the respective treaties were to comprise one arbitrator appointed by the former enemy state concerned, one by the state or states alleging that the human rights provisions had been infringed, and a third member to be selected by mutual agreement. If the two parties were unable to agree upon the appointment of the third member, either party could apply to the Secretary-General of the United Nations to make the appointment. The former enemy states failed to appoint an arbitrator, and the International Court was asked *inter alia* whether, after appointing its own national member to the tribunal, the other party could apply to the Secretary-General to make an appointment; and whether a tribunal consisting of only the two members could proceed to hear the dispute. The Court held[1] that the strict wording of a treaty could not be ignored in order to make it "effective". A tribunal constituted in the way suggested would not be the tribunal provided for in the treaty. The Secretary-General had no power to appoint a third member until the national members of the tribunal had been appointed.

To avoid the frustration of agreements to arbitrate, a number of similar formulae have been adopted to provide for the appointment of arbitrators in the face of the non-co-operation of one of the parties to a dispute. Article 21 of the European Convention for the Peaceful Settlement of Disputes of 1957 reads:

> "If the nomination of the members of the Arbitral Tribunal is not made within a period of three months from the date on which one of the parties requested the other party to constitute an Arbitral Tribunal, the task of making the necessary nominations shall be entrusted to the Government of a third State, chosen by agreement

---

20. This formula was adopted in the Agreement of February, 1955, between Britain and Greece regarding the submission of the *Ambatielos* claim to arbitration, 12 U.N.R.I.A.A. 87.   1. I.C.J. Rep. 1950, p. 221.

between the parties, or, failing agreement within three months, to the President
of the International Court of Justice. Should the latter be a national of one of the
parties to the dispute, this task shall be entrusted to the Vice-President of the Court,
or to the next senior judge of the Court who is not a national of the parties."

Substantially the same approach was employed by the International Law
Commission in its 1958 Draft Code on Arbitral Procedure. And since the
Peace Treaties case a variety of agreements entered into by the specialised
agencies and other organisations within the U.N. orbit have included
similar provisions for the constitution of arbitration tribunals to settle
disputes arising under the particular treaty. Despite these developments,
it should be realised that a vast number of pre-existing arbitration agreements remain vulnerable to parties who obstinately refuse to participate
in the machinery for arbitration.

c THE ROLE OF ARBITRATION

It is not easy to estimate either the role of arbitration or its significance.
For certain types of case it is clear that arbitration has been largely super-
seded by judicial settlement. If there had been no International Court, the
Anglo-Norwegian Fisheries case would no doubt have been submitted to
arbitration; and the same can be said for territorial disputes like the *Eastern
Greenland* and the *Minquiers and Ecrehos* cases.

On the other hand, arbitration can provide a less formal process which
may be considered more appropriate for minor cases. An isolated act of
interference with a fishing vessel operating inside a fishing zone in a
limited area could readily be submitted to arbitration.[2] An alteration in
the whole method of delimiting national waters as provided for in the
Norwegian decrees giving rise to the *Fisheries* case would be a matter of
fundamental importance upon which the parties might wish the International Court to pass judgment.

As only states can be parties to cases before the International Court,
arbitration is the only judicial proceeding which the parties themselves
can initiate that can give a binding award in a dispute involving an international organisation:[3] hence the reason for the inclusion of clauses in a
wide variety of treaties (usually of economic or technical assistance)
entered into by the specialised agencies and other U.N. bodies providing
for the submission of disputes arising out of the treaty or out of operations
conducted under the treaty to arbitration. Similarly, a number of quasi-
international disputes involving oil companies and concessionary states

---

2. E.g. the sort of incident that occurred in the case of the *Red Crusader*, a British fishing
vessel, seized by the Danish authorities for allegedly fishing within the fishing zone surrounding the Faroe Islands: this particular dispute was in fact submitted to a fact-finding Commission of Enquiry: (1962) 35 I.L.R. 485.

3. A number of treaties between international organisations and states (e.g. the Headquarters Agreement between the U.N. and the United States) contain provision for the
submission of disputes arising between them over interpretation of the treaty to the Court
by way of its advisory procedure, it being agreed that the Court's opinion should be
accepted as binding. This approach is made additionally cumbersome by the fact that the
resolution of a competent organ is required to set in motion the advisory process.

have been submitted to arbitrations having an international character.[4]

Arbitration is certainly better suited to the settlement of a large number of outstanding claims between two states than recourse to the Court. Often the arbitration commission is able to lay down certain guiding principles and then limit its task to applying those principles to the particular facts of individual claims. Reference has already been made in the previous chapter to the *Lusitania* claims between the United States and Germany which were decided in this way;[5] and to the claims between the United States and Italy under the 1947 Italian Peace Treaty.[6] While commissions of this type were common in the inter-war years, they have largely been superseded by the tendency of states to *negotiate* settlements of all outstanding claims; the task of allocating sums to individual claimants being left to national claims commissions.

One final comparison of arbitration with judicial settlement needs to be made because it ties in with what has already been said on the subject of so-called legal and political disputes. The argument was raised during debates in the 6th Committee of the eighth session of the General Assembly on one of the International Law Commission's drafts on arbitral procedure that arbitration was being defined in terms too closely resembling judicial settlement by the International Court. Reference was made to the origins of arbitration as a form of conciliation, and to the fact that many treaties during the inter-war years defined the undertaking to arbitrate to include political, or non-justiciable, disputes.

Certainly the theory was held in many quarters in the 'twenties and the 'thirties that the Permanent Court was appropriate for legal disputes and arbitration for non-legal disputes. Legal disputes (i.e. disputes about rights) under the General Act of 1928 were to be submitted to the Court, unless the parties agreed to settle the dispute by arbitration. Political disputes (disputes about interests) were to be subject to a system of conciliation, and, if that failed, to arbitration. However, it was recognised that a political dispute would involve legal issues, and such issues were to be decided in accordance with the rules laid down in Article 38 of the Court's Statute; but if there were no rules applicable (i.e. where the issue involved a conflict of interests) the tribunal "shall decide *ex aequo et bono*".

Although the Statute of the International Court, like that of the Permanent Court, does enable the parties to agree to the Court deciding *ex aequo et bono*, this option appears as an alternative to its normal jurisdiction. Article 38 (1) states that the Court "whose function is to decide in accordance with international law such *disputes* as are submitted to it, shall apply" international conventions, international custom, general principles of law, etc., but paragraph (2) goes on to provide that paragraph (1) "shall not prejudice the power of the Court to decide a case *ex aequo et bono*, if the parties agree thereto." States can only submit cases to the Court in accordance with the Statute, and this compartmentalisation

---

4. E.g. the *Abu Dhabi* and *Aramco* arbitrations, discussed above, pp. 429–432.
5. See above, p. 466.   6. See above, p. 405.

would seem to rule out the possibility of states seeking a decision from the Court in accordance partly with Article 38 (1) and partly with 38 (2). The only alternative in the context of the Court would seem to be to submit the issues separately, an excessively legalistic and probably an expensive and time-consuming exercise.

In this respect, arbitration offers a more satisfactory solution. The jurisdiction of a tribunal is governed not by a Statute, but by the *compromis*, the agreement between the parties in which they have defined its jurisdiction. In the *compromis* which is the "fundamental law" upon which the tribunal's powers are based, the parties can so define the issues as to obtain a decision on certain matters based upon principles of law, and an award, or even a recommendation, based upon political considerations on matters over which the parties' disagreements are extra-legal.[7] And if an award of this nature is required, it is more likely that the parties would wish to select their own arbitrators, than have the tribunal constituted for them as would be the case with the Court.

Even though arbitration has advantages over judicial settlement in relation to political disputes, it cannot be claimed that it has managed to establish itself as an acceptable procedure for their settlement. States prefer to retain control over their disputes rather than risk an unfavourable outcome in third party adjudication. And the rapid development in the role played by international organisations in the field of international relations has provided more attractive alternatives for dispute adjustment or for exerting political pressure towards the desired solution. While taking into account legal factors, the organs of the United Nations are an ideal setting for the advancement of political considerations in support of a particular claim. But to the powers of the United Nations the discussion will turn in the following chapters.

3 THE INTERNATIONAL COURT OF JUSTICE

A. Organisation of the Court

a THE JUDGES AND THEIR APPOINTMENT

The Court consists of fifteen judges, no two of whom may be nationals of the same state (Art. 3 (1)).[8] These judges must be "persons of high moral character, who possess the qualifications required in their respective countries for appointment to the highest judicial offices, or are jurisconsults of recognised competence in international law" (Art. 2). The judges are elected by the General Assembly and by the Security Council from a list of persons nominated by the national groups in the Permanent

---

7. There would seem to be no obstacle to a *compromis* granting to the arbitral tribunal the sort of powers the Permanent Court declined to exercise in the *Free Zones* case, above, p. 477.

8. Unless otherwise stated, references are to the Statute of the International Court.

Court of Arbitration, or in the case of members of the United Nations (who are automatically parties to the Statute)[9] not represented in that Court by national groups appointed by their governments under the same conditions as those laid down in the 1907 Hague Convention (Art. 4). In making their nominations (which may be no more than four persons, not more than two of whom shall be of their own nationality) each national group is "recommended to consult its highest court of justice, its legal faculties and schools of law, and its national academies and national sections of international academies devoted to the study of law" (Arts. 5 (2) and 6).

In the election itself, the General Assembly and the Security Council "shall proceed independently of one another" (Art. 8). In compliance with this provision, judges are elected once their name appears on the list of successful candidates in both the Council and the Assembly. Although the Statute provides for a joint conference of three members of each body to resolve any deadlock after the Council and Assembly have had three election meetings (Arts. 11 and 12), differences over the election of particular candidates have largely been avoided or settled by a willingness to compromise.

One consequence of the joint responsibility of the Security Council in the election procedure has been to establish the practice that permanent members of the Council should have one of their nationals on the Court. Although this practice was broken in 1967 with the ending of Wellington Koo's association with the Court (there is now no Chinese national on the Court), there is no reason to suppose that it should not be continued as far as the other permanent members are concerned.

While this understanding has arisen *de facto*, the Statute itself (Art. 9) requires that the electors should "bear in mind not only that the persons to be elected should individually possess the qualifications required, but also that in the body as a whole the representation of the main forms of civilisation and of the principal legal systems of the world should be assured." Under the present distribution, judges of the Court are from the following states: Peru, Soviet Union, United Kingdom, Japan, United States, Italy, Pakistan, Mexico, Senegal, France, Lebanon, Philippines, Sweden, Poland and Nigera.

b INDEPENDENCE

The term of appointment of the judges, who may be re-elected, was established at nine years (the elections being held every third year when five places on the Court are contested) (Art. 13 (1)) to reinforce the principle of impartiality and freedom from governmental influence. Before taking up his duties every member of the Court is required to take a solemn declaration to "exercise his powers, impartially and conscientiously" (Art. 20). To avoid any conflict of duty, no member of the Court may "exercise any political or administrative function, or engage

---

9. See below, p. 487.

in any other occupation of a professional nature" (Art. 16); nor can he act as agent, advocate or counsel in any case, nor participate in any decision in a case in which he has already played a part as agent, counsel or advocate, or in any other capacity (Art. 17).

To this notion of impartiality and independence the appointment of *ad hoc* judges provides a major departure. Not only does the fact that a judge is a national of one of the parties before the Court not debar him from continuing to sit, but in cases where a party has no national on the Court it may appoint a national judge for the purposes of the case (Art. 31). The existence of *ad hoc* judges is not easily justified. On the occasions when they have been appointed they have *invariably* given judgment in favour of their own state (though this is certainly the *tendency* among national judges already members of the Court when their own state is involved in litigation). It cannot be said that the presence of their own national is an incentive, albeit a minor one, to states to submit to the jurisdiction of the Court, unless one accepts the principle that a national judge is in the position of an additional advocate for the cause of his own state. But this notion would appear to be totally inconsistent with the concept of impartiality which must be fundamental to any definition of the judicial office.

c THE ESTABLISHMENT OF THE COURT

The officers of the Court comprise two categories, those who are members of the Court, and those who form the Registry of the Court.

The officers who are judges are the President and Vice-President. They are both elected by the Court for three years and may be re-elected (Art. 21). The President, or in his absence,[10] the Vice-President, acts as chairman of the Court in its judicial capacity, and also as the general overseer of its administration. The President is therefore required to take up residence at the seat of the Court in the Hague (Art. 22 (2)).

The Registry comprises the Registrar, a Deputy-Registrar, and the other non-judicial officers of the Court. Both the Registrar and the Deputy-Registrar are appointed for seven years (and can be re-elected) by the Court from among candidates proposed by members of the Court (Statute, Art. 21 (2), Rules of the Court, Art. 14). Other officials are appointed by the Court on proposals submitted by the Registrar (Rules, 17 (1)), although temporary staff may be taken on by the Registrar on his own initiative. All officials must be proficient in English and French, the official languages of the Court.

B. Access to the Court

Before any state can submit to the jurisdiction of the Court and become a party to a case before the Court, it must have access to the

---

10.   And note also, Art. 45.

Court. In this respect not all states are in the same position. There is a distinction between states which are parties to the Statute and those which are not; and a further difference arises from the way in which a state becomes a party.

a MEMBERS OF THE UNITED NATIONS

Under Article 93 (1) of the U.N. Charter all members of the Organisation are *ipso facto* parties to the Statute. Hence, by gaining admission to the United Nations a state becomes bound not only by the provisions of the Charter, but also by those of the Statute.

b NON-MEMBERS OF THE UNITED NATIONS

Such states may obtain access to the Court in two ways:

i *By becoming a party to the Statute under Article 93 (2) of the Charter*

The conditions upon which this step may be taken are to be "determined in each case by the General Assembly upon the recommendation of the Security Council." In 1946 the Swiss Government requested the Secretary-General to inform them of the conditions that would be laid down. A committee of experts set up by the Security Council recommended that there should be deposited with the Secretary-General a declaration by the state concerned, accepting the provisions of the Statute, agreeing to the obligation of compliance with the Court's decisions under Article 94 of the Charter, and undertaking to pay an equitable proportion of the expenses of the Court. Subject to these conditions Switzerland and a number of other states (San Marino, Liechtenstein and, prior to its admission to membership in the United Nations, Japan) have become parties to the Statute. States becoming parties in this manner are entitled to nominate candidates for election to the Court, and to take part in the subsequent election in the General Assembly in accordance with a resolution of the Assembly (No. 264 of 1948).

ii *Access for states not parties to the Statute*

Under Article 35 (2) of the Statute, the Court shall be open to states not parties to the Statute in accordance with conditions to be laid down by the Security Council. The conditions, laid down in a Council resolution of October, 1946, are that the state concerned shall previously have deposited with the Registrar a declaration accepting the jurisdiction of the Court (either specifically, over a particular dispute, or generally, over any group or over all disputes) in accordance with the Charter, the Statute and the Rules of the Court, and more especially undertaking to comply with decisions of the Court in accordance with Article 94 of the Charter. Such state shall contribute towards the expenses of the Court in all cases to which it is a party (Art. 35 (3)). A number of states availed themselves of this procedure for gaining access to the Court before later becoming members of the United Nations. The only declarations now in existence for non-parties to the Statute are by the Federal Republic of Germany in respect of a number of treaties to which it is a party, and by the Republic of Vietnam (South Vietnam) in respect of the Peace Treaty with Japan.

C. The contentious jurisdiction of the Court

It is a fundamental principle of international law that "no State can, without its consent, be compelled to submit its disputes with other States either to mediation or to arbitration, or to any other kind of pacific settlement."[11] As consent is the basis of the jurisdiction of an international tribunal, discussion of the jurisdiction of the International Court must centre on the means available for such consent to be given. And for this purpose it is necessary to distinguish between the Court's contentious and its advisory jurisdiction. The reason for this difference is that whereas the contentious procedure of the Court can only be employed against a respondent state which has at some time submitted to the Court's jurisdiction, *prima facie* all that is required to obtain an advisory opinion from the Court is a favourable majority in a political organ with authority to set in motion the advisory procedure. The principle of consent thus plays only a minor role in the context of the Court's advisory jurisdiction.

The contentious jurisdiction of the Court may be classified under three headings: conventional (i.e. by express agreement between the parties); under the principle of *forum prorogatum* (i.e. by tacit agreement); and compulsory (i.e. by declaration accepting the Court's jurisdiction *vis-à-vis* any other state accepting the same obligation). In addition, however, when exercising its contentious jurisdiction, the Court has the power to take certain measures of an incidental nature which will be considered together under the heading of incidental jurisdiction.

a CONVENTIONAL JURISDICTION

The jurisdiction of the Court is stated by Article 36 (1) of its Statute to comprise *inter alia* "all matters specially provided for . . . in treaties or conventions in force."[12] There are a variety of methods whereby states may grant jurisdiction by express agreement.

---

11. *Eastern Carelia* case, P.C.I.J. Rep., Ser. B, No. 5, p. 27.
12. The reference to matters specially provided for in the U.N. Charter is almost certainly a drafting error. Under Article 36 of the Charter, the Security Council may recommend "appropriate procedures or methods of adjustment", bearing in mind that "legal disputes should as a general rule be referred by the parties to the International Court". However, a Council resolution cannot of itself give the Court jurisdiction over the dispute: see the comments in the *Corfu Channel* case, I.C.J. Rep. 1948, at p. 32.

i *Special agreement*

A special agreement is similar to the arbitral *compromis*. It is an agreement whereby the parties undertake to submit a given dispute to the Court. The Court's jurisdiction is defined within the compass of the agreement,[13] and the Court becomes seised of the dispute (i.e. the proceedings are deemed to have commenced) at the moment the agreement is notified to the Court (Statute, Art. 40). Cases that have been brought before the Court in this way include the *Minquiers and Ecrehos* case[14] and the *Frontier Land* case;[15] in the *Corfu Channel* case Albania and the United Kingdom entered into a special agreement[16] after the Court already had jurisdiction on the basis of *forum prorogatum*.

ii *By a disputes clause in a treaty*

Many treaties, both bilateral and multilateral, contain clauses granting jurisdiction over disputes to the International Court or to its predecessor, the Permanent Court.

1 *Treaties for the general settlement of disputes*

Both the 1928 General Act and the 1957 European Convention for the Pacific Settlement of Disputes contain general obligations under which the parties accepted the jurisdiction of the Permanent Court and the International Court respectively. Similar treaties can be found whereby two states agree to settle their disputes amicably. For example, in the *Electricity Company of Sofia* case, Belgium submitted its claim against Bulgaria to the Permanent Court, relying alternatively on the two states' acceptance of the Court's compulsory jurisdiction and on the provisions of the Treaty of Conciliation, Arbitration and Judicial Settlement between them.[17]

2 *Treaties dealing with other matters but including a provision for the settlement of disputes arising under the treaty*

There are a multitude of treaties of this type, and a number of cases have been heard by the Court under the terms of such treaties. For example, the *Northern Cameroons* case,[18] in which the Republic of the Cameroons sought a declaration that the United Kingdom had failed to carry out its obligations under the Trusteeship Agreement with respect to that territory, was submitted to the Court under the terms of Article 19 of the Agreement. Article 19 provided that if "any dispute whatever should arise between the Administering Authority and another Member of the United Nations relating to the interpretation or application of the provisions of this Agreement, such dispute, if it cannot be settled by

---

13. *Lotus* case, P.C.I.J. Rep., Ser. A, No. 10, p. 12; *Minquiers and Ecrehos* case, I.C.J. Rep. 1953, at p. 59.
14. I.C.J. Rep. 1953, p. 47. 15. I.C.J. Rep. 1959, p. 209.
16. For a list of such cases heard by the Permanent Court, see P.C.I.J. Rep., Ser. E, No. 16, p. 43.
17. (1939), P.C.I.J. Rep., Ser. A/B, No. 77. See also the *Haya de la Torre* case, I.C.J. Rep. 1951, p. 71, below, p. 500. 18. I.C.J. Rep. 1963, p. 15.

negotiation or other means, shall be submitted to the International Court of Justice".

3   Treaties enabling a particular dispute to be referred to the Court

Where the agreement does not provide for the case to be submitted to the Court and therefore does not set out the terms for the submission, but only *enables* a party to make application to the Court, the agreement is not a special agreement but an ordinary basis of conventional jurisdiction subject to the normal procedural rules.[19] In the *Asylum* case,[20] the so-called Agreement of Lima referred to the fact that the Plenipotentiaries of Peru and Colombia had been unable to "reach an agreement on the terms in which they might refer the dispute jointly to the International Court" but went on to state that they had nevertheless agreed that "proceedings before the recognised jurisdiction of the Court may be instituted on the application of either of the parties".

In all cases other than those instituted by notification of a special agreement, proceedings are commenced by the unilateral application of one of the parties to the Court in accordance with Article 32, paragraphs 2 and 3, of the Rules of Court.

iii   Where the treaty, although conferring jurisdiction on the Permanent Court, remains in force after 1945

In order to preserve the large number of provisions conferring jurisdiction on the Permanent Court, Article 37 of the Statute of the International Court laid down that whenever "a treaty or convention in force provides for reference of a matter to a tribunal to have been instituted by the League of Nations,[1] or to the Permanent Court of International Justice, the matter shall, as between the parties to the present Statute, be referred to the International Court of Justice." In order for a treaty conferring jurisdiction on the Permanent Court to bestow jurisdiction on the International Court it is essential: (1) that the treaty should still be in force; and (2) that the parties to the treaty should also be parties to the Statute.

As far as (1) is concerned, there is normally no difficulty: it is obvious enough whether or not a treaty is still in force. In the *Haya de la Torre* case,[2] it was not contested that the Protocol of Friendship and Co-operation between Colombia and Peru of 1934 was sufficient to give jurisdiction to the International Court. However, in the various *South-West Africa* cases the Court had to decide whether Article 37 could apply to various parts of the Mandate between South Africa and the League of Nations with respect to the administration of South-West Africa. In line with its general approach that the United Nations was entitled to

---

19. Cp. the procedures as set out in the Rules of the Court, Arts. 32–41.
20. I.C.J. Rep. 1950, p. 266.
1.   A number of treaties entered into at the time when the League was already in being but before the creation of the Permanent Court used a formula of this type.
2.   I.C.J. Rep. 1951, p. 71. See also the *Ambatielos* case, I.C.J. Rep. 1952, at p. 39.

exercise the supervisory functions formerly vested in the League, the Court held in the first of the cases that the Mandate did grant it jurisdiction. "According to Article 7 of the Mandate, disputes between the mandatory State and another Member of the League of Nations relating to the interpretation or the application of the provisions of the Mandate, if not settled by negotiation, should be submitted to the Permanent Court of International Justice. Having regard to Article 37 of the Statute of the International Court of Justice, and Article 80 (1) of the Charter,[3] the Court is of opinion that this clause in the Mandate is still in force and that, therefore, the Union of South Africa is under an obligation to accept the compulsory jurisdiction of the Court according to those provisions."[4]

The question raised by (2), that is, whether or not the states concerned are also parties to the Statute, would also appear to be free from difficulty. However, the issue was complicated by the Court's decision in the *Aerial Incident* case[5] on the similar provision of Article 36 (5) of the Statute dealing with declarations, accepting the compulsory jurisdiction of the Permanent Court, which are "still in force". It was held that a declaration could not remain in force if the declarant state was not already a party to the Statute of the International Court at the time the Permanent Court was dissolved. The reasons for this decision will be considered later:[6] for the moment the important aspect of the decision is how far it affects the application of Article 37.

This issue was placed squarely before the Court in the *Barcelona Traction* case.[7] Subject to an obligation on a party making application to follow certain procedures, Article 17 of the Spanish-Belgian Treaty of Conciliation, Judicial Settlement and Arbitration of 1927 allowed either party an ultimate right to commence proceedings before the Permanent Court. Belgium, having complied with the procedures required by the Treaty, had made application to the Court. Among the objections raised to the Court's jurisdiction by Spain was the contention that, as Spain had only been admitted to membership of the U.N., and thus became a party to the Statute, after the dissolution of the Permanent Court, there had been a period of nine years in which the final part of Article 17 of the 1927 Treaty had ceased to operate. The Court held, however, that "the ordinary rule of treaty law must apply", namely "that unless the treaty or provision concerned expressly indicates some difference or distinction, such phrases as 'the parties to the Statute', or 'the parties to the present convention', [etc.] . . . apply equally and indifferently to cover all those States which at any given time are participants, whatever the date of their several ratifications, accessions . . ., etc."

---

3. Under Article 80 (1) subject to certain exceptions, "nothing in this Chapter shall be construed in or of itself to alter in any manner the rights whatsoever of any states or any peoples or the terms of existing international instruments to which Members of the United Nations may respectively be parties."
4. I.C.J. Rep. 1950, at p. 138.   5. I.C.J. Rep. 1959, p. 127.
6. See below, pp. 511–523.   7. I.C.J. Rep. 1964, p. 6, at pp. 26 *et seq.*

Nor would the Court accept the argument that Article 17 could be made operative again only by the express agreement of the parties. It considered the "case of the reactivation of a jurisdictional clause by virtue of Article 37 to be no more than a particular case of the familiar principle of consent given generally and in advance". If a state joined an international organisation the constitution of which included an obligation that members should submit to the compulsory jurisdiction of their disputes arising within the organisation's sphere of competence, admission to membership would involve implied consent to that obligation. Similarly, "states joining the United Nations or otherwise becoming parties to the Statute, at whatever date, knew in advance (or must be taken to have known) that, by reason of Article 37, one of the results of doing so would, as between themselves and other parties to the Statute, be the reactivation in relation to the present Court, of any jurisdictional clauses referring to the Permanent Court, in treaties still in force, by which they were bound."[8]

b FORUM PROROGATUM

The Court may also exercise jurisdiction in cases in which the respondent state tacitly consents to submit to the jurisdiction. The question whether, at the outset of the proceedings, the Court has jurisdiction under some treaty or under the parties' declarations of acceptance of the Court's compulsory jurisdiction (if any have been made) becomes irrelevant, because any imperfection in the basis of jurisdiction is cured by the tacit acceptance by the parties of the Court's jurisdiction.

The usual process whereby jurisdiction is conferred in this way is by the respondent state refraining from contesting the Court's jurisdiction once the proceedings have been instituted. As the Permanent Court pointed out, "the submission of arguments on the merits, without making reservations in regard to the question of jurisdiction, must be regarded as an unequivocal indication of the desire of a state to obtain a decision on the merits of a suit". But it is clear that refraining from contesting the jurisdiction is not the only means of perfecting the Court's jurisdiction. The Court, in the same judgment from which the above passage is quoted, stated that "the consent of a state to the submission of a dispute to the Court may not only result from an express declaration, but may also be inferred from acts conclusively establishing it."[9]

If a state is subject to the jurisdiction of the Court with respect to certain types of dispute, it is obliged to contest the jurisdiction of the Court if an application is made commencing proceedings against it. In such a situation jurisdiction already exists *ratione personae* (i.e. in respect of the parties). It may be perfected *ratione materiae* (i.e. in respect of the subject matter) by the respondent state appearing without contesting the

8. I.C.J. Rep. 1964, at pp. 34-36. Despite the obvious reasonableness of this line of argument, it had been rejected by the Court in relation to Article 36 (5) of the Statute in the *Aerial Incident* case, see below, p. 512.

9. *Minority Schools* case, P.C.I.J. Rep., Ser. A, No. 15, at p. 24.

jurisdiction. But if the jurisdiction does not exist *ratione personae*, if the respondent state is not subject to the jurisdiction at all, it would seem that it is under no obligation to appear to contest the Court's jurisdiction.

For the Court to exercise jurisdiction in a case of this type, something more is required than an application by the claimant state together with the purely negative fact that the respondent state raises no objections to the Court's jurisdiction. The Court has relied upon what is often referred to as the *doctrine of successive acts.* In addition to the unilateral application, there must be some positive response from the respondent state.

In the *Corfu Channel* case,[10] the United Kingdom, in pursuance of a resolution of the Security Council recommending that the dispute be submitted to the Court, made application to the Court, and notice of this application was communicated to the Albanian Government. The Albanian Government, in its reply, set out a number of reasons why it considered that it would be within its rights to argue that the United Kingdom was not entitled to bring the case before the Court by unilateral application, but then stated that "notwithstanding this irregularity", because of its "devotion to the principles of friendly collaboration between nations and of the pacific settlement of disputes", it was prepared to appear before the Court. The Court held that this letter constituted "a voluntary and indisputable acceptance of the Court's jurisdiction." It was true that the consent of the parties conferred jurisdiction on the Court, but neither the Statute nor the Rules of Court required that the consent should be expressed in any particular form. There was "nothing to prevent the acceptance of jurisdiction, as in the present case, from being effected by two separate and successive acts, instead of jointly and beforehand by a special agreement."[11]

This procedure of unilaterally applying to the Court in circumstances where the respondent state is in no respect subject to the Court's jurisdiction is only possible because Article 32 (2) of the Rules of Court lays down that the application should, only *as far as possible*, specify the provision on which the applicant founds the jurisdiction of the Court. Following the *Minority Schools* case, a number of judges who disapproved of the notion of *forum prorogatum* attempted to have the equivalent provisions of the Rules of the Permanent Court altered to make it compulsory for the applicant state to specify the basis of the Court's jurisdiction. The refusal of a majority of judges of the Permanent Court to sanction such an alteration, and the affirmation by judges of the International Court of the propriety of a unilateral arraignment of a state not subject to the Court's jurisdiction, has thus provided an additional basis of jurisdiction.

Prima facie the principle of *forum prorogatum* would seem to be potentially useful as a means whereby the government of a state can submit to the jurisdiction without the need to go through the formal procedures that might be required under its own constitution in order to enter into a

10. I.C.J. Rep. 1947–8, p. 15.   11. *Ibid.*, pp. 27–28.
Rⅱ

treaty, or to make a declaration under Article 36 (2) of the Statute, accepting the Court's jurisdiction. Despite this apparent use, it cannot be said that the principle has proved in practice a fertile basis of jurisdiction in cases heard by the Court.

In the *Anglo-Iranian Oil Company* case, the United Kingdom invited the Iranian Government, as an alternative basis of jurisdiction, to agree to appear before the Court in conformity with Iran's obligations under the U.N. Charter to settle its disputes by peaceful means.[12] As the Iranian Government contested the Court's jurisdiction based upon the Iranian declaration of acceptance, the United Kingdom subsequently acknowledged that the Iranian Government "must be taken to have declined to confer jurisdiction on the Court on the basis of *forum prorogatum*."[13]

During the 1950s a number of applications were made to the Court by states in the hope of inducing other states, not otherwise subject to the jurisdiction of the Court, to submit to the jurisdiction with respect to the particular case. In 1954, for example, the United States made application to the Court against both Hungary and the Soviet Union in respect of the treatment in Hungary of certain U.S. aircraft and their crews. Neither Hungary nor the Soviet Union had accepted the Court's jurisdiction in any form. However, the applications were invitations to both governments, on being notified of the applications by the Registrar, to submit to the jurisdiction by taking "the necessary steps to enable the Court's jurisdiction over both parties to the dispute to be confirmed." The Hungarian Government notified the Registrar that it was "unable to submit in this case to the jurisdiction" of the Court. In its reply to the Registrar, the Soviet Union stated that it regarded as "unacceptable" the proposal of the United States that the International Court should examine the case. The Court, therefore, ordered that the two cases should be removed from the list.[14]

c COMPULSORY JURISDICTION

The compulsory jurisdiction of the Court depends upon a prior declaration of acceptance under Article 36 (2) of the Statute, which reads:

> "The states parties to the present Statute may at any time declare that they recognise as compulsory *ipso facto* and without special agreement, in relation to any other state accepting the same obligation, the jurisdiction of the Court in all legal disputes concerning:
> a. the interpretation of a treaty;
> b. any question of international law;
> c. the existence of any fact which, if established, would constitute a breach of an international obligation;
> d. the nature or extent of the reparation to be made for the breach of an international obligation."

---

12. I.C.J. *Pleadings*, pp. 17–18.   13. *Ibid.*, p. 145.

14. I.C.J. Rep. 1954, p. 99 and p. 103 respectively. See the similar applications against Czechoslovakia and the Soviet Union by the United States, I.C.J. Rep. 1956, p. 6 and p. 9 respectively; and the application by the United Kingdom against Argentine with respect to sovereignty over certain Antarctic territories, *ibid.*, p. 12.

Although this jurisdiction is generally referred to as "compulsory" (indeed that term is used in Article 36 (2) itself), it is only compulsory once the declaration is made and within the limits of that declaration. As there is no obligation on a state, even if a party to the Statute, to make such a declaration, there is no such thing as truly "compulsory" jurisdiction.

Article 36 has been the subject of much judicial interpretation and juristic discussion and it is necessary to consider a number of the issues that have been raised.

i *The enumeration of types of dispute*

It is interesting to note that, although Article 36 (2) is based upon the same numbered paragraph of the Statute of the Permanent Court, it is in fact shorter. One consequence of this reduction in length has been to render redundant sub-paragraphs (a), (c) and (d), all of which are covered by the general words of (b), "any question of international law". In the original text the sub-paragraphs were spelt out because the introductory words allowed the declaration to be in respect of "all or any" of them. With the omission of the "or any" the reason for retaining (a), (c) and (d) disappeared.

ii *The nature of the obligation created by a declaration*

Questions of estoppel apart, a state can usually resile from a statement of intention, or of its rights, or of its views on a particular matter. On the other hand, bilateral or multilateral undertakings like treaties cannot be terminated unless in accordance with their terms or with the consent of the other party or parties. While a declaration under Article 36 (2) is *made unilaterally*, the use of the expression "in relation to any other state accepting the same obligation" suggests that the *effect* of such a declaration is to create a series of bilateral relations with other states that have made declarations of acceptance. Can a state be made respondent in a case on the strength of a declaration of acceptance which it has denounced in violation of the terms of the declaration?

It is clear that once an application has been made to the Court under an effective declaration of acceptance, the subsequent lapse or withdrawal of the acceptance cannot deprive the Court of jurisdiction. In the *Nottebohm* case,[15] the Court was called upon to consider the effect, if any, of the subsequent lapse of the Guatemalan declaration of acceptance. Liechtenstein's application to the Court was made in December 1951. The Guatemalan acceptance expired on 26th January, 1952. It was argued on behalf of Guatemala that as from midnight 26th/27th January the Court no longer had jurisdiction to hear the dispute. It is hardly surprising that the Court took the view that, once it was validly seised of the dispute, it could exercise its powers. In its own words, an "extrinsic fact such as the subsequent lapse of the Declaration, by reason of the

---

15. I.C.J. Rep. 1953, at pp. 120–123.

expiry of the period or by denunciation, cannot deprive the Court of the jurisdiction already established."

It is also clear that a state cannot be arraigned before the Court on the strength of a declaration that has already lapsed or been denounced in accordance with its terms. But what if a state were to denounce in violation of the terms of the acceptance because it realised that an application was about to be made? The view has been expressed that "once a state has denounced a title of jurisdiction, and especially a declaration accepting the compulsory jurisdiction, it is politically inconceivable that another state would seek to invoke the denounced instrument as the basis for the introduction of . . . proceedings."[16] Such an extreme opinion hardly seems tenable. If states are willing to make application to the Court in circumstances where the other party is not obviously subject to the jurisdiction of the Court (e.g. on the basis of a Security Council resolution,[17] or relying on an extended and rather artificial notion of the term treaty[18]), why should a state be deterred by the fact that the declaration has just been denounced? However, what is important is not whether a state is likely to make application to the Court in such circumstances, but what attitude the Court would adopt if an application were made.

The answer to this question would depend upon the Court's analysis of the nature of the bond between states accepting its compulsory jurisdiction. Light might be shed on its likely approach by some of its comments in the *Right of Passage* case.[19] Portugal, though a party to the Statute by reason of its membership of the U.N., accepted the Court's compulsory jurisdiction for the first time on 19th December, 1955, and on 22nd December it filed an application against India to establish recognition of alleged rights of passage between Portuguese territory on the coast, and two Portuguese possessions further inland which were entirely surrounded by Indian territory. On receipt of the *application*, the Court notified India by telegram that it had been made; but official notification of the existence and terms of the Portuguese *declaration* was not transmitted by the Secretary-General to the Indian Government until 19th January, 1956. It was objected by India that the three days gap between the declaration and the application had not been sufficient time for the Secretary-General to transmit copies of the declaration to other parties to the Statute as required by Article 36 (4); and that, until that step had been taken, there could be no legal relationship between Portugal and those parties. This contention the Court rejected in terms which have a bearing on the problem under discussion. "The contractual relation between the parties and the compulsory jurisdiction of the Court resulting therefrom are established . . . by the fact of the making of the Declaration. . . . A state accepting the jurisdiction of the Court must expect that an Application may be filed against it before the Court by a new declarant state on the

16.   Rosenne, *The Law and Practice of the International Court*, Vol. 1, p. 417.
17.   As in the *Corfu Channel* case, see above, p. 488, fn. 12.
18.   As in the *Anglo-Iranian Oil Company* case, see above, p. 359.
19.   I.C.J. Rep. 1957, p. 125.

same day on which that state deposits with the Secretary-General its Declaration of Acceptance. For it is on that very day that the consensual bond, which is the basis of the Optional Clause, comes into being between the states concerned."[20]

If a "contractual relation", or a "consensual bond", was created between the state making a declaration and all other parties that had made declarations accepting the Court's jurisdiction at the moment such declaration was made, it would seem to follow that the declarant state is bound by the terms of its declaration. If the declaration does not include a provision for denunciation, then *prima facie* a unilateral act of withdrawal would not be effective. It may be that other parties to the Court's compulsory jurisdiction would not object to a denunciation, particularly if the state concerned gave reasonable notice of its intentions. In that case, however, the effectiveness of the denunciation would depend upon the acquiescence of other states, and not upon any power of unilateral denunciation.

In practice a large number of states have included a right of unilateral determination in their declarations. In the *Right of Passage* case, the Court considered a power of denunciation in an extreme form contained in the Portuguese declaration. In the declaration the Portuguese Government reserved the right "to exclude from the scope of the present declaration, at any time during its validity, any given category or categories of disputes, by notifying the Secretary-General of the United Nations and with effect from the moment of such notification." In the Court's view, as it was not claimed by Portugal that this provision was intended to act rectroactively to deprive the Court of jurisdiction in an application that had already been made, there was no basis for the Indian objection that the provision was incompatible with the object and purpose of the Optional Clause.[21]

Before leaving the subject of the Portuguese declaration and the *Right of Passage* case, it is interesting to notice the unsettling effect they had on other states that had accepted the compulsory jurisdiction.[1] It was feared by a number of states that other states, which were parties to the Statute but which had not accepted the Court's compulsory jurisdiction, might make an unexpected declaration of acceptance with a view to bringing a particular dispute before the Court. In order to guard against such a possibility, the United Kingdom altered its own declaration of acceptance to exclude "disputes in respect of which any other party to the dispute has accepted the compulsory jurisdiction of the International Court of Justice only in relation to or for the purposes of the dispute; or where the acceptance of the Court's compulsory jurisdiction on behalf of any other Party to the dispute was deposited or ratified less than twelve months prior to the filing of the application bringing the dispute before the Court." A similar restriction was adopted by India, and the French

---

20. *Ibid.*, at p. 146.   21. *Ibid.*, at p. 142.
1. Though the possibilities were obvious enough, and had been pointed out (e.g. by Waldock in 1955–6 B.Y.B.I.L. at p. 280), it was only the *Right of Passage* case that brought home to states the disadvantage of their position *vis-à-vis* non-declarant states.

declaration of 1959 excluded "disputes with any state which, at the date of occurrence of the facts or situation giving rise to the dispute, has not accepted the compulsory jurisdiction of the International Court of Justice for a period at least equal to that specified in this declaration" (i.e. 3 years).[2]

iii *Reciprocity*

Under Article 36 (3) of the Statute, a declaration may be made *inter alia* unconditionally, or on condition of reciprocity on the part of a number of other states. In origins, the idea behind this provision was that states could make their acceptance of the Permanent Court's jurisdiction subject to a condition that it was not to become operative until certain specified, or a particular number of, states had accepted the jurisdiction. However, in view of the fact that the great majority of acceptances of the jurisdiction of the International Court are expressly made subject to a general condition of reciprocity, it seems necessary now to define reciprocity in totally different terms.

In the *Interhandel* case, the Court stated that reciprocity "in the case of Declarations accepting the compulsory jurisdiction of the Court enables a Party to invoke a reservation to that acceptance which it has not expressed in its own Declaration but which the other Party has expressed in its Declaration."[3] And the trend has been to equate this *condition* of reciprocity with the *principle* of reciprocity inherent in Article 36 (2) of the Statute which refers to "any other state accepting the same obligations". Indeed, the Court has on occasion treated them as identical.[4]

However, a close analysis of the principle of reciprocity suggests that this identification may be logically erroneous. Reciprocity in this sense simply denotes that the jurisdiction of the Court depends upon the terms which the parties to the dispute have incorporated in their declaration of acceptance, and exists within the "area" common to both declarations. In *effect*, this hypothesis will normally enable one party to "rely" upon the reservations contained in the other party's declaration, but it is not necessarily identical with the condition of reciprocity.

Two cases may be contrasted. In the *Electricity Company of Sofia*,[5] Belgium made application to the Permanent Court to commence proceedings against Bulgaria. The Bulgarian acceptance of the Court's jurisdiction was unconditional, but the Belgian declaration of March, 1926, applied only to "disputes arising after the ratification of the present Declaration with regard to situations or facts subsequent to this ratification". It was accepted by both parties, and by the Court, that Bulgaria could rely upon the terms of the Belgian reservation.[6] It is clear that

---

2. The present French declaration has omitted the "for a period at least equal to that specified in this declaration", the tense of "has" being changed to "had".
3. I.C.J. Rep. 1959, at p. 23.
4. E.g. in the *Right of Passage* case, I.C.J. Rep. 1957, at p. 145.
5. (1939), P.C.I.J. Rep., Ser. A/B, No. 77.
6. Though on the facts it was held that the dispute, and the situation giving rise to it, arose after the critical date, and, therefore, within the Court's jurisdiction; see below.

whether the matter was approached as a condition, or as a principle, of reciprocity, the conclusion would have been the same. The area common to both declarations was restricted by the Belgium time limitation, so that from either point of view, Bulgaria was in effect relying upon it.

In contrast, in the *Norwegian Loans* case,[7] the Court had to consider whether Norway, the respondent state, could rely upon a reservation contained in the declaration of acceptance made by France, the applicant state. The reservation in question purported to exclude disputes "relating to matters which are essentially within the national jurisdiction as understood by the government of the French Republic". The Court correctly analysed the principle of reciprocity based upon Article 36 (2) of the Statute. It pointed out that, as two declarations were involved, jurisdiction was conferred upon the Court only to the extent to which the two declarations coincided. As the French acceptance was within narrower limits than the Norwegian, the "common will" of the parties which was the basis of the Court's jurisdiction, existed within the narrower limits indicated by the French declaration.[8] However, the two reservations placed side by side only excluded matters within the national jurisdiction as understood by the French Government, so that it was not possible for Article 36 (2) to operate at all,[9] certainly not to the extent of enabling the Norwegian Government to exclude the subject matter of the dispute from the Court's jurisdiction on the ground that it fell within *Norway*'s national jurisdiction.

How, then, was the Court able to reach the conclusion that Norway, could rely on the French reservation to the extent of enabling it to classify the dispute as being within Norwegian domestic jurisdiction? The Court's explanation was that both declarations included a condition of reciprocity. "In accordance with the condition of reciprocity to which acceptance of the compulsory jurisdiction is made subject in both Declarations and which is provided for in Article 36, paragraph 3, of the Statute, Norway, equally with France, is entitled to except from the compulsory jurisdiction of the Court disputes understood by Norway to be essentially within its national jurisdiction."[10]

Hitherto this significant distinction between the principle of reciprocity inherent in Article 36 (2) and a condition of reciprocity incorporated in most declarations of acceptance has not been clearly defined by the Court, and has been largely ignored in juristic writings. In fact many jurists[11] have expressed the opinion (and even the Court itself has suggested[12]) that there is no difference between the principle of reciprocity and the

---

7. I.C.J. Rep. 1957, p. 9.   8. *Ibid.*, at p. 23.

9. The relevance of Article 36 (2) would seem to be to render the reservation void, on the ground that the two states had obviously not accepted the same obligation, but the Court held that, as the validity of the reservation had not been raised, it did not have to consider the point. See further, below p. 503.

10. I.C.J. Rep. 1957, at p. 24.

11. E.g. Hudson, *The Permanent Court*, 2nd ed., at p. 465; Waldock, 32 B.Y.B.I.L., at pp. 254-5; Briggs, 93 H.R., at p. 267.

12. See above, fn. 4, p. 498.

condition of reciprocity. Not only is such a view hardly reconcilable with the Court's statements and reasoning in the *Norwegian Loans* case, but it also requires that the condition of reciprocity contained in most declarations of acceptance made by states should be regarded as mere surplusage.

One final comment may be made on the limits of reciprocity, whether under Article 36 (2) or expressly imposed in the declarations of acceptance. It cannot be invoked to enable a temporal limitation in the earlier declaration of one party to be attached to the subsequent and unconditional declaration of the other party. In the *Interhandel* case,[13] the United States declaration of 1946 excluded from the Court's jurisdiction disputes arising prior to the date of the declaration. On 26th July, 1948, the United States finally rejected the representations of the Swiss Government on behalf of the Swiss company, Interhandel. On 28th July, the Swiss Government accepted the jurisdiction of the Court without making any reservation as to time. Could the United States apply the past disputes reservation in their own declaration to the Swiss acceptance date? This suggestion was emphatically rejected by the Court. Reciprocity enabled one party to "rely" upon a restriction contained in the declaration of the other party, but no more. It could not justify a state's claim to rely upon a restriction which was not included in the declaration of the other party.[14]

iv *Reservations*

During the early years of the Permanent Court, the question whether a state could validly append reservations to a declaration of acceptance was a matter of controversy. Article 36 (3) of the Statute, which was in identical terms to the provision in the present Statute, laid down that declarations could be made "unconditionally or on condition of reciprocity on the part of several or certain states, or for a certain time." It was argued that it was implicit in this provision that only limitations in accordance with its terms were admissible. However, it became so common to include a wide range of reservations to declarations that their validity was no longer questioned. At the San Francisco Conference, the sub-committee that dealt with the Statute considered that, as Article 36 (3) had been consistently interpreted to allow reservations, there was no need to amend it to make express provision for them.

As to the types of reservation, these vary from provisions intended to exclude disputes arising out of a war or other hostile relations,[15] to reservations by a group of states to retain for their mutual settlement disputes arising *inter se*,[16] or to reservations by individual states designed

---

13. I.C.J. Rep. 1959, p. 6.   14. *Ibid.*, at p. 23.
15. E.g. the general clauses introduced into the declarations of many Commonwealth states designed primarily, though not exclusively, to exclude matters arising out of the Second World War; and see the much wider reservation in the present Israeli declaration.
16. E.g. the limitation in declarations by Commonwealth states reserving disputes between them to methods of settlement to be agreed amongst themselves.

to prevent a specific dispute coming before the Court.[17] None of these forms of reservation have been matters of controversy either in juristic writings or in cases before the Court. However, more detailed examination is necessary of two types of reservation which have given rise to juristic and judicial discussion and controversy.

1 The so-called automatic reservation

The term "automatic" has been adopted to denote reservations which purport to reserve the issue of their applicability to the sole determination of the reserving state. Thus, in the French declaration of 1947, which was replaced in 1959, matters essentially within the national jurisdiction as understood by the French Government were excluded from the acceptance of the Court's jurisdiction. The United Kingdom declaration of 1957 (replaced in 1958, which declaration was in turn replaced in 1963) excluded *inter alia* disputes "relating to any question which, in the opinion of the Government of the United Kingdom, affects the national security of the United Kingdom or of any of its dependent territories." However, perhaps the most frequently cited example of an automatic reservation is that contained in the United States declaration. Often referred to as the Conally amendment, it provides that the declaration shall not apply to "disputes with regard to matters which are essentially within the domestic jurisdiction of the United States of America as determined by the United States of America".

It has been strenuously argued that such a reservation is invalid.

First, it is arguable that it is inconsistent with the principle of reciprocity inherent in Article 36 (2) of the Statute. Unless both states, parties to a case before the Court, have included an automatic reservation in their declarations of acceptance, they are in no sense accepting the same obligation. However, this lack of mutuality of obligation may be rectified if both declarations contain a condition of reciprocity, because this will amount to an express recognition of the right of one party to adopt for its own benefit an automatic reservation in the acceptance of the other party. Such a view was implicitly endorsed by the Court in the *Norwegian Loans* case, the relevant part of which judgment was discussed above.[18]

Secondly, it may be doubted whether an automatic reservation is compatible with Article 36 (6) of the Statute which provides that in the event of a dispute as to whether the Court has jurisdiction, the matter should be settled by the decision of the Court. This principle, the inherent power of a tribunal to interpret the text establishing its jurisdiction, is a fundamental principle of international jurisprudence. The assumption upon which an automatic reservation is based is that the reserving state should have the power in the first instance to decide whether the Court has jurisdiction.[19]

---

17. E.g. the Australian reservation relating to the Continental Shelf and pearl fishing designed to forestall any attempt at unilateral application by Japan.   18. P. 499.
19. The invalidity of the French and United States reservations upon this ground was asserted by Judge Lauterpacht in the *Norwegian Loans* and *Interhandel* cases respectively.

Thirdly, quite apart from the conflict with Article 36 (6), there would seem to be a fundamental inconsistency between an automatic reservation and the concept of compulsory jurisdiction. In the *Nottebohm* case,[20] it was stated by the Court that a subsequent withdrawal or lapse of a declaration could not offset the Court's right to exercise jurisdiction once it became seised of a dispute. And, in the *Right of Passage* case,[1] the Court held that, as long as the clause in the Portuguese declaration containing a power of denunciation with immediate effect over any specific dispute or class of disputes was not intended to operate retroactively to withdraw from the Court's jurisdiction a case of which it was already seised, no issue of the clause's incompatibility with the objects and purpose of the Optional Clause arose. However, the effect of a determination by a state under an automatic reservation that the dispute falls outside the Court's jurisdiction is tantamount to a claim to withdraw from the Court a dispute of which it has already been validly seised.

Although it may appear difficult to counter these arguments against the validity of an automatic reservation in theory, an answer would seem to be possible on the basis of the Court's essentially practical approach to the issue. In the *Norwegian Loans* case, it upheld a Norwegian determination that the dispute fell within that state's national jurisdiction on the ground that the validity of the French reservation had not been questioned by the parties. In consequence, the Court held that it had before it "a provision which both Parties to the dispute regard as constituting an expression of their common will relating to the competence of the Court."[2]

While states continue to claim and to allow the condition of reciprocity as part of the scheme of compulsory jurisdiction; and as long as objections are not made on the diplomatic level to the inclusion of automatic reservations in declarations accepting the Court's jurisdiction, theoretical arguments concerning the invalidity of such reservations cannot be considered conclusive. In the same way as the practice of states has established the validity of reservations in general, the practice of states seems to have accepted the specific validity of automatic reservations.

And this essentially pragmatic solution is reinforced by the unlikelihood of a successful challenge to their validity being made, or, if it were made, of having the desired effect. If the automatic reservation is contained in the declaration of the applicant state, the respondent state would no doubt be anxious to rely upon its right to make use of the reservation under the condition of reciprocity.[3] This was in fact what happened in the *Norwegian Loans* case.[4]

But even if the reservation is contained in the declaration of the respon-

---

20. See above, p. 495.   1. See above, pp. 496–497.
2. I.C.J. Rep. 1957, at p. 27.
3. If there is no condition of reciprocity in both declarations, there would not be the mutality required by Article 36 (2) as the two parties would not have accepted the same obligation. *Vis-à-vis* each other the two parties would not be subject to the compulsory jurisdiction of the Court at all: see above, p. 499.
4. See above, *ibid.*

dent state, it may not be in the interests of the applicant state to challenge the reservation's validity. Among the chief exponents of the invalidity view there is a sharp difference of opinion between those who consider that the invalid reservation can be ignored leaving the rest of the declaration effective,[5] and those who argue that such a reservation is fundamental to the whole declaration which must therefore be considered as totally vitiated by the invalidity of the reservation.[6] The former argument is based upon the proposition that the state concerned intended to accept the jurisdiction of the Court; and the latter upon the contention that as the declaration would never have been made without such a reservation,[7] it is hardly possible to disregard the reservation and treat the rest of the declaration as effective. Be that as it may, as the consequence of successfully challenging the validity of the reservation could be a decision that the *entire* declaration was invalid, an applicant state might well be reluctant to take the risk.

However, if the issue of validity should be raised before the Court, the more probable consequence is that the Court would avoid drastic solutions: it would be unlikely to hold either an automatic reservation, or a declaration containing an automatic reservation, invalid. Nevertheless, if it is to uphold such a reservation, the Court would have to counter the formidable theoretical arguments against the reservation's validity which have already been considered. How might the Court approach this task?

First, the contention that such a reservation is inconsistent with the principle of reciprocity contained in Article 36 (2) of the Statute is not destructive of the *validity* of the reservation. It can only mean that *prima facie* the state making the reservation has not accepted the same obligation, so that *vis-à-vis* a state that has not made an automatic reservation in substantially similar terms, there is no common area of jurisdiction. This discrepancy can be rectified, as pointed out above, by the presence of a condition of reciprocity in both declarations. This mutual understanding between the parties, the Court held in the *Norwegian Loans* case, was sufficient to enable Norway to take advantage of the French reservation to the extent of categorising the dispute as falling within Norwegian national jurisdiction.

Secondly, Article 36 (6) of the Statute only reserves to the Court its ultimate power of deciding its own jurisdiction. In the same way as an arbitral tribunal could only determine its jurisdiction within the limits set by the treaty or *compromis* creating the tribunal, so the International Court can only exercise jurisdiction within the limits defined by the Statute and by the issue as presented to it by the parties. And there would

---

5. E.g. Judge Klaestad in the *Interhandel* case, I.C.J. Rep. 1959, at p. 77 who argued that, as the United States intended to accept the Court's jurisdiction, it should be treated as having done so.

6. E.g. Judge Spender in the *Interhandel* case, *ibid.*, at p. 57; and Judge Lauterpacht, *ibid.*, at p. 101, and in the *Norwegian Loans* case, I.C.J. Rep. 1957, at p. 58.

7. As is almost certainly the case with the United States declaration: see Judge Lauterpacht's survey of its history in the *Interhandel* case, I.C.J. Rep. 1959, at p. 105 *et seq.*

seem to be no fundamental reason why the parties either by express agreement or by tacit acceptance should not accept the right of either of them to decide the jurisdictional issue. The Court in the *Norwegian Loans* case accepted the Norwegian categorisation of the dispute as essentially within Norway's national jurisdiction on the ground that neither party had objected to the validity of the French reservation. If tacit acceptance may be evidenced by the pleadings in a case, why should it not be evidenced by the presence of a condition of reciprocity in the parties' declarations of acceptance and by the absence of a protest against an automatic reservation when the existence of the declaration containing it is first notified to a state by the Secretary-General?

Such a solution to the problem raised by the "same obligation" aspect of Article 36 (2) is only possible providing one accepts the possibility of the revision of a treaty provision by state practice even to the extent of producing a result not compatible with the strict wording of the provision. An alteration in the application of a treaty provision of this type is not without precedent (e.g. the approach of the Security Council to Article 27 (3) of the Charter[8]). As long as states that have accepted the Court's jurisdiction are prepared to go along with this apparent revision · of the Statute, it is unlikely that the Court would adopt such a drastic course as to hold a declaration containing an automatic reservation, or the reservation itself, invalid.

Thirdly, the contention that the Court, in keeping with the views expressed in the *Nottebohm*[9] and *Right of Passage*[10] cases, would refuse to allow a state the power to withdraw from the Court a case of which it was already validly seised could be countered with a similar argument to that used in the previous paragraphs. Acquiescence in the existence of automatic reservations and of the reciprocal rights conferred by conditions of reciprocity in declarations of acceptance creates a situation essentially different from the situations considered by the Court in those two cases. Certainly the Court case saw no difficulty in accepting the "withdrawal" of the *Norwegian Loans* case from its jurisdiction by the Norwegian determination in reliance upon the French reservation.

There is, however, an alternative argument that has been raised in favour of recognising the validity of an automatic reservation. It is said that a determination by a state that a matter is within its domestic or national jurisdiction, or is a matter of national security, must be made in good faith, and that the Court has a power, in accordance with Article 36 (6), to decide whether the determination was so made. A determination not made in good faith should be treated as a nullity.

The drawback to this approach is that it is rejected both by those who argue against the validity of an automatic reservation and, though with some inconsistency, by the United States, the most notable upholder of the reservation.

The late Judge Lauterpacht, who was perhaps the principal protagonist

---

8. See below, p. 545.   9. Above, p. 495.   10. Above, p. 496.

of the invalidity view, denied that a legal obligation to act in good faith could be attached to an automatic reservation. "The legal obligation of a Government", he said, "to avail itself of its freedom of action in a manner consistent with good faith has a meaning, in terms of legal obligation, only when room is left for an impartial finding whether the duty to act in accordance with good faith has been complied with. But in the case now before the Court any such possibility has been expressly excluded. The Court has no power to give a decision on the question whether a state has acted in good faith in claiming that a dispute covers a matter which is essentially within its domestic jurisdiction. If the Court were to do so, it would be arrogating to itself a power which has been expressly denied to it."[11]

To some extent the reasoning of this pronouncement is circular. If the question to be decided is whether an automatic reservation can be interpreted to include a requirement that a determination made under it should be in good faith, it is not conclusive on the point that the reservation itself entitles the state to make a determination. The real issue is whether, once a determination is made, it is open to the Court to decide whether it is an effective determination, i.e. whether it has been made in good faith. The determination that a matter is within a state's domestic jurisdiction may not be correct according to international law, but this factor is only relevant in so far as it tends to show that the determination was not made in good faith. It is not the correctness of the determination which is in issue, because that is a matter for the state itself, but whether the determination was sufficiently reasonable to be classified as made in good faith.

Once it is established that there is nothing in the terminology of automatic reservations which excludes the possibility of interpreting them in the light of the requirement of good faith, the Lauterpacht view would seem to depend solely upon the attitudes of states which have included such reservations in their declarations of acceptance. In a passage immediately following that quoted above from his opinion in the *Norwegian Loans* case, Judge Lauterpacht said that "it is abundantly clear from the evidence which is generally available that the authors of the 'automatic reservation' have reserved for the Governments concerned the right to judge whether in invoking it in a particular case they have complied with the obligation to act in good faith. They have repeatedly declared that their own sense of international duty and propriety, public opinion within and outside their countries, and their reputation and prestige in the world would constitute a restraining factor of great potency in shaping their decision. But they have denied to the Court the power to determine the legality of that decision from the point of view of the obligation to act in good faith or otherwise."[12]

This approach seems to place too much reliance upon the attitude of

---

11. *Norwegian Loans* case, Sep. Op., I.C.J. Rep. 1957, at pp. 52–53.
12. I.C.J. Rep. 1957, at p. 53.

the state making the reservation. It is obviously a relevant factor, but it cannot be considered as conclusive. An erroneous view of the law does not become correct by unilateral repetition. However, while consistency does not necessarily strengthen a case, inconsistency can certainly weaken it. Since Judge Lauterpacht made his comments in the *Norwegian Loans* case, the United States has vacillated in its interpretation of its own automatic reservation. As respondent in the *Interhandel* case, it claimed that its right to determine that certain aspects of the dispute fell within its domestic jurisdiction was not subject to "review or approval by any tribunal".[13] In the *Aerial Incident* case, on the other hand, the United States, as applicant, put forward the view that the automatic reservation did not authorise nor empower "this Government or any other Government on a basis of reciprocity, to make an arbitrary determination that a particular matter is domestic, when it is evidently one of international concern and has been so treated by the parties."[14] However, when the United States decided to discontinue the case against Bulgaria, it purported to withdraw this argument on the ground that it was "not valid".[15] Nevertheless, it can hardly be argued that either theoretical or practical considerations rule out the possibility of the Court holding that a determination under an automatic reservation should be made in good faith.

In view of the present uncertainty over automatic reservations, it is not possible to state categorically what view the Court would take if the validity issue were placed squarely before it. However, past history does suggest that a decision that the reservation itself or the declaration containing it is invalid, would be unlikely. Basing itself on the tacit consent of states, the Court could uphold the reservation despite the arguments based upon alleged inconsistencies between the effects of the reservation and the provisions of the Statute. Alternatively, or in addition, the Court could claim and put into practice a power to review the good faith of any determination made by a state purporting to rely upon the reservation. There would be obvious political dangers for the Court to act in this way, because, despite inconsistencies in American practice, the right of unilateral determination is still viewed in many quarters in the United States as fundamental to its acceptance of the Court's compulsory jurisdiction. The questioning by the Court of the good faith of a determination under the reservation could lead to a cancellation of the declaration altogether. It would be a matter of some difficulty to decide whether the cause of compulsory jurisdiction is served better by limiting the effect of the reservation and thus risking the loss of the United States as a declarant under Article 36 (2), or by allowing states to take advantage of a right of unilateral determination whether to allow a case against them to proceed.

2 *Time limitations*

Time can affect declarations of acceptance in a number of ways. A declaration takes effect on the date it is transmitted to the Secretary-

---

13. *Pleadings*, at p. 452.   14. *Pleadings*, at p. 323.   15. *Ibid.*, at p. 677.

General of the United Nations, or at a later date if one is specified, or if the declaration is conditional upon the happening of some event (such as ratification of the declaration by the state making it or the making of a similar declaration by another state or group of states). Declarations are often made for a specified period "and thereafter until terminated". However, the matter that requires examination in the present context is the effect of a time exclusion clause in a declaration of acceptance.

These exclusion clauses are worded in a variety of ways, but they may be said to fall into two main categories:

> (x) a single clause of the type found in the Unites States declaration which applies only to disputes "hereafter arising" (i.e. after the 14th August, 1946, the date on which declaration was made), or in a number of declarations which are limited to disputes arising after a specified date, often the date on which the state made an earlier declaration of acceptance;[16]
>
> (xx) a "double" clause of the type found in the declarations of many Commonwealth states which apply only to disputes arising after the specified date "with regard to situations or facts subsequent to that date",[17] or of the type, which are probably similar in effect, to be found in declarations that apply to disputes "which may arise with regard to situations or facts" subsequent to the date specified.[18]

Jurisdictional issues raised by temporal limitations of these types are complex. In the first place, they can normally be decided only after a careful examination of the circumstances of the case.[19] Secondly, it is no easy task to specify precisely when a "dispute" arose, and it is even less easy to decide when situations or facts out of which a dispute has arisen occurred. The first matter has consequences for the procedure to be adopted when objection is made to the Court's jurisdiction *ratione temporis* (i.e. it is alleged that the dispute, or the facts or situations from which it stemmed, occurred outside the period common to both declarations).[20] The second must be considered in some detail in the light of the Court's attitude towards objections to its jurisdiction on such grounds.

In the *Phosphates in Morocco* case,[1] the facts were as follows:

1906 General Act of Algeciras, and the

1911 Franco-German Convention to which Italy later acceded together laid down an "open-door" economic policy for Morocco including the regulation of mining concessions;

1918–19 Phosphate prospecting licences were issued to a number of French nationals and later assigned to T, an Italian national;

1920 State monopoly of phosphates established;

1925 T's rights were denied recognition by the Moroccan Mines Department;

---

16. E.g. successive Pakistan declarations which apply to disputes arising after 24th June, 1948, the date on which the first Pakistan declaration was communicated to the Secretary-General.

17. As, for example, in the United Kingdom, Australian, Canadian and Indian declarations.

18. As in the Swedish declaration.   19. See below, pp. 516 *et seq.*

20. See below, pp. 516–517.   1. (1938), P.C.I.J. Rep., Ser. A/B, No. 74.

> 1931 New French declaration accepting jurisdiction over "any disputes which may arise after the ratification of the present declaration with regard to situations or facts subsequent to such ratification".

The basis of the Permanent Court's decision, that the Italian Government had failed to answer the French argument that the facts and situations giving rise to the dispute were earlier than the 1931 exclusion date, cannot be faulted. The monopoly was created in 1920, contrary it was alleged to France's treaty obligations; it was true that this created an illegal situation which continued until after the French declaration of 1931, but this situation could not be considered in isolation from the "facts", i.e. the legislation creating the phosphate monopoly, from which it arose. Nor could it be argued that the rejection of T's petition to the Mines Department for recognition of his rights constituted an uncompleted violation of international law which only became definitive as a result of a final confirmation of the French attitude in certain diplomatic correspondence of 1933. The decision of the Mines Department was in itself an internationally unlawful act; it was a definitive act which by itself involved international responsibility. The dispute, and the facts and situation out of which it had arisen, were clearly anterior to the period covered by the French declaration of acceptance, and thus fell outside the Court's jurisdiction.

The Court made little attempt to analyse either when the dispute arose (did it arise in 1920 with the passing of the legislation? or with the rejection of T's petition in 1925?) or what situations or facts were sufficiently closely connected with the dispute to be covered or excluded by the French declaration of acceptance. Although specific findings on these issues were not necessary in the circumstances of the case, this reluctance to come to grips with the complex issues involved has characterised the approach of both the Permanent Court and the International Court in later cases.

The *Electricity Company of Sofia* case[2] arose out of the following circumstances:

> 1898 a concession to generate electricity granted to a French company;
> 1908 transfer of the company's rights to a Belgian company;
> 1914–18 company nationalised for the duration of the war;
> 1919 restored by the Treaty of Neuilly;
> 1925 award of arbitral tribunal laying down prices for electricity;
> 1926 Belgian acceptance of the Court's jurisdiction "in any disputes arising after the ratification of the present declaration with regard to situations or facts subsequent to this ratification";[3]

---

2. (1939), P.C.I.J. Rep., Ser. A/B, No. 77.
3. The Bulgarian declaration contained no temporal limitation.

1934   coal tariff imposed by the State Mines Administration against which the company protested, and proceedings in the local courts went against the company;

1936   imposition of a discriminatory income tax.

Unlike the earlier case, this case required the Court to consider the limitation in respect of past facts or situations, because it was clear that the dispute itself did not arise until after 1926. The Court laid down the proposition that the "only situations or facts which must be taken into account from the standpoint of the compulsory jurisdiction accepted in the terms of the Belgian declaration are those which must be considered as being the source of the dispute", and then explained that no such relation existed "between the present dispute and the awards of the Mixed Arbitral Tribunal. The latter constitute the source of the rights claimed by the Belgian company, but they did not give rise to the dispute, since the parties agree as to their binding character and that their application gave rise to no difficulty until the acts complained of."[4]

It is clear that this approach severely limits the potentially corrosive effect of these double exclusion clauses on the Court's jurisdiction. What the Court did in the *Electricity Company* case was to substitute notionally the words "caused by" for the words "with regard to" in the Belgian declaration of acceptance. In a way this step is hardly surprising in view of the considerable uncertainty in the meaning of the expression "with regard to situations or facts". Any wider interpretation would allow a state to escape altogether from the obligations accepted by the declaration. In a sense the dispute in the *Phosphates in Morocco* case was "with regard to" the treaties of 1906 and 1911; and in the *Electricity* case "with regard to" the arbitral awards of 1926. And if one equates the "with regard to" formula with the similar exclusion of disputes "concerning situations or facts" which might have arisen prior to a given date,[5] and were to adopt a wide interpretation of such an exclusion, it would be possible to argue that the original grant of the concession in the *Electricity* case was a fact or situation which "concerned" the dispute that later arose. However, the Court has adopted the reasonable attitude that if a state wishes to restrict almost to vanishing point the obligations apparently assumed under its declaration by a temporal limitation which seemingly is ancillary to the substance of the declaration, it should do so in unequivocal terms.

The present Court's reluctance to allow a time limitation to impede the exercise of jurisdiction is strikingly illustrated by the *Interhandel* case.[6]

1940   Prior to 1940 it was common ground between Switzerland, the applicant state, and the United States that the General

---

4. *Ibid.*, at p. 82.   5. See, for example, the Belgian declaration.
6. I.C.J. Rep. 1959, p. 6.

Aniline and Film Company (G.A.F.), one of the largest producers of photographic supplies and textile auxiliaries in the United States, was controlled by German interests through a Swiss company. In 1940 it was claimed by Switzerland that the link between the Swiss company and German interests was severed when the company was re-organised as Interhandel.

1942   The United States Government vested 90 per cent of G.A.F. shares in a receiver as "enemy property".

1954–6 The American view that G.A.F., through Interhandel, was controlled by or benefited German interests was rejected by the Swiss authorities who conducted two separate investigations into the alleged German ties of Interhandel.

1946   The Washington Accord of 25th May between the U.S., the U.K., France and Switzerland *inter alia* provided for the unblocking of Swiss assets in the United States, and for the liquidation by Switzerland of German property situated in Switzerland.

On 26th August, the United States accepted the compulsory jurisdiction of the Court with respect to disputes "hereafter arising".

1946–8 Protracted diplomatic correspondence as to the "enemy" or "neutral" character of Interhandel.

1948   In January the Swiss Authority for Review, set up under the Washington Accord to determine the nature of assets in Switzerland, "definitively" recognised the non-enemy character of the assets of Interhandel.

In May, for the first time, the Swiss Government requested the restitution to Interhandel of G.A.F.'s assets in the United States.

In July the United States rejected this demand for restitution in a communication which it described as "its final and considered view".

The Court held that the dispute had not arisen before 26th August, 1946, the date of the U.S. declaration of acceptance. The subject matter of the dispute as presented to the Court was the claim for restitution, which had not become a clearly defined issue between the parties until July, 1948, when the Swiss request of May was peremptorily rejected by the United States.

This approach by the majority of the judges was strongly criticized by the minority on the grounds that to distinguish between the disagreement over the character of Interhandel and the dispute over the restitution of assets was "unrealistic and somewhat artificial".[7] Nevertheless, the majority decision is not without merit. Although the claim for restitution

---

7. Judge Hackworth, *ibid.*, at p. 33.

of assets developed from, and depended on, the controversy over the character of Interhandel, the release of the G.A.F. assets was not sought until after the exclusion date. It is likely that, if the United States had employed a double exclusion clause of the type to be found in the Belgian or French declarations discussed in relation to the *Phosphates* and *Electricity Company* cases, the pre-existence of the controversy over the character of Interhandel would have prevented the Court exercising jurisdiction. But, as has been stated before, if a party accepts the Court's jurisdiction subject to a restriction in respect of time, it is hardly surprising that the Court will construe the time limitation strictly in favour of the jurisdiction which the declaration purports to accept.

v *Transfer of jurisdiction from the Permanent Court*

Under Article 36 (5) of the present statute, declarations made under Article 36 of the Statute of the Permanent Court "and which are still in force shall be deemed, as between the parties to the present Statute, to be acceptances of the compulsory jurisdiction of the International Court of Justice for the period which they still have to run and in accordance with their terms." The straightforward application of this provision is clear enough. For example, the 1930 declaration of Canada (to remain in force for ten years and thereafter until terminated), that of 1937 by Colombia (limited only to disputes subsequent to an earlier declaration of 1932), and similar declarations by a number of other South American states, are sufficient to bestow jurisdiction on the Interantional Court by reason of Article 36 (5).

In each case, however, the state concerned was an original member of the United Nations, that is, it became a party to the Statute of the present Court before the dissolution of the Permanent Court in 1946. But what was the position of a state which did not become a party to the Statute until after the dissolution of the Permanent Court? What happened to its declaration of acceptance of the jurisdiction of the Permanent Court at the moment of dissolution if it was not yet a party to the new Statute for Article 36 (5) to operate?

These questions were directly in issue in the *Aerial Incident* case[8] in which Israel sought damages from Bulgaria for the shooting down of an Israeli airliner and for the consequent loss of life. Bulgaria contested the Court's jurisdiction *inter alia* on the ground that the Bulgarian declaration of 1921 by which it had accepted the jurisdiction of the Permanent Court had ceased to be in force on the dissolution of that Court in April 1946. The declaration of 1921 could not therefore be said to be in force within the meaning of Article 36 (5) of the Statute of the International Court when Bulgaria became a party to the Statute by reason of its admission to membership in the United Nations in 1955.

The Court upheld the Bulgarian objection. *In the first place* it was clear from the evidence that Article 36 (5) was intended to deal with the impending termination of numerous acceptances of jurisdiction with the

---

8. I.C.J. Rep. 1959, p. 127.

termination of the Permanent Court: the provision, therefore, was only intended to deal with parties to the new Statute. *Secondly*, on the wording of Article 36 (5), it could only apply to declarations still in force, and there was no suggestion that it could suspend earlier declarations until a state had become a party to the new Statute. *Thirdly*, if Bulgaria's admission to membership were to have the effect of "reactivating" its declaration of acceptance, it would mean that such admission would be subject to different legal consequences from the admission of other states.

In normal circumstances this decision by the Court would be regarded as conclusive. However, in view of the fact that the Court in the *Barcelona Traction* case[9] largely adopted the views of the dissenting minority in the earlier *Aerial Incident* case and applied them to the parallel situation under Article 37, some further comment is necessary. The decision of the Court in the later case *on the first ground* of the decision in the earlier case is totally inconsistent with its earlier pronouncements. It was held that Article 37 was intended to deal with a host of treaty provisions that would otherwise become inoperative. *On the third ground*, too, the later decision adopted a contrary view. Admission to membership of the United Nations involved an acceptance of all the obligations of the Charter and the Statute, including the obligation to accept transfers of titles of jurisdiction from the Permanent Court to the International Court. The only basis for a distinction between the two provisions would seem to be in relation to *the second ground* of the Court's decision in the earlier case. "In force" in Article 37 applies to the treaty containing the title of jurisdiction, and whether the treaty remains in force or not depends upon its terms and not upon the continued existence of a provision contained in it for the settlement of disputes. However, the same expression in Article 36 (5) can only apply to the declaration itself, and the Court in the earlier case took the view that a declaration could not remain in force if there was no Statute to which the declaring state was a party to support the declaration.

Even though this ground for distinguishing the two provisions of the Statute is all that it is possible to deduce from the reasons given by the Court in the two cases, and therefore probably represents the law, it is far from being a satisfactory distinction, nor is it certain that the decision in the *Aerial Incident* case would be treated as conclusive on Article 36 (5) if a similar situation were once more to come before the Court.[10] The strong Joint Dissenting Opinion of Judges Lauterpacht, Spender and Wellington Koo in that case was emphatic that "having regard both to the ordinary meaning of their language and their context, the words 'which are still in force' refer to the declarations themselves, namely to a period of time, limited or unlimited, which has not expired, regardless of any prospective or actual date of the dissolution of the Permanent Court.

---

9. I.C.J. Rep. 1964, p. 6.

10. It is interesting to note that for a while the United States seemed likely to continue its claim against Bulgaria in the *Aerial Incident* case, apparently believing that it could put forward further arguments that would persuade the Court to alter its mind on the interpretation of Article 36 (5).

So long as the period of time of declarations made under Article 36 of the Statute of the Permanent Court still has to run at the time when the declarant state concerned becomes a party to the Statute of the International Court of Justice, those declarations fall within the purview of Article 36 (5)."[11] And when one turns to the decision of the Court in the *Barcelona Traction* case, it is clear that the Court in effect accepted the validity of the view of the joint dissenting opinion on this point. The Court stated that, in preserving existing conventional jurisdiction, Article 37 was not intended to prevent the operation of causes of extinction other than the disappearance of the Permanent Court. In that sense it was "correct to say that regard must be had not only to whether the treaty or convention is still in force, but also to whether the jurisdictional clause it contains is itself, equally, still in force." The "sole relevance of the date of admission to the United Nations, if it was subsequent to the dissolution, is whether there still remained in existence any jurisdictional clause in respect of which Article 37 could take effect."[12]

Despite the comments by the Court accepting the earlier decision as "confined entirely"[13] to the question of the applicability of Article 36 (5), it is difficult to avoid the conclusion that the *Barcelona Traction* decision is entirely inconsistent with it. There is no convincing logical reason for distinguishing between the two provisions of the Statute, and, of the two conflicting views, that adopted in the later case is much to be preferred. By becoming a member of the United Nations and a party to the Statute, a state is clearly accepting obligations under Article 36 and 37 of the Statute if it had once granted jurisdiction to the Permanent Court in an instrument which still had a period of time to run. If it was not prepared to accept the transfer of obligations, it should take appropriate steps to terminate its earlier declaration or treaty obligation accepting the compulsory jurisdiction of the Court.

d INCIDENTAL JURISDICTION

In carrying out its normal functions, the International Court is entitled to exercise a variety of jurisdictional powers, usually of a subsidiary or procedural nature. Because of the variety of these powers, they cannot all be considered; nor are they readily classified in any useful manner even for information purposes. For want of any satisfactory alternative, it is proposed to deal with the more important aspects of the Court's incidental jurisdiction in the chronological order in which they are likely to occur in the course of litigation.

i *Interim measures of protection*

Under Article 41 (1) of the Statute, the Court has "power to indicate, if it considers that circumstances so require, any provisional measures which ought to be taken to preserve the respective rights of either party."

---

11. I.C.J. Rep. 1959, at p. 164.   12. I.C.J. Rep. 1964, at p. 34.
13. *Ibid.*, at p. 29.

And this provision is reinforced by Article 61 of the Rules of Court which deals specifically with what it terms "Interim Protection". Paragraph 3 of the Article requires that the President shall convene the Court "forthwith", and empowers him, "if need be", to take "such measures as may appear to him necessary in order to enable the Court to give an effective decision" on the request for protection.

It is clear that both the President's power in the first place, and the power of the Court when convened, depend upon the likelihood of action being taken by one of the parties that will affect the rights of the other party. Thus the President can only suggest measures of protection if the threatened rights will be prejudiced in the short period before the Court can act. The Court is similarly limited by the fact that it can only act when there is a genuine need to protect the rights of a party that are actually threatened. Although the time when this threat is most likely to occur is at the outset of the proceedings, it is conceivable that the need for protection will only arise at a later stage. It is clear from Article 61 of the Rules that the Court's powers are sufficiently flexible to meet this eventuality. Even if an earlier request for protection is rejected, it is expressly provided that a party can make a fresh request based on new facts, or that, because of a change in circumstances, the Court may revoke or modify an earlier decision indicating interim measures of protection.

The wording of Article 41 of the Statute is so wide that it could be taken to mean that the Court has a power to indicate interim measures of protection even though it has no jurisdiction on the merits of the claim. Such an interpretation would clearly be absurd. On the other hand, it would be equally absurd for the Court first to have to decide whether it did have jurisdiction over the merits of the dispute before it could act under Article 41. By the time a hearing on the jurisdictional issues had taken place and a decision on them been given, the rights of one of the parties might already have been seriously prejudiced.

Between the two extremes, however, there lies one obvious compromise. Providing there seems to be some basis for exercising jurisdiction over the dispute, the Court can with propriety make use of its powers under Article 41. In other words, the Court is entitled to make a preliminary finding that it might have jurisdiction over the claim as a basis for indicating provisional measures.

That this is only partly true of the approach of the Court to the problem is apparent from the granting of interim measures in the *Anglo-Iranian Oil Company* case.[14] There was a difference of opinion between the majority of the Court and the two judges who dissented on the degree of likelihood necessary that the Court would have jurisdiction over the claim on the merits before interim measures could be granted. The majority view was to the effect that the existence of a possible title of jurisdiction, irrespective of whether it was an adequate basis of jurisdiction,

---

14. I.C.J. Rep. 1951, p. 89.

was sufficient for the Court to exercise its powers under Article 41. Undoubtedly, there is something to be said for the proposition that, as long as there is a possibility of the Court having jurisdiction, it should be entitled to protect the rights in issue in the case. However, in the light of prevailing attitudes of states to the Court's jurisdiction, it may be wondered whether the power to indicate interim measures of protection in cases where the possibility of the Court holding that it has jurisdiction on the merits is remote is anything but harmful to the image and to the best interests of the Court. In order to safeguard the position of the Court, the minority view has much to commend it: that interim measures should only be granted where "there exist weighty arguments in favour of the challenged jurisdiction".

ii *The power to determine its jurisdiction*

As has already been stated,[15] the rule laid down in Article 36 (6) of the Statute, which provides that in the event of a dispute as to whether the Court has jurisdiction, the matter shall be settled by the decision of the Court, is not limited to jurisdictional disputes arising out of declarations under Article 36 (2). Being a reiteration of a general principle of law that applies throughout the field of international adjudication, it is applicable to all cases of contested jurisdiction. This point was made most forcibly in the *Nottebohm* case, in which the Court asserted that since the *Alabama* case, "it has been generally recognised, following the earlier precedents that, in the absence of any agreement to the contrary, an international tribunal has the right to decide as to its own jurisdiction". This principle of international law was equally applicable to the International Court, so that, even without Article 36 (6), the Court was competent to adjudicate on its own jurisdiction.[16]

Objections to the Court's jurisdiction can take a variety of forms, and the jurisprudence on the subject is considerable. Furthermore, there is often difficulty in classification: some objections are clearly of a preliminary nature; others are not; while some, though preliminary in nature, cannot be resolved without a hearing of the merits of the case. Some are objections to the jurisdiction; others raise issues of admissibility (that local remedies have not been exhausted, or that the applicant state has no *locus standi*) or of competence (that the dispute, or the remedy sought, is not one that falls within the competence of a judicial tribunal).

1 *Objections to the Court's jurisdiction*

Because of the principle of *forum prorogatum* it is essential that objections to the Court's jurisdiction *stricto sensu* (i.e. on the ground that the dispute does not fall within the parties' declarations of acceptance) should be made at the earliest possible moment. This requirement is in any case made obligatory by Article 62 (1) of the Rules which provides that a preliminary objection must be filed at the latest before the expiry of the time limit

---

15. Above, p. 501.   16. I.C.J. Rep. 1953, at pp. 119–20.

fixed for the delivery of the respondent state's first pleading.[17] In the majority of cases it will be possible for the Court to determine whether it has jurisdiction before hearing the merits of the dispute. However, in certain cases, for example, in the case of a time limitation in one of the declarations of acceptance, it may not be possible to decide the jurisdictional issue without hearing the evidence of the parties in full.[18] In such a case the objection is "joined to the merits" without prejudice to the position of the party making the objection.

2 *Objections to the admissibility of the claim*

There are a variety of grounds upon which a respondent state might claim that a case is not admissible:

(x) *That the claim, although clearly of an international nature, is still not admissible before the Court*

Two examples of reasons why the claim might not be admissible are a failure to exhaust local remedies,[19] or a failure to fulfil the procedures required by the treaty bestowing jurisdiction upon the Court. As objections of this type are not strictly speaking objections to the jurisdiction, the procedure to be followed need not be governed by Article 62 of the Rules, even though the normal practice has been to include objections of this type when raising preliminary objections to the jurisdiction. It is certainly more helpful to the Court to have notice of them along with jurisdictional objections. Furthermore, if objections to the admissibility are not included in the first set of pleadings at the latest, the Court might well take the view that the respondent state has waived its right to insist upon, for example, the exhaustion of local remedies.

(xx) *That the claim is not one that the claimant state is entitled to bring*

The most obvious example of a situation where a state is held not to have the requisite *locus standi* to present the claim occurs if it is established that the nationality of claims rule is not satisfied. However, as the absence of the necessary *locus standi* in such a case is often intimately related to the circumstances in which international law recognises a breach of obligation owed to the applicant state, an objection raised upon this ground is only partly of a preliminary character. The normal procedure is to join the objection to the merits.

The dual nature of an objection of this type may be illustrated by reference to the *Barcelona Traction* case.[20] The Belgian claim against Spain was presented on behalf of Belgian shareholders in a Canadian company whose rights, it was alleged, had been prejudiced by the activities of the Spanish authorities. Spain objected that the claim was not admissible for

---

17. The order of pleadings is set down in Article 41 of the Rules.
18. E.g. in the *Right of Passage* case, I.C.J. Rep. 1960, at p. 33.
19. As in the *Interhandel* case, I.C.J. Rep. 1959, p. 6.
20. I.C.J. Rep. 1964, p. 6, esp. at pp. 41 *et seq*.

want of capacity on the part of the Belgian Government in view of the fact that the Barcelona company did not possess Belgian nationality. While the objection was clearly preliminary in the sense that, if it was correct, Spain had no case to answer, the issue could be put in an alternative form. It could be asked "whether international law recognises for the shareholders in a company a separate and independent right or interest in respect of damage done to the company by a foreign government; and if so to what extent and in what circumstances, and, in particular, whether those circumstances (if they exist) would include those of the present case." Viewed in this light, it was clear that "the question of the *jus standi* of a government to protect the interests of shareholders as such, is itself merely a reflection, or consequence, of the antecedent question of what is the juridical situation in respect of shareholding interests, as recognised by international law." In other words, a finding on the preliminary objection would be tantamount to a decision on the merits. The proper course for the Court was to join the objection to the merits.

However, it is clear that the *locus standi* principle is not limited to non-compliance with the nationality of claims rule. The argument that it is not the applicant state which is entitled to complain at the respondent's conduct is of more general application. Indeed, it appears to have been crucial in the controversial *South-West Africa* cases submitted to the Court by Ethiopia and Liberia against South Africa, the allegation being that South Africa had failed to carry out the obligations imposed upon it by the Mandate under which it had agreed with the League of Nations to administer the territory.

The South African Government raised the preliminary objection that Ethiopia and Liberia had no *locus standi* to present the case. The only basis of jurisdiction was Article 7 (2) of the Mandate, which provided that the Mandatory agreed that "if any dispute whatsoever should arise between the Mandatory and another Member of the League of Nations relating to the interpretation or the application of the provisions of the Mandate, such dispute, if it cannot be settled by negotiation, shall be submitted to the Permanent Court of International Justice." The South African argument was that, although both Ethiopia and Liberia had been members of the League, they were no longer members, as the League had been dissolved in 1946. In line with an earlier series of advisory opinions[1] which had established the transfer of the supervisory powers of the League to the United Nations, the Court rejected this argument. As long as South Africa continued to administer the territory by virtue of the Mandate, the rights of former members of the League under the Mandate also survived.[2]

When the case was heard on the merits,[3] South Africa made no further submission on the *locus standi* issue. There must have seemed no point in doing so for the pronouncements of the Court in the hearing of the

---

1. And particularly that of 1950: I.C.J. Rep. 1950, p. 121.
2. I.C.J. Rep. 1962, at pp. 335 *et seq.*   3. I.C.J. Rep. 1966, p. 6.

preliminary objections gave to Article 7 of the Mandate the widest possible application. The Court had said that "the manifest scope and purport of the provisions of this Article indicate that the Members of the League were understood to have a legal right or interest in the observance by the Mandatory of its obligations both toward the inhabitants of the Mandated Territory, and toward the League of Nations and its Members."[4]

Nevertheless, because of a shift in the balance of opinion brought about by minor changes in the membership of the Court,[5] the Court of its own volition raised a second issue relating to the *locus standi* of the two applicant states. This issue had not been expressly raised at the first hearing, though it was certainly covered by the Court's pronouncements on the effects of Article 7 of the Mandate. The approach of the majority on the hearing of the merits was to distinguish between two types of obligation under the Mandate agreement. Those duties imposed upon the Mandatory relating to the conduct of the Mandate and to the treatment accorded to the Mandated Territory and its inhabitants were owed principally towards the League and its organs. On the other hand, there were also obligations, similar to those imposed by treaties of commerce, which were in the nature of special rights conferred directly upon individual members of the League or their nationals. Despite its earlier pronouncements, the Court now concluded that the obligations which the applicants alleged had been broken fell within the former category, and that the legal interest in seeing that they were performed was vested exclusively in the League and not in individual members. In the Court's view, the legal right or interest in the subject-matter of a dispute "must be clearly vested in those who claim them, by some text or instrument, or rule of law".[6] In the present case, no such rights or interests were vested in individual members of the League. Nor was the wide jurisdictional clause in Article 7 of the Mandate of any assistance to the applicants' case. Many declarations accepting the compulsory jurisdiction of the Court were similarly widely phrased. But this fact did not absolve a complainant state from the need to show that it had an interest in the claim it was presenting.[7]

(xxx) *That the claim is outside the Court's competence*

One major ground for arguing that the Court is not competent to hear a case is that the dispute is political and not legal. This rather complex issue has already been discussed, and it will be necessary to add further comment when dealing with the Court's advisory jurisdiction. It is not an argument that has been any obstacle to the Court in the exercise of its contentious jurisdiction. If objection were made on this ground, it would be similar to an objection to the jurisdiction, though not identical with such an objection. It is tantamount to saying that, though the dispute falls

---

4. I.C.J. Rep. 1962, at p. 343.
5. See the comments by Cheng in (1967) 20 C.L.P., pp. 193–9.
6. I.C.J. Rep. 1966, at p. 32.   7. *Ibid.*, at p. 42.

within the Court's jurisdiction *ratione personae, materiae* and *temporis*, it is not a dispute upon which a judicial tribunal should properly give, or is competent to give, a decision.

This notion that a judicial tribunal, or the International Court in particular, has a proper function, and that it is not competent to determine a case falling outside that function provided a basis for the decision in the *Northern Cameroons* case.[8] The Court was asked by the Republic of the Cameroons to declare that the United Kingdom had not properly carried out its duties as laid down in the Trusteeship Agreement under which it had formerly administered the Northern Cameroons. However, in the Court's view such a decision, if it were to hear the merits of the case, would be pointless. Under a U.N. plebiscite the Northern Cameroons had voted for incorporation in Nigera: this incorporation had been effected by a General Assembly resolution bringing an end to the Trusteeship Agreement. The applicant state was not seeking to have either the plebiscite declared invalid, or the resolution void. "The function of the Court is to state the law, but it may pronounce judgment only in connection with concrete cases where there exists at the time of the adjudication an actual controversy involving a conflict of legal interests between the parties. The Court's judgment must have some practical consequence in the sense that it can affect existing legal rights or obligations of the parties, thus removing uncertainty from their legal relations. No judgment on the merits in this case could satisfy these essentials of the judicial function."[9]

iii *Intervention*

Intervention by a third state in proceedings already instituted before the Court may occur in two ways:

1 *Where that state has a legal interest that might be affected by the decision*

Under Article 62 of the Statute, the Court has jurisdiction to decide upon a request by a state that wishes to intervene in a case on the ground that it has an interest of a legal nature which might be affected by the decision. A request for permission to intervene must be filed with the Registry at the latest before the commencement of the oral proceedings (Article 64 of the Rules).

2 *Where the construction of a convention to which other states are parties is in question*

Article 63 imposes upon the Registrar a duty to notify all parties to a Convention, other than those taking part in the case, that the Convention is in issue before the Court. Such states have a *right* to intervene if they so wish, though if they do intervene, the Court's decision will be equally binding upon them.

---

8. I.C.J. Rep. 1963, p. 15.   9. *Ibid.*, at pp. 33–34.

iv *Interpretation or revision of a judgment*

Once a decision is reached by the Court it is final (Article 60 of the Statute), and binding upon the parties (Article 94 (1) of the U.N. Charter). However, Article 60 goes on to state that in the event of a dispute as to the meaning or scope of the judgment, the Court shall construe it upon the request of any party. The main limitations upon this power are (1) that there must be a dispute (a state cannot ask for clarification until a dispute arises); and (2) that the Court cannot go beyond the scope of its original judgment.[10]

"An application for revision of a judgment may be made only when it is based upon the discovery of some fact of such a nature as to be a decisive factor, which fact was, when the judgment was given, unknown to the Court and also to the party claiming revision, always provided that such ignorance was not due to negligence" (Article 61 (1) of the Statute). Article 61 also imposes time limits upon the making of such application: within six months of the discovery of the new fact, and in any case not after the lapse of ten years from the date of the judgment.

D. The Court's advisory jurisdiction

a THE RIGHT TO REQUEST AN ADVISORY OPINION

The right to request an advisory opinion is not granted to individual states, but only to a number of organs of the United Nations and to all but one of the specialised agencies. The grant of the right is governed by Article 96 of the Charter which envisages two possibilities:

(i) an original right which is bestowed directly on the General Assembly and the Security Council; and
(ii) a derivative right which may be bestowed upon other organs of the U.N. and specialised agencies by the General Assembly.

Article 96 (2) expressly limits any such grant by the Assembly to legal questions arising within the scope of the activities of the organ or agency concerned, though this limitation is probably unnecessary as no organ would be entitled to request an opinion on a matter outside its sphere of competence. It would seem to follow that a similar limitation should be implied into Article 96 (1) dealing with the original right, though, for practical purposes, this might be of importance only in the case of the Security Council, as the Assembly has the widest competence over the whole range of U.N. activities.

The following U.N. organs have been authorised to request opinions: ECOSOC, Trusteeship Council, Interim Committee of the General Assembly, and the Committee on Applications for Review of Adminis-

---

10. *Asylum* case, I.C.J. Rep. 1950, at p. 403.

trative Tribunal Judgments. The first three are authorised in relation to legal questions arising within the scope of their activities, though, in the case of ECOSOC, this competence is extended to cover questions concerning the relationships of the U.N. and the Specialised Agencies. The Committee on Applications for Review's authority is limited to matters arising under Article 11 of the Statute of the U.N. administrative Tribunal.

The only specialised agency that has not been authorised to request an opinion is U.P.U. In all but Financial Agencies (the Bank, the Fund, I.D.A. and I.F.C.), the request can be made by the Assembly or Conference of the Agency, or by the executive organ with the Assembly's or the Conference's approval (except in the case of the I.C.A.O. in which the Council does not need such authorisation from the Assembly). Although the Fund or the Bank, etc., can request an advisory opinion, the likelihood of their doing so is small, because disputes over interpretation of the relevant articles of association or agreement are specifically made subject to the determination of the Executive Directors and appeal to the Board of Governors. In addition the I.A.E.A. has been granted the power to request an advisory opinion, though there exists some doubt as to the validity of this grant. Although within the U.N. orbit, it is doubtful whether the I.A.E.A. is a specialised agency as such.[11]

b JURISDICTION IN ADVISORY CASES

Prima facie, all that is required in order to obtain an advisory opinion from the Court is a favourable majority from the General Assembly or, on a matter within its sphere of competence, from some other appropriate organ of the U.N. or of a specialised agency. However, Article 65 (1) of the Statute which governs the Court's advisory jurisdiction does suggest two limitations upon this apparently wide competence.

i *An advisory opinion may only be given on a legal question*

As has already been stated, the Court's jurisdiction over non-legal disputes is severely restricted, and does not exist at all in relation to its compulsory jurisdiction under Article 36 (2), or to its advisory jurisdiction as Article 65 (1) is limited to "legal questions" only.[12]

ii *The Court may decline to give an opinion*

Article 14 of the Covenant of the League of Nations, by stating that the Court "may . . . give an advisory opinion" allowed the Court a discretion whether or not to answer a question submitted to it. And Article 65 (1) of the present Statute is similarly permissive.

While the contentious jurisdiction is clearly consensual in basis, so that a state can decide either in advance or latterly whether to submit to the Court's jurisdiction in certain types of dispute, there is no such formal limitation on the Court's advisory competence. It is the existence of this

---

11. See below, p. 608.   12. See above, pp. 474–478.

discretion which provides the Court with a means of ensuring compliance with what might be termed the jurisdictional proprieties.

The following considerations and criteria have been advanced and either accepted or rejected by the Court as reasons why the Court should decline to give an opinion:

1   *That the Court should not decide upon the merits of a dispute between states*

It would be contrary to the whole conception of the Court's powers if it could hear in its advisory capacity a dispute over which it would have no jurisdiction as a contentious case. To an extent, at least, the need for the Court to observe the essentially consensual basis of its jurisdiction has been recognised. In the *Eastern Carelia* case,[13] the Court was asked by the Council of the League whether a statement, made by the Russian delegation and annexed to the Treaty of Dorpat between that state and Finland, was conclusive on the status of Eastern Carelia. Russia was not at the time a member of the League and had rejected all suggestions that the League might intercede in the dispute. The Court declined to give an opinion on the ground that answering the question would be "substantially equivalent to deciding the dispute between the parties"; it felt that it could hardly depart from the fundamental principle that "no State can, without its consent, be compelled to submit its disputes with other states either to mediation or to arbitration, or to any other kind of pacific settlement."[14]

2   *That the non-co-operation and absence of consent of a party or of parties involved does not prevent the Court giving an opinion*
   (a) *if the question asked relates to the competence of the U.N. or of any of its constituent or associated organs; or*
   (b) *if the question concerns the procedure of settlement and not the substance of the dispute;*
   (c) *but, in any case, the Court, being the principal judicial organ of the U.N., should in principle participate in the activities of the Organisation by giving an answer to questions submitted to it.*

The extent of the limitation placed upon the Court's power to give an opinion by the *Eastern Carelia* case depends largely upon whether the consent of the parties is essential, or whether it is essential only when the question submitted to the Court concerns the substance of the dispute between the parties. Any doubt on this issue was resolved by the Permanent Court itself in the *Frontier between Turkey and Iraq* case.[15] The Treaty of Lausanne provided that if Turkey and Britain were unable to reach agreement on the disputed frontier within nine months, the dispute was to be referred to the League of Nations. The Court was asked whether the Treaty gave the Council of the League the right to make a

---

13. P.C.I.J. Rep., Ser. B., No. 5.   14. *Ibid.*, at pp. 27–29.
15. (1925), P.C.I.J. Rep., Ser. B., No. 12.

binding award in the case once the states concerned had failed to reach agreement. Turkey objected to the Court hearing the questions submitted to it and refused to take part in the proceedings. The Court took the view that the refusal of Turkey to co-operate in the hearing was no reason for it refusing to give an opinion. The circumstances of the present case were different from those of the *Eastern Carelia* case, "since the question before the Court referred not to the merits of the affair but to the competence of the Council, which had been duly seised of the affair and could un-doubtedly ask for the Court's opinion on points of law."[16] Because the report of the Court's decision in the *Frontier* case on this point is so brief it is not clear whether the reasons given for departing from the *Eastern Carelia* principle (i.e. that the question did not refer to the merits, and that it related to the competence of the Council) were alternatives, or needed to exist in conjunction.

In the *Peace Treaties* case,[17] however, the present Court apparently treated such reasons as alternatives. It will be recalled that allegations were made by a number of members of the United Nations that Bulgaria, Roumania and Hungary were failing to carry out certain human rights provisions of their respective Peace Treaties. The Treaties provided for the creation of arbitral tribunals to hear such disputes, but the three former enemy states refused to appoint arbitrators to implement these proce-dures. The allegations were also discussed in the General Assembly which submitted to the Court a series of questions dealing with the settlement procedures under the Treaties. The three states objected to the Court's answering the questions on the ground that the Court could not proceed without their consent. In rejecting this objection, the Court commented that the present case was "profoundly different" from the circumstances of the *Eastern Carelia* case, and relied upon the fact that the present request concerned "the applicability to certain disputes of the procedures for settlement instituted by the Peace Treaties" and that answering it would not be equivalent to deciding the main point of the dispute between the parties.[18] In other words, the fact that the request did not relate to the merits of the dispute was, by itself, a sufficient ground for distinguishing the *Eastern Carelia* decision.

But this is not all that was said by the Court in the *Peace Treaties* case. It had already suggested that the question of consent was now largely irrelevant to the exercise of its advisory functions "even where the request for an opinion relates to a legal question actually pending between states. The Court's reply is only of an advisory character: as such, it has no binding force. It follows that no state, whether a member of the United Nations or not, can prevent the giving of an advisory opinion which the United Nations considers to be desirable in order to obtain enlightenment as to the course of action it should take. The Court's opinion is given not to states, but to the organ which is entitled to request

---

16. *Ibid.*, Ser. E, No. 2, at p. 164.   17. I.C.J. Rep. 1950, p. 65.
18. *Ibid.*, at p. 72.

it; the reply of the Court, itself an 'organ of the United Nations', represents its participation in the activities of the Organisation, and, in principle should not be refused."[19]

The only possible limitation which the Court suggests exists upon its duty to reply to a question submitted to it is that the question must be one which the U.N. considers desirable in order to obtain enlightenment as to the course of action it should take. This is not to say that the Court cannot still decline to give an opinion, but the grounds upon which it should decline are restricted almost to the point of disappearance. As long as the U.N. considers that the advice is relevant to its course of action is a far wider basis for the Court to disregard the *Eastern Carelia* principle than the suggestion in the *Frontier* case that the question should relate to competence of the organ concerned.

3 *That the Court should decline to give an opinion where the request, although it asks a legal question, raises serious political issues*

As has already been stated, the Court in its advisory capacity has, in theory at any rate, no jurisdiction at all over non-legal questions. However, it is arguable that even a legal question may have such important political implications that the Court should decline to answer it. This contention was hardly considered at all in litigation before the Permanent Court,[20] but it has been raised frequently in cases before the International Court.

The significant role that the United Nations has come to play as an arena for diplomatic manœuvring and political wrangling has given added significance to certain issues of interpretation of the Charter. Indeed, the experience of the United Nations suggests that the use of the process of the Court's advisory jurisdiction has been but another form of political pressure to be exerted against a minority. Over two major issues, that of admission to membership of the U.N., and of the powers of the Organisation to create peace-keeping forces, it is difficult to escape the conclusion that the political factors involved far outweighed the significance of any answer the Court could give by a simple process of treaty interpretation.

During the first ten years of the United Nations one of the most vexed issues concerned the admission of new members. A variety of legal or entirely political reasons were given by members of the Security Council when voting on applications for admission.[1] The motives behind the disputes became more and more obviously "cold-war" politics designed to "keep potential supporters of the other side out at any cost". At one stage the Soviet Union let it be known that it would not vote against applications from Finland and Italy only if Bulgaria, Hungary and Roumania were admitted to membership at the same time.

---

19. *Ibid.*, at p. 71.
20. The only references being in the *Frontier between Turkey and Iraq* case (1925), Ser. B, No. 12, p. 8 (telegram from Turkish Foreign Minister to the Registrar of the Court) and in Judge Anzilotti's S.O. in the *Customs Union* case, Ser. (1931), P.C.I.J. Rep, A/B, No. 41, esp. at pp. 61–69.   1. See below, pp. 537–539.

It was this suggestion of a "package deal" which decided the General Assembly to ask the Court for its opinion on two specific questions. Was a member state voting on an application for membership entitled to take into account conditions other than those laid down in Article 4 (1) of the Charter? And, in particular, was a member state entitled to subject its affirmative vote to the additional condition that other applicants be admitted to membership at the same time?

The argument that the first question was a political one and fell outside the Court's jurisdiction was rejected: the Court would not "attribute a political character to a request which, framed in abstract terms, invites it to undertake an essentially judicial task, the interpretation of a treaty provision."[2] The Court went on to hold that the conditions laid down in Article 4 (1)—that "an applicant must (1) be a State; (2) be peace-loving; (3) accept the obligations of the Charter; (4) be able to carry out these obligations; and (5) be willing to do so"—were exhaustive. It inevitably followed that it was not open to a member of the United Nations to subject its affirmative vote to the condition that other States be admitted to membership at the same time as the applicant whose admission was being considered.[3]

While it is true that by stating the question in abstract terms as a matter of treaty interpretation, the General Assembly is submitting to the Court a "legal question" (i.e. a question within the Court's jurisdiction), it need not follow that, providing the question is "abstract", the Court should always answer it. The Court has a discretion in what legal questions it answers: as a matter of "propriety" it may decline to give an opinion. The International Court has consistently refused to consider the political implications of the dispute in relation to which a particular question is submitted to it. Once the issue of jurisdiction is decided (i.e. whether the question is "legal"), the secondary issue of propriety is largely ignored.

In the *Expenses* case[4] the Court was asked whether the costs of the United Nations Emergency Force, set up in 1956 to police the withdrawal of foreign troops from Egyptian territory, and of the force created to deal with civil strife that broke out in the Congo in 1960,[5] constituted expenses of the organisation that could be apportioned between members of the U.N.[6] The legal issues concerned the powers of the Organisation under the Charter, but these issues were inextricably bound up with differing political philosophies towards the peace-keeping role of the United Nations.

Objections were raised in the General Assembly to the submission of the matter to the Court. In the words of one representative, the "problem which the resolution sought to solve had important political aspects which militated against its solution by legal means. . . . Nothing could be gained by seeking the advisory opinion of the International Court."[7] However,

---

2. Admissions case, I.C.J. Rep. 1948, at p. 61.   3. *Ibid.*, at p. 62–63.
4. I.C.J. Rep. 1962, p. 151.   5. See below, pp. 563–572, 577–582.
6. In accordance with Art. 17 of the Charter.
7. (Afghanistan), G.A.O.R., 16th Sess. 5th Committee, 897th Mtg., para. 26; see also the statement of Roshchin (U.S.S.R.) *ibid.*, para. 7.

the majority view that the difference of opinion on the question submitted to the Court was "very clearly of a legal nature, however much the whole problem may be complicated by other considerations of a political kind"[8] prevailed.

Despite this admission by the majority that the question was complicated by political considerations the Court saw no obstacles to its giving an answer. While accepting that "even if the question is a legal one, which the Court is undoubtedly competent to answer, it may nonetheless decline to do so", the Court held that only "compelling reasons" would lead it to refuse to give its opinion. However, it rejected the existence of political factors as constituting sufficiently compelling reasons. "It is true that most interpretations of the Charter of the United Nations will have political significance, great or small. In the nature of things it could not be otherwise. The Court, however, cannot attribute a political character to a request which invites it to undertake an essentially judicial task, namely, the interpretation of a treaty provision."[9]

In a sense it is not surprising that the Court, as the judicial organ of the United Nations, wishes to play its part in the work of the Organisation. And political factors need not deter it from playing a role. The real problem is that legal solutions do not necessarily answer political problems. And if the Court's opinion is disregarded because one side or the other is not willing to accept a legal solution, the Court's prestige is likely to suffer. The *Admissions* case had no effect on the voting habits of members of the Security Council. In fact, the deadlock over membership was eventually broken by a package deal on a much larger scale than that which led to the submission of the matter to the Court in the first place, and which the Court ruled was contrary to Article 4 (1) of the Charter. And in the *Expenses* case, the recalcitrant minority felt no more obliged to pay their "debts" to the Organisation for peace-keeping expenditures after the Court had given its opinion than before.

It might be argued that the Court should be less ready to exercise its advisory jurisdiction in cases in which the legal issues are inextricably bound up with major political controversies. The consequence of such a change in attitude might be a reduction in the use of the advisory procedure, but a reduction would be equally likely to follow the persistent disregard of the Court's opinions. A more satisfactory solution would be for the Court to frame its opinions in the form of advice rather than as definitive statements of legal principle. Although this approach would be totally at variance with past practice, it would at least enable the Court to examine situations in their political context and not as legal abstractions. Members of the U.N. might also feel freer to take into account or disregard the advice thus given when deciding on their course of action without the charge being made that those unwilling to accept the Court's advice are in some way "bringing the Court into disrepute".[10]

---

8. Hodges (U.K.) Plenary Mtg. 1068, para. 115.   9.   I.C.J. Rep. 1962, at p. 155.
10.   Much of the material for the sections dealing with the Court's advisory jurisdiction is taken from (1966) 15 I. & C.L.Q. 325–368

E. The obligation of compliance and the enforcement of judgments

a DECISIONS IN CONTENTIOUS CASES

i *Customary international law*

It is a general principle of law that a decision of a competent tribunal is binding upon the parties to the litigation. This principle applies equally to arbitral awards as it does to decisions of the International Court, although members of the United Nations have specifically undertaken to comply with any decision of the Court in a case to which they are parties (Article 94 (1) of the Charter).

The enforcement of decisions of an international tribunal, however, poses unique problems. Securing compliance with the judgments of a municipal court is an executive matter. In the international community, however, there is no readily available means of execution available to the successful litigant if the other party refuses to abide by the decision. To an extent, it is true, a state that is willing to submit a claim to judicial determination in the first place is likely to be ready to abide by that determination. This consideration was the reason why the San Francisco Conference paid so little attention to the problems of non-compliance when drafting the new Statute in 1945. Nevertheless, in the light of the hotly contested proceedings that have often taken place in relation to the Court's compulsory jurisdiction, it is obviously possible for a state to become an unwilling party to litigation; and an unwilling party is less likely to abide by a subsequent decision it considers inimical to its interests.

The classic means of remedying an international wrong was self-help. In view of the Charter provisions regulating the use of force in any form it would seem that self-help can only be used if states have first of all attempted to settle their dispute by peaceful means. *A fortiori*, self-help would be available once the stage of a binding award by a judicial tribunal had been reached.

But what other limits are there on the right of self-help? The finer points are best left to the final chapter on the use of force by states, but it is clear that force may not be used against the territorial integrity of a state (Article 2 (4) of the Charter).

In the *Corfu Channel* case,[11] the Court held that the presence of mines in the area of the Channel within Albanian territorial waters ought to have been known to Albania, so that the Albanian authorities were under a duty to warn shipping of the hazard. However, the existence of the danger did not justify the subsequent operations by British minesweepers under the protection of a large force of British naval vessels within Albanian territorial waters. "The Court can only regard the alleged right of intervention as the manifestation of a policy of force, such as has, in

---

11. I.C.J. Rep. 1949, p. 4.

the past, given rise to most serious abuses and such as cannot, whatever be the present defects in international organisation, find a place in international law. . . . Between independent States, respect for territorial sovereignty is an essential foundation of international relations. . . . To ensure respect for international law, of which it is the organ, the Court must declare that the action of the British Navy constituted a violation of Albanian sovereignty."[12]

It is clear, for example, that a state could not seize a public ship belonging to its judgment debtor as security for payment of an award made by an international tribunal. However, if the subject matter of the dispute were a piece of territory, there is no reason why the successful litigant should not seize what a Court has decided rightfully belongs to it because that state is in no sense violating the territorial integrity of another state.

A more fruitful opportunity for the "enforcement" of an award of compensation is likely to be by the blocking or seizure of assets belonging to the debtor state. This opportunity would obviously be available in the case of assets situated within the territory of the "judgment creditor".[13] It may also be possible for a state to obtain possession of assets situated abroad by instituting proceedings against them in the courts of the *situs*, or by some other process.[14]

In a case where the international tribunal's award of compensation was in respect of an injury to a national of a claimant state, would it be possible for the national himself to seek enforcement by proceedings in municipal courts? The answer should, in principle, be in the negative. The claim in which the award was made was on the international plane; to that litigation the injured national was in no sense a party. Neither under the municipal law of most states, and certainly not by international law, has the injured individual any entitlement to the compensation due to his state.[15] It is hardly likely that municipal law would allow an individual to recover the sums due before they had been handed over to the state of nationality.

The case of *Socobel* v. *The Greek State*[16] concerned an attempt by a Belgian company to attach assets of the Greek Government in settlement of a debt alleged to be due to it as a result of a judgment of the Permanent Court.[17] That Court in a claim presented by Belgium on behalf of Socobel decided that certain arbitral awards in favour of the company were binding on Greece. Under one of the awards Socobel was entitled to a payment of compensation by the Greek government. After the Second World War when funds allocated to Greece under the Marshall

---

12. I.C.J. Rep. 1949, at p. 35.
13. For this reason *inter alia* it is not likely that, particularly among the major commercial nations of the world, an award of compensation by an international tribunal would not be met: otherwise "self-help" in the form of seizure of assets would be readily available.
14. For the unusual situation that arose in the *Monetary Gold* case, I.C.J. Rep. 1954, p. 19, see Rosenne, *Law and Practice of the International Court*, Vol. I, pp. 142–8.
15. See under English law, *Civilian War Claimants' Association* v. *R.*, [1932] A.C. 14.
16. (1951), 18 I.L.R. 3.   17. P.C.I.J. Rep., Ser. A/B, No. 78.

Plan were paid into a Belgian bank, the Belgian company instituted these proceedings. The Belgian tribunal rejected the defence of sovereign immunity on the ground that immunity from execution did not extend to the economic activities of a state. There was no means of enforcing the private law arbitration, but did the judgment of the International Court create any right against the assets? It was held that, even if certain procedural difficulties could be overcome concerning the enforcement of an award of the International Court, the company was faced with the insuperable obstacle that it had been in no way a party to the decision it was seeking to have enforced.

ii *Organisational enforcement*

In the final analysis compliance with decisions of the International Court depends principally upon the political pressures that exist within the world community. Once a state has decided to procrastinate or to avoid complying with an award, the outcome depends upon how much political pressure can be brought to bear on the defaulter. Such pressure may take the form of cutting off economic aid or of outlets for the exports of that state; withdrawal of technical assistance missions; breaking off of diplomatic relations, and so on. Whether these pressures are sufficient to secure compliance depends upon the circumstances of the particular case.

The political significance of this "post-adjudicative" phase as it has been called is emphasised by the fact that reference to it within the U.N. framework is to be found not in the Statute of the Court but in the Charter of the Organisation. As it is an additional weapon in the diplomatic armoury, it is hardly surprising that the U.N. should have a role to play in this phase of dispute settlement. And it is similarly appropriate that responsibility for assisting the "judgment creditor" should be vested in the Security Council, the executive arm of the Organisation. Hence Article 94 (2) of the Charter provides that, if "any party to a case fails to perform the obligations incumbent upon it under a judgment[18] rendered by the Court, the other party may have recourse to the Security Council, which may, if it deems necessary, make recommendations or decide upon measures to be taken to give effect to the judgment."

The powers bestowed upon the Council in this context are *sui generis* in that any action that the Council may take must be based upon the existing determination of the legal position of the parties. Disputes with which the Council would be likely to deal in the exercise of its functions under Chapters VI and VII of the Charter[19] will normally concern a legal situation about which there is still controversy, and therefore perhaps room for compromise. Nevertheless, it is likely that even when acting under Article 94 the Security Council will view its powers in the light of those specifically bestowed under those chapters of the Charter. Indeed,

---

18. Does a judgment include an order for interim measures of protection? See Rosenne, *op. cit.*, Vol. I, pp. 156-9.

19. See below, pp. 563-572.

the choice of the expressions "make recommendations or decide upon measures" would seem to be an implied reference to the framework within which the Council generally acts under the Charter.

Although the reference in Article 94 is to the Security Council, this limitation would not appear to prevent a party having recourse to other institutional means of securing compliance with, or an agreed solution based upon, a judgment. As will be discussed in a later chapter, the General Assembly has a competence throughout the whole field of U.N. activities, including a secondary responsibility for the maintenance of international peace and security.[20] And, if a judgment of the Court relates to a dispute between members of a regional organisation,[1] or relates to a subject matter within the competence of an organisation with a special field of interest (e.g. G.A.T.T.),[2] there would be no barrier to the parties employing these alternative forums for bringing about compliance with the judgment.

b ADVISORY OPINIONS

The binding effect of the Court's advisory opinions has posed problems both of a practical and of a theoretical nature. In retaining the advisory part of the Court's functions, the framers of the Charter and the Statute were careful to stress the non-obligatory nature of advisory opinions. Nevertheless, there has always existed a widespread feeling that such weighty pronouncements by the Court have some higher moral value and deserve greater attention than is usually accorded to mere "legal advice".

It is clear beyond question that an advisory opinion, unless it is given compulsive effect by prior agreement, can give rise to no direct obligations on States: it is, as the Court stated in the *Peace Treaties* case, "only of an advisory character" and "as such, it has no binding force."[3] However, the question was inevitably asked, what was the status of a pronouncement of the relevant legal principles if "it has no binding force"? It is in their attempts to answer this question that upholders of the Court's prestige, and of the authority even of its advisory opinions, have all too often been led into a fruitless and circuitous process of reasoning.

As has already been stated, the binding nature of a judicial award has a different connotation under international law from what it has under municipal law. Municipal systems provide a "due process" for the enforcement of judgments, but the enforcement of the decisions of an international tribunal will usually depend on the political circumstances of the states involved and the attitudes of other interested parties. Thus, although it is only possible to talk of the obligation "to comply in good faith with the . . . decisions of the Court" expressed in Article 94 of the

---

20. See below, pp. 577–582, 592–593.

1. See the role of O.A.S. in the *Arbitral Award* case, I.C.J. Rep. 1960, p. 192, discussed in Rosenne, *op. cit.*, pp. 159–61.

2. See below, pp. 592–609.   3. I.C.J. Rep. 1950, at p. 71.

Charter in connection with decisions of the Court in contentious cases, the process of enforcement is, in the final analysis, the same as that applicable in order to secure compliance with an opinion given by the Court in its advisory capacity.

If political pressure is to be exerted against States in order to obtain general compliance with an advisory opinion, there must exist some obligation to comply. This obligation of compliance is said to be based upon two principal duties; a direct moral duty and an indirect legal duty. As Judge Azevedo pointed out in the *Peace Treaties* case, the fact that an advisory opinion "did not produce the effects of the *res judicata* . . . is not sufficient to deprive [such an] opinion of all the moral consequences which are inherent in the dignity of the organ delivering the opinion, or even of its legal consequences."[4]

This reference to legal consequences is not difficult to explain. If the Court does make a pronouncement on what the law is in a particular field, even if, being an advisory opinion, it is not "binding" *per se*, it is arguable that such a pronouncement must be "binding" as an authoritative statement of international law. It can hardly be claimed that it is logically satisfying to regard advisory opinions as in one sense "not binding" and in another as "binding" at one and the same time. Judge Lauterpacht acknowledged this dilemma when he said that "it may not be easy to characterise precisely in legal terms a situation in which South Africa declines to act on an Advisory Opinion which it was not legally bound to accept but which gave expression to the legal position as ascertained by the Court."[5]

It is thus not possible to give any absolute answer to questions relating to the nature of and the obligations created by advisory opinions. Many of the difficulties stem from the types of issue upon which the Court's advice is requested. However, this factor will be considered under the heading of the role of the Court, to which the discussion must now turn.

F. The role of the Court

a CONTENTIOUS JURISDICTION

The underlying philosophy of the attempts to encourage the adjudication of international disputes, at least until the outbreak of the Second World War, was the belief that arbitration or judicial settlement could be a more attractive alternative to the use of force. The steps in this direction that commenced with the first Hague Convention for the Peaceful Settlement of Disputes in 1899, continued with the creation of the Permanent Court of International Justice in 1920 and culminated with the

---

4. *Ibid.*, at p. 80.
5. *Hearing of Petitioners from S.-W. Africa* case, I.C.J. Rep. 1956, at p. 47; and see the careful analysis of advisory opinions by Judge Zoricic in the *Peace Treaties* case, I.C.J. Rep. 1950, at pp. 101–2.

General Act of Geneva in 1925 were the fruits of these attempts. The Second World War was seen as proof that means of peaceful settlement were not in themselves sufficient without a proscription on the use of force and some means of enforcing the proscription. The U.N. Charter was designed to provide both these requirements.

The Charter is primarily concerned with disputes likely to endanger international peace and security,[6] and the parties to such a dispute are required, first of all, to seek a solution by "negotiation, enquiry, mediation, conciliation, arbitration, judicial settlement, resort to regional agencies or arrangements, or other peaceful means of their own choice" (Article 33 (1)). However, the Security Council itself may at any stage of such a dispute recommend appropriate procedures or methods of adjustment (Article 36 (1)) and in making these recommendations it is required to "take into consideration that legal disputes should as a general rule be referred by the parties to the International Court" (Article 36 (3)).

Despite the existence of this provision and of the fact that the Court is the principal judicial organ of the U.N. (Article 92), the Charter is perhaps more of a discouragement than an incentive to judicial settlement. The dispute settlement machinery of the Charter provides a new arena. for diplomatic exchanges and for the advancement of legal arguments without fear of a final determination upon their validity.

The law-making process in the international community is, it will be recalled,[7] primarily based upon the practice of states. This process has one fundamental factor in its favour. The speed of change in the world community must be reflected in the legal rules upon which the community is based. As long as states remain the primary determinants of these rules, the rules may remain uncertain, but there is little danger of their beoming static. Adjudication, on the other hand, even though it deals only with a specific dispute, is usually based upon some principle of law, and for that reason tends to introduce a static element into international law.

In the same way as the Court's pronouncements can put a brake upon the future development of the law, they can also play a quasi-legislative role. If there exist conflicting views of the law on a particular matter, a decision by a court based upon one of those views is in practical terms legislative in effect. Although the decision itself is binding only upon the parties to the dispute, the basis of the decision, i.e. the formulation of the law, is in theory at least binding upon all states. It is a strongly held view among Communist states and among a number of new states, particularly in Asia, that the weakness of judicial settlement lies as much in the law upon which it is based as it is upon the principle of third party adjudication.

Against this unpromising background, it is hardly surprising that advance acceptance of the Court's compulsory jurisdiction is limited to approximately a third of the states which are parties to the Statute. A

---

6. See below, pp. 569–572; in situations where there is an actual threat to the peace, breach of the peace or act of aggression, the case is no longer a matter of "pacific settlement".

7. See above, pp. 5–26.

glance at the reports of the Court reveals how few are the cases which are submitted for its consideration. And in many of those which are submitted between states that have "consented" to the Court's jurisdiction, the jurisdictional issue of whether the dispute is in fact covered by the parties' declarations of acceptance is hotly contested.

It is doubtful whether the contentious jurisdiction of the Court contributes anything to the settlement of disputes the continuation of which would be likely to lead to a breach of international peace. Where jurisdiction is contested, a final decision against the wishes of one of the parties is of limited value. The *Corfu Channel* award was never met; and the *Right of Passage* decision was overtaken by events when Indian forces occupied Portuguese territory on the sub-continent. The only entirely satisfactory decisions are those reached in cases where the parties have either expressly or tacitly agreed to submit the case to the Court. And in such circumstances, the role of the Court is scarcely distinguishable from that of a permanently established arbitral tribunal.

b ADVISORY JURISDICTION

As has already been explained, the Court's advisory jurisdiction has been in a number of respects the more controversial. States that are fundamentally opposed to judicial settlement can avoid any dispute to which they are a party coming before the Court as a contentious case. However, consent has but a limited relevance to the exercise of the Court's advisory jurisdiction.

The reason why consent has become an issue at all in relation to the Court's advisory functions is the type of question submitted to the Court. A number of U.N. organs have a wide power of setting in motion the advisory procedures. Should any dispute arise over a provision of the Charter, or the powers of the organisation itself, then the General Assembly, though in certain circumstances at least also the Security Council, can ask for guidance from the Court. If a dispute were to arise over the relationship between the U.N. and one of the Specialised Agencies, ECOSOC is specifically empowered by the General Assembly to refer the matter to the Court. And matters falling exclusively within the competence of a particular agency (other than U.P.U.) can be submitted to the Court by the agency itself.

The liberty whether or not to request an advisory opinion is a very flexible alternative to a constitutional provision that the advisory procedure must be employed for the authoritative interpretation of a disputed text. The furthest that the General Assembly has been prepared to go is to "recommend" that the various organs of the U.N. and the specialised agencies "should, from time to time, review the difficult and important points of law within the jurisdiction of the International Court of Justice which have arisen in the course of their activities and involve questions of principle which it is desirable to have settled . . . and . . . should refer them to the . . . Court . . . for an advisory opinion."[8]

---

8.   G.A. Res. 171 (III) of 14th November, 1947.

534

Despite this exhortation, the Court's advisory jurisdiction has not been invoked with any great frequency. In an earlier Chapter[9] it was explained that member states of international organisations on the whole prefer to avoid rigid, and therefore restrictive, interpretations of their constitutions. Hence they tend to regard interpretation by the organs of the organisation concerned preferable to interpretation by the International Court. Illustrative of this reluctance to have recourse to the Court is the fact that, apart from the General Assembly, no other organ has set in motion the advisory procedure.

The motives which in a particular case have led the General Assembly to submit issues to the Court are not easily ascertained, unless one accepts the notion that all requests are made with the genuine intention of obtaining legal advice. In some cases the *bona fides* of member states need not be doubted. The *Reparations* case[10] involved an important issue of international law upon which the differences of opinion were basically juridical and not political.[11] A number of other cases, like that concerning the competence of the General Assembly to admit a state to membership in the absence of a recommendation of the Security Council,[12] or that concerning the power of the U.N. Administrative Tribunal to make an award binding on the Assembly,[13] were illustrations of situations in which the Assembly wished to demonstrate that the legalistic arguments of the minority were palpably wrong.

However, while it is true that whatever the issues involved, political factors do feature in the considerations involved in the decision by the Assembly to request an advisory opinion, and in the motives of states voting in favour of, or against, the resolution embodying the request, there have been situations in which one suspects that political considerations exerted a paramount influence on the attitudes of member states. The disruption of the uneasy amity that had existed between members of the alliance which secured the military defeat of Germany and Japan in the Second World War, posed grave problems for the post-war world. And as the guardian of the recently established peace, the United Nations suffered acutely from the wranglings between the former allies—the Communist states on the one hand and the western powers on the other.

On two principal occasions, the powers of states under provisions of the Charter, and the powers of individual organs of the United Nations, became major political issues in the "cold war". The first main controversy was provided by problems of membership;[14] and the second by the relationship of the Security Council to the General Assembly and the role of the Secretary-General as far as peace-keeping operations were concerned.[15] Once the actual text of the Charter became the focal point of a global ideological conflict between the two major power *blocs* it can

9. Chapter 9, at pp. 378–379.   10. I.C.J. Rep. 1949, p. 174.
11. It is the only G.A. resolution requesting an advisory opinion that has ever been adopted unanimously.
12. I.C.J. Rep. 1950, p. 4.   13. I.C.J. Rep. 1954, p. 47.
14. See below, pp. 537–539.   15. See below, pp. 563–582, 585–588.

hardly be supposed that the majority of states believed that a strictly legal interpretation of the disputed provisions of the Charter could serve either to resolve, or even to relieve, the tensions. Indeed, the refusal of states to act in accordance with the opinions given by the Court in the *Admissions* case and in the *Expenses* case suggests that a major reason in each situation for requesting an advisory opinion was to exert an additional form of political pressure against a recalcitrant minority.

CHAPTER TWELVE

INTERNATIONAL ORGANISATIONS—I
MEMBERSHIP, STRUCTURE AND VOTING*

The origins of the League of Nations and, therefore, of the United Nations which was established to replace it, can be traced to four main sources.

First, in order of importance, was the Concert of Europe, the theory and the reality of the nineteenth-century hegemony of the Great Powers which met together from time to time to settle the major political problems of the day. This hegemony was recognised in the Council of the League, and has been perpetuated in the permanent membership granted to the United States, the Soviet Union, China, Britain and France, in the Security Council of the United Nations.

Secondly, the various agencies created by governments to improve international co-operation in telegraphs and postal services, in health and hygiene, and in river and railway transport, provided an example of joint endeavour on an international scale. Although few of these agencies took advantage of the opportunity of co-ordination under the direction of the League offered by Article 24 of the Covenant, a number of them became, or were the forerunners of, the specialised agencies of the United Nations.

Thirdly, the staffs of many of these agencies were in the nature of permanent international civil servants. The experience gained in such employment, together with the similar experience of the staffs recruited for shorter periods to organise and run major international conferences, provided the background for the establishment and tradition of the Secretariat of the League and of the United Nations.

Fourthly, and this influence is least in importance, and the most difficult to estimate, is the effect of the various writers and influential groups who, prior to 1919 and again during the Second World War, initiated studies and plans for future international organisation. Perhaps their most significant contribution was the proposal that the League of Nations should have a permanent official with the diplomatic prestige of the "world chancellor". Nothing as grandiose would ever have proved acceptable to the states which drafted the Covenant of the League, but the

---

* For a convenient collection of constitutional texts, see *International Organisation and Integration*, Sijthoff/Leyden, 1968.

creation of the post of Secretary-General owed something to the proposals formulated by these unofficial bodies.

I MEMBERSHIP OF INTERNATIONAL ORGANISATIONS

Membership of international organisations can be divided into three categories: original members, members subsequently admitted, and associate members.

a ORIGINAL MEMBERSHIP

The normal type of original membership is that of states which attended the conference called to draft the constitution of the organisation, and which subsequently ratified the constitution in accordance with its provisions. Article 3 of the U.N. Charter provides that the original members of the Organisation shall be states which, having participated in the San Francisco conference on international organisation, "sign the present Charter and ratify it". Similarly, the original members of the International Monetary Fund are described by Article 2 of the Fund Agreement as "those of the countries represented at the U.N. Monetary and Financial Conference whose governments accept membership" before a specified date. Original membership of regional organisations is of course also limited by geographical factors.

b SUBSEQUENT MEMBERSHIP
i *The United Nations*

Admission to membership in the United Nations is governed by Article 4 of the Charter, which is divided into two paragraphs. In the first, it is stated that membership is "open to all other peace loving states which accept the obligations contained in the present Charter and, in the judgment of the Organisation, are able and willing to carry out these obligations." The second provides that the admission of "any such state" is to be effected by "a decision of the General Assembly upon the recommendation of the Security Council."

During the period from 1946 until 1955, throughout which the "cold war" between the Soviet Union and the "western" powers was at its height, political wranglings prevented the admission of a large number of applicants. The reasons given by members of the Security Council were sometimes disguised in legal terms; for example, that a state's independence was in doubt (Jordan, Ceylon), that it was not peace-loving or willing to carry out its obligations under the Charter (Albania, Bulgaria, Hungary, Roumania), or that it would not be able to carry out such obligations (Mongolia). On other occasions, political motives were openly confessed: for example, that the applicant had remained neutral in the war against Germany (Ireland, Portugal), or that a vote would be withheld from two states (Finland, Italy) if they and three others (Bulgaria, Hungary, Roumania) were not admitted together. In practice, states believed likely to favour the western standpoint had their applications "vetoed" by the Soviet Union, while communist states failed to obtain the necessary number of votes in a Council which at that time was still largely "pro-western".

The General Assembly attempted to exert pressure on the Council in order to fulfil the United Nations' aim of universality of membership, and on two occasions tried to make use of the International Court by asking for an advisory opinion on the legal effects of the paragraphs of Article 4.

On the first occasion[1] involving the interpretation of paragraph (1), the Assembly asked the following questions:

> "Is a Member of the United Nations which is called upon, in virtue of Article 4 of the Charter, to pronounce itself by its vote, either in the Security Council or in the General Assembly, on the admission of a State to membership in the United Nations, juridically entitled to make its consent to the admission dependent on conditions not expressly provided by paragraph 1 of the said Article? In particular, can such a member, while it recognises the conditions set forth in that provision to be fulfilled by the State concerned, subject its affirmative vote to the additional condition that other States be admitted to membership in the United Nations together with that State?"

The majority of the Court held that the conditions laid down in Article 4 (1)—that "an applicant must (1) be a State; (2) be peace-loving; (3) accept the obligations of the Charter; (4) be able to carry out these obligations; and (5) be willing to do so"—were exhaustive. It inevitably followed that it was not open to a member of the United Nations to subject its affirmative vote to the condition that other states be admitted to the United Nations at the same time as the applicant, the admission of which was being considered.

Despite the view expressed by the Court, the members of the Security Council still failed to agree upon the large majority of outstanding applications. Two years later, in 1950, the General Assembly made another attempt to find a way out of the deadlock. According to Article 4 (2), it was for the Assembly to reach a decision on the admission of a state, and only for the Council to "recommend" an applicant. As a recommendation could be either favourable or unfavourable, was it not possible for the Assembly to admit a state despite an *unfavourable* recommendation from the Security Council? It was more than likely that this possibility had been intended by the San Francisco Conference, because the Committee which had drafted Article 4 expressly adopted such an interpretation and included it in the Conference records. True, the Security Council had either made a favourable recommendation, or no recommendation at all, but was not the failure to make a favourable recommendation the equivalent of an unfavourable recommendation?

The issue was submitted to the International Court[2] in the following terms:

---

1. I.C.J. Rep. 1948, p. 57.   2. I.C.J. Rep. 1950, p. 4.

"Can the admission of a State to membership in the United Nations, pursuant to Article 4, paragraph 2, of the Charter, be effected by a decision of the General Assembly when the Security Council has made no recommendation for admission by reason of the candidate failing to obtain the requisite majority or of the negative vote of a permanent Member upon a resolution so to recommend?"

By a large majority, the Court was of opinion that the General Assembly had no power to act in the absence of a recommendation by the Security Council that an applicant should be admitted to membership. The evidence of the records of the San Francisco Conference was irrelevant, because the intention of the parties to a treaty was to be deduced from the words used, provided that those words were unambiguous. In this case, the words used were not ambiguous. They required both a "recommendation" of the Security Council and a "decision" of the General Assembly; and it was clear that the recommendation of the Security Council was "the condition precedent to the decision of the Assembly by which the admission is effected."

In 1955, following an easing of international tension after the death of Stalin, the deadlock over admission to membership was broken by a "package deal" involving the "bloc" acceptance of sixteen hitherto unsuccessful applicants, a solution contrary to the expressed opinion of the majority of the Court in the first of the advisory opinions on Article 4. This political compromise seems to make a mockery of the legal interpretation of paragraph 1. The question whether the Court should involve itself in issues of a political nature has already been discussed,[3] but, in the present context, it is at least worth mentioning the forceful joint dissenting judgment of Judges Basdevant, Winiarski, McNair and Read.[4] In their view, "resolutions which embody either a recommendation or a decision in regard to admission are decisions of a political character; they emanate from political organs; by general consent they involve the examination of political factors, with a view to deciding whether the applicant state possesses the qualifications prescribed by paragraph 1 of Article 4". As the "main function of a political organ is to examine questions in their political aspect", it followed that members of such an organ were "entitled to base their arguments and their vote upon political considerations", even when the matter under discussion was an application for admission to the United Nations. Indeed, the very conditions of membership laid down in Article 4 (1) could not be assessed without the application of a political judgment based upon political factors. Their conclusion that a member of the Organisation when called upon to vote on an application for membership could legitimately base its reasons for voting in a particular way upon factors not mentioned in paragraph 1 bears more in relation to reality than the other too legalistic view adopted by the majority of the Court, and disregarded by the Security Council in its subsequent practice.

---

3. Above, pp. 524–526.   4. I.C.J. Rep. 1948, at pp. 82–93.

ii *Other international organisations*

1   *The specialised agencies*

In general, states members of the United Nations can become members of any of the Specialised Agencies by formal notification of acceptance of the obligations of membership. In some cases, the notification is to be made to the Secretary-General or Director-General of the Agency concerned (as with the I.T.U.[5] and the I.L.O.[6]), or to the Secretary-General of the United Nations (as in the case of I.M.C.O.[7] or W.H.O.[8]). But at least as often a government of a particular state is designated to act as depository for ratifications or acceptances of the constitution. Acceptances of the U.N.E.S.C.O. constitution have to be notified to the United Kingdom;[9] of the I.A.E.A.,[10] I.C.A.O.,[11] I.M.F.,[12] and W.M.O.[13] constitutions to the United States.

In the case of the financial agencies, the Fund is regarded as the "parent" body, so that subsequent membership of the International Bank is open to members of the Fund at such times and in accordance with such terms as the Bank may prescribe;[14] and, in turn, membership of the International Finance Corporation is open to members of the Bank.[15]

The procedures governing the admission of members other than states qualifying as original members or already members of the United Nations may be divided into two categories. On the one hand, there are those agencies in which a vote of approval, usually in the form of a qualified majority, by the existing members is sufficient. The majority most often required is two-thirds (as with the F.A.O.,[16] I.T.U.,[17] U.P.U.,[18] and W.M.O.[19]), although the I.C.A.O. constitution requires four-fifths,[20] while the W.H.O. constitution provides for admission by a simple majority of the Health Assembly.[1] On the other hand, there are a number of agencies in which the procedure is further qualified, either by the need for a prior recommendation by the executive organ of the agency[2] (as in the case of I.M.C.O., where the co-operation of the I.M.C.O. Council is required,[3] or of U.N.E.S.C.O. under the constitution of which there

---

5.   Art. 19 (2).   6.   Art. 1 (3).   7.   Arts. 6 and 57.   8.   Art. 79 (b).
9.   Art. 13.   10.   Art. 21 (c).   11.   Art. 92.   12.   Art. 20 (2)
13.   Art. 33. New admissions to the U.P.U. have to be channelled through the Swiss Government: Art. 11 (3).
14.   I.B.R.D., Agreement, Art. 2 (1).
15.   I.F.C. Agreement, Art. 2 (1). See also I.D.A. Agreement, Art. 2 (1).
16.   Art. 2 (2).   17.   Art. 1 (2) (c).   18.   Art. 11 (4).
19.   Art. 3 (c).   20.   Art. 93; but see below, fn. 2.   1.   Art. 6.
2.   Or by a right of veto granted to an organ of another institution. For example, Art. 2 of the relationship agreement between the U.N. and I.C.A.O. gives the U.N. General Assembly the power to recommend the rejection of an application from any state not qualifying for admission under Articles 92 and 93 of the I.C.A.O. constitution. The Assembly recommendation is binding on I.C.A.O. If no recommendation is made within a certain period, the Organisation may proceed to admit the applicant in accordance with Article 93. A similar power is granted to the Economic and Social Council of the United Nations in the U.N.E.S.C.O. relationship agreement, Art. 2.
3.   Art. 8.

must be a prior recommendation by the Executive Board[4]), or by the need for the participation of certain states or representatives in the majority vote (as with the I.L.O. in which the two-thirds majority must include "two-thirds of the government delegates present and voting"[5]).

2 Regional organisations

Admission to membership in regional organisations is, with few exceptions, only possible with the unanimous agreement of existing members. Article 10 of the North Atlantic Treaty states that the parties may "by unanimous agreement, invite any other European state in a position to further the principles of this Treaty and to contribute to the security of the North Atlantic area to accede to this Treaty." Similarly, by Article 237 of the Treaty of Rome, any European state may become a member of the European Economic Community, provided the Council reacts favourably to the application "by means of a unanimous vote." Although couched in different languages, the Eastern European equivalents to N.A.T.O. and the E.E.C.—the Warsaw Pact and COMECON —contain similar provisions requiring unanimous consent to the admission of new members. Thus, Article 9 of the Warsaw Pact, while stating that the treaty should be open to accession by other states, "irrespective of their social and political structure", goes on to lay down that such "accessions shall come into effect with the consent of the states parties to the Treaty after the instruments of accession have been deposited with the Government of the Polish People's Republic."

Among exceptions to the application of the unanimity rule are the Organisation of American States and the Council of Europe. Provided a state is "geographically eligible", Articles 2 and 3 of the Organisation's Charter seem to allow membership as of right.[6] By Article 4 of the Statute of the Council, any European state which is deemed "able and willing to fulfil the provisions of Article 3" (requiring all members to "accept the principles of the rule of law and of the enjoyment by all persons within its jurisdiction of human rights and fundamental freedom") may be invited to become a member by the Committee of Ministers. In Article 20 (c) it is laid down that resolutions of the Committee relating to admission to membership or associate membership shall require a two-thirds majority.

c ASSOCIATE MEMBERS

The main reason for having associate membership is to enable states or other territorial units to co-operate in the functioning and benefits of

---

4. Art. 2 (2).   5. Art. 1 (4).
6. Though this position will be altered when the Protocol of Amendment to the Charter of the O.A.S. signed in February, 1967, receives sufficient ratifications to bring it into force. According to the new Article 7 (the present Articles 2 and 3 will be renumbered 4 and 5), the General Assembly of the O.A.S., upon the recommendation of the Permanent Council, shall decide both by a two-thirds majority, whether the applicant shall be permitted to sign and ratify the Charter.

an organisation to which for one reason or another they are not eligible to belong. The United Nations Charter makes no provision for associate membership, but some of the specialised agencies, notably the I.T.U.[7] W.H.O.,[8] and I.M.C.O.,[9] do have associate members. In these cases, associate membership is open to territories which, not being states, cannot become full members of the agency concerned. Part IV of the Treaty of Rome deals specifically with the association of overseas countries and territories which have special relations with Belgium, France, Italy and the Netherlands. These provisions do not create "associate membership" as such,[10] but are intended to apply the rules of the Treaty to states which, being situated outside Europe, could not become members of the Community. Article 238 of the Treaty uses similar language in stating that the Community may conclude "with a third country, a union of states or an international organisation agreements creating an association embodying reciprocal rights and obligations, joint actions, and special procedures." The creation under this Article of a type of associate membership has taken place because of the wish of certain states to enjoy some of the economic benefits of the Community, without becoming involved in its organisational and political structure.

2. STRUCTURE AND VOTING: THE DOCTRINE OF THE EQUALITY OF STATES

The theory of state equality appeared early in writings on international law. It was perhaps inevitable that the premise of naturalist philosophy, that all men were equal, should be transposed into the field of international relations. The doctrine of the legal equality of states has its most obvious applications on the international plane in the principle that no state can without its consent be made a party to arbitration or to the judicial settlement of its disputes; and on the municipal plane in the privileges and immunities accorded to foreign sovereigns and their diplomatic representatives. Yet running counter to these manifestations of equality are a number of developments arising from the fact of inequality. While in the narrow field of what might be termed "international administration", and in the making of a number of "law-making" conventions, almost entirely devoted to certain aspects of the conduct of war, there was a practical application of the principle of the equality of states, throughout the century preceding the First World War, the political future of Europe was in the hands of the major powers. And, as has already been pointed out, this contrast between the hegemony of the great powers on the one hand, and the theoretical equality of states on the other was preserved in the respective membership and functions of the Council and the Assembly of the League of Nations.

7. Art. 1 (3).   8. Art. 8.   9. Art. 9.
10. Cp. Art. 4 of the U.P. Convention.

A. The United Nations

a THE SECURITY COUNCIL

i *Structure*

Under Article 23 of the Charter, the Security Council consists of formerly eleven, but now fifteen members, of which five (China, France, the Soviet Union, the United Kingdom and the United States) are permanent members. The non-permanent members are elected for two-year terms by the General Assembly, and the elections are "staggered", so that five states are elected to the Council each year. Article 23 also lays down that, in making the choice, the Assembly shall pay special regard "in the first instance, to the contribution of Members of the United Nations to the maintenance of international peace and security and to the other purposes of the Organisation, and also to equitable geographical distribution." At the eighteenth session of the Assembly, a resolution[11] was passed which set out the basis upon which this "equitable geographical distribution" should operate: five from African and Asian states; one from Eastern European states; two from Latin-American states; and two from Western European and other states.

ii *Voting*

Article 27 sets out the voting procedure. Each member of the Council is to have one vote. Decisions of the Council on procedural matters are to be made by an affirmative vote of nine members (formerly seven when the membership of the Council was eleven), but decisions "on all other matters" shall be made by an affirmative vote of nine members (formerly seven) "including the concurring votes of the permanent members."

In addition to a privileged position by reason of their permanent membership of the Council, the five states also have a privileged position with regard to voting. Decisions on non-procedural matters can only be adopted with their approval. The most vexing problem that has faced the Council in this context is the distinction between procedural and non-procedural matters, because the distinction can often be politically vital. For example, a decision by the Council to set up a sub-committee is in one sense a matter of procedure (Article 29 which empowers the Council to establish "such subsidiary organs as it deems necessary" comes under the general heading of "Procedure" within Chapter V of the Charter), but in view of the powers of investigation that might be delegated to such a sub-committee, its creation will often have serious political repercussions. Should not the preliminary "decision" that the draft resolution under discussion be treated as a procedural matter require a positive vote including the concurring votes of the permanent members of the Council? This was certainly the view of the Sponsoring Powers at San Francisco

---

11. Res. 1991, of 17th December, 1963: this resolution was the one upon which the amendment increasing the number of members of the Council was based.

(China, U.S.S.R., U.K., and U.S.A.) because they issued the so-called "Four Power Statement", to which France later adhered, stating that "the decision regarding the preliminary question as to whether or not such a matter is procedural must be taken by a vote of seven members of the Security Council, including the concurring votes of the permanent members." It is often suggested that this statement was the origin of the "double veto" whereby a permanent member can prevent any matter being classified as procedural against its will, and further that the statement, not having been acquiesced in by non-permanent members, is not binding on the Council as a whole. It is true that the statement is not "binding" in this sense, but it is difficult to interpret the actual terms of Article 27 itself to give any other meaning. By paragraph 2 decisions on procedural matters require only the affirmative vote of nine members (seven at the time of the "Four Power Statement"), but, by paragraph 3, decisions "on *all other matters*", including therefore on the preliminary question, require the concurring votes of the permanent members.

Even if the "double veto" has a firm legal foundation in the wording of Article 27, it cannot be denied that it is open to abuse. A permanent member of the Security Council can, if this possibility is taken to its logical conclusion, prevent the adoption of any resolution by the Council, whatever the nature of the resolution. A means of escaping from such an unsatisfactory position is offered by the power of the President of the Council to make a ruling on whether or not the draft resolution before the Council is procedural. Under the Rules of Procedure of the Council (Rule 30) a presidential ruling stands unless reversed by a majority of nine members of the Council. In this way, the "veto" can be by-passed.

An illustration of what is usually regarded as a proper use of the presidential power occurred in 1950 when a resolution was before the Council to invite a Chinese Communist representative to attend meetings of the Council to discuss the threatened invasion of Formosa. The Chinese representative on the Council attempted to have the preliminary question of whether the resolution was procedural or not submitted first, but was ruled out of order by the President. After a vote of 7 to 3 in favour, the resolution was declared adopted despite the negative votes of both the Chinese and American representatives. When the Chinese representative challenged this ruling, the President applied Rule 30, and his ruling was upheld with China in a minority of one. The attitude of the President can be supported on the ground explained by the Yugoslav representative in the course of the debate. He noted the right of a permanent member to insist upon its right of veto in a vote on the preliminary question, but regarded the Chinese position in this instance to be inconsistent with the previous practice of the Council, as the right to insist upon a qualified majority on the preliminary issue "is confined to questions the procedural nature of which is in doubt". But the question of inviting states parties to the dispute to deliberations of the Council had been expressly mentioned as a procedural matter in the Four Power Statement, and this interpretation had never been challenged.

However, there have been occasions upon which the power of the President may have been misused in order to prevent an "inconvenient" negative vote by a permanent member having the effect of preventing the adoption of a resolution. It is true that such occasions have been rare,[12] because all the permanent members of the Council have an interest in retaining their right of veto intact, but the power should be handled with care. The veto was not written into the Charter as the price of Russsian participation in the United Nations: it was a right also insisted upon by the United Kingdom and the United States. It is part of the Charter, and can only be eradicated by some future agreement among the permanent members, but such a step does not seem likely in the foreseeable future. And to attempt to undermine it by misuse of the presidential ruling would undermine the principle of great power hegemony upon which the Council and the Charter is based.

iii *Abstention and absence*

Although Article 27 (3) of the Charter makes it compulsory for a member of the Council to abstain in decisions under Chapter VI and Articles 52 (3), if that member is a party to the dispute, the wording of Article 27 (3) makes it clear that in all other cases of a non-procedural nature, the concurring vote of the permanent members is required. Any lack of emphasis in the English text is remedied by the equally authoritative French, Spanish, Russian and Chinese text, all of which refer to the concurring vote of "all the permanent members".

Nevertheless, as has been mentioned on a number of earlier occasions, the practice has become established of regarding an abstention by a permanent member as not affecting the validity of a resolution which otherwise satisfies the requirements of Article 27. Although statements were made at early meetings of the Council that the abstention in question was in no way to be considered as a precedent, by 1949, it was possible for the United Kingdom representative to make the following statement to the Political Committee of the General Assembly:[13]

> "Since July 1946, a practice has been created in the Security Council whereby a permanent member can, by abstaining from the vote, permit the Council to take action which that member does not affirmatively support, provided that such action has been approved by the affirmative votes of seven members. That procedure has been explicitly sanctioned by all five permanent members on various occasions. It should be noted, specifically, that during the discussion on the question of Indonesia in July 1947, the then President of the Council, the representative of Syria, stated: 'I think it is now jurisprudence in the Security Council—and the interpretation accepted for a long time—that an abstention is not considered a veto, and the concurrent votes of the permanent members mean the votes of the permanent members who participate in the voting. Those who abstain intentionally are not

---

12. E.g. over the Laos question in 1959, discussed in (1960) 54 A.J.I.L. 118–31.
13. G.A.O.R. (III), *Ad hoc* Political Committee, Mtgs. 6th April–10th May, p. 200. See generally (1951) 60 Yale L.J. 209–57.

considered to have cast a veto. That is quite clear.' Irrespective of the strictly legal position, it is unwise to abandon a practice whereby the permanent members of the Council were attempting to avoid hampering decisions by exercising their veto."

This practice of "disregarding" the abstention of a permanent member is based upon the acquiescence of a member actually present at the time of voting, and it cannot therefore provide an exact precedent for the situation where a member of the Council is in fact absent from the meeting. The question of absence became of the greatest importance in 1950 when the Council, in the absence of the Soviet representative, passed the resolutions sanctioning the creation of a force to operate in the name of the United Nations, but under the control of the United States, on behalf of South Korea which had been invaded by Communist forces from the north.

Prior to 1950 a number of resolutions had been passed by the Council in the absence of a member, but in each case the affirmative vote of the absent member was not necessary to the validity of the resolution. In 1946, for example, the Soviet delegate was absent when a resolution was adopted to invite an Iranian representative to the Council. Before putting the resolution to the Council, the Chinese President stated that "since this is a purely procedural question, a decision can be taken even in the absence of the U.S.S.R. representative." Subsequently the Soviet Union challenged the legality of this resolution, but was met with the contention that, as the resolution was purely procedural, the Soviet vote was irrelevant. As one representative observed, the power of veto could not be "extended" beyond the terms of the Charter by a permanent member "simply absenting itself from the Council's deliberations."[14]

Even the argument that the Soviet Union, by being in breach of Article 28, which requires that each member of the Council shall be represented "at all times" at the seat of the Organisation in order that the Council might "function continuously", had in some way "abandoned the Charter" so that it had lost its right to complain that what the Council did in its absence, hardly seems justification for the remaining members to disregard other provisions of the Charter.[15] However, even

14. S.C.O.R. (I), No. 2, p. 128.
15. There is a similarity between this argument and that submitted to the International Court in the *Peace Treaties* case. The Court had held (I.C.J. Rep. 1950, p. 65) that the Peace Treaties with Bulgaria, Hungary and Roumania imposed a duty on those states to appoint an arbitrator to the commissions envisaged by the Treaties to deal with breaches of the human rights provisions contained in the Treaties. Once arbitrators had been appointed by these states and by the Allied and Associated powers complaining of infringements of the Treaties, the two arbitrators thus appointed to the Commission set up under each Treaty were to appoint by agreement between them a third member of the Commission. If they could not agree, the Secretary-General of the United Nations had the power to make the appointment of the third member. It was contended that, because the three states refused to make an appointment to the Commission, the Secretary-General could nevertheless appoint a member to each Commission; and that the Commissions comprising the member appointed by the complaining Allied Power, and the Secretary-General's appointee could adjudicate on the disputes. The Court (I.C.J. Rep. 1950, p. 221) rejected this argument. The failure of the three former enemy states to appoint members to the

if doubt must remain as to the formal validity of resolutions passed in the absence of a permanent member when its concurring vote is necessary, it does not follow that the army which fought in Korea could not legally be considered as a United Nations force. But that is an issue which will be considered in the following chapter.

b THE GENERAL ASSEMBLY AND THE OTHER PRINCIPAL ORGANS
i *Structure*

According to Article 7 of the Charter, in addition to the Security Council and the General Assembly, there are established also as "principal organs" the Economic and Social Council (ECOSOC), the Trusteeship Council, the International Court and the Secretariat. Although termed "principal organs", both ECOSOC, and the Trusteeship Council operate under the control of the General Assembly, to which they submit reports on their activities. The subsidiary nature of ECOSOC's position is made clear by Article 60 which states that responsibility for the discharge of the functions of the United Nations in the field of international economic and social co-operation "shall be vested in the General Assembly and, under the authority of the General Assembly, in the Economic and Social Council." Similarly, under Article 85, the function of the United Nations with regard to trusteeship agreements for all areas except those designated as strategic areas (where the supervision is exercised by the Security Council) shall be exercised by the General Assembly; and the Trusteeship Council, operating under the authority of the General Assembly, shall assist the Assembly in carrying out its functions.

The General Assembly comprises all members of the United Nations, but ECOSOC and the Trusteeship Council are organs of limited membership. ECOSOC now consists of twenty-seven members, elected, nine to retire each year, by the General Assembly. Although Article 61 makes no provisions for "permanent membership" or "geographical distribution", both criteria are applied by the Assembly in the practice of ECOSOC elections. The permanent members of the Security Council are always elected to the Economic and Social Council, and geographical and other factors play their part in the election of other members. Thus, when the membership of ECOSOC was increased recently from eighteen to twenty-seven, the General Assembly decided that, "without prejudice to the present distribution of seats in the Council", the nine additional members were to be elected, seven from African and Asian states, one from Latin American states, and one from Western European or other states.[16] On the other hand, membership of the Trusteeship Council is more closely controlled by the provisions of

Commissions was a breach of an international obligation, but it did not absolve the other parties to the Treaties from complying with their terms if they wished to make use of the procedures for settling disputes available under each Treaty.

16. G.A. Res. 1991 (XVIII).

Article 86. In theory, it is based upon the principle that administering and non-administering states should be equally represented on the Council, but the position is complicated by the fact that the permanent members of the Security Council are given permanent membership of the Trusteeship Council. As the number of administering authorities dwindles, far from it being necessary for the General Assembly to elect additional non-administering members to the Council, the number of administering states is now outnumbered by the number of non-administering permanent members of the Security Council. The Trusteeship Council consists therefore of two administering states, Australia and the United States, and of the other four permanent members of the Security Council.

It is perhaps worth mentioning in the present context that political considerations also influence the selections for office in the other two "principal organs", the Court and the Secretariat. The only limitation upon the election of judges (apart from the need that a candidate should obtain "an absolute majority of votes in the General Assembly and in the Security Council"), is that, by Article 9 of the Statute of the Court, the electors are to bear in mind, not only the necessary legal prowess of the persons to be elected, but also that "in the body as a whole the representation of the main forms of civilisation and of the principal legal systems of the world should be assured." In practice, as in ECOSOC, a national of each of the permanent members of the Security Council has been elected to the Court, although since the termination of Wellington Koo's long association with the Court, no Chinese national has been elected to the bench. Similarly, while the Secretary-General of the United Nations is a "neutral", acceptable to all the permanent members of the Security Council, the senior appointments of the Secretariat, at Under-Secretary level, have always been filled by nationals of the major powers.

ii *Voting*

Voting in the General Assembly is governed by Article 18 of the Charter. Each member is to have one vote, and in all matters except for "important questions" decisions are to be by a majority of members "present and voting". Important questions, which require a two-thirds majority of the members of the Assembly present and voting, expressly include recommendations with respect to the maintenance of international peace and security, the elections of members to the Security Council, ECOSOC, and the Trusteeship Council, admission of new members of the United Nations, suspension or expulsion of members, the operation of the trusteeship system, and budgetary matters. It is possible, as happened over the issue of the representation of Communist China in the United Nations, for the General Assembly, by a simple majority, to classify a question as "important" and therefore to make it subject to the two-thirds rule. On the other hand, all decisions of ECOSOC and the Trusteeship Council, in both of which each member is entitled to one vote, are by simple majority.

B. The specialised agencies

a STRUCTURE

If one regards the General Assembly and the Security Council as the "chief organs" of the United Nations (which, in practical terms, is an accurate description, despite the fact that they are only two of a number of "principal organs" within the meaning of Article 7 of the Charter), this pattern of an assembly or conference comprising representatives from all the members of the organisation and of an executive body of limited membership is to be found in all the specialised agencies.

i *The Assembly or Conference*

The exception to the straightforward representation of each member state in the plenary organ of the agency concerned is provided by the I.L.O., which has a unique tripartite structure of delegates representing governments, employers and workers. In the General Conference of the I.L.O., each member is represented by two government delegates, one employers' delegate and one workers' delegate.[17]

The division between government, labour and industry is very much the product of pre-1914 social and economic thought, and was seen by the creators of the I.L.O. as an answer to the Communist International. However, the theory of tripartism has tended to break down in the face of two developments. In the first place, even in non-communist states, the extent to which the government has become the most significant employer makes the division unreal (though workable). Secondly, the admission of communist states, in which the government exercises complete control over all aspects of the economy, to membership has made it almost impossible to maintain the distinction. Disputes among members of the organisation over the acceptance of non-governmental representatives from communist states has centred on the application of Article 3 (5) of the constitution, which requires members to nominate non-government delegates in agreement with the industrial organisations "which are most representative of employers or workpeople, as the case may be, in their respective countries." It was argued that, as the industrial organisations in these states were in no sense independent of the State Administration and the Communist Party, the effect of the I.L.O. constitution was to allow the governments concerned four delegates to the conference. Although, on a report of the Credentials Committee, non-government representatives have been admitted to the Conference, there has been continued opposition to their serving as non-government representatives on various committees set up by the Conference.

---

17. Art. 3 (1).

ii *The executive organ*

Although the name of the executive board, and the number of its members, varies from one agency to another, there is a possible line of distinction between those organisations in which states of particular importance in the field in which the agency operates are given preference in the system of election, and those organisations where a system of preference would serve no particularly useful purpose. The Governing-Body of the I.L.O. consists of 48 persons, 24 of whom are to represent governments, 12 employers, and 12 workers; but of the 24, "ten shall be appointed by the Members of chief industrial importance".[18] In electing the members of the Council of I.C.A.O., the Assembly of that organisation is to "give adequate representation" first to "the states of chief importance in air transport" and secondly to states "which make the largest contribution to the provision of facilities for international civil air navigation"; after taking into account these two criteria, the I.C.A.O. Assembly is to ensure that "all the major geographic areas of the world are represented on the Council."[19] Similarly, by Article 18 of the I.M.C.O. Constitution:

> "In electing the members of the Council, the Assembly shall observe the following principles:
> (a) six shall be governments of States with the largest interest in providing international shipping services;
> (b) six shall be governments of other States with the largest interest in international seaborne trade;
> (c) six shall be governments of States not elected under (a) or (b) above, which have special interests in maritime transport or navigation and whose election to the Council will ensure the representation of all major geographic areas of the world."

In both I.B.R.D. and I.M.F., five of the "Executive Directors" are appointed directly by the states with the largest quotas (i.e. contributions to the agency concerned).[20] In contrast, the constitutions of F.A.O.,[1] U.N.E.S.C.O.,[2] W.H.O.,[3] W.M.O.[4] and I.T.U.[5] contain no direction to elect states of particular significance to the Executive organ of those agencies, although the U.N.E.S.C.O., W.H.O. and I.T.U. constitutions contain references to equitable geographical distributon or some such criterion.

b VOTING

i *Weighted voting*

Unlike the organs of the United Nations, and most of the specialised agencies, the voting systems operated in the financial agencies are based upon the weighting of the votes of the states contributing most to the organisation's capital. For example, in the I.M.F., each member is entitled to 250 votes plus one additional vote for each part of its quota

---

18. Art. 7.   19. Art. 50 (b).   20. I.B.R.D., Art. 5 (4) (b); I.M.F., Art. 12 (3) (b).
1. Art. 5 (1).   2. Art. 5 (2).   3. Art. 24.   4. Arts. 8 (i) and 13.
5. Art. 9 (1) (1).

equivalent to 100,000 U.S. dollars.[6] In the executive organ (the "executive directors"), each director casts the number of votes which together were cast for or against his appointment by the state or group of states he is deemed to represent.[7] As a result of this system of weighted voting, the five largest members of the Fund are entitled to cast between them about fifty per cent of the votes, and the United States alone accounts for half of that total.

ii *Qualified majorities*

Qualified majorities are required in the plenary organs of a number of agencies as exceptions to the basic simple majority rule. By Article 17 (2) of the I.L.O. constitution for example, unless otherwise expressly provided, all matters are to be decided by a simple majority of the votes cast by the delegates present. However, in a number of important issues a two-thirds majority vote is required—in budgetary matters, in order to adopt a Labour Convention or Recommendation, admission of new members, etc. Most of the agencies follow this pattern of different articles requiring a two-thirds majority instead of a simple majority for specific matters,[8] although W.H.O. has a provision similar to Article 18 of the Charter setting out a number of "important questions" for which a two-thirds majority is required, and enabling additional categories of "important questions" to be added by simple majority.

iii *The need to be approved by a certain member or group of members*

The additional qualification that a particular vote, in order to be effective, requires the concurrence of certain members is not to be found very often in the constitutions of the Specialised Agencies. However, in a number of cases, the amendment procedures of an organisation require not only a qualified majority, but also the agreement of certain members. This is the position in the I.L.O. constitution: Article 36 provides that amendments "which are adopted by the Conference by a majority of two-thirds of the votes cast by the delegates present shall take effect when ratified or accepted by two-thirds of the Members of the Organisation including five of the ten Members which are represented on the Governing Body as Members of chief industrial importance." A similar effect is achieved by the equivalent provisions in the Fund and Bank agreements which, in all but a few more important matters that require acceptance by all members, lay down that an amendment must be accepted by three-fifths of the members, having four-fifths of the voting powers.[9] Under this provision, the United States is given a right of veto of all amendments (since it is entitled to well over twenty per cent of the votes), while the United Kingdom in conjunction with two or three of the next largest contributors could also block any proposed amendment.

---

6. Art. 12 (5) (a).   7. Art. 12 (3) (i).
8. E.g. U.N.E.S.C.O., Art. 4 C. (8); I.C.A.O., Art. 48 (c). Cp. W.M.O., Art. 11 (b).
9. I.B.R.D., Art. 8; I.M.F., Art. 17.

C. Regional organisations

Because of the variety of organisations and the differences in structure, it is not possible to provide more than the barest outline of some of the more interesting features of the constitutions of a number of regional organisations. For this reason, institutions basically concerned with mutual defence created by a group of states (N.A.T.O., the Organisation of American States, the Arab League and the Warsaw Pact) will be largely disregarded.

a COUNCIL OF EUROPE

The most advanced constitutional structures are to be found amongst the European institutions. The earliest departure from the traditional type of organisation based upon an Assembly where each member state is entitled to equal representation and voting power is to be found in the Statute of the Council of Europe. In the Consultative Assembly of the Council, members are entitled to a representation (and therefore voting strength) according to the population of each state. Thus, France, (West) Germany, Italy and the United Kingdom are entitled to eighteen representatives, states of less population, like Belgium and the Netherlands, seven, and the smallest states, like Iceland or Luxembourg, three each.[10] Furthermore, the representatives are not government representatives at all, for Article 25 of the Statute provides that the Consultative Assembly shall consist of representatives elected by the parliament of each member, or appointed in such manner as that parliament shall decide. The representatives have therefore been representatives of national parliaments and more particularly of the political parties that are represented in the national parliaments.

Although the fact that the Assembly does not comprise state representatives as such makes for freedom of debate, it must be remembered that the real decisions of the Council of Europe (which in any case is not endowed with wide powers) are made by the Committee of Ministers.[11] The Committee is an organ of the traditional type. Each member is entitled to one representative and one vote. On important issues, the vote has to be unanimous; though on a number of matters (the adoption of the budget, or of rules of procedure, or financial and administrative regulations, recommendations for the amendment of all but the most important provisions of the Statute) the Committee may proceed by a two-thirds majority; while on questions "arising under the rules of procedure or under the financial and administrative regulations" a decision may be reached by a "simple majority vote."[12]

10. Art. 26.
11. Art. 13 lays down that the Committee of Ministers is "the organ which acts on behalf of the Council of Europe".
12. Art. 20; resolutions of the Assembly normally require a two-thirds majority: Art. 29.

b THE EUROPEAN COMMUNITIES

The three European Communities (the Coal and Steel Community—E.C.S.C.; the Economic Community—E.E.C.; and EURATOM) of the "six" (Belgium, France, (West) Germany, Italy, Luxembourg, and the Netherlands) are examples of the most advanced "supra-national" constitutional structures. They are also the most complex, because in many cases action is only possible with the co-operation of more than one of the organs of the Community concerned. Furthermore, although the structure of the Communities is similar, it is not identical, because, although there is now one Commission, one Council and one Assembly for all three Communities, the powers exercised by each organ vary between one Community and another.

i *The commission* (formerly the High Authority of E.C.S.C. the Commission of E.E.C., and the Commission of EURATOM)

Because the Coal and Steel Community was intended to deal with an area of industrial production that needed strong remedies if it was to survive, and also because its scope was more limited than the Economic Community, the High Authority of E.C.S.C. was given far greater powers than those allotted to the Commissions of E.E.C. and EURATOM. Comprising nine members, eight by agreement among the Member Governments, the ninth co-opted, the High Authority could act by majority vote even to the extent of making decisions binding on both member governments and commercial undertakings involved in the coal and steel industries.

The E.E.C. Commission had nine members, "appointed by the Governments of Member States acting in common agreement" (Arts. 157 (1) and 158 of the Rome Treaty), but it shared the responsibility of "ensuring the achievement of the purposes stated in this Treaty" (a responsibility in the E.C.S.C. resting solely with the High Authority) with the other institutions of the Community, particularly with the Council (see Art. 155). Whereas the High Authority had power to make binding decisions, the Commission would normally "formulate recommendations", often for final decision by the Council (see Arts. 14 (2) (c); 20; 33; and 43). The EURATOM Commission, apart from the fact that it comprised only five members, was very similar in most respects to the E.E.C. Commission, except for its position under Articles 134–135 of the EURATOM Treaty which relate to questions of liaison, the creation of a Scientific and Technical Committee, etc.

By a treaty[13] signed in Brussels in April, 1965, and which came into force in July, 1967, the three treaties setting up the Communities were amended to provide for a single Commission for all three. The new Commission consists of fourteen members "appointed by mutual agreement between the Governments of the Member States", and is to exercise

---

13. (1965) 4 I.L.M. 776.

"the powers and competences" devolving upon the High Authority and the two Commissions under the three earlier treaties.

ii *The Council* (formerly the Special Council of E.C.S.C. and the Councils of E.E.C. and EURATOM)

By Article 27 of the E.C.S.C. Treaty, it was provided that each state should appoint one of the members of its government to the Special Council. In a number of cases—establishment of production quotas when demand has fallen (Art. 58 (1)), restriction of exports in time of shortages (Art. 59 (5)), etc.—the Council's approval was necessary before the High Authority could act; and in others it was the Council which could act alone—making various amendments to the Treaty, or the fixing of minimim and maximum customs rates. The voting procedures were set out in Article 28. A unanimous decision required the votes of all of the members of the Council. A two-thirds majority was occasionally required by specific provisions of the Treaty (e.g. by Art. 56 (1)). All other decisions of the Council were taken by a majority vote of the total membership, which had to include the vote of one of the states which produced "at least one-sixth of the total value of coal and steel produced in the Community."

The Councils of E.E.C. and EURATOM were virtually identical. Unlike the position in E.C.S.C., the main control of the two Communities was in the Council's hands, for the usual procedure was for the Council to act on proposals put to it by the Commission. Decisions on the most important matters had to be unanimous (although abstention was allowed). Amongst such matters were alterations to the number of members of the Commission (Art. 157 (1)); fixing of external tariffs during the first two stages (Art. 20); and decisions on the common agricultural policy during the first two stages (Art. 43). Certain provisions of the Treaty required a qualified majority—e.g. reduction of internal tariffs during the third stage (Art. 14 (2) (c)), fixing of external tariffs after the second stage (Art. 20), decisions on the common agricultural policy after the second stage (Art. 43 (2)). Where decisions of the Council required such a majority, Article 148 stated that the votes of its members were to be weighted as follows: Belgium (2), Germany (4), France (4), Italy (4), Luxembourg (1), Netherlands (2). Where the Treaty required a previous proposal from the Commission, any twelve votes in the Council would constitute the necessary majority, but in all other cases the twelve votes had to include a favourable vote by at least four members. In cases where no provision was made for unanimous approval by members of the Council or for a qualified majority, decisions were made by a majority vote of the members.

By the treaty of April, 1965, a Council was established to replace the previous three organs, and, as in the case of the Commission, the Council is to exercise "the powers and competences" devolving upon the institutions it replaces. To bring the voting procedures of the E.C.S.C. at least partly into line with the other Communities, Article 28 of the E.C.S.C. Treaty was amended (see Art. 8 (2) of the 1965 Treaty).

It is clear that the intention of those who drafted the Treaty of Rome was that, as the E.E.C. progressed, decisions of the Council should no longer require unanimity, but could be reached by a majority, albeit a qualified majority, vote. It is the increasing "supra-national" nature of the Treaty which has brought the theory of the Community into conflict with President De Gaulle's "independent line" in French foreign and domestic policies. In fact, rather than submit to the possibility that French agriculture in particular should be subject to the majority vote of the Council, President De Gaulle showed such reluctance in the process from the second to the third stage of the common agricultural policy that it was feared that there might be a break up in the Community as envisaged by the Treaty of Rome. As part of a compromise, certain "arrangements" were made in January, 1966,[14] between the members of the Community, although the terms of the arrangement regarding majority voting hardly conceals the fundamental differences between France and the other members of the Community. It is worth setting out the first three paragraphs of this "arrangement":

> "1. In the event of decisions that can be adopted by majority on the proposal of the Commission, when very important interests of one or several partners are at stake, the members of the Council will attempt, within a reasonable period of time, to arrive at solutions that could be adopted by all members of the Council in respect of their mutual interests and those of the Community, in accordance with Article 2 of the Treaty.
> 2. With regard to the preceding paragraph, the French delegation considers that, when very important interests are concerned, discussion must be continued until unanimous agreement has been reached.
> 3. The six delegations acknowledge that a difference of opinion remains on what should be done in the event that conciliation cannot be fully attained."

Paragraph 5 expressly sets out a number of matters, upon which all members are agreed, that should be decided by "common agreement".

c THE ASSEMBLY OF THE THREE COMMUNITIES

The role of the Assembly is to exercise a supervisory control over the working of the Treaties. This supervision is carried out by its right of discussion and to make suggestions, and by its ultimate power to force the resignation of the Commission. This power is set out in Article 144 of the Treaty of Rome: if a motion of censure is adopted by a two-thirds majority of the votes cast, representing a majority of the members of the Assembly, "the members of the Commission shall resign their office in a body."

Representation in the Assembly is as follows: Belgium (14), Germany (36), France (36), Italy (36), Luxembourg (6), Netherlands (14). As the Assembly was in effect a reorganisation of the former Common Assembly of E.C.S.C., representatives were to be appointed, as before, by national

---

14. 5 I.L.M. 316.

parliaments "from among their members in accordance with the procedure laid down by each member state". However, whereas the E.C.S.C. Treaty had made it discretionary whether a member introduced a system of election of representatives, the Treaty of Rome amended the E.C.S.C. Treaty in introducing a mandatory provision—the Assembly "shall draw up proposals for elections by direct universal suffrage in accordance with a uniform procedure in all member states." In 1960, the Assembly approved a proposed Convention for implementing this provision, though no further action has yet been taken.

D. The reality of the doctrine of the equality of states

The "sovereign equality" of states is stated by Article 2 (1) of the United Nations Charter to be the first principle upon which the Organisation is based. The concept of sovereign equality produces practical manifestations in the jurisdictional sphere. In the words of the Permanent Court in the *Eastern Carelia* case,[15] it is "well established in international law that no state can, without its consent, be compelled to submit its disputes with other states either to mediation or to arbitration, or to any other kind of pacific settlement." Because of the principle of the equality of states, municipal courts have adopted the rule that they will not exercise jurisdiction over a foreign sovereign, at any rate in his public capacity. And, as was pointed out in Chapter 1, the equality of states has a more fundamental application: it would seem that some form of consent, or at least non-objection, is necessary for the development of rules of international law binding upon a particular state.

However, the legal notion of equality, of unfettered state sovereignty, is limited in practical terms. Rules of international law develop because states do observe certain practices in their mutual relations. And the need to co-operate in a variety of fields—in international peace and security, in economic and social matters—has led states to accept limitations both upon their freedom of action and upon their national equality in relation to other states which have more to contribute to the common goal. The results of this need to co-operate can be seen in the structure and voting procedures of the organisations that have been discussed.

Smaller states will often be prepared to accept the privileged position of the few in the interests of a sufficient degree of co-operation to offset their own lack of privilege. The obvious illustration is the Security Council in which certain states are given both permanent membership and a privileged voting position. But a similar situation is to be found in I.C.A.O. and I.M.C.O., and more particularly in the financial institutions where the price of participation by the wealthier western states was a system of weighted voting and a large measure of say in the workings and management of the agencies.

Article 148 of the Treaty of Rome which sets out the voting procedures

---

15. (1923) P.C.I.J. Rep., Ser. B, No. 5, at p. 27.

of the E.E.C. is in many ways a microcosm of the attitude of states to the surrender of sovereignty to a supra-national organisation. Some decisions are possible by a majority, in more important matters by a system of weighted voting which is intended to reflect the significance of each member's contribution to the Community. However, certain issues are regarded as of such fundamental importance that no member, not even the smallest, is prepared to accept as binding a majority vote: in such cases, the Treaty requires the unanimous consent of the parties.

CHAPTER THIRTEEN

INTERNATIONAL ORGANISATIONS—II FUNCTIONS AND POWERS RELATING TO INTERNATIONAL PEACE AND SECURITY

1 THE ROLE OF THE UNITED NATIONS

A. The Security Council

The primary purpose of the United Nations set out in Article 1 (1) of the Charter is to "maintain international peace and security", an object which stems from the opening passage of the preamble stating the determination of the "peoples of the United Nations . . . to save succeeding generations from the scourge of war". The "primary responsibility" for carrying out this aim is entrusted to the Security Council as agent for the members of the Organisation[1] and those members "agree to accept and carry out decisions of the Security Council in accordance with the present Charter."[2] The means whereby the Council carries out its tasks are set out in Chapters VI and VII of the Charter.

a PLACING A MATTER BEFORE THE COUNCIL

i *The process of seising the Council*

In order for the Council to consider a question, it must first be "seised" of that question. The process by which the Council is "seised" of a question may conveniently be considered as divided into two stages: ·

1 *The request that the Council should consider the question*

Such a request may be made by any of the parties to a dispute, provided that, if a party is not a member of the United Nations, it must accept in advance, "for the purposes of the dispute, the obligations of pacific settlement" contained in the Charter. In addition, a member of the Organisation may bring to the attention of the Council "any situation" which "might lead to international friction or give rise to a dispute" (Arts. 35 and 34):

There are a number of cases where states have directed their notification

---

1. Art. 24 (1).   2. Art. 25.

of a dispute or other situation not direct to the Council, but to the Secretary-General, thus giving him a choice of action. It would then be for the Secretary-General to bring the matter to the attention of the Council if he thought fit (acting under Art. 99).

The General Assembly also may call the attention of the Council to situations likely to endanger international peace and security (Art. 11 (3)) and, in cases where enforcement action is necessary, it *must* refer the matter to the Council (Art. 11 (2)).

2 The placing of the matter on the agenda

It is for the Council to decide as a procedural matter whether or not to place a particular dispute on its agenda. It may be that the Council is not satisfied that the matter constitutes a threat to international peace and security or a situation likely to lead to international friction, in which case it will decide that it has no competence to consider the matter.

ii The timing of placing a matter before the Council

The time at which a dispute is submitted to the Council may, therefore, be taken out of the hands of the parties if the Assembly or the Secretary-General takes the initiative. However, even if the timing is left to the parties, their discretion is not entirely unfettered. Although Article 33 (1) states that the "parties to a dispute, the continuance of which is likely to endanger the maintenance of international peace and security, shall, first of all, seek a solution by negotiation, inquiry, mediation, conciliation, arbitration, judicial settlement, resort to regional agencies or arrangements, or other peaceful means of their own choice", in practice resort to the Security Council has become as much an important alternative to the traditional modes of peaceful settlement as it has become a last measure if all else fails. It is true that the stage at which the assistance of the Council is invoked may depend on whether a dispute gets out of hand and becomes an obvious threat to international peace and security, but, if the parties to a dispute, the continuation of which is likely to endanger international peace and security, fail to settle it by the processes set out in Article 33 (1), Article 37 (1) *requires* them to refer the dispute to the Council.

If a matter is placed on the agenda, the Council is under a duty, imposed by Article 32, to invite any member of the United Nations not a member of the Security Council, or any state not a member of the United Nations, which is a party to the dispute "to participate, without vote, in the discussion relating to the dispute". It is also possible, under Article 31, for a member of the Organisation which is not represented on the Council to "participate, without vote, in the discussion of any question brought before the Security Council whenever the latter considers that the interests of that member are specially affected".

b THE POWERS OF THE COUNCIL

Once a matter is formally before the Council by being placed on its agenda, the Charter itself suggests two main divisions in the type of action which the Council might undertake. Available to it are its powers of pacific settlement under Chapter VI, and its powers in relation to threats to the peace, breaches of the peace and acts of aggression under Chapter VII. However, to restrict a discussion of the Council's powers within the Charter framework of Chapter VI and VII would result in a totally mis-leading impression of the Council's role.

In the first place, as the Security Council has avoided the practice of referring in its resolutions to the provision or provisions of the Charter under which the Council is claiming to act, it is often difficult to assign the Council's actions specifically to either Chapter VI or Chapter VII. As analysis of the workings of the Council would probably reveal that, as disagreements amongst the permanent members have prevented the operation of the provisions of Chapter VII in the way envisaged by the San Francisco conference, the provisions of Chapter VI have been extended, often by analogy with the provisions of Chapter VII, to cover situations which the framers of the Charter would have considered as falling more properly within Chapter VII.

Secondly, there have been situations in which the Council's actions could not have been justified by reference to any particular Charter pro-vision but owed their validity to the powers granted to the Council by necessary implication from the functions assigned to it under the Charter. For example, the U.N. operation in the Congo (O.N.U.C.), which is dealt with in more detail below, was created by the Security Council, but for a time ultimate operational control was assumed by the General Assembly because of disagreements among the permanent members of the Council. Under Article 11 (2) of the Charter, however, any question relating to the maintenance of international peace and security "on which *action* is necessary shall be referred to the Security Council by the General Assembly". In the *Expenses* case[3] (in which the International Court was requested to give an opinion *inter alia* on the validity of the General Assembly's apportionment of the expenses of O.N.U.C. as part of its normal budgetary functions under Article 17 (2)), the Court held that Article 11 (2) precluded the Assembly from taking action that was exclusively within the province of the Security Council under Chapter VII of the Charter, but that O.N.U.C. was not such an action.[4] It follows from this conclusion either that Chapter VII envisages two types of action, one "preventive or enforcement measures" directed against a state, and the other action that is not directed against any state (the first alone being exclusively within the province of the Council); or, alterna-tively (or perhaps in addition), that O.N.U.C. fell outside the powers of the Council under Chapter VII altogether. If this was the case, although the operation might initially have been created under Chapter VI of the Charter, it later developed into an action involving the use of force that seems totally inconsistent with the concept of "Pacific Settlement" within that Chapter. Having excluded both Chapter VI and Chapter VII as

---

3. I.C.J. Rep. 1962, p. 151.   4. *Ibid.*, at pp. 165 and 177.

bases for O.N.U.C., the only alternative would be to suggest that the Council has a residual power to take measures for the maintenance of international peace and security which are not spelt out in the Charter.

With this general framework in mind, it is now possible to consider in more detail the powers of the Council. Because of the gradual disappearance of many of the distinctions between Chapters VI and VII in the practice of the Council, the discussion will start from the standpoint of the type of action taken rather than from the Charter provision upon which such action is based.

i *Preliminary powers: provisional measures and investigation*

Certain powers exercised by the Council are apparently of a preliminary nature. For example, under Chapter VII, Article 40 provides that the Council, in order to prevent an aggravation of the situation, can, before making a determination of the existence of any threat to the peace, breach of the peace, or act of aggression, "call upon the parties concerned to comply with such provisional measures as it deems necessary or desirable". Although the Charter only grants expressly the power to decide upon provisional measures in cases under Chapter VII, it is obvious that a situation may be aggravated by the acts of the disputing states or other entities even in circumstances where the Council is exercising its functions under Chapter VI. The absence of a provision similar to Article 40 in Chapter VI has not deterred the Council from calling upon the parties concerned to cease any conduct likely to exacerbate a dispute.

Although intended to be preliminary and temporary in effect, provisional measures may serve as a basis for the settlement of the dispute without further need for Council action, either directly because compliance with the Council's call results in the removal of the source of friction between the parties, or indirectly where the removal of the immediate cause of conflict in compliance with the Council's demands leads to a gradual easing of tension and creates an atmosphere in which the dispute can more readily be settled. Similarly, the other main basis of preliminary action by the Council, the power of investigation, because of its temporising and clarifying effect, may have a long term significance in bringing about the settlement of the dispute.

The Charter itself (Article 34) limits investigation to disputes or situations which might "lead to international friction or give rise to a dispute" and for the specific purpose of determining "whether the continuance of the dispute or situation is likely to endanger the maintenance of international peace and security," thus excluding from its operation any situation involving an actual breach of the peace or act of aggression under Chapter VII. However, even if such a strict interpretation of Article 34 is correct, it is surely only of academic interest. In order best to decide what action to take even under Chapter VII it would seem reasonably necessary for the Council to be able to investigate the circumstances of the alleged breach of the peace or act of aggression. If a power of investigation is not expressly granted under Chapter VII, it may readily be implied.

ii *The implementation of the Council's decisions by individuals acting on its behalf*

If the Security Council wishes to implement a particular policy it will often be obliged to assign the carrying out of that policy to individuals or groups of individuals from the United Nations secretariat or to sub-committees comprising representatives of states members of the Council.

The provisions of Chapter VII of the Charter dealing with the availability of armed forces to operate under the direction of the Security Council also made provision for a specially constituted Military Staff Committee. However, whereas the placing of armed forces at the disposal of the Council is dependent, under Article 43, upon agreements being entered into with the contributing states (and no such agreements have been made), Article 47 lays down that there *shall be* established a Military Staff Committee. The consequence has been a Committee with no practical role to perform. Apart from a minimal function in connection with the Korean war, the existence of the Committee has been largely disregarded. When the Security Council authorised the creation of forces to help restore internal order in the Congo and in Cyprus, responsibility for carrying out the Council's mandate was entrusted to the Secretary-General. It did not follow that the Secretary-General himself had to superintend personally the carrying out of the task entrusted to each force. In the case of the Congo, he was empowered to delegate supervision of the day to day operations to a military commander and he kept in close touch with events through a senior member of the Secretariat acting as U.N. Special Representative.

The Council has from the earliest days of the U.N. appointed individuals to act on its behalf in various troubled parts of the world. Perhaps the best remembered instance of such an appointment was Count Bernadotte's role as U.N. Mediator in Palestine in 1948. While engaged in trying to bring about a cease-fire between Arab and Jewish forces, Count Bernadotte was assassinated, but the 1949 armistice agreements were eventually brought about with the assistance of the Acting Mediator.

While it is clear that the appointment of various individuals, or instructing the Secretary-General, to carry out specific tasks fall within the implied powers of the Security Council to fulfil its responsibilities in the field of international peace and security, the Council has an express power under Article 29 to "establish such subsidiary organs as it deems necessary for the performance of its functions". The most notable examples of the use of this power have been sub-committees created to carry out the Council's investigating function under Article 34. For example, the civil war largely fomented, it was alleged, by guerrillas from Yugoslavia, Bulgaria and Albania, that raged in the northern areas of Greece during the years immediately following the Second World War, was the subject of a report (dated 27th May, 1947) of a Commission set up by the Security Council for the specific purpose of investigating the situation in Greece. A more ambitious "subsidiary organ" was the observer group set up in 1958 to look into the Lebanese complaint that the United Arab Republic was infiltrating men and material into the Lebanon in an effort to subvert the Lebanese government.

Because of the voting provisions of Article 27 under which the Security Council operates, there has been much confusion over whether setting up a committee of investigation or other similar body falls within Article 29 (in the section of Chapter V of the Charter headed "Procedure") or whether it must be considered as subject to a non-procedural vote as falling within Article 34 which is part of Chapter VI. In so far as practice within the Council since 1955 (when "cold war" tensions relaxed sufficiently to allow a more rational approach to a number of problems) provides any reliable guide, there is a discernable trend that the Council is seeking to distinguish between committees or other subsidiary organs with a purely fact finding role, and a commission having the full powers of investigation of the Council itself under Article 34. Such a distinction, however difficult to draw in some circumstances, has the merit of being in accord with the report of the Interim Committee of the General Assembly of 1948 with which the Assembly attempted to bring pressure to bear on the Security Council over its application of the veto provisions of the Charter. The report suggested that among procedural matters not subject to the veto should be included steps "incidental to the establishment of a subsidiary organ: appointment of members, terms of reference, interpretation of terms of reference, reference of questions for study, approval of rules of procedure." However, as the report went on to point out, "the approval of the terms of reference of such subsidiary organs should require the unanimity of the permanent members if the subsidiary organ were given authority to take steps which, if taken by the Security Council, would be subject to the veto, or if the conferring of such authority would constitute a non-procedural decision." In other words, it would be a purely procedural matter for the Council to ask for all available details from the parties to a dispute, or to appoint a sub-committee to consider the evidence presented by the parties, but it would be a non-procedural matter if the Council itself, or a sub-committee acting on its behalf, were to undertake positive investigation (for example, by "on the spot" inspection) of the veracity of the parties' complaints.

iii *Implementation of Council resolutions by action taken on behalf of the U.N. by member states*

1 *Action under Chapter VII*

The bases in the Charter for Security Council action under Chapter VII may be summarised as follows:

1. the power to call upon the parties to comply with provisional measures (Article 40);
2. the power to determine that a situation amounts to a threat to the peace, breach of the peace, or act of aggression (Article 39), and once such a determination has been made, either

3. to make recommendations to maintain or restore international peace and security (Article 39); or
4. to decide what measures not involving the use of armed force are to be employed to give effect to the Council's decisions (Article 41); or if such measures would be inadequate or have proved to be inadequate,
5. to take such action by air, sea or land forces as may be necessary to maintain or restore international peace and security (Article 42).

The tendency has been to regard all action by the Council, or under the auspices of the Council, within Chapter VII of the Charter as "enforcement action" as distinct from any measures the Council might take under Chapter VI relating to pacific settlement. However, Chapter VII itself is headed "Action with respect to threats to the Peace, Breaches of the Peace, and Act of Aggression", and it is possible to imagine situations of such a type where the remedial action need not be "enforcement" action at all. Indeed, the only occasions upon which the expression "enforcement measures" (Article 50) or "enforcement action" (Article 53 (1)) appear in the Charter are in the context of action *against* a state. On a straightforward interpretation of the Charter, therefore, it is at least arguable that Chapter VII could apply to both enforcement action and action not directed against any state in particular. And such a possibility is not ruled out by the specific powers granted by Articles 39–42. Action falling short of enforcement measures would *seem* to be possible under Article 39 (the power to make recommendations); Article 40 (provisional measures directed to the parties involved); Article 41 (the power to make decisions not involving the use of armed force); and Article 42 (providing that there is a distinction between enforcement action against a state, and other action involving air, sea and land forces).

While such a view is theoretically possible, what must now be considered is whether the practice of the Council in any way supports the distinction between enforcement and other action under Chapter VII.

(a)   Action amounting to enforcement action

The intervention, with the authority of the Security Council, of United States and other forces in the name of the United Nations on behalf of South Korea in 1950, was made possible by the fortuitous absence of the Soviet Union from the Council. Although doubts therefore exist as to the validity of the resolutions of the Council passed in the absence of a permanent member whose concurring vote was essential in accordance with Article 27,[5] the procedure adopted by the Council to enable action to be taken on behalf of the Organisation does illustrate how the Council may act under Chapter VII despite the absence of forces at its immediate command. Without such forces, the Council could not order members of the Organisation to provide assistance to the Republic of

---

5. See above, pp. 546–547.

Korea. But Article 39 is worded generally enough to enable the Council to recommend such action:

> "The Security Council shall determine the existence of any threat to the peace, breach of the peace, or act of aggression and shall make recommendations, or decide what measures shall be taken in accordance with Articles 41 and 42, to maintain or restore international peace and security."

When the United States representative and the U.N. Commission in Korea both reported the invasion of South Korea by forces from the North, the Council determined that this action constituted "a breach of the peace" and called for an immediate cessation of hostilities.[6] When this call went unheeded, the Council passed a second resolution[7] recommending that members of the U.N. should "furnish such assistance to the Republic of Korea as may be necessary to repel the armed attack and to restore international peace and security in the area". A third resolution[8] established the Unified Command and recommended that member states providing military forces and other assistance pursuant to the two earlier resolutions should "make such forces and other assistance available to a unified command under the United States": the United States was requested to "designate the commander of such forces" and to "provide the Security Council with reports as appropriate on the course of action taken under the unified command".

Although the theory of enforcement action would seem to be that of concerted action by members of the Organisation, such a limitation is not expressly stated in the Charter nor need it necessarily be implied. It is clearly open to the Council to issue directives to a single state either to desist from a particular course of action, or to take a particular course of action. For example, because the supply of oil appeared likely to be decisive in the attempts by the world community to prevent Southern Rhodesia from establishing its independence, the Council, in a resolution of April 1966,[9] called upon the Portuguese Government to refrain from pumping oil to Rhodesia through the pipeline at Beira; upon other states to divert any vessels flying their flag from carrying oil destined for Rhodesia; and upon the United Kingdom Government "to prevent by the use of force if necessary the arrival at Beira of vessels reasonably believed to be carrying oil for Rhodesia". Implementation of the Council's policy was thus left primarily to the government of the United Kingdom.

(b) *Action not amounting to enforcement action*

While the action of the Unified Command in Korea was action against a particular entity, and therefore clearly fell within Article VII, is it possible for the Security Council to create a force to undertake a peace keeping role within the framework of Chapter VII without involving the Organisation in enforcement measures?

---

6. U.N. Doc. S/1501.   7. S/1511.   8. S/1588.
9. S/RES/221: see 60 A.J.I.L. 925.

In July, 1960, the breakdown of internal law and order only a few days after the Congo became independent brought a telegram from the Congolese President and the Prime Minister requesting the "urgent dispatch of military assistance". The Security Council adopted a resolution[10] authorising "the Secretary-General to take the necessary steps, in consultation with the Government of the Republic of the Congo, to provide the Government with such military assistance as may be necessary, until, through the efforts of the Congolese Government with the technical assistance of the United Nations, the national security forces may be able, in the opinion of the Government, to meet fully their tasks." The force comprised troops from a number of African, Asian and European states supported by services (notably the airlift of contingents and supplies) provided by European states and the United States. It was clearly of a military nature, but it had as its primary task the restoration of internal order within a state. Even when authority was finally given by the Security Council for O.N.U.C. to use force in the face of constant harrassment by rebel troops of the province of Katanga which had purported to secede from the Congolese Republic, the authority was couched in the most cautious terms. The resolution concerned[11] urged the United Nations to "take immediately all appropriate measures to prevent the occurrence of civil war in the Congo, including arrangements for cease-fires, the halting of all military operations, the prevention of clashes, and the use of force, if necessary, in the last resort." In considering the constitutional power of the Security Council to mount such an operation, the International Court in the *Expenses* case[12] stated that it was not necessary to express an opinion as to which article or articles of the Charter were the basis of the Council's resolutions, but it could be said that the operations of O.N.U.C. "did not include a use of armed force against a state which the Security Council, under Article 39, determined to have committed an act of aggression": the operation "did not involve 'preventive or enforcement measures' against any state under Chapter VII."[13]

As has already been suggested, the Court, in choosing these words, seems to have been drawing a distinction between enforcement action under Chapter VII, and other action involving a use of force that is not directed against any state, but which nevertheless falls within Chapter VII. While there is some support for such a distinction in the Charter, it does not necessarily follow that O.N.U.C. was a "Chapter VII" operation not amounting to enforcement action. For it to satisfy this description, it must be possible to justify the creation of the force in terms of the express provisions of Chapter VII, or, alternatively, if some other basis can be found for the establishing of the force, it must be possible to justify its continuation within the framework of Chapter VII.

Article 39 cannot be ruled out of consideration entirely as far as the creation of the force is concerned, even though in two important respects

---

10. S/4387.   11. S/4722 of 21st February, 1961.
12. I.C.J. Rep. 1962, p. 151.   13. *Ibid.*, at p. 177.

the Council avoided using terminology appropriate to Article 39. It is arguable that if the Council intended to make use of Article 39 it would have determined that there existed a threat to the peace or breach of the peace in its original resolution of 14th July, 1960. Furthermore, although Article 39 itself empowers the Council, once such a determination is made, to make either *recommendations* or *decisions*, the July resolution was a *decision* to "authorise" the Secretary-General to take the "necessary steps." The powers of decision provided for in Article 39 are those available under Articles 41 and 42, so that it can hardly be claimed that the term "decides" in the original resolution was a decision in the sense in which that expression is employed (i.e. in contrast to a recommendation) in Article 39. A "decision to authorise" is patently not a basis of obligation under Article 25 of the Charter binding on all members of the Organisation. But can it be regarded as a "recommendation" in the absence of any intial determination of the existence of a threat to the peace or breach of the peace? Although the existence of an initial relationship between the resolution of 14th July and Article 39 is, therefore, doubtful, there is more support for the view that O.N.U.C. was later continued by the Council acting under Article 39. Resolution of February 1961, which referred to the "prevalence of conditions . . . which threaten international peace and security", the Council *urged* the United Nations to take "all appropriate measures" including "the use of force, if necessary, in the last resort".

Although it is possible to regard the general powers of Article 39 as applicable to enforcement procedures (as in the case of the Korean operation), and to a use of force not amounting to enforcement action, various other views have been expressed as to the constitutional basis of O.N.U.C. Because it is not possible to state categorically that Article 39 was *the* basis of the operation, some comment is necessary on the relevance of other provisions of Chapter VII.

Article 40 has the strong support of the Secretary-General himself who expressed the view that the operation was carried out by implication under Article 40, which was in turn dependent upon an "implicit finding under Article 39."[14] While it has already been suggested that provisional measures decided upon by the Security Council *can* in practice be effective to resolve a dispute or take the danger out of a situation, it is clear that such measures must nevertheless be "provisional" in order to fall within Article 40. The original resolution authorising the Secretary-General to provide the Congolese Government with military assistance was "provisional" in the sense that it was hoped that the government itself would soon be able to take over the maintenance of internal law and order, but that hardly qualifies the assistance as a "provisional measure" prior to "making recommendations or deciding upon the measures provided for in Article 39." It is true that parts of a number of the Council's early resolutions made demands that were in the nature of provisional measures

---

14. S.C.O.R. (XV) 920th Mtg., p. 19. This opinion was adopted by Schachter in (1961) 55 A.J.I.L. 1.

(notably the repeated calls for the withdrawal of Belgian troops from the Congo), but these were ancillary to the creation of the force itself (at least in the view of a majority of members of the Council).[15]

Article 41 relating to measures *not* involving the use of armed force is the least appropriate provision of the Charter, and can therefore be disregarded.

Article 42 poses problems. In the first place, it concerns action *by the Council*: in the absence of forces at its immediate call as envisaged by Article 43, it is doubtful whether the Council can take action at all under Article 42.

Secondly, action under Article 42 (as with measures under Article 41 or recommendations under Article 39) requires a prior determination that a threat to the peace, a breach of the peace, or an act of aggression has occurred (Article 39). However, the omission of any express statement by the Council that it was dealing with a "threat to international peace and security" until the resolution of 21st February, 1961, would not in itself be fatal to the application of Article 42 if the initial resolution of 14th July, 1960, was by implication based upon the existence of such a threat. But this initial resolution was careful to restrict its pronouncements to the breakdown of internal law and order and to the undesirable presence of Belgian troops whose attempts to assist in the restoration of internal order were strongly resented. The most that the International Court in the *Expenses* case was prepared to acknowledge was that the resolution of July 1960 "was clearly adopted with a view to maintaining international peace and security":[16] the Court was not willing to base the Congo operation upon the existence of a threat to international peace and security, even if O.N.U.C. subsequently had to deal with such a threat.

Thirdly, it is clear from the records of the San Francisco Conference that measures taken under Article 42 (and indeed under Article 41 which is complementary to Article 42) were envisaged as being in the nature of enforcement action directed against a state responsible for a breach of the peace or act of aggression. It is doubtful whether Article 42 can be interpreted as applying to two separate types of action—enforcement action directed against a state, and other action not directed against any particular state—on the basis of the International Court's rather ambiguous categorisation of O.N.U.C. as not involving "preventive or enforcement measures" against any state.[17]

However, while it is possible to provide a constitutional basis for O.N.U.C. within Chapter VII without being obliged to regard it as an enforcement action, in view of the general nature of the International Court's statements in the *Expenses* case, it may be necessary to look beyond Chapter VII in order to justify the creation of the Congo force in accordance with the Charter.

---

15. Though probably not shared by the Soviet Union in view of its attempt to have Belgium condemned for armed aggression: its amendment (S/4386) to this effect was rejected by the Council.

16. I.C.J. Rep. 1962, at p. 175.   17. *Ibid.*, at p. 177.

As will be explained later, because U.N.E.F. from the outset, and O.N.U.C. for a period at a subsequent stage in the operation, were subject to the control of the General Assembly, their validity depended, in the case of U.N.E.F. exclusively, and in the case of O.N.U.C. partially, upon the competence of the Assembly in the field of international peace and security. The main restriction on the powers of the Assembly is contained in Article 11 (2) of the Charter which states, *inter alia* that any "question on which action is necessary shall be referred to the Security Council". The word "action" in itself is hardly a precise expression, but the Court took the view that, as the Charter clearly bestowed a secondary responsibility in relation to international peace and security on the Assembly, "action" in this context could only mean "such action as is solely within the province of the Security Council", i.e. action "which is indicated by the title of Chapter VII of the Charter, namely 'Action with respect to threats to the peace, breaches of the peace, and acts of aggression."[18] If O.N.U.C. was not action "indicated by the *title* of Chapter VII", it may not be permissible to argue that its creation and maintenance fall within the ambit of Chapter VII at all. But where else in the Charter is provision made for the undertaking of peace-keeping operations?

2   Action under Chapter VI

The powers of the Council relating to the pacific settlement of disputes are stated in the most general terms, but they may be summarised as follows:

1. The Council may call upon the parties to a dispute to settle it by peaceful means (Article 33 (2)); or, if the parties so request, the Council may make recommendations with a view to pacific settlement (Article 38).

2. The Council may investigate any dispute or situation which might lead to international friction or give rise to a dispute (Article 34).

3. The Council *may* at any stage in a dispute or situation the continuation of which is likely to endanger international peace and security, recommend appropriate procedures or methods of adjustment (Article 36 (1)), bearing in mind that legal disputes should as a general rule be referred to the International Court (Article 36 (3)).[19]

4. But, once the Council deems that the continuance of a dispute is *in fact* likely to endanger the maintenance of international peace and security, it *shall* decide whether to take action under Article 36 or to recommend such terms of settlement as it may consider appropriate (Article 37 (2)).

So widely stated are the Council's powers of recommendation under Articles 36 (1) and 37 (2) that the creation of a force with a peace-keeping role would appear to be within their compass. When the Council created a force (UNFICYP) in March 1964 to prevent civil strife between the Greek and Turkish communities in Cyprus, the Council spelt out the connection with Chapter VI of the Charter by describing the situation as

---

18. *Ibid.*, at p. 165.
19. Though a recommendation by the Council under Article 36 is not sufficient to give the Court jurisdiction over a dispute between parties that have not accepted, or will not recognise, the Court's competence: see above, p. 488, fn. 12.

"likely to threaten international peace and security", and by "recommending" the creation of the force.[20]

While it is clear that the Council itself saw the Cyprus force as falling within its power under Chapter VI, there is perhaps a logical difficulty in ascribing any type of force, whether it is called a peacekeeping force, or a "police force", to a Chapter in the Charter headed "Pacific Settlement of Disputes". However, this difficulty is more apparent than real. There is no reason why a force should not be created that is ancillary to the actual settlement of the dispute. In the case of both O.N.U.C. and UNFICYP, the Security Council initially saw as its object the normalisation of internal conditions: it was concerned with whether the situation was *likely* to endanger the maintenance of international peace and security, not with the present existence of a threat to the peace. The creation of a peace-keeping force was essentially the setting up of a subsidiary organ to act through the Secretary-General, under the ultimate control of the Council. Once internal order was restored, the parties, whether states or other entities, to the dispute or situation would then be in a position to seek a solution by peaceful means, either directly, or through the good offices of the Council.

It is possible to argue, therefore, that at its inception, O.N.U.C. could be considered as operating under Chapter VI. After receiving the original telegram from the Congolese President and the Prime Minister, the Secretary-General reported the matter to the Council in terms closely following the text of Article 99 of the Charter which deals with Secretary-General's power to bring to the attention of the Council "any matter which, in his opinion, may threaten international peace and security". The majority view in the Council, and the view of states contributing forces, was that the forces were to form a "police force" to assist the Congolese government in maintaining law and order until Congolese units were able to "meet fully their tasks". It was only at a later stage when the Council was faced with the complexities of the problem posed by the need to restore law and order in the face of foreign mercenaries, of Katangese determination to maintain their secession from the Congo, and of dissension in the ranks of the Congolese army, that the character of the operation changed. The resolution of February 1961 (which spoke in terms of the "prevalence of conditions which seriously imperil peace and order, and the unity and territorial integrity of the Congo, and threaten international peace and security") and that of November, 1961 (which authorised the Secretary-General "to take vigorous action, including the requisite measures of force", and called upon all Member States to refrain from any acts or omissions supporting directly or indirectly "activities against the United Nations often resulting in armed hostilities against the United Nations forces and personnel") were clearly no longer consistent with any theory that O.N.U.C. was operating under Chapter VI of the Charter.

---

20. S/5575: reproduced (1964) 3 I.L.M. 371.

While it is possible for the Security Council to establish a peace-keeping force under Chapter VI (and it certainly is the accepted view that it did so in creating UNFICYP), and theoretically possible that O.N.U.C. at its inception was such an operation, practical facts militate against this conclusion. Debates in the Council assumed that the Congo crisis was a "Chapter VII situation" and repeated references to Articles 25 and 45 of the Charter, relating to the binding nature of Security Council decisions and measures taken under such decisions, emphasise the nature and quality of the action being undertaken in the views of the members of the Council and of the Secretary-General.

3 Action under powers impliedly granted by the Charter

While it is possible to classify the Unified Command in Korea within the provisions of Chapter VII of the Charter, and perhaps UNFICYP in terms of Chapter VI, O.N.U.C. does not fit neatly into any particular provisions of the Charter (though Article 39, perhaps together with Article 40, most nearly provide a satisfactory constitutional basis), nor, it would seem, obviously into Chapter VII of the Charter. In the absence of agreements under Article 43 for the provision of troops and other forces to operate directly under the Security Council should it wish to invoke Article 42, the concept of action by the U.N. has been substantially modified in practice. There have been frequent attempts to justify actions taken by the Council under one provision or another of the Charter, but it cannot be claimed that such efforts have been altogether successful. Perhaps the main reason why the Council has itself usually refrained from specifying the provisions of the Charter upon which it purported to act is that its operations seem to cut across the "compartments" suggested by Chapters VI and VII, and clearly do not classify readily into the actual provisions of Chapters VI and VII. Only with difficulty can O.N.U.C. be explained in terms of Chapter VII, and then at the apparent disregard of the International Court's statement that the operation was not of the type "indicated by the title" of that Chapter. Chapter VI is ruled out because of the attitudes of the states members of the Council, and of the Secretary-General, all of whom viewed the crisis as falling outside the scope of the Council's powers of peaceful settlement.

But even if the Congo operation is not strictly justifiable in terms of either Chapter VI or Chapter VII of the Charter, it does not follow that the creation and maintenance of O.N.U.C. was in any sense an invalid act by the Council. The International Court in the *Expenses* case was careful to point out that "when the Organisation takes action which warrants the assertion that it was appropriate for the fulfilment of one of the stated purposes of the United Nations, the presumption is that such action is not *ultra vires* the Organisation."[1] The Court could, however, have stated the position more forcibly in the specific context of international peace and security, because, in addition to stating the maintenance

---

1. I.C.J. Rep. 1962, at p. 168.

of international peace and security as the first purpose of the United Nations, Article 1 (1) of the Charter also sets out as part of this purpose the taking of "effective collective measures for the prevention and removal of threats to the peace, and for the suppression of acts of aggression or other breaches of the peace". Provided that the proposed action is otherwise in accordance with the Charter, it is clearly within the powers of the Security Council, though not expressly stated, necessarily to be implied, to recommend "collective measures" to be taken by member states in assisting the Council to exercise its primary responsibility for the maintenance of international peace and security. If O.N.U.C. can not be justified within the precise provisions of Chapter VI and VII of the Charter, it may well be argued that the operation is justifiable as a "collective measure" within Article 1 (1).[2]

iv *The power of the Council to bind member states*

One of the major causes of the Council's reluctance to acknowledge that its actions are undertaken under powers not granted by Chapter VII is its insistence that when acting under Chapter VII, its decisions have binding force. According to Article 25 of the Charter, members of the Organisation "agree to accept and carry out the decisions of the Security Council in accordance with the present Charter." If the effect of Article 25 is to make decisions of the Council "binding", does this rule apply to all paragraphs of a resolution which make use of the expression "the Security Council . . . *decides* . . ."? It is hardly to be supposed that the Security Council can extend its powers by the use of a particular form of words. It must follow, therefore, that only decisions made in accordance with other provisions of the Charter have this binding effect for members of the Organisation. As a general proposition, Chapter VI deals principally with the power of the Council to recommend certain types of action, while Article 39 of Chapter VII enables the Council to make either recommendations, or decisions under Articles 41 and 42, once the Council has determined the existence of any threat to the peace, breach of the peace or act of aggression. However, it has already been suggested that the powers of the Security Council under Article 42 are dependent upon the implementation of the provisions of Article 43: until agreements are entered into by states for the provision of forces for use by the Council, the Council is unable to make any decisions based upon Article 42. On the other hand, Article 41 does not depend upon the prior implementation of Article 43 for its efficacy; but its wording is not entirely free from doubt. The Article grants to the Council power to "*decide* what measures not invoking the use of armed force are to be employed to give effect to its decisions", but goes on to state that the Council may "*call upon*" member states to apply such measures. Does a call by the Council to

---

2. The chief exponent of this view is Halderman: see *The United Nations and the Rule of Law*, pp. 91–125.

member states that they should implement its decisions under Article 41 create an obligation under Article 25?

In this context, it is necessary to consider the Council's resolution of 16th December, 1966,[3] imposing an embargo on trade with Southern Rhodesia. The resolution took the unusual form of including a specific reference to Articles 39 and 41 of the Charter. The Council determined that "the present situation in Southern Rhodesia constitutes a threat to international peace and security" and decided that "all States Members of the United Nations shall prevent" the import from and export to Rhodesia of a large number of items. The Council avoided the possible ambiguity contained in Article 41 (i.e. the contrast between the decision to take certain measures and the call upon member states to implement such measures) by purporting to impose an obligation directly by the use of a decision that all states "shall prevent" trade in certain commodities with Rhodesia. To reinforce further its claim to be exercising mandatory powers, the Council also reminded "Member States that the failure or refusal by any of them to implement the present resolution shall constitute a violation of Article 25 of the Charter". However, as stated above, a resolution of the Security Council does not become binding simply because the Council uses the appropriate terminology with a view to making it binding if the resolution is not properly subject to the Council's powers of decision under the Charter.

It would seem that the intention of the San Francisco conference which drafted the Charter was that action decided upon by the Council, once it had determined the existence of a threat to the peace, breach of the peace or act of aggression (that is, action under Articles 41 and 42) would create obligations for members of the Organisation under Article 25. The United Kingdom clearly held this view, because by the United Nations Act of 1946 it was provided, *inter alia*, that if the Security Council called upon Britain under Article 41 of the Charter to apply any measures to give effect to any of the Council's decisions, H.M. Government might by Order in Council make such provision as appeared necessary for enabling the measures to be effectively applied. But are member states obliged to carry out all decisions of the Council which relate to Article 41?

The Dumbarton Oaks proposals[4] upon which the Charter was based provide evidence of a distinction between action under Article 41 and decisions to which Article 25 was to apply. Article 25 of the Charter appeared as Chapter VI, Section B, paragraph 4, of the proposals and was in substantially similar terms. Much of Article 39 was contained in Chapter VIII, B, 2, except that the Council was to be given powers to "*decide* upon the measures to be taken to maintain or restore peace and security", with no reference to measures in accordance with subsequent provisions of Chapter VIII, Section B (as with Article 39 which refers to

---

3. S/RES/232 (1966): reproduced 6 I.L.M. 141; see also S/RES/253 (1968): 7 I.L.M. 897.
4. The proposals are set out in (1945) 39 A.J.I.L., docs. sect., pp. 46–56.

Articles 41 and 42). The original text of what is now Article 41 avoided the ambiguity latent in the use of the expression, the Council may "decide" what measures are to be employed "to give effect to its decisions", by stating that the Council should be "empowered" to determine what measures should be employed to give effect to its decisions. In the Dumbarton Oaks proposals, therefore, Article 41 was the means of carrying out decisions "to maintain or restore peace and security" under what is now Article 39. The use of the expression "the Security Council may decide" in Article 41 might have had the unforeseen consequence of widening the scope of Article 25. Under the Dumbarton Oaks proposals, the meaning was clear: decisions could only be made if their object was the maintenance or restoration of peace and security. Under the Charter it is possible to envisage a decision under Article 39 designed to maintain or restore international peace and security, reinforced by a decision under Article 41 which is not limited to the present maintenance or restoration of international peace and security, but which it is hoped will (in time) give effect to the earlier decision.

In its discussions of the Palestine question in 1948,[5] the Security Council was faced with what action to take on a proposed partition plan. Even if a solution imposed by the Council might in general terms help the restoration of international peace and security, the majority of U.N. members would have agreed with the view of the U.S. representative that Articles 41 and 42 only enabled the Council to take action directly related to, and not simply with the ultimate object of, restoring international peace and security. In the words actually used by Mr. Austin:[6] "The Security Council, under the Charter, can take action to prevent aggression against Palestine from outside. The Security Council, by these same powers, can take action to prevent a threat to international peace and security from inside Palestine. But this action must be directed solely to the maintenance of international peace. The Security Council's action, in other words, is directed to keeping the peace and not to enforcing partition."

The restrictive view of Article 41 is reinforced by a further reference to Article 39. Under Article 39, once the Security Council has determined the existence of a threat to the peace, breach of the peace or act of aggression, it can, *inter alia*, decide what measures shall be taken in accordance with Article 41 to maintain or restore international peace and security. In other words, the threat to the peace under the first part of Article 39 must, in order to justify action under Article 41, be of such a degree as to place the continuation of peace in jeopardy, so that action is immediately necessary in order to maintain international peace and security. The Rhodesian situation is hardly a threat to the peace in the sense of requiring immediate remedial action. Indeed, the Council in its second resolution[7]

---

5. S.C.O.R. (III), Nos. 16-35, pp. 264-92; conveniently extracted in Sohn, *Cases on U.N. Law*, pp. 482 *et seq.*   6. Sohn, *op. cit.*, at p. 485.
7. S/RES/217 (1965): reproduced (1966) 5 I.L.M. 167.

after Rhodesia's Unilateral Declaration of Independence characterised this action by the "illegal authorities" as "extremely grave" but determined that the "continuance" of the situation would only "in time" constitute a threat to international peace and security. The fact that Rhodesia had maintained its independence for twelve months without more than a few terrorist incidents occurring, and those within its own borders, suggests that the situation was no more an *immediate* threat to the peace in December, 1966, than it had been in November, 1965. Furthermore, as the Charter itself implies, and as was accepted in the debates on the Palestine question in 1948, the Security Council's powers, even under Article 41, are restricted to measures directly designed to maintain international peace and security. Action designed to help maintain international peace and security by imposing a settlement on the parties to a dispute or situation (in this case, preventing Rhodesia from acquiring independence without guarantees of majority rule) cannot be imposed, or furthered by the imposition of sanctions, within Chapter VII of the Charter, but at most can be the subject of recommendations by the Council.

Because of the powers of the Security Council to impose obligations upon member states to undertake certain types of action in accordance with Article 25, the right of decision was severely limited by the Charter. Decisions could only be made following the determination of the existence of a threat to the peace, breach of the peace or act of aggression, and if the decision were to use force the forces had first to be made available to the Council by the agreement of member states. Because such forces were never made available as envisaged by Article 43, the trend has been for the Council to operate more by conciliation and compromise than by the imposition of sanctions on the recalcitrant.

One specific consequence of this development has been to create uncertainty as to the relationship between a U.N. force and the state on the territory of which the force is to operate. It was generally accepted at San Francisco, and has not been doubted since, that a state or other authority against which preventive or enforcement action is being taken has no right to object to the entry of U.N. forces into its territory. What is less clear is the position of forces created by the Organisation by means other than the procedure laid down in Article 43 of the Charter.

Although Article 42 is dependent on the availability of forces at the disposal of the Council, there is no legal barrier to the implementation of enforcement procedures by means of forces made available as a result of some *ad hoc* arrangement. Leaving aside the controversy of the legality of resolutions taken by the Security Council in the absence of a permanent member, the Unified Command in Korea was created by the offer of troops from various states on the basis of a Council recommendation (clearly in pursuance of Article 39) that members of the Organisation should "furnish such assistance to the Republic of Korea as may be necessary to repel the armed attack and to restore international peace and security in the area". The fact that the Unified Command, having driven back the invading North Korean armies, carried the war into North Korean territory was not considered in itself to be an illegal act.

What was in doubt in the Korean war was the *political* wisdom of extending the hostilities. Because the creation of all U.N. forces in the absence of the prior agreements envisaged by Article 43, is dependent upon the continued co-operation of contributing states, the objects of the force have to be defined in terms designed to eliminate controversy. One means of eliminating controversy is to base the force not only upon the consent of contributing states (which is of course essential), but also on the consent of the state on the territory of which the force is to operate. The Council in the same way as it has avoided, or has been obliged by political factors to refrain from, using its enforcement powers, has relied upon the agreement of the territorial state to the presence of peace-keeping forces. Thus, in the case of O.N.U.C., even if it is possible to regard it as an operation mounted under Chapter VII (though not equivalent to enforcement action), the force was established in the Congo with the consent of the Congolese Government.[8]

B. The General Assembly

As it was the Security Council which was to be given primary responsibility for the maintenance of international peace and security, and precise powers for the pacific settlement of disputes and for meeting threats to the peace, breaches of the peace and acts of aggression, the San Francisco conference did not attach great significance to the secondary role of the General Assembly. The powers of the Assembly were not, therefore, spelt out with any precision: the relevant provisions of Chapter VI speak in terms of discussion and recommendation. But, as will be shown, it is the general nature of the Assembly's powers which eventually enabled it to assert a much more important role in the field of international peace and security than that intended for it by those who drafted the Charter.

a PLACING A MATTER BEFORE THE ASSEMBLY

Any matter relating to international peace and security may be brought before the Assembly by any Member of the United Nations (Article 11 (2)), or by the Security Council (also Article 11 (2)), or by a state which is not a member of the Organisation provided that "it accepts in advance, for the purpose of the dispute, the obligations of pacific settlement provided in the present Charter" (Article 35 (2)).

Unlike the Security Council, the General Assembly is not organised to function continuously, but is only required to meet in "regular annual sessions". Should an international crisis require consideration by the Assembly, Article 20 goes on to provide that special sessions may be

---

8. For the position of U.N.E.F., see below, p. 580, fn. 11.

"convoked by the Secretary-General at the request of the Security Council or of a majority of the Members of the United Nations".

b THE POWERS OF THE ASSEMBLY

The powers of the General Assembly in the field of international peace and security are expressed in the widest terms. They may be summarised as follows:

> 1. The General Assembly *may consider the general principles of co-operation in the maintenance of international peace and security,* including the principles governing disarmament and the regulation of armaments, *and may make recommendations with regard to such principles* to members of the Organisation, or to the Security Council, or to both (Article 11 (1)).
> 2. The General Assembly *may discuss any questions relating to the maintenance of international peace and security, and,* except while the Security Council is exercising in respect of any dispute or situation the function assigned to it in the Charter, *may make recommendations with regard to any such questions* to the State or States concerned or to the Security Council or to both; BUT *any such question on which action is necessary shall be referred to the Security Council* (Article 11 (2)).
> 3. Except when the Security Council is exercising its functions, the Assembly *may recommend measures for the peaceful adjustment of any situation* which it deems likely to impair the general welfare or friendly relations among nations (Article 14).
> 4. The Assembly has an overall power, unhampered by any restriction contained in Article 11 (Article 11 (4)), to *discuss any questions or any matters within the scope of the present Charter,* and, except while the Security Council is exercising its functions, *may make recommendations* to member States or to the Security Council or to both *on any such questions or matters* (Article 10).

i *The Uniting for Peace resolution*

It will be recalled that the creation of the Unified Command in Korea by the Security Council was possible solely because of the fortuitous absence of the Soviet representative. It was realised by the General Assembly that, as disagreements among the permanent members would leave the Council powerless to act in a future case of the Korean type, the Organisation as a whole would be reduced to impotence if the Assembly did not examine methods whereby it could assume some of the responsibilities of the Security Council.

As a result of its deliberations, the Assembly adopted three closely connected resolutions, the first of which is usually termed the *Uniting for Peace* resolution.[9] By the first paragraph the General Assembly resolved that

> "if the Security Council because of lack of unanimity of the permanent members, fails to exercise its primary responsibility for the maintenance of international peace and security in any case where there appears to be a threat to the peace, breach of the peace, or act of aggression, the General Assembly shall consider the matter immediately with a view to making appropriate recommendations to members for collective measures, including in the case of a breach of the peace or act of aggression the use of armed force when necessary, to maintain or restore international peace and

---

9. G.A. Res. 377 (v).

security. If not in session at the time, the General Assembly may meet in emergency special session. . . . Such emergency special session shall be called if requested by the Security Council on the vote of any seven members, or by a majority of the Members of the United Nations. . . ."

The argument favoured by the large majority of members who voted for the resolution was that the General Assembly could, as a general proposition, do anything by recommendation that the Security Council could do by recommendation or decision. The foundation of this argument was the wide scope of Article 10 of the Charter which enables the Assembly to discuss and make recommendations on any matter "within the scope of the present Charter". Two limitations upon the application of Article 10 are that the recommendations may be directed at the Security Council or Member States (or both) but not at non-members, and that, according to Article 12 (1), the Assembly may not make any recommendations, unless so requested by the Council, in relation to any dispute or situation in respect of which the Security Council is exercising "the functions assigned to it in the present Charter". Neither limitation has any relevance to the *Uniting for Peace* resolution which deals exclusively with recommendations to member states and would only be invoked if, because of a lack of unanimity among the permanent members, the Council was *not* exercising the functions assigned to it by the Charter.

As the introductory outline of the power of the Assembly shows, Article 10 is reinforced by the provisions of Articles 11 and 14 which deal specifically with the maintenance of international peace and security. The main difficulty in applying any of these provisions in the way suggested by the *Uniting for Peace* resolution is the existence of the statement at the end of Article 11 (2) that any question relating to international peace and security on which "action" is necessary shall be referred to the Security Council. However, before considering the precise effect of this part of Article 11, it is first necessary to consider the creation of the U.N. Emergency Force (U.N.E.F.) and the view of the International Court towards the legality of this action by the Assembly.

ii *The United Nations Emergency Force*

Following the outbreak of war between Israel and Egypt in 1956, and the subsequent military operation undertaken by France and the United Kingdom, the Security Council was unable to adopt effective measures because of the negative votes of the latter two states. The Council made use of the procedure suggested by the Uniting for Peace resolution for the calling of an emergency special session of the General Assembly, in spite of the existence of an express power to do so by means of Article 20 of the Charter. However, although it is clear enough that the emergency session of the Assembly was called under the *Uniting for Peace* resolution, it is doubtful whether U.N.E.F. was created within the framework suggested by that resolution.

The method adopted by the Assembly to deal with the crisis was first, by Resolution 997 (ES—I) of 2nd November, 1956, to call upon the parties, *inter alia*, to cease fire and withdraw to their previous positions; secondly, by Resolution 998, to request the Secretary-General to submit to the Assembly "within forty-eight hours a plan for the setting up, with the consent of the nations concerned, of an emergency international U.N. Force to secure and supervise the cessation of hostilities"; and then, by Resolution 1000, the Assembly formally established the Force and authorised the "Chief of Command" nominated to "recruit, from the observer corps of U.N.T.S.O.,[10] a limited number of officers" and also from various member states other than the permanent members of the Security Council "the additional number of officers needed". In Resolution 1001, the Assembly expressed its approval of "the guiding principles for the organisation and functioning" of the Force as set out in the Secretary-General's report and authorised the Secretary-General "to continue discussions with governments of Member States concerning offers of participation in the Force, toward the objective of its balanced composition".

iii *The limitations upon the Assembly's power*

While the Uniting for Peace Resolution was designed to provide the U.N. with some means of taking action to meet a threat to the peace, breach of the peace, or act of aggression in circumstances where the Security Council was unable to exercise its functions, U.N.E.F. was created to undertake an essentially passive and supervisory role. It was, in the terms of Resolution 998 already quoted, given the task of securing and supervising the cessation of hostilities: it was not intended forcibly to "separate" the combatants (indeed it would have been totally inadequate for such a purpose). However, although there are obvious distinctions between the type of force envisaged by the Uniting for Peace Resolution and the Force actually created in 1956, the legality of the creation of both types of Force by the General Assembly depends largely upon the consideration of the same factors.

The main argument against the legality of the creation of U.N.E.F. by the General Assembly was that *action* in the field of international peace and security was the sole prerogative of the Security Council. As Article 24 (1) only conferred "primary responsibility" on the Security Council, so that by implication from this provision secondary, or residual, responsibility for the maintenance of international peace and security lay with the General Assembly, the validity of the argument depended upon the interpretation to be placed upon that part of Article 11 (2) which states that any question relating to the maintenance of international peace and security upon which action is necessary must be referred to the Security Council. In relation to U.N.E.F., the International Court in the *Expenses* case held that Article 11 (2) was no obstacle to the measures adopted by

10. For the U.N. Truce Supervision Organisation, see Bowett, *United Nations Forces*, pp. 63, 74–77.

the General Assembly because "action" must be interpreted to mean "coercive or enforcement action", that is "action that is solely within the province of the Security Council." There were many types of action which the Assembly could take in the field of international peace and security as a normal feature of the functioning of the United Nations. The Court specifically mentioned in this context the creation of subsidiary organs under Article 22 of the Charter with powers of "investigation, observation and supervision", although "the way in which such subsidiary organs are utilised depends on the consent of the state or states concerned".[11]

Because the Court based its justification of the Assembly's powers in relation to U.N.E.F. on an interpretation of Article 11 (2) as referring to enforcement action, the impression has been created that the Assembly cannot recommend action to meet a threat to the peace, breach of the peace, or act of aggression as envisaged by the *Uniting for Peace* resolution. However, too much should not be read into the words used by the Court, which was concerned with the status of U.N.E.F. and not with a definitive interpretation of the effects of Article 11 (2).

In the first place, the Court itself seemed uncertain as to which provision of the Charter empowered the Assembly to create a peace-keeping force, and equally uncertain as to the application of the last part of Article 11 (2) to other provisions of Chapter IV. At one stage of its judgment, the Court suggested that Article 11 (2) enabled the Assembly, by means of recommendations to states, or to the Security Council, or to both, to organise peace-keeping operations, at the request, or with the consent, of the states concerned, but added that this power "is a special power which in no way derogates from its general powers under Article 10 or Article 14, *except as limited* by the last sentence of Article 11, paragraph 2."[12] However, the way in which Chapter IV of the Charter is set out makes it difficult to accept the Court's view that a part of Article 11 (2) can limit either Article 14, which itself only refers to the limitation contained in Article 12, or Article 10, particularly in view of the fact that Article 11 (4) states that the powers of the General Assembly as set out in Article 11 "shall not limit the general scope of Article 10". Indeed, in relation to Article 14, the Court at a later stage of its judgment appeared to contradict its earlier view by pointing out that the powers of the Assembly in Article 14 "are not made subject to the provisions of Article 11."[13]

---

11. I.C.J. Rep. 1962, at p. 165. The question of consent is relevant not only to the formation of the force but also to its operation on the territory of a state. Unless a U.N. force is created by the Security Council acting within its mandatory powers under Chapter VII (and the scope for such action is circumscribed by the absence of troops under Article 43), the force will require the consent of the state on the territory of which it is to operate. This fact was vividly illustrated in the case of U.N.E.F. which was withdrawn from Egyptian territory in 1967 on the eve of the "June War" between Israel and a number of Arab states because of the request by Egypt to the Secretary-General that the Force should be withdrawn. The Special Report of the Secretary-General on the withdrawal of U.N.E.F. is given in (1967) 6 I.L.M. 557.

12. *Ibid.*, at p. 165.   13. *Ibid.*, at p. 172.

Secondly, it is doubtful whether action in Article 11 (2) does mean enforcement action, because to interpret the provision in this way would be to render it meaningless. Enforcement action can only be given any precise meaning in the context of Article 50 which refers to "enforcement measures against any state taken by the Security Council" and the whole tenor of Chapter VII is that enforcement measures against a state are mandatory in effect under Articles 41 and 42 of the Charter. But the General Assembly cannot take enforcement action in this sense; it can only *recommend* a particular course of action. The *Uniting for Peace* resolution does not attempt to claim that the Assembly has a power of imposing anything akin to "mandatory sanctions". Under that resolution it was envisaged that the General Assembly, if faced with what appeared to be a threat to the peace, breach of the peace, or act of aggression, should consider the matter immediately "with a view to making appropriate *recommendations* to Members for collective measures, including *in the case of a breach of the peace or act of aggression* the use of armed force when necessary, to maintain or restore international peace and security". It will be recalled that in the context of the powers exercised by the Security Council mention was made of the International Court's pronouncement that "when the Organisation takes action which warrants the assertion that it was appropriate for the fulfilment of one of the stated purposes of the United Nations, the presumption is that such action is not *ultra vires* the Organisation",[14] and of the fact that the first of the purposes of the U.N. stated in the Charter was to maintain international peace and security. The method of maintaining international peace and security stated in Article 1 (1) refers to the taking of "effective collective measures for the prevention and removal of threats to the peace, and for the suppression of acts of aggression or other breaches of the peace", but this provision does not place any restriction on the means whereby the U.N. is to organise such collective measures. As the General Assembly is empowered to discuss and make recommendations upon any question or matter within the scope of the Charter, it would be surprising if these powers did not include recommendations in furtherance of the objects stated in Article 1 (1) of the Charter.

Finally, however, it would seem that there was no need for the Court to indulge in an interpretation of Article 11 (2) that creates as many problems as it solves. The final part of Article 11 (2) only provides that, if action is necessary, the matter should be referred to the Security Council. It does not lay down that the Assembly shall not take action. Indeed the last part of Article 11 (2) is clearly complementary to Article 12 which provides that when the Security Council is exercising its functions under the Charter, the General Assembly shall not make any recommendations with regard to the dispute or situation unless requested to do so by the Council. In other words, if action is needed, the matter should be referred first to the Security Council which has primary responsibility

---

14. *Ibid.*, at p. 168.

for the maintenance of international peace and security, but once it has
been referred to the Council, and the Council ceases to exercise its functions with respect to the matter (either because it is unable to do so, e.g.
because of lack of unanimity among the permanent members, or because
it is willing for the Assembly to deal with the matter and requests the
Assembly to do so), there is no provision preventing the Assembly from
taking *action* within the powers granted to it under the Charter. In the
Dumbarton Oaks proposals, the relationship between the last part of
Article 11 (2) and Article 12 was unmistakable, because Chapter V,
Section B, paragraph 1, stated in part that any question on which action
was necessary should be referred to the Security Council by the General
Assembly and that the General Assembly should not on its own initiative
make recommendations on any matter relating to international peace and
security which was being dealt with by the Security Council. It is submitted that, apart from the question whether the last part of Article 11 (2)
applies to other provisions of Chapter IV of the Charter, the separation
of the equivalent provision of the Dumbarton Oaks proposals into separate
articles of the Charter does not alter their relationship. Article 12 lays
down that the Assembly should not make recommendations with regard
to a dispute or situation (although there is no prohibition on discussion)
if the Security Council is exercising its functions. In this way the primary
responsibility of the Security Council is maintained. But what if a matter
relating to international peace and security, which has not been considered
in the existing circumstances by the Security Council, is before the
General Assembly? If the situation is sufficiently grave to require action
by the Assembly (action which the Assembly can take only by recommendation), then all that Article 11 (2) requires is that the Security Council
should be given an opportunity of fulfilling its primary responsibilities in
the field of international peace and security.

C. The role of the Secretary-General

The various peace-keeping forces created by the U.N. have not followed
the pattern envisaged by those who framed Chapter VII of the Charter.
Not only were forces not available to the Security Council under Article
43, but ultimate control of the force (with the exception of the Unified
Command in Korea) was exercised through the Secretary-General, and
not through the Military Staff Committee of the Council. However,
significant though the Secretary-General's part was in the creation and
carrying out of the tasks of the various U.N. forces, this aspect of his
work is but one example of the significant role assumed by the Secretary-
General of the United Nations in the field of international peace and security.

a THE ORIGINS OF THE POST OF SECRETARY-GENERAL

It will be recalled that, at the beginning of the previous Chapter,
reference was made to a number of influences which helped in the creation

of, and helped determine the constitutional structure of, the League of Nations. The influence which is the least capable of precise assessment was that of private organisations who published plans for future world government. Perhaps the most notable feature of such plans was the idea of a "world chancellor". The states who signed the Covenant of the League settled for something far less dramatic—a Secretary-General with a general power to "act in that capacity at all meetings of the Assembly and of the Council" of the League.

The first Secretary-General of the League was a notable British civil servant, Sir Eric Drummond, who brought to the post the public reserve and tradition of the British civil service. He saw himself not as the mouthpiece of "the League" in its struggle against contumacious members, but as a "behind the scenes" counsellor to member states. In many ways, the role of the United Nations Secretary-General owes more to the example of the Director of the International Labour Office, the dynamic Albert Thomas, than to the work of Sir Eric Drummond. Despite the lack of definition of his position (the constitution of the I.L.O. laid down that the Director should, subject to the instructions of the Governing Body, be responsible for the efficient conduct of the I.L. Office and for such other duties as may be assigned to him). Albert Thomas was continually upholding the rights of the I.L.O. and reminding members of their obligations. Unlike Sir Eric, Albert Thomas attempted to create a "world public opinion" by appealing publicly to a wider audience than the governments of member states.

b THE APPOINTMENT OF THE SECRETARY-GENERAL

Article 97 of the Charter provides that the Secretary-General shall be appointed by the General Assembly upon the recommendation of the Security Council. At the San Francisco conference, it was originally accepted that the term of appointment should be laid down as three years in the Charter in the belief that the future permanent members of the Security Council would consider a recommendation of a candidate for the post of Secretary-General to be a procedural matter. When it became clear, however, that the major powers intended to insist upon their right to veto any particular nomination, the Netherlands delegate to the conference moved for the rescission of the earlier decision on the three year term, for otherwise the Secretary-General would "work in the knowledge that his chances of re-election would be small if he were to incur the displeasure of one of the permanent members".[15]

As a consequence of the application of Article 27 (3) to the appointment of the Secretary-General, the effect of Article 97 which speaks in terms of appointment by the Assembly upon the Council's recommendation has been altered. The practice has been for the security Council to agree upon a candidate and for the Assembly to appoint that candidate, so that the appointment is in effect that of the permanent members' nominee.

15. U.N.C.I.O. Docs. Vol. 7, p. 204.

No term of office having been set down in the Charter, the employment of the Secretary-General is subject to the provisions of a General Assembly resolution of 1946.[16] Under this resolution the first Secretary-General (Trygve Lie) was appointed for a five year term, the appointment to be open for renewal for a further five years. At the end of Lie's first term of office in 1950, there was a complete deadlock in the Security Council over the appointment of a successor. The Soviet Union refused to accept Lie on account of his handling of the Korean situation, while the United States was equally adamant that the U.S. representative in the Council would vote against any alternative candidate. In the absence of any recommendation from the Security Council, the General Assembly resolved that Lie should remain in office for a further three years.[17] The Assembly took this step, not by extending the term of office laid down in the 1946 resolution, but by reference to the principle of "effectiveness". The Charter, to be effective, required the uninterrupted exercise of the functions of the Secretary-General. As the appointment of a Secretary-General in accordance with Article 97 was not possible, the Assembly claimed that it possessed residuary powers in relation to the position of Secretary-General, and under the Charter in general. While no such power was granted to the Assembly by the Charter, it could also be argued that there was nothing in the Charter to prevent the Assembly taking such a course.

One other aspect of Article 97, or rather of what Article 97 does not include, concerns a proposal, much favoured by the major powers, that there should be five deputies to the Secretary-General, all elected by the procedure required for the appointment of the Secretary-General himself. It was clearly the intention of the future permanent members to secure these valuable political posts for their own nominees. There were such objections at the San Francisco conference, however, that the proposal was dropped. Although nationals of permanent members of the Security Council have, as a matter of practice, obtained important posts within the Secretariat, there is a significant "psychological" difference in their position as appointees of the Secretary-General rather than as formal appointments by the political organs of the U.N. Furthermore, the fact that the Secretary-General alone is subject to appointment by the United Nations as a whole (even if in practice the role of the permanent members of the Security Council is decisive) enhances his position and prestige in relation to other officials of the Secretariat, and in his dealings with members of the Organisation.

c THE FUNCTIONS AND POWERS OF THE SECRETARY-GENERAL

The functions of the Secretary-General may be divided very broadly into two categories:

---

16. G.A. RES/11 (I).   17. G.A. RES/492 (v).

i *Administrative functions*

Article 97 refers to the Secretary-General as the "Chief Administrative Officer" of the Organisation, and, in this capacity, he carries out the functions of a civil servant. Although the work itself is carried out by staff of the Secretariat, it is the Secretary-General who is responsible for the organisation of meetings of U.N. bodies, the circulation of reports, and the general preparation that makes for the smooth running of the U.N. machine.

ii *Political functions*

1 *Position under the Charter*—The presence of members of the Secretariat throughout the organs of the U.N. provides the Secretary-General with a valuable co-ordinating and organising position upon which to base his political effectiveness. But before discussing how the Secretary-General can make use of this aspect of his position, it is first necessary to consider his legal position within the framework of the Charter.

Under Article 98, the Secretary-General shall act as Chief Administrative Officer of the Organisation in all meetings of the General Assembly, the Security Council, ECOSOC and the Trusteeship Council. In addition, Article 99 provides that the Secretary-General may bring to the attention of the Security Council "any matter which in his opinion may threaten the maintenance of international peace and security". The effect of Article 99 when coupled with Article 98 is to give the Secretary-General an important position, almost that of an additional member of the Security Council (though not a voting member). Trygve Lie wrote of Article 99 that it conferred upon the Secretary-General "world political responsibilities which no individual, no representative of a single nation, ever had before."[18]

2 *Implied power of investigation*—At an early stage in the practice of the U.N., Trygve Lie successfully asserted that it followed from Article 99 that if the Secretary-General could bring any matter to the notice of the Council, he must have the power of investigation to ascertain the necessary facts. The significance of this aspect of the Secretary-General's position may be demonstrated by reference to the circumstances in which the Secretary-General made this claim. The civil war in Greece was the matter of debate on a United States resolution that the Security Council should establish a commission of investigation. Although the resolution was subsequently adopted, the Secretary-General warned that if the commission were not established, he reserved his right in accordance with the Charter to make "such enquiries or investigations" as he thought necessary in order to decide whether at a later stage he should bring any aspect of the crisis once more to the attention of the Council.

3 *Delegated authority*—While a power of investigation may be implied from the right granted to the Secretary-General under Article 99, additional powers may also be implied from the Secretary-General's position

---

18. *In the Cause of Peace*, p. 39.   19. S.C.O.R. (I–2), No. 16, 70th Mtg., p. 404.

as a servant of the U.N. As a servant, it is obvious that he may accept a delegation of authority from U.N. organs. Dag Hammarskjold was a most willing representative of the General Assembly and of the Security Council in carrying out tasks entrusted to him. In 1955 he travelled to Peking in pursuance of a General Assembly resolution requesting him to obtain the release of a number of American airmen held by the Chinese.[20] In 1956 the General Assembly authorised the Secretary-General to obtain compliance with the Assembly's call for a withdrawal of foreign troops from Egypt, and requested him to organise an emergency U.N. force and to send it to Egypt.[1] In 1960, the initial Security Council resolution in the Congo crisis authorised the Secretary-General to "take the necessary steps" to provide the Congolese government with the required military assistance.[2] And, in 1964, the creation of UNFICYP was left by the Security Council to the Secretary-General to organise "in consultation with" the governments of Cyprus, Greece, Turkey, and Britain.[3]

4 *Implied authority to pursue existing policies*—Hammarskjold was not content to leave the initiative in measures relating to international peace and security to the political organs of the United Nations. As early in his period of office as 1957, he had claimed the right to act in the absence of authority from the Council or the Assembly should this appear necessary in order to fill "any vacuum that may appear in the systems which the Charter and traditional diplomacy provide for the safeguarding of peace and security".[4] But the significance of these words can be overestimated. In the absence of remedial action by the political organs of the U.N., Hammarskjold may have been prepared to address himself to the parties to the dispute, to act as a conciliator, and even to encourage the adoption of a particular policy. But only when faced with an existing operation which, because of disagreements among the states concerned, was failing to carry out its appointed tasks did Hammarskjold continue the operation on his own initiative.

In the Lebanon crisis of 1958, the Security Council created an observer group (U.N.O.G.I.L.)[5] to investigate the Lebanese complaint of intervention by the U.A.R. in its internal affairs. A month later, in the face of increasing infiltration by U.A.R. personnel and military equipment, the Lebanese Government sought American assistance, and a force of U.S. marines was landed in the Lebanon. The Security Council was unable to agree upon the adoption of any further measures to deal with the crisis, but Hammarskjold, on his own initiative, increased the size of U.N.O.G.I.L.,[6] a move which helped bring about a normalisation of the situation and the withdrawal of U.S. troops.

Similarly, in the course of the Congo operation, Hammarskjold became involved in a bitter argument with the Congolese Government which claimed that the O.N.U.C. should bring an end to the secession of

20. G.A. RES/906 (IX).
 1. See above, p. 579.   2. See above, p. 566.   3. See above, p. 570.
 4. G.A.O.R. (XII) 690th. Plen. Mtg., paras. 72–73.   5. S/4023 (XIII).
 6. See the Secretary-General's Statement, S.C.O.R. (XIII), 837th Mtg., para. 10–16.

Katanga by the direct use of force. The Secretary-General's view was that he had no mandate to authorise the conquest of Katanga, and this was indeed the view of the majority of Security Council members, but the Council was unable to agree upon the terms of a resolution clarifying the Secretary-General's position. All that he could do in such a situation was to interpret his existing mandate as best he could. Hammarskjold later explained to the General Assembly that, as "agent of the Organisation", he welcomed positive advice, but if such advice was not forthcoming—as had happened in the Security Council—when his "line of implementation had been challenged", then he had no choice but to follow his own conviction guided by his view of the authority he had been given.[7] It was argued, notably by the Soviet Union, that in acting thus the Secretary-General had assumed functions which the Security Council was alone entitled to exercise. This argument against the constitutionality of O.N.U.C., at least in its later stages, was rejected by the International Court. In the light of "a record of reiterated consideration, confirmation, approval and ratification" in a number of resolutions by the Security Council and the General Assembly of the actions of the Secretary-General, it was "impossible to reach the conclusion" that the Congo operation "usurped or impinged upon the prerogatives conferred by the Charter on the Security Council".[8]

5 *Significance of the office*—It is not altogether an easy task to estimate the significance of the role of Secretary-General in the field of international peace and security. To an extent the role will depend upon the personality of the holder of the office: U Thant sees his part in more passive terms than Dag Hammarskjold. But the Secretary-General is also limited by the part the United Nations as an organisation can play in any particular situation. The Suez and Congo crises did not involve a "confrontation", even indirectly, between the United States and the Soviet Union so that the U.N. could usefully assist in maintaining or restoring international peace and security. But in situations like the Cuba crisis of 1962, and the present position in Vietnam, in which the two major powers are directly or indirectly at loggerheads, the U.N. is powerless to act in the absence of a change to a less intransigent policy on the part of the two states.

Within the restrictions placed upon his role by the present international situation, the Secretary-General has an important part to play as spokesman for the U.N. The prestige of the office enables the Secretary-General to make public pronouncements in an attempt to influence the course of events. Hammarskjold in particular gained prestige from the fact that he came to be regarded as the mouthpiece not only of the Organisation, but also of the smaller states in the U.N. He was able to act externally on behalf of the Organisation, and internally as a make-weight in the balance of influence between the major powers.

Inside the U.N. itself, the Secretary-General took advantage of his

---

7. See also Hammarskjold's comments in *The International Civil Servant in Law and in Fact*, esp. at pp. 23-25. 8. I.C.J. Rep. 1962, at pp. 176-7.

co-ordinating functions exercised through the Secretariat to fill in short-comings in the organisational structure of the Organisation. When, in 1956, the General Assembly decided to recommend the creation of U.N.E.F. it was obviously impossible for a large body of states to consider anything more than the most general matters of policy. Furthermore, the Charter provided no machinery, like the Military Staff Committee of the Security Council, whereby the Assembly could administer a peace-keeping operation. It was the Secretary-General, and his power of appointment of individuals in any capacity to the Secretariat, who was able to provide a solution to both the Assembly's difficulties. So successful was the experiment of allowing the Secretary-General to oversee the carrying out of U.N.E.F.'s tasks that, in the Congo and in Cyprus, a similar approach was adopted by the Security Council, though for somewhat different reasons. In the Assembly a general consensus among such a large membership is only possible in the most wide terms. In the Security Council a general consensus is often all that is possible before disagreement occurs among the permanent members. In the Assembly, rather than work by majority, it is felt better to work by near unanimity; and in the Council it is necessary to agree upon a resolution that is acceptable to all the permanent members. Providing that there is general agreement on the need for action of some kind, it is felt better to leave the implementation of the course of action to the Secretary-General than to risk friction over matters of detail.

2   REGIONAL ORGANISATIONS

Chapter VIII of the U.N. Charter was designed to enable states to assist in the maintenance of international peace and security through the activities of regional organisations. Thus, under Article 52 (1) it is stated that nothing contained in the Charter precludes the existence of "regional arrangements or agencies" for dealing with matters in the field of international peace and security, providing that their activities are "consistent with the Purposes and Principles of the United Nations". To an extent, Chapter VIII envisages regional agencies playing a part both in the pacific settlement of disputes (Article 52 (2) and (3)) and in the taking of enforcement action, though no such action is to be taken by regional agencies without the authorisation of the Security Council (Article 53 (1)).

The majority of regional organisations operating in the field of international peace and security have been directed not so much at the objectives mentioned in Chapter VIII but at the implementation of Article 51, which falls within Chapter VII of the Charter and makes clear that nothing in the Charter "shall impair the inherent right of individual or collective self-defence" until the Security Council has taken the necessary steps to maintain international peace and security. This emphasis is illustrated by the fact that Article 1 of the North Atlantic Treaty, in which the parties undertake to settle their disputes by peaceful means, in no sense creates a regional arrangement for the settlement of disputes as envisaged by Article 52 of the Charter, while Article 5 of the Treaty, in which the parties agree that an armed attack against one or more of them in Europe or North America shall be considered an attack against them all, makes specific reference to the right of collective self-defence "recognised by Article 51 of the Charter". Article 5 goes on to state that any such attack and the measures taken by N.A.T.O. to meet the attack shall be reported immediately to the Security Council, and that once the Security Council has taken the action "necessary to restore and maintain international peace and security" the measures taken by N.A.T.O. "shall be terminated". It is this claim to be able to take action "necessary to restore and maintain international peace and security" which reveals the principal weakness of the parties' contention that N.A.T.O. (and similar defence pacts) falls exclusively under Article 51 of the Charter. Taking action to *restore* peace might well go beyond the legitimate bounds of self-defence. When such action is envisaged, of course, a regional defence organisation should comply with Article 54 which lays down that the Security Council "shall at all times be kept fully informed of activities undertaken or in contemplation under regional arrangements",[9] not an obligation which the parties would be particularly anxious to fulfil.

The main reason for the inclusion of Chapter VIII in the Charter was the existence of the Organisation of American States with wide powers of pacific settlement and collective security among its members. With the advent of the U.N. Charter, it became necessary to redraft the constitution of the O.A.S. This redrafting is to be found in three main agreements,[10] the main constitution which is contained in the Bogota Charter, the Inter-American Treaty of Reciprocal Assistance (the Rio Treaty) and the American Treaty of Pacific Settlement (the Bogota Pact).

Article 1 of the O.A.S. Charter specifically states that it is a "regional agency" within the United Nations, and Article 4 proclaims a series of "essential purposes" partly in order to "fulfil its regional obligations" under the U.N. Charter. Similarly Article 20 of the O.A.S. Charter requires the submission of disputes amongst member states to "peaceful procedures" as set out in the Charter, before being referred to the Security Council of the United Nations.

However, the collective security arrangements stated in the Bogota Charter and elaborated in the Rio Treaty do not altogether conform with Chapter VIII of the U.N. Charter. Article 3 (1) of the Rio Treaty is similar in terms to the North Atlantic Treaty ("armed attack by any state against an American state shall be considered as an attack against all the American States"), and there is an undertaking to assist in meeting the attack "in the exercise of the inherent right of individual or collective self-defence recognised by Article 51 of the Charter of the United Nations". But Article 6 of the Rio Treaty is much wider in scope:

---

9. See below, pp. 684–687.
10. For the proposed redrafting of the O.A.S. Charter that awaits sufficient ratifications to bring it into force, see (1967) 6 I.L.M. 310,

"If the inviolability or the integrity of the territory or the sovereignty or political independence of any American state should be affected by an aggression which is not an armed attack or by an extracontinental or intracontinental conflict, or by any other fact or situation that might endanger the peace of America, the Organ of Consultation shall meet immediately in order to agree on the measures which must be taken in case of aggression to assist the victim of the aggression or, in any case, the measures which should be taken for the common defense and for the maintenance of the peace and security of the continent."

It is Article 6 of the Rio Treaty, which is substantially reproduced in Article 25 of the Bogota Charter, that has been the basis of actions by the O.A.S. apparently inconsistent with Article 53 (1) of the U.N. Charter which states that, though the Security Council shall, where appropriate, make use of such regional agencies for enforcement action under its authority, no enforcement action may be taken by regional agencies without the authorisation of the Council. The cause of the friction has been the attempted use of the O.A.S. by the United States to maintain in modern form the Monroe Doctrine. According to President Monroe, the United States should consider any attempt by European powers "to extend their system to any portion of this hemisphere as dangerous to our peace and safety". Nearly a century and a half later, Secretary of State Dulles introduced a resolution to the tenth O.A.S. Conference at Caracas which stated *inter alia* that "the domination or control of the political institutions of any American state by the international communist movement, extending to this Hemisphere the political system of an extracontinental power, would constitute a threat to the sovereignty and political independence of the American states, endangering the peace of America."[11]

For the past decade Central America has been the object of revolutionary movements stemming from the successful establishment of the Castro régime in Cuba. In a region also producing right wing military dictatorships, the result has been a testing period for United States policy, for the solidarity of the O.A.S., and for the relationship between the O.A.S. and the Security Council.

In 1960, following charges by Venezuela that the military dictatorship in the Dominican Republic had been committing acts of aggression against Venezuela, and flagrant and widespread violations of human rights in its own territory, the sixth meeting of consultation of American Foreign Ministers agreed to the breaking of diplomatic relations, and to a partial interruption of economic relations, with the Dominican Republic. It was also agreed that the O.A.S. should "transmit to the Security Council of the United Nations full information concerning the measures agreed upon".[12] The United States did not feel enthusiastic about taking such measures against an anti-Communist régime, but fell in with the mood of the other states in the hope that support would be forthcoming for

---

11. Quoted: Whiteman, *Digest of International Law*, Vol. 5, p. 425.
12. Sixth Mtg. of Consultation, *Final Act*, O.E.A., Ser. C/II 6. (1960) p. 6.

United States action against Cuba. The Communist members of the Security Council (Russia and Poland) were similarly placed in a predicament. While favouring action against the Dominican Republic, they nevertheless saw the undesirability of allowing the O.A.S. a free hand in imposing sanctions uncontrolled by the Security Council, and therefore by the Soviet veto. While protesting that the measures taken by the O.A.S. constituted enforcement action within Article 53 of the Charter, they nevertheless were prepared merely to abstain in the vote on a joint United States, Argentine and Ecuador resolution in which the Security Council simply "took note" of the actions by the O.A.S.[13] The main argument in favour of the view that the measures adopted by the O.A.S. did not fall within Article 53 of the U.N. Charter was expressed by the United Kingdom representative as follows:[14]

> "In the opinion of the United Kingdom Government, it is common sense to interpret the use of this term in Article 53 as covering only such actions as would not normally be legitimate except on the basis of a Security Council resolution. There is nothing in international law, in principle, to prevent any State, if it so decides, from breaking off diplomatic relations or instituting a partial interruption of economic relations with any other State. These steps, which are the measures decided upon by the Organisation of American States with regard to the Dominican Republic, are acts of policy perfectly within the competence of any sovereign state. It follows, obviously, that they are within the competence of the members of the Organisation of American States acting collectively."

The O.A.S. has relied upon this interpretation of its relationship with the Security Council under Article 53 in a series of diplomatic and economic measures against Cuba, despite Soviet protests that such actions could not be undertaken without the authorisation of the Council. As a consequence, however, it has even been suggested that Article 53 (1) may be treated as obsolete because its provisions have been disregarded in practice. Such a view is not supportable. If the United States and its supporters in the O.A.S. are prepared to act in defiance of the U.N. Charter it is difficult to imagine how sanctions are to be applied for breach of their obligations under the Charter, but it does not follow that the obligations cease to exist. Even those states outside the O.A.S. which support, or at least do not wish to criticise publicly, U.S. actions, do so, not on the ground that Article 53 (1) has in some way "ceased to exist", but on the ground that it does not apply *in the circumstances*.

---

13. S/4491 (1960).   14. S.C.O.R. (XV) 893rd Mtg., p. 16.

CHAPTER FOURTEEN

INTERNATIONAL ORGANISATIONS— III

FUNCTIONS AND POWERS RELATING TO ECONOMIC AND SOCIAL MATTERS INCLUDING HUMAN RIGHTS

1 ECONOMIC AND SOCIAL MATTERS

As early as 1941, the Atlantic Charter had set out the aims of the Allies, who were already referring to themselves as "the United Nations", and amongst these aims was the "desire to bring about the fullest collaboration between all nations in the economic field, with the object of securing for all improved labour standards, economic advancement, and social security." This object re-appeared as one of the Purposes of the new United Nations organisation (Article 1 (3) of the Charter), and was reinforced by the terms of Article 55 which provides that in order to create "conditions of stability and well-being which are necessary for peaceful and friendly relations among nations" the U.N. "shall promote" *inter alia* "higher standards of living, full employment, and conditions of economic and social progress"; "solutions of international economic, social, health, and related problems"; and "universal respect for, and observance of, human rights and fundamental freedoms".

A. The General Assembly

As the section dealing with the powers of the Assembly in the field of international peace and security[1] showed, Chapter IV of the Charter defines those powers in the most general terms. In the specific context of economic and social matters, Article 13 provides that the Assembly "*shall initiate studies and make recommendations*" in order to promote, *inter alia*, international co-operation in the economic, social, cultural, educational, and health fields. It will also be recalled that Article 10 was not limited to the maintenance of international peace and security, but

---

1. Above, pp. 577 *et seq.*

empowered the Assembly to discuss and make recommendations on any question or matter "within the scope of the present Charter".

Even though the administration of activities in relation to economic and social matters is in the hands of the Economic and Social Council (ECOSOC), it is clear that the General Assembly has an overall responsibility, and this responsibility is spelt out in more detail in Chapters IX and X of the Charter. In Article 60 it is stated that ECOSOC acts "under the authority of" the Assembly; Article 66 (1) talks of ECOSOC "carrying out" recommendations of the Assembly; and Article 66 (3) refers to the functions of ECOSOC as being those specified in the Charter or assigned to it by the Assembly. From the wide range of ECOSOC's activities, however, it is obvious that the General Assembly's responsibilities could not involve a close scrutiny of the extensive work carried out in the economic and social fields. Such control as the Assembly does exercise is left in the hands of three of its Committees (the Second, which deals with Economic and Financial matters; the Third, which deals with Social, Humanitarian and Cultural activities; and the Fifth, whose tasks concern Administrative and Budgetary matters), and of the Advisory Committee on Administrative and Budgetary Questions.

B. The Economic and Social Council

ECOSOC has been described as "an organ of very wide terms of reference but of limited powers".[2] Article 55[3] sets out these terms in the broadest manner, and, by Article 56, all members of the U.N. "pledge themselves to take joint and separate action in co-operation with the Organisation for the achievement of the purposes set forth in Article 55." Despite this undertaking, ECOSOC has never developed more than a power to encourage members to co-operate in economic and social matters. Because of the less involved attitude of states towards such matters, ECOSOC's power to make recommendations even to members of the Organisation (Art. 62 (1)) has proved far less valuable in relation to economic and social matters than has the Assembly's power to make recommendations in the context of international peace and security.

The types of recommendation made by ECOSOC vary greatly in content. Recommendations to states may be designed to increase aid to developing countries; those to the General Assembly may be to suggest the preparation or signature of a draft convention; while recommendations to a specialised agency may relate to a problem peculiarly the concern of that particular agency. Often these recommendations are the result of studies initiated by ECOSOC under Article 62 (1).

Perhaps the most striking undertaking that ECOSOC has initiated is the programme of technical assistance, which after 1950 became the

---

2. Bowett, *The Law of International Institutions*, p. 53.   3. See previous page.

Expanded Programme for Technical Assistance (E.P.T.A.). The object of the scheme was the channelling of expert assistance, available through the specialised agencies, to under-developed countries. A Committee of ECOSOC (T.A.C.) dealt with the overall policy of the programme, while the functioning of the programme was organised by a Technical Assistance Board (T.A.B.) on which the specialised agencies were represented. Funds were provided partly through the normal budgets of the participating bodies, and partly, in the case of more ambitious projects, through the U.N. Special Fund. In 1966, E.P.T.A. and the Special Fund were merged to form the U.N. Development Programme, and the direction of the Programme placed in the hands of a Governing Council of thirty-seven members created from the former T.A.C. and Governing Council of the Special Fund.

In general, ECOSOC's functions may be divided into two categories—those arising out of Article 62 (making and initiating studies and reports, and making recommendations, often based upon such studies) and those stemming from Article 63 (2) (the co-ordination of the activities of the specialised agencies). In order to assist with the carrying out of its functions under Article 62, the Economic and Social Council has made use of its power, as set out in Article 68, to create a number of Commissions. The Commissions number amongst them four regional economic commissions, to deal with Europe, Asia and the Far East, Latin America and Africa. Their duties are concerned with initiating and participating in concerted action to raise the economic activity of the region concerned, and to investigate the economic problems of the states of the region. The other Commissions deal with a variety of matters: there is a Social Commission, one for Human Rights, another dealing with the Status of Women, a more specialised Commission entrusted with the serious problems arising out of Narcotic Drugs, and so on.

While ECOSOC can undertake studies and make recommendations, its primary role is that of an instrument of co-ordination. Article 57 (1) of the Charter refers to the "various specialised agencies, established by inter-governmental agreement and having wide international responsibilities, as defined in their basic instruments, in economic, social, cultural, educational, health and related fields" and states that they "shall be brought into relationship with the U.N. in accordance with the provisions of Article 63". Under Article 63 (1), it is for ECOSOC to "enter into agreements with any of the agencies referred to in Article 57, defining the terms on which the agency concerned shall be brought into relationship with the United Nations" (though these agreements are subject to approval by the General Assembly).

The agreements entered into with the specialised agencies have certain similarities in that they set out the status and precise relationship of the particular agency to ECOSOC and to the U.N. as a whole. There are a variety of provisions allowing for reciprocal rights to be represented at meetings, to propose agenda items, and to cover the mutual exchange of information. Only recently, however, has ECOSOC attempted to bring some degree of uniformity into the budgets presented to the U.N. by the agencies. Though the broad outline of co-ordination procedures are to be found in the special agreements, the very magnitude of ECOSOC's tasks will be appreciated when it is realised that the Council is also empowered (by Article 71) to make "suitable arrangements for consultation with non-governmental organisations which are concerned with matters within its competence". The Administrative Committee on Co-ordination (A.C.C.), on which the heads of all the specialised agencies sit, has proved a valuable instrument in assisting ECOSOC carry out its functions in relation to the specialised agencies, but the need for improvement has not gone unrecognised. ECOSOC has to deal with a large number of organisations and other bodies operating in the social and economic field. It also has to deal with an international community of more than 120 members. In addition, there has been a continuous, and ever more rapid, growth in the activities and diversification of international institutions operating in the field. It remains to be seen whether moves in the U.N., which gained momentum with the opening address of the Secretary-General to ECOSOC in 1964, in which he stressed the need for more effective collaboration, will be able to improve the procedures with which ECOSOC is expected to carry out its formidable duties.

C. The Specialised Agencies and Similar Bodies

To the lawyer, two of the more interesting features of the specialised agencies are their constitutional structures, which were dealt with in Chapter 12, and their powers to make recommendations to states in the form of draft agreements regulating matters as varied as conditions of employment or safety standards at sea or in the air, an aspect of their functions that will be dealt with in the course of this chapter. However, while it may not be necessary to go into details of the functions of these agencies in order to discuss their quasi-legislative powers, a brief outline of the work, and the field of competence, of these institutions is essential to an understanding of their role in the field of international economic and social co-operation.

a INTERNATIONAL LABOUR ORGANISATION (I.L.O.)
i *Origins*
International consultation in the labour field was not unknown in the years before the First World War, but the devastations of war gave new impetus to the movement in favour of a more permanent structure to channel international co-operation. In addition, western Europe was haunted by the spectre of international Communism, and the I.L.O. was in part the socialist and liberal answer to the threat of the Communist International. Originally linked to the League of Nations, the I.L.O. Constitution was amended at the Montreal Conference of 1946 to make way for its

future relationship with the United Nations. The agreement whereby the U.N. recognised the I.L.O. "as a specialised agency responsible for taking such action as may be appropriate under its basic instrument for the accomplishment of the purposes set forth therein" was entered into in December, 1946.

ii *Objects*

The objects of the I.L.O. referred to in Article 1 (1) of its Constitution are set out in the preamble of this instrument, and were elaborated upon in the so-called Declaration of Philadelphia of May, 1944. One of the most quoted tenets of the 1944 Declaration is the statement that "poverty anywhere constitutes a danger to prosperity everywhere", but the preamble to the constitution states more specifically the need to improve the conditions of work, "by the regulation of the hours of work, including the establishment of a maximum working day and week, the regulation of the labour supply, the prevention of unemployment, the provision of an adequate living wage, the protection of the worker against sickness, disease and injury arising out of his employment, the protection of children, young persons and women, provision for old age and injury, protection of the interests of workers when employed in countries other than their own, recognition of the principle of equal remuneration for work of equal value, recognition of the principle of freedom of association, the organisation of vocational and technical education and other measures."

iii *Processes*

The methods whereby the I.L.O. operates are set out in the constitution. Under Article 10 (1), the function of the I.L. Office (the Secretariat) "shall include the collection and distribution of information on all subjects relating to the international adjustment of conditions of industrial life and labour, and particularly the examination of subjects which it is proposed to bring before the Conference with a view to the conclusion of International Conventions, and the conduct of such special investigations as may be ordered by the Conference or by the Governing Body." (Article 12 (1) imposes on the I.L.O. the duty to co-operate "with any general international organisation" entrusted with the task of co-ordinating the activities of international organisations with "specialised responsibilities", and also to co-operate with those organisations with "specialised responsibilities" in related fields. Article 12 (3) enables the I.L.O. to make "suitable arrangements" for consultation with "non-governmental international organisations, including international organisations of employers, workers, agriculturalists and co-operators".

iv *Conventions and recommendations*

The object of this consultative process is the formulation of Conventions and Recommendations for the regulation of conditions of employment and related matters. Both Conventions and Recommendations are adopted by a majority of two-thirds of the votes cast by the delegates present in the Conference (as the I.L.O. Assembly is called); and in framing either type of instrument the Conference "shall have due regard to those countries in which climatic conditions, the imperfect development of industrial organisation, or other special circumstances make the industrial conditions substantially different" (Article 19 (2) and (3)). In the case of Conventions, Article 19 (5) lays down that they are to be communicated to members for ratification. Members undertake that they will within one year, or at the latest within eighteen months from the closing of the session of the Conference, bring Conventions before the state authorities competent to take whatever legislative or other action is appropriate. If the appropriate authorities "consent" to the Convention the Member should communicate its ratification to the Director-General of the I.L.O., and also "take such action as may be necessary to make effective the provisions of the Convention". If such consent is not obtained, the Member is obliged only to report to the Director-General of the I.L.O. at appropriate intervals, "the position of its law and practice in regard to the matters dealt with in the Convention, showing the extent to which effect has been given, or is proposed to be given, to any of the provisions of the Convention by legislation, administrative action, collective agreement or otherwise, and stating the difficulties which prevent or delay the ratification of such Convention." The procedure with respect to Recommendations is similar except that they are designed to encourage states to bring their standards into line with those laid down in Recommendations; there is no question of "ratifying" them, and while there is an obligation on members to inform the Director-General of the present state of their law, Members do not have to give reasons for their failure to ratify.

On the other hand, ratification of a Convention involves a Member in the possibility of representations being made by an industrial association of employers or of workers (Art. 24) or of complaints being filed by other Members (Art. 26 (1)) that the Member has not secured effective observance of a particular Convention. In the case of a representation under Article 24, the most that the Governing Body (as the I.L.O. "Council" is called) is to publish the representation and any reply by the Member concerned if that is considered unsatisfactory (Article 25). In the case of a complaint under Article 26 (1), however, in addition to seeking a statement from the government concerned, the Governing Body may appoint a Commission of Inquiry to consider the complaint and report thereon (Art. 26 (3)). The "offending" state, if the findings of the Commission are unacceptable, may refer the complaint to the International Court (Art. 29 (2)), which, in a decision that is final (Art. 31), may "affirm, vary or reverse any of the findings or recommendations of the Commission of Enquiry" (Art. 32). If the Member fails to carry out the recommendations of the Commission, or of the Court, "the Governing Body may recommend to the Conference such action as it may deem wise and expedient to secure compliance therewith" (Art. 33).

b FOOD AND AGRICULTURE ORGANISATION (F.A.O.)

i *Origins*

F.A.O. was the first of the U.N. Specialised Agencies to be created (at Quebec in 1945), and, like the I.L.O., its antecedents can be traced back to before the First World War. In fact, it was the direct successor of the International Institute of Agriculture, an inter-governmental body created by an international conference in 1905 as a clearing house for information on matters of common interest in the field of agriculture.

ii *Objects and functions*

The functions of the Organisation are set out in Article 1 of its constitution, and they may be divided in the manner suggested by the paragraphs of that Article into three categories.

Article 1 (1) states that F.A.O. shall "collect, analyse, interpret, and disseminate information relating to nutrition, food and agriculture" (the term "agriculture" being taken to include "fisheries, marine products, forestry and primary forestry products").

Article 1 (2) refers to F.A.O.'s duty to "promote and, where appropriate, . . . recommend national and international action" with respect to research, to the spread of knowledge, to the conservation of natural resources and the adoption of improved methods of agricultural production, and the improvement of the processing, marketing, and distribution of food and agricultural products. At the lowest level, the carrying out of these functions (suggesting fields of research, spreading public knowledge, etc.) is but an extension of the duties imposed by paragraph 1. However, at a more significant level, F.A.O. is concerned in the working of the various international commodity agreements, and its rules of procedure refer specifically to the F.A.O. Council's right to examine "current developments" in relation to commodity arrangements with a view to recommending appropriate action. F.A.O. has established a Committee on Commodity Problems and has entered into a number of "relationship" agreements with Commodity Councils, but has never succeeded in exercising any degree of control over the Councils, the operations of which have remained largely autonomous.[4]

Perhaps F.A.O.'s most important contributions to international action within its sphere of competence have been in taking over and expanding the process of convention-making that was part of the work of the International Institute of Agriculture. There are similarities in the F.A.O. constitution to the provisions of the I.L.O. constitution relating to recommendations. The F.A.O. Conference (that is, the "Assembly" of the Organisation) may, by a two-thirds majority of the votes cast, "approve and submit" to member states "conventions and agreements concerning questions relating to food and agriculture" (Art. 14 (1)); and, under Article 14 (2), the Council can, by a similar majority, approve and submit to member states, (a) agreements of purely regional importance, and (b)

---

4. For the Commodity Agreements, see below, p. 609.

conventions or agreements supplementary to those coming into force under paragraphs 1 or 2 (a). Unlike the position in the I.L.O., the F.A.O. constitution does not lay down specific provisions for the ratification and enforcement of conventions. Article 14 (4) simply states that any convention or agreement, supplementary convention or agreement, shall come into force for each contracting party as the convention or agreement may prescribe. The only duty is that imposed upon associate members, and that is that they shall submit such conventions or agreements to the authority having responsibility for their international relations (Art. 14 (5)). However, all members and associate members have to submit periodic reports *inter alia* "on the action taken on the basis of recommendations made and conventions submitted by the Conference" (Art. 11 (1)), and the Conference can approve the publication of such reports "together with any reports relating thereto adopted by the Conference" (Art. 11 (3)).

Under *Article 1 (3)* of the constitution, F.A.O. is also under a duty to "furnish such technical assistance as governments may request", and to organise, in co-operation with the governments concerned, such missions as may be needed to carry out the obligations of membership of F.A.O. In addition to undertaking missions on its own account, F.A.O. has played its part in the development of the U.N. Technical Assistance Programme. Of particular importance has been its work in the field of international action to prevent the spread of, and the worst effects of, various plant and animal pests and diseases.

c WORLD HEALTH ORGANISATION (W.H.O.)

i *Origins*

Prior to 1945, there already existed a number of international bodies operating in the field of health. W.H.O. took over the functions of the Health Organisation of the League of Nations, the International Office of Public Hygiene situated in Paris, the Health Division of U.N.R.R.A., and converted a number of regional bureaux into its regional offices (e.g. the Pan American Sanitary Bureau).

ii *Objects and functions*

Article 1 of the W.H.O. constitution states as the objective of the Organisation "the attainment by all peoples of the highest possible level of health". In order to achieve this objective, a wide range of functions are allotted to W.H.O. under Article 2. A reading of Article 2 will demonstrate that it is not an easy matter to separate W.H.O.'s various functions into convenient categories, although it is possible to distinguish certain broad divisions in the methods whereby the Organisation can operate.

1 *Co-ordination of activities*

According to Article 2 (a), W.H.O. is to "act as the directing and co-ordinating authority on international health work" and Article 2 (b) states that the Organisation is to "establish and maintain effective collaboration with the United Nations, specialised agencies, governmental health administrations, professional groups and such other organisations as may be deemed appropriate". In addition to assisting member states to reach agreement on the means to combat common problems, W.H.O. has achieved an harmonious and fruitful relationship with a variety of non-governmental organisations involved in matters of health.

2 *Advice and services*

Article 2 also states that W.H.O. is to "promote and conduct research in the field of health", and to "establish and maintain such administrative and technical services as may be required, including opidemiological and statistical services". In these and other ways, the Organisation can "provide information, counsel and assistance in the field of health".

In order to "furnish appropriate technical assistance", W.H.O. has conducted a series of programmes designed to control or eradicate diseases in various parts of the world. In this connection it has figured largely in co-operation with other specialised agencies (notably with F.A.O. over nutrition and food hygiene, and with I.L.O. over industrial injuries) and in the programme of Technical Assistance.

3 *Health regulations and conventions*

The W.H.O. constitution creates two types of "legislative" process.

(*a*) *Regulations*

The Health Assembly has authority (Article 21) "to adopt regulations concerning:

(a) sanitary and quarantine requirements and other procedures designed to prevent the international spread of disease;
(b) nomenclatures with respect to diseases, causes of death and public health practices;
(c) standards with respect to diagnostic procedures for international use;
(d) standards with respect to the safety, purity and potency of biological, pharmaceutical and similar products moving in international commerce;
(e) advertising and labelling of biological, pharmaceutical and similar products moving in international commerce."

Under Article 22, such regulations come into force for all members after notice has been given of their adoption by the Health Assembly, unless a member notifies the Director-General of the Organisation that it has rejected, or made reservations to, the regulations within the period allowed by the notice.

(*b*) *Conventions or agreements*

The Assembly also has a power similar to that of I.L.O. and F.A.O. of adopting, by a two-thirds majority vote, conventions or agreements "which shall come into force for each Member when accepted by it in accordance with its constitutional processes" (Art. 19). Under Article 20, each Member undertakes that it will within eighteen months of the adoption of a convention or agreement "take action relative to the acceptance of such convention or agreement". If a Member does not accept the convention or agreement, it must furnish a statement of the reasons for non-acceptance.

d UNITED NATIONS EDUCATIONAL, SCIENTIFIC AND CULTURAL ORGANISATION (U.N.E.S.C.O.)

i *Objects*

The *raison d'être* of U.N.E.S.C.O., as stated in the prefatory declaration of its constitution, is that its members "believing in full and equal opportunities for education for all, in the unrestricted pursuit of objective truth, and in the free exchange of ideas and knowledge, are agreed and determined to develop and to increase the means of communication between their peoples and to employ these means for the purposes of mutual understanding and a truer and more perfect knowledge of each other's lives". And the purpose of the Organisation, contained in Article 1 (1), is "to contribute to peace and security by promoting collaboration among the nations through education, science and culture".

ii *Functions*

It is clear from Article 1 that U.N.E.S.C.O.'s functions are primarily directed at encouraging co-operation among its members. Although illiteracy is a problem of the greatest magnitude in many parts of the world, U.N.E.S.C.O., with limited financial resources, is not in a position to do more than arrange teacher training programmes, assist in the planning of courses with standardised (and therefore cheaper) textbooks, and matters of a similar nature. It cannot create, finance, and run, with its own personnel, ambitious schemes in different regions of the world.

U.N.E.S.C.O.'s efforts in attempting to encourage mutual understanding among its members have not been restricted to arranging "cultural exchanges" or providing fellowships for individual specialists in the educational field to work in less fully developed countries. It has in a less obvious way encouraged and helped to guide the rewriting of history books used in schools in an attempt to make them more accurate in detail and less nationalistic in their approach.

The General Conference of U.N.E.S.C.O. has a power to adopt both recommendations (by a majority vote) and conventions (by a two-thirds majority). In both cases, Member States are under a duty to submit them to the "competent authorities" in the state within a period of one year from the close of the session of the Conference at which they were adopted (Art. 4 (4)). In addition, under Article 8, Member States are under a duty to report periodically to the Organisation *inter alia* on the action taken upon such recommendations and conventions. Perhaps the most notable achievements of U.N.E.S.C.O. acting in pursuance of its powers under Article 4 (4) have been the Universal Copyright Convention, designed to protect writers and artists against the unauthorised reproduction of their work in other countries, and the Convention for the Protection of Cultural Property in the Event of Armed Conflict.

e WORLD METEOROLOGICAL ORGANISATION (W.M.O.)
i *Origins*
The constitution of W.M.O. was drawn up by a conference of the International Meteorological Organisation which had been established as early as 1878. I.M.O. came into existence in 1950, and in 1951 I.M.O. transferred to W.M.O. all I.M.O.'s work, obligations and assets.

ii *Objects*
The purposes of W.M.O. are to "facilitate world wide co-operation in the establishment of networks of stations for the making of meteorological observations", to promote the rapid exchange of weather information, to encourage research, and to "further the application of meteorology to aviation, shipping, agriculture, and other human activities" (Art. 2).

iii *Functions*
Practical co-operation in day to day problems is largely channelled through six regional associations, but W.M.O. has also established a number of technical commissions comprising experts to advise the W.M. Congress in fulfilling the purposes of the Organisation under Article 2 and its functions under Article 8. Article 9 lays down that the members "shall do their utmost" to implement decisions of the Congress (which in most cases have to be by a two-thirds majority (Art. 11)), but if any member "finds it impracticable to give effect to some requirement in a technical resolution adopted by Congress, such Member shall inform the Secretary-General of the Organisation whether its inability to give effect to it is provisional or final, and state its reasons therefor."

f INTERNATIONAL TELECOMMUNICATION UNION (I.T.U.)
i *Origins*
The I.T.U. traces its ancestry to the International Telegraph Union which was established in 1865. I.T.U. took its present name in 1932 and its present form under a convention which came into force in January, 1949, as reformulated in a new Convention becoming operative in January, 1967.

ii *Objects*
The purposes of the Union, as set out in Article 4 (1), are to extend co-operation in the use and improvement of telecommunication; to promote the development of technical facilities and their most efficient operation; and to harmonise the actions of nations in the attainment of those ends. In carrying out these tasks the Union shall in particular work to avoid harmful interference between radio stations of different countries, *inter alia* by the allocation and registration of radio frequencies; undertake studies,

formulate recommendations and opinions, and collect and publish information for the benefit of all members and associate members; foster the development and improvement of equipment and networks in new or developing countries; and promote the adoption of measures for co-operating in ensuring the safety of life (Art. 4 (2)).

iii *Structure and functions*

Because the I.T.U. plays a leading role in the field in which it operates (unlike other agencies which have so far been considered which play a much less significant part in co-operation between states), its constitution is a much more detailed document, and expressly creates a larger number of permanent bodies through which the Union operates. Although space is too limited to consider the intricacies of its structure, it is worth mentioning that the constitution provides for a Plenipotentiary Conference, Administrative Conferences, an Administrative Council, and four permanent organs, comprising the International Frequency Registration Board, whose difficult task it is to reduce radio interference from other stations to a minimum, a General Secretariat, and two Consultative Committees, one for Radio and the other for Telegraph and Telephone.

The only "legislative" powers contained in the constitution concern the sets of Regulations (dealing with Telegraph, Telephone, Radio and Additional Radio Regulations) which form part of the I.T.U. Convention. According to Article 7, rr. 52–53, ordinary administrative conferences may revise the Regulations, voting being by simple majority. Under Article 15, r. 205, members and associate members "shall inform the Secretary-General of their approval of any revision of these Regulations by competent administrative conferences". In practice the majority of revisions are accepted by most members, although some states do occasionally find it necessary to make reservations with respect to certain amendments.

g UNIVERSAL POSTAL UNION (U.P.U.)

i *Origins and objects*

U.P.U. was established by the Berne Convention of 1874 (although it was only in 1878 that it adopted its present name). It is a "Union" of national postal administrations, originally open to all administrations which wished to accede to the convention, but now subject to a formal admissions procedure. Its aim is "to secure the organisation and improvement of the postal services and to promote in this sphere the development of international collaboration" (Art. 1 (2)).

ii *Functions*

While much of its work has been concerned with the speeding of mail services by studies in automation, and in reducing the cost, or at least reducing increases in the cost of mail services (for example, by consultation with international airlines), U.P.U. also deals with the regulatory side of inter-state mail. Letter post is regulated by the provisions of the U.P.U.

convention (Art. 22 (3)), but a number of other Agreements (regulating Insured Letters and Boxes, Postal Parcels, Postal Money Orders and Travellers' Cheques, etc.) are only binding upon members that have acceded to them (Art. 22 (4)). In order to implement the Convention and these Agreements, the Postal Administrations of member states draw up "by common consent" detailed rules and procedures known as "Detailed Regulations". It is thus clear that both formal "Acts of the Union" (i.e. the Convention and the Agreements) and the less formal "Detailed Regulations" require ratification, or, in the case of the Regulations, a clear acceptance of their terms, before they become binding.

h INTERNATIONAL CIVIL AVIATION ORGANISATION (I.C.A.O.)
i *Objects and functions*

The Chicago Convention of 1944 did more than establish I.C.A.O. in Part II of the Convention; it also restated the general principles of air navigation and of international air transport. The objects of I.C.A.O. are "to develop the principles and techniques of international air navigation and to foster the planning and development of international air transport" (Art. 44). As a consequence, I.C.A.O. is the forum within which problems of the Convention as a whole are discussed, and the agency for the development of air communications on both a multilateral and a bilateral basis (the final act of the Chicago Conference laid down a standard form of bilateral agreement for establishing international air routes which has been widely used).

ii *Standards and recommended practices*

One unusual feature of I.C.A.O. is the fact that its "legislative" functions are performed by the Council, a body of limited membership, whereas in the other agencies dealt with so far, such functions have been assigned to the "Assembly" or "Conference" at which all members are represented. Article 54 (l) refers to the adoption of "standards" and "recommended practices" (both termed "Annexes"), which the Council may adopt by a two-thirds majority vote (Art. 90). Annexes become effective within three months of being submitted to I.C.A.O. members, or at the end of such longer period as the Council may prescribe, unless

(i) a majority of members of I.C.A.O. register their disapproval with the Council (Art. 90); or

(ii) if a state finds it impracticable to comply, it must notify the Organisation of the differences between its own practices and those established by international standard: it is then for the Council to notify members of the discrepancy (Art. 38). The main distinction suggested by the Assembly of I.C.A.O. at its first meeting in 1947 between "standards" and "recommended practices" is that uniform application of the former is recognised as necessary for the safety or regularity of international air navigation so that members of I.C.A.O. must conform to them; while application of the latter is regarded as desirable, so that member states are to endeavour to conform with them.

i INTER-GOVERNMENTAL MARITIME CONSULTATIVE
ORGANISATION (I.M.C.O.)

i *Objects and functions*

The constitution of I.M.C.O. was adopted in 1948, but it did not secure sufficient ratifications to enter into force until ten years later, the first Assembly of the Organisation meeting in January, 1959. Article 1 states the purposes of I.M.C.O. in fairly wide terms *inter alia* as the provision of "machinery for co-operation, among Governments in the field of governmental regulation and practices relating to technical matters of all kinds affecting shipping engaged in international trade, and to encourage the general adoption of the highest practicable standards in matters concerning maritime safety and efficiency of navigation", the encouragement of "the removal of discriminatory action and unnecessary restrictions by Governments affecting shipping engaged in international trade", and the provision of facilities "for the exchange of information among Governments". Because of the possible interference from I.M.C.O. in the maritime policies of states, the name of the organisation was designed to emphasise its "consultative" nature, and Article 2 of its constitution lays down that its functions are to be "consultative and advisory".

ii *Conventions and safety regulations*

One of the most important aspects of the Organisation's work is dealt with in Article 3 (b): it is to "provide for the drafting of conventions, agreements, or other suitable instruments, and to recommend these to Governments and to intergovernmental organisations, and to convene such conferences as may be necessary". Nevertheless, because of the vital significance of shipping policies to maritime states, the constitution of I.M.C.O. leaves the adoption of any conventions I.M.C.O. might recommend to the discretion of its members. The process of recommendation is based upon the work of the Organisation's Maritime Safety Committee whose task it is to submit to the Assembly, through the Council, "proposals made by members for safety regulations or for amendments to existing safety regulations, together with its comments or recommendations thereon" (Art. 30 (a)). It is for the Assembly to "recommend to members for adoption regulations concerning maritime safety, or amendments to such regulations, which have been referred to it by the Maritime Safety Committee through the Council" (Art. 16 (i)).

j INTERNATIONAL MONETARY FUND (I.M.F.)

i *Origins and objects*

The United Nations Monetary and Financial Conference of 1944 (usually referred to as the Bretton Woods Conference after the place in the United States where it was held) drew up the Articles of Agreement of the Fund which came into existence in December, 1945. The purposes of the Fund are stated in Article 1 to be, *inter alia*, the promotion of international monetary co-operation, the facilitation of the expansion and balanced growth of international trade, the promotion of exchange stability, assistance in establishing a multilateral system of payments and in eliminating foreign exchange restrictions, the making available of the Fund's resources in order to enable members to correct "maladjustments" in their balance of payments, and shortening the duration and lessening the degree of disequilibrium in the balance of payment of members.

ii *Functions*

The Fund agreement imposes the obligation upon members to maintain the par value of its currency "in terms of gold as a common denominator or in terms of the United States dollar of the weight and fineness in effect on July 1, 1944" (Art. 4 (1) (a)). Exchange transaction must take place within a closely defined margin of the par value (Art. 4 (3)), and members undertake to "collaborate with the Fund to promote exchange stability, to maintain orderly exchange arrangements with other members, and to avoid competitive exchange alterations" (Art. 4 (4) (a)). A change in the par value of a member's currency may be made only on the proposal of the member and only after consultation with the Fund, but such proposal may only be made by a member in order "to correct a fundamental disequilibrium" (Art. 4 (5)).

The I.M.F. possesses no "legislative" power in the sense that term has been employed in relation to other specialised agencies. It can call on member states to furnish it with information on a variety of aspects of the national economy (Art. 8 (5)), and it is concerned with breaches of the undertakings assumed under the Fund Agreement by its members. But the Fund is primarily concerned with providing assistance to deal with the short term balance of payments problems of its members. Members can, within defined limits, "borrow" from the Fund by purchasing either with gold or their own currency, the currency of other members. The fund has also developed a system of what might be termed "guarantees" in the form of "stand-by agreements" which enable a member to draw up to a stipulated amount over a specified period. However, while the Fund can express its views on the subject, it is not geared to deal with, or cure, chronic balance of payments crises among its members: it deals only in short term palliatives.

k INTERNATIONAL BANK FOR RECONSTRUCTION AND DEVELOPMENT (I.B.R.D.)

In addition to signing the Agreement under which the I.M.F. was established, the Bretton Woods Conference also drew up the Agreement for the creation of the International Bank. Under Article 1, the purposes of the Bank include assisting in the reconstruction and development of territories of members by facilitating the investment of capital, promoting private foreign investment by means of guarantees or participation in loans, promoting long-range balanced growth of international trade and maintaining equilibrium in balance of payments by encouraging international investment, and arranging loans made or guaranteed by the Bank to give priority to the more useful and urgent projects. In other words, while the Fund is directly concerned with the balance of payments problems, albeit on a short-term basis, the Bank is only concerned with such problems in so far as increased productive investment would tend, it was hoped, to eradicate chronic balance of payments crises among its members.

Although the Bank is legally a separate entity from the Fund, the two institutions are closely related. The voting structure is substantially the same; membership is linked; and the representatives of states are usually the same persons. Similarly, neither institution is endowed with the power to draw up conventions of a law-making type for acceptance by its members. The Bank primarily enters into agreements with states for the direct loan of capital, or for the guaranteeing of a loan subscribed to from another source.

l INTERNATIONAL FINANCE CORPORATION (I.F.C.)

One drawback of the International Bank is that it is geared to provide loans to governments but not directly to private industry in the absence of a government guarantee. To fill what many states considered to be a gap in the Bank's activities, the I.F.C. was established in 1956 "to further economic development by encouraging the growth of productive private enterprise in member countries, particularly in the less developed areas, thus supplementing the activities of the International Bank". Article 1 then goes on to specify that the Corporation shall, *inter alia*, "in association with private investors, assist in financing the establishment, improvement and expansion of productive private enterprises which would contribute to the development of its member countries by making investments, without guarantee of repayment by the member government concerned, in cases where sufficient private capital is not available on reasonable terms".

Although the I.F.C. is "an entity separate and distinct from the Bank" (Art. 4 (6) (a)) and has a separate relationship agreement with the United Nations, its Board of Governors and Board of Directors comprise the Governors and Directors of the Bank (Article 4 (2) (b) and (4) (b)), and it is entirely dependent upon the Bank for most of its ancillary services. Membership is restricted solely to members of the Bank (Art. 2 (1)), and suspension from membership or ceasing to be a member of the Bank, automatically has the same effect with regard to the Corporation (Art. 5 (3)).

m INTERNATIONAL DEVELOPMENT ASSOCIATION (I.D.A.)

The I.D.A. came into existence in 1960 under an agreement which is substantially the same as that which created the I.F.C. Thus, while the I.D.A. is a separate and distinct entity, it is linked as closely to the I.F.C. as the I.F.C. is with the Bank. The purpose of the Association is to supplement the Bank's activities by making available to the less developed areas of the world included in its membership "finance to meet their important developmental requirements on terms which are more flexible and bear less heavily on the balance of payments than those of conventional loans" (Art. 1).

n INTERNATIONAL ATOMIC ENERGY AGENCY (I.A.E.A.)

Although termed an "Agency", the I.A.E.A. is not regarded as a "specialised agency" in the sense in which that term is applied to the other institutions described in this section. Because its function is concerned with enlarging the contribution of atomic energy, something that can as easily be converted to military purposes, to "peace, health and prosperity" (Art. 2), its primary duty is to submit reports to the General Assembly, and, where appropriate, to the Security Council, rather than to ECOSOC (Art. 3. B. (4)). It has a relationship with the United Nations, therefore, of a rather different kind.

In addition to its role in encouraging research and in exchanging scientific and technical information, the Agency is also a supplier of facilities, plant and equipment, including fissionable materials, to areas that are lacking in such items. Under Article 12 the Agency can lay down safeguards to be observed by states making use of equipment and material that it has supplied and these standards may also be applied by the Agency to any state's activities in the field of atomic energy if that state so wishes (Art. 3. A. (6)). In ensuring the observance of its safeguards, including the requirement that no equipment or material should be diverted to military purposes, the I.A.E.A. may send inspectors to the territory of the states being assisted by the Agency (Art. 12, A. (6), B. and C).

D. Universal institutions not falling within the U.N. framework

a GENERAL AGREEMENT ON TARIFFS AND TRADE (G.A.T.T.)

While the Bretton Woods Conference, in creating the Fund and the Bank, dealt with two aspects of international economic relations, it did not provide any machinery for the liberalisation of world trade. After a period of discussion, proposals were worked out for the creation of an International Trade Organisation and, as an interim measure, for a General Agreement on Tariffs and Trade. However, whereas G.A.T.T. quickly came into force, the obligations of the I.T.O. constitution proved unacceptable to the great majority of states, and the Organisation never came into being.

As its name implies, G.A.T.T. is a treaty[5] rather than a constitution, and the participants are parties to the treaty who attend conferences and not members of an institution who attend meetings of its organs. However, G.A.T.T. has a permanent secretariat and has set up a Council of Representatives (comprising heads of the permanent missions to G.A.T.T.) who carry on the work of G.A.T.T. between conferences.

---

5. A treaty, that is, in the international law sense; under the municipal law of a number of states it was classified as a less formal agreement not requiring ratification by their normal treaty-making constitutional processes.

The Treaty lays down a general most favoured nation clause among its participants (who have to be "admitted" by a two-thirds majority vote). If applied strictly, such a clause would have the effect of eliminating discrimination, but in order to make the obligations under G.A.T.T. acceptable, the Treaty includes a wide range of "escape clauses". Some are designed to maintain the traditional relationships between a number of European states and their former colonial territories. It is also possible to restrict greatly increased imports if these are likely to cause serious injury to domestic producers.

b INTERNATIONAL COMMODITY AGREEMENTS

Because of fluctuations of price in a number of leading commodities (mainly agricultural) from one year to the next, attempts have been made to stabilise prices within defined limits to ensure a fair balance between the interests of importing and exporting states. These agreements fall on the periphery of international organisations because, although they create a certain institutional structure, the organs are designed to help implement the provisions of agreements which are effective for comparatively short periods. Furthermore, as happened in the case of the International Wheat Agreement, the fact that the terms of the agreement are only operative over short periods makes for fluctuations in membership. The United Kingdom, although the most important importer of wheat, refused to accept the terms of the agreements renegotiated in 1953 and 1956. Commodity agreements exist also for sugar, coffee, tin, olive oil, and for tea, although this last agreement is not an intergovernmental agreement, but one made with associations of tea producers.

E. Regional organisations

A number of regional organisations include, as secondary objectives, the encouragement of economic and social co-operation. The O.A.S. attempted to place its economic aims on a more ambitious footing by the "Alliance for Progress", an agreement of the American states signed in 1961. Based upon mutual co-operation and backed by United States aid, it was intended to make use of the various bodies working on economic development in the region (including the U.N. Economic Commission for Latin-America). The Organisation of African Unity has as its first stated purpose the promotion of "the Unity and solidarity of the African States" (Art. II (1) (a)), but it has spent more of its time dealing with the eradication of all forms of colonialism (sub-paragraph (d)) than with co-operation to achieve a better life for the peoples of Africa (sub-paragraph (b)). The O.A.U. is basically a simple structure of which the principal organs are an Assembly of Heads of State and Government and a Council of Ministers (Art. VII). Even though Article XX provides for a number of Specialised Commissions in the economic, social, health, scientific and technical fields, the type of organisation and resources at its disposal do not make it an effective body for operations in the economic and social field in a continent as divided and undeveloped as Africa. Similarly, the Arab

League is far more a vehicle of Arab nationalism in the political sphere, than a means of co-operation in the economic sphere, although in accordance with Article 2 of the Pact which created the League, a number of trade and payment agreements have been entered into and a Financial Organisation created.[6]

a ORGANISATION FOR EUROPEAN ECONOMIC CO-OPERATION (O.E.E.C.) RECONSTITUTED IN 1961 AS THE ORGANISATION FOR ECONOMIC CO-OPERATION AND DEVELOPMENT (O.E.C.D.)

The Marshall Plan, instituted by the United States for the reconstruction of Europe after the Second World War, was made possible by the allocation of funds by the United States under the Economic Co-operation Act of April, 1948. The efforts of the states of Western Europe were channelled through the O.E.E.C. which came into being at about the same time.

The object of O.E.E.C. was to liberalise trade among its members by the expansion of production and the lowering of tariffs. Committees were established to consider both general problems (for example, trade or manpower) and the difficulties of specific industries (coal, steel, electricity, etc.), and their surveys and reports made significant contributions to the policies of member states. O.E.E.C. was also responsible for the creation of a number of separate agencies, like the European Atomic Energy Agency and, perhaps more important at the time, the European Payments Union which between 1950 and 1958 (when it was replaced by the European Fund) contributed greatly to the settlement of trade transactions between member states.

With the creation of the European Communities and the consequent movement away from trade liberalisation across the tariff wall created by the E.E.C., it was felt that changes would be required in the structure and functions of O.E.E.C. Its reconstruction as O.E.C.D., and the opening of membership to non-European states (Canada, the United States, Japan), has not led to any significant development in its role. It provides a meeting place for members of E.F.T.A. and the E.E.C., and for the members of N.A.T.O. in an economic setting, but these are scarcely reasons for continuing the existence of an organisation which has fulfilled its most useful role—the post-war reconstruction of Europe. Meeting places for the various groups of states are available elsewhere, so that perhaps all that remains to justify O.E.C.D. are the Atomic Energy Agency, the European Fund and the Development Assistance Committee[7] which were created under the aegis of O.E.E.C., and the continued value of O.E.C.D. reports.

---

6. On both the African and American continents, small groups of states have set about creating "common markets" or free trade areas; e.g., Central African Economic and Customs Union (text in (1965) 4 I.L.M. 699); Economic Community of East Africa (1966) 5 I.L.M. 633); Caribbean Free Trade Association (1968) 7 I.L.M. 935). And for the proposed Latin American Free Trade Association, see (1965) 4 I.L.M. 651. At the time of writing it was not possible to assess the importance of these groupings to the economic life of the states concerned.

7. D.A.C. tries, with some success, to co-ordinate aid projects to developing countries. Interestingly enough, a number of states, like Australia, are members of D.A.C. even though not members of O.E.C.D.

b THE EUROPEAN COMMUNITIES

i *European Coal and Steel Community (E.C.S.C.)*—After the Second World War, various proposals were mooted for some sort of unification of the states of Western Europe. The Council of Europe was a very tentative step towards greater unity, but it was essentially a consultative organisation with no "supra-national" power.

The main impetus towards European union was the feeling, strongly held by France and its neighbours to the north, that a closer relationship between them would prove an obstacle to a resurgence of uncontrolled German militarism as well as a considerable benefit to their economic development. The first co-operative effort was an implementation of the Schumann plan that the French and German coal and steel industries should be placed under unified control. In the event, six states (France and Germany, together with Italy, Belgium, Holland and Luxembourg) formed the European Coal and Steel Community which came into being in 1952.

The purpose of E.C.S.C., as stated by Article 2 of its constituent treaty, is to contribute to the expansion of the economy, the development of employment, and the improvement of the standard of living in the participating countries through the creation of a common market in coal and steel. In carrying out its purpose, import and export duties, price discrimination, subsidies and restrictive practices were declared incompatible with the establishment of a common market in coal and steel and therefore prohibited (Art. 4). As it was for the High Authority of the Community (since July, 1967, the joint Commission of the three Communities) to ensure the achievement of the purposes set out in the treaty (Art. 8), one of the major tasks of the High Authority was to supervise the compliance by states and individual industrial concerns with the provisions of Article 4. The Court of the European Communities has heard a number of cases brought by firms alleging that the High Authority had exceeded its powers as laid down in the E.C.S.C. treaty.

The E.C.S.C. undoubtedly proved a striking success as an example of what close and integrated co-operation could achieve in a limited field. A "common market" was achieved by the ending of tariffs and subsidies within the Community. Uneconomic works and mines were phased out and mobility of labour was accomplished by close co-operation in the field of social security. But E.C.S.C. was not without its drawbacks. By the second half of the 1950s coal's position was being undermined by other fuels, and it was obviously going to be increasingly difficult to pursue a unified policy in isolation. This need for integration in other fields, when added to economic benefits and political idealism, proved irresistible.

ii *European Economic Community (E.E.C.)*—Although envisaged originally as a common market, E.E.C. as defined by the Treaty of Rome of 1957 was a more ambitious project, aiming ultimately at a form of politica union. For that reason it was called E.E.C. and not the Common Market. The principles upon which the Community is based are set out in Articles 2 and 3 of the Treaty. According to Article 2, it shall be the aim of the

Community, by establishing a common market and progressively approximating the economic policies of Member States, to promote throughout the Community harmonious development of economic activities, continuous and balanced expansion, increased stability, accelerated raising of the standard of living and closer relations among Member States. To achieve these purposes, the activities of the Community set out in Article 3 include the elimination of customs duties and restrictions on imports and exports between member states; the establishment of a common tariff and commercial policy towards outside states; the abolition as between member states of obstacles to the freedom of movement of persons, services and capital; the inauguration of a common agricultural policy and a common transport policy; the standardising of the municipal law of member states to the degree that is necessary for the functioning of the Common Market; the creation of a European Social Fund for the wider employment of workers; and the establishing of a European Investment Bank to facilitate the economic expansion of the Community.

The detailed provisions of Parts II, III and IV of the Treaty give specific effect to the principles stated in Article 3. Under Part V, which deals with the institutions of the Community, the Commission fills the role (though its powers are more restricted, usually by the need to co-operate with the other organs of the Community) of the former High Authority of E.C.S.C. Thus the Commission, *inter alia*, shall, with a view to ensuring the functioning and development of the Common Market, ensure the application of the provisions of this Treaty (Art. 155). However, the less prominent role of the Commission under the E.E.C. Treaty than of the commission acting as the High Authority of E.C.S.C. is illustrated by a comparison between Article 33 of the E.C.S.C. Treaty and Article 169 of the Rome Treaty. The former places the onus on states or industrial enterprises or associations to challenge the validity of decisions of the Commission acting as the High Authority before the Court of the Communities, while the latter makes the Court an essential instrument in the enforcement of opinions of the Commission that a state has failed to fulfil its obligations under the Treaty.

In addition to the greater restrictions upon action by individual organs of the Community, and the necessity of unanimity amongst the members of the "six" before each succeeding stage of the Community's development is entered, the E.E.C. also differs substantially from E.C.S.C. in that the E.E.C. Treaty is drafted in more general terms. Because its progress is not defined so carefully by the Rome Treaty, E.E.C. remains on the one hand a more flexible institution, but on the other its policies are more open to disruption by disagreements among its members. The adoption of a common agricultural policy nearly caused a split between France and the other members, particularly Germany, and a number of problems (notably in relation to transport, social security and movement of goods) have only been tackled in a very limited way. It is undoubtedly true that the prosperity of the members of the Community has increased, but this prosperity may have been achieved partly at the expense of states outside the Community. The contribution of the E.E.C. to the general economic welfare of Europe has yet to be demonstrated, and a positive contribution may only be possible if membership of the Community is substantially enlarged.

iii *European Atomic Energy Community (EURATOM)*—The third of the Communities, EURATOM, is in all respects the smallest. It has a limited field of operation, and this field is even more restricted by the fact that individual member states have continued with their own efforts at nuclear power in addition to their contributions to EURATOM. Thus, the emphasis in the work of EURATOM has been not on the creation of "conditions necessary for the speedy establishment and growth of nuclear industries" (as stated in Article 1 of the EURATOM Treaty), but in the more general activities provided for in Article 2—the development of research, dissemination of information, establishment of safety standards, co-operation with other states and international organisations, etc. Also on a smaller scale were the institutions of EURATOM. Until the fusion of the executives of the three Communities of 1967, the Commission of EURATOM had only five members, instead of the nine members of the E.E.C. Commission. The eventual fusion of the three Communities, towards which the creation of joint institutions was a first major step, may give impetus to a joint fuel policy among the members of the Communities in which atomic energy will play a significant role.

c THE EUROPEAN FREE TRADE ASSOCIATION (E.F.T.A.)

At the time the E.E.C. was created, the United Kingdom attempted to bring about a free trade area among all O.E.E.C. members, with the E.E.C. representing the "six". Although the British suggestion found favour with states which were not involved in the creation of the E.E.C., the "six" were not prepared to involve their own Common Market with its plan for a common external tariff in a free trade area with no external tariff policy. The fears of the dangers arising from absence of a common external tariff were increased by the knowledge that Britain was anxious to retain all the advantages of its preference trade with the Commonwealth.

Although the members of E.E.C. were not interested in a free trade area, Britain did obtain sufficient support from six other European states outside the Community to bring about the creation of E.F.T.A. As E.F.T.A. is primarily concerned with a general reduction of tariffs amongst its members, in which it has achieved a considerable measure of success, it has only a limited organisational structure—a Council on which each state is represented and which takes most of its decisions by unanimous agreement, and a number of committees.

E.F.T.A. plays a relatively minor role in the trade even of its members, most of which trade principally with the members of E.E.C. or, in the case of the United Kingdom, with states outside Europe altogether. Its relative unimportance to the United Kingdom may be illustrated by the action of the British Government in October, 1964, in imposing a fifteen per cent surcharge on import duties without consulting its E.F.T.A. partners.

d COUNCIL FOR MUTUAL ECONOMIC ASSISTANCE (COMECON)

Regional organisations have undoubtedly reached a more advanced stage of development among the states of Western Europe where a greater degree of "community spirit" has emerged from the destruction of two world wars. On the other side of the "iron curtain", the Soviet Union and its satellites created an informal Council for Mutual Economic Assistance in 1949 as a propaganda counterpart to O.E.E.C. and the Marshall Plan. For most of the first decade of its existence, COMECON was of little significance, but following the Hungarian uprising in 1956, COMECON came to be used as a vehicle for the integration of the economies of the east European states. In 1959 COMECON was given its own Charter which came into force in 1960. Under this Charter the Consultative Body of Representatives has the power "with the concurrence of those member countries of the Council concerned" to make recommendations on any question of economic or scientific and technical co-operation (Art. 4). Among the functions of the Council enumerated under Article 3 is included the preparation of recommendations regarding the most important questions of economic relations resulting from the respective plans for the development of the national economy of the member countries of the Council with a view to co-ordinating these plans. In its work the Council is dependent upon the activities of a large number of Permanent Commissions, comprising officials and experts. Most of the Commissions are involved in one sector of the economy only —one with coal, another with electricity, a third with transport, and so on, but there is also an Economic Commission, the task of which is to work out the overall economic issues of co-operation and integration.

2 HUMAN RIGHTS

It will be recalled that Article 55 of the Charter requires the U.N. to promote "universal respect for, and observance of, human rights and fundamental freedoms". After the First World War, there had been a variety of "minority provisions" designed to safeguard human rights in the Peace Treaties, and the Upper Silesian Convention had even established an arbitral tribunal with the right of individual access. The German seizure of large areas of central Europe had put an end to the working of the various treaty provisions, but the widespread Nazi persecutions of the period from 1933–45 gave impetus to a new move to establish respect for human rights as a corner stone of the post-war world. While there was some measure of agreement that the Charter of the U.N. should state amongst its aims the promotion of human rights, express references to the safeguarding of such rights were either of a general nature (as under Art. 55 and 56), or ancillary to other purposes (as under Art. 73 and 76 relating to the inhabitants of non-self-governing and trusteeship territories). The legal effect of the Charter upon human rights is therefore limited, although as a basis for political action and future legal development the Charter is undoubtedly of the greatest significance.

A. The United Nations

a THE GENERAL ASSEMBLY

The General Assembly has a general power to discuss any questions or any matter within the scope of the present Charter or relating to the powers and functions of any organs provided for in the present Charter, and may make recommendations to Members of the Organisation on any such questions or matters (Art. 10), a power which is framed so widely as to include questions or matters relating to human rights. More specifically, Article 13 (1) (b) lays down that the Assembly shall initiate studies and make recommendations for the purpose of promoting international co-operation in the economic, social, cultural, educational, and health fields, and assisting in the realisation of human rights and fundamental freedoms for all without distinction as to race, sex, language, or religion.

In this context, perhaps the Assembly's most notable contribution to the concept of human rights was the Universal Declaration of Human Rights of December, 1948. While in no sense imposing legal obligations upon members of the U.N., the terms of the Declaration do represent, in its own words, "a common standard of achievement for all peoples and all nations, to the end that every individual and every organ of society, keeping this declaration constantly in mind, shall strive by teaching and education to promote respect for these rights and freedoms and by progressive measures, national and international, to secure their universal and effective recognition and observance, both among the peoples of member states themselves and among the peoples of territories under their jurisdiction."

b THE ECONOMIC AND SOCIAL COUNCIL

The process of implementing the U.N.'s obligations under the Charter in the field of human rights and fundamental freedoms is primarily the task of ECOSOC and of its Commission on Human Rights. In addition to drafting the Universal Declaration, the Commission has also drawn up a number of conventions designed to put into practice the ideals of the Declaration, although until recently these conventions have never progressed beyond the draft stage. In December, 1966, however, two Covenants (one dealing with Economic, Social and Cultural Rights, the other with Civil and Political Rights) were opened for signature by the United Nations.[8]

c THE TRUSTEESHIP COUNCIL

The Trusteeship Council, under the authority of the General Assembly, has the task of supervising the carrying out of the objectives laid down in

---

8. For the texts, see 6 I.L.M. 360, 368.

Article 76 of the Charter, including the encouragement of respect for human rights and for fundamental freedoms. In relation to Trusteeship territories, Article 87 states that the General Assembly and under its authority, the Trusteeship Council, in carrying out their functions may, *inter alia*, consider reports submitted by the administering authority, accept petitions and examine them in consultation with the administering authority, and arrange periodic visits to the territories concerned. In relation to non-self-governing states, Article 73 of the Charter sets out a general declaration of principle that "the interests of the inhabitants of these territories are paramount" and under this Article Members of the U.N. also "accept as a sacred trust the obligation to promote to the utmost . . . the well being of the inhabitants of these territories". Although it is doubtful whether Article 73 imposes any sort of legal obligation upon states responsible for the administration of non-self-governing territories, it has nevertheless been taken as a political justification for strong diplomatic pressure within the United Nations for the speedy granting of independence to these territories. The General Assembly, because of the importance many of the newer states placed upon "decolonialisation", has established a separate committee to give effect to the Assembly's Declaration on the Granting of Independence to Colonial Countries and Peoples of 1960.

B. European developments under the Council of Europe

Article 1 (a) of the Statute of the Council of Europe states the aim of the Council to be the achievement of "a greater unity between its Members for the purpose of safeguarding and realising the ideals and principles which are their common heritage and facilitating their economic and social progress". The Council is clearly, therefore, an organisation concerned with realising a greater degree of unity amongst its members. However, its powers are limited. The Committee of Ministers can only make recommendations to member governments, while the Consultative Assembly, comprising representatives elected by national Parliaments, can only deliberate, resolve and recommend. Only in the case of recommendations is there any legal effect and this is limited to a requirement that the Committee of Ministers should consider them and decide what action, if any, to take on them.

Article 1 (b) of the Statute also provides that the aim of the Council shall be pursued, *inter alia*, "by agreements and common action in economic, social, cultural, scientific, legal, and administrative matters, and in the maintenance and further realisation of human rights and fundamental freedoms". The Council has taken the initiative in drafting a number of agreements (there were well over thirty by the end of 1965) for bringing about a standardisation and mutual application of social security schemes, professional and university qualifications, patents, etc.

The mention of human rights in Article 1 is reinforced by the provisions of Article 3 which lays down that every member of the Council "must accept the principles of the rule of law and of the enjoyment by all persons within its jurisdiction of human rights and fundamental freedoms". This emphasis is borne out by the attention paid to human rights by the Council in drafting and supplementing the Convention for the Protection of Human Rights and Fundamental Freedoms of 1950.

a THE EUROPEAN CONVENTION ON HUMAN RIGHTS

The Convention states in Article 1 that the parties "shall secure to *everyone* within their jurisdiction" the rights and freedoms set out in the Convention. Section 1 (Arts. 2–18) sets out and defines the rights and freedoms—the right to life; prohibition of torture or degrading treatment or punishment; prohibition of slavery; the right to liberty; the right to a fair hearing; prohibition against retroactive penal legislation; the right to respect for family life; freedom of thought and religion, of expression, and so on. A number of exceptions are stated, notably in Article 15 which allows derogation from the obligations of the Convention, "in time of war or other public emergency threatening the life of the nation" but only "to the extent strictly required by the exigencies of the situation".

i *The European Commission of Human Rights*

Not only did the Convention impose obligations upon states party to it, but it also created a system for enforcing breaches of the Convention. The Commission, which comprises the number of members equal to the number of parties to the Convention, no two members being of the same nationality (Art. 20), has jurisdiction to consider:

(a) any alleged breach of the Convention by a party to the Convention referred to the Commission by any other party (Art. 24); and

(b) petitions "from any person, non-governmental organisation or group of individuals claiming to be the victim of a violation by one of the High Contracting Parties of the rights set forth in this Convention, provided that the High Contracting Party against which the complaint has been lodged has declared that it recognises the competence of the Commission to receive such petitions" (Art. 25),

provided that all domestic remedies have been exhausted, and that the matter has been referred to the Commission within six months of the date on which the final decision was taken (Art. 26). In addition to the restriction contained in Article 26, the Commission must not deal with any petition that is anonymous, or is based upon a matter that has already been considered by the Commission or has already been submitted to another procedure of international investigation (Art. 27).

In the event of the Commission accepting a petition as admissible, it shall by means of a sub-commission of seven members, including one member appointed by each of the parties (Art. 29):

(a) "with a view to ascertaining the facts, undertake together with the representatives of the parties an examination of the petition and, if need be, an investigation, for the effective conduct of which the states concerned shall furnish all necessary facilities";

(b) "place itself at the disposal of the parties concerned with a view to securing a friendly settlement of the matter on the basis of respect for Human Rights as defined in this Convention" (Art. 28).

If the Commission succeeds in effecting a friendly settlement, it shall draw up a report to be sent to the states concerned, to the Committee of Ministers and to the Secretary-General of the Council of Europe for publication (Art. 30). If a solution is not reached, the Commission is required to report to the Committee of Ministers, stating its opinion as to whether the facts disclose a breach of the Convention by the state concerned and make such proposals to the Committee as it thinks fit (Art. 31). Under Article 32, if the matter is not referred to the Court of Human Rights within three months of the transmission of the report to the Committee of Ministers, the Committee can itself decide by a two-thirds majority whether there has been a violation of the Convention. If it does so decide, the Committee shall prescribe a period during which the state concerned must take the measures required by the Committee's decision. If the state does not comply with the decision, the Committee, again by a two-thirds majority, shall decide "what effect shall be given to its original decision and shall publish the Report." The last paragraph of Article 32 states that parties to the Convention undertake to regard as binding on them any decision which the Committee of Ministers may take under the preceding paragraphs.

ii The European Court of Human Rights

The judges on the Court are equal in number to the members of the Council of Europe and it is also provided that no two judges shall be of the same nationality (Art. 38). For the consideration of each case, the Court shall consist of a chamber of seven judges, including as an *ex officio* member the judge who is a national of any state concerned in the action, or, if there is no such judge, a person of its choice who shall sit in the capacity of judge (Art. 43).

The jurisdiction of the Court shall extend to all cases concerning the interpretation and application of the Convention which the parties to the Convention or the Commission shall refer to it (Art. 48) provided:

(a) that the parties have declared that they recognise as compulsory the jurisdiction of the Court (Art. 46); and

(b) that if the case is referred to the Court by a party to the Convention, that party must be either the state the national of which is alleged to be the victim, or the state which referred the case to the Commission, or the state against which the complaint has been lodged (Art. 48).

But, in any event, the Court may only deal with a case after the Commission has acknowledged the failure of efforts for a friendly settlement, and within three months of the Commission's report to the Committee of Ministers (Art. 47).

Once a case is before the Court, the Court has the power to "afford just satisfaction to the injured party" (Art. 50). The Court's decision is final (Art. 52), and the parties to the Convention undertake to abide by the decision of the Court in any case to which they are parties (Art. 53). It is for the Committee of Ministers of the Council of Europe to supervise the carrying out of the Court's decision (Art. 54).

b THE WORKING OF THE CONVENTION

Although it is possible for one state to refer to the Commission an alleged breach of the Convention by another state (perhaps the best known illustration of this occurring was in the complaint by Greece of the action of the British authorities and troops in Cyprus prior to the Cyprus settlement of 1960 when the complaint was dropped), by far the majority of complaints are those made by individual petition under Article 25. Applications by one state against another are referred immediately to the state which is alleged to have broken its obligations under the Convention, but individual applications are so voluminous that each complaint is first considered by a group of three members of the Commission whose task it is to disallow at the initial stage petitions that appear obviously vexatious or unfounded. If the group is unanimous in favour of admissibility, the matter is submitted to the Government of the state concerned for its observations. If the group is not unanimously in favour of admitting the claim, the report is considered by the Commission as a whole. In cases of doubt, the Commission may hold a preliminary enquiry, even involving an oral hearing, before pronouncing upon the admissibility of the claim.

Whether the complainant is a state or an individual, it is the task of the Commission to act as a conciliator (for this reason its deliberations, unlike those of the Court, are held in camera). Only if its efforts prove unsuccessful is it required to submit a report which may involve a finding that there has been a breach of the Convention. Should the matter then go before the Court, it can only do so (providing of course the state or states concerned have accepted the Court's jurisdiction) at the instance of a state concerned or of the Commission. The "victim" has no right of access to the Court. It has proved a difficult question as to how the "victim" can be the subject of proceedings to which he is not a party. If his claim is submitted by the state of which he is a national, at least he can be "represented" by his own state, but what if he is a national of the "defendant" state, or even of a state not a party to the Convention at all?

The solution which most obviously presents itself is that the Commission should present the claim on the victim's behalf. To an extent the Commission is inevitably placed in the position of having to present the case to the Court, but it has so far resisted the pressure that it should in any sense "represent" the individual alleging that he has suffered as a result of a breach of the Convention. In the words of one writer, the Commission "has taken the view that it does not appear as *advocate* for the individual, for so to do would be detrimental to the objectivity and impartiality which it must retain if, in the earlier stages when the matter is before the Commission, it is to be able to act as conciliator in trying to effect an amicable settlement": the role of the Commission, therefore, is "that of an *amicus curiae* more than a 'party' ".[9]

But even if, in the course of "assisting" the Court (to use the expression adopted in the Commission's own rules of procedure), the Commission is, and sees itself as, the means whereby the claim is presented to the Court, without actually "presenting" the case on behalf of the claimant, it cannot redress the balance arising from the fact that the defendant state has the right to be heard by the Court. The most the Commission has felt itself able to accomplish is to allow the individual concerned to submit written observations on the substance of its report, a practice which, as it enables the individual indirectly to present legal arguments to the Court, goes beyond his position as a potential witness as to facts. In the *Lawless* case,[10] the defendant state, the Irish Republic, raised a number of preliminary objections to the procedure adopted by the Commission in obtaining the observations of the claimant, Lawless. The Court rejected the Irish contentions, pointing out that it had to "bear in mind its duty to safeguard the interests of the individual, who may not be a party to any court proceedings." It was, therefore, "in the interests of the proper administration of justice that the Court should have knowledge of and, if need be, take into consideration, the applicant's point of view."[11] Accordingly, in the proceedings on the merits of the dispute,[12] the Commission was careful to present to the Court not only its own view of the law but also the view of the law held by the applicant where that view differed from the view of the Commission.

c THE SIGNIFICANCE OF THE EUROPEAN CONVENTION

While the Convention has undoubtedly contributed to the adoption of a number of statements of human rights in the constitutions of newly emergent states, its impact is still uncertain. In Europe itself the effect of the Convention is greatest in those states where under their constitutional law treaties are part of municipal law. However, even in those states, the significance of the Convention should not be over-rated. The Convention is the common denominator of the extent to which a number of "like-minded" states could agree on certain basic human rights. To a large extent the Convention reproduces the rights which the contracting states believe are already accepted within their own municipal law. As the local remedies rule requires that an individual alleging a breach of the Con-

---

9.   Bowett, *op. cit.*, p. 245.   10.   (1960) 31 I.L.R. 276.
11.   *Ibid.*, at p. 289.   12.   *Ibid.*, at p. 290.

vention should first seek redress in the courts of the state concerned, the field in which a successful complaint can be made to the Commission is restricted to a limited number of situations where the Commission's view of the Convention differs from the interpretation put upon it by the state. Examples of blatant breaches of the Convention will be rare. Accordingly, it is hardly a matter of surprise that approximately ninety-five of every hundred petitions received by the Commission are dismissed at the first investigation, and of the remainder only a handful have ever reached the Court of Human Rights though the Convention was signed as long ago as 1950. Of the remaining cases, it is probably true to say that, as breaches of the Convention will largely arise through differences of interpretation or inadvertence, adverse comment of the defendant state by the Commission will normally result in some arrangement being reached between the parties. It is in this area that the operation of the enforcement provisions of the Convention have their most beneficial effects.

CHAPTER FIFTEEN

INTERNATIONAL ORGANISATIONS— IV
THE PLACE OF LAW IN INTERNATIONAL ORGANISATIONS

This final chapter on international organisations is designed to serve a dual role. It will cover several topics not dealt with hitherto, but it will also bring together the threads of earlier chapters in an attempt to estimate the part played by legal principles in the working of international institutions.

The role of law within an organisation will vary enormously both with the type of organisation and with the aspects of the work or structure of the organisation being dealt with. To take an obvious illustration of the first circumstance, in tightly drawn constitutions like the treaties which created the European Communities, the powers of the various organs of the institution are carefully defined, and, in the case of the Communities, the task of interpreting their constitutional texts is placed in the hands of a judicial body—the Court of the Communities. By way of contrast, the powers of the various organs of the U.N. often overlap; they are in few cases clearly defined, and nowhere is provision made for the submission of disputes over the Charter to judicial determination. While submission in the case of disputes over the Community treaties is the norm, submission of similar disputes in the case of the U.N., whether to the International Court for an advisory opinion, or to some other specially created judicial body, is the exception. And as far as variations between different aspects of the working of the same institution are concerned, one has only to look at the contrast that exists between the infrequent involvement of the International Court in the interpretation of the U.N. Charter, and the important part played by the U.N. Administrative Tribunal in relations between the Organisation and individual members of the Secretariat.

I CONSTITUTIONAL INTERPRETATION IN GENERAL

Despite the fact that judicial determination is resorted to infrequently by the various organs of the U.N., it does not follow that legal principles have no part to play in the day-to-day operations of the Organisation,

Even in the most acrimonious debates in its political organs, reference to legal considerations (the wording of the Charter, the previous practice of the organ concerned, etc.) is usually in evidence. As has already been discussed in an earlier chapter,[1] the principal difference between a political organ and a judicial body when called upon to consider a disputed constitutional text is that the approach of the former is likely to be more flexible.

In that chapter, a number of illustrations were given—the Security Council's adaptation of Article 27 (3) of the Charter to prevent abstentions by a permanent member having the effect of "vetoing" resolutions of a non-procedural nature;[2] the straightforward interpretative approach of the International Court in its advisory opinion in the *Competence of the General Assembly* case, dealing with Article 4 (2) of the Charter;[3] and the different attitudes to the relationship between the I.L.O. and the League of Nations as far as membership was concerned,[4] etc. However, one further example is worth considering, the *Constitution of I.M.C.O.* case,[5] because it does demonstrate how divergent the approaches of a political organ and a judicial body might be in a particular case.

Under the I.M.C.O. constitution, provision was made (Art. 28 (a)) for the election by the Assembly of the Organisation of a Maritime Safety Committee of fourteen members, being "Governments of those nations having an important interest in maritime safety, of which not less than eight shall be the largest ship-owning nations". The eight members elected under this part of Article 28 (a) were from the ten leading shipping nations according to the registered gross tonnage given in *Lloyd's Register of Shipping* for 1958; the two states omitted being Liberia, which had the third largest amount of shipping registered, and Panama the eighth largest. There were extra-legal reasons why a majority of members (almost all of them being traditional maritime states like the United Kingdom, Norway and the Netherlands) were not prepared to support the candidature of states operating "flags of convenience". While the traditional maritime states allowed registration primarily or even exclusively on the basis of national ownership, states like Liberia and Panama attracted the registration of large amounts of "non-national" shipping. The hostility towards these states was, therefore, principally economic in origin. Registration and other costs being lower, ships operating under flags of convenience were able to compete on most favourable terms with the shipping fleets of the traditional maritime states.

Of course, political discrimination could not in itself justify the operation of the election procedures in this way: there would also have to be some legal justification for the course adopted. According to the United Kingdom, Liberia and Panama were not entitled to automatic inclusion upon the Maritime Safety Committee because the use of the word "elected" gave the Assembly a freedom of choice over which states were

---

1. Chapter 9, pp. 378–379.   2. Above, p. 379.   3. Above, pp. 374–375.
4. Above, p. 379.   5. I.C.J. Rep. 1960, p. 150.

to be represented on the Committee. The only limitations upon the choice were that all fourteen states to be elected should have an "important interest in maritime safety", and that the first eight should qualify under the uncertain test of being "the largest ship-owning nations". The reason why this test was uncertain, the United Kingdom pointed out, was that it could not be interpreted literally. Communist states apart, few states "owned" the vessels operating under the national flag. Nor did it necessarily mean registered tonnage because in states like Liberia and Panama the majority of ships were owned by foreign nationals. The Assembly had, therefore, been justified in voting upon each candidate in the order of the *Lloyd's Register of Registered Gross Tonnage*, but was not bound automatically to appoint the eight states having the largest registered tonnage.

Had there been a sufficient majority of opinion within I.M.C.O. favouring the rejection of Liberia and Panama as members of the Safety Committee, no doubt the United Kingdom view would have prevailed. The voting on Liberia's candidature was 11 in favour, 14 against, with three abstentions. In other words, the United Kingdom had the positive support of only half the members of the Organisation. In addition, the United States, by far the most important maritime state whatever criteria were adopted, supported the Liberian cause. With the members so evenly divided on the issue, a compromise was reached whereby the U.N. General Assembly was asked to request an advisory opinion from the International Court on whether the Maritime Safety Committee elected in accordance with the United Kingdom's interpretation of Article 28 (a) was in fact validly constituted.

The Court, by a large majority, held that the election had not conformed with Article 28 (a). Despite the use of the term "elected", it was clear that the I.M.C.O. Assembly had no discretion in appointing the eight because the constitution clearly stated that "not less than eight *shall be* the largest ship-owning nations". And the expression "largest ship-owning nations" could only refer to registered tonnage because there was no practicable alternative test (indeed use had been made of the *Lloyd's Register* in connection with other provisions of the constitution such as the assessment of contributions to the I.M.C.O. budget). There certainly was no reason for rejecting registered tonnage as the criterion because of a lack of a "genuine link" between ships flying "flags of convenience" and the state in which such vessels were registered.

There is one important lesson to be learnt from this case. The decision of the Court in favour of the Liberian view was to render the opposing interpretation invalid. In an earlier advisory opinion the Court had emphasised that the "political character of an organ cannot release it from the observance of treaty provisions established by the Charter when they constitute limitations on its powers or criteria for its judgment", and that to "ascertain whether an organ has freedom of choice for its decisions reference must be made to the terms of its constitution."[6] However, if

---

6. I.C.J. Rep. 1948, at p. 64.

the Court had not been consulted, if a majority of the I.M.C.O. Assembly had accepted the validity of the election, the election would in no sense have been "invalid". Like most organs within an international institution, the I.M.C.O. Assembly is entitled to act as the final arbiter in the interpretation of its own powers. The misuse of its power by the Assembly (for example, if it were to disregard entirely the limitations of its constitution to the detriment of minority interests) might lead to the break up of the Organisation. The continued existence of any organisation will depend upon the good faith of the majority in abiding by a reasonable interpretation of the constitution.

2 THE CONSTITUTIONAL FRAMEWORK OF THE UNITED NATIONS SECRETARIAT: AN INTERNATIONAL CIVIL SERVICE

The public service of a state requires certain standards of integrity and loyalty in the national interest. To a large extent, the fact that those employed are usually nationals of the state concerned will ensure the necessary loyalty. Obviously enough, the task of creating an international civil service in which the loyalty of the officials is not divided between the organisation they serve and the state of which they are nationals is a formidable challenge.

a APPOINTMENT OF STAFF

It will be recalled that the attempt to have Deputy Secretaries-General chosen by the same process as the Secretary-General was resisted by the smaller powers. As a consequence, all staff are appointed by the Secretary-General under regulations established by the General-Assembly (Art. 101 (1) of the U.N. Charter). These regulations provide, *inter alia*, that the "paramount consideration in the appointment, transfer or promotion of the staff shall be the necessity for securing the highest standards of efficiency, competence and integrity", and that due regard "shall be paid to the importance of recruiting the staff on as wide a geographical basis as possible" (Reg. 4. 2).

There still remains a difference between Under-Secretaries and other members of the Secretariat. In the past, the heads of the more important departments have by understanding been nationals of the permanent members of the Security Council.[7] Today, there are about twenty-five

---

7. This is very much a simplification. The General Assembly in Res. 13 (I) of 13th February, 1946, approved the Preparatory Commission's plan for a secretariat divided into eight units, each headed by an Assistant Secretary-General. A Russian became head of the Political Department; an American head of Administrative and Financial services; a Briton was appointed to the Economic Department; a Frenchman to the Department of Social Affairs; and a Chinese to the Trusteeship Department. Dissatisfaction with the working of the organisational structure led Trygve Lie to plan changes, but these were not implemented before Hammerskjold became Secretary-General. Hammerskjold carried out a reorganisation of his own. All senior posts became Under-Secretaries, and the structure of the departments was changed: see Bailey, *The Secretariat of the United Nations*, esp. pp. 68-76.

Under-Secretaries and the problem of specific nationality has assumed less political significance. Their period of appointment is set at five years (though it is subject to prolongation or renewal) (Reg. 4. 5 (a)). The same regulation divides other personnel into those on permanent and those on temporary appointments. It is this nucleus of permanent officials which sets the standard of an international civil service.

This standard is partly psychological; a sense of being servants of an international organisation first and foremost. Even though the United Nations has only been in existence for a quarter of a century, it is possible to regard this sense as being a tradition, a tradition created by, and inherited from, the League of Nations. As a distinguished commentator wrote in 1943, basing his analysis on the experience of the League, the "international outlook required of the international civil servant is an awareness made instinctive by habit of the needs, emotions and prejudices of the people of differently-circumstanced countries, as they are felt and expressed by the peoples concerned, accompanied by a capacity of weighing these . . . elements in a judicial manner before reaching any decision to which they are relevant".[8] In the words of Staff Regulation 1. 1, members of the Secretariat "are international civil servants. Their responsibilities are not national but exclusively international. By accepting appointment, they pledge themselves to discharge their functions and to regulate their conduct with the interests of the United Nations only in view."

b PROTECTION FROM EXTERNAL INTERFERENCE

In order to secure and safeguard the international outlook and loyalties of the Secretariat, it is important that individual members should be protected from outside interference. Article 100 of the Charter provides the basis of this protection by imposing an obligation on members of the Secretariat (including the Secretary-General) that they "shall not receive instructions from any government or from any other authority external to the Organisation", and an obligation on member states "to respect the exclusively international character of the responsibilities of the Secretary-General and the staff and not to seek to influence them in the discharge of their responsibilities". However, this provision is only a basis; the legal protection of the Secretariat has been assured by a number of developments.

i *Diplomatic protection*

If a person is injured while on the territory of a foreign state, should all else fail in his attempt to obtain redress, he can seek the diplomatic protection of the state of which he is a national. Similarly, for a member of the staff of an international organisation, it is a necessary attribute of his primary allegiance to that organisation that, in the last resort, he should be able to seek the protection of the organisation he serves rather than of the state of which he is a national.

---

8. Jenks, in *Public Administration Review*, No. 2, 1943, p. 95.

Although this proposition was clearly a desirable development, there was the practical difficulty to be overcome that the constitutions of international organisations did not make express provision for the making of claims against states on the international plane. This issue was raised in a critical form following the assassination in 1948 of Count Bernadotte, the U.N. mediator in Palestine, and of his French aide, Colonel Sérot. The incident led to the submission to the International Court of a request for an advisory opinion[9] on two questions:

"I In the event of an agent of the United Nations in the performance of his duties suffering injury in circumstances involving the responsibility of a state, has the United Nations, as the Organisation, the capacity to bring an international claim against the responsible *de jure* or *de facto* government with a view to obtaining the reparation due in respect of the damage caused (a) to the United Nations, (b) to the victim or to persons entitled through him?

"II In the event of an affirmative reply on point 1 (b), how is action by the United Nations to be reconciled with such rights as may be possessed by the state of which the victim is a national?"

The significance of the Court's replies to these questions in the context of the international personality of the United Nations has already been considered.[10] It is sufficient to recall that the Court reached the conclusion that the Organisation was "a subject of international law and capable of possessing international rights and duties" including the "capacity to maintain its rights by bringing international claims." Nor could it be doubted that the Organisation had the capacity to bring a claim against a state which had broken obligations that it owed to the Organisation. Under this heading it was possible to envisage claims being made for the loss of the services of a valuable servant and for the cost of replacing him, or for the amount spent by the Organisation in pension payment or medical bills.

But how was it possible to justify a claim by the United Nations presented on behalf of the victim in respect of his own injuries, or on behalf of his dependants? The Court demonstrated that the nationality of claims rule, which in any case did not always apply strictly to claims brought by states, was based upon the theory of a breach of an international obligation owed to the national state. This was "precisely what happens when the Organisation, in bringing a claim for damage suffered by its agent, does so by invoking the breach of an obligation towards itself." The obligation arose from the purposes and functions of the Organisation which often found it "necessary to entrust its agents with important missions to be performed in disturbed parts of the world. . . . In order that the agent may perform his duties satisfactorily he must feel that this protection is assured to him by the Organisation. . . . To ensure the independence of the agent, and, consequently, the independent action of the Organisation itself, it is essential that in performing his duties he need not have to rely on any other protection than that of the Organisation. . . . In particular, he should not have to rely on the protection of his

---

9.   *Reparations* case, I.C.J. Rep. 1949, p. 174.   10.   Above, pp. 86–87.

own state. If he had to rely on that state, his independence might well be comprised, contrary to the principle applied by Article 100 of the Charter."[11]

While the Court was willing to imply a power for the U.N. to present claims on behalf of an agent's dependents, and saw no theoretical obstacle in the nationality of claims rule, it was unable to offer any satisfactory means of resolving the practical difficulty that could arise if the national state also pressed claims on behalf of the victim or his family. This competition could not result in the state responsible for the injury being liable for the same damages twice over. The remedy was for a general convention to be adopted to reduce or eliminate the risk of competition between the Organisation and the national state, or for agreements to be reached with the national state to meet the needs of the particular case.

One final query that was raised concerned the situation where the injured agent was a national of the state alleged to be responsible. The Court believed that this consideration presented no problem. "The ordinary practice whereby a state does not exercise protection on behalf of its nationals against a state which regards him as its own national does not constitute a precedent which is relevant here. The action of the Organisation is in fact based not upon the nationality of the victim but upon his status as agent of the Organisation. Therefore, it does not matter whether or not the state to which the claim is addressed regards him as its own national, because the question of nationality is not pertinent to the admissibility of the claim."[12]

ii *Pressure from the host state*

Whatever organisation is concerned, relations between the organisation and its staff on the one hand and the state in which the permanent seat of the organisation is established on the other are bound to be of importance to the proper functioning of the organisation. And in no case are relations of more fundamental importance than in the case of the United Nations which has its permanent headquarters in New York. While it is difficult to estimate the extent to which an organisation is affected or influenced by the environment of its headquarters, it can safely be stated that the United Nations in New York is a different body from what it would have been if it had made its home, for example, at the seat of the former League of Nations in Geneva.

While headquarters' agreements between organisation and host state do provide elaborate codes of immunities and privileges for staff of the organisation,[13] these undertakings in themselves are not sufficient to eradicate all means whereby the host state might exert pressure on the organisation or its staff. Despite the existence of the 1947 agreement between the United Nations and the United States, events in the early 1950s brought the Secretary-General and the U.S. Government into con-

---

11. I.C.J. Rep. 1949, at p. 183.　　　12.　*Ibid.*, at p. 186.
13. For details, see above, pp. 210–212.

flict with regard to the degree of control the host state could exercise over the political affiliations of its nationals serving in the Secretariat.

Following the break down in relations between the Soviet Union and its former western allies particularly after 1948, the climate of political opinion in the United States become violently anti-communist. Allegations of subversion were made, first against members of the Federal public service, and then attention was turned to a number of U.S. nationals working for the U.N. Among official agencies engaged in an investigation of these allegations was a Federal Grand Jury. Several members of the U.N. staff, subpoenaed to appear, had refused to testify, claiming the benefit of the amendment to the U.S. Constitution providing exemption from giving evidence that might lead to self-incrimination.

Strong pressure was exerted on the Secretary-General against the continued employment in the Organisation of U.S. nationals who were alleged to be disloyal to the United States. The Secretary-General sought the advice of a Commission of Jurists. Their report,[14] while stressing the "independence" and the "sole responsibility to the General Assembly" of the Secretary-General "for the selection and retention of staff", added a second consideration which they considered as of equally paramount importance, i.e. that in "exercising his responsibility . . . the Secretary-General should . . . refrain from engaging or . . . remove from the staff any person whom he has reasonable grounds for believing to be engaged or to have been engaged, or to be likely to be engaged in, any subversive activities against the host state." The correct procedure, the Commission advised, in cases where there had been a refusal to testify was to dismiss the individual staff member concerned, because invocation of the right to refuse to testify could only be justified if the testimony should it be given would reveal that the individual had engaged in conduct subversive of the interests of the United States.

The decision of the Secretary-General to suspend the officials concerned demonstrates the susceptibility of an organisation to pressures from the host state if those pressures are exerted with determination. The Commission itself referred to the need for "tact and discretion on the part of both the international body and its staff on the one hand, and the 'host country' on the other, if conflict is to be avoided and the international body is to be able to perform its proper functions." It is now generally regarded, as was argued by a number of member states at the time, that the American actions constituted an improper interference with the Organisation. However, in the face of the refusal of the U.S. Government to issue passports to certain of its nationals to travel abroad on behalf of the U.N., and of cases of obstruction of access to U.N. premises, the Secretary-General was placed in an invidious position. By dismissing the staff concerned he was at least trying to restore a sufficiently harmonious relationship with the host state to enable more normal functioning of the Organisation as a whole.

---

14. Reproduced in (1953) 47 A.J.I.L. (docs. section) 97.

iii *Relations between the Secretary-General and members of the staff of the Secretariat*

The decision of the Secretary-General to dismiss the various U.S. nationals against which allegations of subversion had been made brought into prominence another potential source of danger to the status of the international civil servant and to the morale of the service in which he is employed. Individuals of the required calibre are not going to leave their home state to work for an international organisation unless their employment is guaranteed against arbitrary dismissal, even if the reason given is the interests of the organisation concerned. Protection from unfair treatment at the hands of the Secretary-General is indirectly also protection from the external pressures that might be exerted against officials of the Organisation by member states.

Following the example of the League of Nations, the permanent administrative tribunal of which was reconstituted as the I.L.O. Administrative Tribunal, the U.N. created its own administrative tribunal in 1949. Comprising seven members of different nationalities elected by the General Assembly, the U.N. Administrative Tribunal is "competent to hear and pass judgment upon applications alleging non-observance of contracts of employment of staff members of the Secretariat of the United Nations or of the terms of appointment of such staff members." Article 2 (1) of the Tribunal's Statute then goes on to interpret "contracts" and "terms of appointment" as including "all pertinent regulations and rules in force at the time of the alleged non-observance".

The degree of protection which the Tribunal can provide to staff members is limited by the fact that the Tribunal's jurisdiction is limited. For example, it is not open to the Tribunal to call in question the exercise of administrative discretion, unless there has been a misuse of power. This residual control is based upon the *détournement de pouvoir* of French administrative law. It can be said that there has been such a *détournement* "if an administrative power or discretion has been exercised for some object other than that for which power or discretion was conferred".[15]

In a number of the cases heard by the Tribunal arising out of the conflict of 1952–3 between the U.S. Government and the Secretary-General, the argument was raised by the applicants that the Secretary-General had been prompted by the desire to placate the government of a member state exerting pressure on him in a manner contrary to Article 100 (2) of the Charter. The approach adopted by the Tribunal may be illustrated by two cases involving personnel on "temporary-indefinite" contracts of service. Under the Staff Regulations (Reg. 9. 1 (c)), the Secretary-General had a wide discretion to terminate these appointments "if, in his opinion, such action would be in the interest of the United Nations."

In the case of *Kaplan*[16], all the applicant could claim was that he had showed "outstanding professional ability" and that, after adverse com-

---

15. Brown and Garner, *French Administrative Law*, p. 123.
16. (1953) 20 I.L.R. 506.

ments had been made about him by the State Department for refusing to testify before the Grand Jury, he had been dismissed. The Tribunal held that, the Secretary-General being vested with this discretion to terminate if such action would be in the interests of the United Nations, it was not for the Tribunal to substitute its opinion for that of the Secretary-General. The only ground upon which it could rescind the decision would be if there had been a misuse of power. As no evidence had been adduced establishing improper motivation, the claim must fail.

The *Kaplan* case is in striking contrast to the *Crawford* case[17] in which the Secretary-General let it be known in the course of the proceedings before the Tribunal that one of the reasons for terminating the applicant's appointment was her refusal to answer a question put to her by the Internal Security Sub-Committee of the U.S. Senate which was engaged on a similar investigation to that of the Federal Grand Jury. The question, concerning who had asked her to join the Communist party in 1935, had been similar to a question she had refused to answer in an affidavit to the F.B.I. in 1939, long before she entered the service of the United Nations. The Tribunal held that her refusal to answer in 1952 could hardly constitute a valid reason for dismissal if refusal to answer a similar question in 1939 was not sufficient to prevent her initial employment by the Organisation. What had made the difference, presumably, was the pressure put on the Secretary-General by the U.S. Government. The Secretary-General had, therefore, been prompted by an improper motive, so that the applicant's claim succeeded.

The *Crawford* case is exceptional. It has been criticised because it did come dangerously near to substituting the Tribunal's opinion for that of the Secretary-General. In order to reach the conclusion that the Secretary-General had acted out of improper motives, the Tribunal first decided that the applicant's dismissal was not based upon reasonable grounds. But, as the Secretary-General was given a power to terminate the appointment because it was in the interests of the U.N. to do so, it is clear that he was never intended to have to show "reasonable grounds". Not only is the approach of the Tribunal in the *Crawford* case unlikely to be followed with any frequency because its correctness in law is in doubt, but, as a purely practical matter, it is unlikely that the Secretary-General will often divulge his reasons for believing the action to be in the interests of the U.N. And, as the *Kaplan* case shows, without evidence of why the Secretary-General took such action, there is little chance of the applicant being able to establish improper motive.

The Tribunal has a wider jurisdiction with respect to permanent appointments. The reason is that the Staff Regulations place greater restrictions upon the powers of the Secretary-General to terminate the appointments of permanent staff of the Organisation. At the time of the 1952–3 crisis, the Secretary-General could dismiss permanent staff only in cases of unsatisfactory service or of serious misconduct. The Commission of

---

17. *Ibid.*, p. 561.

Jurists, which advised the Secretary-General over the alleged "un-American" activities of certain U.S. nationals in the Secretariat, suggested that these persons could be dismissed on the ground that their conduct amounted to a fundamental breach of their obligations under Regulations 1 (4) and 1 (8).

Before the Tribunal in the *Gordon* case,[18] the Secretary-General relied upon the contention that the conduct of Gordon and other such personnel constituted both unsatisfactory service and serious misconduct. By implication, therefore, the Secretary-General admitted that he had no power to dismiss staff on a ground not laid down in the Staff Regulations. This admission the Tribunal seemingly endorsed when it commented that the opinion of the Jurists "disregards the nature of permanent contracts and the character of the regulations governing termination of employment laid down by the General Assembly".

As to the main argument put forward by the Secretary-General, the Tribunal distinguished between unsatisfactory services and serious misconduct. It appeared clearly that the word "services" was used in the Staff Regulations and Rules "solely to designate professional behaviour within the Organisation". Gordon's acts were patently not capable of amounting . to "unsatisfactory services". As to serious misconduct, the Staff Regulations provided two procedures: through the initial stage of the Joint Disciplinary Committee or by summary act of the Secretary-General. But this latter alternative was only introduced to meet cases where the misconduct was patent and where the interests of the service required immediate and final dismissal. Such a situation had obviously not arisen in this case. The applicant's refusal to testify before the Senate Sub-Committee had been a legitimate exercise of a constitutional right. The Secretary-General himself had felt so unsure of his position that he had sought clarification from the Commission of Jurists; and he had subsequently granted termination indemnities which were expressly forbidden by the Regulations in cases of summary dismissal. The Tribunal concluded that it was not possible to regard the conduct of Gordon as serious misconduct which alone could justify the Secretary-General in dismissing a staff member summarily without the safeguard afforded by the disciplinary procedure.

iv *Protection from the General Assembly*

In a number of the cases arising out of the refusal by U.S. nationals to testify before various federal investigating committees, compensation was awarded by the Administrative Tribunal. When the General Assembly was called upon to allocate funds in a supplementary allocation for the payment of these sums, the United States contended that the Tribunal's decisions were not binding on the Organisation, and that funds should not therefore be allocated. Obviously, acceptance of this argument would seriously diminish the protection available to staff members through

18. (1953) 20 I.L.R. 493.

recourse to the Tribunal. It would be a less certain remedy against arbitrary dismissal if member states were free to nullify its effects by refusing to provide the necessary funds to satisfy judgments.

The issue was of sufficient importance for the General Assembly to submit it to the International Court for an Advisory Opinion.[19] Had the Assembly the right to refuse to give effect to an award of compensation made by the Tribunal in favour of a staff member whose contract of service had been terminated without his assent?

The Court answered this question in the negative. An examination of the relevant provisions of the Statute of the Tribunal showed that it was established "not as an advisory organ or a mere subordinate committee of the General Assembly, but as an independent and truly judicial body pronouncing final judgments . . . within the limited field of its functions. According to a well-established and generally recognised principle of law, a judgment rendered by such a judicial body is *res judicata* and has binding force between the parties to the dispute." The parties to the dispute in this case were the individual staff member on the one hand and the Organisation (through the Secretary-General) on the other. "When the Secretary-General concludes . . . a contract of service with a staff member, he engages the legal responsibility of the Organisation, which is the juridical person on whose behalf he acts."[20] Nor was it possible to argue that the Assembly did not have the legal authority to create a tribunal able to make awards binding on the Organisation. The "power to establish a tribunal, to do justice as between the Organisation and the staff members, was essential to ensure the efficient working of the Secretariat, and to give effect to the paramount consideration of securing the highest standards of efficiency, competence and integrity. Capacity to do this arises by necessary intendment out of the Charter."[1]

While interference with awards of the Tribunal by the Assembly and indirectly with the rights of staff members, was thus prevented, there is a second possible method whereby the Assembly might more directly tamper with the rights of such personnel. As the Staff Regulations are made by the Assembly (Art. 101 (1) of the Charter), they may also be amended by the Assembly. What is the effect of such an amendment upon serving staff members?

The jurisprudence of the U.N. Tribunal distinguishes between provisions of the Regulations of a contractual nature and those of statutory nature: "all matters being contractual which affect the personal status of each staff member, e.g. the nature of his contract, salary, grade; all matters being statutory which affect in general the organisation of the International Civil Service, and the need for its proper functioning, e.g. general rules that have no personal reference."[2] Contractual elements cannot be changed without the agreement of the parties, but the statutory elements of the Regulations may be changed at any time by the General Assembly, and these changes are binding on staff members.

---

19. I.C.J. Rep. 1954, p. 47.   20. *Ibid.*, at p. 53.   1. *Ibid.*, at p. 57.
2. The Tribunal's own words in the *Kaplan* case, 20 I.L.R., at p. 508.

The effect of this distinction is to create the doctrine of acquired or vested rights. Indeed, although such a principle would seem to be a general principle of law operating independently of express provision, it is in fact also incorporated into the Staff Regulations, Regulation 12. 1 of which provides that the Regulations "may be supplemented or amended by the General Assembly, without prejudice to the acquired rights of staff members."

Of course, the degree of protection afforded by this notion of acquired rights will depend upon precisely where the line dividing contractual and statutory regulations is drawn. In this respect the *Kaplan* case[3] provides an unsatisfactory guide. When Kaplan was appointed, the Staff Regulations then in force did not permit the Secretary-General to terminate a temporary appointment without stating his reasons for doing so. The Regulations were subsequently amended to allow the Secretary-General a discretionary power to terminate if, in his opinion, such action was in the interests of the United Nations. In terminating Kaplan's appointment, the Secretary-General purported to act under the new regulation. The Tribunal upheld the validity of the dismissal, *inter alia*, on the ground that Kaplan had no vested right in the terms upon which appointments might be terminated. In other words, such terms were non-contractual.

It can hardly be claimed that a distinction along the lines suggested by this case is satisfactory. It might be justifiable on the ground that Kaplan's appointment was not permanent, so that the terms upon which he could be dismissed were of less importance. But there is nothing in the Tribunal's judgment to suggest that the Tribunal saw any difference between the positions of permanent and of non-permanent members of staff. To apply the ruling on this point in the *Kaplan* case to permanent staff would be highly prejudicial to their status. It is surely of fundamental importance to a person making a career in the Secretariat to have the terms under which he might be dismissed clearly laid down in his contract of service. By treating such provisions in the Staff Regulations as non-contractual the Tribunal places the permanent staff member at the mercy of the whims of a majority of the General Assembly. As alterations to the Regulations dealing with dismissal have been made by the Assembly, it can hardly be claimed that the *Kaplan* decision is in the best interests of the international civil service.

3 JUDICIAL CONTROL WITHIN THE EUROPEAN COMMUNITIES

Although the European Communities have been described in the context of international organisations, they possess a number of characteristics more usually found in a federal state. They exhibit the obvious hallmark of most international institutions—creation by a group of states which

3.   20 I.L.R. 506.

constitute the members of the organisation. It is also true that most of the functions of statehood remain vested in the individual states. But within the sphere of operations of the three Community treaties, there are many features common to the constitutional structure of a federation. And nowhere is this similarity more apparent than in the type of case heard by the Court of Justice of the European Communities, in which groups of manufacturers or other industrial organisations, member states of the Communities, or the various organs of the Communities can be involved as parties.

a ORGANISATION AND COMPOSITION OF THE COURT

The treaties which established the three Communities provided for a Court of Justice as one of the four institutions of each Community. Under the *Convention relating to Certain Institutions common to the European Communities* of March, 1957, the Court of E.E.C. was reconstructed to serve all three Communities. However, while the Court itself became a single institution, its jurisdiction, being based on the three separate treaties, varies with the treaty with which the particular case is concerned.

Under Article 165 of the E.E.C. treaty,[4] the Court consists of seven judges and sits as such in exercising *pleine juridiction*. Although it may set up *chambres* of three or five judges for certain purposes (for *instruction*, or to decide certain categories of case), it must sit in plenary session to hear cases submitted by a member state, or by one of the institutions of the Community, or by courts of member states requiring an authoritative preliminary decision on any question of interpretation of the Rome treaty. Under Article 167,[5] the judges are to be chosen from persons whose independence can be fully guaranteed and who fulfil the conditions required for the exercise of the highest judicial functions in their respective countries or who are legal experts of universally recognised and outstanding ability. They are appointed by agreement between the governments of member states for a period of six years; retirement is "staggered" so that three retire at a time and the other four three years later. They are eligible for reappointment. It is for the judges to appoint one of their number as President of the Court.

The Court is assisted in its work by two Advocates-General appointed in the same way and on the same terms as the judges. Their principal duty is to present publicly, with complete impartiality and independence, reasoned conclusions on cases submitted to the Court (Art. 166).[6] However, this general responsibility is more precisely defined in the Rules of Procedure. The Advocate-General will be heard if a party raises a new legal argument in the course of proceedings; or if a preliminary objection is raised or a preliminary issue has to be decided; he can put questions to the agents, legal advisers or counsel appearing on behalf of the parties, and

---

4. EURATOM, Art. 137; and E.C.S.C. Art. 32 as amended in 1957.
5. EURATOM, Art. 139; E.C.S.C. Art. 32 (b) as amended.
6. EURATOM, Art. 138; E.C.S.C. Art. 32 (a).

so on. If there is to be an *instruction* (investigation) stage, the Advocate-General dealing with the case must be heard by the Court upon what measures of instruction are necessary (examination of witnesses, inspection of documents, etc.) and what facts have to be proved.

b JURISDICTION

The jurisdiction of the Court is complex, partly because of the complex structure of the Communities, and partly because the method of redress is available to different persons in different cases.

i *Claims that a member state has failed to fulfil its obligations under the relevant treaty*

The procedure to be followed in such cases vividly illustrates these difficulties. Under the E.C.S.C. treaty (Art. 88), it was the High Authority which had the power to decide whether the actions of a state were compatible with its obligations under the treaty. It was then for the state to take proceedings before the Court within two months of the decision being notified to have the decision annulled. In contrast, under Article 169 of the E.E.C. treaty,[7] if the Commission considers that a member state has failed to fulfil its obligations, it shall issue a reasoned opinion on the matter after giving the state concerned the opportunity to submit its comments. If the state does not comply with the terms of the opinion within the period laid down by the Commission, it is then open to the Commission to refer the case to the Court. Since the unification of the High Authority of E.C.S.C. and the Commissions of E.E.C. and EURATOM into a single Commission, it is the unified Commission which now acts, but, until there is a complete fusion of the three communities, the Commission is only entitled to exercise the powers formerly available to the relevant organs under the three treaties.

A difference also exists between the procedures to be followed in claims presented by other states that a state has failed to fulfil its treaty obligations. Under Article 89 of the E.C.S.C. treaty any dispute among member states concerning the application of the treaty may be submitted to the Court at the request of one of the states party to the dispute; and, by agreement between the states concerned, the Court may be granted jurisdiction over "any difference between Member States in connection with the objects of the present Treaty". Under Article 170 of the E.E.C. treaty,[8] any member state which considers that another has failed to fulfil its obligations under the treaty may refer the matter to the Court. But, before doing so, it must first refer the matter to the Commission, which is obliged to give the disputants the opportunity of presenting both written and oral submissions and replies and then to give a reasoned opinion on the matter. This procedure is a form of an "arbitration", but the Commission's opinion is in no sense final because any or either of the States involved is still free to institute proceedings before the Court.

---

7. EURATOM, Art. 141.   8. EURATOM, Art. 142.

Although no provision is made by the three principal treaties for individuals to apply to the Court, such jurisdiction may be bestowed by supplementary agreement, certainly in the case of E.C.S.C. Under Article 43 of the E.C.S.C. treaty the Court may exercise jurisdiction in any other case covered by an additional provision of the treaty. "Additional provision" has taken to include annexes to the treaty, various additional protocols and the transitional provisions. Hence, in *Humblet* v. *Belgian State*,[9] the Court assumed jurisdiction in a claim presented by an E.C.S.C. official who claimed that it was a breach of the Protocol on Privileges and Immunities for the Belgian authorities to take his own tax free salary into account when assessing his wife's liability to tax.

ii *Legality of the acts of the various institutions*

Certain acts have binding force. Article 189 of the Rome Treaty[10] prescribes that Regulations, which are of general application, are binding in every respect; that Directives are binding on the member state to which they are addressed, though the means of implementation are left to domestic agencies; and that Decisions, to whomsoever they are addressed, are binding in every respect. Recommendations and opinions have no binding force. In contrast, decisions and recommendations of the Commission acting in the capacity of the former High Authority of E.C.S.C. are binding: decisions in all respects, but recommendations only with regard to the objectives specified, and not to the means of implementation.[11]

The Court of the Communities has jurisdiction to supervise the legality of the acts[12] both of the Council and the Commission acting under the E.E.C. treaty and of the Commission acting under the E.C.S.C. treaty. In the case of E.E.C. (Art. 173)[13], the proceedings may be instituted by a member state, by the Council or by the Commission; or a natural or legal person may appeal against a decision directed to him or against a decision which, although in form directed to someone else, is of direct concern to himself. Article 33 of the E.C.S.C. treaty empowers the Court to decide upon applications made by one of the member states or by the Council; enterprises (which can include individuals[14]) or associations "engaged in production in the sphere of coal and steel" or, for certain purposes, "engaged in distribution other than sale to domestic consumers or to small craft industries" (Art. 80)[15] can apply to the Court against decisions and recommendations concerning them that are individual in character, and they have a more limited right of appeal against general decisions and recommendations affecting them.[16]

---

9. (1960), 29 I.L.R. 56.   10. EURATOM, Art. 161.
11. E.C.S.C., Art. 14
12. Or of a failure to act where the relevant treaty imposes a duty to act.
13. EURATOM, Art. 146.
14. Implicit in *Nold* v. *High Authority* (1959), 27 I.L.R. 321.
15. For the interpretation of the expressions "enterprises and associations", see Valentine, *The Court of Justice of the European Communities*, Vol. 1, pp. 153 *et seq.*
16. See *ibid.*, pp. 157 *et seq.*

The most important factors concerning proceedings instituted against acts of the Council or of the Commission for annulment (*recours en annulation*) are the grounds upon which the application can be made and upon which the Court can exercise its powers. Both the E.C.S.C. treaty (Art. 33) and the E.E.C. treaty (Art. 173)[17] stipulate four grounds for quashing such acts:

(1) lack of competence (*incompétence*);
(2) violation of a substantial procedural requirement (*violation des formes substantielles*);
(3) violation of the Treaty or of any rule of law concerning its application;
(4) misuse of powers (*détournement de pouvoir*)

These grounds are virtually identical with those upon which the French *Conseil d'Etat* will review administrative action. It will readily be understood that both in French law and in Community law, the grounds are by no means mutually exclusive. For example there have been many situations which could very well have been considered under any of the first three grounds.

1   *Lack of competence*

The nearest approach to this concept in English law is the doctrine of *ultra vires*, the notion that a particular organ or entity can only act validly within the powers granted to it. In practice, the Court of the Communities has not made great use of this ground for annulling acts of the various institutions mainly because grounds 2 and 3 are in many situations equally applicable, and perhaps more readily established.

A case in which the Court did make use of *incompétence* was that of *Netherlands Government* v. *The High Authority*.[18] Article 70 of the E.C.S.C. treaty provided that transport rates for coal and steel within member states should either be published or brought to the knowledge of the High Authority. Purporting to be acting in pursuance of this provision, the High Authority issued a number of Decisions specifying the details which it required to be brought to its knowledge. These Decisions were challenged by the Netherlands and Italian Governments. The Court held from the absence of any specific power to prescribe the extent and form of such publication, etc. (such a power being expressly granted in the parallel provision dealing with price lists and conditions of sale applied by enterprises within the Community) that the High Authority was without competence to enforce Article 70 by means of Decisions.

2   *Violation of a substantial procedural requirement*
3   *Violation of the treaty*

As the procedural requirements that must be satisfied for the Commission or the Council of the Communities to act are in many cases

---

17. EURATOM, Art. 146.   18. (1960) 29 I.L.R. 163.

specifically laid down in the relevant treaty, a failure to comply with such requirements would constitute a violation of the treaty. It is hardly surprising, therefore, that the Court has not always drawn a clear distinction between headings (2) and (3). Furthermore, there have been occasions when the failure to comply with either (2) or (3) has been considered so fundamental as to make the act a complete nullity. The attitude of the Court in such circumstances has been to hold that, being a nullity, such an "act" does not need annulling (in fact, it could not be annulled).

A case which illustrates both the overlapping of (2) and (3) and also the consequence of a fundamental failure to comply with them was *Société des Usines à Tubes de la Sarre* v. *The High Authority*.[19] The plaintiff enterprise had submitted its investment plan to the High Authority for approval. Under Article 54 of the E.C.S.C. treaty, the High Authority could notify its disapproval by means of an Opinion, but it was also provided that such an Opinion was to have the force of law and accordingly was subject to a right of appeal to the Court. The applicants instituted proceedings impugning the unfavourable Opinion given by the High Authority on the ground that the Opinion had failed to state reasons for the refusal as required by Article 15. The Court upheld the applicant's contention, but the process of reasoning, and the basis of the decision are of considerable interest. The Court accepted the view of the advocate-general that no reasons had been given, so that conditions imposed by the treaty had not been complied with. While certain of the formalities did not affect the nature or existence of the act, the giving of reasons was "an essential element, indeed a constitutive part of such an act". However, as a consequence of this defect, the Court did not have to annul the act for either a failure to comply with the treaty, or a violation of a fundamental procedural requirement, because the "absence of supporting reasons implies the non-existence of an Opinion."

There is no legal or practical reason why the Court should have to distinguish precisely and logically between the first three grounds of challenge. It is largely immaterial to a successful applicant whether he has persuaded the Court that the defect in the act challenged arose out of a violation of a substantial legal requirement or out of a violation of the treaty.

In *Italian Government* v. *The High Authority*,[20] the Court had to consider the applicant's claim that, for a variety of reasons, a new system of price listing introduced by the High Authority at the beginning of 1954 was invalid. One of the grounds (that in fixing the prices for the Italian market, the High Authority had not acted with the agreement of the Italian Government as required by s. 30 of the Convention containing Transitional Provisions) was not raised at the outset of the proceedings, and an objection was made to its admissibility. The objection was rejected. Even if the challenge had not been made on this ground by the applicant, it would have been necessary for the Court to have considered it *proprio*

---

19. (1957), 29 I.L.R. 77.   20. (1954), 22 I.L.R. 737.

motu because, if the argument were well founded, an annulment for violation of the treaty or for violation of a substantial procedural requirement
would have been justified. In the course of giving its judgment, the Court
took the view that the failure to agree on the prices with the Italian
Government, and a failure to consult with the Consultative Committee
as was also required by the treaty, should both be treated as violations of
substantial procedural requirements rather than as violations of the treaty,
but its earlier pronouncement clearly shows that the distinction is of no
great significance.

4 *Détournement de pouvoir*

It will be recalled from the discussion of the jurisdiction of the U.N.
Administrative Tribunal that a *détournement de pouvoir* occurs when an
administrative act is performed in accordance with the terms in which a
power is granted but for some improper motive. Although the claim that
a misuse of power had occurred was raised with great frequency in the
early days of the E.C.S.C., no applicant ever succeeded in having an act
annulled on that ground. Apart from the difficulty of establishing that a
body has acted for some ulterior and improper reason, the Court has
refused to annul an act, even if the existence of such a motive can be
proved, providing that the main purpose of the act was for the purposes
envisaged by the grant of the power.

In the case *French Government* v. *The High Authority*,[1] the Court had to
deal with the situation arising out of the consistent selling of steel by
enterprises at prices below those laid down by the High Authority. The
High Authority had later passed Decisions allowing price variations within
certain narrow limits. It was alleged by the applicant that the motive
behind these Decisions had been the reluctance of the High Authority to
enforce a price scheme that had been so widely disregarded. The Court
refused to annul the Decisions. "Even if the Decisions in question have
been partially inspired by the intention to introduce a new system better
suited than the previous one to be observed by the enterprises, one cannot
conclude from this that the purpose of the Decision was to legitimate the
infractions previously committed. At any rate, it is evident that the
Decisions were especially destined to pursue the objectives referred to in
the Treaty. Even if among the motives which do justify the action of the
High Authority, there had been an unjustified one, namely, the intention
to avoid punishing the guilty enterprises, the Decisions would not, because
of that, be vitiated by *détournement de pourvoir*, inasmuch as they do not
infringe upon the essential objective, which is the prohibition of unfair
competitive practices and of discriminations."

One reason why the plea of *détournement* was frequently raised in early
proceedings under the E.C.S.C. treaty is the limitation contained in
Article 33 that "the investigation by the Court may not include an
evaluation of the situation resulting from the economic facts and circum-

---

1. (1954), 25 I.L.R. 388.

stances in the light of which such Decisions or Recommendations were taken, except where the High Authority is alleged to have committed a *détournement de pouvoir* or to have patently misconstrued the treaty or any rule of law concerning its application." Despite the apparent meaning of this provision, an allegation of a *détournement* or patent misconstruction alone will not be sufficient to enable the Court to examine the High Authority's evaluation of the economic circumstances upon which its decision is based. From the outset the Court of E.C.S.C. took the view that the allegation must be supported at least by *prima facie* evidence.[2] If such evidence were not required there was the obvious danger that assertions would be made of a *détournement* or of a patent misconstruction with the sole object of being able to call in question the High Authority's economic evaluation.

iii *Other proceedings against the Communities or their institutions*
1 *Appeals against penalties*
    Institutions of the Communities have wide powers to impose penalties upon member states and private enterprises. Acting under Article 172 of the Rome Treaty,[3] the E.E.C. Council granted the Court *pleine juridiction* "to adjudicate in proceedings instituted against decisions by which the Commission has fixed a fine or a penalty; it may cancel, reduce or increase the fine or the penalty imposed." Article 36 of the E.C.S.C. treaty directly made fines and penalties imposed under the provisions of the treaty subject to the Court's jurisdiction.
    The significance of the *pleine juridiction* is that the Court is thus endowed with the widest powers both over the fines and over the act or acts giving rise to this imposition. In this context, the jurisdiction clearly includes a power to annul acts that are vitiated by any of the grounds considered under heading (b).

2 *Non-contractual liability of the Communities*
    The three Community treaties grant jurisdiction to the Court to hear cases arising out of the wrongful acts of the Community or of its servants. However, the manner in which this is accomplished differs.
    Article 40 of the E.C.S.C. treaty enables the Court to award damages against the Community in the event of an injury caused by a *faute de service* on the part of the Community, or against an employee of the Community for a *faute personnelle* committed by that employee in the performance of his duties. The Court may only make an award of compensation against the Community in the latter situation if the injured party is unable to obtain the damages awarded from the employee. In contrast, Article 178 of the Rome Treaty[4] grants the Court jurisdiction to hear cases

---

2. *Netherlands Government* v. *High Authority* (1955), 22 I.L.R. 750, at pp. 753–4, on the reason for alleging a patent misconstruction.
3. EURATOM, Art. 144 (b) grants jurisdiction directly to the Court over "appeals instituted by persons or undertakings against penalties imposed on them by the Commission".   4. EURATOM, Art. 151.

concerning compensation as provided for in Article 215[5] which lays down that, as regards non-contractual liability, E.E.C. shall, in accordance with the general principles common to the laws of Member States, compensate for any injury caused by its institutions or by its employees in the performance of their duties.

The difference between Article 40 of the E.C.S.C. treaty and Article 215 of the E.E.C. treaty will be better understood if the provisions are considered against the general background of the liability of public authorities under French administrative law.

In the first place, the distinction between wrongful acts of the Community and wrongful acts by its employees is not that between the liability for personal torts and vicarious responsibility known to English law. It is made clear under the E.C.S.C. treaty that it is the individual community official who can be made liable before the Court for a *faute personnelle*: the responsibility of the community will not be vicarious, but only as guarantor if the community official is unable to meet the damages out of his own pocket.

Under the French *droit administratif*, the Court responsible for dispensing "administrative justice", the *Conseil d'Etat*, originally had jurisdiction over *faute de service*, but not over *faute personnelle*. *Faute de service* is a wrongful act caused by administrative inefficiency or error, in other words, a fault of the system or within the system. A *faute personnelle* occurred when the responsibility lay not with the system or its operation, but was caused by the wrongful and unauthorised acts of a public servant or servants. In such a case, the remedy lay against those responsible personally in the ordinary courts. However, such a distinction was not altogether satisfactory. It was unreasonable that a public authority should be able to escape liability by showing that its employees had been acting in an unauthorised manner. The *Conseil d'Etat* therefore evolved the doctrine of *cumul* under which an authority would nevertheless still be responsible as long as the official, though acting in an unauthorised manner, was taking advantage of his official position and power.

This notion of an employee taking advantage of his position is rendered in the treaties as *"dans l'exercice de ses fonctions"*. However, while under French law *fautes personnelles* of this type enabled the *Conseil d'Etat* to exercise jurisdiction and to grant damages against the public authority as an alternative remedy to an action in the ordinary courts against the errant official, the E.C.S.C. treaty only contemplates a grant of jurisdiction to the Court of the Communities: the award is still to be made against the official. On the other hand, Article 215 of the E.E.C. treaty clearly envisages an award against the Community to make good any damage caused by its institutions or by its employees in the performance of their duties. By granting jurisdiction to the Court of the Communities and by giving the Court power to award damages against the Community in respect of the wrongful acts of its officials in the performance of their functions, the

---

5. EURATOM, Art. 188.

E.E.C. treaty is closer to the law and practice of the French *Conseil d'Etat*. Hitherto the Court of the Communities has not been called upon to consider a *faute personnelle*, though it has had occasion to deal with alleged *fautes de service*. One case in particular, *Société Fives Lille Cail & others* v. *The High Authority*,[6] provides a striking illustration of a failure of the administrative machine. The applicants claimed that the High Authority should continue to pay reimbursements to them for transport costs in obtaining shipbreaking scrap. Payments had been made by an Office set up in Brussels in 1954 by the High Authority to deal with the subsidising of the high costs of obtaining scrap. In 1960, on discovering the basis upon which these payments had been made, the High Authority declared that the payment went far beyond the subsidy scheme which the Office had been authorised to operate, and refused to allow any further such disbursements. In the case as presented to the Court, the applicants sought, *inter alia*, damages for an alleged *faute de service*. While disallowing the claim for damages on the ground that it had not been shown that the damages flowed from the wrongful act, the Court nevertheless held that a *faute* had occurred. The promises had been made by the Office "only by reason of the fact that the High Authority failed to exercise sufficient control over the functioning of the subsidy machinery. . . . In fact, the importance of the payments made . . .—in all more than half a million dollars—were certainly of a nature to have attracted attention had the High Authority exercised sufficient supervision. . . . In any event, by the very fact of having authorised the subsidy system, whatever its form, the High Authority should have kept it under its control. . . ."[7]

3 Contractual liability of the Communities

All three treaties contain clauses in identical terms to Article 42 of the E.C.S.C. treaty conferring jurisdiction on the Court to hear disputes arising out of any contract entered into by the Community which contains a clause granting such jurisdiction.

As the normal means of litigating a case arising out of a contract to which one of the Communities is a party will be before the courts of one of the member states, the main importance of Article 42 has been to enable the Court of the Communities to hear disputes arising out of the contracts of service of E.C.S.C. officials. Under the E.E.C. treaty, an additional provision was included (Art. 179) whereby the Court "shall have jurisdiction to determine actions between the Community and its employees within the limits and under the conditions laid down in Service Regulations or arising out of the system applicable to employees."[8] The system referred to was that of individual contracts with each employee, but the basis of employment has been the Service Statute in the case of E.C.S.C. since 1955 and of E.E.C. since 1962.

In actions alleging, for example, wrongful dismissal, the Court will be

---

6. [1962] C.M.L.R. 251.   7. *Ibid.*, at pp. 281-2.
8. EURATOM, Art. 152.

guided by the same basic motion of *légalité* which underlies both the four grounds of challenge of the other administrative acts of organs of the Communities and the whole concept of French administrative jurisdiction. Hence the challenge may be on the grounds of *incompétence, vice de forme, violation de la loi*, and *détournement de pouvoir*, though in the case of individuals there are two obvious differences in emphasis. In the first place, a *détournement* is more likely to occur in situations involving personal relationships. Secondly, the likelihood is that *violations de la loi* will arise in the wider sense that has been developed by the French *Conseil d'Etat* embracing what in English law would be designated failures to comply with the rules of natural justice.

In the case of *Mirossevich v. The High Authority*,[9] the plaintiff moved to Luxemburg from Rome to take a post as a translator with the High Authority. There was some dispute as to the terms of the appointment, but the Court held that it was subject to a probationary period of one month. During the probationary period she was only asked to translate three documents, the longest being a mere seven pages in length. At the end of the period she was informed that her capabilities did not measure up to the standard required. The plaintiff challenged the Decision not to offer her a contract as a translator on two main grounds. She claimed that, during her probationary period, she had never been allowed to demonstrate her ability; and that there had been a *détournement de pouvoir* in that the real reason for her not being appointed to the permanent staff had been the wish of the head of the section in which she worked to appoint one of his friends in her place. The Court held that the Decision must be annulled, because the probationary period had clearly been served under irregular conditions. Despite the fact that the section head had secured the appointment of his friend, the Court was of the opinion that there was not sufficient evidence to establish a *détournement de pouvoir* in respect of the plaintiff.

iv *Proceedings by the Communities against their servants*

Not only has the Court jurisdiction over claims presented by officials against the Community which employs them, it also has jurisdiction in certain specified circumstances over proceedings brought by a Community against its servants.

(1) Under the Service Regulations of E.E.C. made under Article 179 of the Rome Treaty,[10] an official may be required to make good, in whole or in part, any damage suffered by the Communities (i.e. by the E.E.C. or EURATOM; the action in case of a *faute personnelle* by a servant of E.C.S.C. must be brought against the individual concerned) as a result of serious *fautes personnelles* committed in the course of, or in connection with, the performance of his duties. The procedure is for the appointing authority to establish that a *faute* has occurred by means of a Decision to

---

9. Valentine, *op. cit.*, Vol. 2, p. 727: the report in 23 I.L.R. 627 is inadequate.
10. EURATOM, Art. 152.

that effect. It is for the official concerned to challenge this Decision, if he wishes, before the Court.

(2) Under the E.E.C. treaty, but not under the E.C.S.C. treaty, the Court on the application of the Council or the Commission, may compulsory retire a member of the Commission if

(*a*) he breaks his obligations resulting from his position under Article 157;[11] or
(*b*) he no longer fulfils the conditions required for the performance of his duties or has been guilty of serious misconduct (Article 160).[12]

Acting under Article 157, the Court may also decree forfeiture of pension rights or other benefits in lieu thereof in case of a failure to fulfil the obligations arising from his office.

(3) The Court has a similar jurisdiction to deprive of office or declare to have forfeited their right to a pension or other benefits judges who no longer fulfil the conditions required for appointment or meet the obligations resulting from their office. The decision to this effect must be unanimous among the other judges and the advocates-general (Court Statute, Article 6).

v *Preliminary rulings on issues before the courts of member states*

In view of the extent to which the three Communities, but particularly E.E.C., pervade the everyday affairs of life in the member states, disputes involving issues arising out of the Community treaties can come before the ordinary courts of those members. It would obviously be unsatisfactory for a mass of conflicting jurisprudence to develop among the courts in the different states. Accordingly, provision is made for the submission of certain preliminary issues to the Court of the Communities. Under Article 41 of the E.C.S.C. treaty the Court has jurisdiction to pass on the validity of certain acts of the Commission and the Council acting under the E.C.S.C. treaty when such validity is in issue before a municipal tribunal. The provisions of Article 177 of the Rome Treaty[13] are more detailed. The Court has jurisdiction to give a preliminary ruling on the interpretation of the treaty or on the validity and interpretation of acts passed by institutions of the Community when a request for a ruling is made by a court of a member state before which such an issue is raised. When the municipal court is one the decision of which will not be open to appeal, the court is *required* to refer the issue to the Court of the Communities.

vi *Advisory jurisdiction*

The Court has a restricted jurisdiction to give advisory opinions.

(1) Under Article 95 of the E.C.S.C. treaty the Court is required to

---

11. EURATOM, Art. 126. 12. EURATOM, Art. 129.
13. EURATOM, Art. 150 is similar, but *not* identical.

International Organisations IV

consider any proposals drawn up by the Commission and Council for the amendment of the rules governing the exercise by the Commission of the powers conferred on it by the treaty.

(2) The Court may be asked by the Council, the Commission or any member state to consider the compatibility of any treaty to be entered into by the Community with the provisions of the E.E.C. treaty (Art. 228).

(3) The Court has jurisdiction to pass on the compatibility with the EURATOM treaty of treaties contemplated by member states. Under the treaty, the Commission has the power to declare such treaties incompatible; it is then for the member state concerned to challenge this decision before the Court (Art. 103). Once a treaty has come into operation, however, it is for the Commission to seek the opinion of the Court on whether or not the treaty is compatible with the EURATOM treaty (Art. 104).

c THE WORK OF THE COURT

It will have been noticed that a majority of cases involving challenges to the acts of executive organs have been against the High Authority under the E.C.S.C. treaty. The reason for this feature was the leading role of the High Authority in the work of Community. Its powers were far more extensive than those of the E.E.C. Commission. An obvious illustration of this difference has already been considered. The High Authority had the power to decide for itself in specific cases whether its decisions or other obligations stemming from the E.C.S.C. treaty had been broken. It was then for the state or enterprise thus held to be in default to challenge the validity of the High Authority's acts. In contrast, under the Rome Treaty, the E.E.C. Commission could only express an opinion that a member state had failed to comply with its obligations. Enforcement in cases where a state failed to accept the views of the Commission could only be achieved by the Commission itself bringing the matter before the Court.

Until quite recently the great majority of cases heard by the Court have involved appeals against acts of the various institutions or against member states. However, the year 1967 saw a dramatic decrease in the number of such cases compared with the year before, and an equally dramatic increase in the number of cases submitted by national courts for a preliminary ruling on different aspects of Community law.

The former development is probably symptomatic of a more ready acceptance of the new Commission's authority, and perhaps of a less forceful approach by the Commission in the face of French hostility to the supranational elements in the Commission's authority. It is also possible that, being the creation of a merger between the former High Authority and the Commission of E.E.C. and EURATOM, the new Commission is inclined to place more emphasis on the E.E.C. "way of doing things" (initially, at least, by compromise) than on the authoritarian role which it has inherited from the High Authority.

The timing of the latter development (the sudden increase in the use of the Court's preliminary jurisdiction) is partly the consequence of the time lag between disputes arising and being litigated; but it also signifies the extent to which Community law has permeated the economic life of member states with resulting effects upon the type of cases being initiated before the national courts. For example, during 1967 the Court dealt with numerous disputes concerning the social security benefits of migrant workers and the tax provisions of the E.E.C. treaty; and other cases involved farm levies and the treaty's rules governing competition.

4 TERMINATION OF MEMBERSHIP AND SUSPENSION OF THE RIGHTS OF MEMBERSHIP

It will be remembered from an earlier chapter that precise regulation is made in most international organisations of the process of admission to membership. It will further be recalled that admission problems have often arisen because of, or been intensified by, political factors operating within the international community. Cases of termination of membership (whether by expulsion or withdrawal) or suspension of the rights of membership are likely to be less frequent; and, because of their likely political repercussions, it was found less easy to make adequate provision for such eventualities. However, despite the political pressures likely to influence the outcome, it remains true that disputes over expulsion, withdrawal or suspension cannot be resolved satisfactorily by a complete disregard of legal principle.

a EXPRESS PROVISION

It will be obvious that there are differences between the considerations which arise when there is and when there is not express provision to cover the situation. When provision is made, the member wishing to withdraw, or the Organisation wishing to expel or suspend, should act in accordance with the rules laid down. But how have the constitution-makers approached the problems of drafting suitable provisions?

i *Withdrawal*

The constitutions of a number of organisations contain no "withdrawal clause". This was the case with U.N.E.S.C.O., until its constitution was amended, and is the case with W.H.O., and, more significantly with the U.N., and the three European Communities. However, withdrawal is expressly provided for in the treaties setting up most international organisations. These provisions display a number of similar features:

1 *Membership compulsory for a specified period*

A period of compulsory membership before withdrawal is permitted may be achieved in two ways, although the reasons are probably different.

First, a number of organisations have prohibited withdrawal within a specified period after the treaty has come into force. In the case of

I.C.A.O., the period was 3 years;[14] I.M.C.O., twelve months;[15] I.A.E.A., 5 years,[16] and so on. Secondly it is possible to have a provision restricting the right of withdrawal for a specified period after admission. In the case of F.A.O. notice of withdrawal cannot be given until four years from the date of acceptance of the Convention.[17] The reason behind the first type of provision was presumably to make sure that the Convention, once it came into effect, would have a minimum number of members for a certain period. The second type is less frequently found and presumably intended to ensure that a member will at least make a genuine attempt to participate in the work of the organisation before giving notice.

There is, however, a third category which is probably best described as a combination of both. In the case of N.A.T.O. and W.E.U., the periods after the treaties came into force before withdrawal was possible were set at 20 years[18] and 50 years[19] respectively. Because of the length of these periods, particularly the latter, the effect was to impose a substantial compulsory period of membership not only on original members, but also on most members subsequently admitted to the organisations.

2 Method of withdrawal

The most frequent method is for the constitution concerned to require notice or notice in writing or formal notice, to be given to the Secretary-General of the Organisation. By way of variation, the I.M.C.O. constitution required "written notification . . . to the Secretary-General of the United Nations";[20] and the I.C.A.O. constitution notice of denunciation to the government of the U.S.A.[1] Sometimes the notice has to be given to the depository government (the U.S.A. in the case of I.A.E.A.; Belgium in the case of W.E.U.). In the case of the financial institutions (I.M.F., I.B.R.D., I.F.C. and I.D.A.), the notice has to be transmitted in writing to the agency at its "principal" office.

In most cases, it is expressly provided that it is for the Secretary-General or government concerned, to inform all members of the notice of withdrawal. Failure by the Secretary-General or government to do so would not of course affect the validity of the withdrawal.

3 Period of notice

Although in some cases (for example under the agreements creating the financial institutions)[2] the notice is effective on receipt, many constitutions provide for twelve months' or one year's notice. I.L.O. is exceptional in providing for 2 years;[3] and the Statute of the Council of Europe stipulates that withdrawal will take effect at the end of the financial year if notice is given in the first nine months, or at the end of the following financial year if notice is given in the last three months of the financial year.[4]

---

14. Art. 95 (a).   15. Art. 59 (a).   16. Art. 18 (D).   17. Art. 19.
18. Art. 13. For the French claim to withdraw from the N.A.T.O. command structure, but not from the alliance, see (1968) 62 A.J.I.L. 577, esp. at pp. 605–623.
19. Art. 12.   20. Art. 59 (a).
1. Art. 95 (a).   2. E.g. I.M.F., Art. 15 (1).   3. Art. 1 (5).   4. Art. 7.

4 *Need to fulfil obligations*

As the position with regard to financial obligations for the year in which a state withdraws is far from clear,[5] it is surprising that more organisations have not had included in their constitutions a provision stating that such withdrawal does not affect the state's budgetary obligations for that year (as with F.A.O.[6] and I.A.E.A.[7]). The I.L.O. constitution goes a stage further in making the *effectiveness* of the withdrawal dependent on the member having fulfilled all its financial obligations.[8] The agreements setting up I.M.F.,[9] I.B.R.D.,[10] I.F.C.,[11] and I.D.A.,[12] because of the nature of their operations, contain more detailed provisions for the settling of the credits and debts of members wishing to withdraw.

ii *Suspension*

Suspension is a sanction designed to secure compliance with various of the obligations of membership. Accordingly, in organisations where more adequate sanctioning procedures, for example under the European Communities in which compulsory judicial settlement of disputes accompanied by enforcement of decisions is available, there is no need for a relatively unsophisticated weapon like suspension.

The application of the power of suspension will vary in a number of ways:

1 *It may be discretionary or mandatory*

In many cases, the power vested in the organisation to suspend a member is coupled with a discretion whether or not to exercise it. And even in organisations containing a mandatory provision, the suspension may be waived in certain circumstances. For example, under the U.N. Charter, a state against which preventive or enforcement action has been taken *may* be suspended from the rights and privileges of membership (Art. 5); but in cases where the arrears of financial contributions equal or exceed the amount due for the previous two years, the member in arrears *shall* have no vote in the General Assembly, although the Assembly may nevertheless permit the member to vote if the Assembly is satisfied that the failure to pay is due to conditions beyond the control of the Member (Art. 19). Similarly, Article 13 (4) of the I.L.O. constitution provides that in a case of arrears of a like amount, the member concerned *shall* have no vote in the Conference, in the Governing Body, in any Committee or in elections to the Governing Body, although this suspension may be waived by a two-thirds majority vote of the Conference if the default was due to conditions beyond the control of the member.

Automatic suspension without an "escape clause" is unusual. Where it

---

5. Is the withdrawing state liable for all contributions, for part only, or for none? Does liability depend upon whether assessment is made at the beginning of the year, before withdrawal, or at the end of the year, after withdrawal?

6. Art. 19. 7. Art. 18 (E). 8. Art. 1 (5). 9. Schedule D.

10. Art. 6 (4). 11. Art. 5 (4). 12. Art. 7 (4).

does occur it is invariably restricted in its operation to special circumstances. Under Article 2 (3) of the U.N.E.S.C.O. treaty, members suspended from the exercise of the rights and privileges of membership of the United Nations *shall*, upon the request of the latter, be suspended from the rights and privileges of membership of U.N.E.S.C.O. And Article 88 of the I.C.A.O. Constitution requires the Assembly to suspend a member from voting in the I.C.A.O. Assembly and Council if it is in default under the provisions of the constitution relating to the settlement of disputes.

The value of suspension as a sanction must be doubted. It might be of some use as a threat with which to cajole an unco-operative member, but as an automatic consequence on the occurrence of a particular situation it is probably more harmful than beneficial.

It will be remembered that the International Court in the *Expenses* case[13] declared that the costs of U.N.E.F. and O.N.U.C. constituted expenses of the Organisation and were, therefore, subject to the General Assembly's powers of apportionment among member states under Article 17 (2) of the Charter. Despite the Court's opinion, a minority of members, including France and the Soviet Union, continued their refusal to pay. By the start of the 1964 Session of the Assembly, several states were in arrears by an amount greater than the total of their contributions for the previous two years. Article 19 of the Charter was, therefore, clearly applicable to them; nor was there any ground for such states to claim that the non-payment was through circumstances beyond their control, so that the Assembly had no basis upon which to allow them to vote. The existence of Article 19 in mandatory form was obviously an embarrassment to the Assembly in its attempts to reach a compromise over the problem of financing previous or future peace-keeping operations. The solution the Assembly adopted on the applicability of Article 19 was to treat it as a discretionary provision and to refuse to deprive states in arrears of their vote in the Assembly, a solution which might be justifiable on political grounds but possible only by a violation of legal principle.

2   *Basis of suspension and extent of loss of rights*

In a majority of cases in which provision for suspension is made, there is distinction drawn between a failure to fulfil financial obligations and cases of non-compliance with more fundamental obligations or of persistent violations of the constitution. In the former situation the loss of rights is usually partial; in the latter total.

Under the Statute setting up the I.A.E.A. (Art. 19), the sanction in a case of arrears of financial contributions equalling or exceeding the total amount due for the previous two years is loss of all voting rights in the Agency; in the case of persistent violations of the Statute the member concerned may be deprived of all privileges and rights of membership. Slightly different is the Statute of the Council of Europe which distinguishes between a failure to fulfil financial obligations when the Committee of Ministers *may* suspend the right of representation of the member

---

13.   I.C.J. Rep. 1962, p. 151.

concerned on the Committee and in the Consultative Assembly (Art. 9), and seriously violating the underlying obligations of membership[14] in which case the member may be suspended from all rights of representation (and also asked to withdraw). The U.N. Charter, as has already been mentioned, contains provision for loss of voting rights in the General Assembly in a case of failure to pay financial contributions when the amount owing equals or exceeds the total due over the previous two years (Art. 19), and for total deprivation of rights and privileges in the case of a state against which preventive or enforcement action has been taken (Art. 5).

Among the more stringent suspension provisions are those contained in the Articles of Agreement of the I.M.F. and the International Bank. Article 15 (2) (a) of the Fund Articles (Article 6 (2) of the articles of the Bank is similar, but not identical) stipulates in a case of a member state failing to fulfil any of its obligations, the Fund may declare the state ineligible to use the resources of the Fund. Because of the nature of the work. Because of the nature of the work of the financial institutions, a potential sanction of this type is likely to be most effective.

Neither the constitution of W.M.O. (Art. 31) nor that of W.H.O. (Art. 7) distinguish between a failure to fulfil financial obligations and other obligations in allowing the plenary organ of the organisation concerned to suspend the defaulting member. However, it is interesting to note that while suspension in W.M.O. is from "exercising rights and enjoying privileges", in W.H.O. it is from "voting privileges and services" on such conditions as the Health Assembly "thinks proper". In other words, the Assembly has a discretion as to the extent of loss of rights and services.[15]

3 Organs empowered to suspend and period of suspension

In most cases the organ entrusted with the power of suspension is the Congress or Assembly (i.e. the plenary organ) of the institution concerned. A major exception to this pattern is the application of Article 5 of the U.N. Charter. Suspension from the rights and privileges of membership in the U.N. of a state against which preventive or enforcement action has been taken is by the General Assembly *on the recommendation of the Security Council.*

Express provision is not always made for the ending of the period of suspension. And where it is made, there is no pattern discernible. Article 7 of the W.H.O. Constitution makes the suspension last until the voting privileges and services are restored by the Assembly. Under Article 5 of the U.N. Charter, the rights and privileges of membership may be

---

14. The actual provision refers to a member "seriously violating Article 3". Under Article 3 every member "must accept the principles of the rule of law and of the enjoyment by all persons within its jurisdiction of human rights and fundamental freedoms, and collaborate sincerely and effectively in the realisation of the aim of the Council as specified in Chapter I."

15. Under an amendment to the W.H.O. constitution a member may be suspended or excluded for deliberately practising a policy of racial discrimination.

restored by the Security Council to a state against which preventive or enforcement action has been taken.

iii *Expulsion*

The constitutions of a number of international organisations contain an exclusion clause enabling a decision to be reached expelling a state from membership. The way in which this power is prescribed varies greatly.

Under the U.N. Charter (Art. 6), in cases of persistent violations of the principles of the Charter, the state responsible can be expelled from the organisation by the General Assembly upon the recommendation of the Security Council. The Statute of the Council of Europe (Art. 8) provides that a member that has seriously violated the fundamental principles upon which the Council is based may be asked to withdraw by the Committee of Ministers: if this request is refused, the Committee may decide that the state concerned has ceased to be a member.

In contrast, under the Articles of Agreement of the International Bank (Art. 6 (2)), suspension matures automatically into expulsion at the end of one year unless the member is restored to good standing by a majority of the Governors of the Bank exercising a majority of the total voting power. In the case of I.M.C.O., Article 11 of its constitution in effect grants a power of exclusion to the General Assembly of the United Nations by laying down that no state may remain a member of I.M.C.O. contrary to a resolution of the General Assembly. Article 2 (4) of the constitution of U.N.E.S.C.O. makes exclusion from the Organisation automatic if the member concerned has been expelled from the United Nations.

b WHERE NO PROVISION IS MADE
i *Withdrawal*

A majority of organisations have included a specific provision governing the right of a member state to withdraw. However, the issue of whether a state can withdraw in the absence of such a provision has proved a subject of controversy and importance. The reason why there has been controversy is that in three important cases (those of W.H.O., of U.N.E.S.C.O., until its constitution was amended in 1954, and of the U.N. itself), states have attempted to withdraw despite the absence of an express liberty to do so.

When the United States ratified the W.H.O. constitution in 1947, it did so subject to the terms of a Joint Resolution of Congress reserving a right to the United States to be able to withdraw on giving one year's notice. The Secretary-General of the United Nations to whom the ratification had been communicated referred the matter to the first session of the World Health Assembly. The Assembly, despite some misgivings, decided to accept the United States' acceptance of the constitution, even though the consequence, in strict legal theory, was to grant to the United States a right of withdrawal not available to any other member.

During the period from February, 1949, to August, 1950, the states of

Communist Europe notified the Director-General of W.H.O. of their withdrawal from the Organisation. In reply to the first purported withdrawal, that of the Soviet Union, the Director-General had refused to accept the Russian communication as valid because there was no provision allowing withdrawal in the W.H.O. constitution. This stand was subsequently endorsed by the Organisation's Executive Board and Assembly. Although the states concerned no longer attended meetings of the organisation and took no part in its activities, they were nevertheless treated as members. They were regularly invited to conferences, they were circulated with papers and information, and they remained on the list of members (although classified as "inactive"). When in 1955 the states intimated their wish to rejoin the Organisation, the Executive Board and the Assembly both took the view that, as the states were already members, there was no need to admit them to membership. The most important issue was of course that of outstanding financial obligations. The Assembly proposed that the Organisation should accept a payment of five per cent of the amounts due for the years in which the states had not been "actively participating in the work of the Organisation".

A similar problem arose, although on a much smaller scale, when a number of states (Poland, Hungary and Czechoslovakia) purported to withdraw from U.N.E.S.C.O. at the end of 1952 and the beginning of 1953. The period of absence only lasted until late 1954. The attitude of the Organisation was similar to that earlier adopted to "withdrawals" from W.H.O. in that the states concerned continued to be treated as members. On their resumption of participation in the activities of the Organisation, a compromise was affected similar to that later adopted by W.H.O. Despite objections by the states concerned, the amounts paid in settlement of past financial liabilities (the states had in fact been in arrears for some time before their "withdrawals") were treated as covering the periods of non-participation as well as their earlier indebtedness. Despite this reaffirmation of legal principle based upon the doctrine of *pacta sunt servanda*, the binding nature of treaties, a number of states recognised the unsatisfactory position that non-recognition of these "withdrawals" created. It was no encouragement to states to resume co-operating in the work of an organisation if they were to be saddled with financial obligations for the period of their withdrawal. Far better was a realistic acceptance of the position by amending the constitution to allow for unilateral withdrawal. In 1954, such a step was taken by U.N.E.S.C.O.

The reason why the W.H.O. and U.N.E.S.C.O. constitutions had not originally made any reference to withdrawal was in deference to the attitude adopted by those who drafted the U.N. Charter. Withdrawal was dealt with by Committee 1/2 of the San Francisco Conference and the Committee's report was included in the First Commission's report to the plenary meetings of the Conference. Although the report was approved virtually without comment, it is doubtful how far it may be called in aid as an "interpretation" of the Charter. The relevant passage of the Committee's commentary stated in part that "the Charter should not make express provision either to permit or to prohibit withdrawal from the Organisation." The Committee deemed that "the highest duty of the nations which will become Members is to continue their co-operation within the Organisation for the preservation of international peace and security. If, however, a Member because of exceptional circumstances feels constrained to withdraw, and leave the burden of maintaining international peace and security on the other Members, it is not the purpose of the Organisation to compel that Member to continue its co-operation in the Organisation."[16]

The validity of a purported withdrawal has only become an issue in relation to one state, namely Indonesia. In January, 1965, the Indonesian Government informed the Secretary-General that, because of the election of "neo-colonialist" Malaysia to a non-permanent seat on the Security Council, it had no alternative left but to withdraw from the Organisation even though such a step was "revolutionary" and "unprecedented". In February, the Secretary-General cautiously replied stating that copies of the "withdrawal" had been circulated to member states, and noting Indonesia's intention to consider itself still bound by the "principles of international co-operation . . . enshrined in the . . . Charter".

The general reaction of member states was to avoid controversy, although the United Kingdom did place on record a protest at the Indonesian action. Leaving aside the basic issue of the validity of withdrawal in any circumstances, even if one accepted the possibility of withdrawal in "exceptional circumstances" as suggested by Committee 1/2 of the San Francisco Conference, the British Government was convinced that the election of Malaysia to the Security Council could not be considered as in any sense "exceptional".

The only steps taken in consequence of Indonesia's action were that it was replaced on a number of subsidiary organs and bodies within ECOSOC, and the General Assembly refrained from making a budgetary assessment with respect to Indonesia.

In September, 1966, following a change in government within the country, Indonesia notified the Secretary-General that it had "decided to resume full co-operation with the United Nations and to resume participation in its activities". When the General Assembly met, the President of the Assembly summarised the position by saying that "the Government of Indonesia considers that its recent absence from the Organisation was based not upon a withdrawal from the United Nations but upon a cessation of co-operation. The action so far taken by the United Nations on this matter would not appear to preclude this view. If this is also the general view of the membership, the Secretary-General would give instructions for the necessary administrative actions to be taken for Indonesia to participate again in the proceedings of the Organisation." As no objections were made, Indonesia was allowed to resume its place in the Assembly.

It could be argued that, if Indonesia had withdrawn as was claimed in

16.   7 U.N.C.I.O. 430-1.

1965, it could not have "resumed" its place in the organisation; it should have been "readmitted", presumably by the General Assembly upon the recommendation of the Security Council in accordance with Article 4 of the Charter. The settlement of Indonesia's financial obligations by an "appropriate payment" in respect of the period of its "withdrawal" was clearly designated to preserve the interpretation that Indonesia had never ceased to be a member.

The Indonesian case only provides limited assistance in defining the scope of withdrawal in the absence of an express provision in the Charter. As with W.H.O. and U.N.E.S.C.O., member states were divided between the feeling that withdrawal should not be encouraged and the knowledge that it is difficult to force a state to participate in the work of an organisation against its wishes. Nevertheless, the reaction of the United Kingdom probably reflects majority opinion in recognising that the existence of Committee 1/2's report makes it impossible to deny altogether a right to withdraw. Once this right is recognised, the issue of what conditions would justify a withdrawal is of less significance. To allow withdrawal is to recognise the futility of treating as members states which have, for all practical purposes, withdrawn. It is of no value to attempt to limit that right of withdrawal to "special circumstances" because such a test is too imprecise. But if the circumstances are spelt out with precision, the situation is essentially similar to having no withdrawal clause for a state wishing to leave the organisation for some other reason.

Attempts are often made to regard the constitution of an international organisation as being juridically identical to an ordinary treaty and to apply the same principles of law to both. Nowhere can this analogy be more harmful than in the present context when dealing with the principle of *pacta sunt servanda*. The dynamic nature of international organisations their constant changes and development, make the analogy inappropriate. Treaties are static instruments; constitutions of international organisations dynamic. Withdrawal is obviously to be discouraged, but as the work and effectiveness of each organisation is based upon co-operation, withdrawal may be a preferable alternative to non-co-operation.

It seemed to be implicit in the handling of Indonesia's resumed participation in the work of the U.N. that if it had effectively withdrawn from the Organisation, it could only have been readmitted by the formal admission procedure laid down in Article 4 of the Charter. But there is no convincing reason why this proposition should be accepted. On its terms alone, Article 4 does not obviously apply to readmission. In fact, there would appear to be less obstacle to the application of Article 110 (4).[17] And once one accepts that an original state that has withdrawn is not obliged to be "re-admitted", there is no good reason for applying Article 4 to states subsequently admitted that have withdrawn. Whether Indonesia had withdrawn or only temporarily ceased to participate in the work

---

17. The I.L.O. Constitution (Art. 1 (6)) expressly provides for readmission by the same alternatives as admission.

of the Organisation, there would have been no legal obstacle to its "re-admission" by the informal method adopted.

ii *Suspension and expulsion*

In accepting the terms of the constitutional treaty establishing an organisation, a state agrees to be bound by the terms of that constitution. Even if withdrawal in the absence of a specific provision permitting such action may be justified, there is less reason for supporting punitive action in the form of suspension or expulsion in the absence of express provision.

There is the isolated example of the expulsion of Cuba from O.A.S. in January, 1962. A number of members abstained from voting, doubting the validity of such a step. When increasing hostility to the policies of Portugal and more particularly South Africa led the I.L.O. Conference to press for similar action to be taken against the latter in 1961, it is significant that the Organisation proceeded with more regard to legal niceties. The 1961 Conference requested the Governing Body to advise the Republic of South Africa to withdraw. Eventually, in 1964, the Conference adopted two constitutional amendments, the first of which provided specifically for "suspension from participation in the International Labour Conference" of any Member which has been "found by the United Nations to be flagrantly and persistently pursuing . . . a declared policy of racial discrimination", and the second for expulsion or suspension of any member of I.L.O. which the United Nations had suspended from the rights and privileges of membership. In neither case was the consequence to be automatic: it was to be imposed by a vote concurred in by two-thirds of the delegates attending the session, including the two-thirds of the Government delegates present and voting.

The steps taken within the I.L.O. do suggest that, in the absence of an express provision enabling suspension or exclusion, such action has no legal effect, even if it might have the practical consequence of excluding the state concerned from the benefits of membership.[18]

iii *Non-ratification of constitutional amendments*

A majority of constitutions contain provisions governing amendment procedures, but few expressly cover the position of states which do not ratify amendments. In cases where the procedure laid down is not "legislative", that is, where the amendment will not bind states not ratifying, the problems will be less serious.

Under Article 94 (a) of the I.C.A.O. constitution, amendments approved and ratified in accordance with that provision are only to come into effect with respect to states which have ratified them. The only real problem of having a provision of this type is that, once an amendment is made,

---

18. In the face of increasing hostility South Africa gave notice of withdrawal from the I.L.O. See also the General Assembly's Second Committee's report on South Africa and U.N.C.T.A.D. in (1969) 8 I.L.M. 209.

different rules may apply to different members of an organisation. In practice, however, non-ratification by a large minority will be most unlikely unless the matter is of fundamental importance; and non-ratification by a small number of members will cause little inconvenience unless the alteration is of sufficient importance. To protect the Organisation against the difficulties that would arise in such a situation, Article 94 (b) of the I.C.A.O. Convention provides that if the amendment is of a nature to justify this course, the Assembly in its resolution recommending adoption of the new provision, may provide that any state which does not ratify the amendment within the specified period after it has come into force shall thereupon cease to be a member of an Organisation and party to the Convention.

It is reasonable that an organisation should be able to protect itself in this way. It is equally reasonable that the member which finds that it is bound by significantly different obligations from those governing the relations of other members of an organisation should, if it so wishes, be allowed to withdraw, even in the absence of a specific provision permitting withdrawal.

If this is the position with respect to constitutional amendments which are not binding on all members, *a fortiori* withdrawal should be possible in an organisation amendments to the constitution of which are legislative in effect. Article 108 of the Charter provides that amendments "shall come into force for all Members of the United Nations when they have been adopted by a vote of two thirds of the members of the General Assembly and ratified in accordance with their respective constitutional processes by two-thirds of the Members of the United Nations, including all the permanent members of the Security Council." Amendments effected in accordance with this procedure are clearly legislative in effect: they come into force "for all Members" of the Organisation. It will be recalled that the United Nations Charter makes no provision for withdrawal, although Committee 1/2 of the San Francisco Conference reported that withdrawal might be permissible in "exceptional circumstances". The report went on to discuss in general, and not very satisfactory terms, what the Committee meant by "exceptional circumstances". Among them it included an unacceptable amendment of the Charter: a member would not be "bound to remain in the Organisation if its rights and obligations . . . were changed by Charter amendment in which it has not concurred and which it finds itself unable to accept".

It is believed that this "understanding" of the position by the Committee is representative of the legal position in any organisation in which there is no provision prohibiting withdrawal and no evidence suggesting that withdrawal is not contemplated. In the case of W.H.O. no provision was made for withdrawal, though the International Health Conference of 1946 which approved the constitution added a declaration concerning withdrawal following the entry into force of an amendment unacceptable to a member state. This declaration was in terms identical to the section of the report of Committee 1/2 of the San Francisco Conference quoted above. But, even without this declaration, it is arguable that a right of withdrawal should exist in the circumstances envisaged.

5 DISSOLUTION AND SUCCESSION OF INTERNATIONAL ORGANISATIONS

Whether the constitution of an international organisation makes express provision for its dissolution is, as in the case of withdrawal, primarily a political decision. An organisation, like the United Nations which is designed to achieve universality and to secure permanently international peace and security is not likely to have in its constitution a withdrawal clause, and even less likely to have elaborate procedures for its own dissolution.

In international practice, dissolution alone has been an unusual phenomenon: it has usually been effected in conjunction with a transfer of rights to a new organisation. Before dealing with the "succession" problem, however, it is necessary to separate and to discuss the issues that arise in connection with the act of dissolution.

a DISSOLUTION WITHOUT SUCCESSION

The League of Nations had continued to operate during the period of the Second World War through its Secretary-General and a Supervisory Commission created by the Assembly of the League in 1939. With the creation of the United Nations, the problem arose of how to extinguish the League. A proposal was circulated to states members of the League suggesting that a resolution of the League Assembly would be an appropriate and expeditious means of dissolving the Organisation. As no objections were made to this procedure, the Assembly duly resolved that the Secretary-General and a "Board of Liquidation" should have full powers to wind up the affairs of the League, and that the Assembly itself, the Council and the other organs would cease to exist on the day following the close of the Assembly's session.

While this method had obvious practical advantages, it does raise a number of legal problems. A treaty can be terminated by agreement of the parties. It is possible to regard a unanimous decision of an international organisation to dissolve as evidence of such agreement, but what if the decision is not reached without opposition? For practical purposes a large majority in favour of dissolution may be sufficient, but the legal position is less clear. If the reason for the dissolution is replacement by a new entity to assume the functions of the organisation being wound up, it might be possible to rely upon a plea of change of circumstances which the majority is admitting to exist. In any case, it is most unlikely that a minority would take their opposition to the act of dissolution to the extreme of refusing to acquiesce in the organisation's demise.

If there is to be no succession, dissolution raises the question of what to do with the assets of the organisation. It is thought that the administration of the liquidation set out in the articles of association of the financial agencies provide a useful guide to the approach likely to be adopted.[19] The basis of the provisions is that the organisation's debts to external creditors should be paid first and that assets remaining after such payments should then be distributed among member states. Of course, it is possible that states might participate in more than one capacity. For example, a state may have made a loan to the organisation as well as contributed as a member to the budget of the organisation. In respect of the first transaction, the state is entitled to priority, but not in respect of the second.

In winding up an organisation, it is presumed that arrangements would be made for the equitable termination of the contracts of employment of the secretariat of the organisation. Any sums agreed upon to be paid in lieu of notice, or to be paid under the award of an administrative tribunal, would be debts of the organisation ranking in priority to distribution of assets among member states.

The reason for the detailed provisions covering "liquidation" in the case of the financial agencies is obvious enough. All the agencies are creditors or debtors of large funds. Most other organisations have only to cover current expenditure in their budgets. Hence repayment of any surplus funds will no doubt easily be calculated on the basis of the rate of contribution of each state to the organisation's budget. Minor variations are readily adopted if the assets include accumulated income or there have been recent increases in membership.

b SUCCESSION

i *Transfer of assets*

The usual procedure in cases where a new organisation is to succeed to the assets, rights and duties of the organisation being dissolved is for the two institutions to effect the transfer by formal treaty. For example, in July, 1946, the Secretary-General of the League of Nations and the U.N. Secretary-General's representative at Geneva entered into a series of agreements on behalf of their respective organisations for the transfer of the assets, services and facilities of the League in Switzerland to the United Nations.[20] Later agreements between the two officials dealt with the transfer of various charitable and other funds to the control of the United Nations.[21] Similarly, when U.N.R.R.A. went into liquidation in 1948, it entered into an agreement with the United Nations for the transfer of its residual net assets to the U.N. for the account of U.N.I.C.E.F.[1] Pending dissolution, the affairs of the Administration were placed in the hands of an Administrator for Liquidation.

ii *Transfer of functions*

While a transfer of assets is primarily a matter for the organisations concerned, the transfer of functions raises more acutely the issue of

---

19. E.g., I.M.F. Schedule E; I.B.R.D., Article 6 (5).
20. 1 U.N.T.S., pp. 109, 119, 131, 135.
21. 4 U.N.T.S. 443, 449; 5 U.N.T.S. 389, 395.   1.   27 U.N.T.S. 349.

whether states affected or likely to be affected by the exercise of the functions to be transferred need consent to the transfer. If the question of the transfer of supervision over the mandate system of the League of Nations to the United Nations is examined, the legal dilemma will readily be appreciated.

South-West Africa was administered by South Africa under a mandate agreement with the League. Supervision of the carrying out of the mandate was vested in the Council of the League to which annual reports had to be submitted by South Africa in accordance with Article 22 of the Covenant of the League and Article 6 of the mandate. In a resolution of 18th April, 1946, the Assembly of the League had recognised that, "on the termination of the League's existence, its functions with respect to the mandated territories will come to an end"; had noted that the U.N. Charter embodied "principles corresponding to those declared in Article 22 of the Covenant"; and had also taken note "of the expressed intentions of the Members of the League now administering territories under Mandate to continue to administer them for the well-being and development of the peoples concerned in accordance with the obligations contained in the respective Mandates, until other arrangements have been made between the United Nations and the respective mandatory Powers." But there was no express transfer of functions to the United Nations.

As will be remembered, South Africa was the only administering power which refused to enter into a trusteeship agreement with the United Nations to supersede its mandate. Disputes have arisen with regard to South Africa's obligations under the mandate, and these controversies have been the subject matter of a number of advisory opinions by the International Court. In the first case,[2] the Court was asked three questions: about the continued existence of the mandate, about the applicability of Chapter XII of the Charter dealing with supervision of trusteeship agreements to mandates, and about the competence of South Africa acting alone to modify the status of South-West Africa. The Court had no difficulty in answering the first and third questions. It had been obvious to all concerned that the mandates continued to exist, even after the dissolution of the League. It was envisaged that they should be replaced by trusteeship agreements but there was no obligation upon a mandatory to enter into such an agreement. On the other hand, the fact that the mandatory continued to be bound by the mandate implied that it could not unilaterally alter the status of the mandated territory.

The question of the applicability of Chapter XII, however, was juridically different: it did not depend upon any clear interpretative approach to the mandate agreement. The mandate imposed certain obligations upon the mandatory to submit reports to the League Council. The mandate continued to exist, but the supervisory organ had disappeared. The United Nations, it is true, had within its framework an organ (i.e. the General

---

2. Status of South-West Africa, I.C.J. Rep. 1950, p. 128.

Assembly) designed to supervise a similar régime for non-self-governing territories, but no provision had been made for it to assume the functions of the League Council in respect of the mandate system.

In linking the obligation to submit to supervision contained in a mandate to the U.N. system for supervising trusteeship territories, the Court was undoubtedly calling in aid the principle of "effectiveness",[3] that treaties should be interpreted in order that they should be effective. This "necessity" that the mandates should be adequately supervised prompted the Court to apply Chapter XII of the Charter to cover the supervision of mandate as well as trusteeship territories. But how can this be reconciled with the Court's opinion to the effect that the territory remained under the mandate and that the Charter imposed no obligation upon the mandatory power to enter into a trusteeship agreement?

The purpose for questioning this part of the Court's judgment is to illustrate the legal difficulty that will always arise if one entity attempts to assume functions previously bestowed upon another institution which has ceased to exist. If the Charter had contained express provision governing transfer of supervisory functions, no problem would have arisen. The agreement of the mandatory power would be implicit in its ratification of the Charter.

South Africa's agreement to *a* transfer of functions can probably be implied from its statements to the effect that, pending international recognition of the incorporation of South-West Africa as part of South Africa, South Africa would consider itself bound by the terms of the mandate including the obligation to submit an annual report on its administration of the territory. However, this "agreement" fell far short of a recognition of, or assent to, a total succession by the United Nations to the authority previously exercised by the League. As Judge McNair said in dissenting from the Court on this issue, he could find no "legal ground on which the Court would be justified in replacing the Council of the League by the United Nations for the purposes of exercising the administrative supervision of the Mandate and the receipt and examination of reports. It would amount to imposing a new obligation upon the Union Government and would be a piece of judicial legislation. In saying this, I do not overlook the competence of the General Assembly . . . under Article 10 of the Charter, to discuss the Mandate for South-West Africa and to make recommendations concerning it, but that competence depends not upon any theory of implied succession but upon the provision of the Charter."[4]

Despite the view of the majority of the Court a succession of one organisation to the functions of another depends upon the consent not only of a majority, but also of any state affected by the exercise of the functions. That consent may certainly be implied from the conduct of the state

---

3. Though the Court never admitted that this was what it was doing, presumably because in the same year it had been careful to limit application of the principle: *Peace Treaties* case, *ibid.*, p. 221.

4. *Ibid.*, at pp. 161-2.

concerned, but an acknowledgment of the general position of the successor need not imply acceptance of its right to exercise all the powers of the former authority. By dealing with the General Assembly as the appropriate U.N. organ with which to discuss the future of South-West Africa, South Africa was not assenting to a total exercise by the Assembly of the various functions of the League Council.

However, even if there has been an assent to, amounting to a total acceptance of, the successor's authority, there still remains the problem of identifying the means for the exercise of the functions, for it may be that the procedures of the two organs are not identical. In the disputes over South-West Africa, for example, the ultimate authority of the League Council was exercised through decisions based upon the unanimity rule; the nearest equivalent in the General Assembly was the two-thirds majority required for important questions under Article 18 of the Charter.

In 1955 this question of voting differences was submitted to the International Court.[5] In holding that it was correct for the General Assembly to regard questions relating to reports and petitions as important questions, the Court pointed out that it was not possible for the Assembly to adopt procedures identical to those of the League Council. Referring to its advisory opinion of 1950, the Court commented that when it "stated in its previous Opinion that in exercising its supervisory functions the General Assembly should conform 'as far as possible to the procedure followed in this respect by the Council of the League of Nations', it was indicating that in the nature of things the General Assembly, operating under an instrument different from that which governed the Council of the League of Nations, would not be able to follow precisely the same procedures as were followed by the Council. Consequently, the expression 'as far as possible' was designed to allow for adjustments and modifications necessitated by legal or practical considerations."[6]

Nevertheless, adjustments and modifications cannot justify an *extension* of the powers assumed from the previous authority. In a third request for an advisory opinion on South-West Africa,[7] the Court was asked whether the General Assembly's Committee on South-West Africa could grant oral hearings to petitioners on matters relating to South-West Africa. The Permanent Mandates Commission of the League had not done so, principally because the Council had been reluctant to authorise such hearings in the face of opposition from the mandatory powers. In the Court's view it was true that the "degree of supervision to be exercised by the General Assembly should not . . . exceed that which applied under the Mandates system",[8] but there was no reason to interpret this statement as implying that the Assembly should be restricted to measures which had actually been applied by the League of Nations. There was no provision

---

5. I.C.J. Rep. 1955, p. 67.   6. *Ibid.*, at pp. 76–77.
7. I.C.J. Rep. 1956, p. 23.
8. A quotation from the first advisory opinion, I.C.J. Rep. 1950, at p. 138.

contained in the League Covenant, in the Mandate agreement, or in the U.N. Charter which prohibited the adoption of such a course by the League Council or by the General Assembly if it was necessary for the maintenance of effective international supervision of the administration of the mandated territory.

CHAPTER SIXTEEN

THE USE OF FORCE BY STATES

The extent to which a state is entitled to use force in the conduct of its international relations raises a profusion and a confusion of politico-legal problems which are scarcely capable of analysis, let alone solution. Nevertheless, no account of the contemporary legal framework within which these relations are conducted would be complete without some attempt to postulate the legal rules that exist, or are alleged to exist, and the political pressures that are exerted within, and perhaps outside, these rules.

In no area is international law more vulnerable to the taunt that "it doesn't really work" than in the context of the rules which are claimed to exist prohibiting or restricting the use of force. The reason why this type of assertion is made is partly due to the fact that widespread publicity is given to instances of the use of force by states, while peaceful inaction or co-operation, that is, the normal situation in the relations of states, merits scarcely a mention in the news media. However, the making of such an assertion discloses a fundamental misunderstanding of the role of international law. It has already been demonstrated that legal principles are only allowed to be the sole determinants within a limited area (i.e. mainly within the jurisdictional competence of the International Court). The more important the issue, the less tractable it is to anything other than political compromise in which the part played by legal rules is correspondingly limited. And if one assumes that states will only have recourse to force as a last resort when they consider their vital interests most gravely threatened or affected, the role of legal principle may well vanish altogether, even though the states concerned will often advance reasons which purport to establish the legality of their actions within the existing or supposed legal order.

I THE RIGHT TO WAGE WAR

a THE HISTORICAL BACKGROUND

Although Grotius and other writers of the late Middle Ages and early modern times attempted to distinguish between the just and unjust war, the modern state system, built as it was on the basis of the theory of state sovereignty, treated the right to wage war as inherent in the concept of sovereignty. As to resort to war was the right of every state, it was variously defined in the widest terms. In the opinion of Vattel, war was the condition in which nations prosecute their rights by force.[1] According to Washington, J., of the U.S. Supreme Court in *Bas* v. *Tingy*, war was "an external contention by force between . . . two nations".[2] "War is essentially a struggle between states, involving the application of force", was Wheaton's view.[3]

Definitions of this type clearly illustrate the prevailing attitude towards war that existed at the end of the eighteenth century and throughout the nineteenth century. Even though there were various situations in which isolated instances of the use of force (in cases of so-called pacific blockade, reprisals, and even acts of intervention) were generally not regarded as amounting to "war", there was nevertheless a trend towards regarding any use of force and war as identical. For example following the blockade of Venezuelan ports by Britain, Germany and Italy in 1902, it was felt necessary by Britain and Venezuela to include in their protocol of 1903 a provision which, after reciting that "inasmuch that it may be contended [as it was by the United States] that the establishment of a blockade of a Venezuelan port by British naval forces has, *ipso facto*, created a state of war between Britain and Venezuela and that any treaty existing between the two countries has been thereby abrogated", went on to confirm the existence of their treaties.

b THE COVENANT OF THE LEAGUE OF NATIONS

It was a widely held belief at the time that the First World War had been caused "by accident"; that, if states had only had a forum in which to discuss their problems, misunderstandings would have been cleared up and war would have been avoided. The Covenant of the League of Nations was designed to provide such a forum. The right to resort to force was restricted. Under Article 12 (1) member states agreed that, if there arose between them any dispute likely to lead to a rupture, they would submit the matter either to arbitration or judicial settlement, or to inquiry by the Council, and they agreed in no case to resort to war until three months after the award by the arbitrator or the judicial decision, or the report by the Council. This three month "cooling period", it was believed, would prevent the "accidental" outbreak of hostilities.

c THE PACT OF PARIS AND THE PRACTICE OF STATES

The Covenant in no sense "abolished" war. The nearest it came to such a proscription was in Article 10 whereby members of the League undertook "to respect and preserve as against external aggression the territorial integrity and existing political independence of all Members of the League". However, this provision was subsequently reinforced by the Kellogg–Briand Pact of 1928, in accordance with Article 1 of which some

---

1. *The Law of Nations* (1758), Classics of International Law, ed., p. 235.
2. 4 Dallas 37, at p. 40 (1800). 3. *International Law*, 7th ed., p. 68.

sixty-three states solemnly declared in the names of their respective peoples that they condemned "recourse to war for the solution of international controversies" and renounced it "as an instrument of national policy in their relations with one another."

Although Article 10 of the Covenant talked of "aggression", the extent of the limitations upon the use of force that existed at the outbreak of the Second World War depended upon the definition of "war" in the Covenant and, more particularly, in the 1928 Pact of Paris. Given the wide meaning attributed to the term during the nineteenth and at the beginning of the twentieth century, the latter instrument amounted to a nearly total prohibition on the use of force in the relations of its signatories *inter se*.

The practice of states during the 1930s was more equivocal. It is true that the Italian invasion of Abyssinia led to the recommendation by the Council of the League that economic sanctions be imposed upon Italy. However, the ineffectiveness of the sanctions demonstrated the reluctance of a majority of League members to guarantee the carrying out of the obligations of the Covenant. Even less were those states prepared to become involved in the war between Japan and China stemming from the initial attack by Japan upon the Chinese province of Manchuria in 1931. Although the Lytton Commission of Enquiry rejected all Japanese justifications for that state's aggressive acts, the members of the League took no positive act beyond a general policy of non-recognition of the new "state" of Manchunko which Japan purported to establish out of the Chinese province.

Symptomatic of the reluctance of states to treat continued hostilities as "war" contrary to the Covenant and the Pact was the attitude of the British Government. A case before the English Court of Appeal[4] concerned the cancellation of a charterparty under a term in the contract enabling either party to cancel "if war breaks out involving Japan". The commercial arbitrator found that at the date of cancellation (18th September, 1937) and for some time previously serious fighting had been in progress between Japan and China over large areas of the territory of the latter. In reply to an inquiry from the plaintiffs' solicitors, however, the British Foreign Office stated that "the current situation in China is indeterminate and His Majesty's Government are not at present prepared to say that a state of war exists."

d THE NUREMBURG TRIBUNAL

As will be discussed shortly, the United Nations Charter deliberately avoided the use of the term war. In an attempt to prevent semantic controversy, the Charter made use of general expressions like "the threat or use of force" or "threats to the peace" or "breaches of the peace". Although the charter of the International Military Tribunal which was created to deal with the major Nazi war criminals postdated the Charter of the United Nations, the duty of the Tribunal was to apply the law as it

---

4. *Kawasaki Kisen* v. *Bantham Steamship Co.*, [1939] 2 K.B. 544.

was claimed to have existed at the end of the 1930s. Hence its jurisdiction was defined in such a manner as to comply with the outlawing of war in the Kellogg-Briand Pact. The charter of the Tribunal defined as *crimes against peace* the "planning, preparation, initiation or waging of a war of aggression, or a war in violation of international treaties, agreements or assurances".

It cannot be claimed that all the Tribunal's decisions on this issue were logically convincing. It decided that certain of the accused had "planned and waged aggressive wars against twelve nations". However, the invasion of Austria,[5] described by the Tribunal as a "premeditated aggressive step in furthering the plan to wage aggressive wars against other countries", was carried out almost entirely without bloodshed. Even if one accepts the Tribunal's finding that the "ultimate factor was the armed might of Germany ready to be used if any resistance was encountered", the *anschluss* with Austria was scarcely classifiable as a resort to war within the scope of the expression as understood or applied in 1938.

The basic law of the Tribunal, as set out in its charter, to a large extent avoided the issue of whether the absorption of Austria constituted the "waging" of aggressive war by coalescing the crime charged as one of "planning and waging". Hence it was possible to consider the *anschluss* as part of the planning stage of the overall design to wage aggressive war. As the Tribunal said in the course of its judgment in the trial of Von Papen, there was "no evidence that he was a party to the plans under which the occupation of Austria was a step in the direction of further aggressive action, or even that he participated in plans to occupy Austria by aggressive war if necessary."[6]

Similar doubts could be raised with respect to the German seizure of Czechoslovakia and occupation of Denmark. In both cases the take over was accomplished without the outbreak of hostilities under the terms of agreements with the governments of the states concerned. However, the agreement with Czechoslovakia was only signed after Hitler threatened to bomb Prague out of existence; and, in the case of Denmark, it was known that German troops would have invaded the country if agreement to their entry had not been forthcoming.

2 THE UNITED NATIONS CHARTER AND THE CONCEPT OF AGGRESSION

Although speaking in terms clearly referrable to the Paris Pact, the Nuremberg Tribunal based its decisions on the notion that the Covenant and the Pact were specific conventional instances of a wider principle of customary law outlawing "aggressive war". The U.N. Charter accepted this principle but defined it in such a way as to leave no doubt that the principle could be broken even though no force had been used providing that the same result was achieved by the threat of force. Thus Article 2 (4) of the Charter provides that all members of the Organisation "shall refrain in their international relations from the threat or use of force against the

---

5. 22 I.M.T. 433-6.   6. *Ibid.*, 573.

territorial integrity or political independence of any State". This provision clearly accords with the finding of the Tribunal that the occupation of Denmark by Germany in 1940, though accomplished with the "agreement" of the Danish Government, was nevertheless contrary to the proscription of the use of force already existing under customary international law.

However Article 2 (4) goes beyond prohibiting the threat or use of force against territorial integrity or political independence by adding "or in any other manner inconsistent with the purposes of the United Nations". The Purposes of the Organisation are set out in Article 1. They are so widely drawn that, assuming for the moment that a state retains a right to use force unless it is otherwise prohibited from doing so, it is by no means easy to determine when a particular use of force, not directed against territorial integrity or political independence, would be covered by this additional proscription. If one takes the first two Purposes —to maintain international peace and security, and to develop friendly relations among nations based on respect for the principle of equal rights and self-determination of peoples—it can be seen how potentially all-embracing is the formula adopted by Article 2 (4). Any use of force by a state outside its own borders is likely to be inconsistent with the general purpose of maintaining international peace and security or of promoting friendly relations among nations.

While the Charter places an imprecise but nevertheless wide prohibition on the use of force by states, it also explicitly provides for a major exception to the general prohibition. As will be discussed shortly, Article 51 preserves what it terms "the inherent right of individual or collective self-defence if an armed attack occurs against a Member of the United Nations". At this stage all that is necessary is to notice that the terminology of Article 51, although apparently precise, has given rise to controversy because self-defence under customary international law was almost certainly wider in application than this provision suggests. Despite the differences between the Charter and the earlier instruments like the Covenant and the Paris Pact, there nevertheless remains a "twilight zone" between permissible and impermissible coercion. And because of the existence of this area of uncertainty, the process whereby the international community determines whether the Charter obligations have been broken becomes a matter of the greatest significance.

As the organ having the primary responsibility for the maintenance of international peace and security, the Security Council of the United Nations has the power under Article 39 of the Charter to "determine the existence of any threat to the peace, breach of the peace or act of aggression" and to "make recommendations, or decide what measures shall be taken . . . to maintain or restore international peace and security." The measures that the United Nations can take once such a determination has been made have already been considered.[7] In the present context, what is

---

7.   Above, Chapter 13. States can of course use force if they have been so authorised by a resolution of the Security Council or of the General Assembly.

important is the meaning to be attributed to the expressions "threat to the peace", "breach of the peace" or "act of aggression" upon which the determination must depend.

It is hardly surprising that in any given situation a member of the Security Council when called upon to decide whether what has occurred constitutes an act within the compass of Article 39 will be motivated primarily by its own political interests and attitudes. To take an extreme illustration of the influence likely to be exerted by political and ideological considerations, the Soviet-Marxist doctrine of aggression depends upon distinguishing between the ends to be achieved by the use of force. A war is never "unjust" or "aggressive" if it is a war of liberation waged, not with a view to conquest, but to free a people from their colonialist masters, or to defend a people from imperialist conquest. Such a conquest might be achieved either by direct military action or by subversion. Hence, the Russian invasion of Czechoslovakia in 1968 was justifiable, in Soviet Communist ideology, *inter alia* upon the alleged basis of protecting the Czech people from subversive imperialist elements which had permeated, and were taking advantage of the status of, the Czech Communist party.

In an attempt to restrict the influence of political factors in deciding whether a particular use of force constituted a breach of the Charter, a great deal of time during the 1950s was spent by the International Law Commission and by the Sixth Committee and by Special Committees of the General Assembly on the problem of defining aggression. Although, of course, Article 39 refers to threats to the peace and breaches of the peace as well as to acts of aggression, the approach was to consider the problem from the point of view of the respect for territorial integrity and political independence requirement of Article 2 (4). In other words, it was assumed that, as a broad generalisation, a threat to the peace or breach of the peace inconsistent with the main obligations of Article 2 (4) could constitute aggression. Other possible threats or breaches were of less importance and need not therefore be covered by any prescriptive formula.

The definitions advanced fell within three main categories:

a DEFINITIONS BY LISTING ACTS CATEGORISED AS AGGRESSIVE

This approach has been consistently favoured by the Soviet Union since its proposals were written into the 1933 London Convention on the Definition of Aggression.

b DEFINITIONS IN GENERAL TERMS

Definitions of this type suffer from the obvious handicap that their very generalisations come little nearer to guiding the "decision-maker" than the use of the term "aggression" itself.

c DEFINITIONS COMBINING (A) AND (B)

An example of this form of definition is that submitted jointly to the General Assembly by Iran and Panama.[8] It first described aggression in

---

8. For a convenient text, see Stone, *Aggression and World Order*, pp. 202–3.

general terms as "the use of armed force by a state against another state for any purpose other than the exercise of the inherent right of individual or collective self-defence or in pursuance of a decision or recommendation of a competent organ of the United Nations." Then, it continued, "in addition to any other acts which such international bodies as may be called upon to determine the aggressor may declare to constitute aggression, the following are acts of aggression in all cases": these acts included invasion; armed attack against the territory, population, or armed forces of a state; blockade; or the "organisation, or the encouragement of the organisation, by a state, of armed bands within its territory or any other territory for incursions into the territory of another state, or the toleration of the organisation of such bands in its own territory, or the toleration of the use by such armed bands of its territory as a base of operations or as a point of departure for incursions into the territory of another state, as well as direct participation in or support of such incursions."

It can be seen that as soon as the attempted definition passes from the general to the particular considerable difficulty is found in drafting descriptions to cover every eventuality. And the closer the definition comes to covering all possibilities, the greater the measure of disagreement among states as to whether a specific activity does constitute aggression. Furthermore, the usefulness of any definition is likely to be minimal unless it provides some answer to when the use of force may be legitimately classified as "self-defence". If one accepts (as most states publicly appear to acknowledge) that any use of force needs to be justified (i.e. is *prima facie* "illegal"), the problem is seen in a different light. It is not "aggression" alone that requires definition, but also "non-aggression", which usually means self-defence.

Before turning to the role of self-defence, however, it is apparent from the discussion so far that, even if aggression is not capable of definition in terms that are at the same time useful and sufficiently precise, some *description* is necessary of the circumstances in which aggression is alleged to have taken place.

It is possible to accept a declaration of war against another state; any attack upon or invasion of the territory of that state; the imposition of a blockade of its ports or airspace; etc., as constituting *prima facie* an illegal use of force.

There is also general support for the proposition that the encouragement of armed bands by allowing them to operate across one's borders against the territory of another state constitutes aggression. The civil war that raged in northern Greece after the end of the Second World War was fomented by Communist guerrillas operating from the territory of Greece's northern neighbours. In its Resolution No. 193 of 1948, the General Assembly declared that the "continued aid given by Albania, Bulgaria and Yugoslavia to the Greek guerrillas endangers peace in the Balkans and is inconsistent with the purposes and principles of the Charter".

The Soviet definition of aggression submitted to the General Assembly

Special Committee in 1956[9] referred to the situations already considered, but it also went on to deal with what it termed "indirect", "economic" and "ideological" aggression. In varying degrees these proposals were, and remain, more controversial.

So-called "indirect" aggression related to acts of subversion, encouraged or promoted, by one state against another. It goes beyond aggression by armed bands because it involves no large scale use of the territory of the "aggressor" and repeated crossing of the border between the states concerned. Whether such activities do amount to aggression in the present stage of development of international law must remain doubtful. It is even less likely that economic or propaganda activities directed against another state can be considered as constituting aggression.

3   SELF-DEFENCE

a   CUSTOMARY INTERNATIONAL LAW

Under most municipal legal systems self-help and self-defence have a role to play in the preservation of rights recognised by the legal system concerned. The precise role will depend upon the degree of sophistication of the law-preserving agencies operating within the system. Where these agencies are ineffective, the part allotted to self-defence or self-help will be correspondingly large.

While there is an analogy to be drawn between rights available to individuals in private law and the rights available to states in international law, it is an analogy which at the most provides an imprecise guide and should not, therefore, be taken to logical extremes. Hence it is possible to accept in general terms that "self-defence operates to protect essential rights from irreparable harm in circumstances in which alternative means of protection are unavailable; its function is to preserve or restore the legal *status quo*, and not to take on a remedial or repressive character in order to enforce legal rights" (this latter function being that of self-help).[10] But it is important to realise that "essential rights" in the present context may be very much different when applied to a state under international law than to an individual under municipal law.

As has already been stated, advanced municipal systems can lay down precise rules for the application of the doctrine of self-defence. Being an entirely legal concept, it is subject in any particular case to determination by a court of law. There can be no precise formulation of the concept under international law, nor is there much likelihood of judicial determination on the issue of whether the plea of self-defence has rightfully been raised. It is the responsibility of the international community as a whole to ensure that the plea of self-defence is not advanced as an excuse for the illegal use of force. This responsibility is implicit in the requirement

---

9.   See Stone, *Aggression and World Order*, at pp. 201–2.
10.   Bowett, *Self-Defence in International Law*, p. 11.

of Article 51 of the U.N. Charter that measures taken by members in the exercise of the right of self-defence shall be immediately reported to the Security Council. However, the notion that self-defence could not be arbitrarily employed by states as an excuse for recourse to war had already been accepted prior to 1945. Before both the Nuremberg and Tokyo Tribunals it was argued on behalf of the accused German and Japanese leaders that under the Kellogg–Briand Pact states were entitled to determine conclusively whether their actions had been in self-defence. The contention was emphatically rejected. In the words of the Tokyo Tribunal, under "the most liberal interpretation of the Kellogg–Briand Pact, the right of self-defence does not confer upon the state resorting to war the authority to make a final determination upon the justification for its action. Any other interpretation would nullify the Pact; and this Tribunal does not believe that the Powers in concluding the Pact intended to make an empty gesture."[11]

In order that the world community should be able to classify a particular act as being one taken in self defence it is obviously necessary to have some objective standard of what constitutes a legitimate exercise of the right of self-defence. It is in the light of this need that the description quoted above, which speaks in terms of the protection of "essential rights", may be considered.

i *The rights to be protected*

Customary international law grants to states a variety of "rights" (that treaty obligations should be honoured by other states; that its nationals and their property should be respected; etc.). However, it is clear that a state is not free to use force to safeguard each and every right to which it is entitled. A state is certainly entitled to protect:

1 *Territorial integrity*

The infringement of its territory has always been considered as the most obvious justification for a state to act in its own defence. Both the Covenant of the League and the Charter of the U.N. imposed specific duties designed to protect "territorial integrity".

2 *Political independence*

Both Article 10 of the Covenant and Article 2 (4) of the Charter coupled together respect for territorial integrity and respect for political independence. In many instances an attack against the former will involve an attack against the latter, but there may be situations in which by encouraging or promoting political agitation one state may endanger the political independence of another without necessarily infringing its territorial integrity.

3 *Freedom of navigation for its ships*

Freedom of transit on the high seas is a right which a state is entitled to claim for ships flying its flag. A ship which is entitled to exercise freedom

---

11. I.M.T. for the Far East, p. 68.

of navigation is also entitled to protect that freedom from interference, even to the extent of using force.

In the *Corfu Channel* case,[12] the International Court held that a British naval force was entitled to assert a right of passage through an international strait, even though such passage involved navigating inside Albanian territorial waters. It did not affect the issue that the vessels had been at "action stations" in order to be able to retaliate if fired upon as had occurred during previous voyages through the channel. Implicit in this decision is a recognition that a ship exercising lawful rights of passage is entitled to use force in self-defence.

However it is less certain whether or how far a plea of self-defence can extend to:

4 The protection of nationals abroad

In the past, there have been many instances of a state asserting the right to intervene on the territory of other states in circumstances where the lives or property of its nationals have been in jeopardy. Such claims are advanced less frequently today than in the nineteenth century and during the early part of the present century, but it is by no means certain that the trend is firmly established towards considering the use of force in such circumstances as illegal.

It is reconcilable with the theory of *self*-defence by a state only if one is prepared to extend the underlying concept of diplomatic protection that a state, by taking up a claim on behalf of its nationals, is in fact asserting its own rights. Imminent danger to the nationals of a state may by this fiction be considered as an imminent danger to the state concerned.

Because, as will be discussed shortly, self-defence depends upon the existence of imminent danger, and is restricted by the principle that the action taken should be proportionate to the injury to be prevented, self-defence in the case of nationals is more likely to arise when the threat is to the person of the individuals rather than when it is directed against their property. Hence one finds the U.S. delegate to the Havana Conference of 1928 asking rhetorically what steps the U.S. Government was entitled to take if there was a break down in law and order in a foreign state and a consequent danger to the lives of U.S. nationals, but answering himself in somewhat wider terms by stating that "in such a case a government is fully justified in taking action of a temporary character for the purpose of protecting the lives *and property* of nationals."[13]

5 The protection of a state's economic welfare

Although a state is undoubtedly vitally affected by its economic and trading activities, other states (treaty obligations apart) are under no duty to trade with it. If they refuse to trade, or impose restrictions upon trade with it, it is doubtful whether the "injured" state has legal grounds for

---

12. I.C.J. Rep. 1949, p. 4.
13. Hyde, *International Law Chiefly as Interpreted and Applied by the United States* (2nd ed.), Vol. I, p. 252.

complaint. Admittedly the law in this area is inchoate. There are suggestions in the practice of states that an unjustified refusal to trade with the
deliberate intention of harming the state concerned may be sufficient
reason for that state to take retaliatory measures, otherwise of an illegal
kind, against the property of the state imposing the boycott. It is hardly
likely, however, that a plea of self-defence could excuse the use of force in
such circumstances. Despite various proposals that have been advanced
defining aggression to include "economic aggression", no such principle
has yet been accorded recognition or acceptance as a rule of international
law.

ii *Circumstances giving rise to the right to act in self-defence*

1 *The need to act must be instant and overwhelming*

During the nineteenth century, when there existed no clear limitation
upon the right of states to go to war, a plea of self-defence was not necessary to justify one state waging war against another state. However, force
not amounting to war was *prima facie* wrongful,[14] though international law
did recognise, in varying degrees, a number of different excuses for such
limited use of force. Providing the use of force could be excused as a
reprisal, or perhaps even as a pacific blockade, the states concerned
could continue to regard their relations, both legally and publicly, as
those of friendly states, while the conduct of the state employing force
could not be characterised as illegal. Among the legitimate excuses for
hostile measures falling short of war was included the plea of necessity of
which self-defence was only a special application.

Because of the close correlation between the two concepts, it is hardly
surprising that pleas of "necessity" or of "self-defence" will arise out of
similar situations, and that often it may be difficult to decide which of
them is the more appropriate in the circumstances. In no case is this confusion more apparent than in the *Caroline* incident[15] which is generally
treated as the classic illustration of the exercise of the right of self-defence.

For more than half a century following the War of Independence, there
were strong pressures within the United States demanding the termination
of British rule in Canada. By 1837 the United States Government no
longer professed territorial designs against its northern neighbour, but
there were still groups operating within both Canada and America, the
aim of which was the instigation of a rebellion against the Crown.
Although the U.S. Secretary of State instructed governors of states
bordering on Canada "to arrest the parties concerned if any preparations
are made of a hostile nature against a foreign power in amity with the
United States", there had not been time to put a stop to the activities of
the s.s. *Caroline* which was engaged in ferrying recruits, supplies and arms
to a band of 1,000 men established on Canadian territory. A British force
crossed to the U.S. side of the border, set the *Caroline* on fire and cast the

---

14. Because the States were at peace: there was of course nothing wrongful in going to war.   15. Moore, *Digest*, Vol. 7, pp. 919 *et seq.*

vessel adrift so that it fell to its destruction over the Niagara Falls. During the attack on the vessel, two U.S. citizens were killed. Subsequently, one of the British subjects who had taken part in the raid was arrested in the United States and charged with murder and arson.

Strong protests were made by the British Government at this arrest on the ground that the individual concerned had participated in a justifiable attack against a hostile expedition emanating from American territory. The U.S. Secretary of State acknowledged that such an action could be justified providing the British Government could show the "necessity of self-defence, instant, overwhelming, leaving no choice of means, and no moment for deliberation". This "necessity" the British minister, Lord Ashburton, claimed existed, but in a spirit of compromise he added the British Government's apologies for the infringement of U.S. territory. The U.S. Secretary of State replied to the effect that, as the parties were agreed as to the principles of law, but differed as to their application to the incident, and as an apology had been made, the subject would be "the topic of no further discussion" between their two governments.

The significance of the *Caroline* incident, and of the statement of principle by the U.S. Secretary of State, has been widely exaggerated. Although the situation was in some respects closely analogous to that giving rise to action in self-defence, it had one important point of distinction. It was never alleged that the U.S. authorities were in any way responsible, either by positive act of encouragement or omission to prevent, for the activities of the *Caroline*. Hence the operation carried out by the British force raised two entirely different questions, though they were questions which the diplomatic exchanges tended to confuse. In the first place, at the international level, could the British justify the incursion on to American territory? And, secondly, on the municipal plane, could individuals taking part in the raid plead the purpose and circumstances of the operation as a defence to criminal proceedings in the American Courts?

A plea of self-defence was hardly available to the British authorities on the international plane because no breach of its international duties was alleged against the U.S. Government. In the circumstances, all that they could argue was that the exigencies of the situation demanded immediate and extraordinary action. To violate the territory of an "innocent" state could only be justified on the grounds of necessity, i.e. if the necessity was "instant, overwhelming, leaving no choice of means, and no moment for deliberation". In fact, it is interesting to recall that the Law Officers in giving their opinion on the matter were careful to avoid altogether the expression "self-defence" preferring the wider concept of "self-preservation". Self-preservation is a term which has been largely discarded in the terminology of international law, its place being taken, if at all, by "necessity".

The principal argument advanced by the British Government after the arrest of the individual who, it was alleged, had participated in the attack on the *Caroline* was that, as he had been acting as an agent of the British Government, he could not be personally accountable in the American

Courts for his actions. However, the British Government at the outset had been reticent about their connection with the operation. In reply to the initial American protest over the sinking of the *Caroline*, the British Minister in Washington referred to the violence which "Her Majesty's subjects in Upper Canada had already severely suffered"; with which they were still threatened; and which "naturally and necessarily . . . impelled them to consult their own security, by pursuing and destroying the vessel".

In the Note of 1841 in which the "instant, overwhelming", test first appeared, the Secretary of State almost certainly still had in mind the original British argument that Her Majesty's subjects were entitled to take action for their own protection. What was justifiable among states on grounds of "necessity" could perhaps be justified among individuals as a plea of self-defence. But any extension of self-defence to the preservation of public order must be allowed, if at all, within strictly defined limits. Hence the American demand that the British Government should show "a necessity of self-defence, instant, overwhelming, leaving no choice of means, and no moment for deliberation". The Secretary of State in the course of the same communication observed that the right of self-defence was *necessary for the preservation* of both individuals and nations. This similarity with the principle of necessity as understood in American municipal law may be further illustrated by reference to the charge made to the jury in the contemporaneous case of *U.S.* v. *Holmes.*[16] The issue "does not become 'a case of necessity' unless all ordinary means of self preservation have been exhausted. The peril must be instant, overwhelming, leaving no alternative but to lose our own life, or to take the life of another person."

The similarity between the language used in the two cases can be of assistance to an understanding of the *Caroline* incident. Self-defence had already emerged as a definite principle of the common law, but the existence of necessity as a defence still remains a matter of controversy. If necessity did exist as an independent defence to a charge arising out of a use of force by an individual, it was certainly only within the most limited ambit. It is surprising, therefore, that if the Secretary of State had considered the case as one of self-defence he should have employed language in keeping with the Anglo-American concept of necessity, but almost certainly too restrictive if applied to the common law notion of self-defence.

Nor should too much be read into the fact that the British Government accepted the formulation of the law put forward by the U.S. Secretary of State. It could hardly have seemed worthwhile cavilling at the use of the expression "necessity of self-defence" instead of the "self-preservation" employed by the Law Officers. Being reluctant to exacerbate matters by alleging a breach of a duty of prevention by the American authorities

---

16. Fed. Cas. No. 15383 (1842): for a convenient text, see Brett and Waller, *Cases and Materials in Criminal Law*, 2nd ed., pp. 75-78.

(which might have enabled the authorities in Canada a more general power to take preventive action across the border), the Foreign Office was content to justify the attack within the terms of the American formulation of the law and to add an apology with a view to facilitating a final settlement.

In the final analysis, the traditional rules of international law allowed a state to employ force, short of actually declaring war, in defence of certain of its rights if these were threatened by a breach of duty on the part of another state. The interests which it could protect in this way were sufficiently wide to suggest that a plea of self-defence was less restricted than one might suppose on an initial reading of the views expressed by the U.S. Government in the *Caroline* case. A use of force in a situation where there had been no breach of duty by the state against which action was taken could only be justified on the exceptional grounds of necessity, or self-preservation as it was often termed. The *Caroline* case itself illustrates this point. And to take another example, the sinking of the French fleet at Oran at the time of the French surrender in 1940 could perhaps be justified by the British Government on the basis that it was impelled to act by "necessity" as it could not risk the possibility of the ships being used by the Germans.

2 The force used must be proportionate to the harm threatened

Whether the action taken is in self-defence or is based on "necessity", it is generally accepted that the degree of force must be commensurate with the harm to be averted. In the course of the *Caroline* dispute, in the communication in which he put forward his "instant, overwhelming" test, the American Secretary of State emphasised that even if "the necessity of the moment" justified the incursion into American territory, the British Government still had to show that the Canadian authorities had done "nothing unreasonable or excessive; since the act justified by the necessity of self-defence must be limited by that necessity, and kept clearly within it".

Because of its basis in municipal law principles relating to self-defence, the test of proportionality tends to be regarded in absolute terms. It is argued that the use of force in self-defence must approximate in degree to that employed by the aggressor. The consequence of this tendency is that the essentially imprecise nature of the rules of international law is lost sight of. Nowhere is this more apparent than in the largely unrealistic debates on whether today nuclear weapons can be employed as a means of self-defence against an attack by conventional weapons.

In the very different conditions of a court-orientated municipal system, it is possible for a rule to develop based upon essentially legalistic distinctions. Hence in the allied defence of provocation to a charge of murder at common law, the English Courts have established that "fists might be answered with fists, but not with a deadly weapon".[17] In the international

---

17.   Per Devlin, J., in *R.* v. *Duffy*, [1949] 1 All E.R. 932, at p. 933.

community, however, the categorisation of an act as lawful self-defence depends upon the general community reaction, and by its very nature this reaction is incapable of providing a precise formulation of a rule of law in itself, or a precedent upon which such a formulation might be based.

Of course, the very imprecision of the rules gives states a considerable latitude in interpreting and acting upon them. While this fact might appear particularly unfortunate in a field as vital as the use of force, the remedy is not in the hands of the writer on international law to attempt to define exact criteria for the legality of the use of force in self-defence. It is, therefore, fanciful to test the degree of force used by the amount of force it is designed to counter. Thus it is probably more in keeping with reality to adopt the proposition that the amount of force should be commensurate with the objectives that a plea of self-defence might reasonably entitle a state to achieve.

If self-defence is judged from this standpoint a number of controversial issues are readily resolved. There is no set rule that retaliation with nuclear weapons even on a limited scale is out of proportion to an attack with conventional weapons. Providing the use is restricted so that it achieves no more than the objects which the attacked state is entitled to achieve there is no reason why it cannot be justified as lawful self-defence.

A state that is subject to continual harassment by a neighbouring state, for example, could legitimately strike against the base-camp or centre of organisation of the raids even though this attack might necessarily be on a much larger scale than each individual raid, or even than the sum total of the raids. The object to be achieved is the prevention of raids in the future or a reduction in their number and effectiveness. The test is still, however, essentially relative. It may be for example that the amount of force necessary to prevent further raids altogether would be out of proportion to the continuing threat. The state concerned would be obliged to settle for an operation on a smaller scale with more limited objectives, such as the hampering of future attacks by destroying supply dumps, bases or training camps used by personnel participating in the raid.

b THE EFFECTS OF THE U.N. CHARTER

i *In general*

Customary international law allowed a state a wide and largely ill-defined right to employ force in its own defence. There was no significant reason why it should have been defined more precisely until limits were placed upon the freedom of states to pursue a policy based upon force as an instrument of national policy. The Kellogg-Briand Pact, by restricting the right to wage *war*, increased the importance of achieving an adequate definition of self-defence. However, it was only with the much wider prescriptions contained in the Charter that it became necessary to distinguish between self-defence and other forms of coercion falling short of war—like reprisals, for instance.

While it was true that the traditional law did recognise that a state could employ self-defence to prevent or restrict the effectiveness of hostile acts against its territory, and reprisals as retaliation against previous acts as a deterrent for the future, such a distinction was of little practical significance. The Charter obligations relating to the peaceful settlement of disputes and to the maintenance of international peace and security, and the specific undertaking to refrain from the threat or use of force against the territorial integrity of any state, make any use of force by a state *prima facie* illegal. But because Article 51 specifically reserves to states the "inherent right of self-defence", the distinction between self-defence and reprisals has assumed fundamental importance.

In 1964 British aircraft undertook an attack against a small fort situated in Yemeni territory just across the border from the South Arabian Federation for the defence of which Britain had treaty obligations. The borders of the Federation had been violated on a number of occasions by Yemeni forces and aircraft. Damage had been caused and loss of life had occurred in these attacks. The British selected the fort as a military installation with only a small civilian population who were warned by pamphlets dropped from the air of the impending attack so that they could leave if they wished. Criticism of the attack was based on the allegation that it was essentially a retaliation or reprisal. This allegation was hotly denied by the British Government. Before the Security Council the British representative accepted that there was "a clear distinction to be drawn between two forms of self-help. One, which is of a retributive or punitive nature, is termed 'retaliation' or 'reprisals'; the other, which is expressly contemplated and authorised by the Charter, is self-defence against armed attack." He pointed out that "legitimate action of a defensive nature . . . may sometimes have to take the form of a counter-attack", and then re-asserted the basis of the British argument that the fort in question "was not merely a military installation, but was known to be a centre for aggressive action against the Federation. To destroy the fort with the minimum use of force was, therefore, a defensive measure which was proportionate to and confined to the necessities of the case".[18]

This problem of distinguishing between self-defence and other forms of self-help is not confined to cases of reprisals. A better known example arose in the *Corfu Channel* case.[19] It will be recalled that the Court held that a British naval force had been entitled to assert its right of passage through the channel even though it involved passing through Albanian territorial waters, and the "innocence" of the passage was not destroyed by the fact that the ships were at "action stations". In view of previous incidents, they were entitled to be prepared to fire back in self-defence if attacked. Following the damage to two of the ships from mines, however,

---

18. Lauterpacht, *British Practice in International Law* (1964), pp. 109–113. See also the Security Council reaction (9 I.L.M. 445) to the Israeli raid on Beirut airport as a "reprisal" for the earlier attack by Lebanese based "commandos" on an Israeli airliner in Switzerland. Even under customary international law a reprisal was illegal if it involved a disproportionate amount of force: see the *Naulilaa* case, above pp. 392–393. A reprisal might be permissible as a last resort in a case of "necessity", in which case the degree of force would depend upon the "necessity" for action.

19. I.C.J. Rep. 1949, p. 4. For the Cuban Quarantine, see above pp. 267–273.

a large British force was assembled to protect a mine-sweeping operation carried out inside Albanian territorial waters. The Court refused to accept that this operation could be justified on the ground of self-protection or self-help. "Between independent states, respect for territorial sovereignty is an essential foundation of international relations. The Court recognises that the Albanian Government's complete failure to carry out its duties after the explosions, and the dilatory nature of its diplomatic notes, are extenuating circumstances for the action of the United Kingdom Government. But to ensure respect for international law, of which it is the organ, the Court must declare that the action of the British Navy constituted a violation of Albanian sovereignty."[20]

ii *Article 51 in particular*

Article 51 provides *inter alia* that nothing "in the present Charter shall impair the inherent right of individual or collective self-defence if an armed attack occurs against a Member of the United Nations, until the Security Council has taken the measures necessary to maintain international peace and security". However straight-forward this provision might appear at first sight, it has nevertheless been the subject of continuing controversy. Indeed, on closer examination it will be noticed that Article 51 contains a number of ambiguities. These ambiguities are perhaps best considered in the context of the issues which have been the most debated.

1 *"Anticipatory" self-defence*

Because Article 51 refers solely to situations where an armed attack has actually occurred, it has been argued that the Charter only reserves the right of self-defence to this limited extent. Supporters of this view have inevitably been led into tortuous distinctions between different situations to decide whether each situation qualifies as an "armed attack". Once a missile is launched, it may be said that the attack has commenced; but does it also apply to the sailing of an offensive naval force? Does the training of guerrillas and other irregular forces for use against another state constitute an armed attack?

Such legalistic arguments, as has been stated before in other contexts, are likely to be self-defeating. Unless a rule of international law is based upon the practice of states or is sufficiently general to fit in with both that practice and the reasonable demands of states likely to be faced with the need to act, it is probable that it will not be observed. And in the international community, rules based solely upon the legal niceties of treaty construction without adequate recognition by states are unlikely to meet those demands.

However, there would appear to be no need to adopt such an unrealistic approach to Article 51, because it is possible to reconcile its wording with the reasonable interests of states. It has already been pointed out that Article 51 retains the "inherent right of self-defence" independently of

---

20. I.C.J. Rep. 1949, at p. 35.

other provisions of the Charter in cases of an armed attack. In cases where there is no armed attack but where, under the traditional rules of international law, there existed a wider right of action in self-defence, the right of self-defence, which Article 51 recognises is inherent, still continues to exist, though made subject to the restrictions contained in the Charter.

Before taking action in circumstances other than those of an armed attack, the Charter imposes upon states the obligation to settle their disputes by peaceful means, and empowers the Security Council to take the steps necessary to ensure the maintenance of international peace and security. But if there appears no likelihood of the various procedures proving adequate or *a fortiori* if they have been tried and found wanting, states retain a residual power to act in self-defence even in circumstances where no armed attack has occurred.

The pre-emptive attack launched by Israel principally against the United Arab Republic in June, 1967, is an excellent illustration of the circumstances in which a right of anticipatory self-defence might still be claimed. It had long been the stated object of most of the Arab states to "liberate" the areas of Palestine under the sovereignty of the State of Israel. In their opinion Israel did not exist as a state. Right of passage for its vessels through the Suez Canal was denied, and more recently passage through the Straits of Tiran had been obstructed. On the eve of the Israeli attack, a propaganda campaign threatening annihilation of Israel reached a peak, and the U.A.R. President demanded the withdrawal of the small contingent of U.N.E.F. that was supervising the 1956 Egypt/Israel cease-fire line. To all outward appearances an invasion of Israel was imminent.

In addition to this threat, Israel could claim that the procedures available under the Charter had proved inadequate. The Security Council's resolutions concerning the free passage of Israeli shipping had been consistently flouted. The last part of U.N.E.F. was being withdrawn because its presence was dependent upon the consent of the territorial state, and that state had withdrawn its consent.

The principal Israeli attack was against Egypt from which the main threats had emanated. Within hours the Egyptian air force had been destroyed as a viable fighting force by a series of air attacks which caught most Egyptian aircraft on the ground. Simultaneously Israeli land forces struck against the Egyptian army in Sinai, and in less than a week had advanced to the banks of the Suez Canal. Large numbers of Egyptian troops, cut off from supplies, perished in the vast areas of desert.

Thus far at any rate, it is possible to accept the Israeli action as necessary on the grounds of self-defence. By largely destroying the Egyptian air force, the Egyptian army threatening Israel's vulnerable southern border had its effectiveness reduced, and, by the land attack in the Sinai, the threat was removed altogether.

Such an interpretation of the Charter has the merit of according with the practice of states and the generally accepted view of international law at the time when Article 51 was drafted. The Tokyo Tribunal had no hesitation in deciding that the Dutch declaration of war upon Japan in

December, 1941, was justifiable on the grounds of self-defence. At that time Japan had not attacked Dutch territories in the Far East, but its war aims, including the seizure of these territories, had been made known. As the Tribunal stated, the fact that the Netherlands, "being fully apprised of the imminence of the attack, in self-defence declared war against Japan . . . and thus officially recognised the existence of a state of war . . . cannot change that war from a war of aggression on the part of Japan".[1] It is hardly likely that those who drafted Article 51 would have been prepared to disregard the lessons of recent history and to insist that a state should wait for the aggressor's blow to fall before taking positive measures for its own protection. There is no need to read Article 51 in such a way; and it would be totally unrealistic to do so.

2   *Territorial integrity and political independence*

Prior to the Charter it was by no means clear how far a war undertaken in self-defence could justify action directed against the territorial integrity and political independence of the aggressor. The view of the states which defeated Germany and Japan in the Second World War was that they were entitled to occupy the territory of the enemy states and to take over the administration of those territories in order to establish democratic government and institutions on a firm foundation. It is believed that this principle, that an aggressor is not entitled to claim the benefit of what is now contained in Article 2 (4) of the Charter, is also accepted by the provisions of the Charter.

According to Article 51, nothing contained in the Charter (e.g. not even Article 2, paragraphs 3 and 4) is to impair the inherent right of individual or collective self-defence if an armed attack occurs against a member of the United Nations. It is true that Article 51 was included in the Charter primarily because the states of Latin-America were anxious lest the Charter should derogate from the right of states to establish regional security pacts similar to that which they themselves had signed at Chapultepec a few months before. Nevertheless, in the wording of Article 51 there is an undoubted parallel with the then current use of "United Nations" as meaning any of the states allied in the war against Germany and Japan. Hence the right of self-defence is retained for all Members whenever another of the United Nations is subject to an armed attack. Similarly, Article 1 of the Charter states as the primary purpose of the United Nations the maintenance of international peace and security by taking "effective collective measures for the prevention and removal of threats to the peace, and for the suppression of acts of aggression or other breaches of the peace". The notion of collective measures and of collective self-defence by all of the United Nations reflects that period of time when the allies regarded themselves as fighting on behalf of world order against the fascist aggressors who were not *ex hypothesi* counted amongst the United Nations.

---

1.   I.M.T. for the Far East, p. 995.

While it is possible to argue consistently with the wording of the Charter that Article 2 (4) is no barrier to action taken against an aggressor which has mounted an armed attack against any state, it is less certain whether or how far, in cases falling short of an armed attack, Article 2 (4) must be respected. A state which has reasonable grounds for believing that its existence is threatened, is entitled to protect itself even to the extent of launching an attack into the territory of the state from which the threat emanates. A state's "territorial integrity" does not extend so far as to enable it to prepare, free from all interference, an invasion against a neighbouring state. The rights granted to a state by Article 2 (4) must be read in conjunction with its obligations under the Charter. Territorial integrity does not denote inviolability if what a state is preparing is a breach of the peace or act of aggression.

However, territorial integrity and political independence would obviously be applicable to prevent a state, initially acting in self-defence to meet a threat from another state, from annexing, whether in whole or in part, the territory of that other state. The obligation contained in Article 2 (4) sets the limit for, and is itself limited by, the right of self-defence: the two are complementary. The factor which harmonises them is the notion of proportionality. A *threat* of an attack will never justify the threatened state taking over the government of the alleged "aggressor" in order to oblige it to "mend its ways". It will seldom, if ever, justify the seizing of territory belonging to the "aggressor".

The success of the Israeli campaigns in the "June War" of 1967—in the Sinai against Egypt, and as far as the west bank of the River Jordan against the state of Jordan—left Israel in occupation of large areas of foreign territory. The political justification for retaining these areas, initially at any rate, was that, unless the Arab states were willing to recognise Israel's right to exist and to undertake to respect Israel's territorial integrity and political independence, Israel was not prepared to relinquish the territory taken and to return to the previous, extremely vulnerable, boundaries between itself and its Arab neighbours. To this type of situation, legal principles provide inadequate criteria against which to measure the conduct of the states concerned. The retention of large areas of foreign territory may not be legally justifiable on the ground of self-defence against possible future attacks; but it is undoubtedly a strong bargaining counter in any political adjustment of the situation.

While doubts exist about the "proportionality" of retaining foreign territory as a possible discouragement against future attacks by the states the territory of which is thus occupied, self-defence clearly could not justify a purported annexation of such territory. In an earlier chapter[2] it was pointed out that the prescription on the use of force contained in the Charter required that annexation no longer be considered a basis for the acquisition of territory. Certainly a plea of self-defence, even if it could legally justify the temporary retention of the territory of threatening

---

2. Chapter 5.

neighbours (a possibility which is doubtful enough in itself), could never justify a state incorporating such territory permanently under its national sovereignty. More recent Israeli claims, notably to annex those parts of Jerusalem formerly held by Jordan, are clearly incapable of legal justification.

3   *Collective self-defence and regional organisations*

Article 51 was introduced into the draft of the Charter at a late stage at the insistence of a number of states, notably those of South America, which had entered into collective security pacts and which wished therefore to ensure that the legality of these agreements was not brought into doubt by the provisions of the Charter. To these states the most significant aspect of self-defence was that it could justify collective action. As the Colombian representative said at the San Francisco Conference in 1945, "an aggression against one American state constitutes an aggression against all the American states, and all of them exercise their right of legitimate defence by giving support to the state attacked, in order to repel aggression. This is what is meant by the right of *collective self-defence*."[3]

By referring to the "inherent right of individual *or collective self-defence*", Article 51 has provided a legal basis upon which a number of regional security systems have flourished. However, the wording of the Article has not been without its interpretative problems. Can the notion of collective defence be said to be "inherent"? And can there be such a thing as "collective self-defence"?

In many ways the development of the concept of collective security has been the history of the Monroe doctrine. Throughout the nineteenth century, the notion that European states should not interfere with the affairs of the American Republics provided a moral justification for the assertion of what was in reality a United States "sphere of interests" policy. With the present century, however, American politicians felt the need to rationalise their attitudes in legal terms. This change in approach apparently occurred over a relatively short period of time, and owed much to Elihu Root and to President Wilson.

In a speech to the Second Pan American Scientific Congress in December, 1915, the Secretary of State, Lansing, stated that "if the sovereignty of a sister Republic is menaced from overseas, the power of the United States and, I hope and believe, the united power of the American Republics will constitute a bulwark which will protect the independence and integrity of their neighbour from unjust invasion or aggression." Four years later, Article 21 of the Covenant of the League of Nations brought legal respectability to this aspect of United States policy by excepting from the effects of other obligations of the Covenant "regional understandings like the Monroe doctrine". At the Peace Conference, President Wilson explained that the "Covenant provides that the members of the League will mutually defend each other in respect of their political and territorial integrity. This Covenant, is, therefore, the highest tribute to the

---

3.   12 U.N.C.I.O. 687.

Monroe Doctrine, for it is an international extension of that principle by which the United States said that it would protect the political independence and territorial integrity of other American states."[4]

Nevertheless, the suspicion still persisted that the Monroe doctrine was designed to serve essentially United States interests. A variety of pronouncements served to enhance the impression that the defence of interests at stake was principally that of the United States. It was not until the advent of the Second World War that the notion of self-defence assumed an essentially collective nature. The 1940 Declaration of Habana stated that "any attempt on the part of a non-American state against the integrity or inviolability of the territory, the sovereignty or the political independence of an American state shall be considered as an act of aggression against the states which sign this declaration." This concept of collective security was re-iterated in the Act of Chapultepec of 1945 and later in the Charter of the Organisation of American States.

Even if one accepts that the practice of states did recognise a right of collective self-defence, how widely does that right extend?

Article 5 of the North Atlantic Treaty provides that an armed attack against one or more of the parties to the Treaty in Europe or North America, "shall be considered an attack against them all; and consequently they agree that, if such an armed attack occurs, each of them, in the exercise of the right of individual or collective self-defence recognised by Article 51 of the Charter of the United Nations, will assist the Party or Parties so attacked by taking forthwith, individually and in concert with the other Parties, such action as it deems necessary, including the case of armed force, to restore and maintain the security of the North Atlantic area." In order to comply with the provision of Article 51 of the Charter that the right of self-defence is not impaired until the Security Council has taken effective action, Article 5 of the Treaty then goes on to state that any "such armed attack and all measures taken as a result thereof shall immediately be reported to the Security Council. Such measures shall be terminated when the Security Council has taken the measures necessary to restore and maintain international peace and security."[5]

It has been contended that the first part of Article 5 contains a possible conflict. As action taken in self-defence will not *necessarily* restore international peace and security, a state might have to go beyond the legitimate exercise of its own right of self-defence in order to take part in an operation designed to achieve the further objective of restoring peace or security even in a particular area.

This conflict is more apparent than real. As far as regional organisations are concerned, measures amounting to self-defence may be taken pending action by the Security Council, but the position with regard to action going beyond the limits of self-defence is less clear. If the action amounts to enforcement action (i.e. action against a particular state), then prior

---

4. Hackworth, *Digest*, Vol. 5, pp. 441, 443.
5. Article 4 of the Warsaw Pact is in similar terms.

authorisation is required from the Security Council (Art. 53 (1)). But "activities" not amounting to enforcement action against a particular state do not need such authorisation: Article 54 only requires that the Security Council "shall at all times be kept informed of activities undertaken or in contemplation under regional arrangements or by regional agencies for the maintenance of international peace and security."

It will be recalled that, in the context of the relationship between the powers of the Security Council and the General Assembly, a distinction was drawn between enforcement action and action not directed against any state.[6] Is it not possible to distinguish between Article 53 (1) and Article 54 by a similar line of reasoning? The meaning of "activities" by regional organisations which only require to be notified to the Council is not made any clearer by reference to the records of the San Francisco Conference. The Dumbarton Oaks proposals more clearly contrasted the two equivalent provisions (Section C, paras. 2 and 3) because, at that stage, what is now Article 51 had not even been contemplated. The inclusion of Article 51 has tended to obscure such a distinction, but is believed that it should not be allowed to do so. In fact, Article 51 can be disregarded because whereas Articles 53 and 54 deal specifically with regional organisations, Article 51 falls within a different Chapter of the Charter (Chapter VII dealing with threats to the peace, breaches of the peace and acts of aggression), and is, therefore, of general application. The confusion has only been caused because in practice the right to act in collective self-defence is a right claimed by regional organisations. Hence the tendency has been to contrast Article 51 with Article 53 and to disregard or overlook the contrast between Articles 53 and 54.

The reason why collective self-defence and regional security are so closely associated is that, politically at least, a state has a greater interest in the security of its neighbours than in the security of some geographically remote state. It is even possible to argue that a right of collective self-defence only exists when an attack on state A infringes the rights of state A and also the rights of states B and C which seek to come to its aid. Geographical proximity to state A would obviously constitute one basis for states B and C claiming a right to join with state A in repelling the attack. And there would seem to be no reason why the existence of a "defensive alliance" between states A, B and C should not give states B and C a sufficient interest in the security of state A.[7] However, the requirement that the action in self-defence should be proportionate to the rights to be protected and the harm to be prevented would certainly prevent a purely punitive action against the attacking state. The action must be limited to securing state A from the existing danger.

If the relationship between A, B, and C is both geographical and contractual their position might qualify as a regional arrangement or agency.

---

6. Above, pp. 564–569.
7. There would, of course, be nothing to prevent state A seeking outside help from any source in operations for its own protection carried out on its own territory.

In addition to their right to act collectively in self-defence, they would also be entitled to act in accordance with Articles 53 and 54 of the Charter. And if one does read Article 54 as covering "anything not amounting to enforcement action", the powers of states organised as a regional agency for the maintenance of international peace and security are extensive. It is true that, even thus organised, states cannot without the authorisation of Security Council embark upon a punitive operation against a state they categorise as an "aggressor"; but as the earlier discussion of the powers of the General Assembly revealed, there is an extensive range of activities of a collective nature that, in the light of the International Court's pronouncements in the *Expenses* case,[8] cannot be said to amount to enforcement action.

Article 5 of the North Atlantic Treaty will only contain a "real" conflict for those writers who contend that N.A.T.O. as a whole is based exclusively upon Article 51 of the Charter. The power to take measures to restore security to the North Atlantic area could readily include action not justifiable on the grounds of self-defence. However, even if one accepts that N.A.T.O. is primarily an organisation for the purposes of collective self-defence, there is no reason for rejecting the notion that it is also entitled to exercise powers appropriate to a regional agency. In restoring security, N.A.T.O. would be equally entitled to act in accordance with Articles 53 and 54 as with Article 51.

4 CIVIL WAR

a IN GENERAL

It will already be apparent that international law provides an imprecise framework for the regulation of the use of force by states. Despite the number of major conventions of which the U.N. Charter is the most important, the legal prescriptions provide major loopholes for the state employing force to claim some semblance of justification for its actions. It is true that, given the political will to act, a state will more readily be dissuaded by questions of power rather than by considerations of law. Nevertheless, the existence of a plausible legal excuse may assist the creation of a favourable public opinion amongst the population of the state employing force or deter other states from taking a strongly disapproving attitude towards the action. In no situation is the absence of precise rules of law more apparent than in that loosely categorised as a civil war; and in no situation are the harmful consequences of these deficiencies more apparent.

Unless it has entered into treaty arrangements prohibiting the stationing of foreign troops on its territory, a state is entitled to agree to the establishment of foreign bases within its borders. There is no reason why the foreign forces should not assist the territorial state in defending itself (indeed, defence is usually the stated reason for their presence). And there

---

8. I.C.J. Rep. 1962, at p. 177; see also above, pp. 588–591.

would seem to be no reason why the government of the state should not request the state sending the forces for their assistance in putting down civil disturbances. Similarly, there is nothing in the practice of states which suggests that an established government is not entitled to seek military assistance from other states in order to restore internal order. The United Kingdom has sent troops to prevent an attempted *coup d'état* in Brunei, to put down military mutinies in east Africa, and to help in the suppression of "terrorism" in Malaya. The United States has placed forces within reach of Nicaragua and Guatemala in 1960, and of the Dominican Republic in 1961, at the request of the states concerned in case assistance was required in the putting down of insurrection. And in 1963 a force of American marines, landed ostensibly to protect American lives in the Dominican Republic, took part in the crushing of a widespread revolt against a military government which had itself seized power by force.

The situation in the Dominican Republic in 1963 was complicated by the fact that the Council of the O.A.S. recommended the dispatch of an inter-American peace force to the Republic. The United States agreed that it would withdraw any of its troops that were not required as part of the O.A.S. force. Nevertheless, the Dominican crisis does demonstrate that in a situation as uncertain and unstable as that which existed in the Republic, and which exists in many other parts of the world, support of the existing government is an unsatisfactory criterion for interfering in the internal affairs of another state. A state is entitled to choose its own government free from external interference, and there comes a stage when support for an existing government is in effect to deny the citizens of the state concerned the right to change their government.

Various attempts have been made to call in aid traditional principles relating to the status of insurgency and belligerency in order to distinguish between the extremes of riots on the one hand and large scale and highly organised rebellion on the other. There is some evidence to support the proposition that state practice acknowledges the right of a state to provide military assistance to the established government if the "rebels" are unrecognised. It would follow from this proposition that a state has no right to intervene once the rebellion has reached the stage of a "civil war", that is, once the rebels are sufficiently organised within a particular area to be considered as insurgents. But even if this general trend in state practice does represent international law, it is far from providing a ready basis for solving a number of other problems. For example, if the initial assistance does not succeed in "nipping the revolution in the bud" and the rebels do manage to establish themselves in an organised form, does the assistance, or any increase in the extent of the assistance, become "illegal"? And by what standards does one judge the degree of independent organisation that the rebels have to achieve? Express recognition of belligerency is no longer common practice, but a variety of pronouncements by states may be taken to amount to an implied recognition of insurgent status. But the difficulty remains of deciding what evidentiary value is to be placed upon these political acts tantamount to recognition.

The situation is likely to become more complex if the claim is raised by the intervening state and the existing government that the revolt was cited and supported from foreign territory. The almost inevitable consequence in this type of situation is that "intervention" is followed by "counter-intervention", and what might have commenced as a civil rebellion ends up as a quasi-international war fought on the territory of one state. In this process of political action and reaction rules of international law can play little part. The rules are too imprecise to give an adequate answer. The states involved are too preoccupied with their political aims and interests to allow legal principles to operate. Both sides will, if needs be, define such principles that exist to suit their own standpoint. And from the conflicting practice one is still left with the same imprecise general principles which were inadequate to resolve the issues in dispute at the outset.

b THE VIETNAM WAR
i The historical background to the 1954 Geneva Conference

Nowhere are these uncertainties in the law and difficulties in interpreting and applying state practice more apparent than in the circumstances of the present conflict in Vietnam. As the following historical outline will show, the situation at each stage of the development of the conflict has been legally ambiguous.

What is now Vietnam (i.e. the territory occupied in the north by the government of the Democratic Republic of Vietnam, and in the south by the government of the Republic of Vietnam) was formerly three provinces forming part of what was loosely referred to as French Indo-China. At the end of the Second World War, the liquidation of Japanese authority in Vietnam was entrusted to Chinese forces in the north and to British forces in the south. On the 1st January, 1946, French military and civilian authorities were allowed to resume control in the south; but, when the Chinese withdrew from the north in February, the French discovered that the major part of the north was already under the control of the pro-Communist Viet Minh, members of which were also actively engaged against French authority in the south.

An agreement was reached with the Viet Minh whereby French troops were to be allowed to enter the north unopposed in return for French recognition of the Democratic Republic as a state within the French Union. The Republic was to comprise the northern province, but a referendum was to be held in the two southern provinces on whether the whole of Vietnam was to be incorporated in the new state.

Despite this agreement, sporadic fighting continued. It was soon apparent that there could be no accommodation between the two sides. The Viet Minh aimed at a unified Vietnam under Communist domination, while the French were anxious to re-establish as much of their former authority in Indo-China as possible. By the end of 1946 the fighting had assumed the proportions of a full scale civil war.

In an attempt to provide a rallying-point for nationalist, but anti-Communist, forces, the French brought back from exile Bao Dai, the former Emperor of the central province of Annam. Under the Elysée Agreement of 1950 between Bao Dai and the French President, Vietnam was constituted an Associate State within the French Union. Defence and foreign relations were to be controlled by France, and French bases in Vietnam were to remain. Immediately this agreement was signed, a number of states, including the United States and the United Kingdom recognised the new status of Vietnam and recognised the government of Bao Dai as the government of Vietnam. By this time, however, Communist China and the Soviet Union had already recognised the government of the Democratic Republic as the government of Vietnam.

The British recognition of the régime of Bao Dai did not go uncriticised in Parliament or in the Press. It was argued, and it became increasingly apparent that such a view was correct, that the régime could only control the major cities and that, even in the southern half of the country, the villages were largely in the hands of the Viet Minh. With the increasing support given to the Viet Minh by Communist China, and to the French by the United States, the civil war came to be regarded from abroad as a conflict between pro-Communist and anti-Communist forces.

Nevertheless, the war did not lose entirely its initial impetus as a "war of liberation" by the Viet Minh against French colonial rule. It was this factor more than any which weighed against the régime of Bao Dai. Despite the increase in American assistance that the recognition of Bao Dai had made politically possible,[9] the forces of the French Union came under increasing pressure.

In early 1954, the foreign ministers of France, the United Kingdom, the U.S.S.R., and the U.S.A. met for more than three weeks at Berlin. They proposed that a meeting should be held at Geneva towards the end of April to discuss the Korean and Indo-China questions. Before the Geneva Conference was held, the military situation of the French forces deteriorated further. A large French force was besieged at Dien Bien Phu, and its situation was so serious that the suggestion was made in Washington that American air power should be used in an attempt to raise the siege.

Opposition to this project particularly by the United Kingdom was partly instrumental in the idea being abandoned. However, the United Kingdom did express interest in less extreme American ideas for the collective defence of the region. It was upon the basis of these proposals that S.E.A.T.O. was created later in the year.[10]

---

9. Large-scale support for the French was politically difficult for the U.S. Government because it would have been criticised in America as support for French imperialism. Once the régime of Bao Dai was established the amount of support for the war could be increased because it could be claimed that it was being sent directly to an independent state struggling against Communist aggression.

10. For the relevance of S.E.A.T.O., see below, p. 703.

ii *The 1954 Geneva Conference*

In the meanwhile, however, the Geneva Conference was held. In fact it resolved itself into two conferences, one dealing with Korea, the other with Indo-China. From the western viewpoint, the latter conference could hardly have commenced under more unfavourable circumstances. The day of the first plenary meeting coincided with the capitulation of the French forces at Dien Bien Phu. The Agreement on the Cessation of Hostilities in Viet-Nam subsequently adopted recognised the fact that French authority in the north had virtually collapsed by providing for a "provisional" demilitarised zone five kilometres in width roughly along the 17th parallel; French forces were to withdraw to the south, the Viet Minh to the north.

The nature of this Agreement was principally that of a general armistice. It was signed on behalf of the military commanders of the two sides—the French Union forces and the People's Army of Viet-Nam. It provided for a line of demarcation, on each side of which the demilitarised zone was established. This line was described as "provisional". In other words, the Agreement resembled the traditional concept of a general armistice in that it was a cessation of hostilities pending a final political settlement.

The final political settlement in most cases of international wars has usually been a peace treaty. In the case of the civil wars in Indo-China, the political solution envisaged for Cambodia, Laos and Vietnam was not identical in each case. With respect to Laos, it was probably to be some form of arrangement subsequently to be agreed upon. Article 14 of the Laos Cessation of Hostilities Agreement simply stated that, "pending a political settlement", the fighting units of the communist Pathet Lao were allowed to adopt one of a number of courses specified. Article 14 of the Viet-Nam Agreement, on the other hand, dealt with the conduct of civil administration "pending the general elections which will bring about the unification of Viet-Nam." In other words, the political settlement envisaged for Vietnam was to be the holding of elections leading to unification of the country.

The Viet-Nam Agreement also imposed strict limitations upon any military build-up in either "regrouping zone" as the North and South were termed. The introduction into Vietnam of any troop reinforcements and additional military personnel was prohibited (Art. 16). The introduction of replacements for arms, munitions and other war material, such as combat aircraft, naval craft, armoured vehicles, etc., except for that used up or worn out during the period of hostilities, was prohibited (Art 17). The establishment of new military bases was prohibited (Art. 18); no military base was to be established under the control of a foreign state, and the two parties were to ensure that the zones assigned to them would not adhere to any military alliance and would not be used for the resumption of hostilities or to further an aggressive policy (Art. 19).

Supervision of the carrying out of the agreement was placed in the hands of an International Control Commission. This Commission was to comprise representatives of Canada, India and Poland, presided over by the Indian representative (Art. 34). Provision was made for mobile inspection teams to ensure the proper carrying out of the regroupment (Art. 35); in addition, Article 36 (d) set out the general task of the Commission as to "supervise at ports and airfields as well as along all frontiers of Viet-Nam the execution of the provisions of the agreement on the cessation of hostilities, regulating the introduction into the country of armed forces, military personnel and of all kinds of arms, munitions and war material." The Commission was granted power to make recommendations to the two parties. When dealing with questions concerning violations, or threats of violations, which might lead to a resumption of hostilities, namely, a refusal by the forces of one side to carry out the regroupment plan, or a violation by the forces of one of the parties of the regrouping zone, territorial waters or air space of the other, decisions of the Commission must be unanimous (Art. 42); otherwise they can be by the President's casting vote if the other two members disagree (Art. 41). If a party refuses to put into effect a recommendation made by the Commission, the parties or the Commission *shall* inform the members of the Geneva Conference. If the Commission fails to reach unanimity in cases covered by Article 42, it shall submit majority and minority reports to the members of the Conference (Art. 43).

The fact that this armistice agreement has a broader basis (hence the interest of the members of the Geneva Conference in implementation of the Commission's recommendations) is clear from the final declaration of the Geneva Conference. The Conference "took note" of the agreements for the cessation of hostilities in Cambodia, Laos and Vietnam, and of the clauses in the Agreement on Viet-Nam prohibiting the introduction into that country of foreign troops, arms and ammunition, and the establishment of foreign military bases. It "recognised" that the "essential purpose of the Agreement relating to Viet-Nam is to settle military questions with a view to ending hostilities and that the military demarcation line is provisional and should not in any way be interpreted as constituting a political or territorial boundary." The Conference then declared that, "so far as Viet-Nam is concerned, the settlement of political problems, effected on the basis of respect for the principles of independence, unity and territorial integrity, shall permit the Viet-Namese people to enjoy the fundamental freedoms, guaranteed by democratic institutions established as a result of the general elections by secret ballot. In order to ensure that sufficient progress in the restoration of peace has been made, and that all the necessary conditions obtain for free expression of the national will, general elections shall be held in July, 1956, under the supervision of representatives of member States of the International Control Commission, referred to in the agreement on the cessation of hostilities."

While it is possible to categorise the Agreement on the cessation of hostilities as an armistice, and, therefore, an international undertaking binding on the two sides, the status of the Conference's "Final Declaration" is less readily defined. Even if it does amount to a treaty creating binding obligations, it would not affect the government of South Vietnam which refused to accept it. That government, while objecting to the principle of partition contained in the agreement for the cessation of hostilities, nevertheless undertook "to make and support every effort to re-establish a real and lasting peace in Viet-Nam", and "not to use force to resist procedures for carrying the cease-fire into effect". And the United States, though not prepared to join with the other members of the Conference in the issue of the Final Declaration, issued a Statement of its own in which it "took note" of the agreements on the cessation of hostilities, "declared" that it would refrain from the threat or the use of force to disturb them, in accordance with Article 2 (4) of the U.N. Charter, and would "view any renewal of the aggression in violation of the aforesaid agreements with grave concern and as seriously threatening international peace and security"; and reiterated an earlier statement that in the case of "nations now divided against their will, we shall continue to seek to achieve unity through free elections supervised by the United Nations to insure that they are conducted fairly."

For the other members of the Geneva Conference, the Final Declaration, to which they assented but did not actually sign, was more a statement of policy than it was an international treaty. This view certainly seems to be that later accepted by the United Kingdom Government. In the Narrative of events contained in the official government record dealing with the Indo-China conflict that was presented to Parliament in December, 1965, it was stated that the "Final Declaration, in contrast to the three Agreements, was not a formal instrument in the usual treaty form. It was not signed and appears to have the character properly of a statement of intention or policy on the part of those member States of the Conference who approved it."[11]

iii *The Geneva Accords and the Status of Vietnam*

The fragile nature of the 1954 settlement soon became apparent. At the time of the Conference the French had publicly declared their intention of withdrawing their troops from Cambodia, Laos and Vietnam at the request of the governments concerned. French troops were gradually withdrawn from the whole of Indo-China so that their ability to carry out obligations assumed by France under the Agreements for the Cessation of Hostilities dwindled and finally disappeared. As far as Vietnam was concerned, the position was made worse by the fact that the government of Vietnam in the South refused to assume the legal obligations of the French Command, although it did express willingness to co-operate with the Commission.[12]

---

11. H.M.S.O.: Misc. No. 25 (1965), Cmnd. 2834, p. 16, para. 41.
12. The legal status of the International Control Commission is thus ambiguous. The I.C.C. was set up by the Cease-Fire Agreement, one of the parties to which has ceased to have any influence or legal interest in Vietnam. Much of the Agreement has been disregarded, and its legal significance is doubtful. Nevertheless, the parties have continued to base some of their legal arguments upon the continued applicability of the Agreement, most notably in relation to the I.C.C.

The most serious consequence of the Vietnamese government's refusal to consider itself bound by the Final Declaration of the Conference, which it had at the time refused to accept, was that it later declared itself free of any obligation to enter into consultations for the holding of free elections throughout Vietnam. The intransigence of the South Vietnamese Government increased when in October, 1955, Bao Dai was replaced as Head of State by President Ngo Dinh Diem. While paying lip-service to the goal of reunification, the new government reiterated the claim that free elections would be impossible in the North of the country, ruled as it was by a Communist government. Charges and counter-charges followed between North and South. Diem, it was alleged, was in breach of the provisions of the Geneva Accords[13] prohibiting discrimination against former opponents. The South replied that such charges were false and had in fact been made with a view to covering up for the subversion being carried on by Communist agents operating in the South.

The Geneva Accords and the subsequent failure of the South to co-operate in the holding of elections had only indirect effects upon the status of Vietnam. It is clear that, at the time of the Geneva Conference, Vietnam was regarded as a single territorial unit. Recognition had been accorded to the government of Ho Chi Minh or to that of Bao Dai on the basis that the government so recognised was the government of all of Vietnam. In other words, the situation was that of a civil war in which two sides were striving for control of the state. It differed from the "classic" civil war situation in that the new state was created at a time when a civil war was already being fought. In other words, one of the factual attributes of statehood—that there should be a stable government obeyed by a majority of the population—was almost certainly not present when Vietnam was first recognised, although recognition was accorded to the new state on the basis that the government which was recognised at the same time, was a government having control of the country.

The Geneva Accords did not directly disturb this situation. By recognising the provisional nature of the military demarcation line and expressly rejecting the notion that it should in any way be interpreted as constituting a political or territorial boundary, they accepted as fundamental the notion that Vietnam was a single state. It was a state divided temporarily until it could be re-unified through the holding of nation-wide elections.

Nevertheless, the *physical* division of the country did have indirect effects once the South Vietnamese refusal to participate in elections made it inevitable that the provisional demarcation line was likely to remain indefinitely. In the North, the division created a quasi-state under the authority of a government which, despite rival claims that the government in the South was the government of the whole of Vietnam, made good its control over the whole of the administrative zone allotted to it under the cease-fire.

---

13.   The three cease-fire agreements and the Final Declaration together are often referred to as the Geneva Accords.

Although the physical division established a similar entity in the South, the position there was by no means so clear. The régime in the South never succeeded in obtaining the support of all non-Communist groups in the population. Indeed the seizure of power by President Diem in 1955 was followed by eight years of increasingly unpopular government. There was, therefore, widespread unrest and disorder on the purely internal level. In the wider context, however, the failure of the Diem régime to unite the non-Communist elements meant that the claims of the Democratic Republic in the North to be the only true government of the whole of Vietnam posed a very real threat to the continued existence of South Vietnam.

It is this combination of factors, the internal and the external, which has given the Vietnam war its hybrid characteristics—a civil war on two levels (i.e. within Vietnam as a whole, or solely within the South) and its international ramifications (the alleged attempt by the North to take over the South by force). The ultimate object of the North has always remained what it claims is the rightful unification of the country under the people's (i.e. Communist) control. This object was also the short-term goal at the time of the Geneva Conference, and it remained so as long as there was a possibility of elections being held. As the hope of elections faded, Communist policy shifted towards the more immediate objective of establishing a means of opposing and subsequently controlling the government in the South. In 1960, with this aim in view, the National Liberation Front was formed in the South as an essentially governmental organisation, with the Viet Cong as its military branch, to serve as a focal point for dissent from the Saigon government.

In the face of this attempt by the Communists to take over the South, the United States sought to render assistance to the Saigon government. Insurrection in the South was supported by the North and met with American supplies of arms and military materials (or vice versa depending on which side's claims one accepts). The large-scale infiltration of military units from the North led to the involvement of American combat troops, and to the subsequent bombing of supply routes, including ports, and of military installations in the North (or vice versa, again according to one's view-point).

In simplified form, the United States has based its claim to intervene on the grounds that South Vietnam is a separate state which is being subjected to armed attack by the North, and that the United States is entitled to assist the government of South Vietnam as an exercise in collective self-defence.

The North Vietnamese argument, on the other hand, has not been entirely consistent. Although the government of the Democratic Republic has throughout maintained that the Saigon government was a puppet régime and in no way representative of the people, the "people" in question have variously been described as those of Vietnam (implying that the government in Hanoi is the true government of Vietnam) or those of South Vietnam (thus suggesting that South Vietnam is a separate entity,

the true government of which is the N.L.F.). Although the latter contention has been that more frequently advanced since 1960, the North Vietnamese have been unwilling to abandon altogether their psychologically
and legally useful claim that Vietnam and its people are "one and the
same". In so far as the Hanoi government has acknowledged that regular
North Vietnamese army units are operating in the South, its justification
has been based upon the assertion that the United States has been guilty of
aggression against the people of Vietnam. Although American bombing
raids on the North in August, 1964, and from February, 1965, until
November, 1968, have been categorised as armed attacks on the territory
of the independent State of North Vietnam, the military activities of the
United States in the South have not been so precisely classified. In a sense,
the North Vietnamese wish to "have the best of both worlds". They wish
to be able to say that the war in the South is a civil war of national independence waged by the N.L.F. against the Saigon régime which has been
"created" and supported by the United States. But they also wish to be
able to claim that the war is a war of national liberation by all the people
of Vietnam, by the people of the North as well as of the South.

The American contention that the South was a separate state was
believed necessary because if it was claimed that the renewal of fighting in
Vietnam after 1954 was a continuation of the earlier conflict, the hostilities
would be of the character of a civil war. And, if it was a civil war, the
United States' attitude had traditionally been that there was a duty upon
other States not to intervene in such a struggle. By regarding the post-1954
developments as crystallising the division of North and South into separate
states, it was possible to treat the support given by the North to the insurrection in the South as constituting aggression against the State of South
Vietnam in reply to which international law allowed a use of force.

As has been stated already, international law in this area has not
developed rules of great precision. It is not possible to regard the whole
problem as being answerable by classifying the situation as either "two
states/aggression", or "civil war/non-intervention". In many respects the
North and the South have the characteristics of states, but it does not
follow that they are states for all purposes. Indeed as will already have been
realised, the war itself has similar dual characteristics: it has features of a
civil war, but it also has other aspects that have more in common with
wars waged across international boundaries.

The general trend amongst writers[14] has been to conclude that North
and, more significantly, South Vietnam are *de facto* states. The use of such
an expression as *"de facto* States" can be dangerously misleading. It was
pointed out in an earlier chapter that while recognition of governments
de facto or *de jure* was commonplace, states were either recognised or not
recognised. A state has a certain status under international law, and that is

---

14. E.g. Hawkins in *The Viet-Nam War and International Law*, p. 163; Moore in (1967)
61 A.J.I.L. 1; Legal Adviser, Department of State, in *The Legality of United States Participation in the Defense of Viet-Nam*, mentioned below, p. 698.

ex hypothesi de jure. The nearest to *de facto* recognition of an entity approximating to a state, is recognition of the government as *de facto* exercising authority in a particular area. And such recognition has importance in the municipal law of the recognising state rather than under international law. On the international plane *de facto* recognition has evidentiary value in relation to the area and extent of the control exercised by the entity concerned, but it cannot constitute it a state.

The question of whether or not South Vietnam *is* a state is complicated by the fact that much of the evidence supporting its claim could equally support an alternative claim that the Saigon government represented the whole of Vietnam. Even the fact that the Republic of Vietnam has been admitted as a member of most of the U.N. specialised agencies is not conclusive. As the Democratic Republic of Vietnam is not also a member, the Republic itself is not necessarily regarded as the "state of South Vietnam". Furthermore, it will be recalled that references to "states" in constitutional provisions governing admission to international organisations have never been strictly applied. The Ukraine and Byelorussia are members of the U.N.; and both these Soviet Republics and Monaco are members of a number of the specialised agencies although none of them can be considered as a state for the general purposes of international law.

It would seem likely therefore that South Vietnam is not a state, although it has many of the factual characteristics of statehood. It does not follow from the conclusion that South Vietnam is not a state that the whole of Vietnam *is* a state. The present legal status of the North and of the South, as of Vietnam as a whole, is uncertain. However, although it is not possible to classify South Vietnam as a state, the American involvement in the conflict does not ineluctably have to be regarded as illegal intervention in a civil war.

A *de facto* boundary such as that which separated North and South Vietnam has some international status particularly as it continued to operate for administrative purposes long after other parts of the cease-fire agreement came to be ignored. In the words of one commentator,[15] although hostilities across "a cease-fire or armistice line within the territory of a state . . . by the government in control of one side, claiming title to rule the entire State, seems on its face to be civil strife, if such lines have been long continued and widely recognised, as have those in Germany, Palestine, Kashmir, Korea, Viet Nam and the Straits of Formosa, they assume the character of international boundaries. Hostilities across them immediately constitute breaches of *international* peace, and justify 'collective defence' measures."

Although it is possible to agree in principle with the proposition that breach of a temporary cease-fire line within the territory of a state will normally constitute a renewal of civil strife while hostilities across a more permanent demarcation line may be considered as a breach of international peace by the zone or authority attacked and its allies, such an analysis of

---

15. Quincy Wright in 1959 A.S.I.L. Proceedings, at p. 151.

the legal position still falls short of providing a ready answer to the Vietnam conflict. It is not possible to state with certainty that what has taken
place has been a clear case of a largely peaceful situation being upset by an
unjustified attack launched across the cease-fire line. It is the complicated
issues of fact that must now be considered.

iv *Has the South been the victim of aggression from the North?*

Under the Agreement for the Cessation of Hostilities, the troops of the
two sides were to withdraw to their own area of control as laid down in
the Agreement. Thus French Union troops withdrew from the parts of
the North that they still occupied to places south of the demilitarised zone.
However, there was a considerable difference between the regular forces
of the French Union and the part regular and part irregular army of the
Viet Minh. Many citizen soldiers or guerrillas no doubt welcomed the
cease-fire as an opportunity to return to their homes. In the case of many
of the guerrillas operating in the South, that home was south of the line of
demarcation.

On the strength of this development, which must surely have been
foreseen, the United States Government alleged that the North Vietnamese had, from the outset, broken the armistice. In the Department of
State 1966 publication, *The Legality of United States Participation in the
Defense of Viet Nam*, it was stated that from the beginning, "the North
Vietnamese violated the 1954 Geneva Accords. Communist military
forces and supplies were left in the South in violation of the Accords."[16]
This alleged fact was put forward as one excuse for the failure of the South
to consult with the North on the holding of free elections throughout
Vietnam. It was further alleged that conditions in the North were "such as
to make impossible any free and meaningful expression of popular will."

Despite these allegations, it is difficult to avoid the conclusion that the
first major "breach" of the Accords was the refusal of the South to comply
with the understanding relating to the holding of elections. However, as
has already been explained, it is doubtful to what extent the South Vietnamese were ever bound by either the cease-fire agreement or the Final
Declaration of the Geneva Conference, or how far the latter instrument
created legal obligations even for those members of the Conference which
assented to it. But even if a legal obligation was created obliging the
South Vietnamese to participate with the North in the holding of elections,
it can hardly be claimed breach of such an obligation *legally* entitled the
North to encourage and support subversion and rebellion against the
government of the South.

Dissatisfaction with the régime in the South and with its refusal to
co-operate in the holding of elections gave rise to opposition from both
anti-Communist and pro-Communist groups. Both participated in rioting
and demonstrations against the Saigon government; in addition there was
widespread renewal of guerrilla warfare by pro-Communists. By 1961,

---

16. (1966) 54 Dept. of State Bulletin 474; convenient text in 60 A.J.I.L. 565, at p. 576.

this warfare had intensified to such an extent that "the United States found it necessary in late 1961 to increase substantially the numbers of . . . military personnel and the amounts and types of equipment introduced . . . into South Viet Nam."[17] In 1962, a majority of the Legal Committee of the International Control Commission reached the conclusion that there was evidence showing that armed and unarmed personnel, military and other supplies had been sent from the North to the South with the object of "supporting, organising, and carrying out hostile activities, including armed attacks, directed against the Armed Forces and Administration of the Zone in the South" in violation of the cease-fire agreement. The Committee also concluded that the South was in violation of the Agreement in receiving American military aid, and that, by the establishment of American bases and by the introduction of American personnel, the South and the United States had in effect entered into a military alliance contrary to the Agreement.[18]

"Violations" and "counter-violations" continued. Prior to 1964, it was the American view that the majority of personnel infiltrated from the North were former residents of the South who had been trained in guerrilla warfare. From 1964, having "apparently exhausted their reservoir of Southerners who had gone North",[19] the Communists began infiltrating regular units of the North Vietnamese army. By March, 1966, the American estimate was that there were nine regiments of such troops fighting in the South. The American reply to this build-up was two-fold: American troop commitments were increased and, in February, 1965, American aircraft commenced bombing operations over North Vietnam.

In this process of "escalation" as it is popularly termed, legal arguments are frequently adopted to justify the step being taken without regard to the over-all position. But is it possible to analyse the confused history of the conflict in legal terms? The original régime in the South of Bao Dai was very much a puppet of the French. By this policy the French were able partly to disguise a war of independence as a civil war between opposing national groups. The Geneva settlement was clearly envisaged as being of a temporary nature. Despite repeated subsequent references to it as creating a series of legal obligations for the various States involved, it is doubtful whether it should be regarded as a binding treaty or series of treaties. The Viet Minh was the only authority later involved which was a party to the armistice, while the other states or authorities made sure that they did not restrict their future conduct. The South Vietnamese and the Americans expressly refused to be bound by the settlement, while the tenor of the Final Declaration was such as to make its legal status extremely doubtful.

It is true that the existence of the armistice line does support the view that hostilities fomented and supported, and later conducted, across it do constitute an attack entitling the "victim" to act in self-defence. However,

17. *Ibid.*, at p. 577.   18. A text of the Report is contained in Cmnd. 1755.
19. 60 A.J.I.L., at p. 566.

the *raison d'être* of the line and the failure of the "victim" to implement the terms for political settlement contained in the armistice would be factors justifying the renewal of a conflict under traditional international law. The U.N. Charter would make a renewal of warfare on an international scale illegal, but its relevance to civil warfare is uncertain. While the Organisation can act in cases of threats to international peace and security, and a civil war can clearly constitute such a threat, it is doubtful whether a party renewing a civil war would be deemed an aggressor.

Between civil war on the one hand and international conflict on the other, there is a "twilight area" of hostilities having characteristics analogous to both. State practice has not displayed a sufficient measure of consistency to determine which rules of international law are most appropriate. Hence it is possible to regard North Vietnamese actions against the South as, at the same time, a legal renewal of a civil war *and* an attack across an international boundary justifying force being used, and assistance from outside being sought, by the "victim". In the present stage of development of international law, the practice of states is not sufficiently well-defined to enable a conclusion to be reached on whether the North Vietnamese or the American view is correct.

v *The justification of American assistance to South Vietnam*

Despite North Vietnamese allegations to the contrary, an anti-Communist régime has existed in Saigon independently of the United States military presence. Even though this régime may not have enjoyed the massive support of the population of South Vietnam, nevertheless it has had a factual existence, and a sufficient degree of international recognition as a government, to act on behalf of the "Southern Zone" of Vietnam. To some extent, therefore, the United States can rightfully claim that the presence of its forces has been at the invitation and with the consent of a "lawful" government. But how is this question of consent relevant?

1 *If the war is a civil war confined to South Vietnam*

It is often asserted that a state is not entitled to intervene in a civil war occurring on the territory of another state. However, such a rule does not seem to be supported by the prevailing practice of states. Even under traditional rules of international law, a duty of neutrality arose only in circumstances in which the rebels had achieved such a degree of authority and control in a defined area as to be recognised as belligerents. And even this rule suffered from the obvious defect that recognition, being a political act, could be granted or withheld at will. In such circumstances, it is hardly surprising that non-intervention did not establish itself as an all-embracing formula covering the position of all other states in their attitude to a civil war waged within an individual state.

Because the prescriptions upon the use of force contained in the Covenant of the League, the Kellogg–Briand Pact, and the U.N. Charter relate to the international plane, there is no conventional rule prohibiting a state from answering the call of another state to provide it with troops to operate solely within the territory of the latter. A state can ask for the stationing of foreign troops on its territory to protect it from possible external aggression, or to help it keep or restore internal law and order. There are of course degrees of disturbances threatening the law and order of a state, and there is general acceptance by states (at least if the express pronouncements of their representatives are any criterion) that force should not be employed to assist the government of a state faced with a rival régime established in control of a defined area of state territory. This approach does not mean that the traditional duty of neutrality should be observed; it is doubtful whether today in such a situation a rule is recognised whereby a state would be prohibited from providing arms and other supplies to either of the contesting parties. The present century has seen frequent illustrations of rival claimants to exercise the powers of government being overtly supplied from abroad. In the Spanish Civil War, the major European powers adopted an agreed policy of non-intervention, but the Nationalist armies of General Franco owed their success to the assistance provided by Fascist Germany and Italy, while the Republican side had the support of Soviet Russia.

In the context of the Vietnam war, there are sharp differences of opinion about the facts of the situation. The United States Government is reluctant to abandon its argument that the conflict arises out of North Vietnamese aggression. But, if it were to do so, it would no doubt seek to rely upon the proposition that its military presence was requested by the government of South Vietnam. Neither the United States nor South Vietnam is barred from this action by the provisions of the Geneva Accords prohibiting the introduction of military equipment and of foreign troops and bases into Vietnam because neither is bound by the Accords.

The Communist reply to this analysis based upon the organisational structure of the N.L.F. as the rival government is insufficient to destroy the validity of the case favouring the United States. While it is possible to state that a government need not, in order to continue to exist, have to remain in control of the entire area of the state's territory, in order to be recognised initially, it must have control over a defined area. The government in Saigon may not have control over the whole of Vietnam, but it has always controlled certain areas. The N.L.F., on the other hand, has never had a regular "seat of government" and defined area of authority. The N.L.F. has been essentially an "underground" movement, constantly moving its headquarters to avoid detection. Despite opposition to its authority, the régime in Saigon has remained the "established" government; while its opponents have never established themselves with sufficient definition to achieve the status of a belligerent in a civil conflict.

While the above analysis provides the basis for concluding that American action is not contrary to international law, it must be admitted that the line of reasoning is based upon practical realities rather than upon legal niceties. A use of force on the international plane is *prima facie* unlawful. However, the employment of force on the territory of another state and confined to that territory is not on the international plane if the state concerned consents to such action. The rules of international law limiting the right of the established government of a state to agree to the use of force by another state have not sufficiently crystallised, except possibly in the extreme case where a rival government exists with authority in a definite area of state territory. As there was no limitation upon the freedom of the South Vietnamese Government in Saigon to invite American troops, there was no illegality in their involvement in the war.

2   *If the war is a war across international boundaries*

Once it is accepted that international law does not prohibit a state from seeking the presence on its territory of foreign troops, it is clear that, within that territory, those troops can assist in repelling incursions by hostile forces. Therefore, so long as the operations in defence of the territorial state are conducted within its borders, the issue of in what circumstance a right of collective self-defence exists is largely academic.

The extent of this right will only become crucial if action is taken outside the territory of the state concerned. In such a situation, the foreign troops cannot base their claim to act upon the consent of the state being defended, because the action being taken is no longer confined to its territory. That state can only act on its own account to the extent that international law recognises the right to take preventive action in self-defence. And, as the foreign state supplying the troops can no longer rely upon the consent of the territorial state, it must be able to show that it is acting in collective self-defence.

In Vietnam, the United States can claim to act within the South on the basis of the consent and approval of the government of the South. American bombing of the North, however, can only be justified upon some general ground recognised by international law. The United States Government claims that it is, together with the government of South Vietnam, exercising the right of collective self-defence.

It has already been suggested[20] that a right of collective self-defence might be limited to situations in which the states concerned have a "legal interest" over and above that of the international community as a whole in each other's territorial integrity and political independence. Geographical proximity provides the most obvious "interest" that requires protection. The practice of states seems to suggest that a treaty arrangement might be sufficient, but the correctness of this suggestion is doubtful. In most cases, such treaties have some claims to be based upon a regional connection, and, as they usually relate to circumstances in which an "armed attack" has occurred, they may be no more than a form of advance consent to the operation of troops of other states of the alliance on the territory of each member state.

The United States' contention that it is acting in collective self-defence with South Vietnam lacks any real foundation. In refusing to join with the other states represented at the Geneva Conference of 1954 in issuing the

---

20.   Above, pp. 686–687.

Final Declaration, the United States made its own individual declaration in which it stated that it "would view any renewal of the aggression in violation of the aforesaid agreements with grave concern and as seriously threatening international peace and security." As part of its policy of containing or discouraging "Communist aggression", the United States became a member of S.E.A.T.O. Under Article IV (1) of the South-East Asia Collective Defence Treaty, signed later in the year of the Geneva Conference, each party[1] recognised that "aggression by means of armed attack in the treaty area against any of the Parties or against any State or territory which the Parties by unanimous agreement may hereafter designate, would endanger its own peace and safety", and agreed that it would "in the event act to meet the common danger". A protocol to the Treaty provided that the parties unanimously designated Cambodia, Laos "and the free territory under the jurisdiction of the State of Viet Nam" as states or territories referred to in Article IV (1)

It was recognised by Article IV (3) that "no action on the territory of any state designated by unanimous agreement under paragraph 1 of this Article or on any territory so designated shall be taken except at the invitation or with the consent of the government concerned", so that the Treaty would appear to be principally a form of political guarantee rather than the basis of a legal power. In fact, it is difficult to understand how the parties to a treaty can, by designating areas outside their own territory, create for themselves, even with the agreement of the governments of the areas concerned, a power to exercise a right of collective self-defence in respect of those areas. If the agreement of the "victim" is not sufficient to entitle foreign troops invited to assist it to exercise a right of "preventive self-defence", the prior agreement of states wishing to exercise that right can hardly make up for this deficiency. A right of collective self-defence enabling action to be taken outside the territory of the "victim" will only exist if the other participating states have a sufficient legal interest in the defence of the victim. That interest cannot be created by the "unanimous agreement" of those states.

But is it possible that the presence of a state's troops in the territory of a "victim" in itself is sufficient to create such an interest? If, for example, the existence of the North Atlantic Treaty does not in itself give the United States a sufficient legal interest in the defence of the United Kingdom, does the presence of American troops and bases create such an interest? It would be unrealistic if international law did not recognise that a close alliance involving the stationing of the troops of one state in the territory of another did not give the former a sufficient legal interest in the defence of the latter.

But even this situation is not identical with that of Vietnam. The American claim is that U.S. troops were sent there to meet a pre-existing "armed attack". In other words, the legal interest only arose after the

---

1. The parties to the Treaty were Australia, France, New Zealand, Pakistan, Philippines, Thailand, the United Kingdom and the United States.

alleged aggression took place. Although it is clear that, before American bombing of the North commenced, U.S. military bases were established in the South and were subject to attack, the "aggression" was initially directed not at South Vietnam and the United States and other members of the S.E.A.T.O. alliance collectively, but at the government of South Vietnam alone. It is doubtful, therefore, whether the United States can claim that, in conjunction with South Vietnam, it is exercising the right of collective self-defence.

One final aspect of the attacks upon the territory of the North is the question of whether they would have been lawful if carried out by South Vietnam alone. It will be recalled that such action in self-defence must be necessary and proportionate to the object to be achieved. In so far as it is possible to make any deductions from the conflicting evidence, the necessity of action to stop the increasing infiltration of men and supplies may be said to have been established. But what of the proportionality requirement? The force employed was significantly greater than that being used by the alleged aggressors. Nevertheless, the proportionality test can only be meaningfully applied if the yard-stick to be employed is the objective to be achieved. In this sense, it is perhaps possible to argue that severe limitation upon the operations of the North Vietnamese in the South was an objective not disproportionate to the widespread bombing of supply routes, including ports, in the North.

5 CONCLUSION

The problem of the trained lawyer is that he will approach international law with the prejudices of a lawyer. Despite its claim to be "law", international law is in many ways an unfamiliar discipline, and it does not assist understanding of its role for the lawyer to grasp at the features which resemble most closely other types of legal system.

Some of the more obvious dangers of a "legalistic" approach may be categorised:

(i) the attempt to deduce precise rules as if judicial settlement were the normal process of determining international disputes;

(ii) the tendency to characterise action as illegal which departs from a rule without considering whether the departure is, through its political acceptability, likely to produce a change in the rule;

(iii) the failure to realise that "legality" is not the ultimate test of state conduct, and that all states are motivated primarily by political motives: even the decision to abide by legal principles is in itself a political decision.

In short, the legal mind is prone to regard all situations as capable of analysis in legal terms entirely detached from their legal implications. In de Visscher's words, the "man of law is naturally liable to misunderstand the character of political tensions and the conflicts to which they give rise. He is inclined to see in them only 'the object of litigation', to cast in the terms of legal dialectic what is in the highest degree retractory to reasoning, to reduce to order what is essentially unbridled dynamism, in a word to depoliticise what is undiluted politics."[2]

Of course, not all issues in the conduct of international relations are of such importance that the states concerned are reluctant to allow the system of international law free play, or to operate subject to their control. In many of the areas covered by this book, the members of the international community have a paramount interest in the observance of the rules of international law because those rules help eliminate unnecessary tensions. In this context, the final topic, the use of force by states, is the least typical. The provisions of the Charter aimed at prohibiting the use of force illustrate a community interest, largely shared by the individual members of that community, in the eradication of force as a means of settling disputes. However, there will arise situations in which the community interest is not shared by an individual state or group of states. Does the state, or do the states, concerned act in accordance with the interests of the community in abiding by the rule of international law, or should it, or they, act to serve their own best interests?

To the lawyer, there might seem to be only one answer. But this is to place too much significance upon the part of international law in international relations. When a government seeks advice on a particular course of action from its advisers, one question that might be raised is the legality of the action. The answer given by the legal adviser will be one sort of advice, but even a negative opinion will not necessarily be decisive. Only in the comparative rarity of the judicial settlement of a dispute is it likely that the legal answer will be conclusive.

---

2. *Theory and Reality in Public International Law*, Eng. trans., at p. 79.

INDEX

EXTRADITION—*continued*
  English law—*continued*
    foreign states—*continued*
      treaty, dependent on, 322, 323, 324, 325
      trial of extradition crime only, 332–334
      waiver of protection, 334
    international law of, 347
      principle of speciality, 348
    jurisdiction—
      state where crime takes effect, 169
      surrender by state with territorial compet-
        ence, 322
    meaning, 322
    municipal law and, 323 *et seq.*
    political asylum, claims for, 328, 329, 350
    political offenders, of, 324, 325, 326, 341, 342
      international definition of offences, 348–350
      overthrow of government, relevance of,
        327, 329, 330, 344
      personal motives for crime, 331
    treaties, dependent on, 322, 323, 324, 325, 340, 347

FALKLAND ISLANDS,
  sovereignty over, 138*n.*, 140

FEDERATION,
  international status of, 75

FISCAL REGULATIONS,
  enforcement of—
    contiguous zone, in, 243, 244, 245, 246
    territorial waters, in, 235

FISHERIES,
  conservation of, 255
  contiguous zones, rights in, 155, 157, 158, 244, 245, 255
  high seas, on, 252, 255
  servitudes, 147, 148
  vessels, innocent passage, right of, 234, 235
  zones, claims to, 155, 157, 158, 244, 245, 255

FOOD AND AGRICULTURE ORGANISA-
  TION (F.A.O.),
  executive organ, 550
  functions, 598
  membership, 540
    withdrawal, 648, 649
  objects, 598
  origins, 598
  W.H.O., co-operation with, 600

FORCE,
  use of—
    aggression, concept of, and U.N. Charter, 667
    international law, in, 664
    Security Council, decisions involving, 564, 568, 572–576
    self-defence, in, 668, 670, 671 *et seq.*
    proportionate to harm, 677
    war, right to wage, 664–667

FOREIGN ARMED FORCES,
  territorial jurisdiction, exemption from, 171
  American law, under, 212
    civilian components, 215
    dependants, 216
    internal discipline, 213
    offences other than disciplinary, 213
  English law, under, 191
  N.A.T.O. Status Agreement, 191, 213–216, 225

other legal systems, 224, 225
Warsaw Pact, under, 225

FOREIGN OFFICE CERTIFICATE,
  status, as to, in claims to immunity, 51, 58, 59, 177, 183, 192

FOREIGN SOVEREIGN,
  immunity of, 170, 171, 172, 192, 216, 556
  American law, under, 192, 196
    public ships of, 192–197
    title, questions of, 198
    waiver of, 199–201
  English law, under–
    governmental agencies, 174
    personal, 172
    property, extended to, 173–176
    public ships, of, 171, 172–175, 176
    submission to jurisdiction, effect of, 178–180, 185
    waiver of, 178–180, 185
  other legal systems, under, 216
    public ships, 219–221
  territorial jurisdiction, exemption from, 170, 171, 172, 192

FOREIGN STATES,
  immunity of, 170–172, 216
  American law, under, 192 *et seq.*
    agreement to waive, 200
    armed forces, 212
    claim for, procedure as to, 194–197
    commercial activities, in, 192, 195, 197, 200, 201
    consular officers, 208
    diplomatic and other staff, 201 *et seq.*
    execution, 197
    governmental agencies, 198
    international organisations, 209
    political units within a state, 198
    property of, 192–194
    public corporations, 198
    public ships of, 192–197
    quasi-diplomatic privileges and im-
      munities, 208
    restrictions by executive on, 195–197
    sovereign of, 192
    submission to jurisdiction, 199, 200
    Tate letter, effect of, 195–197, 218, 220
    trading operations, as to, 200
    waiver of, 199–201
  English law, under, 172 *et seq.*
    armed forces, 191
    claims to, establishment of, 176
    consular officers of, 188
    diplomatic and other staff, 180 *et seq.*
    execution, 179
    governmental agencies of, 174, 176, 179
    international organisations, 189
    property of, 173–176
    public ships of, 171, 172–175, 176
    quasi-diplomatic privileges and im-
      munities, 188
    sovereign of, 172, 176
    submission to jurisdiction, effect of, 178–180, 185
    waiver of, 178–180, 185
  other legal systems, 216
    commercial activities, in, 217 *et seq.*
    diplomatic immunities, 222
    public ships of, 219
    state agencies of, 221

FOREIGN STATES—*continued*
territorial jurisdiction, exemption from, 170
et seq.

FORMOSA,
sovereignty over, 141

FRANCE,
municipal law—
customary international law as part of, 68
treaty rules, relationship with, 70
territorial claims, 134, 135

GENERAL AGREEMENT ON TARIFFS
AND TRADE (G.A.T.T.),
objects and functions of, 608
reciprocity as basis of, 380

GENERAL ASSEMBLY,
disputes—
notification of, 559, 576
powers as to. *See* powers of, *infra.*
Security Council, reference to, 559, 569
special sessions, convocation of, 576, 577
ECOSOC, responsibility for, 593
human rights, 615
International Court of Justice—
advisory opinion, request for, 520, 534
expenses of peace-keeping, as to, 525,
560, 561, 650
membership applications, as to, 525, 538
judges, election of, 485
Statute, parties to, 487
membership of, 547
suspension, 649, 651
withdrawal, 653–656
peace-keeping operations of, 568, 569, 578,
582
powers of—
economic matters, as to, 592
emergency special session, to call, 577
maintenance of peace and security, as to,
530, 569, 577—582
Security Council, on default of, 569, 577–
582
social matters, as to, 592
subsidiary organs, creation of, 580
summary of, 577
Uniting for Peace resolution as to, 577–581
structure, 547, 549
trusteeship system, overall control of, 84, 85
U.N.E.F., establishment of, 568, 569, 578–580
U.N. Secretariat—
protection of, 632, 633
staff regulations, amendment of, 633, 634
Uniting for Peace resolution, 577–581
voting, 548

GENEVA CONVENTION,
counterfeiting, suppression of, 175
drugs, on, 170
fishing and conservation, on, 256
high seas, on, 252–254, 257–264, 279, 399
hot pursuit, doctrine of, 246 *et seq.*
territorial sea, on, 154, 155, 157, 160, 233 *et
seq.*
contiguous zone, as to, 243–246, 264, 265

GERMAN DEMOCRATIC REPUBLIC,
international status of, 74, 78, 79
non-recognition of, 78, 79, 98, 99, 101*n.*
American law, effect under, 119
English law, effect under, 115–117

GERMAN FEDERAL REPUBLIC,
Act of State doctrine, 71
municipal law—
customary international law as part of, 69
treaty rules, relationship with, 69

GOOD OFFICES,
arbitration distinguished, 478
meaning, 478
settlement of international disputes by, 464,
478

GREENLAND,
Ihlen Declaration, 362, 372
sovereignty over uncolonised areas, 136, 139,
142, 143

GULFS. *See* BAYS.

HAGUE CONVENTIONS (1899 and 1907),
peaceful settlement of international disputes,
for, 479, 480

HIGH SEAS,
approach, right of, 264
claims to areas of, 139
conservation of resources, 255
contiguous zones. *See* CONTIGUOUS ZONES.
flag, verification of, 257, 263
hot pursuit, doctrine of, 246–251
interference on, grounds for, 257 *et seq.*
international peace and security, maintenance
of, 264
concerted action for, 271
regional organisations, by, 271, 272
United Nations, by, 271
jurisdiction on, 251 *et seq.*
conservation, 255–257
flag, verification of, 257, 263
international peace and security, threats to,
264, 271
municipal courts, of, 273
civil, 274
criminal, 273
pacific blockade, 269
piracy, 257–262
pollution, 252
security, protection of, 264
self-defence, 264, 269
self-preservation, 253, 254
slave-trading, 257, 262
meaning, 252
naval manœuvres on, 252, 254
nuclear tests on, 252, 254
pacific blockade, 252, 269
Rhodesian oil supplies, of, 252, 271
piracy, 257
pollution of—
oil, by, 252–254
radio-active materials, by, 254
quarantine, imposition of, 252, 267–271, 272,
273
rocket ranges, use for, 254
seizure, right of—
constructive presence in territorial waters,
245
flag, vessel without, 263, 273
hot pursuit, engaged in, 245, 246 *et seq.*
pirate ship or aircraft, 261, 273
self-defence, 258, 269
collective, 270

MUNICIPAL LAW—*continued*
English, *See* ENGLISH LAW.
extradition and, 323 *et seq.*
immunity from territorial jurisdiction under—
consular officers, 222
diplomatic, 222
foreign armed forces, 224
foreign sovereign, of, 216
foreign states, of, 216
international organisations, 223
public ships, of, 219
state agencies, 221
international law—
contrary to, 53–56
contrasted, 1
relationship between, 44 *et seq.*
international organisations, status under, 88
international tribunals, before—
primacy, question of, 45
validity, question of, 46, 54
recognition and, 114 *et seq.*
effects of, under, 120
unrecognised state or government, position of, 114, 119, 120
source of international law, as, 6, 28, 29, 37–39
treaties, ratification of, 362
United States of America, of. *See* AMERICAN LAW.

NATIONAL WATERS. *See* INTERNAL WATERS.

NATIONALISATION,
compensation for corporations, 419, 420
Cuba, in, validity of, 442
foreign-owned property, of, 433, 440 *et seq.*, 472

NATIONALITY,
acquisition of—
adoption, by, 299–302
birth, by, 290
illegitimate child, 290n., 299
jus sanguinis, 290, 291, 292, 408
jus soli, 291, 408
change of sovereignty, on, 296
change of status, by, 299
citizenship, right to, 293, 295
illegitimate child, by, 290n., 299
international law, whether concerned with, 314, 315
legitimation, 299
marriage, by, 292–294
naturalisation, by, 294–296
administrative procedure, 296
collective, 296
judicial process, by, 296
residence qualification, 294, 408
"public interest", in, 295, 296
registration as citizen, right to, 293, 295, 296
state conferring, a matter for, 314, 315
transfer of territory, by, 296
aircraft, of, 307, 308, 310
claims, of, 403. *See also* NATIONALITY OF CLAIMS.
corporations, of, 312, 313, 413
diplomatic protection, right of, 288, 289, 309, 403
corporations, 313
domestic jurisdiction and, 314, 315

internal purposes, for, 288
jurisdiction based on, 303
civil, 170, 303
conflicts of, 304
alien, temporary allegiance of, 305
allegiance, duty of, 305, 306
dual nationality, 304, 305
national and territorial law, between, 304
criminal, 303
victim a national, 306
link between individual and state, 289, 305, 308, 309, 315, 407–410, 412, 415, 416
loss of, 299 *et seq.*
acquisition of new nationality, by, 292–294, 300
allegiance to foreign state, by, 300
desertion from armed forces, by, 300
expatriation, by, 301, 302
involuntary, 301
marriage, by, 292–294, 301
naturalised citizens, by, 302, 303
operation of law, by, 300
voluntary renunciation, 300
principles governing, 288
ships, of, 307, 308–315

NATIONALITY OF CLAIMS,
contractual obligations, breach of, 425, 426–434, 440
corporations—
aliens, owned and operated by, 413–416
incorporation as basis of protection, 413, 417, 419
minority shareholders aliens, 419
nationalised, compensation where, 419, 420
seat of control test, 415, 416
shareholders, claims on behalf of—
foreign corporations, in, 417–419
minority interests, 419
nationality of, 414, 415, 416, 516, 517
indirect wrongs, responsibility for, 420 *et seq.*
individuals, 413 *et seq.*, 460
alien seamen, claims by flag ship for, 403n., 460n.
continuity of nationality, 404
dual nationality—
claimant and respondent states, 404
claimant and third state, 405–407
dominant nationality, test of, 404–407
estoppel, nationality by, 30, 411–413
foreign nationals, claims on behalf of, 403
national by birth, link with claimant state of, 408, 409
naturalised person, link with claimant state of, 407, 408, 409
residence in respondent state, 407
residence in third state, relevance of, 409
International Court, *locus standi* before, 517, 518
local remedies, exhaustion of, 444 *et seq.*
officials, tortious acts of, 425, 434
U.N. officials, protection of, 627, 628

NATURALISATION
nationality acquired by, 294–296, 408
claims, as basis of, 407, 408, 409

NAURU,
international status of, 83, 84, 86

NETHERLANDS,
Act of State doctrine, 71, 72

NETHERLANDS—*continued*
municipal law—
  customary international law as part of, 66
  treaty rules, relationship of, 69

NEW GUINEA,
international status of, 83, 86
sovereignty over, 143

NON-SELF GOVERNING TERRITORIES,
independence, promotion of, 616
international status of, 79 *et seq.*, 142, 143
sovereignty over, 143
treaties, parties to, 358

NORTH ATLANTIC TREATY ORGANISA-
TION,
collective self-defence, 599, 685, 687
membership, 541, 648
status of visiting forces, 188, 213–216, 225

NORWAY,
domestic jurisdiction, dispute within, 502–505
territorial waters, fisheries within, 151, 152–
154

NUCLEAR WEAPONS,
high seas, tests on, 252, 254
self-defence, use in, 677, 678
testing in self-preservation, 255n.

NUREMBERG TRIBUNAL, 92, 131, 371,
400, 666, 667

OCCUPATION,
acquisition by, 132
intention to occupy as sovereign, 133
possession, taking of, 132
prescription contrasted, 135

ORGANISATION FOR ECONOMIC
CO-OPERATION AND DEVELOP-
MENT (O.E.C.D.),
functions, 610
O.E.E.C. reconstituted as, 610

ORGANISATION FOR EUROPEAN ECO-
NOMIC CO-OPERATION (O.E.E.C.),
objects, 610
O.E.C.D., reconstituted as, 610

ORGANISATION OF AFRICAN UNITY,
609

ORGANISATION OF AMERICAN STATES
(O.A.S.),
Alliance for Progress, 609
Bogota Charter, 589, 590
collective security, for, 589
constitution of, 589
Cuba, measures against, 252, 267–271, 272,
273, 590, 591, 656
membership, 541
pacific settlement, for 589
Rio Treaty, 589, 590
U.N., relationship with, 589–591

OUTER SPACE,
air space, boundary between, 286
exploration of, 287
jurisdiction in, 286, 287
legal régime of, 287

PACIFIC ISLANDS,
international status of, 83

PALESTINE,
partition of, 574
Security Council, powers of, 562, 574
U.N. mediator in, 562

PANAMA CANAL,
international status of, 146, 228
jurisdiction of riparian state, 228

PERMANENT COURT OF INTER-
NATIONAL JUSTICE,
decisions of, *ex aequo et bono*, 278
jurisdiction—
  advisory, 516–518
  disputes clause in treaty referring to, 490–
492
  domestic, reservation as to, 316
  International Court, transfer to, 511–513
  post-1945, in force, 490–492
  treaty, acceptance by, 489

PIRACY,
aircraft, committed by, 257, 258, 260, 260n.,
261, 273
"hi-jacking" contrasted, 260
high seas, on, 252, 257 *et seq.*
  limited to acts on, 260, 261
individual liability under international law,
91, 92
insurgents, acts of, 258–260
meaning, 257, 258
political motives, relevancy of, 258–260
port, committed in, 261
slave-trading, whether, 262, 263
territorial waters, in, 260, 261

PORTS,
foreign ships, jurisdiction over, 227, 228
  civil cases, in, 233, 240
  criminal cases, in, 230
  internal discipline, matters of, 232, 237
international traffic, for, access to, 228, 229,
233
piracy committed in, 261
public ships, immunity of, 230, 233. *See also*
SHIPS.
warships, access to, 230

POSIVITISM,
consensual theory, support of, 24, 27, 28
sovereignty, absolute nature of, 4
writers, 40

PRESCRIPTION,
acquisition by, 133, 137
consolidation distinguished, 137, 138
meaning, 137
practical application of, 135
protest, relevance of, 134
sovereignty extinguished by, 140

PRINCIPALITIES,
international status of, 76, 77, 81

PRIVATE INTERNATIONAL LAW,
civil jurisdiction, 170
  territorial waters, in, 241
recognition, effectiveness of foreign law and,
115, 116, 118
relevant foreign law repugnant to international law, 53

PROTECTED STATES,
international status of, 81, 82
sovereignty over, 143